# PUBLIC ADMINISTRATION

## Concepts and Cases

### FIFTH EDITION

Richard J. Stillman II

*George Mason University*

**HOUGHTON MIFFLIN COMPANY**     Boston     Toronto

Dallas     Geneva, Illinois     Palo Alto     Princeton, New Jersey

*Sponsoring Editor:* Margaret Seawell
*Project Editor:* Susan Yanchus
*Design Coordinator:* Martha Drury
*Production Coordinator:* Frances Sharperson
*Manufacturing Coordinator:* Holly Schuster
*Marketing Manager:* Karen Natale

*For my wife, Kathleen*
*my daughter, Shannon Marie*
*my son, Richard J. III*

Printed in the U.S.A.

Library of Congress Catalog Card Number: 91–71958

ISBN: 0–395–59015–9

ABCDEFGHIJ–D–987654321

# Contents

# Preface

As the study of public administration enters its second century, fundamental concepts of bureaucracy like public budgeting, administration power, implementation, personnel motivation, and decision making; trends in government such as privatization; and contemporary issues of administration ethics and priorities remain key areas of research. The fifth edition of *Public Administration* introduces students to these and other topics that are part of the essential framework of the public sector.

## Format and Approach

The methodological format and design of the first four editions remain intact in the fifth edition. The approach seeks to interrelate many of the authoritative conceptual works in public administration with contemporary case studies.

By pairing a reading with a case study in each chapter, the text serves four important purposes:

1. The concept-case study method permits students to read firsthand the work of leading administrative theorists who have shaped the modern study of public administration. This method aims at developing in students a critical appreciation of the classic administrative ideas that are the basis of modern public administration.
2. The text encourages a careful examination of practical administrative problems through the presentation of contemporary cases—often involving major national events—that demonstrate the complexity, the centrality, and the challenge of the current administrative processes of public organizations.
3. The book seeks to promote a deeper understanding of the relationship between the theory and practice of public administration by allowing readers to test for themselves the validity of major ideas about public administration in the context of actual situations.
4. Finally, the concept-case method develops a keener appreciation of the eclectic breadth and interdisciplinary dimensions of public administration by presenting articles—both conceptual and case writings—from a wide variety of sources, using many materials not available in the average library.

The immense quantity of literature in the field has always made selecting the writings a challenge. My final choice of writings is based on affirmative answers to the following four central questions:

1. Do the writings focus on the central issues confronting public administrators?
2. Do the writings, individually and collectively, give a realistic view of the contemporary practice of public administration?
3. Do the individual conceptual readings and case studies relate logically to one another?

4. Are the writings interesting and long enough to convey the true sense and spirit intended by the authors?

The arrangement of the selections follows an order of topics used by many instructors in the field, moving from a definition of public administration to increasingly specific issues and problems. Many subjects (such as headquarters-field relationships, position classification, enforcement, government regulation, productivity, and personnel recruitment), though not treated separately, are discussed within various chapters under other headings (refer to the topic index for additional cross-references).

A diagram may help readers to understand the design of the book more clearly.

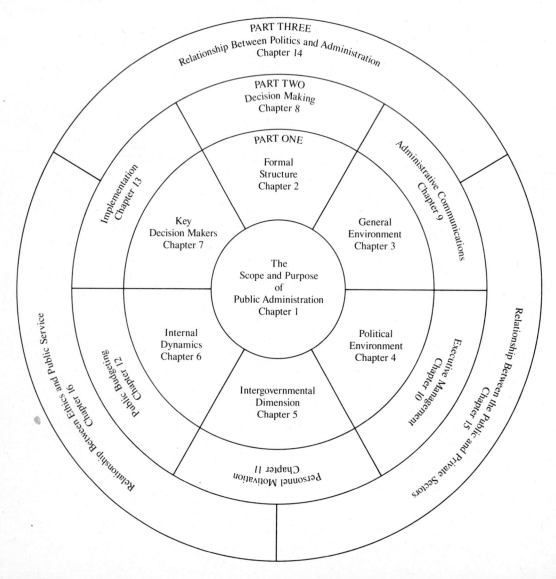

At the center of this schematic figure is Chapter 1, which discusses "The Scope and Purpose of Public Administration," perhaps the most difficult, central intellectual problem in public administration today. The first ring outward is Part One, "The Environment of Public Administration." These six chapters present concepts and cases pertaining to the broad environment surrounding public administration and the work of public administrators. The second ring is Part Two, "The Multiple Functions of Public Administrators." These six chapters focus on the major activities, roles, and responsibilities of practicing administrators in the public sector. The exterior ring is Part Three; these three chapters discuss "Enduring and Unresolved Relationships" in public administration, ones especially critical during the last decade of the 20th century for the field as a whole.

## New Material in the Fifth Edition

Readings and cases have been carefully selected with an eye to readability and contemporary appeal to ensure that the text stays current and continues to reflect the ideas and events shaping public administration today. In this edition, special attention has been paid to ensuring the accessibility of writings for students: contemporary topics and issues that students want and need to know about make up more than half (17 of 32) of the new selections.

Seven new readings appear in this edition:

Reading 1: "The Study of Public Administration" (Woodrow Wilson)

Reading 5: "American Federalism: Madison's Middle Ground" (Martha Derthick)

Reading 6: "Hawthorne and the Western Electric Company" (Elton Mayo)

Reading 10.2: "Management by Groping Along" (Robert D. Behn)

Reading 12: "The Politics of Public Budgets" (Irene S. Rubin)

Reading 13: "Implementation Theory and Practice: Toward a Third Generation" (Malcolm L. Goggin, Ann O'M. Bowman, James P. Lester, and Laurence J. O'Toole, Jr.)

Reading 15: "The Public and Private Spheres in Historical Perspective" (Thomas K. McCraw)

Eleven case studies are also new to this edition:

Case Study 2: "The Rise of U.S. Bureaucracy" (Richard J. Stillman II)

Case Study 5: "Achieving a Negotiated Compensation Agreement in Nuclear Waste Disposal Siting: The MRS Case" (E. Brent Sigmon)

Case Study 6: "Personnel Changes in City Government" (Curtis Copeland)

Case Study 7: "Politics, Professionals, and the President: Developing an Executive Tax Initiative" (Timothy J. Conlan, Margaret T. Wrightson, and David R. Beam)

Case Study 8: "The Decision to Liberate Kuwait" (Bob Woodward)

Case Study 10: "The MOVE Disaster" (Jack H. Nagel)

Case Study 12: "County Prison Overtime" (Tom Mills)

Case Study 13: "Planning for Early Intervention in HIV Infection: Judith Kurland and the Boston Department of Health and Hospitals" (Esther Scott)

Case Study 14: "Mayor Dinkins: Every Day a Test" (Sam Roberts)

Case Study 15: "Close Encounters or How to Create a Workable Partnership in Downtown" (Margaret F. Reid)

Case Study 16: "The $150 Billion Calamity" (David Maraniss and Rick Atkinson)

Revised and expanded introductions, alerting students to the main ideas that follow, open each selection. Also updated are the review questions, key terms, and suggestions for further reading that conclude each chapter, as well as the subject and topic indexes.

## The Instructor's Guide

The *Instructor's Guide* complements the text by offering insights, practical suggestions, and resources for teaching introductory and graduate students. The guide is organized as a set of memoranda from myself to the instructor. Each memo addresses a separate important topic, such as "How to use case studies in the classroom." The guide also includes sample quizzes, exams, and course evaluation forms. Appendices include the Federalist Papers, nos. 10 and 51, the Declaration of Independence, and the Constitution.

## Acknowledgments

Various people have contributed to this book either by helping to shape its focus in the early stages or by reviewing the finished manuscript. Special thanks are due: Charles T. Barber, University of Southern Indiana; Stephen Brooks, University of Akron; Margaret Gilkison, University of Wisconsin-Eau Claire; Fred A. Kramer, University of Massachusetts-Amherst; Wendell C. Lawther, University of Central Florida; John Moore, University of California-Santa Barbara; Michael Munger, University of Texas-Austin; Alan Shank, State University of New York-Geneseo; and Shui Yan Tang, University of Southern California.

Several faculty colleagues at George Mason University offered invaluable suggestions and ideas for preparing this fifth edition, especially Wayne F. Anderson, Timothy J. Conlan, James P. Pfiffner and my chair, Louise White. Thanks must also go to my editors at Houghton Mifflin for their generous support and enthusiastic encouragement throughout this difficult writing and editing assignment, particularly Jean Woy, Margaret Seawell, and Susan Yanchus. The students, both graduate and undergraduate, whom I have taught over the last two decades have shaped this text in more ways than I can calculate—or thank them for: To these and many others, I owe a debt of gratitude for their assistance.

R.J.S. II

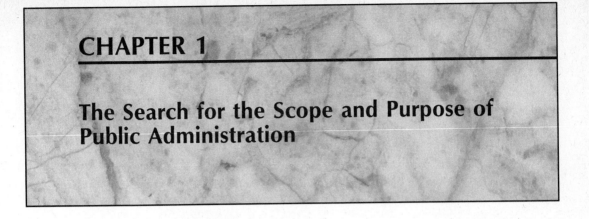

# CHAPTER 1

## The Search for the Scope and Purpose of Public Administration

*O*ur own politics must be the touchstone for all theories. The principles on
which to base a science of administration for America must be principles
which have democratic policy very much at heart.

*Woodrow Wilson*

## Introduction

A definition of the parameters of a field of study, that is, the boundaries,
landmarks, and terrain that distinguish it from other scientific and humanistic
disciplines, is normally considered a good place to begin any academic subject.
Unfortunately, as yet, no one has produced a simple definition of the study of
public administration—at least one on which most practitioners and scholars
agree. Attempting to define the core values and focus of twentieth-century
public administration provides lively debates and even deep divisions among
students of the field.

A major difficulty in arriving at a precise and universally acceptable definition arises in part from the rapid growth in the twentieth century of public
administration, which today seems to be all-encompassing. Public administrators are engaged in technical, although not necessarily mundane details: they
prepare budgets for a city government, classify jobs in a post office, have
potholes patched and mail delivered, or evaluate the performance of a city's
drug treatment centers. At the same time, they are also concerned with the
major goals of society and with the development of resources for achieving
those goals within the context of a rapidly changing political environment. For
instance, if an engineering staff of a state agency proposes to build a highway,
this decision appears at first glance to be a purely administrative activity.
However, it involves a wide range of social values related to pressing concerns

such as community land-use patterns, energy consumption, pollution control, and mass transit planning. Race relations, the general economic well-being of a community, and the allocation of scarce physical and human resources affect even simple administrative decisions about highway construction.

Public administration does not operate in a vacuum but is deeply intertwined with the critical dilemmas confronting an entire society. The issue then becomes: How can a theorist reasonably and concisely define a field so interrelated with all of society?

The rapidly increasing number and scope of activities involving public administration have led theorists to develop a variety of definitions. Consider eight offered during the last decade by leading textbook writers:

> Public Administration is the production of goods and services designed to serve the needs of citizens-consumers.
>
> > Marshall Dimock, Gladys Dimock, and Douglas Fox,
> > *Public Administration* (Fifth Edition, 1983)

> We suggest a new conceptual framework that emphasizes the perception of public administration as *design,* with attendant emphasis on participative decision making and learning, purpose and action, innovation, imagination and creativity, and social interaction and "coproduction."
>
> > Jong S. Jun,
> > *Public Administration* (1986)

> In ordinary usage, public administration is a generic expression for the entire bundle of activities that are involved in the establishment and implementation of public policies.
>
> > Cole Blease Graham, Jr., and
> > Steven W. Hays,
> > *Managing the Public Organization* (1986)

> Traditionally, public administration is thought of as the accomplishing side of government. It is supposed to comprise all those activities involved in carrying out the policies of elected officials and some activities associated with the development of those policies. Public administration is . . . all that comes after the last campaign promise and election-night cheer.
>
> > Grover Starling,
> > *Managing the Public Sector* (Third Edition, 1986)

Public administration:
1. is a cooperative group effort in a public setting.
2. covers all three branches—executive, legislative, and judicial—and their interrelationships.
3. has an important role in the formulation of public policy, and is thus part of the political process.
4. is different in significant ways from private administration.

5. is closely associated with numerous private groups and individuals in providing services to the community.

> Felix A. Nigro and Lloyd G. Nigro,
> *Modern Public Administration* (Seventh Edition, 1989)

Public administration is the use of managerial, political, and legal theories and processes to fulfill legislative, executive, and judicial governmental mandates for the provision of regulatory and service functions for the society as a whole or for some segments of it.

> David H. Rosenbloom and Deborah D. Goldman,
> *Public Administration: Understanding Management, Politics, and Law in the Public Sector* (Second Edition, 1989)

. . . Public administration is centrally concerned with the organization of government policies and programs as well as the behavior of officials (usually nonelected) formally responsible for their conduct.

> Charles H. Levine, B. Guy Peters, and Frank J. Thompson,
> *Public Administration: Challenges, Choices, Consequences* (1990)

The practice of public administration involves the dynamic reconciliation of various forces in government's efforts to manage public policies and programs.

> Melvin J. Dubnick and Barbara S. Romzek,
> *American Public Administration: Politics and the Management of Expectations* (1991)

Generally, these attempts at defining public administration seem to identify it with the following: (1) the executive branch of government (yet it is related in important ways to the legislative and judicial branches); (2) the formulation and implementation of public policies; (3) the involvement in a considerable range of problems concerning human behavior and cooperative human effort; (4) a field that can be differentiated in several ways from private administration; and (5) the production of public goods and services. However, trying to pin down public administration in more specific detail becomes, according to specialists such as Harold Stein, a fruitless endeavor. The many variables and complexities of public administration make almost every administrative situation a unique event, eluding any highly systematic categorization. As Harold Stein writes: "public administration is a field in which every man is his own codifier and categorizer and the categories adopted must be looked on as relatively evanescent."[1]

For some writers like Frederick C. Mosher, the elusiveness of a disciplinary core for public administration gives the subject its strength and fascination, for students must draw upon many fields and disciplines, as well as their own

[1]Harold Stein, *Public Administration and Policy Development: A Case Book* (New York: Harcourt Brace Jovanovich, 1952), p. xxv.

resources, to solve a particular administrative problem. As Mosher writes: "Perhaps it is best that it [public administration] not be defined. It is more an area of interest than a discipline, more a focus than a separate science. . . . It is necessarily cross-disciplinary. The overlapping and vague boundaries should be viewed as a resource, even though they are irritating to some with orderly minds."[2]

But for others like Robert S. Parker, the frustrations of dealing with such a disorderly discipline mitigate against its being a mature, rewarding academic field of study. "There is really no such subject as 'public administration,' " writes Parker. "No science or art can be identified by this title, least of all any single skill or coherent intellectual discipline. The term has no relation to the world of systematic thought. . . . It does not, in itself, offer any promising opportunity to widen or make more precise any single aspect of scientific knowledge."[3]

Despite Parker's pessimistic assessment of the present and future status of public administration, the search for a commonly accepted definition of the field, both in its academic and professional applications, continues by many scholars.

Indeed, defining public administration—its boundaries, scope, and purpose—has become, in recent decades, a preoccupation and difficulty confronting public administration theorists. The field's "identity crisis," as Dwight Waldo once labeled the dilemma, has now become especially acute because a plethora of models, approaches, and theories now purport to define what public administration is all about.

To help us understand public administration today, it is useful to study the rationale for creating this field, as outlined in an essay written in 1887 by Woodrow Wilson, a young political scientist at the time. Wilson (1856–1924) is better known as the twenty-eighth President of the United States (1913–1921), father of the League of Nations, Commander-in-Chief during World War I, and author of much of the new freedom progressive reform legislation. Wilson is also credited by scholars with writing the first essay on public administration in the United States and therefore is considered by many as its American founder. His short but distinguished essay, "The Study of Administration," was published a century after the U.S. Constitution's birth. Wilson had just begun his academic career, teaching political science at Bryn Mawr College in Pennsylvania, after earning his Ph.D. at Johns Hopkins University. The editor of a new journal (*Political Science Quarterly*) asked Wilson to contribute an essay on this developing subject. At that time, public administration had been a well-established discipline in Europe, but was largely unknown in America.

Geographic isolation, agrarian self-sufficiency, the absence of threats to national security, and limited demands for public services, among other things,

[2]Frederick C. Mosher, "Research in Public Administration," *Public Administration Review*, 16 (Summer 1956), p. 177.

[3]Robert S. Parker, "The End of Public Administration," *Public Administration*, 34 (June 1965), p. 99.

had allowed the United States to get along reasonably well during its first century of existence without the self-conscious study of public administration. However, many events were forcing Americans to take notice of the need for public administration. By the late nineteenth century, technologic innovations such as the automobile, telephone, and light bulb and growing international involvement in the Spanish-American War, combined with increasing public participation in a democratic government, created urgent needs for expanded, effective administrative services. As a consequence, we also required an established field of administrative study. Wilson wrote his essay at the time when civil service reform had been instituted in the federal government (the Civil Service Act or "the Pendleton Act," named for its legislative sponsor, had been passed in 1883). Much of Wilson's centennial essay was, not surprisingly, a plea for recognizing the central importance of administrative machinery, especially a well-trained civil service based on merit, rather than politics, to operate a modern democratic government.

Just as the *Federalist Papers,* authored by James Madison, Alexander Hamilton, and John Jay had a century before advocated the passage of the U.S. Constitution, Wilson called in 1887 for the necessity of this new field "to run a constitution" during its second century. His essay strived to encourage the development of public administration and to underscore the importance of effective administration for the Constitution's survival in the future.

But how could Americans graft public administration into their Constitution, which had not mentioned this subject? For Wilson—and modern students of the field—this was the critical issue. In developing public administration—both practically and academically—Wilson's basic difficulty was to reconcile the notions of constitutional democracy with inherent concerns for popular control and participation with theories of efficient, professional administration, and their stress on systematic rules and internal procedures as distinct from democratic oversight and influence. For Wilson, this inevitable conflict could be settled by dividing government into two spheres—"politics," in which choices regarding what government should do are determined by a majority of elected representatives, and "administration," which serves to carry out the dictates of the populace through efficient procedures relatively free from political meddling.

Although modern administrative scholars generally reject the possibility or desirability of drawing any hard-or-fast line between politics and administration, or what most call "the politics-administrative dichotomy," the issues Wilson raised are enduring and important. Read the essay for yourself and see how you judge the validity of Wilson's arguments.

How did Wilson define public administration and why did he believe it was so critical to the future of the United States? Are his arguments for its basic rationale and value still valid?

Why did Wilson distinguish between "politics" and "administration" as important terms for creating public administration? In your opinion, is such a "politics-administration dichotomy" practical and workable? What are the advantages and disadvantages of using such a dichotomy today as a way to advance this field of study?

What sources did Wilson believe the U.S. should draw on in developing this new field? And what sources should Americans avoid in shaping their administrative enterprise? And why?

What issues and challenges did Wilson pose for administrative study and practice? Are these still priorities for the 1990s?

# The Study of Administration

## WOODROW WILSON

I suppose that no practical science is ever studied where there is no need to know it. The very fact, therefore, that the eminently practical science of administration is finding its way into college courses in this country would prove that this country needs to know more about administration, were such proof of the fact required to make out a case. It need not be said, however, that we do not look into college programmes for proof of this fact. It is a thing almost taken for granted among us, that the present movement called civil service reform must, after the accomplishment of its first purpose, expand into efforts to improve, not the *personnel* only, but also the organization and methods of our government offices: because it is plain that their organization and methods need improvement only less than their *personnel.* It is the object of administrative study to discover, first, what government can properly and successfully do, and, secondly, how it can do these proper things with the utmost possible efficiency and at the least possible cost either of money or of energy. On both these points there

Reprinted with permission from *Political Science Quarterly,* 2 (June 1887): 197–222.

is obviously much need of light among us; and only careful study can supply that light.

Before entering on that study, however, it is needful:

I. To take some account of what others have done in the same line; that is to say, of the history of the study.
II. To ascertain just what is its subject-matter.
III. To determine just what are the best methods by which to develop it, and the most clarifying political conceptions to carry with us into it.

Unless we know and settle these things, we shall set out without chart or compass.

## I.

The science of administration is the latest fruit of that study of the science of politics which was begun some twenty-two hundred years ago. It is a birth of our own century, almost of our own generation.

Why was it so late in coming? Why did it wait till this too busy century of ours to demand attention for itself? Administration is the most obvious part of government; it is government in action; it is the executive, the operative, the most visible side of government, and is of course as old as government itself. It is government in action, and one might very naturally expect to find that government in action had arrested the attention and provoked the scrutiny of writers of politics very early in the history of systematic thought.

But such was not the case. No one wrote systematically of administration as a branch of the science of government until the present century had passed its first youth and had begun to put forth its characteristic flower of systematic knowledge. Up to our own day all the political writers whom we now read had thought, argued, dogmatized only about the *constitution* of government; about the nature of the state, the essence and seat of sovereignty, popular power and kingly prerogative; about the greatest meanings lying at the heart of government, and the high ends set before the purpose of government by man's nature and man's aims. The central field of controversy was that great field of theory in which monarchy rode tilt against democracy, in which oligarchy would have built for itself strongholds of privilege, and in which tyranny sought opportunity to make good its claim to receive submission from all competitors. Amidst this high warfare of principles, administration could command no pause for its own consideration. The question was always: Who shall make law, and what shall that law be? The other question, how law should be administered with enlightenment, with equity, with speed, and without friction, was put aside as "practical detail" which clerks could arrange after doctors had agreed upon principles.

That political philosophy took this direction was of course no accident, no chance preference or perverse whim of political philosophers. The philosophy of any time is, as Hegel says, "nothing but the spirit of that time expressed in abstract thought"; and political philosophy, like philosophy of every other kind, has only held up the mirror to contemporary affairs. The trouble in early times was almost altogether about the constitution of government; and consequently that was what engrossed men's thoughts. There was little or no trouble about administration,—at least little that was heeded by administrators. The functions of government were simple, because life itself was simple. Government went about imperatively and compelled men, without thought of consulting their wishes. There was no complex system of public revenues and public debts to puzzle financiers; there were, consequently, no financiers to be puzzled. No one who possessed power was long at a loss how to use it. The great and only question was: Who shall possess it? Populations were of manageable numbers; property was of simple sorts. There were plenty of farms, but no stocks and bonds; more cattle than vested interests.

• • •

There is scarcely a single duty of government which was once simple which is not now complex; government once had but a few masters; it now has scores of masters. Majorities formerly only underwent government; they now conduct government. Where government once might follow the whims of a court, it must now follow the views of a nation.

And those views are steadily widening to new conceptions of state duty; so that, at the same time that the functions of government are every day becoming more complex and difficult, they are also vastly multiplying in number. Administration is everywhere putting its hands to new undertakings. The utility, cheapness, and success of the government's postal service, for instance, point towards the early establishment of governmental control of the telegraph system. Or, even if our government is not to follow the lead of the governments of Europe in buying or building both telegraph and railroad lines, no one can doubt that in some way it must make itself master of masterful corporations. The creation of national commissioners of railroads, in addition to the older state commissions, involves a very important and delicate extension of administrative functions. Whatever hold of authority state or federal governments are to take upon corporations, there must follow cares and responsibilities which will require not a little wisdom, knowledge, and experience. Such things must be studied in order to be well done. And these, as I have said, are only a few of the doors which are being opened to offices of government. The idea of the state and the consequent ideal of its duty are undergoing noteworthy change; and "the idea of the state is the conscience of administration." Seeing every day new things which the state ought to do, the next thing is to see clearly how it ought to do them.

This is why there should be a science of administration which shall seek to straighten the paths of government, to make its business less unbusinesslike; to strengthen and purify its organization, and to crown its duties with dutifulness. This is one reason why there is such a science.

But where has this science grown up? Surely not on this side of the sea. Not much impartial scientific method is to be discerned in our administrative practices. The poisonous atmosphere of city government, the crooked secrets of state administration, the confusion, sinecurism, and corruption ever and again discovered in the bureaus at Washington forbid us to believe that any clear conceptions of what constitutes good administration are as yet very widely current in the United States. No; American writers have hitherto taken no very important part in the advancement of this science. It has found its doctors in Europe. It is not of our making; it is a foreign science, speaking very little of the language of English or American principle. It employs only foreign tongues; it utters none but what are to our minds alien

ideas. Its aims, its examples, its conditions, are almost exclusively grounded in the histories of foreign races, in the precedents of foreign systems, in the lessons of foreign revolutions. It has been developed by French and German professors, and is consequently in all parts adapted to the needs of a compact state, and made to fit highly centralized forms of government; whereas, to answer our purposes, it must be adapted, not to a simple and compact, but to a complex and multiform state, and made to fit highly decentralized forms of government. If we would employ it, we must Americanize it, and that not formally, in language merely, but radically, in thought, principle, and aim as well. It must learn our constitutions by heart; must get the bureaucratic fever out of its veins; must inhale much free American air.

If an explanation be sought why a science manifestly so susceptible of being made useful to all governments alike should have received attention first in Europe, where government has long been a monopoly, rather than in England or the United States, where government has long been a common franchise, the reason will doubtless be found to be twofold: first, that in Europe, just because government was independent of popular assent, there was more governing to be done; and, second, that the desire to keep government a monopoly made the monopolists interested in discovering the least irritating means of governing. They were, besides, few enough to adopt means promptly.

• • •

The English race . . . has long and successfully studied the art of curbing executive power to the constant neglect of the art of perfecting executive methods. It has exercised itself much more in controlling than in energizing government. It has been more concerned to render government just and moderate than to make it facile, well-ordered, and effective. English and American political history has been a history, not of administrative development, but of legislative oversight,—not of progress in governmental organization, but of advance in law-making and political criticism. Consequently, we have reached a time when administrative study and creation are imperatively necessary to the well-being of our governments saddled with the habits of a long period of constitution-making. That period has practically closed, so far as the establishment of essential principles is concerned, but we cannot shake off its atmosphere. We go on criticizing when we ought to be creating. We have reached the third of the periods I have mentioned,—the period, namely, when the people have to develop administration in accordance with the constitutions they won for themselves in a previous period of struggle with absolute power; but we are not prepared for the tasks of the new period.

Such an explanation seems to afford the only escape from blank astonishment at the fact that, in spite of our vast advantages in point of political liberty, and above all in point of practical political skill and sagacity, so many nations are ahead of us in administrative organization and administrative skill. Why, for instance, have we but just begun purifying a civil service which was rotten full fifty years ago? To say that slavery diverted us is but to repeat what I have said—that flaws in our Constitution delayed us.

Of course all reasonable preference would declare for this English and American course of politics rather than for that of any European country. We should not like to have had Prussia's history for the sake of having Prussia's administrative skill; and Prussia's particular system of administration would quite suffocate us. It is better to be untrained and free than to be servile and systematic. Still there is no denying that it would be better yet to be both free in spirit and proficient in practice. It is this even more reasonable preference which impels us to discover what there may be to hinder or delay us in naturalizing this much-to-be desired science of administration.

What, then, is there to prevent?

Well, principally, popular sovereignty. It is harder for democracy to organize administration than for monarchy. The very completeness of our most cherished political successes in the past embarrasses us. We have enthroned public opinion; and it is forbidden us to hope during its reign for any quick schooling of the sovereign in executive expertness or in the conditions of perfect functional balance in government. The very fact that we have realized popular rule in its fullness has made the task of *organizing* that rule just so much the more difficult. In order to make any advance at all we must instruct and persuade a multitudinous monarch called public opinion,—a much less feasible undertaking than to influence a single monarch called a king. An individual sovereign will adopt a simple plan and carry it out directly; he will have but one opinion, and he will embody that one opinion in one command. But this other sovereign, the people, will have a score of differing opinions. They can agree upon nothing simple: advance must be made through compromise, by a compounding of differences, by a trimming of plans and a suppression of too straightforward principles. There will be a succession of resolves running through a course of years, a dropping fire of commands running through a whole gamut of modifications.

In government, as in virtue, the hardest of hard things is to make progress. Formerly the reason for this was that the single person who was sovereign was generally either selfish, ignorant, timid, or a fool,—albeit there was now and again one who was wise. Nowadays the reason is that the many, the people, who are sovereign have no single ear which one can approach, and are selfish, ignorant, timid, stubborn, or foolish with the selfishnesses, the ignorances, the stubbornnesses, the timidities, or the follies of several thousand persons,—albeit there are hundreds who are wise. Once the advantage of the reformer was that the sovereign's mind had a definite locality, that it was contained in one man's head, and that consequently it could be gotten at; though it was his disadvantage that that mind learned only reluctantly or only in small quantities, or was under the influence of someone who let it learn only the wrong things. Now, on the contrary, the reformer is bewildered by the fact that the sovereign's mind has no definite locality, but is contained in a voting majority of several million heads; and embarrassed by the fact that the mind of this sovereign also is under the influence of favorites, who are none the less favorites in a good old-fashioned sense of the word because they are not persons but preconceived opinions; *i.e.,* prejudices which are not to be reasoned with because they are not the children of reason.

Wherever regard for public opinion is a first principle of government, practical reform must be slow and all reform must be full of compromises. For wherever public opinion exists it must rule. This is now an axiom half the world over, and will presently come to be believed even in Russia. Whoever would effect a change in a modern constitutional government must first educate his fellow-citizens to want *some* change. That done, he must persuade them to want the particular change he wants. He must first make public opinion willing to listen and then see to it that it listen to the right things. He must stir it up to search for an opinion, and then manage to put the right opinion in its way.

The first step is not less difficult than the second. With opinions, possession is more than nine points of the law. It is next to impossible to dislodge them. Institutions which one generation regards as only a makeshift approximation to the realization of a principle, the next generation honors as the nearest possible approximation to that principle, and the next worships as the principle itself. It takes scarcely three generations for the apotheosis. The grandson accepts his grandfather's hesitating experiment as an integral part of the fixed constitution of nature.

Even if we had clear insight into all the political past, and could form out of perfectly

instructed heads a few steady, infallible, placidly wise maxims of government into which all sound political doctrine would be ultimately resolvable, *would the country act on them?* That is the question. The bulk of mankind is rigidly unphilosphical, and nowadays the bulk of mankind votes. A truth must become not only plain but also commonplace before it will be seen by the people who go to their work very early in the morning; and not to act upon it must involve great and pinching inconveniences before these same people will make up their minds to act upon it.

And where is this unphilosophical bulk of mankind more multifarious in its composition than in the United States? To know the public mind of this country, one must know the mind, not of Americans of the older stocks only, but also of Irishmen, of Germans, of Negroes. In order to get a footing for new doctrine, one must influence minds cast in every mould of race, minds inheriting every bias of environment, warped by the histories of a score of different nations, warmed or chilled, closed or expanded by almost every climate of the globe.

• • •

## II.

The field of administration is a field of business. It is removed from the hurry and strife of politics; it at most points stands apart even from the debatable ground of constitutional study. It is a part of political life only as the methods of the counting-house are a part of the life of society; only as machinery is part of the manufactured product. But it is, at the same time, raised very far above the dull level of mere technical detail by the fact that through its greater principles it is directly connected with the lasting maxims of political wisdom, the permanent truths of political progress.

The object of administrative study is to rescue executive methods from the confusion and costliness of empirical experiment and set them upon foundations laid deep in stable principle.

It is for this reason that we must regard civil service reform in its present stages as but a prelude to a fuller administrative reform. We are now rectifying methods of appointment; we must go on to adjust executive functions more fitly and to prescribe better methods of executive organization and action. Civil service reform is thus but a moral preparation for what is to follow. It is clearing the moral atmosphere of official life by establishing the sanctity of public office as a public trust, and, by making the service unpartisan, it is opening the way for making it businesslike. By sweetening its motives it is rendering it capable of improving its methods of work.

Let me expand a little what I have said of the province of administration. Most important to be observed is the truth already so much and so fortunately insisted upon by our civil service reformers; namely, that administration lies outside the proper sphere of *politics*. Administrative questions are not political questions. Although politics sets the tasks for administration, it should not be suffered to manipulate its offices.

This is distinction of high authority; eminent German writers insist upon it as of course. Bluntschli, for instance, bids us separate administration alike from politics and from law. Politics, he says, is state activity "in things great and universal," while "administration, on the other hand," is "the activity of the state in individual and small things. Politics is thus the special province of the statesman, administration of the technical official." "Policy does nothing without the aid of administration"; but administration is not therefore politics. But we do not require German authority for this position; this discrimination between administration and politics is now, happily, too obvious to need further discussion.

There is another distinction which must be worked into all our conclusions, which, though but another side of that between administration and politics, is not quite so easy to keep sight of; I mean the distinction between *constitutional* and administrative questions, between those governmental adjustments which are essential to constitutional principle and those which are merely instrumental to the possibly changing purposes of a wisely adapting convenience.

One cannot easily make clear to every one just where administration resides in the various departments of any practicable government without entering upon particulars so numerous as to confuse and distinctions so minute as to distract. No lines of demarcation, setting apart administrative from non-administrative functions, can be run between this and that department of government without being run up hill and down dale, over dizzy heights of distinction and through dense jungles of statutory enactment, hither and thither around "its" and "buts," "whens" and "howevers," until they become altogether lost to the common eye not accustomed to this sort of surveying, and consequently not acquainted with the use of the theodolite of logical discernment. A great deal of administration goes about *incognito* to most of the world, being confounded now with political "management," and again with constitutional principle.

Perhaps this case of confusion may explain such utterances as that of Niebuhr's: "Liberty," he says, "depends incomparably more upon administration than upon constitution." At first sight this appears to be largely true. Apparently facility in the actual exercise of liberty does depend more upon administrative arrangements than upon constitutional guarantees; although constitutional guarantees alone secure the existence of liberty. But—upon second thought—is even so much as this true? Liberty no more consists in easy functional movement than intelligence consists in the ease and vigor with which the limbs of a strong man move. The principles that rule within the man, or the constitution, are the vital springs of liberty or servitude. Because dependence and subjection are without chains, are lightened by every easy-working device of considerate, paternal government, they are not thereby transformed into liberty. Liberty cannot live apart from constitutional principle; and no administration, however perfect and liberal its methods, can give men more than a poor counterfeit of liberty if it rest upon illiberal principles of government.

A clear view of the difference between the province of constitutional law and the province of administrative function ought to leave no room for misconception; and it is possible to name some roughly definite criteria upon which such a view can be built. Public administration is detailed and systematic execution of public law. Every particular application of general law is an act of administration. The assessment and raising of taxes, for instance, the hanging of a criminal, the transportation and delivery of the mails, the equipment and recruiting of the army and navy, etc., are all obviously acts of administration; but the general laws which direct these things to be done are as obviously outside of and above administration. The broad plans of governmental action are not administrative; the detailed execution of such plans is administrative. Constitutions, therefore, properly concern themselves only with those instrumentalities of government which are to control general law. Our federal Constitution observes this principle in saying nothing of even the greatest of the purely executive offices, and speaking only of that President of the Union who was to share the legislative and policy-making functions of government, only of those judges of highest jurisdiction who were to interpret and guard its principles, and not of those who were merely to give utterance to them.

This is not quite the distinction between Will and answering Deed, because the administrator should have and does have a will of his own in the choice of means for accomplishing his work. He is not and ought not to be a mere passive instrument. The distinction is between general plans and special means.

There is, indeed, one point at which administrative studies trench on constitutional ground—or at least upon what seems constitutional ground. The study of administration, philosophically viewed, is closely connected with the study of the proper distribution of constitutional authority. To be efficient it must discover the simplest arrangements by which responsibility can be unmistakably fixed upon officials; the best way of dividing authority without hampering it, and responsibility without obscuring it. And this question of the distribution of authority, when taken into the sphere of the higher, the originating functions of government, is obviously a central constitutional question. If administrative study can discover the best principles upon which to base such distributions, it will have done constitutional study an invaluable service. Montesquieu did not, I am convinced, say the last word on this head.

To discover the best principle for the distribution of authority is of greater importance, possibly, under a democratic system, where officials serve many matters, than under others where they serve but a few. All sovereigns are suspicious of their servants, and the sovereign people is no exception to the rule; but how is its suspicion to be allayed by *knowledge?* If that suspicion could but be clarified into wise vigilance, it would be altogether salutary; if that vigilance could be aided by the unmistakable placing of responsibility, it would be altogether beneficent. Suspicion in itself is never healthful either in the private or in the public mind. *Trust is strength* in all relations of life; and, as it is the office of the constitutional reformer to create conditions of trustfulness, so it is the office of the administrative organizer to fit administration with conditions of clear-cut responsibility which shall insure trustworthiness.

And let me say that large powers and unhampered discretion seem to me the indispensable conditions of responsibility. Public attention must be easily directed, in each case of good or bad administration, to just the man deserving of praise or blame. There is no danger in power, if only it be not irresponsible. If it be divided, dealt only in shares to many, it is obscured; and if it be obscured, it is made irresponsible. But if it be centred in heads of the service and in heads of branches of the service, it is easily watched and brought to book. If to keep his office a man must achieve open and honest success, and if at the same time he feels himself entrusted with large freedom of discretion, the greater his power the less likely is he to abuse it, the more is he nerved and sobered and elevated by it. The less his power, the more safely obscure and unnoticed does he feel his position to be, and the more readily does he relapse into remissness.

Just here we manifestly emerge upon the field of that still larger question,—the proper relations between public opinion and administration.

To whom is official trustworthiness to be disclosed, and by whom is it to be rewarded? Is the official to look to the public for his meed of praise and his push of promotion, or only to his superior in office? Are the people to be called in to settle administrative discipline as they are called in to settle constitutional principles? These questions evidently find their root in what is undoubtedly the fundamental problem of this whole study. That problem is: What part shall public opinion take in the conduct of administration?

The right answer seems to be, that public opinion shall play the part of authoritative critic.

But the *method* by which its authority shall be made to tell? Our peculiar American difficulty in organizing administration is not the danger of losing liberty, but the danger of not being able or willing to separate its essentials from its accidents. Our success is made doubtful by that besetting error of ours, the error of trying to do too much by vote. Self-government does not consist in having a hand in everything, any more than housekeeping consists necessarily in cooking dinner with one's own hands. The cook must be trusted with a large discretion as to the management of the fires and the ovens.

In those countries in which public opinion has yet to be instructed in its privileges, yet to be accustomed to having its own way, this question as to the province of public opinion is much more readily soluble than in this country, where public opinion is wide awake and quite intent upon having its own way anyhow. It is pathetic to see a whole book written by a German professor of political science for the purpose of saying to his countrymen, "Please try to have an opinion about national affairs"; but a public which is so modest may at least be expected to be very docile and acquiescent in learning what things it has *not* a right to think and speak about imperatively. It may be sluggish, but it will not be meddlesome. It will submit to be instructed before it tries to instruct. Its political education will come before its political activity. In trying to instruct our own public opinion, we are dealing with a pupil apt to think itself quite sufficiently instructed beforehand.

The problem is to make public opinion efficient without suffering it to be meddlesome. Directly exercised, in the oversight of the daily details and in the choice of the daily means of government, public criticism is of course a clumsy nuisance, a rustic handling delicate machinery. But as superintending the greater forces of formative policy alike in politics and administration, public criticism is altogether safe and beneficent, altogether indispensable. Let administrative study find the best means for giving public criticism this control and for shutting it out from all other interference.

But is the whole duty of administrative study done when it has taught the people what sort of administration to desire and demand, and how to get what they demand? Ought it not to go on to drill candidates for the public service?

There is an admirable movement towards universal political education now afoot in this country. The time will soon come when no college of respectability can afford to do without a well-filled chair of political science. But the education thus imparted will go but a certain length. It will multiply the number of intelligent critics of government, but it will create no competent body of administrators. It will prepare the way for the development of a sure-footed understanding of the general principles of government, but it will not necessarily foster skill in conducting government. It is an education which will equip legislators, perhaps, but not executive officials. If we are to improve public opinion, which is the motive power of government, we must prepare better officials as the *apparatus* of government. If we are to put in new boilers and to mend the fires which drive our governmental machinery, we must not leave the old wheels and joints and valves and bands to creak and buzz and clatter on as the best they may at bidding of the new force. We must put in new running parts wherever there is the least lack of strength or adjustment. It will be necessary to organize democracy by sending up to the competitive examinations for the civil service men definitely prepared for standing liberal tests as to technical knowledge. A technically schooled civil service will presently have become indispensable.

I know that a corps of civil servants prepared by a special schooling and drilled, after appointment, into a perfected organization, with appropriate hierarchy and characteristic discipline, seems to a great many very thoughtful persons to contain elements which might combine to make an offensive official class,—a distinct, semi-corporate body with sympathies divorced from those of a progressive, free-spirited people, and with hearts narrowed to the meanness of a bigoted officialism. Certainly such a class would be altogether hateful and harmful in the United States. Any measures calculated to produce it would for us be measures of reaction and of folly.

But to fear the creation of a domineering, illiberal officialism as a result of the studies I am here proposing is to miss altogether the principle upon which I wish most to insist. That principle is, that administration in the United States must be at all points sensitive to public opinion. A body of thoroughly trained officials serving during good behavior we must have in any case: that is a plain business necessity. But the apprehension that such a body will be anything un-American clears away the moment it is asked, What is to constitute good behavior? For that question obviously carries its own answer on its face. Steady, hearty allegiance to the policy of the government they serve will constitute good behavior. That *policy* will have no taint of officialism about it. It will not be the creation of permanent officials, but of statesmen whose responsibility to public opinion will be direct and inevitable. Bureaucracy can exist only where the whole service of the state is removed from the common political life of the people, its chiefs as well as its rank and file. Its motives, its objects, its policy, its standards, must be bureaucratic. It would be difficult to point out any examples of impudent exclusiveness and arbitrariness on the part of officials doing service under a chief of department who really served the people, as all our chiefs of departments must be made to do.

• • •

The ideal for us is a civil service cultured and self-sufficient enough to act with sense and vigor, and yet so intimately connected with the popular thought, by means of elections and constant public counsel, as to find arbitrariness or class spirit quite out of the question.

## III.

Having thus viewed in some sort the subject-matter and the objects of this study of administration, what are we to conclude as to the methods best suited to it—the points of view most advantageous for it?

Government is so near us, as much a thing

of our daily familiar handling, that we can with difficulty see the need of any philosophical study of it, or the exact point of such study, should it be undertaken. We have been on our feet too long to study now the art of walking. We are a practical people, made so apt, so adept in self-government by centuries of experimental drill that we are scarcely any longer capable of perceiving the awkwardness of the particular system we may be using, just because it is so easy for us to use any system. We do not study the art of governing: we govern. But mere unschooled genius for affairs will not save us from sad blunders in administration. Though democrats by long inheritance and repeated choice, we are still rather crude democrats. Old as democracy is, its organization on a basis of modern ideas and conditions is still an unaccomplished work. The democratic state has yet to be equipped for carrying those enormous burdens of administration which the needs of this industrial and trading age are so fast accumulating. Without comparative studies in government we cannot rid ourselves of the misconception that administration stands upon an essentially different basis in a democratic state from that on which it stands in a non-democratic state.

After such study we could grant democracy the sufficient honor of ultimately determining by debate all essential questions affecting the public weal, of basing all structures of policy upon the major will; but we would have found but one rule of good administration for all governments alike. So far as administrative functions are concerned, all governments have a strong structural likeness; more than that, if they are to be uniformly useful and efficient, they *must* have a strong structural likeness. A free man has the same bodily organs, the same executive parts, as the slave, however different may be his motives, his services, his energies. Monarchies and democracies, radically different as they are in other respects, have in reality much the same business to look to.

It is abundantly safe nowadays to insist upon this actual likeness of all governments, because these are days when abuses of power are easily exposed and arrested, in countries like our own, by a bold, alert, inquisitive, detective public thought and a sturdy popular self-dependence such as never existed before. We are slow to appreciate this; but it is easy to appreciate it. Try to imagine personal government in the United States. It is like trying to imagine a national worship of Zeus. Our imaginations are too modern for the feat.

But, besides being safe, it is necessary to see that for all governments alike the legitimate ends of administration are the same, in order not to be frightened at the idea of looking into foreign systems of administration for instruction and suggestion; in order to get rid of the apprehension that we might perchance blindly borrow something incompatible with our principles. That man is blindly astray who denounces attempts to transplant foreign systems into this country. It is impossible: they simply would not grow here. But why should we not use such parts of foreign contrivances as we want, if they be in any way serviceable? We are in no danger of using them in a foreign way. We borrowed rice, but we do not eat it with chopsticks. We borrowed our whole political language from England, but we leave the words "king" and "lords" out of it. What did we ever originate, except the action of the federal government upon individuals and some of the functions of the federal supreme court?

We can borrow the science of administration with safety and profit if only we read all fundamental differences of condition into its essential tenets. We have only to filter it through our constitutions, only to put it over a slow fire of criticism and distill away its foreign gases.

• • •

Let it be noted that it is the distinction, already drawn, between administration and politics which makes the comparative method so safe in the field of administration. When we study the administrative systems of France and Germany, knowing that we are not in search of *political* principles, we need not care a pepper-corn for the constitutional or political reasons which Frenchmen or Germans give for their practices when explaining them to us. If I see a murderous fellow sharpening a knife cleverly, I can borrow his way of sharpening the knife without borrowing his probable intention to commit murder with it; and so, if I see a monarchist dyed in the wool managing a public bureau well, I can learn his business methods without changing one of my republican spots. He may serve his king; I will continue to serve the people; but I should like to serve my sover-. eign as well as he serves his. By keeping this distinction in view,—that is, by studying administration as a means of putting our own politics into convenient practice, as a means of making what is democratically politic towards all administratively possible towards each,—we are on perfectly safe ground, and can learn without error what foreign systems have to teach us. We thus devise an adjusted weight for our comparative method of study. We can thus scrutinize the anatomy of foreign governments without fear of getting any of their diseases into our veins; dissect alien systems without apprehension of blood-poisoning.

Our own politics must be the touchstone for all theories. The principles on which to base a science of administration for America must be principles which have democratic policy very much at heart. And, to suit American habit, all general theories must, as theories, keep modestly in the background, not in open argument only, but even in our own minds,—lest opinions satisfactory only to the standards of the library should be dogmatically used, as if they must be quite as satisfactory to the standards of practical politics as well. Doctrinaire devices must be postponed to tested practices. Arrangements not only sanctioned by conclusive experience elsewhere but also congenial to American habit must be preferred without hesitation to theoretical perfection. In a word, steady, practical statesmanship must come first, closet doctrine second. The cosmopolitan

what-to-do must always be commanded by the American how-to-do-it.

Our duty is, to supply the best possible life to a *federal* organization, to systems within systems; to make town, city, county, state, and federal governments live with a like strength and an equally assured healthfulness, keeping each unquestionably its own master and yet making all interdependent and cooperative, combining independence with mutual helpfulness. The task is great and important enough to attract the best minds.

This interlacing of local self-government with federal self-government is quite a modern conception. It is not like the arrangements of imperial federation in Germany. There local government is not yet, fully, local *self*-government. The bureaucrat is everywhere busy. His efficiency springs out of *esprit de corps,* out of care to make ingratiating obeisance to the authority of a superior, or, at best, out of the soil of a sensitive conscience. He serves, not the public, but an irresponsible minister. The question for us is, how shall our series of governments within governments be so administered that it shall always be to the interest of the public officer to serve, not his superior alone but the community also, with the best efforts of his talents and the soberest service of his conscience? How shall such service be made to his commonest interest by contributing abundantly to his sustenance, to his dearest interest by furthering his ambition, and to his highest interest by advancing his honor and establishing his character? And how shall this be done alike for the local part and for the national whole?

If we solve this problem we shall again pilot the world. There is a tendency—is there not?—a tendency as yet dim, but already steadily impulsive and clearly destined to prevail, towards, first the confederation of parts of empires like the British, and finally of great states themselves. Instead of centralization of power, there is to be wide union with tolerated divisions of prerogative. This is a tendency towards the American type—of governments joined with governments for the pursuit of common purposes, in honorary equality and honorable subordination. Like principles of civil liberty are everywhere fostering like methods of government; and if comparative studies of the ways and means of government should enable us to offer suggestions which will practi- cably combine openness and vigor in the administration of such governments with ready docility to all serious, well-sustained public criticism, they will have approved themselves worthy to be ranked among the highest and most fruitful of the great departments of political study. That they will issue in such suggestions I confidently hope.

## CASE STUDY 1

# Introduction

The following story may shed some further insight into the role of public administration in modern society. The story, "The Blast in Centralia No. 5: A Mine Disaster No One Stopped," is an excellent account of a mine disaster that occurred a generation ago in Centralia, Illinois, killing 111 miners. This article is an unusual case study in public administration; not only does the author, John Bartlow Martin, carefully recount the facts of the catastrophe, but he also attempts to understand the reasons behind the disaster. In his search for clues, the writer reveals much about the inner complexities of the administrative framework of our modern society—a coal company sensitive only to profit incentives; state regulatory agencies inadequately enforcing mine safety legislation; federal officials and mine unions complacent about a growing problem; and the miners incapable of protecting themselves against the impending disaster.

This is an example of administrative reality that, for some, will only confirm their suspicions about the inherent corruption of modern administrative enterprises. The victims died, they might argue, because the mine owners were only interested in profits, not in human lives. But is this the correct interpretation? Martin does not blame any one individual or even a group of individuals but stresses the ineffectiveness of the administrative structure on which all the disaster victims were dependent for survival.

After reading this story you will probably be struck by how much modern society depends on the proper functioning of unseen administrative arrangements—for safeguarding our environment; for protecting the purity of our food; for transporting us safely by road, rail, or air; for sending us our mail; or for negotiating an arms limitations agreement at some distant diplomatic conference. All of us, like the miners in Centralia No. 5, rely throughout our lives on the immovable juggernaut of impersonal administrative systems. A functioning, ordered public administration, as this story illustrates, is an inescapable necessity for maintaining the requisites of a civilized modern society.

As you read this selection, keep the following questions in mind:

What does this case study tell us are the central problems and issues facing public administrators in their work? Why is government administration such a complex and difficult task according to this study?

Given the themes and problems in this case study, how would you frame a suitable definition of the field of public administration? Does it "square" with Woodrow Wilson's?

What does the case say about the special *public* obligations of public administrators compared to the obligations of those engaged in private administration?

Finally, if you had actually been one of the leading administrative officials in the case—Driscoll O. Scanlan, Dwight Green, or Robert Medill—what would have been your view of public administration, and how might such a perspective on administration have helped to shape the outcome of the story?

# The Blast in Centralia No. 5: A Mine Disaster No One Stopped

## JOHN BARTLOW MARTIN

Already the crowd had gathered. Cars clogged the short, black rock road from the highway to the mine, cars bearing curious spectators and relatives and friends of the men entombed. State troopers and deputy sheriffs and the prosecuting attorney came, and officials from the company, the Federal Bureau of Mines, the Illinois Department of Mines and Minerals. Ambulances arrived, and doctors and nurses and Red Cross workers and soldiers with stretchers from Scott Field. Mine rescue teams came, and a federal rescue unit, experts burdened with masks and oxygen tanks and other awkward paraphernalia of disaster. . . .

One hundred and eleven men were killed in that explosion. Killed needlessly, for almost everybody concerned had known for months, even years, that the mine was dangerous. Yet nobody had done anything effective about it. Why not? Let us examine the background of the explosion. Let us study the mine and the miners, Joe Bryant and Bill Rowekamp and some others, and also the numerous people who might have saved the miners' lives but did not. The miners had appealed in various directions for help but

got none, not from their state government nor their federal government nor their employer nor their own union. (In threading the maze of officialdom we must bear in mind four agencies in authority: The State of Illinois, the United States Government, the Centralia Coal Company, and the United Mine Workers of America, that is, the UMWA of John L. Lewis.) Let us seek to fix responsibility for the disaster. . . .

The Centralia Mine No. 5 was opened two miles south of Centralia in 1907. Because of its age, its maze of underground workings is extensive, covering perhaps six square miles, but it is regarded as a medium-small mine since it employs but 250 men and produces but 2,000 tons of coal daily. It was owned by the Centralia Coal Company, an appendage of the Bell & Zoller empire, one of the Big Six among Illinois coal operators. . . . The Bell & Zoller home office was in Chicago (most of the big coal operators' home offices are in Chicago or St. Louis); no Bell & Zoller officers or directors lived at Centralia.

There are in coal mines two main explosion hazards—coal dust and gas. Coal dust is unhealthy to breathe and highly explosive. Some of the dust raised by machines in cutting and loading coal stays in suspension in the air. Some subsides to the floor and walls of the tunnels, and a local explosion will kick it back into the air where it will explode and, in turn, throw more dust into the air, which will explode; and as this chain reaction continues the explosion will propagate throughout the mine or until it reaches something that will stop it.

The best method of stopping it, a method in use for some twenty-five years, is rock dusting. Rock dusting is simply applying pulverized stone to the walls and roof of the passageways; when a local explosion occurs it will throw a cloud of rock dust into the air along with the coal dust, and since rock dust is incombustible the explosion will die. Rock dusting will not prevent an explosion but it will localize one. Illinois law requires rock dusting in a dangerously dusty mine. Authorities disagreed as to whether the Centralia mine was gassy but everyone agreed it was exceedingly dry and dusty. The men who worked in it had been complaining about the dust for a long time—one recalls "the dust was over your shoetops," another that "I used to cough up chunks of coal dust like walnuts after work"—and indeed by 1944, more than two years before the disaster, so widespread had dissatisfaction become that William Rowekamp, as recording secretary of Local Union 52, prepared an official complaint. But even earlier, both state and federal inspectors had recognized the danger.

Let us trace the history of these warnings of disaster to come. For in the end it was this dust which did explode and kill one hundred and eleven men, and seldom has a major catastrophe of any kind been blueprinted so accurately so far in advance.

Driscoll O. Scanlan (who led the rescue work after the disaster) went to work in a mine near Centralia when he was 16, studied engineering at night school, and worked 13 years as a mine examiner for a coal company until, in 1941, he was appointed one of 16 Illinois state mine inspectors by Governor Green upon recommendation of the state representative from Scanlan's district. Speaking broadly, the job of a state inspector is to police the mine operators—to see that they comply with the state mining law, including its numerous safety provisions. But an inspector's job is a political patronage job. Coal has always been deeply enmeshed in Illinois politics.

Dwight H. Green, running for Governor the preceding fall, had promised the miners that he would enforce the mining laws "to the letter of the law," and however far below this lofty aim his administration fell (as we shall see), Scanlan apparently took the promise literally. Scanlan is a stubborn, righteous, zealous man of fierce integrity. Other inspectors, arriving to inspect a mine, would go into the office and chat with the company officials. Not Scanlan; he waited outside, and down in the mine he talked with the miners, not the bosses. Other inspectors, emerging, would write their reports in the company office at the company typewriter. Not Scanlan; he wrote on a portable in his car. Widespread rumor had it that some inspectors spent most of their inspection visits drinking amiably with company officials in the hotel in town. Not Scanlan. Other inspectors wrote the briefest reports possible, making few recommendations and enumerating only major violations of the mining law. Scanlan's reports were longer than any others (owing in part to a prolix prose style), he listed every violation however minor, and he made numerous recommendations for improvements even though they were not explicitly required by law.

Scanlan came to consider the Centralia No. 5 mine the worst in his district. In his first report on it he made numerous recommendations, including these: "That haulage roads be cleaned and sprinkled. . . . That tamping of shots with coal dust be discontinued and that clay be used. . . ." Remember those criticisms, for they were made February 7, 1942, more than five years before the mine blew up as a result (at least in part) of those very malpractices.

Every three months throughout 1942, 1943, and 1944 Scanlan inspected the mine and repeated his recommendations, adding new ones: "That the mine be sufficiently rock dusted." And what became of his reports? He mailed them to the Department of Mines and Minerals at Springfield, the agency which supervises coal mines and miners. Springfield is dominated by the Statehouse, an ancient structure of spires and towers and balconies, of colonnades and domes; on its broad front steps Lincoln stands in stone. Inside all is gloom and shabby gilt. The Department of Mines and Minerals occupies three high-ceilinged rooms in a back corner of the second floor. The Director of the Department uses the small, comfortable, innermost office, its windows brushed by the leaves of trees on the Statehouse lawn, and here too the Mining Board meets. In theory, the Mining Board makes policy to implement the mining law, the Director executes its dictates; in practice, the Director possesses considerable discretionary power of his own.

In 1941 Governor Green appointed as Director Robert M. Medill, a genial, paunchy, red-faced man of about sixty-five. Medill had gone to work in a mine at sixteen; he rose rapidly in management. He had a talent for making money and he enjoyed spending it.

He entered Republican politics in 1920, served a few years as director of the Department of Mines and Minerals, then returned to business (mostly managing mines); and then, after working for Green's election in 1940, was rewarded once more with the directorship. Green reappointed him in 1944 with, says Medill, the approval of "a multitude of bankers and business men all over the state. And miners. I had the endorsement of all four factions." By this he means the United Mine Workers and its smaller rival, the Progressive Mine Workers, and the two associations of big and little operators; to obtain the endorsement of all four of these jealous, power-seeking groups is no small feat. As Director, Medill received $6,000 a year (since raised to $8,000) plus expenses of $300 or $400 a month. He lived in a sizable country house at Lake Springfield, with spacious grounds and a tree-lined driveway.

To Medill's department, then, came Driscoll Scanlan's inspection reports on Centralia Mine No. 5. Medill, however, did not see the first thirteen reports (1942–44); they were handled as "routine" by Robert Weir, an unimaginative, harassed little man who had come up through the ranks of the miners' union and on recommendation of the union had been appointed Assistant Director of the Department by Green (at $4,000 a year, now $5,200). When the mail brought an inspector's report, it went first to Medill's secretary who shared the office next to Medill's with Weir. She stamped the report [with date of receipt] . . . and put it on Weir's desk. Sometimes, but by no means always, Weir read the report. He gave it to one of a half-dozen girl typists in the large outer office. She edited the inspector's recommendations for errors in grammar and spelling, and incorporated them into a form letter to the owner of the mine, closing:

"The Department endorses the recommendations made by Inspector Scanlan and requests that you comply with same.

"Will you please advise the Department upon the completion of the recommendations set forth above?

"Thanking you . . ."

When the typist placed this letter upon his desk, Weir signed it and it was mailed to the mine operator.

But the Centralia company did not comply with the major recommendations Scanlan made. In fact, it did not even bother to answer Weir's thirteen letters based on Scanlan's reports. And Weir did nothing about this. Once, early in the game, Weir considered the dusty condition of the mine so serious that he

requested the company to correct it within ten days; but there is no evidence that the company even replied.

This continued for nearly three years. And during the same period the federal government entered the picture. In 1941 Congress authorized the U.S. Bureau of Mines to make periodic inspections of coal mines. But the federal government had no enforcement power whatever; the inspections served only research. The first federal inspection of Centralia Mine No. 5 was made in September of 1942. In general, the federal recommendations duplicated Scanlan's— rock dusting, improving ventilation, wetting the coal to reduce dust—and the federal inspectors noted that "coal dust . . . at this mine is highly explosive, and would readily propagate an explosion." In all, they made 106 recommendations, including 33 "major" ones (a government official has defined a "major" hazard as one that "could . . . result in a disaster"). Four months passed before a copy of this report filtered through the administrative machinery at Washington and reached the Illinois Department at Springfield, but this mattered little: the Department did nothing anyway. Subsequent federal reports in 1943 and 1944 showed that the "major" recommendations had not been complied with. The federal bureau lacked the power to force compliance; the Illinois Department possessed the power but failed to act.

What of the men working in the mine during these three years? On November 4, 1944, on instructions from Local 52 at Centralia, William Rowekamp, the recording secretary, composed a letter to Medill: "At the present the condition of those roadways are very dirty and dusty . . . they are getting dangerous. . . . But the Coal Co. has ignored [Scanlan's recommendations]. And we beg your prompt action on this matter."

The Department received this letter November 6, and four days later Weir sent Inspector Scanlan to investigate. Scanlan reported immediately:

"The haulage roads in this mine are awful dusty, and much dust is kept in suspension all day. . . . The miners have complained to me . . . and I have wrote it up pretty strong on my inspection reports. . . . But to date they have not done any adequate sprinkling. . . . Today . . . [Superintendent Norman] Prudent said he would fix the water tank and sprinkle the roads within a week, said that he would have had this work done sooner, but that they have 20 to 30 men absent each day." (This last is a claim by the company that its cleanup efforts were handicapped by a wartime manpower shortage. This is controversial. Men of fifty-nine—the average wartime age at the mine—do not feel like spending weekends removing coal dust or rock dusting, a disagreeable task; winter colds caused absenteeism and miners are always laying off anyway. On the other hand, the company was interested in production and profits: as Mine Manager Brown has said, "In the winter you can sell all the coal you can get out. So you want top production, you don't want to stop to rock dust.")

At any rate, Rowekamp's complaint got results. On December 2, 1944, he wrote Scanlan: "Well I am proud to tell you that they have sprinkled the 18th North Entry & 21st So. Entry and the main haulage road. . . . Myself and the Members of Local Union #52 appreciate it very much what you have done for us." It is apparent from this first direct move by Local 52 that Scanlan was working pretty closely with the Local to get something done.

But by the end of that month, December 1944, the mine once more had become so dirty that Scanlan ended his regular inspection report, ". . . if necessary the mine should discontinue hoisting coal for a few days until the [cleanup] work can be done." But all Weir said to the company was the routine "The Department endorses. . . ."

Early in 1945 it appeared that something might be accomplished. Scanlan, emerging from his regular inspection, took the unusual step of telephoning Medill at Springfield. Medill told him to write him a letter so Scanlan did:

"The haulage roads in this mine are in a terrible condition. If a person did not see it he would not believe. . . . Two months ago . . . the local officers [of Local Union 52] told me that . . . if [the mine manager] did not clean the mine up they were going to prefer charges against him before the mining board and have his certificate canceled. I talked them out of it and told them I thought we could get them to clean up the mine. But on this inspection I find that practically nothing has been done. . . . The mine should discontinue hoisting coal . . . until the mine is placed in a safe condition. . . . The coal dust in this mine is highly explosive. . . ."

This stiff letter was duly stamped "Received" at Springfield on February 23, 1945. A few days earlier a bad report had come in from Federal Inspector Perz. And now at last Medill himself entered the pic-

ture. What did he do? The Superintendent at Centralia had told Scanlan that, in order to clean up the mine, he would have to stop producing coal, a step he was not empowered to take. So Medill bypassed him, forwarding Scanlan's letter and report to William P. Young, Bell & Zoller's operating vice-president at Chicago: "Dear Bill. . . . Please let me have any comments you wish to make. . . . Very kindest personal regards." From his quiet, well-furnished office near the top of the Bell Building overlooking Michigan Avenue, Young replied immediately to "Dear Bob" [Medill]: "As you know we have been working under a very severe handicap for the past months. The war demand for coal . . . we are short of men. . . . I am hopeful that the urgent demand of coal will ease up in another month so that we may have available both the time and labor to give proper attention to the recommendations of Inspector Scanlan. With kindest personal regards. . . ."

A week later, on March 7, 1945, Medill forwarded copies of this correspondence to Scanlan, adding: "I also talked with Mr. Young on the phone, and I feel quite sure that he is ready and willing. . . . I would suggest that you ask the mine committee [of Local 52] to be patient a little longer, inasmuch as the coal is badly needed at this time."

The miners told Scanlan they'd wait till the first of April but no longer. On March 14 Medill was to attend a safety meeting in Belleville. Scanlan went there to discuss Centralia No. 5 with him. According to Scanlan, "When I went up to his room he was surrounded with coal operators . . . all having whiskey, drinking, having a good time, and I couldn't talk to him then, and we attended the safety meeting [then] went . . . down to Otis Miller's saloon, and I stayed in the background drinking a few cokes and waited until the crowd thinned out, and went back up to his hotel room with him. . . . I told him that the mine was in such condition that if the dust became ignited that it would sweep from one end of the mine to the other and probably kill every man in the mine, and his reply to me was, 'We will just have to take that chance.' " (Medill has denied these words but not the meeting.)

On the first of April the president of Local Union 52 asked Scanlan to attend the Local's meeting on April 4. The miners complained that the company had not cleaned up the mine and, further, that one of the face bosses, or foreman, had fired explosive charges while the entire shift of men was in the mine. There can be little doubt that to fire explosives on-shift in a mine so dusty was to invite trouble—in fact, this turned out to be what later caused the disaster—and now in April 1945 the union filed charges against Mine Manager Brown, asking the State Mining Board to revoke his certificate of competency (this would cost him his job and prevent his getting another in Illinois as a mine manager). Rowekamp wrote up the charges: ". . . And being the Mine is so dry and dusty it could of caused an explosion. . . ."

Weir went to Centralia on April 17, 1945, but only to investigate the charges against Brown, not to inquire into the condition of the mine. He told the miners they should have taken their charges to the state's attorney. Nearly a month passed before, on May 11, Weir wrote a memorandum to the Mining Board saying that the company's superintendent had admitted the shots had been fired on-shift but that this was done "in an emergency" and it wouldn't happen again; and the Board refused to revoke Manager Brown's certificate.

Meanwhile, on April 12 and 13, Scanlan had made his regular inspection and found conditions worse than in February. He told the Superintendent: "Now, Norman, you claim Chicago won't give you the time to shut your mine down and clean it up. Now, I am going to get you some time," and he gave him the choice of shutting the mine down completely or spending three days a week cleaning up. The Superintendent, he said, replied that he didn't know, he'd have to "contact Chicago," but Scanlan replied: "I can't possibly wait for you to contact Chicago. It is about time that you fellows who operate the mines get big enough to operate your mines without contacting Chicago." So on Scanlan's recommendation the mine produced coal only four days a week and spent the remaining days cleaning up. For a time Scanlan was well satisfied with the results, but by June 25 he was again reporting excessive dust and Federal Inspector Perz was concurring: "No means are used to allay the dust." Following his October inspection Scanlan once more was moved to write a letter to Medill; but the only result was another routine letter from Weir to the company, unanswered.

Now, one must understand that, to be effective, both rock dusting and cleanup work must be maintained continuously. They were not at Centralia No. 5. By December of 1945 matters again came to a head. Scanlan wrote to Medill, saying that Local 52 wanted a sprinkling system installed to wet the coal,

that Mine Manager Brown had said he could not order so "unusual" an expenditure, and that Brown's superior, Superintendent Prudent, "would not talk to me about it, walked away and left me standing." And Local 52 again attempted to take matters into its own hands. At a special meeting on December 12 the membership voted to prefer charges against both Mine Manager Brown and Superintendent Prudent. Rowekamp's official charge, typed on stationery of the Local, was followed next day by a letter, written in longhand on two sheets of dime-store notepaper, and signed by 28 miners. . . . At Springfield this communication too was duly stamped "Received." And another Scanlan report arrived.

Confronted with so many documents, Medill called a meeting of the Mining Board on December 21. Moreover, he called Scanlan to Springfield and told him to go early to the Leland Hotel, the gathering place of Republican politicians, and see Ben H. Schull, a coal operator and one of the operators' two men on the Mining Board. In his hotel room, Schull (according to Scanlan) said he wanted to discuss privately Scanlan's report on Centralia No. 5, tried to persuade him to withdraw his recommendation of a sprinkling system, and, when Scanlan refused, told him, "you can come before the board." But when the Mining Board met in Medill's inner office, Scanlan was not called before it though he waited all day, and after the meeting he was told that the Board was appointing a special commission to go to Centralia and investigate.

On this commission were Weir, two state inspectors, and two members of the Mining Board itself, Schull and Murrell Reak. Reak, a miner himself, represented the United Mine Workers of America on the Mining Board. And Weir, too, owed his job to the UMWA but, oddly, he had worked for Bell & Zoller for twenty years before joining the Department, the last three as a boss, so his position was rather ambiguous. In fact, so unanimous were the rulings of the Mining Board that one cannot discern any management-labor cleavage at all but only what would be called in party politics bipartisan deals.

The commission had before it a letter from Superintendent Prudent and Manager Brown setting forth in detail the company's "absentee experience" and concluding with a veiled suggestion that the mine might be forced to close for good (once before, according to an inspector, the same company had abandoned a mine rather than go to the expense entailed in an inspector's safety recommendation). Weir wrote to Prudent, notifying him that the commission would visit Centralia on December 28 to investigate the charges against him and Brown; Medill wrote to the company's vice-president, Young, at Chicago ("You are being notified of this date so that you will have an opportunity to be present or designate some member of your staff to be present"); but Medill only told Rowekamp, "The committee has been appointed and after the investigation you will be advised of their findings and the action of the board"—he did not tell the Local when the commission would visit Centralia nor offer it opportunity to prove its charges.

Rowekamp, a motorman, recalls how he first learned of the special commission's visit. He was working in the mine and "Prudent told me to set out an empty and I did and they rode out." Prudent—remember, the commission was investigating charges against Prudent—led the commission through the mine. Rowekamp says, "They didn't see nothing. They didn't get back in the buggy runs where the dust was the worst; they stayed on the mainline." Even there they rode, they did not walk through the dust. Riding in a mine car, one must keep one's head down. In the washhouse that afternoon the men were angry. They waited a week or two, then wrote to Medill asking what had been done. On January 22, 1946, Medill replied: the Mining Board, adopting the views of the special commission, had found "insufficient evidence" to revoke the certificates of Prudent and Brown.

He did not elaborate. Next day, however, he sent to Scanlan a copy of the commission's report. It listed several important violations of the mining law: inadequate rock dusting, illegal practice in opening rooms, insufficient or improperly placed telephones, more than a hundred men working on a single split, or current, of air. In fact, the commission generally concurred with Scanlan, except that it did not emphasize dust nor recommend a sprinkling system. Thus in effect it overruled Scanlan on his sprinkling recommendation, a point to remember. It did find that the law was being violated yet it refused to revoke the certificates of the Superintendent and the Mine Manager, another point to remember. Weir has explained that the board felt that improvements requiring construction, such as splitting the airstream, would be made and that anyway "conditions there were no different than at most mines in the state." And this is

a refrain that the company and the Department repeated in extenuation after the disaster. But actually could anything be more damning? The mine was no worse than most others; the mine blew up; therefore any might blow up!

The miners at Centralia were not satisfied. "It come up at the meeting," Rowekamp recalls. Local 52 met two Wednesday nights a month in its bare upstairs hall. The officers sat at a big heavy table up front; the members faced them, sitting on folding chairs which the Local had bought second-hand from an undertaker. Attendance was heavier now than usual, the men were aroused, some were even telling their wives that the mine was dangerous. They wanted to do something. But what? The state had rebuffed them. Well, why did they not go now to the higher officials of their own union, the UMWA? Why not to John L. Lewis himself?

One of them has said, "You have to go through the real procedure to get to the right man, you got to start at the bottom and start climbing up, you see? If we write to Lewis, he'll refer us right back to Spud White." Spud White is Hugh White, the thick-necked president of the UMWA in Illinois (District 12), appointed by Lewis. Now, Lewis had suspended District 12's right to elect its own officers during the bloody strife of the early 1930's, when the members, disgusted with what they called his "dictator" methods and complaining of secret payrolls, expulsions, missing funds, stolen ballots, and leaders who turned up on operators' payrolls, had rebelled; in the end the Progressive Mine Workers was formed and Lewis retained tight control of the UMWA. A decade later the Illinois officers of UMWA demanded that he restore their self-government, but Lewis managed to replace them with his own men, including Spud White. By 1946 President White, a coal miner from the South, was consulting at high levels with Lewis, he was receiving $10,000 a year plus expenses (which usually equal salary), and he was maintaining a spacious house on a winding lane in the finest residential suburb of Springfield, a white house reached by a circular drive through weeping willows and evergreens.

Evidently the perplexed miners at Centralia already had appealed to District 12 for help, that is to White. Certainly Murrell Reak, the UMWA's man on the Mining Board and a close associate of White's, had asked Weir to furnish him with a copy of the findings of the special commission: "I want them so I may show the district UMWA. So they in turn may write Local Union down there, and show them that their charges are unfounded or rather not of a nature as to warrant the revocation of mine mgr. Certificate. . . ." Jack Ripon, the bulky vice-president of District 12 and White's right-hand man, said recently, "We heard there'd been complaints but we couldn't do a thing about it; it was up to the Mining Department to take care of it."

And yet in the past the UMWA has stepped in when the state failed to act. One unionist has said, "White could have closed that mine in twenty-four hours. All he'd have had to do was call up Medill and tell him he was going to pull every miner in the state if they didn't clean it up. It's the union's basic responsibility—if you don't protect your own wife and daughter, your neighbor down the street's not going to do it."

Perhaps the miners of Local 52 knew they must go it alone. They continued to address their official complaints to the State of Illinois. On February 26 Rowekamp wrote once more to Medill: "Dear Sir: At our regular meeting of Local Union 52. Motion made and second which carried for rec. secy. write you that the members of local union 52 are dissatisfied with the report of the special investigation commission. . . ." No answer. And so the members of Local 52 instructed Rowekamp to write to higher authority, to their Governor, Dwight H. Green.

It took him a long time. Elmer Moss kept asking if he'd finished it and Rowekamp recalls, "I'd tell him, Elmer, I can't do that fast, that's a serious letter, that'll take me a while." He wrote it out first in pencil and showed it to a couple of the boys and they thought it sounded fine. Then, sitting big and awkward at his cluttered little oak desk in the living room of his home outside town, he typed it, slowly and carefully—"anything important as that I take my time so I don't make mistakes, it looks too sloppified." He used the official stationery of the Local, bearing in one corner the device of the union—crossed shovels and picks— and in the other "Our Motto—Justice for One and All." He impressed upon it the official seal—"I can write a letter on my own hook but I dassen't use the seal without it's official"—and in the washhouse the Local officers signed it. Rowekamp made a special trip to the post office to mail it. It was a two-page letter saying, in part:

Dear Governor Green:
    We, the officers of Local Union No. 52, U. M.

W. of A., have been instructed by the members . . . to write a letter to you in protest against the negligence and unfair practices of your department of mines and minerals . . . we want you to know that this is not a protest against Mr. Driscoll Scanlan . . . the best inspector that ever came to our mine. . . . But your mining board will not let him enforce the law or take the necessary action to protect our lives and health. This protest is against the men above Mr. Scanlan in your department of mines and minerals. In fact, Governor Green this is a plea to you, to please save our lives, to please make the department of mines and minerals enforce the laws at the No. 5 mine of the Centralia Coal Co. . . . before we have a dust explosion at this mine like just happened in Kentucky and West Virginia. For the last couple of years the policy of the department of mines and minerals toward us has been one of ignoring us. [The letter then recited the story of the useless special commission.] We are writing you, Governor Green, because we believe you want to give the people an honest administration and that you do not know how unfair your mining department is toward the men in this mine. Several years ago after a disaster at Gillespie we seen your pictures in the papers going down in the mine to make a personal investigation of the accident. We are giving you a chance to correct the conditions at this time that may cause a much worse disaster. . . . We will appreciate an early personal reply from you, stating your position in regard to the above and the enforcement of the state mining laws.

The letter closed "Very respectfully yours" and was signed by Jake Schmidt, president; Rowekamp, recording secretary; and Thomas Bush and Elmer Moss, mine committee. Today, of these, only Rowekamp is alive; all the others were killed in the disaster they foretold.

And now let us trace the remarkable course of this letter at Springfield. It was stamped in red ink "Received March 9, 1946, Governor's Office." In his ornate thick-carpeted offices, Governor Green has three male secretaries (each of whom in turn has a secretary) and it was one of these, John William Chapman, that the "save our lives" letter, as it came to be called, was routed. Two days later Chapman dictated a memorandum to Medill: ". . . it is my opinion that the Governor may be subjected to very severe criticism in the event that the facts complained of are true and that as a result of this condition some serious accident occurs at the mine. Will you kindly have this complaint carefully investigated so I can call the report of the investigation to the Governor's attention at the same time I show him this letter?" Chapman fastened this small yellow memo to the miners' letter and sent both to Medill. Although Medill's office is only about sixty yards from the Governor's, the message consumed two days in traversing the distance.

The messenger arrived at the Department of Mines and Minerals at 9:00 A.M. on March 13 and handed the "save our lives" letter and Chapman's memorandum to Medill's secretary. She duly stamped both "Received" and handed them to Medill. He and Weir discussed the matter, then Medill sent the original letter back to the Governor's office and dictated his reply to Chapman, blaming the war, recounting the activities of the special commission, saying: "The complaint sounds a good deal worse than it really is. The present condition at the mine is not any different than it has been during the past ten or fifteen years. . . . I would suggest the Governor advise Local Union No. 52, U. M. W. of A., that he is calling the matter to the attention of the State Mining Board with instructions that it be given full and complete consideration at their next meeting."

This apparently satisfied Chapman for, in the Governor's name, he dictated a letter to Rowekamp and Schmidt: "I [*i.e.,* Governor Green] am calling your letter to the attention of the Director of the Department of Mines and Minerals with the request that he see that your complaint is taken up at the next meeting of the State Mining Board. . . ." This was signed with Governor Green's name but it is probable that Green himself never saw the "save our lives" letter until after the disaster more than a year later. Nor is there any evidence that the Mining Board ever considered the letter. In fact, nothing further came of it.

One of the most remarkable aspects of the whole affair was this: An aggrieved party (the miners) accused a second party (Medill's department) of acting wrongfully, and the higher authority to which it addressed its grievance simply, in effect, asked the accused if he were guilty and, when he replied he was not, dropped the matter. A logic, the logic of the administrative mind, attaches to Chapman's sending the complaint to the Department—the administrative mind has a pigeonhole for everything, matters which relate to law go to the Attorney General, matters which relate to mines go to the Department of Mines

and Minerals, and that is that—but it is scarcely a useful logic when one of the agencies is itself accused of malfunction. Apparently it did not occur to Chapman to consult Inspector Scanlan or to make any other independent investigation.

And Jack Ripon, Spud White's second-in-command at the District UMWA, said recently, "If I get a letter here I turn it over to the department that's supposed to take care of it, and the same with Governor Green—he got some damn bad publicity he shouldn't have had, he can't know everything that's going on." Ripon's sympathy with Green is understandable—he must have known how Green felt, for he and Spud White received a copy of the same letter. Ripon says, "Oh, we got a copy of it. But it wasn't none of ours, it didn't tell us to do anything. So our hands was tied. What'd we do with it? I think we gave it to Reak." Perhaps Murrell Reak, the UMWA's man on the Mining Board, felt he already had dealt with this matter (it was Reak who, to Scanlan's astonishment, had joined the other members of the special commission in upholding the Superintendent and Mine Manager in their violations of the law and then had been so anxious to help White convince the members of Local 52 "that their charges are unfounded"). At any rate, Reak apparently did not call the Board's attention to the "save our lives" letter, even though it was a local of his own union which felt itself aggrieved. And White took no action either.

As for Medill, on the day he received the letter he called Scanlan to Springfield and, says Scanlan, "severely reprimanded" him. According to Scanlan, Medill "ordered me to cut down the size of my inspection report," because Medill thought that such long reports might alarm the miners, "those damn hunks" who couldn't read English (Medill denied the phrase); but Scanlan took this order to mean that Medill wanted him to "go easy" on the operators—"it is the same thing as ordering you to pass up certain things." And one day during this long controversy, Medill buttonholed Scanlan's political sponsor in a corridor of the Statehouse and said he intended to fire Scanlan; Scanlan's sponsor refused to sanction it and but for this, Scanlan was convinced, he would surely have lost his job.

But now hundreds of miles away larger events were occurring which were to affect the fate of the miners at Centralia. In Washington, D.C., John L. Lewis and the nation's bituminous coal operators failed to reach an agreement and the miners struck, and on May 21, 1946, President Truman ordered the mines seized for government operation. Eight days later Lewis and Julius A. Krug, Secretary of the Interior, signed the famous Krug-Lewis Agreement. Despite strenuous protests by the operators, this agreement included a federal safety code. It was drawn up by the Bureau of Mines (a part of the U.S. Department of the Interior). And now for the first time in history the federal government could exercise police power over coal mine safety.

Thus far the efforts of the miners of Local 52 to thread the administrative maze in their own state had produced nothing but a snowfall of memoranda, reports, letters, and special findings. Let us now observe this new federal machinery in action. We shall learn nothing about how to prevent a disaster but we may learn a good deal about the administrative process.

"Government operation of the mines" meant simply that the operators bossed their own mines for their own profit as usual but the UMWA had a work contract with the government, not the operators. To keep the 2,500 mines running, Secretary Krug created a new agency, the Coal Mines Administration. CMA was staffed with only 245 persons, nearly all naval personnel ignorant of coal mining. Theirs was paper work. For technical advice they relied upon the Bureau of Mines plus a handful of outside experts. More than two months passed before the code was put into effect, on July 29, 1946, and not until November 4 did Federal Inspector Perz reach Centralia to make his first enforceable inspection of Centralia No. 5. Observe, now, the results.

After three days at the mine, Perz went home and wrote out a "preliminary report" on a mimeographed form, listing 13 "major violations" of the safety code. He mailed this to the regional office of the Bureau of Mines at Vincennes, Indiana. There it was corrected for grammar, spelling, etc., and typed; copies then were mailed out to the Superintendent of the mine (to be posted on the bulletin board), the CMA in Washington, the CMA's regional office at Chicago, the District 12 office of the UMWA at Springfield, the UMWA international headquarters at Washington, the Bureau of Mines in Washington, and the Illinois Department at Springfield. While all this was going on, Perz was at home, preparing his final report, a lengthy document listing 57 violations of the safety code, 21 of them major and 36 minor. This handwritten final report likewise went to the Bureau at Vincennes where it was corrected, typed, and forwarded to the Bureau's office in College Park, Maryland. Here

the report was "reviewed," then sent to the Director of the Bureau at Washington. He made any changes he deemed necessary, approved it, and ordered it processed. Copies were then distributed to the same seven places that had received the preliminary report, except that the UMWA at Springfield received two copies so that it could forward one to Local 52. (All this was so complicated that the Bureau devised a "flow sheet" to keep track of the report's passage from hand to hand.)

We must not lose sight of the fact that in the end everybody involved was apprised of Perz's findings: that the Centralia Company was violating the safety code and that hazards resulted. The company, the state, and the union had known this all along and done nothing, but what action now did the new enforcing agency take, the CMA?

Naval Captain N. H. Collison, the Coal Mines Administrator, said that the copy of the inspector's preliminary report was received at his office in Washington "by the head of the Production and Operations Department of my headquarters staff . . . Lieutenant Commander Stull. . . . Lieutenant Commander Stull would review such a report, discuss the matter with the Bureau of Mines as to the importance of the findings, and then . . . await the final report"—unless the preliminary report showed that "imminent danger" existed, in which case he would go immediately to Captain Collison and, presumably, take "immediate action." And during all this activity in Washington, out in Chicago at the CMA's area office a Captain Yates also "would receive a copy of the report. His duty would be to acquaint himself with the findings there. If there was a red check mark indicating it fell within one of the three categories which I shall discuss later, he would detail a man immediately to the mine. If it indicated imminent danger . . . he would move immediately." The three categories deemed sufficiently important to be marked with "a red check mark" were all major hazards but the one which killed 111 men at Centralia No. 5 was not among them.

These, of course, were only CMA's first moves as it bestirred itself. But to encompass all its procedures is almost beyond the mind of man. Let us skip a few and see what actually resulted. The CMA in Washington received Perz's preliminary report November 14. Eleven days later it wrote to the company ordering it to correct one of the 13 major violations Perz found (why it said nothing about the others is not clear). On November 26 the CMA received Perz's final report and on November 29 it again wrote to the company, ordering it to correct promptly *all* violations and sending copies of the directive to the Bureau of Mines and the UMWA. Almost simultaneously it received from Superintendent Niermann a reply to its first order (Niermann had replaced Prudent, who had left the company's employ): "Dear Sir: In answer to your CMA8-gz of November 25, 1946, work has been started to correct the violation of article 5, section 3c, of the Federal Mine Safety Code, but has been discontinued, due to . . . a strike. . . ." This of course did not answer the CMA's second letter ordering correction of all 57 violations, nor was any answer forthcoming, but not until two months later, on January 29, 1947, did the CMA repeat its order and tell the company to report its progress by February 14.

This brought a reply from the company official who had been designated "operating manager" during the period of government operation, H. F. McDonald. McDonald, whose office was in Chicago, had risen to the presidency of the Centralia Coal Company and of the Bell & Zoller Coal Company through the sales department; after the Centralia disaster he told a reporter, "Hell, I don't know anything about a coal mine." Now he reported to CMA that "a substantial number of reported violations have been corrected and others are receiving our attention and should be corrected as materials and manpower become available." For obvious reasons, CMA considered this reply inadequate and on February 21 told McDonald to supply detailed information. Three days later McDonald replied ("Re file CMA81-swr"): He submitted a detailed report—he got it from Vice-President Young, who got it from the new General Superintendent, Walter J. Johnson—but McDonald told the CMA that this report was a couple of weeks old and he promised to furnish further details as soon as he could get them. The CMA on March 7 acknowledged this promise but before any other correspondence arrived to enrich file CMA81-swr, the mine blew up.

Now, the Krug-Lewis Agreement set up two methods of circumventing this cumbersome administrative machinery. If Inspector Perz had found what the legalese of the Agreement called "imminent danger," he could have ordered the men removed from the mine immediately (this power was weakened since it

was also vested in the Coal Mines Administrator, the same division of authority that hobbled the state enforcers). But Perz did not report "imminent danger." And indeed how could he? The same hazardous conditions had obtained for perhaps twenty years and the mine hadn't blown up. The phrase is stultifying.

In addition, the Krug-Lewis Agreement provided for a safety committee of miners, selected by each local union and empowered to inspect the mine, to make safety recommendations to the management, and, again in case of "an immediate danger," to order the men out of the mine (subject to CMA review). But at Centralia No. 5 several months elapsed before Local 52 so much as appointed a safety committee, and even after the disaster the only surviving member of the committee didn't know what his powers were. The UMWA District officers at Springfield had failed to instruct their Locals in the rights which had been won for them. And confusion was compounded because two separate sets of safety rules were in use— the federal and the state—and in some instances one was the more stringent, in other instances, the other.

Meanwhile another faraway event laid another burden upon the men in the mine. John L. Lewis' combat with Secretary Krug. It ended, as everyone knows, in a federal injunction sought at President Truman's order and upheld by the U.S. Supreme Court, which forbade Lewis to order his miners to strike while the government was operating the mines. (Subsequently Lewis and the UMWA were fined heavily.) The members of Local 52 thought, correctly or not, that the injunction deprived them of their last weapon in their fight to get the mine cleaned up—a wildcat strike. A leader of Local 52 has said, "Sure we could've wildcatted it—and we'd have had the Supreme Court and the government and the whole public down on our necks."

The miners tried the state once more: Medill received a letter December 10, 1946, from an individual miner who charged that the company's mine examiner (a safety man) was not doing what the law required. Earlier Medill had ignored Scanlan's complaint about this but now he sent a department investigator, who reported that the charges were true and that Mine Manager Brown knew it, that Superintendent Niermann promised to consult Vice-President Young in Chicago, that other hazards existed, including dust. Weir wrote a routine letter and this time Niermann replied: The examiner would do his job properly. He said nothing about dust. This letter and one other about the same time, plus Young's earlier equivocal response to Medill's direct appeal, are the only company compliance letters on record.

There was yet time for the miners to make one more try. On February 24, 1947, the safety committee, composed of three miners, wrote a short letter to the Chicago area office of the Coal Mines Administration: "The biggest grievance is dust. . . ." It was written in longhand by Paul Compers (or so it is believed: Compers and one of the two other committee members were killed in the disaster a month later) and Compers handed it to Mine Manager Brown on February 27. But Brown did not forward it to the CMA; in fact he did nothing at all about it.

And now almost at the last moment, only six days before the mine blew up, some wholly new facts transpired. Throughout this whole history one thing has seemed inexplicable: the weakness of the pressure put on the company by Medill's Department of Mines and Minerals. On March 19, 1947, the St. Louis *Post-Dispatch* broke a story that seemed to throw some light upon it. An Illinois coal operator had been told by the state inspector who inspected his mine that Medill had instructed him to solicit money for the Republican Chicago mayoralty campaign. And soon more facts became known about this political shakedown.

Governor Dwight H. Green, a handsome, likeable politician, had first made his reputation as the young man who prosecuted Al Capone. By 1940 he looked like the white hope of Illinois Republicans. Campaigning for the governorship, Green promised to rid the state of the Democratic machine ("there will never be a Green machine"). He polled more votes in Illinois than Roosevelt; national Republican leaders began to watch him. Forthwith he set about building one of the most formidable machines in the nation. This task, together with the concomitant plans of Colonel Robert R. McCormick of the Chicago *Tribune* and others to make him President or Vice-President, has kept him occupied ever since. He has governed but little, permitting subordinates to run things. Reelected in 1944, he reached the peak of his power in 1946 when his machine succeeded in reducing the control of the Democratic machine over Chicago. Jubilant, Governor Green handpicked a ward leader to run for mayor in April of 1947 and backed him hard.

And it was only natural that Green's henchmen helped. Among these was Medill. "Somebody," says Medill, told him he was expected to raise "$15,000

or $20,000." On January 31, 1947, he called all his mine inspectors to the state mine rescue station in Springfield (at state expense), and told them—according to Inspector Scanlan who was present—that the money must be raised among the coal operators "and that he had called up four operators the previous day and two of them had already come through with a thousand dollars . . . and that he was going to contact the major companies, and we was to contact the independent companies and the small companies." Medill's version varied slightly: he said he told the inspectors that, as a Republican, he was interested in defeating the Democrats in Washington and Chicago, that if they found anybody of like mind it would be all right to tell them where to send their money, that all contributions must be voluntary.

After the meeting Scanlan felt like resigning but he thought perhaps Governor Green did not know about the plan and he recalled that once he had received a letter from Green (as did all state employees) asking his aid in giving the people an honest administration: Scanlan had replied to the Governor "that I had always been opposed to corrupt, grafting politicians and that I wasn't going to be one myself; and I received a nice acknowledgement . . . the Governor . . . told me that it was such letters as mine that gave him courage to carry on. . . ." Scanlan solicited no contributions from the coal operators.

But other inspectors did, and so did a party leader in Chicago. So did Medill: he says that his old friend David H. Devonald, operating vice-president of the huge Peabody Coal Company, gave him $1,000 and John E. Jones, a leading safety engineer, contributed $50 (Jones works for another of the Big Six operators and of him more later). No accounting ever has been made of the total collected. The shakedown did not last long. According to Medill, another of Governor Green's "close advisers" told Medill that the coal operators were complaining that he and his inspectors were putting pressure on them for donations and if so he'd better stop it. He did, at another conference of the inspectors on March 7.

Since no Illinois law forbids a company or an individual to contribute secretly to a political campaign we are dealing with a question of political morality, not legality. The Department of Mines and Minerals long has been a political agency. An inspector is a political appointee and during campaigns he is expected to contribute personally, tack up candidates' posters, and haul voters to the polls. Should he refuse, his local political boss would have him fired. (Soliciting money from the coal operators, however, apparently was something new for inspectors.) Today sympathetic Springfield politicians say: "Medill was just doing what every other department was doing and always has done, but he got a tough break." But one must point out that Medill's inspectors were charged with safeguarding lives, a more serious duty than that of most state employees, and that in order to perform this duty they had to police the coal operators, and that it was from these very operators that Medill suggested they might obtain money. A United States Senator who investigated the affair termed it "reprehensible."

What bearing, now, did this have on the Centralia disaster? Nobody, probably, collected from the Centralia Coal Company. But the shakedown is one more proof—stronger than most—that Governor Green's department had reason to stay on friendly terms with the coal operators when, as their policemen, it should have been aloof. As a miner at Centralia said recently: "If a coal company gives you a thousand dollars, they're gonna expect something in return."

Here lies Green's responsibility—not that, through a secretary's fumble, he failed to act on the miners' appeal to "save our lives" but rather that, while the kingmakers were shunting him around the nation making speeches, back home his loyal followers were busier building a rich political machine for him than in administering the state for him. Moreover, enriching the Green machine dovetailed nicely with the personal ambitions of Medill and others, and Green did not restrain them. By getting along with his old friends, the wealthy operators, Medill enhanced his personal standing. Evidence exists that Bell & Zoller had had a hand in getting him appointed Director, and remember, Weir had worked as a Bell & Zoller boss. By nature Medill was no zealous enforcer of laws. As for the inspectors, few of them went out of their way to look for trouble; some inspectors after leaving the Department have obtained good jobs as coal company executives. Anyway, as one inspector has said, "If you tried to ride 'em, they'd laugh at you and say, 'Go ahead, I'll just call up Springfield.' " As one man has said, "It was a cozy combination that worked for everybody's benefit, everybody except the miners." And the miners' man on the Board, Murrell Reak of the UMWA, did not oppose the combination. Nor did Green question it.

As the Chicago campaign ground to a close, down at Centralia on March 18 Federal Inspector Perz was making another routine inspection. General Superintendent Johnson told him the company had ordered pipe for a sprinkler system months earlier but it hadn't arrived, "that there would be a large expenditure involved there . . . they had no definite arrangements just yet . . . but he would take it up with the higher officials of the company" in Chicago. Scanlan and Superintendent Niermann were there too; they stayed in the bare little mine office, with its rickety furniture and torn window shades, till 7:30 that night. No rock dusting had been done for nearly a year but now the company had a carload of rock dust underground and Scanlan got the impression it would be applied over the next weekend. (It wasn't.) Perz, too, thought Johnson "very conscientious . . . very competent." Scanlan typed out his report—he had resorted wearily to listing a few major recommendations and adding that previous recommendations "should be complied with"—and mailed it to Springfield. Perz went home and wrote out his own report, acknowledging that 17 hazards had been corrected but making 52 recommendations most of which he had made in November (the company and the CMA were still corresponding over that November report). Perz finished writing on Saturday morning and mailed the report to the Vincennes office, which presumably began processing it Monday.

The wheels had been turning at Springfield, too, and on Tuesday, March 25, Weir signed a form letter to Brown setting forth Scanlan's latest recommendations: "The Department endorses. . . ." But that day, at 3:26 P.M., before the outgoing-mail box in the Department was emptied, Centralia Mine No. 5 blew up. . . .

The last of the bodies was recovered at 5:30 A.M. on the fifth day after the explosion. On "Black Monday" the flag on the new city hall flew at half staff and all the businesses in town closed. Already the funerals had begun, 111 of them. John L. Lewis cried that the 111 were "murdered by the criminal negligence" of Secretary Krug and declared a national six-day "mourning period" during this Holy Week, and though some said he was only achieving by subterfuge what the courts had forbidden him—a strike and defiance of Krug—nonetheless he made the point that in the entire nation only two soft coal mines had been complying with the safety code; and so Krug closed the mines.

Six separate investigations began, two to determine what had happened, and four to find out why. Federal and state experts agreed, in general, that the ignition probably had occurred at the extreme end, or face, of the First West Entry, that it was strictly a coal-dust explosion, that the dust probably was ignited by an explosive charge which had been tamped and fired in a dangerous manner—fired by an open-flame fuse, tamped with coal dust—and that the resulting local explosion was propagated by coal dust throughout four working sections of the mine, subsiding when it reached rock-dusted areas. . . .

And what resulted from all the investigations into the Centralia disaster? The Washington County Grand Jury returned no-bills—that is, refused to indict Inspector Scanlan and five company officials ranging upward in authority through Brown, Niermann, Johnson, Young, and McDonald. The Grand Jury did indict the Centralia Coal Company, as a corporation, on two counts of "willful neglect" to comply with the mining law—failing to rock dust and working more than 100 men on a single split of air—and it also indicted Medill and Weir for "palpable omission of duty." The company pleaded *nolo contendere*—it did not wish to dispute the charge—and was fined the maximum: $300 on each count, a total of $1,000 (or less than $10 per miner's life lost). The law also provides a jail sentence of up to six months but of course you can't put a corporation in jail.

At this writing the indictments against Medill and Weir are still pending, and amid interesting circumstances. Bail for Medill was provided by Charles E. Jones, John W. Spence, G. C. Curtis, and H. B. Thompson; and all of these men, oddly enough, are connected with the oil and gas division of the Department from which Medill was fired. And one of them is also one of Medill's defense attorneys. But this is not all. Medill and Weir filed a petition for a change of venue, supported by numerous affidavits of Washington County residents that prejudice existed. These affidavits were collected by three inspectors for the oil and gas division. They succeeded in getting the trial transferred to Wayne County, which is dominated by a segment of Governor Green's political organization led locally by one of these men, Spence. Not in recent memory in Illinois has the conviction of a Department head on a similar charge been sustained, and there is little reason to suppose that Medill or Weir will be convicted. Medill performed an act of great political loyalty when he shouldered most of the blame at Centralia, in effect stopping the investi-

gation before it reached others above him, and this may be his reward.

Why did nobody close the Centralia mine before it exploded? A difficult question. Medill's position (and some investigators') was that Inspector Scanlan could have closed it. And, legally, this is true: The mining law expressly provided that an inspector could close a mine which persisted in violating the law. But inspectors have done so very rarely, only in exceptional circumstances, and almost always in consultation with the Department. Scanlan felt that had he closed the Centralia mine Medill simply would have fired him and appointed a more tractable inspector. Moreover, the power to close was not his exclusively: it also belonged to the Mining Board. (And is not this divided authority one of the chief factors that produced the disaster?) Robert Weir has said, "We honestly didn't think the mine was dangerous enough to close." This seems fantastic, yet one must credit it. For if Scanlan really had thought so, surely he would have closed it, even though a more pliable inspector reopened it. So would the federal authorities, Medill, or the company itself. And surely the miners would not have gone to work in it.

Governor Green's own fact-finding committee laid blame for the disaster upon the Department, Scanlan, and the company. The Democrats in the Illinois joint legislative committee submitted a minority report blaming the company, Medill, Weir, and Green's administration for "the industrial and political crime . . ."; the Republican majority confessed itself unable to fix blame. After a tremendous pulling and hauling by every special interest, some new state legislation was passed as a result of the accident, but nothing to put teeth into the laws: violations still are misdemeanors (except campaign solicitation by inspectors, a felony); it is scarcely a serious blow to a million-dollar corporation to be fined $1,000. Nor does the law yet charge specific officers of the companies—rather than the abstract corporations—with legal responsibility, so it is still easy for a company official to hide behind a nebulous chain of command reaching up to the stratosphere of corporate finance in Chicago or St. Louis. It is hard to believe that compliance with any law can be enforced unless violators can be jailed.

As for the Congress of the United States, it did next to nothing. The Senate subcommittee recommended that Congress raise safety standards and give the federal government power to enforce that standard—

"Immediate and affirmative action is imperative." But Congress only ordered the Bureau of Mines to report next session on whether mine operators were complying voluntarily with federal inspectors' recommendations. . . .

After the Centralia disaster each man responsible had his private hell, and to escape it each found his private scapegoat—the wartime manpower shortage, the material shortage, another official, the miners, or, in the most pitiable cases, "human frailty." Surely a strange destiny took Dwight Green from a federal courtroom where, a young crusader, he overthrew Capone to a hotel in Centralia where, fifteen years older, he came face to face with William Rowekamp, who wanted to know why Green had done nothing about the miners' plea to "save our lives." But actually responsibility here transcends individuals. The miners at Centralia, seeking somebody who would heed their conviction that their lives were in danger, found themselves confronted with officialdom, a huge organism scarcely mortal. The State Inspector, the Federal Inspector, the State Board, the Federal CMA, the company officials—all these forever invoked "higher authority," they forever passed from hand to hand a stream of memoranda and letters, decisions and laws and rulings, and they lost their own identities. As one strives to fix responsibility for the disaster, again and again one is confronted, as were the miners, not with any individual but with a host of individuals fused into a vast, unapproachable, insensate organism. Perhaps this immovable juggernaut is the true villain in the piece. Certainly all those in authority were too remote from the persons whose lives they controlled. And this is only to confess once more that in making our society complex we have made it unmanageable.

## Chapter 1 Review Questions

1. How did Woodrow Wilson justify the creation of the new field of public administration? Why does he view public administration as being so critical to the future of the United States? Do you agree? What does Wilson conclude are the best ways to develop this new field? Are these ideas still valid?
2. Why does Wilson stress throughout his essay the importance of finding the appropriate relationship between democracy and public administration? What does he mean by that? For example?
3. Did the case, "The Blast in Centralia No. 5," help you to formulate your own view of what the scope and purpose of the field are or should be today? Does the case contradict or support the conclusions about the importance of this field made in the Wilson essay?
4. Based on your reading of the case, what do you see as the central causes of the tragedy in "The Blast in Centralia No. 5"? Why did these causes develop?
5. What reforms would you recommend to prevent the tragedy from reoccurring elsewhere? How could such reforms be implemented?
6. Based on your analysis of "The Blast in Centralia No. 5," can you generalize about the importance of public administration for society? Can you list some of the pros *and* cons of having a strong and effective administrative system to perform essential services in society?

## Key Terms

public administration
politics-administration dichotomy

public opinion
civil service

## Suggestions for Further Reading

The seminal book on the origins and growth of public administration in America remains Dwight Waldo, *The Administrative State: A Study of the Political Theory of American Public Administration* (New York: Ronald Press, 1948), which has been reissued in 1984, with a new preface, by Holmes and Meier Publishers. For other writings by Waldo, see "The Administrative State Revisited," *Public Administration Review,* 25 (March 1965), pp. 5–37, and *The Enterprise of Public Administration: A Summary View* (Navato, Calif.: Chandler and Sharp Publishers, 1980). For a helpful commentary on Waldo's ideas and career, see Brack Brown and Richard J. Stillman II, *A Search for Public Administration* (College Station: Texas A&M University Press, 1986). Also for insightful review of Herbert Simon's influence on the field, read the entire issue of *Public Administration Quarterly* (Fall 1988). For two excellent reassessments of Woodrow Wilson and his influence on the field, read: Paul P. Van Riper, ed., *The Wilson Influence on Public Administration: From Theory to Practice* (Washington, D.C.: American Society for Public Administration, 1990); and Daniel W. Martin, "The Fading Legacy of Woodrow Wilson," *Public Administration Review* (March/April 1988), pp. 631–636.

Much can be learned from the writings of important contributors to the field, like Woodrow Wilson, Frederick Taylor, Luther Gulick, Louis Brownlow, Herbert Simon, and Charles Lindblom. For an excellent collection of many of those classic writings with insightful commentary, see Frederick C. Mosher, ed., *Basic Literature of American Public Administration 1787–1950* (New York: Holmes and Meier, 1981), and for a recent selection of key theorists, read Frederick S. Lane, ed., *Current Issues in Public Administration,* Fourth Edition (New York: St. Martin's Press, 1990). Equally valuable is the four-volume history of public

administration prior to 1900 by Leonard D. White: *The Federalists* (1948); *The Jeffersonians* (1951); *The Jacksonians* (1954); and *The Republican Era* (1958), all published by Macmillan. Some of the important books that document the rise of public administration in the twentieth century are Jane Dahlberg, *The New York Bureau of Municipal Research* (New York: New York University Press, 1966); Robert H. Wiebe, *The Search for Order, 1877–1920* (New York: Hill & Wang, 1967); Don K. Price, *America's Unwritten Constitution* (Baton Rouge, La.: Louisiana State University Press, 1983); John A. Rohr, *To Run a Constitution: The Legitimacy of the Administrative State* (Lawrence: University of Kansas Press, 1986); Barry Karl, *Executive Reorganization and Reform in the New Deal* (Cambridge, Mass.: Harvard University Press, 1963); and Stephen Skowronek, *Building a New American State: The Expansion of National Administrative Capacities, 1877–1910* (New York: Cambridge University Press, 1982). Because Frederick Taylor was so critical to the early development of the field, a noteworthy new biography of his life and work is Hindy Lauer Schachter, *Frederick Taylor and the Public Administration Community: A Reevaluation* (Albany, N.Y.: State University of New York Press, 1990). For a broader biographical treatment of the field's major figures, see Brian R. Fry, *Mastering Public Administration: From Max Weber to Dwight Waldo* (Chatham, N.Y.: Chatham House, 1989).

Numerous shorter interpretive essays on the development of the field include Herbert Kaufman, "Emerging Conflicts in the Doctrines of Public Administration," *American Political Science Review* (December 1956), pp. 1057–1073; David H. Rosenbloom, "Public Administration Theory and the Separation of Powers," *Public Administration Review,* 43 (May/June 1983), pp. 213–227; Laurence J.

O'Toole, Jr., "Harry F. Byrd, Sr. and the New York Bureau of Municipal Research: Lessons from an Ironic Alliance," *Public Administration Review,* 46 (March/April 1986), pp. 113–123; Lynton K. Caldwell, "Novus Ordo Seclorum: The Heritage of American Public Administration," and Barry Karl, "Public Administration and American History: A Century of Professionalism"—both appeared in *Public Administration Review,* 36 (September/October 1976), pp. 476–505. Several excellent essays are also found in Frederick C. Mosher, ed., *American Public Administration: Past, Present, Future* (University, Ala.: University of Alabama Press, 1975); Ralph Clark Chandler, ed., *A Centennial History of the American Administrative State* (New York: Free Press, 1987); as well as the bicentennial issue of the *Public Administration Review* (January/February 1987), entitled, "The American Constitution and Administrative State," edited by Richard J. Stillman II.

The past decade has witnessed an outpouring of new, rich, and diverse perspectives on what public administration is and ought to be. Among the recent, more challenging points of view, which attempt to "reformulate the basics" of the field, are: James A. Stever, *The End of Public Administration: Problems of the Profession in the Post-Progressive Era* (Ardley-on-the-Hudson, N.Y.: Transnational Publishers, 1987); "Minnowbrook II," by H. George Frederickson and Richard T Mayer, eds., *Public Administration Review* (March/April 1989), entire issue; Naomi B. Lynn and Aaron Wildavsky, eds., *Public Administration: The State of the Discipline* (Chatham, N.J.: Chatham House, 1990); Gary L Wamsley, et al., *Refounding Public Administration* (Newberry Park, Calif.: Sage, 1990); Henry D. Kass and Bayard L. Catren, eds., *Images and Identities in Public Administration* (Newberry Park, Calif.: Sage, 1990); and Richard J. Stillman II, *Preface to Public Administration: A Search for Themes and Direction* (New York: St. Martin's Press, 1991). Also, the entire 50th anniversary issue of the *Public Administration Review* (March/April, 1990) contains several fine reflective essays on the current status of the field. For useful comprehensive guides to public administration literature, see Howard E. McCurdy, *Public Administration: A Bibliographic Guide to the Literature* (New York: Marcel Dekker, 1986), as well as Daniel W. Martin, *The Guide to the Foundations of Public Administration* (New York: Marcel Dekker, 1989).

# PART ONE

The Environment of Public
Administration: The Pattern of Public
Administration in America

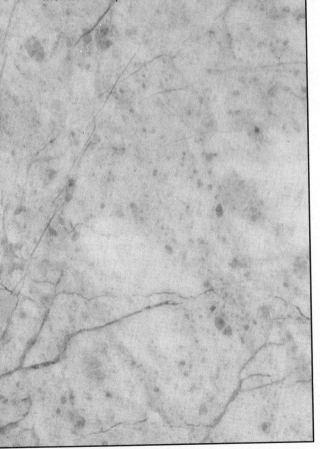

Public administrators are surrounded by multiple environments that serve to shape decisively what they do and how well (or how poorly) they do it. Part One discusses the major conceptual ideas about the key environmental factors that profoundly influence the nature, scope, and direction of contemporary public administration. Each reading in Part One outlines one of these important environmental concepts, and each case study illustrates that concept. The significant environmental concepts featured in Part One include:

**CHAPTER 2**
***The Formal Structure: The Concept of Bureaucracy*** What are the formal elements of the bureaucratic structure that serve as core building blocks in the administrative processes?

**CHAPTER 3**
***The General Environment: The Concept of Ecology*** How does the general administrative environment significantly influence the formulation, implementation, and outcomes of public programs?

**CHAPTER 4**
***The Political Environment: The Concept of Administrative Power*** What is the nature of the political landscape in which public agencies operate, and why is administrative power key to their survival, growth, or demise?

**CHAPTER 5**
***Federalism, Intergovernmental Relations, and Public Administration: The Concept of "Madison's Middle Ground"*** Why do intergovernmental relationships create complex problems for modern American public administrators? What is the structure of these relationships in the 1990s?

**CHAPTER 6**
***Internal Dynamics: The Concept of the Informal Group*** How does the internal environment of organizations affect the "outcomes" of the administrative processes? How can administrators assess and cope with "internal groups?"

**CHAPTER 7**
***Key Decision Makers in Public Administration: The Concept of the Professional State*** Who are the key decision makers in public agencies today? Why are they so vital to shaping public policy?

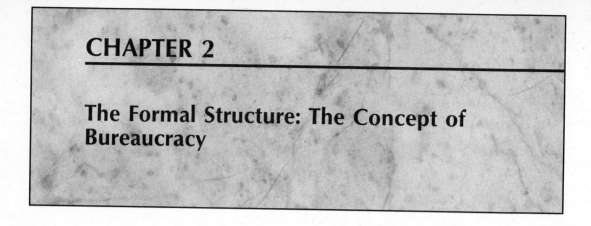

# CHAPTER 2

# The Formal Structure: The Concept of Bureaucracy

*Under normal conditions, the power position of a fully developed bureaucracy is always overtowering. The 'political master' finds himself in the position of the 'dilettante' who stands opposite the 'expert.' . . .*

*Max Weber*

## READING 2

## Introduction

To most Americans, "bureaucracy" is a fighting word. Few things are more disliked than bureaucracy, few occupations held in lower esteem than the bureaucrat. Both are subjected to repeated criticism in the press and damned regularly by political soap box orators and ordinary citizens. "Inefficiency," "red tape," "stupidity," "secrecy," "smugness," "aggressiveness," and "self-interest" are only a few of the emotionally charged words used to castigate bureaucrats.

There may be considerable truth to our dim view of bureaucrats. We also may be justified in venting our spleens occasionally at the irritating aspects of bureaucracy that arise almost daily—we may even experience a healthy catharsis in the process. But this understandably testy outlook should not prevent us from grasping the central importance and meaning of this phenomenon of bureaucracy.

From the standpoint of public administration and social science literature in general, "bureaucracy" means much more than the various bothersome characteristics of modern organizations. The term in serious administrative literature denotes the general, formal structural elements of a type of human organization, particularly a governmental organization. In this sense bureaucracy has both good *and* bad qualities; it is a neutral term rather than one referring to only the negative traits of organizations. It is a lens through which we may dispassionately view what Carl Friedrich has appropriately tagged "the core of modern government."

The German social scientist, Max Weber (1864–1920), is generally acknowledged to have developed the most comprehensive classic formulation of the characteristics of bureaucracy. Weber not only pioneered ideas about bureaucracy but ranged across a whole spectrum of historical, political, economic, and social thought. As Reinhard Bendix observed, Weber was "like a man of the Renaissance who took in all humanity for his province." In his study of Hindu religion, Old Testament theology, ancient Roman land surveying, Junker politics, medieval trading companies, and the Chinese civil service, he sought to analyze objectively the nature of human institutions and to show how ideas are linked with the evolution of political, economic, and social systems. One of his best works, *The Protestant Ethic and the Spirit of Capitalism,* established the critical intellectual ties between the rise of Protestantism and capitalism in the sixteenth and seventeenth centuries. He constantly pressed for answers to enormously complex problems. What is the interplay between ideas and institutions? What distinguishes the Western culture and its ideas? Why has a particular society evolved the way it has?

We cannot summarize here the numerous ideas formulated by Max Weber's fertile mind, but we can examine a few aspects of his thought that bear directly on his conception of bureaucracy. Weber believed that civilization evolved from the primitive and mystical to the rational and complex. He thought that human nature progressed slowly from primitive religions and mythologies to an increasing theoretical and technical sophistication. World evolution was a one-way street in Weber's nineteenth-century view: he visualized a progressive "demystification" of humanity and humanity's ideas about the surrounding environment.

In keeping with his demystification view of progress, Weber describes three "ideal-types" of authority that explain why individuals throughout history have obeyed their rulers. One of the earliest, the "traditional" authority of primitive societies, rested on the established belief in the sanctity of tradition. Because a family of rulers has always ruled, people judge them to be just and right and obey them. Time, precedent, and tradition gave rulers their legitimacy in the eyes of the ruled.

A second ideal-type of authority, according to Weber, is "charismatic" authority, which is based on the personal qualities and the attractiveness of leaders. Charismatic figures are self-appointed leaders who inspire belief because of their extraordinary, almost superhuman, qualifications. Military leaders, warrior chiefs, popular party leaders, and founders of religions are examples of individuals whose heroic feats or miracles attract followers.

Weber postulated a third ideal-type of authority that is the foundation of modern civilizations, namely, "legal-rational" authority. It is based on "a belief in the legitimacy of the pattern of normative rules and the rights of those elevated to authority under such rules to issue commands." Obedience is owed to a legally established, impersonal set of rules, rather than to a personal ruler. Legal-rational authority vests power in the office rather than in the person who occupies the office; thus anyone can rule as long as he or she comes to office "according to the rules."

This third type of authority forms the basis for Weber's concept of bureaucracy. According to Weber, bureaucracy is the normal way that "legal-rational" authority appears in institutional form; it holds a central role in ordering and controlling modern societies. "It is," says Weber, "superior to any other form in precision, in stability, in stringency of its discipline, and in its reliability. It thus makes possible a particularly high degree of calculability of results for the heads of organizations and for those acting in relation to it." It is finally superior in its operational efficiency and "is formally capable of application to all kinds of administrative tasks." For Weber, bureaucracy is indispensable to maintaining civilization in modern society. In his view, "however much people may complain about the evils of bureaucracy it would be sheer illusion to think for a moment that continuous administrative work can be carried out in any field except by means of officials working in offices."

A great deal of Weber's analysis of bureaucracy dealt with its historical development. According to Weber, modern bureaucracy in the Western world arose during the Middle Ages when royal domains grew and required bodies of officials to oversee them. Out of necessity, princes devised rational administrative techniques to extend their authority, frequently borrowing ideas from the church, whose territories at that time encompassed most of Europe. "The proper soil for bureaucratization of administration," writes Weber, "has always been the development of administrative tasks." Bureaucracy grew because society needed to do things—to build roads, to educate students, to collect taxes, to fight battles, and to dispense justice. Work was divided and specialized to achieve the goals of a society.

Weber also identified a monied economy as an important ingredient for the development of bureaucracy. "Bureaucracy as a permanent structure is knit to the presupposition of a constant income for maintenancy. . . . A stable system of taxation is the precondition for the permanent existence of bureaucratic administration." Other cultural factors contributing to the rise of highly structured bureaucracies were the growth of education, the development of higher religions, and the burgeoning of science and rationality.

Weber listed in a detailed fashion the major elements of the formal structure of bureaucracy. Three of the most important attributes in his concept of bureaucracy were the division of labor, hierarchical order, and impersonal rules—keystones to any functioning bureaucracy. The first, specialization of labor, meant that all work in a bureaucracy is rationally divided into units that can be undertaken by an individual or group of individuals competent to perform those tasks. Unlike traditional rulers, workers do not *own* their offices in bureaucracy but enjoy tenure based on their abilities to perform the work assigned. Second, the hierarchical order of bureaucracy separates superiors from subordinates; on the basis of this hierarchy, remuneration for work is dispensed, authority recognized, privileges allotted, and promotions awarded. Finally, impersonal rules form the life-blood of the bureaucratic world. Bureaucrats, according to Weber, are not free to act in any way they please because their choices are confined to prescribed patterns of conduct imposed by legal rules. In contrast to "traditional" or "charismatic" authority, bureaucratic rules provide for the systematic control of subordinates by superiors, thus limiting the opportunities for arbitrariness and personal favoritism.

Weber theorized that the only way for a modern society to operate effectively was by organizing expertly trained, functional specialists in bureaucracies. Although Max Weber saw bureaucracy as permanent and indispensable in the modern world, he was horrified by what he believed was an irreversible trend toward loss of human freedom and dignity:

> It is horrible to think that the world could one day be filled with nothing but those little cogs, little men clinging to little jobs and striving towards bigger ones—a state of affairs which is to be seen once more, as in the Egyptian records, playing an ever-increasing part in the spirit of our present administrative system and especially of its offspring, the students. This passion for bureaucracy . . . is enough to drive one to despair.[1]

And although he despaired over the increasing trend toward bureaucratization in the modern world, Weber also observed the leveling or democratizing effect of bureaucracy on society. As Reinhard Bendix wrote of Weber's idea: "The development of bureaucracy does away with . . . plutocratic privileges, replacing unpaid, avocational administration by notables with paid, full-time administration by professionals, regardless of their social and economic position. . . . Authority is exercised in accordance with rules, and everyone subject to that authority is legally equal."[2]

Over the last fifty years, certain elements in Max Weber's conception of bureaucracy have fueled repeated academic debate and scholarly criticism.[3] Nevertheless, the main outline of his classic formulation is generally accepted as true and significant. For students of public administration, his concept forms one of the essential intellectual building blocks in our understanding of the formal institutional structure of public administration.

As you read this selection, keep the following questions in mind:

Where can you see evidence of Weber's concept of bureaucracy within familiar organizations?

In what respects does Weber's characterization of bureaucracy as a theoretical "ideal-type" miss the mark in describing the practical reality? In what respects is it on target?

[1]As quoted in Reinhard Bendix, *Max Weber: An Intellectual Portrait* (New York: Doubleday and Co., 1960), p. 464.

[2]Ibid., p. 429.

[3]For an excellent discussion of general academic criticism and revision of Weber's ideas, read either Alfred Diamant, "The Bureaucratic Model: Max Weber Rejected, Rediscovered, Reformed," in Ferrel Heady and Sybil L. Stokes, *Papers in Comparative Public Administration* (Ann Arbor, Mich.: Institute of Public Administration, 1962) or Peter M. Blau and Marshall W. Meyer, *Bureaucracy in Modern Society* (New York: Random House, 1971).

How is Weber's bureaucratic model relevant to the previous case, "The Blast in Centralia No. 5"? On the basis of that case as well as your own observations, can you describe some positive and negative features of modern bureaucracy?

# Bureaucracy[1]

MAX WEBER

## 1. Characteristics of Bureaucracy

Modern officialdom functions in the following specific manner:

I. There is the principle of fixed and official jurisdictional areas, which are generally ordered by rules, that is, by laws or administrative regulations.

1. The regular activities required for the purposes of the bureaucratically governed structure are distributed in a fixed way as official duties.
2. The authority to give the commands required for the discharge of these duties is distributed in a stable way and is strictly delimited by rules concerning the coercive means, physical, sacerdotal, or otherwise, which may be placed at the disposal of officials.
3. Methodical provision is made for the regular and continuous fulfilment of these duties and for the execution of the corresponding rights; only persons who have the generally regulated qualifications to serve are employed.

From Max Weber: Essays in Sociology, translated and edited by H. H. Gerth and C. Wright Mills. Copyright © 1946 by Oxford University Press, Inc. Renewed copyright 1973 by Hans H. Gerth. Reprinted by permission of the publisher.
[1]Wirtschaft und Gesellschaft, part III, chap. 6, pp. 650–78.

In public and lawful government these three elements constitute 'bureaucratic authority.' In private economic domination, they constitute bureaucratic 'management.' Bureaucracy, thus understood, is fully developed in political and ecclesiastical communities only in the modern state, and, in the private economy, only in the most advanced institutions of capitalism. Permanent and public office authority, with fixed jurisdiction, is not the historical rule but rather the exception. This is so even in large political structures such as those of the ancient Orient, the Germanic and Mongolian empires of conquest, or of many feudal structures of state. In all these cases, the ruler executes the most important measures through personal trustees, table-companions, or court-servants. Their commissions and authority are not precisely delimited and are temporarily called into being for each case.

II. The principles of office hierarchy and of levels of graded authority mean a firmly ordered system of super- and subordination in which there is a supervision of the lower offices by the higher ones. Such a system offers the governed the possibility of appealing the decision of a lower office to its higher authority, in a definitely regulated manner. With the full development of the bureaucratic type, the office hierarchy is monocratically organized. The principle of hierarchical office authority is found in all bureaucratic structures: in state and ecclesiastical structures as well as in large party organizations and private enterprises. It does not matter for the character of bureaucracy whether its authority is called 'private' or 'public.'

When the principle of jurisdictional 'competency' is fully carried through, hierarchical subordination—at least in public office—does not mean that the 'higher' authority is simply authorized to take over the business of the 'lower.' Indeed, the opposite is the rule. Once established and having fulfilled its task, an office tends to continue in existence and be held by another incumbent.

III. The management of the modern office is based upon written documents ('the files'), which are preserved in their original or draught form. There is, therefore, a staff of subaltern officials and scribes of all sorts. The body of officials actively engaged in a 'public' office, along with the respective apparatus of material implements and the files, make up a 'bureau.' In private enterprise, 'the bureau' is often called 'the office.'

In principle, the modern organization of the civil service separates the bureau from the private domicile of the official, and, in general, bureaucracy segregates official activity as something distinct from the sphere of private life. Public monies and equipment are divorced from the private property of the official. This condition is everywhere the product of a long development. Nowadays, it is found in public as well as in private enterprises; in the latter, the principle extends even to the leading entrepreneur. In principle, the executive office is separated from the household, business from private correspondence, and business assets from private fortunes. The more consistently the modern type of business management has been carried through the more are these separations the case. The beginnings of this process are to be found as early as the Middle Ages.

It is the peculiarity of the modern entrepreneur that he conducts himself as the 'first official' of his enterprise, in the very same way in which the ruler of a specifically modern bureaucratic state spoke of himself as 'the first servant' of the state. The idea that the bureau activities of the state are intrinsically different in character from the management of private economic offices is a continental European notion and, by way of contrast, is totally foreign to the American way.

IV. Office management, at least all specialized office management—and such management is distinctly modern—usually presupposes thorough and expert training. This increasingly holds for the modern executive and employee of private enterprises, in the same manner as it holds for the state official.

V. When the office is fully developed, official activity demands the full working capacity of the official, irrespective of the fact that his obligatory time in the bureau may be firmly delimited. In the normal case, this is only the product of a long development, in the public as well as in the private office. Formerly, in all cases, the normal state of affairs was reversed: official business was discharged as a secondary activity.

VI. The management of the office follows general rules, which are more or less stable, more or less exhaustive, and which can be learned. Knowledge of these rules represents a special technical learning which the officials possess. It involves jurisprudence, or administrative or business management.

The reduction of modern office management to rules is deeply embedded in its very nature. The theory of modern public administration, for instance, assumes that the authority to order certain matters by decree—which has been legally granted to public authorities—does not entitle the bureau to regulate the matter by commands given for each case, but only to regulate the matter abstractly. This stands in extreme contrast to the regulation of all relationships through individual privileges and bestowals of favor, which is absolutely dominant in patrimonialism, at least in so far as such relationships are not fixed by sacred tradition.

## 2. The Position of the Official

All this results in the following for the internal and external position of the official:

I. Office holding is a 'vocation.' This is shown, first, in the requirement of a firmly prescribed course of training, which demands the entire capacity for work for a long period of time, and in the generally prescribed and special examinations which are prerequisites of employment. Furthermore, the position of the official is in the nature of a duty. This determines the internal structure of his relations, in the following manner: Legally and actually, office holding is not considered a source to be exploited for rents or emoluments, as was normally the case during the Middle Ages and frequently up to the threshold of recent times. Nor is office holding considered a usual exchange of services for equivalents, as is the case with free labor contracts. Entrance into an office, including one in the private economy, is considered an acceptance of a specific obligation of faithful management in return for a secure existence. It is decisive for the specific nature of modern loyalty to an office that, in the pure type, it does not establish a relationship to a *person*, like the vassal's or disciple's faith in feudal or in patrimonial relations of authority. Modern loyalty is devoted to impersonal and functional purposes. Behind the functional purposes, of course, 'ideas of culture-values' usually stand. These are *ersatz* for the earthly or supra-mundane personal master: ideas such as 'state,' 'church,' 'community,' 'party,' or 'enterprise' are thought of as being realized in a community; they provide an ideological halo for the master.

The political official—at least in the fully developed modern state—is not considered the personal servant of a ruler. Today, the bishop, the priest, and the preacher are in fact no longer, as in early Christian times, holders of purely personal charisma. The supra-mundane and sacred values which they offer are given to everybody who seems to be worthy of them and who asks for them. In former times, such leaders acted upon the personal command of their master; in principle, they were responsible only to him. Nowadays, in spite of the partial survival of the old theory, such religious leaders are officials in the service of a functional purpose, which in the present-day 'church' has become routinized and, in turn, ideologically hallowed.

II. The personal position of the official is patterned in the following way:

1. Whether he is in a private office or a public bureau, the modern official always strives and usually enjoys a distinct *social esteem* as compared with the governed. His social position is guaranteed by the prescriptive rules of rank order and, for the political official, by special definitions of the criminal code against 'insults of officials' and 'contempt' of state and church authorities.

   The actual social position of the official is normally highest where, as in old civilized countries, the following conditions prevail: a strong demand for administration by trained experts; a strong and stable social differentiation, where the official predominantly derives from socially and economically privileged strata because of the social distribution of power; or where the costliness of the required training and status conventions are binding upon him. The possession of educational certificates—to be discussed elsewhere—are usually linked with qualification for office. Naturally, such certificates or patents enhance the 'status element' in the social position of the official. For the rest this status factor in individual cases is explicitly and impassively acknowledged; for example, in the prescription that the acceptance or rejection of an aspirant to an official career depends upon the consent ('election') of the members of the official body. This is the case in the German army with the officer corps. Similar phenomena, which promote this guild-like closure of officialdom, are typically found in patrimonial and, particularly, in prebendal officialdoms of the past. The desire to resurrect such phenomena in changed forms is by no means infrequent among modern bureaucrats. For instance, they have played a role among the demands of the quite proletarian and expert officials (the *tretyj* element) during the Russian revolution.

Usually the social esteem of the officials as such is especially low where the demand for expert administration and the dominance of status conventions are weak. This is especially the case in the United States; it is often the case in new settlements by virtue of their wide fields for profitmaking and the great instability of their social stratification.

2. The pure type of bureaucratic official is *appointed* by a superior authority. An official elected by the governed is not a purely bureaucratic figure. Of course, the formal existence of an election does not by itself mean that no appointment hides behind the election—in the state, especially, appointment by party chiefs. Whether or not this is the case does not depend upon legal statutes but upon the way in which the party mechanism functions. Once firmly organized, the parties can turn a formally free election into the mere acclamation of a candidate designated by the party chief. As a rule, however, a formally free election is turned into a fight, conducted according to definite rules, for votes in favor of one of two designated candidates. . . . [pp. 196–200]

3. Normally, the position of the official is held for life, at least in public bureaucracies; and this is increasingly the case for all similar structures. As a factual rule, *tenure for life* is presupposed, even where the giving of notice or periodic reappointment occurs. In contrast to the worker in a private enterprise, the official normally holds tenure. Legal or actual life-tenure, however, is not recognized as the official's right to the possession of office, as was the case with many structures of authority in the past. Where legal guarantees against arbitrary dismissal or transfer are developed, they merely serve to guarantee a strictly objective discharge of specific office duties free from all personal considerations. In Germany, this is the case for all juridical and, increasingly, for all administrative officials.

Within the bureaucracy, therefore, the measure of 'independence,' legally guaranteed by tenure, is not always a source of increased status for the official whose position is thus secured. Indeed, often the reverse holds, especially in old cultures and communities that are highly differentiated. In such communities, the stricter the subordination under the arbitrary rule of the master, the more it guarantees the maintenance of the conventional seigneurial style of living for the official. Because of the very absence of these legal guarantees of tenure, the conventional esteem for the official may rise in the same way as, during the Middle Ages, the esteem of the nobility of office rose at the expense of esteem for the freemen, and as the king's judge surpassed that of the people's judge. In Germany, the military officer or the administrative official can be removed from office at any time, or at least far more readily than the 'independent judge,' who never pays with loss of his office for even the grossest offense against the 'code of honor' or against social conventions of the salon. For this very reason, if other things are equal, in the eyes of the master stratum the judge is considered less qualified for social intercourse than are officers and administrative officials, whose greater dependence on the master is a greater guarantee of their conformity with status conventions. Of course, the average official strives for a civil-service law, which would materially secure his old age and provide increased guarantees against his arbitrary removal from office. This striving, however, has its limits. A very strong development of the 'right to the office' naturally makes it more difficult to staff them with regard to technical efficiency, for such a development decreases the career-opportunities of ambitious candidates for office. This makes for the fact that officials, on the whole, do not feel their dependency upon those at the top. This lack of a feeling of dependency, however, rests primarily upon the inclination to depend upon one's equals rather than upon the socially inferior and governed strata. The present conservative movement among the Badenia clergy, occasioned by the anxiety of a presumably threatening separation of church and state, has been expressly determined by the desire not to be turned 'from a master into a servant of the parish.'

4. The official receives the regular *pecuniary* compensation of a normally fixed *salary* and the old age security provided by a pension. The salary is not measured like a wage in terms of work done, but according to 'status,' that is, according to the kind of function (the 'rank') and, in addition, possibly, according to the length of service. The relatively great security of the official's income, as well as the rewards of social esteem, make the office a sought-after position, especially in countries which no longer provide opportunities for colonial profits. In such countries, this situation permits relatively low salaries for officials.

5. The official is set for a *'career'* within the hierarchical order of the public service. He moves from the lower, less important, and lower paid to the higher positions. The average official naturally desires a mechanical

fixing of the conditions of promotion: if not of the offices, at least of the salary levels. He wants these conditions fixed in terms of 'seniority,' or possibly according to grades achieved in a developed system of expert examinations. Here and there, such examinations actually form a character *indelebilis* of the official and have lifelong effects on his career. To this is joined the desire to qualify the right to office and the increasing tendency toward status group closure and economic security. All of this makes for a tendency to consider the offices as 'prebends' of those who are qualified by educational certificates. The necessity of taking general personal and intellectual qualifications into consideration, irrespective of the often subaltern character of the educational certificate, has led to a condition in which the highest political offices, especially the positions of 'ministers,' are principally filled without reference to such certificates. . . . [pp. 202–204]

# 6. Technical Advantages of Bureaucratic Organization

The decisive reason for the advance of bureaucratic organization has always been its purely technical superiority over any other form of organization. The fully developed bureaucratic mechanism compares with other organizations exactly as does the machine with the nonmechanical modes of production.

Precision, speed, unambiguity, knowledge of the files, continuity, discretion, unity, strict subordination, reduction of friction and of material and personal costs—these are raised to the optimum point in the strictly bureaucratic administration, and especially in its monocratic form. As compared with all collegiate, honorific, and avocational forms of administration, trained bureaucracy is superior on all these points. And as far as complicated tasks are concerned, paid bureaucratic work is not only more precise but, in the last analysis, it is often cheaper than even formally un-remunerated honorific service.

Honorific arrangements make administrative work an avocation and, for this reason alone, honorific service normally functions more slowly; being less bound to schemata and being more formless. Hence it is less precise and less unified than bureaucratic work because it is less dependent upon superiors and because the establishment and exploitation of the apparatus of subordinate officials and filing services are almost unavoidably less economical. Honorific service is less continuous than bureaucratic and frequently quite expensive. This is especially the case if one thinks not only of the money costs to the public treasury—costs which bureaucratic administration, in comparison with administration by notables, usually substantially increases—but also of the frequent economic losses of the governed caused by delays and lack of precision. The possibility of administration by notables normally and permanently exists only where official management can be satisfactorily discharged as an avocation. With the qualitative increase of tasks the administration has to face, administration by notables reaches its limits—today, even in England. Work organized by collegiate bodies causes friction and delay and requires compromises between colliding interests and views. The administration, therefore, runs less precisely and is more independent of superiors; hence, it is less unified and slower. All advances of the Prussian administrative organization have been and will in the future be advances of the bureaucratic, and especially of the monocratic, principle.

Today, it is primarily the capitalist market economy which demands that the official business of the administration be discharged precisely, unambiguously, continuously, and with as much speed as possible. Normally, the very large, modern capitalist enterprises are themselves unequalled models of strict bureaucratic organization. Business management through-out rests on increasing precision, steadiness, and, above all, the speed of operations. This, in turn, is determined by the peculiar nature of the modern means of communication, including, among other things, the news service of the press. The extraordinary increase in the speed by which public announcements, as well as economic and political facts, are transmitted exerts a steady and sharp pressure in the direction of speeding up the tempo of administrative reaction towards various situations. The optimum of such reaction time is normally attained only by a strictly bureaucratic organization.*

Bureaucratization offers above all the optimum possibility for carrying through the principle of specializing administrative functions according to purely objective considerations. Individual performances are allocated to functionaries who have specialized training and who by constant practice learn more and more. The 'objective' discharge of business primarily means a discharge of business according to *calculable rules* and 'without regard for persons.'

'Without regard for persons' is also the watchword of the 'market' and, in general, of all pursuits of naked economic interests. A consistent execution of bureaucratic domination means the leveling of status 'honor.' Hence, if the principle of the free-market is not at the same time restricted, it means the universal domination of the 'class situation.' That this consequence of bureaucratic domination has not set in everywhere, parallel to the extent of bureaucratization, is due to the differences among possible principles by which polities may meet their demands.

The second element mentioned, 'calculable rules,' also is of paramount importance for modern bureaucracy. The peculiarity of modern culture, and specifically of its technical and economic basis, demands this very 'calculability' of results. When fully developed, bureauc-

---

*Here we cannot discuss in detail how the bureaucratic apparatus may, and actually does, produce definite obstacles to the discharge of business in a manner suitable for the single case.

racy also stands, in a specific sense, under the principle of *sine ira ac studio.* Its specific nature, which is welcomed by capitalism, develops the more perfectly the more the bureaucracy is 'dehumanized,' the more completely it succeeds in eliminating from official business love, hatred, and all purely personal, irrational, and emotional elements which escape calculation. This is the specific nature of bureaucracy and it is appraised as its special virtue.

The more complicated and specialized modern culture becomes, the more its external supporting apparatus demands the personally detached and strictly 'objective' *expert,* in lieu of the master of older social structures, who was moved by personal sympathy and favor, by grace and gratitude. Bureaucracy offers the attitudes demanded by the external apparatus of modern culture in the most favorable combination. As a rule, only bureaucracy has established the foundation for the administration of a rational law conceptually systematized on the basis of such enactments as the latter Roman imperial period first created with a high degree of technical perfection. During the Middle Ages, this law was received along with the bureaucratization of legal administration, that is to say, with the displacement of the old trial procedure which was bound to tradition or to irrational presuppositions, by the rationally trained and specialized expert. . . . [pp. 214–216]

## 10. The Permanent Character of the Bureaucratic Machine

Once it is fully established, bureaucracy is among those social structures which are the hardest to destroy. Bureaucracy is *the* means of carrying 'community action' over into rationally ordered 'societal action.' Therefore, as an instrument for 'societalizing' relations of power, bureaucracy has been and is a power instrument of the first order—for the one who controls the bureaucratic apparatus.

Under otherwise equal conditions, a 'societal action,' which is methodically ordered and led, is superior to every resistance of 'mass' or even of 'communal action.' And where the bureaucratization of administration has been completely carried through, a form of power relation is established that is practically unshatterable.

The individual bureaucrat cannot squirm out of the apparatus in which he is harnessed. In contrast to the honorific or avocational 'notable,' the professional bureaucrat is chained to his activity by his entire material and ideal existence. In the great majority of cases, he is only a single cog in an ever-moving mechanism which prescribes to him an essentially fixed route of march. The official is entrusted with specialized tasks and normally the mechanism cannot be put into motion or arrested by him, but only from the very top. The individual bureaucrat is thus forged to the community of all the functionaries who are integrated into the mechanism. They have a common interest in seeing that the mechanism continues its functions and that the societally exercised authority carries on.

The ruled, for their part, cannot dispense with or replace the bureaucratic apparatus of authority once it exists. For this bureaucracy rests upon expert training, a functional specialization of work, and an attitude set for habitual and virtuoso-like mastery of single yet methodically integrated functions. If the official stops working, or if his work is forcefully interrupted, chaos results, and it is difficult to improvise replacements from among the governed who are fit to master such chaos. This holds for public administration as well as for private economic management. More and more the material fate of the masses depends upon the steady and correct functioning of the increasingly bureaucratic organizations of private capitalism. The idea of eliminating these organizations becomes more and more utopian.

The discipline of officialdom refers to the

attitude-set of the official for precise obedience within his *habitual* activity, in public as well as in private organizations. This discipline increasingly becomes the basis of all order, however great the practical importance of administration on the basis of the filed documents may be. The naive idea of Bakuninism of destroying the basis of 'acquired rights' and 'domination' by destroying public documents overlooks the settled orientation of *man* for keeping to the habitual rules and regulations that continue to exist independently of the documents. Every reorganization of beaten or dissolved troops, as well as the restoration of administrative orders destroyed by revolt, panic, or other catastrophes, is realized by appealing to the trained orientation of obedient compliance to such orders. Such compliance has been conditioned into the officials, on the one hand, and, on the other hand, into the governed. If such an appeal is successful it brings, as it were, the disturbed mechanism into gear again.

The objective indispensability of the once-existing apparatus, with its peculiar, 'impersonal' character, means that the mechanism—in contrast to feudal orders based upon personal piety—is easily made to work for anybody who knows how to gain control over it. A rationally ordered system of officials continues to function smoothly after the enemy has occupied the area; he merely needs to change the top officials. This body of officials continues to operate because it is to the vital interest of everyone concerned, including above all the enemy.

During the course of his long years in power, Bismarck brought his ministerial colleagues into unconditional bureaucratic dependence by eliminating all independent statesmen. Upon his retirement, he saw to his surprise that they continued to manage their offices unconcerned and undismayed, as if he had not been the master mind and creator of these creatures, but rather as if some single figure had been exchanged for some other figure in the bureaucratic machine. With all the

changes of masters in France since the time of the First Empire, the power machine has remained essentially the same. Such a machine makes 'revolution,' in the sense of the forceful creation of entirely new formations of authority, technically more and more impossible, especially when the apparatus controls the modern means of communication (telegraph, et cetera) and also by virtue of its internal rationalized structure. In classic fashion, France has demonstrated how this process has substituted *coups d'état* for 'revolutions': all successful transformations in France have amounted to *coups d'état*.

## 11. Economic and Social Consequences of Bureaucracy

It is clear that the bureaucratic organization of a social structure, and especially of a political one, can and regularly does have far-reaching economic consequences. But what sort of consequences? Of course in any individual case it depends upon the distribution of economic and social power, and especially upon the sphere that is occupied by the emerging bureaucratic mechanism. The consequences of bureaucracy depend therefore upon the direction which the powers using the apparatus give to it. And very frequently a crypto-plutocratic distribution of power has been the result.

In England, but especially in the United States, party donors regularly stand behind the bureaucratic party organizations. They have financed these parties and have been able to influence them to a large extent. The breweries in England, the so-called 'heavy industry,' and in Germany the Hansa League with their voting funds are well enough known as political donors to parties. In modern times bureaucratization and social leveling within political, and particularly within state organizations in connection with the destruction of feudal and local privileges, have very frequently benefited the interests of capitalism. Often bureaucratization has been carried out in direct alliance with capitalist interests, for example, the great historical alliance of the power of the absolute prince with capitalist interests. In general, a legal leveling and destruction of firmly established local structures ruled by notables has usually made for a wider range of capitalist activity. Yet one may expect as an effect of bureaucratization, a policy that meets the petty bourgeois interest in a secured traditional 'subsistence,' or even a state socialist policy that strangles opportunities for private profit. This has occurred in several cases of historical and far-reaching importance, specifically during antiquity; it is undoubtedly to be expected as a future development. Perhaps it will occur in Germany.

The very different effects of political organizations which were, at least in principle, quite similar—in Egypt under the Pharaohs and in Hellenic and Roman times—show the very different economic significances of bureaucratization which are possible according to the direction of other factors. The mere fact of bureaucratic organization does not unambiguously tell us about the concrete direction of its economic effects, which are always in some manner present. At least it does not tell us as much as can be told about its relatively leveling effect socially. In this respect, one has to remember that bureaucracy as such is a precision instrument which can put itself at the disposal of quite varied—purely political as well as purely economic, or any other sort—of interests in domination. Therefore, the measure of its parallelism with democratization must not be exaggerated, however typical it may be. Under certain conditions, strata of feudal lords have also put bureaucracy into their service. There is also the possibility—and often it has become a fact, for instance, in the Roman principate and in some forms of absolutist state structures—that a bureaucratization of administration is deliberately connected with the formation of *estates,* or is entangled with them by the force of the existing groupings of social

power. The express reservation of offices for certain status groups is very frequent, and actual reservations are even more frequent. The democratization of society in its totality, and in the *modern* sense of the term, whether actual or perhaps merely formal, is an especially favorable basis of bureaucratization, but by no means the only possible one. After all, bureaucracy strives merely to level those powers that stand in its way and in those areas that, in the individual case, it seeks to occupy. We must remember this fact—which we have encountered several times and which we shall have to discuss repeatedly: that 'democracy' as such is opposed to the 'rule' of bureaucracy, in spite and perhaps because of its unavoidable yet unintended promotion of bureaucratization. Under certain conditions, democracy creates obvious ruptures and blockages to bureaucratic organization. Hence, in every individual historical case, one must observe in what special direction bureaucratization has developed.

## 12. The Power Position of Bureaucracy

Everywhere the modern state is undergoing bureaucratization. But whether the *power* of bureaucracy within the polity is universally increasing must here remain an open question.

The fact that bureaucratic organization is technically the most highly developed means of power in the hands of the man who controls it does not determine the weight that bureaucracy as such is capable of having in a particular social structure. The ever-increasing 'indispensability' of the officialdom, swollen to millions, is no more decisive for this question than is the view of some representatives of the proletarian movement that the economic indispensability of the proletarians is decisive for the measure of their social and political power position. If 'indispensability' were decisive, then where slave labor prevailed and where freemen usually abhor work as a dishonor, the 'indispensable' slaves ought to have held the positions of power, for they were at least as indispensable as officials and proletarians are today. Whether the power of bureaucracy as such increases cannot be decided *a priori* from such reasons. The drawing in of economic interest groups or other non-official experts, or the drawing in of non-expert lay representatives, the establishment of local, inter-local, or central parliamentary or other representative bodies, or of occupational associations—these *seem* to run directly against the bureaucratic tendency. How far this appearance is the truth must be discussed in another chapter rather than in this purely formal and typological discussion. In general, only the following can be said here:

Under normal conditions, the power position of a fully developed bureaucracy is always overtowering. The 'political master' finds himself in the position of the 'dilettante' who stands opposite the 'expert,' facing the trained official who stands within the management of administration. This holds whether the 'master' whom the bureaucracy serves is a 'people,' equipped with the weapons of 'legislative initiative,' the 'referendum,' and the right to remove officials, or a parliament, elected on a more aristocratic or more 'democratic' basis and equipped with the right to vote a lack of confidence, or with the actual authority to vote it. It holds whether the master is an aristocratic, collegiate body, legally or actually based on self-recruitment, or whether he is a popularly elected president, a hereditary and 'absolute' or a 'constitutional' monarch. . . . [pp. 228–233]

---

## CASE STUDY 2

# Introduction

How does Max Weber's conceptualization of the formal elements of bureaucracy apply to the United States? What specifically does America's bureaucracy look like? What are its sources of development? Basic design? Formal scope and powers? Do Weber's generalizations fit or fail to fit the American experience?

In light of Weber's ideas about bureaucracy, consider the following interpretative account of the rise of U.S. bureaucracy by the author of this text from his *The American Bureaucracy*. Perhaps this selection is not a case study similar to "The Blast in Centralia No. 5" in Chapter 1, because the writer does not merely recount in detail the facts of a single administrative event as a way of understanding "a slice of administrative reality." Rather, he paints a broad-brush overview of the development of American bureaucracy from 1787 and attempts to explain its unique sources of growth, expansion, and basic formal organizational arrangements. Although not strictly "a case" of a single, isolated event in public administration, it presents a historical interpretation of American experience with bureaucracy that attempts to comprehend the Weberian bureaucratic model in light of its actual evolution and growth in the United States. In short, this essay offers a perspective on Weber's ideas from the standpoint of America's national experience with bureaucracy.

Central to his argument is the thesis that a variety of societal demands over the past 200 years contributed significantly to the shape of diverse types of American bureaucratic institutions. The United States, unlike Europe, has not one, but many bureaucratic forms— the result of numerous experiments of coping with diverse societal challenges since 1787. At its creation as "the first new nation," America required certain minimal "core functions" to operate as a nation, including those necessary to conduct diplomacy, wage war, mint currency, and so forth. Western expansion in the nineteenth century brought about new bureaus and agencies, such as the U.S. Department of the Interior, to foster the country's internal economic and political development. Clientele agencies, such as the Agriculture, Commerce, and Labor departments, arose in the late nineteenth century as responses to specialized needs and pressures of significant occupational groups that were established and influential by that time. In roughly the same era, regulatory agencies and government corporations were created in America to protect public interest(s) in what were deemed vital policy fields and were organized around new institutional formats. The greatest increases in the size and scope of U.S. bureaucracy occurred as a result of the economic challenges of the Great Depression in the 1930s and the hot and cold war defense requirements imposed on the United States in the 1940s and 1950s. Because of the surge in federal block grants, categorical aid, and revenue sharing in the 1960s and 1970s, "overhead staffs" and state/local bureaucracies grew rapidly to administer these "New Frontier," "Great Society," and "New Federalism" programs from the Kennedy, Johnson, and Nixon administrations.

As you read the following selection, try to reflect on such questions as:

How does Stillman's description of America's particular national pattern of bureaucratic development and format compare and contrast with Weber's generalizations?

Why does Stillman argue that at the outset America did not have much of a bureaucracy? Do you agree or disagree?

What stimulated the growth of American bureaucracy, and why are there so many varieties of institutional arrangements of U.S. bureaucracy?

Can you describe "a clientele agency"? And a modern-day example?

# The Rise of U.S. Bureaucracy

### RICHARD J. STILLMAN II

The United States did not always have much of a bureaucracy. Nor did it need one. When the United States began in 1789 as a "new nation," the population was under 4 million (compared with over 250 million today). The average American was a farmer. Nine out of ten people lived directly off the land (now less than 5 percent are farmers). Given the social simplicity and rural autonomy of 1789, few demands

From pp. 29–63 in *The American Bureaucracy* by Richard J. Stillman II. Copyright © 1987 by Nelson-Hall Publishers. Reprinted by permission of the publisher.

were made upon government. No autos meant that no roads had to be built, no drivers' licenses granted, no taxes raised for these purposes. There were no telephones, airlines, or television stations to regulate. No sewage, water, or utilities were provided for homes. Nor were clean air, pure food, and good public health then considered "essentials." Compulsory education through high school was unheard of. Geographic isolation of the "first new nation" prompted little need for a standing army, navy, and air force to defend "global American interests"; nor were there orbiting space shuttles, lunar landings,

COMSAT weather satellites, social security retirement benefits, and medicare/medicaid protection. There was no need of a big bureaucracy to provide such services.

Now our 250 million population is sixty times larger, more heterogeneous, more technologically dependent and interdependent, making greater and more complex demands upon government for a wide variety of goods and services. In particular, urbanization increased dependence upon government activities. In 1789 New York City had a population of 33,000; today it contains more than 8 million people, bringing enormous new demands upon municipal government for basic services. Fire, police, schools, welfare, zoning, water, sewage, and housing are just a few "basics" required by modern urban life. A complex social environment today tends to promote the development of complex bureaucratic services.

# The Growth and Emergence of Organized Functions of Government Bureaucracy

Much as the hull of a ship gradually acquires barnacles, the United States acquired its bureaucratic institutions and services gradually as layers upon layers of responsibilities were added over the course of two hundred years. Different types of social pressures spawned, over a long time, bureaucracy's organizations. These new bureaucratic services or tasks were added gradually and unevenly. Sometimes the buildup of these public bureaucracies was so slow as to be imperceptible; sometimes it was quite swift. First, the basic core bureaucratic service functions were created at the start of the new nation's existence; second, those involved with national economic development evolved in the nineteenth century; third, service-oriented tasks came about in the late nineteenth century; fourth, the rise of regulatory agencies and government corporations services developed in the progressive period of the early twentieth century; fifth, surges in social service organizations arose during the Great Depression; sixth, the development of the large standing defense establishment appeared during World War II and the postwar Cold War era; and seventh, new forms of staff services as well as state and local bureaucracies grew throughout the twentieth century (see figure 2.1).

Each of these basic types of bureaucratic organizations will be examined in turn.

## Creation of the Basic Core Service Functions

At the inception of the U.S. government in 1789, little bureaucracy was needed. Nevertheless, a few public agencies were necessary. Congress created the first executive departments to perform the essential core service functions. Core tasks are those which every nation (or state or municipality) develops in order to be a nation (or state or municipality). The United States set up five units in 1789 to carry out these core functions: the State Department to conduct its external affairs with other nations; the War Department and later the Navy Department (now combined into the Defense Department) to provide protection from threats from other nations; the Treasury Department to collect revenues, pay bills, settle accounts, and establish broad economic policies; the Attorney General's Office (now the Department of Justice) to represent legal cases and offer legal advice to the president and his Cabinet; and the Postal Services Department to run the national mail system, which was and still is essential for internal communications (the U.S. Postal Service now operates as an independent government corporation).

As indicated in figure 2.2, the *department* (with the exception of the Office of the Attorney General, which became a department in 1870) was the key bureaucratic building block from the start. It was the basic organizational arrangement for providing critical national services, and departments still remain the basic organizational building blocks at federal, state, and local levels.

Why? Largely because the founding fathers had had several unhappy experiences throughout the Revolutionary War in conducting administrative business with councils, boards, and legislative committees. These had proved to be slow, unresponsive, and irresponsible. General George Washington, as commander-in-chief of the Continental Armies during the Revolutionary War, continually complained about the inability of these committees to reach agreements and to decide and act expeditiously on critical military matters. When Washington became president, it was no small wonder that he, along with others in Congress who had experienced similar frustrations, instituted departments that were responsible to a single

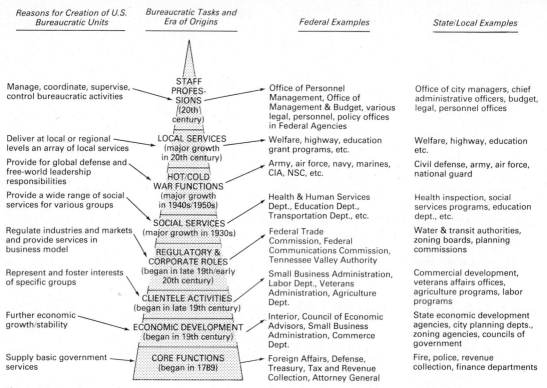

| Reasons for Creation of U.S. Bureaucratic Units | Bureaucratic Tasks and Era of Origins | Federal Examples | State/Local Examples |
|---|---|---|---|
| Manage, coordinate, supervise, control bureaucratic activities | STAFF PROFESSIONS (20th century) | Office of Personnel Management, Office of Management & Budget, various legal, personnel, policy offices in Federal Agencies | Office of city managers, chief administrative officers, budget, legal, personnel offices |
| Deliver at local or regional levels an array of local services | LOCAL SERVICES (major growth in 20th century) | Welfare, highway, education grant programs, etc. | Welfare, highway, education etc. |
| Provide for global defense and free-world leadership responsibilities | HOT/COLD WAR FUNCTIONS (major growth in 1940s/1950s) | Army, air force, navy, marines, CIA, NSC, etc. | Civil defense, army, air force, national guard |
| Provide a wide range of social services for various groups | SOCIAL SERVICES (major growth in 1930s) | Health & Human Services Dept., Education Dept., Transportation Dept., etc. | Health inspection, social services programs, education dept., etc. |
| Regulate industries and markets and provide services in business model | REGULATORY & CORPORATE ROLES (began in late 19th/early 20th century) | Federal Trade Commission, Federal Communications Commission, Tennessee Valley Authority | Water & transit authorities, zoning boards, planning commissions |
| Represent and foster interests of specific groups | CLIENTELE ACTIVITIES (began in late 19th century) | Small Business Administration, Labor Dept., Veterans Administration, Agriculture Dept. | Commercial development, veterans affairs offices, agriculture programs, labor programs |
| Further economic growth/stability | ECONOMIC DEVELOPMENT (began in 19th century) | Interior, Council of Economic Advisors, Small Business Administration, Commerce Dept. | State economic development agencies, city planning depts., zoning agencies, councils of government |
| Supply basic government services | CORE FUNCTIONS (began in 1789) | Foreign Affairs, Defense, Treasury, Tax and Revenue Collection, Attorney General | Fire, police, revenue collection, finance departments |

**Figure 2.1** Modern U.S. bureaucracy

chief executive. The founding fathers had learned one bitter lesson from the Revolution—i.e., some*one* should be held responsible for doing the work of government, and the department format, they saw, was the most effective organizational model to facilitate that end.

The departmental head would be called a secretary (following the British model) and would be appointed, with the consent of the Senate, by the president and would serve at his pleasure. It was this last point that stirred the only real debates in Congress relative to the formation of these early departments. Some representatives argued that only with the consent of the Senate should the president be able to remove Cabinet officials, but the arguments of Congressmen James Madison (Virginia), Fisher Ames (Massachusetts), and others won out. They stressed the need for executive accountability for departmental affairs. One individual, the president, should be held responsible for exec-

utive affairs, and thus the president, not Congress should be entrusted with the power to remove his key assistants. For a period after the Civil War, the Tenure of Office Act of 1867 restricted presidential powers of removal, but since the Supreme Court decision reached in *Myers vs. the United States* (1926), the president has been given an essentially free hand in removing political appointees.

The early departments were created to perform specific tasks, as evidenced by their enabling legislation, that were vital to the nation's well-being (see figure 2.3). The tasks at hand involved the basic work of the new nation. In short, defense, diplomacy, and functional necessities stimulated the creation and subsequent structure of these first bureaucracies. The State Department was established to conduct foreign affairs, maintain embassies and ambassadors abroad, and advise the president on international policies. Thomas Jefferson, the first secretary of state, not only managed diplomatic affairs but had multiple, often

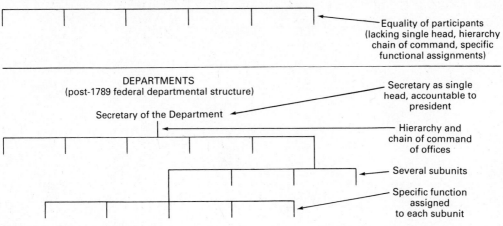

BOARDS or COUNCILS
(pre-1789 basis of U.S. public organizations)

Equality of participants
(lacking single head, hierarchy
chain of command, specific
functional assignments)

DEPARTMENTS
(post-1789 federal departmental structure)

Secretary as single
head, accountable to
president

Secretary of the Department

Hierarchy and
chain of command
of offices

Several subunits

Specific function
assigned
to each subunit

**Figure 2.2**   Departmental structure

unrelated duties (as is the case today with many Cabinet secretaries). He was in charge of issuing copyrights and patents, minting currency, and taking the national census (largely because of Jefferson's interest in these subjects and because no one else wanted to assume responsibility for them). All this Jefferson performed with the assistance of just one chief clerk, seven assistant clerks, and one messenger.[1]

The War Department supervised at first both the army and navy, but in 1798 the navy "spun off" into a separate department in order to prepare for the then-expected naval warfare with Great Britain. Here is an early example of how a crisis precipitated the formation of a new, independent department; in a similar fashion nearly two centuries later, in 1977, the Energy Department, forged from bits and pieces of several smaller agencies, came into existence because of a national energy crisis. Like the State Department, the War and Navy departments were small operations, having few ships, less than 4,000 soldiers, and only eighty civilian employees. The following account by a prominent foreign visitor of his meeting with secretary of war James McHenry in 1796 gives a sense of the informality of these departments' daily operations.

The government officials were as simple in their manners as ever. I had occasion to call upon McHenry, the Secretary of War. It was about eleven o'clock in the morning when I called. There was no sentinel at the door, all the rooms, the

walls of which were covered with maps, were open, and in the midst of the solitude I found two clerks each sitting at his own table, engaged in writing. At last I met a servant, or rather *the* servant, for there was but one in the house, and asked for the Secretary. He replied that his master was absent for the moment, having gone to the barber's to be shaved. Mr. McHenry's name figured in the State Budget for $2,000, a salary quite sufficient in a country where the Secretary of War goes in the morning to his neighbor, the barber, at the corner, to get shaved. I was as much surprised to find all the business of the War Office transacted by two clerks, as I was to hear that the Secretary had gone to the barber's.[2]

While informality was a characteristic of early departmental activities, pronounced differences between the departments were even then apparent. The Treasury Department, partly because of the vigorous personality and leadership of Alexander Hamilton, was given the broadest mandate and widest latitude in its original enabling legislation: "to digest and prepare plans for the improvement and management of revenue"; "to superintend the collection of the revenue"; "to execute such services relative to the sale of the lands belonging to the United States"; and "to perform all such services relative to the finances."[3] And indeed Hamilton exercised broad, sweeping powers in his efforts to raise and collect new sources of national revenues, supervise and di-

**Figure 2.3**    The development of every bureaucracy is rooted in specific public laws approved by the legislature and establishing its missions, structure, and personnel. *Source:* PL 96—465, 94 STAT. 2071—Oct. 17, 1980.

PUBLIC LAW 96–465—Oct. 17, 1980.

94 Stat. 2071

Public Law 96–465
96th Congress

An Act

To promote the foreign policy of the United State by strengthening and improving the Foreign Service of the United States, and for other purposes.

Oct. 17, 190
[H.R. 6790]

*Be it enacted by the Senate and House of Representatives of the United States of America in Congress Assembled,*
SECTION. 1. SHORT TITLE.—This Act may be cited as the "Foreign Service Act of 1980."
SEC. 2. TABLE OF CONTENTS.—The table of contents for this Act is as follows:

Foreign Service
Act of 1980. 22
USC 3901
note.

TABLE OF CONTENTS

rect disbursement of funds, control public debts, and create a national bank. He even drew up the first economic blueprint of national economic growth in his *Report on Manufacturers.* As is also true today, personalities and intellectual capacities of leaders combined with the departmental legal authority and day-to-day responsibilities create wide variations *between* government organizations, even if they can all be broadly defined as departments.

The attorney general, as noted earlier, was different in that his authority was represented by an office, not a department. Until well into the nineteenth century, attorneys general were part-timers. They acted more or less as legal advisors to presidents and as chief litigators for the United States. This tradition continues to this day. Recent attorneys general have been close personal friends, indeed personal attorneys, of presidents they have served—witness two recent appointees, Griffin Bell and William French Smith. Early attorneys general were expected to continue their private legal practices to support themselves. The same was true for local postmasters who worked for the postmaster general. They were also unsalaried and were expected to charge customers for services (a tradition that also holds true today in an altered form, since the U.S. Postal Service is now an independent government corporation and is expected to be a self-supporting enterprise).

For the most part, these core service functions—diplomacy, national defense, finance, legal advice, and internal communications—with minor variations remain today core service functions of U.S. bureaucracy, but with one important difference. Each federal department that performs these basic tasks has multiplied its scope, activities, and size enormously over the past two hundred years.

Figure 2.4 shows the State Department's present organization. It is a far cry from the way it was in Thomas Jefferson's day when it had eight clerks, one messenger, and twenty-five agents! Today State's bureaucracy comprises more than 30,000 persons, staffing 142 embassies around the world, and representing the United States in over 50 international organizations and at more than 800 international conferences annually. The tasks that figure 2.4 shows are only the very "tip of the iceberg" of State's incredibly complex functional responsibilities. Many of these tasks were not even conceived of in 1789. They include descriptors like "combating terrorism," "human rights," "refugee programs," "international

narcotics matters," and "international organization affairs." The same expansion of roles and responsibilities has taken place in other core departments—Treasury, Defense, Justice, and the Postal Service. Though these departments' activities have greatly enlarged, as in the case of the State Department, their basic structures remain much the same as when they were first organized—i.e., having a cabinet secretary in charge, a chain of command, a hierarchy and functionally differentiated activities, and some responsibilities that do not fit in clearly with their overall basic missions.

## National Economic Development in the Nineteenth Century

The first governmental organizations in the United States were created to service the essential core functions of the new nation and were organized in the form of departments and offices. But the nineteenth century saw the emergence of other organizational arrangements. The Interior Department, the only federal department created between 1789 and 1889, was established in 1849 to foster domestic growth and national development. This was the era of rapid westward expansion. As the population shifted west, a new department was necessary to serve new national needs. Proposals to create a "Home Office," along the lines of a British Home Office (essentially a department for domestic affairs), had repeatedly been raised since 1789. However, local pressures to resist federal involvement in this area, coupled with the worries of a growing bureaucracy (even then), had blocked any moves in this direction until 1849, when the need for greater coherence and policy direction became imperative. The Interior Department emerged as an amalgam of bits and pieces of several other agencies then in existence—all involving domestic concerns: Bureau of Indian Affairs (from the War Department); Military Pensions (from War); Patent Office (from State); Census Bureau (from State); and Land Office (from Treasury). Note that the bureau became the organizing principle at Interior. Interior's scattered and somewhat unrelated collection of domestically oriented agencies with a mix of names containing the words *bureau* and *office* remain to a large extent its basic pattern and mode of operation to this very day.

Some of the old functions are still important at Interior (see figure 2.5), such as the Bureau of Indian Affairs or the Bureau of Land Management (formerly

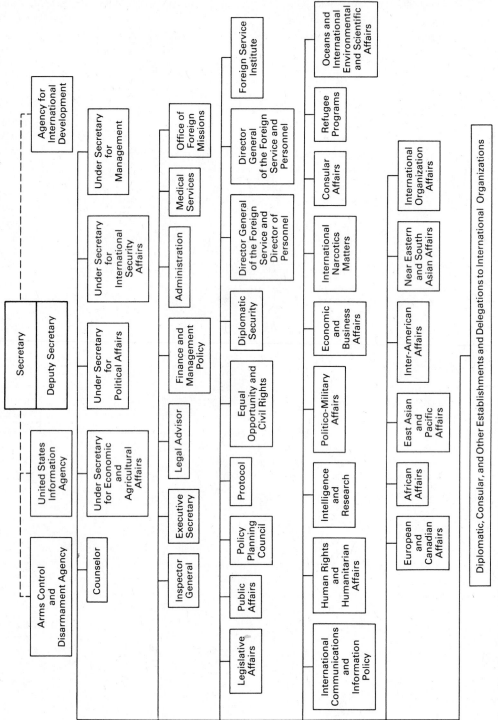

**Figure 2.4**   Department of State. *Source:* U.S. Government Manual, 1990.

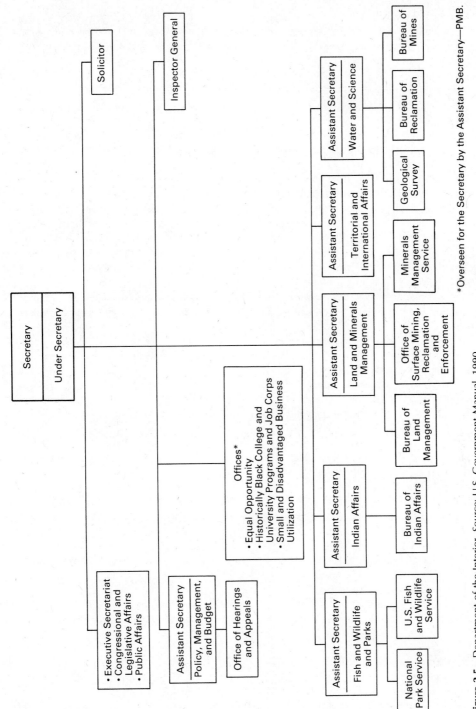

**Figure 2.5**  Department of the Interior. *Source:* U.S. Government Manual, 1990.

*Overseen for the Secretary by the Assistant Secretary—PMB.

Land Office), but many new functions have been added, including the Bureau of Mines, for the inspection of mines and enforcement of safety rules; the National Park Service, for running the national parks; and the U.S. Fish and Wildlife Service, devoted to the protection and improvement of fish and game. Many more functions that were not even envisioned in 1849 are now included in Interior, such as the Ocean Mining Administration.

While the domestically oriented and service-directed tasks have greatly expanded at Interior, its original coupling of disconnected, hodgepodge tasks remains intact. What this organizational pattern created, unlike the original core service departments, was a greater degree of subunit autonomy within its structure (the name *bureau* may therefore designate a greater degree of subunit independence). Generally, oversight from the Cabinet secretary or president of, say, the Land Office within Interior (now the Bureau of Land Management) was less evident even from the start because of the "pulls" of congressional subcommittees and interest groups. Again, this historic pattern holds true today. Even now a president or a secretary of Interior often finds it difficult, if not impossible, to impose long-term policy direction and coherence on diverse Interior service functions such as parks, recreation, wildlife management, resource management, and Indian affairs. Particularly as these domestic functions develop strong domestic constituencies, bureau fragmentation and independence increase.

New service functions were also added to old-line departments in the nineteenth century, along with other varieties of organizational designs. The Civil War and its aftermath forged a diversity of new public activities. The War Department added the Freedmen's Bureau (1866) to aid newly freed slaves; the Treasury added the Internal Revenue Service (1866), the Controller of the Currency (1863), and the Secret Service (1865)—all formed to supervise the collection of revenue and the regulation of currency. The attorney general became an officer with Cabinet rank in 1870 and was put in charge of the Justice Department to handle growing numbers of post-Civil War civil suits, legal controversies over natural resources and taxes. The Justice Department's subunits were called *divisions;* e.g., the Civil Division and the Tax Division. Why this occurred and why their chiefs were called assistant attorneys general is unclear, though here as elsewhere the pressures of dealing

with problems resulting from national growth and development fostered new service functions and an enlarged bureaucracy. Bureaucratic institutions grew quickly in the late nineteenth and early twentieth centuries. But note how the new names utilized to distinguish the subunits in bureaucracy varied widely; e.g., *bureau, service, controller,* and *division.* Each term denoted important subunits within major departments performing specified public tasks, yet the names varied principally because of different departmental traditions. *Divisions* were utilized, for instance, to designate Justice's subdivisions, but not elsewhere. Historic accident and unique departmental traditions caused the multiplication of subunit names and variations of U.S. organizational patterns.

An important deviation from the standard organizational pattern occurred with the creation of the Smithsonian Institution in 1846. In 1829 the will of James Smithson of England bequeathed to the United States his entire estate, "to found at Washington, under the name of the Smithsonian Institution, an establishment for the increase and diffusion of knowledge among men."[4] Congress wanted to accept the gift, but the purpose of the grant did not fit neatly into any of the existing departmental activities. Consequently, Congress created the first independent government agency in the form of a "foundation," vesting control of this agency outside the traditional executive branch chain of command by giving it to the Smithsonian Board of Regents. The board is composed of the chief justice, the vice president, three U.S. senators, three House members, and nine private citizens. The Smithsonian Institution began an important trend of bureaucratic autonomy, for today there are more than sixty independent agencies operating outside the thirteen traditional federal departments (see figure 2.6). Some are large, like the General Services Administration, with multi-billion dollar budgets and thousands of employees. The GSA operates autonomously because Congress and key groups have insisted it maintain its independence (largely to facilitate congressional and interest group control of its affairs). Other independent agencies, like ACTION, which consist of a loose collection of voluntary agencies such as the Peace Corps, Job Corps, Foster Grandparent Program, Volunteers in Service to America (VISTA), and the Drug Use Prevention Program, are quite small by comparison, with only a few thousand employees and a $200-million annual budget.

This chart seeks to show only the more important agencies of the Government.

**The Constitution**

**Legislative Branch**

The Congress

Senate     House

Architect of the Capitol
United States Botanic Garden
General Accounting Office
Government Printing Office
Library of Congress
Office of Technology Assessment
Congressional Budget Office
Copyright Royalty Tribunal
United States Tax Court

**Executive Branch**

**The President**

Executive Office of the President

White House Office
Office of Management and Budget
Council of Economic Advisors
National Security Council
Office of Policy Development
Office of National Drug Control Policy

National Critical Materials Council
Office of the U.S. Trade Representative
Council on Environmental Quality
Office of Science and Technology Policy
Office of Administration
National Space Council

**The Vice President**

Department of Agriculture
Department of Commerce
Department of Defense
Department of Education
Department of Energy
Department of Health and Human Services
Department of Housing and Urban Development

Department of the Interior
Department of Justice
Department of Labor
Department of State
Department of Transportation
Department of the Treasury
Department of Veterans Affairs

**Judicial Branch**

The Supreme Court of the United States

United States Courts of Appeals
United States District Courts
United States Claims Courts
United States Court of Appeals for the Federal Circuit
United States Court of International Trade
Territorial Courts
United States Court of Military Appeals
United States Court of Veterans Appeals
Administrative Office of the United States Courts
Federal Judicial Center

**Independent Establishments and Government Corporations**

ACTION
Administrative Conference of the U.S.
African Development Foundation
Central Intelligence Agency
Commission on the Bicentennial of the United States Constitution
Commission on Civil Rights
Commodity Futures Trading Commission
Consumer Product Safety Commission
Defense Nuclear Facilities Safety Board
Environmental Protection Agency
Equal Employment Opportunity Commission
Export-Import Bank of the U.S.
Farm Credit Administration
Federal Communications Commission
Federal Deposit Insurance Corporation
Federal Election Commission

Federal Emergency Management Agency
Federal Housing Finance Board
Federal Labor Relations Authority
Federal Maritime Commission
Federal Mediation and Conciliation Service
Federal Mine Safety and Health Review Commission
Federal Reserve System, Board of Governors of the Federal Retirement Thrift Investment Board
Federal Trade Commission
General Services Administration
Inter-American Foundation
Interstate Commerce Commission
Merit Systems Protection Board
National Aeronautics and Space Administration
National Archives and Records Administration

National Capital Planning Commission
National Credit Union Administration
National Foundation on the Arts and the Humanities
National Labor Relations Board
National Mediation Board
National Railroad Passenger Corporation (Amtrak)
National Science Foundation
National Transportation Safety Board
Nuclear Regulatory Commission
Occupational Safety and Health Review Commission
Office of Government Ethics
Office of Personnel Management
Office of Special Counsel
Oversight Board
Panama Canal Commission

Peace Corps
Pennsylvania Avenue Development Corporation
Pension Benefit Guaranty Corporation
Postal Rate Commission
Railroad Retirement Board
Resolution Trust Corporation
Securities and Exchange Commission
Selective Service System
Small Business Administration
Tennessee Valley Authority
U.S. Arms Control and Disarmament Agency
U.S. Information Agency
U.S. International Development Cooperation Agency
U.S. International Trade Commission
U.S. Postal Service

**Figure 2.6** The government of the U.S. *Source:* The U.S. Government Manual, 1990.

ACTION's independence set a historic precedent. President Kennedy emphasized at its inception that the Peace Corps' mission should be distinct and separate from such traditional diplomatic agencies as the State Department. Traditional international agencies like State have never wanted to merge with ACTION.

## The Clientele Service Functions

The latter half of the nineteenth century saw the formation of distinctly new forms of U.S. bureaucracy. These responded in large part to new pressures and requirements of society. As Richard Schott has observed, "Whereas earlier federal departments had been formed around specialized governmental functions (foreign affairs, war, finance and the like), the new departments of this period—Agriculture, Labor and Commerce—were devoted to interests and aspirations of particular economic groups. Their emergence testified to the growing specialization and occupational differentiation occurring in American Society."[5] In Schott's view, the growing and powerful economic blocks of interest groups in the late nineteenth and early twentieth centuries spawned new and powerful bureaucracies catering to specific clientele service needs.

The largest and most powerfully organized clientele group of this era was made up of farmers. Three-fourths of Americans at the time were living off the land. The U.S. Department of Agriculture (USDA) was created in 1862. It was at first headed by a commissioner, who then assumed full Cabinet status in 1889 as a departmental secretary. The USDA was established in the same year Congress passed the Morrill Act, which granted land for agricultural colleges to western states, and the Homestead Act, which opened public land to homesteaders. As Leonard White points out, these acts and the USDA "were the three major statutory foundations of federal agricultural policy for nearly a century."[6] At first the functions of the USDA were principally research and education. Development of new farming techniques and dissemination of these methods throughout the country were its early departmental priorities. As the charter of the USDA outlined, its initial goals were "to acquire and diffuse among people useful information on subjects connected with agriculture," "to conduct practical and scientific experiments," and "to appoint persons skilled in the natural sciences pertaining to agriculture."[7] The USDA was a federal bureaucracy that, quite unlike core departments such as State, which saw to the needs of the nation as a whole, catered directly to the needs and interests of a single group, farmers.

Today, although less than 5 percent of Americans live on farms, the USDA has grown into one of the largest federal departments because it conducts a variety of agricultural service functions considerably broader and more pervasive than those outlined by the original charter. As figure 2.7 indicates, over the years the activities of the USDA have expanded into economic forecasting, nutritional programs, food stamps, consumer services, rural development, international affairs, natural resources, and environmental protection. Note how the original scientific and educational programs of the department are now headed only by a director, not an assistant secretary, signaling their relative decline in importance within the overall scheme of current departmental activities. Also, while the USDA's clientele is still predominantly the farm population, the department serves many other groups, such as consumers, international markets, and environmentalists. The number of the USDA's "clienteles" has multiplied during the last century, as have its functional tasks.

## The Rise of Regulatory Agencies and Government Corporations

The late nineteenth and early twentieth centuries saw the development of two other forms of governmental bureaucracies outside the traditional departmental structures: regulatory agencies and government corporations. Regulatory agencies have been viewed by some as "the fourth" or "hidden" branch of government because they play such powerful, yet unpublicized, roles in shaping policies and agendas. Much of the growth of regulatory bureaucracies was, like that of earlier types of federal bureaucracies, the result of new societal needs for public services.

The basic social fabric of the United States was rapidly changing in this era. By the end of the nineteenth century, huge corporate structures, "the trusts," began to control, even monopolize, large segments of markets as diverse as oil, steel, railroads, and other manufacturing enterprises. Trusts had become able to control markets and rig market prices by the late 1800s. Both their enormous economic size and political influence precipitated vigorous demands

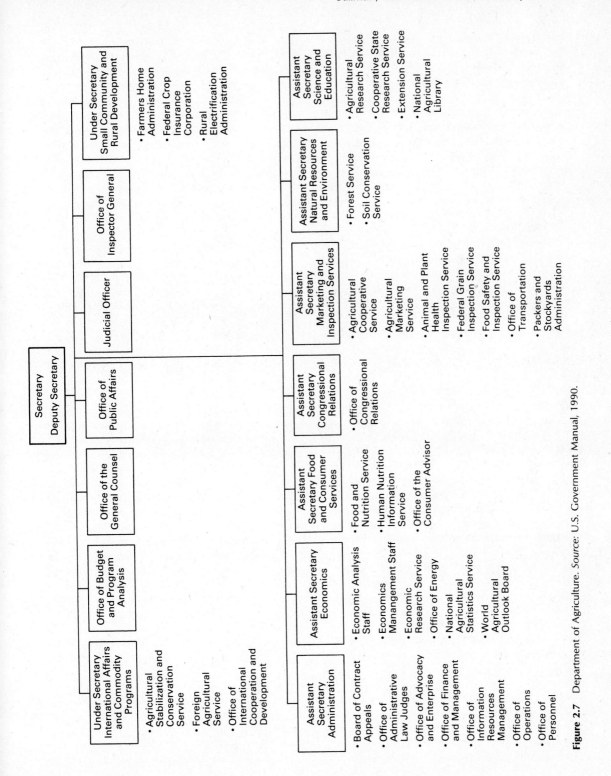

**Figure 2.7**   Department of Agriculture. *Source: U.S. Government Manual, 1990.*

from the public, particularly western farmers and small businesses, that checks be placed on trusts' unrestrained powers.

Government responded with two measures to control these giant corporations. First, trusts were smashed by legislation. The aim of the Sherman Antitrust Act of 1890 was to break up these large trusts by assigning new enforcement powers to the Justice Department. Second, regulatory commissions created permanent legal machinery to oversee and regulate corporate trust activities. Independent regulating began at the federal level in 1887 with the Interstate Commerce Commission (ICC), which was set up to regulate railroad rates, then a major economic issue for western farmers. The monopolistic practices of many railroads servicing the West and Midwest had "squeezed" many farmers, who, in turn, demanded government action. Help came in the form of this new type of bureaucracy, the ICC.

The ICC was modeled on early state regulatory commissions. Three-, five-, or seven-person boards were given legal autonomy and political independence (at least in theory) by being placed outside the formal executive departments. These boards were given quasilegal and executive powers to regulate prices in specific economic markets to curb monopolistic and unfair practices by industrial giants.

Today, almost a century after the creation of the ICC, there are several regulatory commissions. While these commissions regulate a diverse number of economic fields, they have the same independence as the ICC. They now constitute a major and influential part of federal bureaucracy. Some of them are: Nuclear Regulatory Commission, Federal Communications Commission, Federal Home Loan Bank Board, Federal Maritime Commission, Federal Power Commission, Federal Reserve Board, Federal Trade Commission, Commodity Futures Trading Commission, National Labor Relations Board, Securities and Exchange Commission, Consumer Product Safety Commission.

Figure 2.8 shows an organization chart of the Federal Trade Commission, which was established to regulate broad areas of trade practices. Note that its format is essentially the same as the ICC's (though its staff and budget are much smaller). In the words of Professor Marver Bernstein, such commissions involve "location outside an executive department; some measure of independence from supervision by the President or a Cabinet Secretary; immunity from the President's discretionary power to remove mem-

bers of independent commissions from office."[8] It should be added that while Congress has given many regulatory powers to independent commissions, over the years it has also assigned many regulatory functions to regular departments. For example, under the Packers and Stockyards Act of 1921 regulatory functions were assigned to the secretary of agriculture rather than to the Federal Trade Commission. Regulatory activities today are carried out by many executive departments, and not only within independent commissions. Again, historic accident rather than deliberate design frequently determines the location and degree of authority assigned to bureaucracy by Congress.

The Progressive Era also saw the creation of another important form of public bureaucracy: the government corporation. As Harold Seidman, a well-known scholar in this field, has written, the government corporation was "essentially an empirical response to problems posed by increasing reliance on government-created business enterprise and business-type operations to accomplish public purposes."[9] The government corporation was modeled on the private corporation. It had a board of directors, which was given a degree of independence from civil service rules and annual budgetary processes in order to enable it to carry out its corporate activities with greater flexibility in personnel and finances. The corporate format was especially appealing because it *did not* look like, nor was it called by any name resembling, "a public bureaucracy." It was, rather, "a corporation." Given the strong appeal of business values—i.e., values associated with efficiency, economy, and effectiveness—throughout U.S. history, such labeling was highly attractive to the electorate and its representatives. Business values were especially popular during the Progressive Era (the "city manager plan," which modeled local government along business lines, was also created at that time).

The corporate model was an effective device for implementing new programs with speed and efficiency. Government was being asked to perform many new public services. The public wanted these tasks done quickly and efficiently. New roads, schools, and utilities were needed. The government corporation therefore found favor precisely because it could execute these new tasks expeditiously and effectively. When the U.S. government purchased the Panama Railroad Company from the French Canal Company in 1904, a government corporation (the

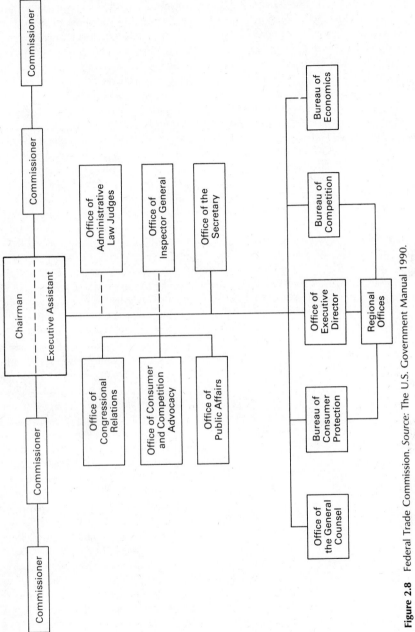

**Figure 2.8**   Federal Trade Commission. *Source:* The U.S. Government Manual 1990.

first one) was created to operate the canal railway. It was notably successful in aiding the building of the canal. Over one hundred government corporations since 1904 have been established to undertake a wide variety of public tasks—from COMSAT, which operates communications satellites, to the Tennessee Valley Authority (TVA), which provides power, irrigation, recreational facilities, and economic development to the Tennessee Valley. Like regulatory commissions, government corporations, at least in theory, are isolated from politics through the appointment of bipartisan directors with overlapping terms. Such neutrality and independence is an important factor in government corporations' flexibility in decision-making and long-term planning capability, especially in fiscal matters, personnel appointments, and capital planning. This rationale was used by President Nixon in 1970 when he proposed to transform the U.S. Postal Service from an executive department into a government corporation. This change was necessary, according to Nixon, "to free it from partisan political pressure" and to "improve its economy and efficiency."[10] The "corporate" form of the post office, and of many other public service organizations as well, is considered a preferable means of delivering services to the public.

Figure 2.9 shows the U.S. Postal Service's corporate format; many other organizations are modeled along much the same lines. Some of them are: St. Lawrence Seaway Development Corporation, Government National Mortgage Association, Commodity Credit Corporation, Federal Crop Insurance Corporation, Federal Home Loan Corporation, Federal Deposit Insurance Corporation, Export-Import Bank, Overseas Private Investment Corporation, and Rural Telephone Bank. As their names signify, they perform many kinds of specific tasks for the public, generally along the lines of those performed by private business. Their work constitutes a major share of federal activities but is largely a "hidden" dimension of government bureaucracy.

## Surges in Social Services in the New Deal and the Great Society

As James Q. Wilson has written, much of our modern bureaucracy is a result of "majoritarian surges of popular demand for more government activity"[11] in the Progressive, New Deal, and Great Society eras. By popular demand, the Progressive Era brought into

existence new varieties of regulatory and governmental corporations, yet the greatest source of civilian growth in U.S. bureaucracy occurred during the New Deal in the 1930s and the Great Society in the 1960s. Both eras ushered in new, diverse types of social service bureaucracies.

The New Deal stimulated unprecedented numbers of bureaucratic services. This was largely in response to an economic crisis—the Great Depression—that gripped the United States in the early 1930s. In 1933, 14 million Americans were out of work—one in four workers. In that same year, 5,000 banks closed their doors and industrial income fell from 85 to 37 billion dollars. Industry was at a standstill; breadlines formed; bankruptcies were common. The average of fifty industrial stocks on the New York Stock Exchange dropped from 252 to 61 between 1929 and 1933. Franklin Roosevelt was inaugurated as president on March 4, 1933. With vast support from the electorate and Congress, he moved quickly to set up a broad array of programs to cope with the economic disaster. The Federal Emergency Relief Administration (1933) was established to direct grants to localities for the support of poor and unemployed persons; the Civilian Conservation Corps (1933) put thousands of young men to work planting forest lands; the Farm Credit Administration (1933) extended farm loans and agricultural credit to bankrupt farmers; the Federal Deposit Insurance Corporation (1933) established protection for bank depositors, and the Works Progress Administration (1933) hired many men and women to build roads, schools, airports, and hospitals. Many other new public agencies were formed to deal quickly with the problems and impacts of this harsh economic emergency.

Most of the measures enacted in Roosevelt's first term were considered temporary. In his second term, however, many permanent public bureaucracies to alleviate or eliminate future economic crises like the Great Depression were created. The social security system created a mandatory retirement benefit program for workers as well as unemployment compensation and welfare programs for the blind, the handicapped, and dependent children, administered through the Federal Security Agency (1939). The Fair Labor Standards Act (1938) established a minimum wage and maximum work hours, and the National Labor Relations Act (1935) created a national system for labor-management collective bargaining that exists to this day. Another New Deal public agency, the

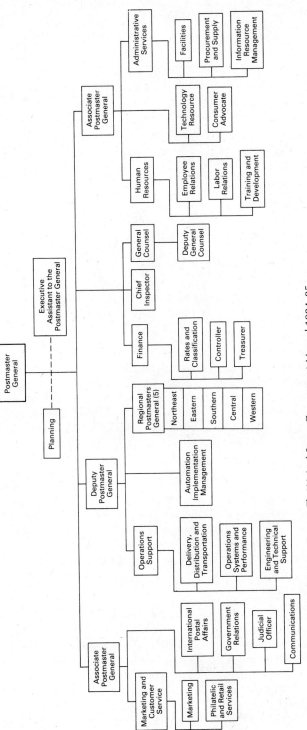

**Figure 2.9**   United States Postal Service. *Source:* The United States Government Manual 1984–85.

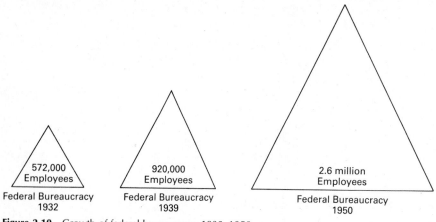

**Figure 2.10**    Growth of federal bureaucracy, 1932–1950

Federal Crop Insurance Corporation (1938), established a system of minimum base prices for farmers—parity payments—that guaranteed farmers minimum base prices for their produce in depressed market years. Through the Rural Electrification Administration (1935), electric power was brought to many isolated households; and the Farm Security Administration (1937) sought to improve the health, safety, and working conditions of farm laborers. These and many other new social services added enormously to the size and scope of the federal bureaucracy. As figure 2.10 shows, the United States developed a large, permanent bureaucracy to carry out these New Deal tasks.

If the New Deal concentrated on finding ways to put people back to work and to provide both "welfare basics" to millions and economic stability to various sectors of the economy, the Great Society in the 1960s sought to extend and expand the scope of these social programs to many areas that had been neglected by the New Deal. After the death of President John F. Kennedy on November 22, 1963, President Lyndon Johnson launched the Great Society, a vigorous new expansion of social service programs. The Medicare Program, for example, established in 1966, guaranteed medical insurance for the aged; the Office of Economic Opportunity (1964) administered "the war on poverty" through various new programs that required "the maximum feasible participation" of the poor; the Department of Housing and Urban Development in 1965 brought together several existing urban-oriented federal agencies and several new ones such as the Model Cities Program, within a new Cabinet-level department, to attack problems of housing and urban development. The Department of Transportation was established in 1966 to coordinate and target mass transit and general transportation policies for the entire nation; several regional commissions, such as the Appalachian Regional Commission, were created to deal with specialized regional economic and social needs. Further, the Great Society saw the rapid expansion of numerous grants-in-aid and categorical programs for the support of specific public programs for hospital, school, and highway construction, largely administered with matching funds through state and local public bureaucracies. Many of these programs are still on the books today.

## Hot War/Cold War Defense Organizations

The unique geographic isolation of the United States combined with its historical liberal opposition to standing professional military forces made large defense bureaucracies both unnecessary and unwanted for the first 150 years of its history. Even the large, bloody battles of the Civil War and World War I were waged mostly with temporary volunteer "citizen soldiers," not with professionals.

All this changed in World War II. The geographic isolation of the United States suddenly disappeared as military threats came to its doorstep. Japan attacked Pearl Harbor on December 7, 1941. Declarations of war from Hitler's Germany and Mussolini's Italy followed. These powerful totalitarian regimes, combined with new arms technology and the weakening of western democracies such as England and France, thrust onto the United States new responsibilities for defending its own interests as well as those of the free world. Overnight new defense agencies became necessary to plan, coordinate, mobilize, and administer the U.S. war effort. Twelve million men and women served in the armed services during World War II, and between 1941 and 1945, 147 new bureaucratic units were established by powerful new institutions, such as the Office of Price Administration, which planned and directed the overall war economy, and local draft boards. As figure 2.10 points out, this war-related activity caused the greatest jump in the overall size of the federal bureaucracy in U.S. history.

After the war many of these new bureaucratic entities, such as the Office of Price Administration, were abolished, but many others remained because of continued threats from the Soviet Union and other communist regimes. The Cold War, which sometimes turned hot in out-of-the-way places such as Korea, meant that during the 1940s and 1950s defense readiness and preparedness were considered a high priority. Large, permanent public bureaucracies were created because of these new long-term defense requirements. The Department of Defense (DoD) was established in 1947 through the merging of the War and Navy departments and the creation of a new subunit, the air force. The National Security Act, which created DoD in 1947, also established the Central Intelligence Agency to collect, coordinate, and disseminate foreign intelligence information vital to U.S. security needs (see figure 2.11). Foreign aid to friendly and neutral nations became an indispensable and undisputed part of U.S. strategic defenses. Military aid, offered to allies in substantial amounts during the 1940s and 1950s, was channeled through DoD's Military Area Assistance Group. Nonmilitary aid was dispensed through the Economic Cooperation Administration (EAC), which in 1961 became the Agency for International Development (AID). ECA and later AID sought to strengthen friendly and neutral countries economically, socially, and politically through a variety of grants, loans, and technical assistance programs.

Cold War defense programs spilled over into domestic issues and public programs. The need to harness science and scientific talent to serve the nation's Cold War needs became a vital preoccupation during this period. The Manhattan Project created the atomic bomb, which had brought a swift and dramatic end to hostilities in World War II, but after the war, Congress was faced with the awesome task of controlling the future use and development of atomic energy. To this end, the Atomic Energy Commission was created in 1946. Basic and applied research was fostered and stimulated through a new grant system that Congress set up in 1950 through the National Science Foundation (NSF). NSF, an independent agency with its own staff of scientific panels whose function was to approve grants for scientific research, became an important new avenue for stimulating research capabilities in universities and private research laboratories. NSF maintained the independence of scientists within their "home" institutions while fostering research into "potential defense spinoffs" through extensive grants and other assistance. Direct links with scientific knowledge and defense department priorities during the 1940s and 1950s were further enhanced by the growing practice of "contracting out" for services to universities, not-for-profit "think tanks" such as the Rand Corporation, and large numbers of private businesses.

Similarly, Cold War pressures to keep pace with the Russians launched the National Aeronautics and Space Administration (NASA) in 1958. The U.S.S.R.'s launching of Sputnik in October 1957 brought the United States overnight into an accelerated and extended space race with the Soviets. NASA throughout the 1960s, and even today, is designated as the "lead" agency in this effort to explore regions beyond the earth. NASA's role and prominence grew largely as a response to Cold War threats from the Soviets; just as AID's, the CIA's, the Atomic Energy Commission's, and NSF's did. Indeed, the spillovers and spinoffs into domestic programs from Cold War concerns were so numerous that it is difficult to describe them all succinctly. For example, the National Defense Highway Act (1955) created a vast, 100-billion-dollar-plus highway program, perhaps the largest public works program in history, stimulated and promoted in part by "defense" concerns (as the legal title of its enabling legislation indicates). The National Defense Education Act of 1958 fostered an influx of loans and grants for mathematics and science education in high

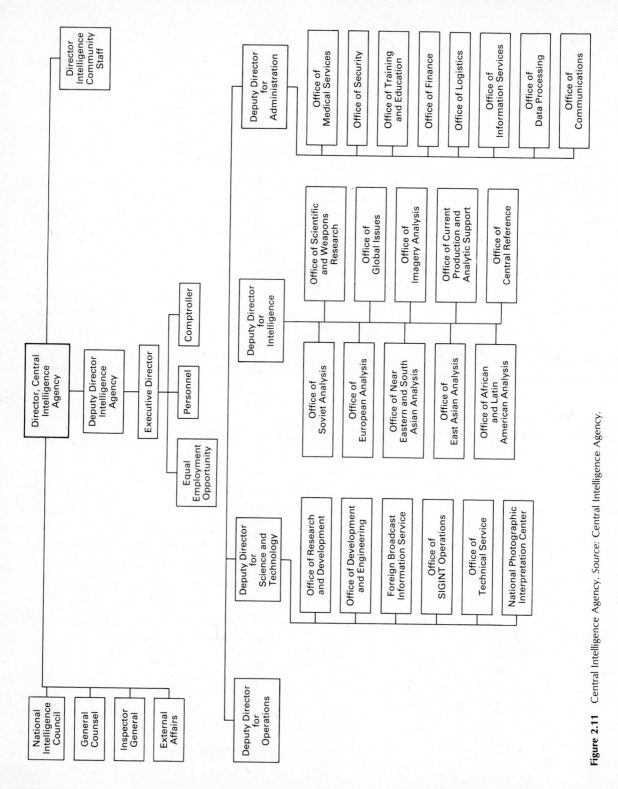

**Figure 2.11** Central Intelligence Agency. *Source:* Central Intelligence Agency.

schools and colleges. This act was prompted by fears that the United States was falling behind the Soviets in these fields. External threats or fears of external threats to the United States have been a major enduring source of the formation, growth, and maintenance of many postwar public bureaucracies and government programs.

## Staff and Local Service Functions

The rise of bureaucratic institutions in the twentieth-century United States spurred the concomitant growth of new layers of bureaucracies to oversee, coordinate, plan, and manage government. One of the earliest staff mechanisms created for these purposes was the General Staff. It was set up by Congress in 1903, upon the advice of Elihu Root, then secretary of war, to better plan and coordinate military activities and to prevent the repetition of the logistical calamities of the Spanish American War. Further, the Budget and Accounting Act of 1921 created an executive budget and added the Bureau of the Budget (first operating under the secretary of the treasury and later within the Executive Office of the President—EOP) as a key instrument for fiscal and budgetary planning. This act (perhaps *the* most critical contribution to federal bureaucracy's development) established the General Accounting Office to provide independent auditing oversight and controls.

The Brownlow Commission Report in 1937, which was the first major study of the organization of the presidency since 1789, recommended to President Franklin Roosevelt a substantial increase in staff assistance for the president. EOP has since grown into a formidable bureaucracy in its own right. Today EOP is the "staff arm" of the president. It consists of several thousand employees, many of them long-term careerists, and comprises a number of powerful policy advisory organizations (see figure 2.12). Some of them are: the Office of Policy Development, which advises the president on domestic policy issues; the National Security Council, which advises on international and defense issues; the Council of Economic Advisers, which set macroeconomic policies; the Office of Management and Budget, which develops the annual executive budget; and the Council on Environmental Quality, which assists in developing national environmental policies.

Staff bureaucracies have further proliferated in each of the thirteen federal executive departments, so that reporting to each Cabinet secretary are many large, specialized offices providing legal advice, policy analysis, personnel and budget recommendations, and much more (refer to the foregoing figures). Congress also has added enormous "overhead staffs" to its legislative advisory and planning capacities. For example, the Congressional Reference Service provides documentary and data reference for

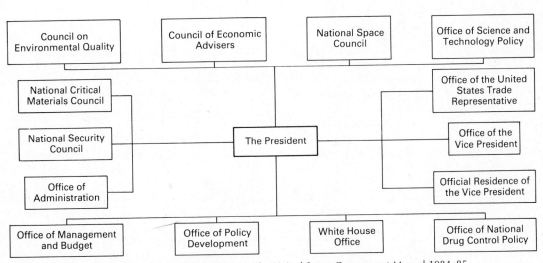

**Figure 2.12** Executive Office of the President. *Source:* The United States Government Manual 1984–85.

congressional activities; the Congressional Budget Office provides budget and economic advice to Congress; the Office of Technology Assessment helps legislators to plan, evaluate, and anticipate future impacts of technology upon U.S. society; the General Accounting Office, already mentioned, is an important source of fiscal and programmatic oversight. Whereas two decades ago Congress had 5,000 employees, it now has more than 20,000 staffers (more than some federal departments, such as the Department of Education, which has fewer employees). Even the judicial bureaucracy has grown rapidly over the last fifteen years. Ironically, members of Congress, who have been the most vocal critics of federal bureaucracy, are part of the fastest-growing bureaucracy since 1970.

Furthermore, more than 1,500 advisory boards and 120 commissions at the federal level report to either the executive or legislative branches, or both, and provide government with a wide array of technical, expert, or lay advice. Most are small and staffed with temporary personnel, but some have important duties and exert strong influence on government. For example, the Advisory Commission on Intergovernmental Relations, through its staff expertise and coordinative role, is immensely important in charting the future course of federalism and urban policies.

Concomitant with the growth of staff services at the federal level has been the rise of local and state bureaucracies during this century. Throughout much of the nineteenth century, local bureaucracies were limited or nonexistent. Most Americans lived on farms or in small towns where private businesses or voluntary cooperation were the chief routes for getting things done—hence volunteer fire brigades, locally "raised" schools, church-supported charities for the poor, aged, and infirm, and privately built and run transit systems, utilities, and housing.

Urbanization, new technologies, industrialization, and demands for new and improved public services brought a rapid growth in state and local bureaucracies throughout the twentieth century. State and local bureaucracies developed around the necessity for core functions, such as police and safety services. Continued economic development, regulatory functions, and corporate forms such as housing and transit authorities added new tasks. Educational needs in particular spurred the development of local public

bureaucracies throughout this century. The urbanization and industrialization of the United States in the early 1900s created the need for an educated workforce and for improved training opportunities. State compulsory education laws enacted largely in the twentieth century required, in turn, the development of massive, complex local education systems to educate the young from kindergarten through high school. State-supported universities and colleges became commonplace by the 1960s. The popularity of the automobile stimulated state highway construction and the establishing of licensing and vehicle facilities and programs. After the Great Depression, state and local welfare bureaucracies, funded increasingly through federal grants, replaced voluntary sources for aiding the poor. Fire and police services expanded in size, scope, and sophistication in response to new technological requirements and to demands for better public protection. Federal categorical grants to localities, combined with block grants and revenue sharing enacted in the 1970s, funneled more fiscal aid to states and localities, spawning the rapid growth of these bureaucratic institutions in a wide variety of areas. Mass transit systems, for example, are found in many medium-sized and large municipalities, thanks to various amounts of discretionary and categorical grants from the federal government (mainly from UMTA, Urban Mass Transit Administration). Food stamps also are locally administered but, for the most part, are federally funded (from the USDA programs). As table 2.1 indicates, since 1950 the most sizable increases in public employment have occurred at state and local levels. Further, much like the federal government, state and local bureaucracies have developed large staffs—"budgeters," "personnelists," and lawyers, as well as expert and lay advisory boards and commissions—to oversee and manage their activities.

As figure 2.13 shows, the formal executive departments as well as the many staffs, commissions, and boards of federal bureaucracies are mirrored in local bureaucracies. Local bureaucracy also has core agencies (fire and police functions), economic development activities, social service agencies, even regulatory and corporate enterprises (zoning and planning boards and housing and transit authorities). These tasks, like those at the federal level, have grown over time and have been sustained both by environmental needs and bureaucratic inertia.

**Table 2.1    Total U.S. Bureaucracy Workforce, 1950–82**

|  | Employment (millions) | | |
|---|---|---|---|
|  | *1950* | *1982* | *Total increase* |
| Federal civilians | 2.1 | 2.9 | +.8 |
| Military | 1.5 (45.6%) | 2.1 (27.6%) | +.6 |
| State | 1.1 (13.9%) | 3.7 (20.5%) | +2.6 |
| Local | 3.2 (40.5%) | 9.4 (50.9%) | +6.2 |
| Total | 7.9 (100.0%) | 18.1 (100.0%) | +10.2 |

*Source:* Statistical Abstracts of the United States, p. 294

## General Characteristics of the Rise of U.S. Bureaucracy: Gradualism, Experimentalism, Majoritarianism, and Complexity

As this essay has underscored, U.S. bureaucracy was not built overnight. It developed gradually, without plan, over nearly two hundred years of history, although, as table 2.2 indicates, there were seven critical periods where spurts of bureaucratic growth occurred: Washington's presidency, the midnineteenth century, the Gilded Age, the Progressive Era, the New Deal, World War II and the Cold War, and the Great Society, where new national experiences, such as war and depression, fostered new demands for public actions and activities.

In each of these eras, however, there was no standard format for public organizations. Rather, there was considerable diversity in formal structures. Americans have been remarkably experimental in creating new types of organizations to fulfill various functional needs. Perhaps no other nation has developed such a wide range of bureaucratic forms—from steeply hierarchical formal executive departments under the strict control of the chief elected official (a president, governor, or mayor) to autonomous agencies outside the structure and au-

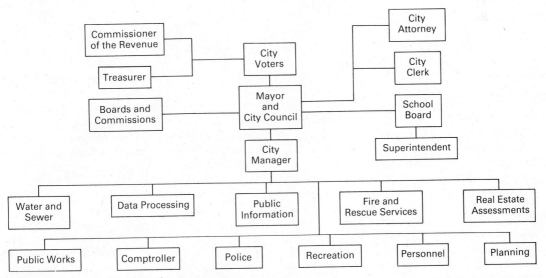

**Figure 2.13**   Organization chart of a city government

**Table 2.2    Rise of U.S. Public Bureaucracy Since 1789: 7 Critical Eras**

| Key Period in Bureaucracy's Development | Public Demands & National Requirements | Major Source of Political Support | Sample Types of Public Agency Est. |
|---|---|---|---|
| Federalist Era 1789–1802 | "Core Functions" of U.S. Government | Early Nationalism & Federalist Party | State Dept., War, Treasury, etc. |
| Mid-nineteenth century | Nation-state economic development | Jacksonian-Democratic-Whig parties | Interior Dept. & various public works projects |
| "Gilded Age"—late nineteenth century | Assistance for farmer, labor, & business | Special interest pressures of agriculture, labor & business | Clientele depts. of agriculture, labor & commerce |
| Populist & progressive eras of late nineteenth & early twentieth century | Regulation of business & new forms of public action | Progressive reform led by presidents Theodore Roosevelt & Woodrow Wilson | Regulatory agencies (FTC, ICC, etc.) and Government corporation (Panama Canal Commission, etc.) |
| New Deal in 1930s | New social regulations and services for coping with Great Depression | Democratic party led by President Franklin Roosevelt & New Deal coalition | Regulatory units like Farm Credit Administration or Federal Deposit Insurance Corp. and new social services like Social Security Administration |
| WW II and Cold War Era in 1940s | Global defense requirements | Wartime and postwar national consensus for strong defense | DOD, CIA, NASA, AID, etc. |
| "Great Society" 1960s | "War on Poverty" & vast new social programs | President Lyndon Johnson and Liberal-Democratic Coalition forged in 1964 election | HHS, HUD, DOT & various new poverty and social programs like Head Start, ACTION, Medicare, etc. |

thority of the executive branch and exhibiting comparatively "flat" organizational forms. Throughout U.S. history, experimentalism has certainly been one of the hallmarks of the rise of bureaucracy. That tradition continues in the 1990s.

Table 2.2 also demonstrates a third important feature of the rise of U.S. bureaucracy: its majoritarian sources. The bulk of U.S. bureaucracy, contrary to the belief of many, was not caused by pressure groups. Rather, there were specific periods when strong surges of majoritarian influence overrode special interests, resulting in the creation of public organizations that promoted national goals in the name of the public interest. The Federalist Era saw the demand for the formation of "the core departments" of the executive branch to carry out the work of "the first new nation." Similar "majoritarian surges" significantly expanded governmental programs during the Progressive, New Deal, World War II and Cold War, and Great Society eras, though certainly for different reasons and with different results. Only throughout the nineteenth century were bureaucratic innovations largely caused by special interest rather than majoritarian surges.

Finally, throughout nearly two centuries in the life of bureaucratic institutions, an increasing complexification of the entire system can be observed. Each succeeding wave of "majoritarian surges" formed a new layer of complexity, which in turn increased the size and diversity of the entire administrative system. Much of the general public's frustration with modern-day bureaucracy may well be caused by a lack of

**Table 2.3    Major Forms and Functions of U.S. Bureaucracy**

| Bureaucratic form | Examples of form | Major functions |
|---|---|---|
| Executive department (all levels) | State Department<br>Education Department<br>Defense Department | Principally implement tasks assigned, with some advisory and regulatory duties |
| Executive offices of president, governor, or mayor (all levels) | Office of Management and Budget, National Security Council, Council of Economic Advisers | Principally advisory roles for chief executive |
| Foundations (mainly federal level) | National Science Foundation | Promotion of research through grants; some advisory roles |
| Institutions and Institutes (mainly federal) | Smithsonian Institution, National Cancer Institute (HHS), Foreign Service Institute (State), Institutes for Environmental Research (Commerce) | Promotion of research-in-house & through grants; education & teaching function |
| Independent agencies (all levels) | ACTION (headed by one person) CIA (headed by one person) General Services Administration (headed by one person), Merit Systems Protection Board (committee governed), Transportation Safety Board (committee governed) | Perform a wide variety of executive quasi-judicial; quasi-legislative and advisory functions *outside* formal executive departments—either single headed or committee governed |
| Commissions on claims (mainly federal) | Indian Claims Commission Foreign Claims Settlement Commission | Largely judicial functions |
| Regulatory agencies (all levels) | Interstate Commerce Commission<br>Federal Trade Commission<br>Nuclear Regulatory Commission | Largely regulatory functions |
| Government Corporations (all levels) | Tennessee Valley Authority<br>U.S. Railway Association<br>Federal Prisons Industries, Inc.<br>Federal Crop Insurance Corporation<br>St. Lawrence Seaway Development Corporation | Carry out a wide variety of functions either within an executive dept. or independent of the executive branch; may be mixed public-private ownership |
| Boards, Councils, and Committees (all levels) | Federal Regional Councils<br>Federal Records Council<br>Water Resources Councils | Largely coordinative and advisory duties |
| Advisory Bodies (all levels) | National Historical Publications Commission<br>Advisory Board of St. Lawrence Seaway Development<br>Advisory Council on Vocational Education | Advisory group of primarily private citizens but legally constituted permanent bodies |
| Intergovernment Units (all levels) | Advisory Commission on Intergovernment Relations<br>Great Lakes River Basin Commission<br>Ozarks Regional Commission<br>Local Council of Government | National and regional planning, coordinating, and advisory bodies |
| Joint Executive-Congressional Units (all levels) | Migratory Bird Conservation Commission<br>Advisory Commission on Low Income Housing | Primarily advise both legislature and executive |
| Legislative Organizations (all levels) | General Accounting Office<br>State Auditor<br>County Auditor | Primarily advisor, research & oversight role for legislature |
| Special Districts (local only) | School District<br>Water & Sewer District<br>Fire District | Performs a wide range of county and municipal services independent of general government |
| Private Organizations, funded and set up by government (all levels) | Rand Corporation<br>Institute for Defense Analysis<br>MITRE<br>Los Alamos Labs<br>County Hospitals | Independent units funded almost entirely by government and chartered by government to perform specific types of contractual service(s) |
| Public Organizations, privately funded with mixed public-private directorship & highly autonomous (all levels) | Federal Reserve Board<br>Corporation for Public Broadcasting<br>Legal Services Corporation | Autonomous public units, largely privately supported, with a wide variety of tasks |

comprehension of such diverse, complex institutions—their functions, structures, or purposes. Understanding these institutions is, of course, the subject of this text.

## Forms, Functions, Policies, and Processes of Contemporary U.S. Bureaucracy

How do the formal elements of U.S. bureaucracy appear today? Table 2.3 summarizes most of the basic forms of present-day federal, state, and local-level bureaucracy. Altogether, these forms represent a composite of two hundred years of U.S. bureaucratic development. The range today, as Harold Seidman notes, is "staggering" and "defies classification."[12] It is a product of gradualism, experimentalism, majoritarianism, and complexification. Who knows for sure whether some of these units can even properly be termed public bureaucracies? For instance, the Rand Corporation, which is a publicly funded, legally chartered private organization, occupies a twilight zone between public and private bureaucracy. Some public bodies are essentially publicly funded but are run like private corporations, as are many local "special district governments." Are these "public" or "private" bureaucracies?

Equally problematic are their functional assignments. As table 2.3 also illustrates, many serve traditional executive roles, carrying out tasks assigned by the chief executive and approved by the legislature and judicial branches, although some fulfill entirely quasi-judicial or quasi-legislative functions. The Indian Claims Commission, for example, acts much like a court. Independent regulatory commissions, such as the Interstate Commerce Commission, have quasi-legislative roles in that Congress has granted to them significant authority to make rules, an essentially legislative function of government. The traditional view that public bureaucracies perform only "executive functions" is wrong. Most agencies are involved in the work of all three branches of government—executive, legislative, and judicial.

The policies that are promulgated as a result of these activities have been well summarized and classified by Theodore Lowi in a four-cell matrix.[13] Lowi sees public sector outputs of administrative units as the making of public policies that *actually* force things to happen to people or groups of people throughout society. Public organizations are not only purposeful but also perform actions that legitimately require actions or inactions on the part of either individuals or the whole environment. The policy outputs of government are unique by comparison with other private or nonprofit organized outputs, according to Lowi, because public agencies have the ability to coerce actions on the part of others. Such coercion may be *immediate* (throwing criminals in jail) or *remote* (administering a sales tax to every customer in an entire state). Lowi uses the polar dimensions of individual vs. environment *and* immediate vs. remote coercion to develop a four-cell matrix in which he summarizes the four basic varieties of public policy outputs of all governmental organizations (see table 2.4).

First, *regulative policies* involve both immediate and individual-oriented outputs of government units, such as ICC actions to stop unfair market competition by businessmen or FCC and Federal Drug Administration (FDA) actions to eliminate fraudulent advertising, or Immigration and Naturalization Service (INS)

**Table 2.4     Varieties of Policy Products of Public Bureaucracies**

|  | Individual effects | Environment effects |
| --- | --- | --- |
| Immediate Coercion | Regulatory Policies, e.g., ICC, FCC, FDA, DEA | Redistributive Policies, e.g., Federal Reserve Board, Internal Revenue Service, Social Security Administration, Federal Housing Administration |
| Remote Coercion | Distributive Policies, Veterans Administration, Agriculture Department, Department of Energy, National Science Foundation | Constituent Policies, e.g., Defense Department, State Department, Justice Department, Office of Management and Budget |

**Table 2.5    Major Formal Processes of U.S. Bureaucracy**

| | Agency by Type of Policy Products | | | |
|---|---|---|---|---|
| | *Regulatory* | *Distributive* | *Redistributive* | *Constituent* |
| Major Types of Formal Processes Involved in Agency Policy-making Roles | Rule making | Distribution of benefits | Adjudication | General program development |
| | Quasi-legislative process of est. agency rules for agency jurisdiction that covers *everyone* | Specific distribution of cash, goods, services to groups, individuals, state or local government with or without restrictions | Determination of whether or not individual can receive benefits that are due under law | Designing new programs to meet constituent service needs |
| | Adjudication | Public sponsored research | Policy development | Program implementation |
| | Quasi-judicial of charging violations of agency rules & effects only *single case one at a time* | In-house or contracted programs for research and development on distributive programs | Creation of new proposals to change or readjust distribution of goods and services to individuals | Carrying out specific legislative statutes and executive orders mandating service activities |
| | Law enforcement | Information gathering and dissemination | Program implementation | Policy revision and creation |
| | Quasi-executive function of selected application of laws and rules to groups and individuals | Collect, process and send out data and information to groups and individuals involving benefits | Carrying out of specifically mandated activities according to legislative standards | Creation or redesign of policies affecting program activities through advice to legislatures and executive |
| | Investigation and review | Initiation of new programs | Advisory processes | Program review and evaluation |
| | Process of examining complaints to see if merits remedying as well as review regulatory actions in order to revise or change rulings | Assists in development of new goods or changes old ones for distribution of benefits | Assisting legislative and executive branches in programming new legislation, revising or proposing new laws, particularly using legislative clearance process | Examination and investigation of programs in order to improve or change actions of agency |

enforcement of immigration laws, or the Drug Enforcement Agency's efforts to combat illicit drug activities. By contrast, *redistributive policies,* according to Lowi's matrix, are immediate but influence society only as a whole. The Federal Reserve Board (FRB) establishes its bank reserve requirements and prime rates, causing, in turn, general inflationary or deflationary trends throughout society. The administration of the progressive income tax by the Internal Revenue Service (IRS) redistributes monies from one group of citizens in society to another, which affects the entire nation. The Social Security Administration (SSA) likewise redistributes monies from younger workers to pensioners, affecting all Americans.

Third, *distributive policies* are those public outputs that are remote *and* individual-oriented. Tariffs influence buying habits of individual consumers but are usually administered far from where these consumers live and work. Similarly, direct government subsidies to industry or to particular social groups, such as farmers or veterans, are distributive forms of public policies, according to Lowi. Finally, the fourth cell of Lowi's matrix contains *constituent policies,* which are both remote and aimed at all of society. DoD's policy outputs are, for the most part, in this category; i.e., defense of the national interests against foreign enemies. No one group of Americans gains more or less (at least in theory) from preserving national integrity, freedom, and liberty. Yet the work of DoD is remote from the daily life of the average citizen.

Obviously, real-world public agencies do not always fit neatly as pure types within the Lowi four-cell matrix. Many agencies promulgate multiple types of public policies at the same time. DoD, for example, may be primarily involved in defending the nation, but it is also very much engaged in distributional and redistributional policy making via its huge $300 billion-plus annual budgets. The EPA regulates air, water, and land quality in the United States, though it also acts to distribute grants to state, local, and private organizations and therefore is very much engaged in distributive policy making. The Department of Agriculture (DoA), which was founded as a clientele department to serve the needs of farmers, can properly be viewed as a distributive agency, but it also regulates the entire food chain to ensure the health and safety of Americans. Most agencies thus contain a mix of Lowi's categories.

However, the formal processes that are found within public agencies that produce these policies depend upon the dominant policy activity of an agency as is indicated in table 2.5. Each variety of policy-making activity tends to have associated with it distinctive internal formal processes and procedures essential for carrying out these policies. As one would expect, regulatory policy-making bodies involve highly legalized internal processes, often associated with the legislative or judicial branches of government, rule making, adjudication, law enforcement, and investigation/review processes. Constituent services require more traditional forms of managerial processes to carry out tasks for their agencies: program development, program implementation, policy revision, program review, and evaluation. Redistributive bureaucracies contain normally a mix of legalistic and managerial processes (adjudication, policy development, program implementation, and advisory). The internal processes of distributive organizations, as one would expect, focus upon those processes that relate directly to the distribution of benefits, publicly sponsored research activities, information gathering and dissemination, and advisory processes. Policy activities, therefore, significantly influence, even determine, the type of formal internal processes found in every agency.

## Notes

1. Leonard D. White, *The Federalists: A Study in Administrative History* (NY: Macmillan, 1948), pp. 22–23.
2. Ibid., p. 147.
3. Frederick C. Mosher (ed.), *Basic Documents of American Public Administration,* 1776–1950 (NY: Holmes and Meier, 1976), pp. 36–38.
4. *The US Government Manual* (Washington, DC, 1980), p. 733.
5. Richard L. Schott, *The Bureaucratic State: The Evolution and Scope of the American Federal Bureaucracy* (NJ: General Learning Press, 1972), p. 9.
6. Leonard D. White, *The Republican Era,* 1869–1901 (NY: Macmillan, 1958), p. 232.
7. Ibid.
8. Marver H. Bernstein, *Regulating Business by Inde-*

*pendent Commission* (Princeton: Princeton University Press, 1955), p. 130.

9. Harold F. Seidman, *Politics, Position and Power,* 2d ed. (NY: Oxford University Press, 1975), p. 254.

10. House Document, pp. 91–313.

11. James Q. Wilson, "The Rise of the Bureaucratic State," *The Public Interest* (Fall 1975), p. 90.

12. Harold F. Seidman, *Politics,* p. 236.

13. Theodore Lowi, "Four Systems of Policy, Politics, and Choice," Inter-University Case Program, Case No. 110 (Syracuse: 1972), p. 27.

## Chapter 2 Review Questions

1. What are the formal elements of Weber's model of bureaucracy? Based on your reading of the case or your own experiences with public bureaucracies, did Weber fail to mention any attributes of bureaucracy in his description?

2. What are the chief causes, based on your reading of Weber and the case study, for bureaucratic growth?

3. Does the case in your view support or contradict Weber's arguments about the monolithic power position of bureaucracy in society? About the nature of bureaucratic rationality? Its hierarchy? Specialization? Narrow latitude of bureaucratic rule enforcement? High degree of efficiency?

4. After reading the foregoing case study, where would you modify Weber's model to account more accurately for the pattern of growth and the characteristics of America's bureaucracy?

5. According to Weber and the case study, is bureaucracy hard to change? What are the main causes of "bureaucratic inertia"? What, according to the case, are the sources prompting change?

6. Think about the case, "The Rise of U.S. Bureaucracy," and what it says about the value of bureaucracy in modern society. Why are bureaucracies important? And yet so disliked? In your view, what should be done about the fundamental public hostility toward bureaucracy?

## Key Terms

ideal-types
traditional authority
charismatic authority
legal-rational authority
bureaucratic hierarchy
tenure in office

objective experts
bureaucratic rules
monied economy
bureaucratic power
bureaucratic secrecy

## Suggestions for Further Reading

For a thoughtful understanding of Weber's background, his intellectual development, and continuing influence, read the introduction of H. H. Gerth and C. Wright Mills, eds., *From*

*Max Weber: Essays in Sociology* (New York: Oxford University Press, 1946); Reinhard Bendix, *Max Weber: An Intellectual Portrait* (New York: Doubleday, 1960); and Marianne Weber, *Max Weber: A Biography* (New York: John Wiley, 1975). For a short but insightful piece, see Alfred Diamant, "The Bureaucratic Model: Max Weber Rejected, Rediscovered, and Reformed," in *Papers in Comparative Administration,* edited by Ferrel Heady and Sybil L. Stokes (Ann Arbor, Mich.: The University of Michigan Press, 1962).

The current literature on bureaucracy is vast but uneven and should be read selectively. Some of the better introductions include Graham Allison, *Essence of Decision: Explaining the Cuban Missile Crisis* (Boston: Little, Brown, 1971); Peter M. Blau and Marshall W. Meyer, *Bureaucracy in Modern Society,* Second Edition (New York: Random House, 1971); Francis E. Rourke, *Bureaucracy, Politics and Public Policy,* Third Edition (Boston: Little, Brown, 1984); Peter Woll, *American Bureaucracy,* Second Edition (New York: W. W. Norton, 1977); Kenneth J. Meier, *Politics and the Bureaucracy: Policy Making in the Fourth Branch of Government,* Second Edition (North Scituate, Mass.: Duxbury Press, 1987); Douglas Yates, *Bureaucratic Democracy: The Search for Democracy and Efficiency in American Government* (Cambridge, Mass.: Harvard University Press, 1982); Harold Seidman and Robert Gilmour, *Politics, Position, and Power,* Fourth Edition (New York: Oxford University Press, 1986); Gary C. Bryner, *Bureaucratic Discretion* (New York: Pergamon Press, 1987); and Richard J. Stillman II, *The American Bureaucracy* (Chicago: Nelson-Hall, 1987). Francis E. Rourke's *Bureaucratic Power in National Politics,* Fourth Edition (Boston: Little, Brown, 1986), is a balanced, up-to-date collection of various excerpts from seminal writings on this subject.

For three excellent historic treatments of the rise of bureaucratic institutions, see the two

volumes of E. N. Gladden, *A History of Public Administration* (London: Frank Cass, 1972); Ernest Barker, *The Development of Public Services in Western Europe, 1660–1930* (New York: Oxford University Press, 1944); and Frederick C. Mosher, *Democracy and the Public Service,* Second Edition (New York: Oxford University Press, 1982). Leonard D. White's four-volume history of American public administration up to 1900 (cited in the previous chapter's "Suggestions for Further Reading") is certainly valuable reading on this topic. Martin Albrow, *Bureaucracy* (New York: Praeger, 1970); Stephen Skowronek, *Building a New American State: The Expansion of National Administrative Capacities, 1877–1920* (New York: Cambridge University Press, 1982); Don K. Price, *America's Unwritten Constitution* (Baton Rouge, La.: Louisiana University Press, 1983); Martin J. Schiesl, *The Politics of Efficiency* (Berkeley, Calif.: University of California Press, 1977); Guy Benveniste, *The Politics of Expertise,* Second Edition (San Francisco: Boyd & Fraser, 1977); Thomas K. McCraw, *Prophets of Regulation* (Cambridge, Mass.: Harvard University Press, 1984); Frederick C. Mosher, *A Tale of Two Agencies* (Baton Rouge, La.: Louisiana University Press, 1984); and Mathew Crenson, *The Federal Machine* (Baltimore: Johns Hopkins University Press, 1975) offer unique and highly original conceptual and historical perspectives, as well as James Q. Wilson's essay, "The Rise of the Bureaucratic State," in *The Public Interest* (Fall 1975).

Serious students of bureaucracy should examine primary materials—executive orders, legislative acts, and official reports. Many key materials are contained in Frederick C. Mosher, ed., *Basic Documents of American Public Administration, 1776–1950* (New York: Holmes and Meier, 1976), and Richard J. Stillman II, ed., *Basic Documents of American Public Administration Since 1950* (New York: Holmes and Meier, 1982). For the best recent defense of bureaucracy, see Charles T. Goodsell, *The Case for Bureaucracy* (Chatham, N.J.: Chatham House, 1983).

Recent works that attempt to view bureaucracy from a comparative perspective are: Joel D. Aberbach, Robert D. Putnam and Bert Rockman, *Bureaucrats and Politicians in Western Democracies* (Cambridge, Mass.: Harvard University Press, 1981); Metin Heper, ed., *The State and Public Bureaucracy* (N.Y.: Greenwood,

1987); and Ali Farazmand, ed., *Handbook of Comparative Development Public Administration* (New York: Marcel Dekker, 1991).

For two excellent recent books devoted to the British experience, see Peter Hennessy, *Whitehall* (New York: Free Press, 1989); and Rosamund M. Thomas, *The British Philosophy of Administration* (Cambridge, England: Center for Business and Public Sector Ethics, 1989).

# CHAPTER 3

## The General Environment: The Concept of Ecology

*A*n ecological approach to public administration builds, then, quite literally from the ground up. . . .

*John M. Gaus*

## Introduction

*Ecology* entered the lexicon of social science and public administration literature long before it became popular in the media and on college campuses in the 1970s as a word synonymous with protecting the natural beauty of the landscape. Originally, the term was derived from the ancient Greek word *oikos,* meaning "living place," and was used extensively by nineteenth-century Darwinian botanists and zoologists to describe how organisms live and adapt to their environments. Sociologists during the 1920s borrowed the ideas of plant and animal ecology and applied the concept to human life; they emphasized the *interdependence* of human life within an increasingly complex organic system and the tendency of living systems to move toward an *equilibrium,* or stabilization of life forms in relation to the surrounding environment.

Ecology was introduced into the public administration vocabulary primarily through the writings of the late Harvard Professor John M. Gaus (1894–1969), one of the early pioneers of public administration; he elaborated on ecology in a series of famous lectures at the University of Alabama in 1945, later published as *Reflections on Public Administration.*

In this work, as well as in his other writings, Gaus was particularly adept at weaving the patterns and ideas of public administration into the total fabric of the issues and events of modern American society. Better than most observers, he showed how public administration, its development, and its activities were influenced by its setting, or its ecology. In his words, ecology "deals with all interrelationships of living organisms and their environment." Thus, "an ecological approach to public administration builds . . . quite literally from the ground up; from the elements of a place—soils, climate, location, for example—to the people who live there—their numbers and ages and knowledge, and the ways of physical and social technology by which from the place and in relationships with one another, they get their living." For Gaus, administrative systems were inextricably intertwined with the fabric of society. In particular, he delineated several important elements that he found useful "for explaining the ebb and flow of the functions of government: people, place, physical technology, social technology, wishes and ideas, catastrophe, and personality." He addressed himself to the importance of these ecological factors in the following selection abridged from his *Reflections on Public Administration.*

Gaus began teaching political science shortly after World War I (prior to Harvard, he taught at the University of Wisconsin) with an early interest in public administration. He interspersed teaching with numerous state and national administrative assignments, and he brought these practical experiences to his classes. Throughout his career, Gaus was fascinated by the interplay of forces between public administration and the larger society.

Gaus shared much in common with Frederick Jackson Turner, an early twentieth-century American historian who poured over maps, soil samples, statistical data of regions, and voting records in his empirical study of the growth of the American nation. Similarly, Gaus asked students of public administration to observe the environment of administration so as to understand how the characteristics of its ecology influence the development of administrative institutions. For Gaus, the term *ecology* was relevant not only to cloistered scholars of administration at work on universal theories of the administrative process, but also to on-the-line practitioners of administration. A conscious awareness of ecological factors permits administrators to respond more wisely to the demands and challenges of the external environment of their organizations. Thus, in the hands of the practitioner, ecology can become a diagnostic tool; it can help in visualizing the major elements in the administrative processes and provide a yardstick for measuring their impact on an organization. However, Gaus was aware that prediction would not be simple: "The task of predicting the consequences of contemporary action, of providing the requisite adjustment, is immensely difficult with the individual or in family life. The difficulty increases with the size and complexity of the unit and expansion and range of variables."

Gaus's concern with ecology of administration was prompted by a special concern with "change." He was a member of the generation rocked by the hardships of a catastrophic economic depression in the 1930s, and he saw the American landscape rapidly being transformed in myriad ways. As he observed, "Change which we have found to be so characteristic of American life, change that has disrupted neighborhoods, that has destroyed cultural stabilities, that has reflected the sweep across the continent, the restless migration to city and back to farm, from one job to another, has brought widely hailed merits. Its merits have been so spectacular, indeed, that we speak of it as progress. . . . Its costs are also becoming clearer, registered in the great dramatic collapses of the depression, more subtly in the defeat, disintegration and frustration of individuals. . . ." Gaus looked to public administration "to find some new source of content, of opportunity for the individual to assert some influence on the situation in which he finds himself." In one essay, "American Society and Public Administration," he stated: "My thesis is that through public instruments some new institutional bases which will enable the individual to find development and satisfaction can be created and some sense of purpose may flower again."[1]

Gaus was both pessimistic and optimistic about the condition of human society. His pessimism welled up when he saw change destroying the patterns of existence familiar to his generation, breaking down the stabilizing institutional arrangements, and confronting individuals with serious economic and personal hardships. Yet Gaus perceived a bright hope in applied social science: through an ecological approach to public administration he believed that new and renewed institutional patterns could be devised for individuals living in an age of change. Ecology in public administration became for Gaus a vital instrument for comprehending, directing, and modulating the forceful shocks of change in contemporary life. In the more than 40 years that have passed since Gaus's studies of ecology were published, younger scholars in the field, such as Fred Riggs, have been active in the wider application of the ecological approach, especially in the newer areas of developmental and comparative public administration.

As you read this selection, keep the following questions in mind:

Why does Gaus argue that knowledge of the general environment is so critical for administrators?

If you were to revise this essay for today's readers, what other environmental factors that affect modern public administration might you add to Gaus's list? (You might include, for example, the generation gap or ethnic or sexual factors.)

In what ways can administrators recognize changes in the general environment?

What might be the price paid for the failure of organizations to respond swiftly and correctly to external environmental change?

As you read Gaus's essay, reflect on its relevance to Case Study 1, "The Blast in Centralia No. 5." How did ecological factors influence the outcome of this case?

---

[1] John Gaus, "American Society and Public Administration," in John M. Gaus, Leonard D. White, and Marshall E. Dimock, *The Frontiers of Public Administration* (Chicago: University of Chicago Press, 1936).

# The Ecology of Public Administration

**JOHN M. GAUS**

The study of public administration must include its ecology. "Ecology," states the Webster Dictionary, "is the mutual relations, collectively, between organisms and their environment." J. W. Bews points out that "the word itself is derived from the Greek *oikos,* a house or home, the same root word as occurs in economy and economics. Economics is a subject with which ecology has much in common, but ecology is much wider. It deals with all the interrelationships of living organisms and their environment."[1] Some social scientists have been returning to the use of the term, chiefly employed by the biologist and botanist, especially under the stimulus of studies of anthropologists, sociologists, and pioneers who defy easy classification, such as the late Sir Patrick Geddes in Britain. In the lecture of Frankfurter's already quoted, the linkage between physical area, population, transport and government is concretely indicated. More recently, Charles A. Beard formulated some axioms of government in which environmental change is linked with resulting public administration. "I present," he stated, "for what it is worth, and may prove to be worth, the following bill of axioms or aphorisms on public administration, as fitting this important occasion.

1. The continuous and fairly efficient discharge of certain functions by government, central and local, is a necessary condition for the existence of any great society.
2. As a society becomes more complicated, as its division of labor ramifies more widely, as

its commerce extends, as technology takes the place of handicrafts and local self-sufficiency, the functions of government increase in number and in their vital relationships to the fortunes of society and individuals.
3. Any government in such a complicated society, consequently any such society itself, is strong in proportion to its capacity to administer the functions that are brought into being.
4. Legislation respecting these functions, difficult as it is, is relatively easy as compared with the enforcement of legislation, that is, the effective discharge of these functions in their most minute ramifications and for the public welfare.
5. When a form of government, such as ours, provides for legal changes, by the process of discussion and open decision, to fit social changes, the effective and wise administration becomes the central prerequisite for the perdurance of government and society—to use a metaphor, becomes a foundation of government as a going concern.
6. Unless the members of an administrative system are drawn from various classes and regions, unless careers are open in it to talents, unless the way is prepared by an appropriate scheme of general education, unless public officials are subjected to internal and external criticism of a constructive nature, then the public personnel will become a bureaucracy dangerous to society and to popular government.
7. Unless, as David Lilienthal has recently pointed out in an address on the Tennessee Valley Authority, an administrative system is so constructed and operated as to keep

alive local and individual responsibilities, it is likely to destroy the basic well-springs of activity, hope, and enthusiasm necessary to popular government and to the following of a democratic civilization."[2]

An ecological approach to public administration builds, then, quite literally from the ground up; from the elements of a place—soils, climate, location, for example—to the people who live there—their numbers and ages and knowledge, and the ways of physical and social technology by which from the place and in relationships with one another, they get their living. It is within this setting that their instruments and practices of public housekeeping should be studied so that they may better understand what they are doing, and appraise reasonably how they are doing it. Such an approach is of particular interest to us as students seeking to cooperate in our studies; for it invites—indeed is dependent upon—careful observation by many people in different environments of the roots of government functions, civic attitudes, and operating problems.

With no claim to originality, therefore, and indeed with every emphasis on the collaborative nature of the task, I put before you a list of the factors which I have found useful as explaining the ebb and flow of the functions of government. They are: people, place, physical technology, social technology, wishes and ideas, catastrophe, and personality. I have over many years built up a kind of flexible textbook in a collection of clippings, articles and books illustrative of each, as any one can do for himself. Such illustrations of the "raw material of politics" and hence administration are in themselves the raw material of a science of administration, of that part of the science which describes and interprets why particular activities are undertaken through government and the problems of policy, organization and management generally that result from such origins.[3]

By illustrating concretely the relation of these environmental factors, a cooperative testing of the theory will be facilitated. The changes in the distribution of the people of a governmental unit by time, age and place throw light on the origins of public policy and administration. At our first census, we were a people 80 per cent of whom lived on farms; at our last census, one hundred and fifty years later, 80 per cent of us did not live on farms. Over a third are now living in a relatively few metropolitan areas; but the growth of these areas is not in the core or mother city; it is in the surrounding suburbs, separate political entities, frequently also separate economic-status and cultural entities, yet sharing with the mother city, which is often absolutely declining in population, the public housekeeping problems of a metropolitan organism for which no—or no adequate—political organization exists. Our population is increasingly one with a larger proportion distributed among the older age classes. These raw facts—too little known and appreciated by citizens, which should be at once placed before them in discussing many of our public questions—in themselves explain much about our functions of government. Coupled with factors of place and technology, they clarify many an issue that is usually expressed in sterile conflicts. For example, the old people in the more frequent large family on a farm of a century ago, where more goods and services were provided on the farm, had a function still to perform and a more meaningful place in the lives of younger generations of the family. In a more pecuniary economy, separated from the family-subsistence economy, ignored in the allocation of the work and rewards of an industrial society, the demand for pensions became irresistible.

The movement of people (by characteristic age and income groups) from the mother city to suburbs (as guided by factors of time-space and cost in the journey to work, the dispersal of shopping centers, the search of industry for land space for straight-line production facilitated by paved roads, trucks and distribution of power by wires, and other technological changes, and changes in what we wish for in residential environment) produces its repercussion in the values of land and buildings, in the tax basis for public services already existent in older areas and demanded in the new, in the differential requirements and capacities-to-pay of people for housing (including the site and neighborhood equipment) and in the adjustment of transport and utility requirements for the ever-changing metropolitan organism.

Thus the factors of people and place are inextricably interwoven. And not merely in crowded urban centers. I have watched the same process of change in sparsely settled areas of farm and forest, and its potent effect on government.

Where there are extensive cut-over areas in the Lake States, where the older farm lands of New England or New York are no longer profitable to agriculture and reforestation is too recent to yield timber crops, in the Great Plains where lands best suited to grazing and with limited rainfall have been subjected to the plough, in the cut-over and eroded lands of the Southern Piedmont, or in the anthracite region of Pennsylvania, physical conditions—the exhaustion of the resource which originally brought settlement—have produced a chain of institutional consequences. Land values and tax payments decline, tax delinquent land reverts to county or state, public schools, roads and other services can no longer be locally financed. Immediate relief through state financial aids or state administered services in turn are inadequate when widespread catastrophic economic depression undermines state revenues. Efforts aimed at restoring a source of production, such as encouragement of cropping timber through favoring taxation or the building up of public forests adequate for permanent wood-using industries, or the restoration of soil, will require a long period of time for efficacy, and equally require an atmosphere

in which political leadership, the careful integration of national, state, local, and individual and corporate policies, and skilled technical personnel can be established and supported steadily. Such an atmosphere, however, is not likely to be present among the frustrate population of such areas, or the better-provided populations of other areas called upon to tax themselves for local units of government in areas which they have never seen or whose problems they do not understand. Thus changes in place, or the use of the resources and products of a place, are coercive in their effect upon public administration.[4]

My own generation has had a great lesson in the importance of change in physical technology in witnessing the adoption of the automobile and the role it has come to play. It may be noted that its widespread use was made possible by the development of paved highways provided necessarily as a public service. Highway expansion and design have been affected by the coercion of political forces created by the physical invention. Groups of automobile users, manufacturers, hotel proprietors, road builders, road machinery and materials suppliers, persons seeking jobs in highway construction and administration and many others, have contended with those using horses, carriage and harness makers and persons opposed to the increased taxation that paved roads would require. The original causes—a combination of physical inventions such as the internal combustion engine and the vulcanization of rubber—get obscured in the ultimate disputes over taxation, jurisdiction, requirement of liability insurance and examination for drivers' licenses, or over the merits or defects of systems of traffic control or the financing of overhead crossings or express highways. The citizen blames "bureaucrats" and "politicians" because the basic ecological causes have not been clarified for him. This process of public function adoption may also be reversed by other changes—as we see, for example, in the abandonment of many publicly financed and constructed canals, when new technologies of transport rendered them obsolete.

Changes in physical technology, however slowly their institutional influences may spread, are more obvious even to the point of being dramatic, to the citizen. But he sometimes forgets the importance of the invention of social institutions or devices, and their continuing influences which coerce us. Thus the pooling and application of the savings of many through the invention of the corporation has set new forces to ripple through the social order, disarranging human relationships and creating new possibilities of large scale enterprise financially capable of utilizing extensive equipment and personnel and creating new relationships between buyer and seller, employer and employee—from which coercions for a new balance of forces, through consumer, labor and investor standards, have resulted.

You will have noted how interrelated all of these factors are in their operation. Perhaps the subtlest one is that for which I have difficulty in finding a satisfactory term. I have used the words "wishes and ideas." What you don't know, it is said, won't hurt you. I wonder whether this is true. If you do know that some new drug, or method of treatment of disease, will prevent the illness or perhaps death of those dear to you, you will have a new imperative for action, even if that action requires a public program. If you know or think you know that a combination of legislative and administrative measures will safeguard your bank deposit or insurance from destruction, that idea will have a coercive effect upon your political action. If you think that public officials are corrupt, that a tariff act or a regulation of a trade is a "racket," that too will influence the political decisions of your time. If you value material well-being, and if that desire takes so definite a form as a house and yard and garden,

there are inevitable consequences in standards of public services that will facilitate the realization of your desire. Down that long road one will find the public insurance of mortgages to achieve lower interest rates and longer-term financing and zoning ordinances.

The originators of ideas and of social as well as physical invention are persons. We students of public administration will do well to study the elements in the influences which Bentham, the Webbs, the city planner Burnham, the health officer Biggs, the pioneers in the New York Bureau of Municipal Research and its Training School for Public Service have wielded. Relevant preparation, longevity, personal or institutional resources for research, sympathetic disciples, frequently some catastrophic situation in which prevailing attitudes were sufficiently blasted to permit the new ideas to be applied, channels of publication and of communication generally, as well as inner qualities of industry and integrity all, or nearly all in some combination, will be found. We each will have touched some one of this kind, perhaps, in our own community; if not a pioneer in original invention, an enlightened civic interpreter, agitator, or organizer. Thus the late Governor Alfred E. Smith had a genius for relating his sense of people's needs, his experience in party and legislative processes and his position as Governor to a political and administrative program in which the special knowledge of many persons was most effectively used in the service of the State of New York.

Catastrophe, especially when leadership and knowledge are prepared with long-time programs into which the immediate hurried relief action can be fitted, has its place in the ecology of administration. It not only is destructive, so that relief and repair are required on a scale so large that collective action is necessary, but it also disrupts, jostles or challenges views and attitudes, and affords to the inner self as well as to others a respectable and face-saving reason for changing one's views as to policy. The atomic bomb gave to many, perhaps, a determining reason for a change of attitude toward international organization. But I incline to the view that the effects of catastrophe on our thinking are relatively short-lived, and confined to relatively smaller institutional changes, and that older forces flood back with great strength to cancel most of the first reaction. A frightened and frustrated society is not one in which really significant changes will take root, unless careful preparation and wise administration of the relief period are available. The night club fire in Boston in recent years in which so many service men from various parts of the country were killed is a tragic example of one role of catastrophe. In the lurid glare of that fire, weaknesses in building codes and the administration of them were revealed. So many vested interests of materials, construction and crafts center in building codes that they are difficult to keep in tune with invention and changing social needs. The fact that many in the fire were from remote places, and were men in the armed services, gave unusually wide reporting of the tragedy for some days, especially as many victims lingered on in hospitals. One result of the shock of the catastrophe was therefore action in cities throughout the world to inspect their places of public amusement and survey their fire-prevention legislation and administration. On a vaster scale, the catastrophe of economic world depression led to a varied array of responses through collective action in which there was much similarity despite regional and ideological differences among the various states of the world, since there were also like ecological factors, common to modern power industry and the price system. World wars illustrate the extent to which a large area of collective action is necessarily adopted under modern conditions of total war—and equally illustrate the tremendous pull of older customary views at the close, when the pressure to remove the controls rises,

and individuals in office are held responsible for the frustrations once borne as a patriotic offering. Wise and fortunate indeed is that community that has so analyzed its problems and needs, and has so prepared to make use of catastrophe should it come by plans for carrying out programs of improvements, that the aftermath of tragedy finds its victims as well cared for as humanly possible and in addition some tangible new advance in the equipment and life of the community. I have seen some communities which, because they had equipped themselves with personnel capable of fresh thinking, had obtained from depression work-relief programs recreation facilities that were their first amenities.

Such an approach as this to our study of public administration is difficult, in that it makes demands upon our powers to observe, upon a sensitive awareness of changes and maladjustment and upon our willingness to face the political—that is, the public-housekeeping—basis of administration. These factors—you may improve upon my selection—in various combinations lie behind a public agency. In their combination will be found the reasons for its existence, and the reasons for attack upon it as well. Only in so far as we can find some essentially public core in the combination can we hope to have an agency free from spoils or abuse of power. The process of growth and formulation of a public policy out of these environmental materials links environment and administration. We may be too responsive to change, or we may fail to achieve our best selves by ignoring what we might do to advantage ourselves by collective action, if we perform this task of politics badly.

"When I pay taxes," wrote Justice Holmes to his friend Sir Frederick Pollock, "I buy civilization." It is no easy task of the citizen in this complicated world to get fair value in what he buys. That task is one of discovery of the causes of problems, of the communication of possible remedies, of the organizing of citizens, of the formulation of law. It is the task, in short, of politics. The task will be more fruitfully performed if the citizen, and his agents in public offices, understand the ecology of government.

## Notes

1. J. W. Bews, *Human Ecology* (London: Oxford University Press, 1935), p. 1.
2. From "Administration, A Foundation of Government," by Charles A. Beard, in *American Political Science Review,* XXXIV, No. 2 (April, 1940), p. 232. Reprinted by permission of the American Political Science Association.
3. The methods as well as the substantive interpretations of Frederick Jackson Turner should be familiar to students of public administration so far as the printed page permits. It was a rich experience to be present as he worked over maps and statistical data of a county, state or region, putting geology, soils, land values, origins of residents, and voting records together for light on the resulting social action.
4. A reverse picture is the sudden demand on the use of ores in the Adirondack region during the world war because of changes in the conditions of ocean shipment. In one remote village a public housing project, to take care of the expanded work force, was a consequence, again, of the catastrophe of war.

---

## CASE STUDY 3

---

# Introduction

The concept *ecology of administration* can be well illustrated by most case studies on public administration, for it would be a rare public administrator who was *not* influenced by at least a few of the major ecological factors that John Gaus outlined in the preceding essay. The theme of ecology runs throughout administrative activities, serving to shape and reshape the course and direction of public policy. The following case study, "Dumping $2.6 Million on Bakersfield," is a good example of how ecological factors can affect public administration and what can happen to administrators who fail to take these external factors into account before initiating a public program.

Michael Aron, a California-based journalist, writes an interesting account of the planning and implementation of a federal program sponsored by the U.S. Department of Health, Education, and Welfare (HEW) to build health clinics for migratory farm workers near the small central California town of Bakersfield. Formulated with good intentions, the program sounded ideal in the initial planning stage, but it nearly failed because inadequate attention was paid to the surrounding social ecology of administration. Aron ably details the ensuing intense struggle between various local forces for control of the health program—the black community, Mexican-American groups, local politicians, and established medical groups. HEW's Washington office and its regional San Francisco office soon became caught in the middle of a conflict that they neither wanted, nor had anticipated.

When reading this selection, keep the following questions in mind:

If you had been the administrator at HEW responsible for the planning of this migratory health program, how would you have assessed the local administrative ecology and better adapted your program to suit its characteristics?

Who were the interest groups, and what were their individual points of view?

In what ways did HEW's own actions in implementing the program intensify the conflict among the major interest groups? In particular, what environmental factors did they fail to recognize in designing and implementing this program?

What were the various viewpoints of the Bakersfield situation *within* HEW? How did these conflicting forces, in turn, influence the course of development of HEW's program?

Do Gaus's ideas on the ecology of administration need adjusting to conform more closely to the current demands and problems confronting modern public administrators, such as those outlined in the case study? If so, specifically in what ways?

# Dumping $2.6 Million on Bakersfield (Or How *Not* to Build a Migratory Farm Workers' Clinic)

## MICHAEL ARON

Like the coming of the railroad, the arrival of big federal money in a small, out-of-the-way California town causes a certain amount of uproar, especially when it is dumped in a bundle by an agency that has to get rid of it quick. In this case, the money comes from the Department of Health, Education, and Welfare, for one of its 131 migrant health programs, and the town that has to fight over the grant is Bakersfield.

But it could just as well have been one of the other 130 migrant health programs, or any federal effort where the bureaucrat is mandated both to spend money fast and also to insure that local people control their own destinies. Controlling your own destiny, in these days of decentralization and revenue sharing, really means that the locals can help decide how to divvy up federal money among themselves. Bakersfield is a consequence of the whole idea of community participation in federal projects, but in this instance, the town only began participating after the money was pumped in—for very obvious reasons and with some very disruptive results.

From "Dumping $2.6 Million on Bakersfield (Or How *Not* to Build a Migratory Farm Workers' Clinic)" by Michael Aron, *The Washington Monthly* (October 1972), pp. 23–32. Reprinted by permission of The Washington Monthly Company.

Our story begins in Washington, D.C., in March, 1970, with the passage by Congress of the Migrant Health Act. Senator Walter Mondale's Migratory Labor subcommittee drafted the legislation, authorizing an $11-million appropriation for migrant programs in fiscal 1970, and it was Mondale, personally, who pressed for insertion of an amendment providing that "persons broadly representative of all elements of the population to be served [be] given an opportunity to participate in the implementation of such programs."

Since this was the time the Nixon Administration was striving to decentralize the "vast" federal bureaucracy, it fell to the regional offices of HEW to implement the legislation. Region IX, headquartered in San Francisco, and responsible for seven Western states (it has since lost Oregon and Washington), proposed four areas with heavy migrant "homebase" populations as possible locations for health projects. Three were in rural California counties, the fourth in the state of Washington. One was Bakersfield, Kern County, California.

HEW's plan was to find a chicano community group in each area to become its delegate agency for day-to-day administration of a project, in the same way that local anti-poverty groups became delegate agencies of the Office of Economic Opportunity. But there was a time problem: the legislation had been passed relatively late in the fiscal year, giving HEW only a few months in which to spend the money or else forfeit it back to Treasury. Compounding the problem was the fact that Bakersfield seemed to have no chicano community groups—20,000 chicanos, but no groups.

With the end of the fiscal year only six weeks away, anxious rural health officials turned their attention to a black group, the Kern County Liberation Movement (KCLM). Born six months earlier in the waning hours of a poor people's workshop and designated a consumers' auxiliary of the local anti-poverty agency, KCLM was little more than a collection of low-income citizens. As its first official act, KCLM had applied to HEW for a $70,000 planning grant to assay the health needs of Bakersfield's black ghetto; that application was still in the pipeline when regional HEW asked KCLM if it would accept $2.6 million to immediately establish a health center.

KCLM responded enthusiastically: certainly they would accept a grant—who wouldn't? In late May, 1970, an official from the Rural Health Office of the Community Health Service of the Health Services and Mental Health Administration (HSMHA) of the Public Health Service of the regional office of HEW flew to Bakersfield to help KCLM prepare a formal application. All this was done very quietly, without fanfare. Final contracts were signed in June, three weeks before the end of the fiscal year.

It wasn't until July that Kern County's health establishment got wind of the news—and when they did, all hell broke loose. The entire roster of local health agencies—the county medical society, the dental society, Kern General Hospital, the county health department, the board of supervisors, the state health department, the California Medical Association; and the congressionally mandated regional planning bodies, Comprehensive Health Planning and Regional Medical Programs—vented their spleen because none had been consulted prior to the awarding of the grant. The medical society had a special reason for bitterness: it had been operating its own federally-funded migrant clinic for years in two old trailers outside of town, and HEW was cutting the budget on that program at the same time it was handing $2.6 million to a bunch of poor people with no experience whatsoever in the administration or delivery of health care.

# Creative Fumbling

For five days the flap over the award commanded headlines in the *Bakersfield Californian* (in sky-blue ink, no less); the paper also editorialized against the grant ("More Fumbling and Bumbling") and even ran a two-part feature on the medical society's "wonderful clinic." Bakersfield's two Republican state assemblymen called press conferences to denounce the award. Congressman Robert Mathias sent an angry telegram to HEW Secretary Elliot Richardson questioning how the department could possibly sanction such behavior on the part of its regional office. "Is this what the Administration means by 'creative federalism'?" Mathias asked. For the next three weeks the Bakersfield health establishment would virtually convulse in an effort to get the grant canceled.

On July 14, Dr. James Cavanaugh, deputy assistant secretary for health, announced a "full review" of the conditions surrounding the awarding of the grant, intimating that the contract would be canceled "if irregularities are detected."

On July 15, Cavanaugh flew from Washington to the regional office in San Francisco. In what is reported to have been a rather stormy session, Cavanaugh and regional officials rewrote the guidelines on community health grants so as to insure consultation with all appropriate state and local agencies. In Washington, meanwhile, Mathias' staff had done some checking and discovered that the Kern County Liberation Movement was not registered with OEO as an official delegate arm of the local anti-poverty agency. Mathias called Cavanaugh to ask if this were sufficiently "irregular" to warrant cancellation of the contract. When Cavanaugh said he didn't think so, Mathias asked if the contract could possibly be renegotiated under the new guidelines just promulgated. Cavanaugh said he doubted it. A Mathias press release the next day called HEW's action "inexcusable" and fixed the blame on "middle-level bureaucrats [who] ignored the letter of the law" (a reference to their failure to consult the congressionally mandated regional planning bodies).

While Mathias was busy reverse pork-barreling in Washington, physicians and politicians in Bakersfield were writing letters to anyone they could think of who might be able to reverse the decision. Let me quote from some of these letters:

Kern General Hospital Administrator Dr. Owen Hatley, to Dr. Vernon Wilson, an HEW official in Rockville, Maryland:

When an independent, unbiased consulting firm, experienced in developing health delivery systems, presents a program for Kern County, then and only then will I support any sponsoring agency in any of these endeavors. Reputable, experienced consulting firms are available, in contrast to falsefront organizations [KCLM] created to obtain desired answers to fuzzy-minded hypotheses conjured up by some social planners.

Congressman Barry Goldwater, Jr. (representing a neighboring district) to Secretary Richardson:

This group [KCLM] has absolutely no experience that would even remotely qualify them for a grant of this magnitude. . . . I request that you immediately investigate this matter and withdraw the grant.

State Assemblyman William Ketchum to HEW Undersecretary John Veneman, his former colleague in the California legislature:

I object to the "cart before the horse" manner in which this has been handled and request that you immediately stop funding . . . [HEW's] "better to spend now than undertake planning" philosophy is a classic symptom of the whole OEO syndrome.

On July 27, KCLM held a press conference to refute the "numerous unfounded charges leveled against us in recent days." Considering the group's relative inexperience, it was an artful performance. One moment they were militant: "The low income community of Kern County wants to see a migrant health center that will meet their needs and they want to see it not after a two- or three-year planning study. Frankly we are *tired* of being studied. We want direct medical services now." The next moment, conciliatory: "Naturally we welcome the cooperation and support of any agencies interested in meeting the common goal of comprehensive health care for the entire community."

In San Francisco, meanwhile, regional HEW was kept busy trying to explain its actions to HEW officials in Washington. An assistant regional director recalls: "Washington was not terribly happy with us, and that's the understatement of the year. Of course, we knew what we were doing all along. We were going to get funding into that area no matter who it upset, and not by the traditional route of currying favor with conservative county medical societies. To get things done, you go do them and fight the political battles after—especially in this Administration. We like to think of ourselves as 'bureaucratic guerrillas' fighting for what we believe in."

By July 29, it was compromise time. Cavanaugh and Mathias flew to Bakersfield together to announce that HEW was suspending project funds for 90 days pending a "restructuring" of the KCLM board of directors. The suspension, Cavanaugh told a press conference, would be lifted only when the board, then made up entirely of "consumers," added professional health-care "providers" to its membership. Cavanaugh's, too, was an artful performance (which may help explain why he is now on the White House staff). He seemed genuinely pained by "this unfortunate misunderstanding." He urged the Bakersfield health establishment to play an "activist" role on the consumer-provider board, and assured his good friends that "this sort of thing will not happen again." Privately, he told Mathias that HEW would consider canceling the grant if KCLM should fail in any way to execute its provisions. And when the man from HEW left town that night, KCLM was still the beneficiary of the potential $2.6 million.

Although project funds were technically suspended, regional HEW began sending "emergency" funds to KCLM to keep it on its feet. The grant had called for expenditures of $391,000 in the first year— $248,000 for staff salaries and the rest for clinic facilities and supplies. (And when they tell you they're putting X million dollars into programs for poor people, remember: professionals, clericals, and private businesses get the money; the poor get services.) Before any of this money could be spent, however, it would be necessary to hire a project director, preferably one who could court the favor of the health establishment and orchestrate a restructuring of the board.

Regional HEW proposed that a young dental school graduate from San Francisco become interim project director until a permanent director could be found. KCLM agreed, and Robert Isman, D.D.S., assumed his duties in August.

Through the fall months Isman worked hard to win

the cooperation of local health agencies, but two things were working against him: his longish hair and what they call in Bakersfield "ultraliberal leanings." City officials, whose own budgets only added up to something like $12 million, simply could not understand why HEW would select such a character to supervise a $2.6-million project. He had no experience, either dental or administrative. He showed up for meetings with bankers and lawyers wearing cutoff jeans and thongs. To this day, people talk about Isman as if his eight months in Bakersfield had been profitably spent dealing hashish on the side.

It took much persuasion and several trips to Bakersfield by regional HEW officials, but in November the KCLM board was restructured to include 10 professional health providers representing various agencies in the county, including the medical society, which put its migrant clinic director on the board but instructed him not to vote. (The argument is sometimes advanced that the medical society joined only to sabotage the project, because free health care for the poor takes money out of the pockets of local physicians and the county hospital; but there's too much conspiracy theory there, or at least not enough money involved to make it credible.)

That the consumers still outnumbered the providers 25 to 10 irked some people, however. Mathias' local aide called the restructuring "a token effort to appease the community." Assemblyman Stacey branded it "a sham and a fraud" and joined the ranks of the countless politicians who at one time or another have accused HEW of "strong-arm tactics."

With the board restructured, everyone expected funding to resume, but HEW suddenly attached new conditions to the lifting of the suspension. KCLM either had to demonstrate broad-based community support, or hire a permanent project director.

In the meantime, forces were still at work trying to get the grant canceled. In December, the medical society applied to HEW for $325,645, ostensibly to expand its existing clinic program, in effect proposing itself as an alternative to KCLM. In Washington, Mathias continued to warn HEW that the project was "doomed to failure" unless local agencies were brought into the fold and given more say in board policy. Quietly, Mathias also asked the Government Accounting Office for a full investigation of the activities of the local anti-poverty umbrella agency, the Kern County Economic Opportunities Corporation.

Three months went by with no progress made

toward filling the project director's job and mounting hostility towards Isman from the establishment. Then in April, 1971, HEW decided to step in and temporarily take over the project itself. Vincent Garza, a Mexican-American public health officer stationed at headquarters, was dispatched to replace Isman as interim project director for 90 days. To complement this action, regional HEW abruptly canceled the dental component of the project, thus insuring Isman's complete removal from the scene. Both sides in Bakersfield welcomed the two moves—the health establishment because Garza was a professional like themselves; KCLM because it meant immediate resumption of funding.

From this point on, the struggle ceases to be one pitting organized medicine and its friends against poor people. As you will see, it evolves into a struggle pitting poor people of one race against poor people of another. There are no Machiavellian plots here, no designs by the establishment to divide and conquer. That's just the way it happens.

## Dude Ranch Junket

Most of the farm workers of Kern County are Mexican-Americans; maybe 20 per cent are Mexican nationals who came north to follow the softfruit season (legally or illegally) and managed to linger longer.

For years, these people have lived in shacks and camps or slept unsheltered on the banks of irrigation canals. Their general health is not good. They get skin diseases from working in fields sprayed with pesticides; they suffer high incidences of venereal disease, eye defects, heart trouble, and nervous disorders; obesity, hypertension, and diabetes are so prevalent that local health authorities believe these conditions to be hereditary in Mexicans; 90 per cent of the children have serious dental problems. "They're learning that an unhealthy body produces nothing," one official said, adding as an afterthought, "They've certainly learned it the hard way." It used to be that when someone got sick, he worked it off or waited it out—unless he got real sick, in which case his family piled him into a car and drove the 20 miles to Kern General Hospital where they would wait for hours in the emergency room hoping that the next intake nurse spoke Spanish. Of course, there was also the medical society's migrant clinic in trailers in Lamont, but it operated only during "the season" (May to

September; the actual season is eight to 10 months), and then only three nights a week from 6 p.m. to 10 p.m. At regional HEW the clinic is still referred to as a "band-aid station."

.The first thing on Garza's agenda when he arrived in Bakersfield was to find a suitable location for a health center. For several days he, an architect, and Mathias' local aide drove around the Lamont-Arvin-Weedpatch area looking for a site—and immediately a conflict arose. KCLM thought they ought to be looking in the Lakeview district, where blacks live. Garza explained that these were *migrant* funds and that it had been HEW's intention all along to put a health center someplace where the campesinos would have easy access to it. But this had not been KCLM's understanding at all; they had been led to believe, they said, that the center would be located in a black neighborhood and that campesinos from all over the county would be encouraged to use it and think of it as their own.

KCLM felt suddenly betrayed. After fighting off the encroachments of the health establishment for almost a year, they now learned that HEW wanted to put the health center in a part of the county where less than one per cent of the population is black. A bitter pill; several KCLM board members chose to resign rather than swallow it.

To sweeten it, perhaps, Garza organized a weekend outing for KCLM board members at a ranch-retreat 80 miles north of Bakersfield and invited the HEW regional director to come along and to bring some of his staff. A good time was presumably had by all, and the regional director soothed ruffled feathers by promising that no matter what happened in the future, KCLM's efforts would not go unrewarded; but folks in Bakersfield took a different view of the outing. Garza returned to Bakersfield on a Monday morning to find himself being blasted on the front page of the *Californian* for his $2,500 dude ranch junket financed by "the taxpayers." (The story was written by the son of the county health superintendent, which says something about small cities.) Three weeks later, Garza left Bakersfield and the Public Health Service and went to Yale on a fellowship.

Garza was replaced in July, 1971, by Charles Pineda, a Mexican-American native of Kern County, the son of a fruit picker and holder of a master's degree in social work. Pineda continued the search for a clinic site and also began to think about recruiting a medical staff.

# Hmm . . . Federal Funding

In September, 15 months after the awarding of the grant, a makeshift clinic was finally opened in Lamont. Pineda had found a young doctor from Los Angeles to become clinic physician ($25,000), had lured an aging South American from a hospital in the Bronx to become medical director ($27,500), and the three of them had talked the medical society into renting its trailers to KCLM until a permanent location could be found ($1,600, which has never been paid). As soon as the medical society clinic shut down for the "winter," KCLM occupied the trailers and began treating its first farmworker patients. Pineda, meanwhile, found an old grocery store in Weedpatch, leased it, and gradually moved the project into it over the next three months.

The clinic in Weedpatch is a shock when you first see it. Somehow the term "migrant health center" leads you to expect a depressing storefront, partitioned in half, and dimly lit, with maybe a purple curtain separating the waiting room from the examining room, and a wizened old doctor inside waiting to grab you in his palsied, age-blotched hands. You walk into the clinic in Weedpatch, however, and your first thought is "hmmm . . . federal funding." The clinic is partitioned all right, but partitioned into a large reception room, two intake offices, five examining rooms, a treatment room, a laboratory, a records library, staff offices, and a lounge. The staff numbers about 25. The equipment is brand new, ultra-modern, and *clean.* When you open your mouth to say "aaahh . . ." in this clinic, you're opening it to an electronic implement coming out of a wall console.

To the campesinos and their families, the clinic is a godsend. It heals them, soothes them, educates them, trains them, employs a few of them—all free of charge, for the time being. HEW wants the clinic to become self-sufficient, so patient billings will begin in the near future; but treatment will still be "free" (sort of) for the 90 per cent who belong to the union's "Robert F. Kennedy Farm Workers' Medical Plan" (for which a small premium is deducted from their paychecks). At last count, the clinic had given treatment to 6,000 patients from 1,200 families, and thanks to the imperatives of bureaucracy, each one now has a detailed record of his medical history, probably for the first time in his life. Ask the campesinos whom they thank for all this, and you get a surprising—no, not surprising—answer. Senator Kennedy, of course. The young one.

## Chicanos in the Wings

But don't get the idea that just because the clinic opened, the infighting ceased. On the contrary, now there was something tangible to fight over.

An interesting bit of correspondence circulated around Bakersfield at this time, copies of an exchange between HEW Secretary Richardson and Senators Walter Mondale and Adlai Stevenson III, past and present chairmen of the Migratory Labor subcommittee. Richardson's letter to the subcommittee requested "clarification of congressional intent" regarding the consumer-participation amendment to the Migrant Health Act. Mondale wrote back: "I was shocked to learn that there is still substantial doubt as to your Department's implementation of an amendment which became effective in March of 1970." Stevenson wrote: "I am extremely concerned that Migratory Health Program relations and guidelines provide the basis for 'meaningful' farm-worker participation, rather than a degree of 'tokenism.' This, of course, requires a policy-making function for the farm-worker participants rather than merely an advisory role."

It was regional HEW that flooded Bakersfield with copies of the exchange. And for a reason. KCLM was still the delegate agency administering the project, but it no longer could be said to represent the true "consumers." Now that the clinic had opened in Weedpatch, the consumers were campesinos. It was *they* who should be doing the community-participating.

This was fine with project director Pineda, a chicano whose father was still out in the fields; it was fine, as well, with the clinic staff, half of whom were Mexican, and others who had to have been sympathetic to the plight of farm workers in the first place in order to have accepted a job in a town as Godforsaken as Weedpatch. KCLM, on the other hand, was naturally upset: first, they had "lost" the clinic itself; now they were faced with possible loss of control over it and forfeiture of their status as a bona fide government delegate agency.

Acting on their own authority, but with behind-the-scenes encouragement from regional HEW, Pineda and several clinic staff members appointed five reasonably intelligent, but non-English-speaking, campesinos to a "campesino board," a kind of shadow cabinet that would wait in the wings ready to take over at the earliest signal from HEW. That they were non-English-speaking meant that they had to rely on people like Pineda to tell them what was going on. This was in October.

On December 14, KCLM voted to fire Pineda. The official reasons are not worth going into—basically they questioned Pineda's competence. The actual reason was that Pineda had been attempting to serve two masters at once, KCLM and the campesinos, and his allegiance to the former seemed to be flagging. Informed of the dismissal, regional HEW immediately ordered him reinstated, saying that KCLM no longer had legal authority to make such a decision (because it no longer represented "consumers").

At its next regular meeting, on December 22, KCLM voted to change its name to the Kern County Health Committee (KCHC). This is not insignificant. It represents a conscious grab at respectability and tacitly acknowledges its new position in the battle configuration. How can you call yourself a liberation movement when you're fighting to preserve a vested interest?

## Culturally Unfit

Two things of consequence happened in January. First, elections for a new campesino board were held in Lamont-Arvin-Weedpatch; four of the five men who had been appointed by Pineda in October won election to the board. (The fifth would have won, too, had he chosen to run.) The board then incorporated itself as Clinica De Los Campesinos, Inc. (CDLC). Second, the clinic's South American medical director failed his state medical board examination, meaning he was without a license to practice in California.

In February, the roof caves in.

On February 14, 24 hours before KCHC was supposed to transfer authority to CDLC, the KCHC board notifies Pineda of his dismissal in a memo listing eight specific grievances, one claiming he hired the South American medical director without consulting the board and another charging him with "loading" the clinic staff with Mexican-Americans.

On February 15: KCHC, citing election "irregularities," rejects the legitimacy of the CDLC board and refuses to transfer control of the project.

On February 16: 200 chicano demonstrators mass in front of the clinic, Pineda and two clinic staff members among them, carrying picket signs and threatening to "shut it down" (in Spanish). The black chairman of KCHC wades into the angry mob and fires the two staff members on the spot. Half of the demonstrators move down the highway to the KCHC administrative office in Lamont. The demonstrations last until midnight without serious incident.

February 17: The clinic has been splattered with paint during the night. There are bullet holes in the plate glass window. KCHC's black chairman appoints himself "acting project director." Regional HEW officials fly down from San Francisco in the hope of restoring order; they put the KCHC chairman on notice that his assumption of the project directorship constitutes a flagrant conflict of interest. Two-thirds of the clinic staff send individual letters to HEW declaring their allegiance to CDLC.

February 18: A provider member of the KCHC board calls the executive secretary of the medical society at midnight and, on behalf of KCHC, pleads for help. The executive secretary calls his 30-year-old assistant, Riley McWilliams, at 2:30 a.m. and orders him to report to KCHC the next day to become interim project director.

February 23: Telegram to KCHC from regional HEW states: actions of KCHC in direct contradiction to agreements; therefore, project funds would be suspended indefinitely and funding to KCHC would terminate on April 15, 1972.

February 24: Local aide sends confidential memo to Mathias in Washington warning of black-brown racial conflict that could engulf the county; says black community promises reprisals if any harm comes to KCHC chairman; surmises that United Farm Workers are involved in demonstrations.

February 26: CDLC writes to Secretary Richardson—letter begins, "Honorable Sire"; informs that Riley McWilliams made project director without HEW approval; ends with veiled threat to close clinic down as "last resort."

February 28: Medical society applies to HEW for $155,891 grant to expand its own clinic; application states, "basic to this proposal is removal of the existing clinic."

February 29: KCHC chairman reports alleged threats to his person.

March 10: CDLC submits application to HEW to take over administration of project; application actually written by four clinic staff members.

March 17: Twelve clinic staff draft joint letter to HEW threatening to resign if CDLC not made delegate agency; claim Riley McWilliams culturally unfit to be project director.

## Bent in the Fields

April 15, the date HEW said it would terminate the project funding to KCHC, came and went, with no word from San Francisco. Three weeks later, the regional director sent letters to KCHC and CDLC proposing a joint luncheon meeting on May 10 at the posh (for Bakersfield) Casa Royale motel. He also sent a letter to the medical society announcing an award of $67,000 to continue their clinic-on-wheels, providing they move it to Buttonwillow, in the southwest part of the county. (Buttonwillow's one physician raised a stink, but that is another story.)

The regional director, the black project officer, and the chicano Public Health Service officer from Los Angeles arrived in Bakersfield the morning of the 10th. At noon they joined the KCHC board for lunch. The CDLC board had been invited to come at 1 p.m., but the hour passed 2 p.m. and the five campesinos had yet to show. Someone suggested that they might have gotten lost, since surely they had never been to the Casa Royale before. Someone else was delegated to go look for them. He found them in their customary positions for that hour, bent over in the fields in 95-degree heat. They said they had not been notified of the meeting. There was reason to think that one of their advisors on the clinic staff had intercepted the letter for reasons she believed to be in their best interests. The meeting proceeded without them. A radical Lutheran minister acted as their unofficial spokesman.

When it was over, an elaborate compromise had been drawn up: 1) the CDLC board would be absorbed into the KCHC board; 2) four providers mutually agreed upon by KCHC and CDLC would join the five campesinos, together to constitute a separate board-within-a-board; 3) the mini-board would serve in a "policy-recommending" capacity and receive the benefit of "whatever training and experience is available"; 4) on or before January 1, 1973, KCHC would transfer administrative control of the project to CDLC, retaining for itself only the role of fiscal intermediary. A fifth provision went unstated, but was well understood nonetheless: in return for its great efforts and considerable sacrifice, KCHC would become

HEW's "umbrella agency" for all future projects in the county.

HEW and KCHC signed the compromise that afternoon. In the evening the five campesinos met with their supporters in the basement of the Lutheran Church in Lamont. Heated debate lasted past midnight, but the campesinos finally decided to sign the compromise. "It was not a victory, it was not a defeat," said CDLC chairman, Natividad Arreolo, weary perhaps in the knowledge that he was due out in the fields again at 4 A.M.

## If Weedpatch Had Movies

That should be the end of the story. You know it's not. In the months since, there have been controversial hirings and firings, protest resignations, accusations of petty theft, and at least one false rumor of a sexual nature deliberately planted to discredit a potential project director. Dr. Garcia, the South American medical director, took his state boards again in June, and the delay in reporting his grade leads to speculation that it is being deliberately held up in channels for political reasons. As of September 1, the young medical society executive was still project director, a fact from which few but the medical society derive any comfort, and yet he is there.

The question remains as to whether KCHC will cede its little fiefdom to the campesinos by January 1, as agreed. HEW says it is committed to seeing the campesinos take over on schedule, and it is hard to imagine what KCHC could possibly gain by holding out. One also can't help but wonder whether the campesinos really are capable of running the project.

The real problem with this project, and, one suspects, with others as well, has been the ease with which political considerations were able to obscure the stated objective, namely, comprehensive health care for farm workers—combined with the fact that HEW would seem to have subordinated the stated objective to an unstated, or at least secondary one, namely, Mexican-American community organization. Thus, it took 15 months of sparring and jockeying before a single patient was seen. And once opened, the clinic had to shorten its hours anytime HEW felt it necessary to suspend funds in order to reprimand this faction or that. The community of 20,000 is still without a dentist because of an essentially political decision.

The medical society seems to think that because doctors can save lives on a surgical table, their expertise necessarily embraces all facets of medicine, including how it should be delivered to people whom the doctors barely understand, can't talk to, and don't especially like—and the medical society fights to preserve the integrity of that idea. The poor people, black and brown, want better medical care than they are accustomed to receiving, but they also want power and respectability and anything else that might foster the illusion that they are swimming into the mainstream, and if a government health project is the only game in town, they'll jump at the chance to play it, and they'll play it as fiercely and seriously as they imagine it to be played elsewhere, and so what if the brothers and sisters have to wait a little longer for something they have never had anyway. And the whites on the clinic staff and the others lurking in the background all the time probably wouldn't be so eager to stir up the waters if only Weedpatch had a movie theater.

The government, through all this, has been like a ship captain steering the project towards shores the crew can't see yet. For the crowd in San Francisco, the project has been, and continues to be, "an interesting social experiment" (an assistant regional director's words), originally conceived to meet a singular need, but taking on added dimensions as it unfolds. Can blacks and browns work together? Are illiterate campesinos capable of self-administration? What adjustments can we make to keep the community from blowing apart? "I would say we've basically been more interested in using the clinic as an instrument of long-range social change than in meeting the short-run health needs of the target community," one HEW official admitted, fully aware that this is the kind of statement bureaucrats get roasted for every day.

To date $400,000 has been spent on the project, a mere fraction of the $13 billion HEW spends every year on health programs. One shudders at the thought of KCLMs and medical societies and campesino-equivalents plotting and maneuvering against each other and intramurally in every community where federal grants have been won; and yet, that is probably what happens, and is happening, all over the country at this moment.

"Kern County?" a project officer asked rhetorically. "Oh, it's not so bad there. These things are usually much worse in urban areas."

# Chapter 3 Review Questions

1. What were the chief elements in the administrative ecology that HEW planners failed to take into account prior to developing the migratory farm workers' health clinic in Bakersfield? If you had been in charge of the project at HEW Regional Headquarters in San Francisco, what would you have done to ensure that the project began properly?

2. What was the role of the local press, politicians, and special interest groups in affecting the outcome of this federally supported program? Can you generalize about the impact of such special interest groups on national programs?

3. Can you distinguish between the institutional factors (such as the budgetary process) and the personnel leadership factors (such as the various persons assigned by HEW to administer the program at the local level) that prevented effective long-term comprehensive planning for this local public program? What reforms would you recommend to enhance better program planning in the future?

4. Compare Case Study 1, "The Blast in Centralia No. 5," with this case. How did the geographical distances in both cases influence the administrative decisions that were made? Can you generalize about the difficulties of effective administrative actions as the *distances* between the administrator and the "administered" expand?

5. Why were there various points of view about the purposes of this program *within* HEW? What were these competing viewpoints? Can you generalize about the difficulties of effective administrative actions as the *levels of bureaucracy* between the administrator and the "administered" expand?

6. After reviewing this case study, how would you modify Gaus's ideas about the nature of modern administrative ecology? In your view, for instance, does he adequately cover the problems of ethnic differences? Class differences? Media influence? Leadership factors? Fragmented government oversight?

# Key Terms

administrative ecology
physical technology
social technology

general environment
wishes and ideas
catastrophe

# Suggestions for Further Reading

Gaus spent much of his life thinking about the ecology of public administration; therefore you would do well to begin by reading the entire book from which the reading in this chapter was reprinted, *Reflections on Public Administration* (University, Ala.: University of Alabama Press, 1947). In recent years comparative administrative scholars are perhaps the ablest group carrying on Gaus's investigations in this area; see Fred Riggs, *The Ecology of Administration* (New York: Asia Publishing House, 1967), as well as Ferrel Heady, *Public Administration: A Comparative Perspective,* Fourth Edition (New York: Marcel Dekker, 1991).

Biographies and autobiographies offer some of the finest observations on the interplay between social forces and public administration, and the five most outstanding ones are Louis Brownlow, *A Passion for Anonymity* (Chicago: University of Chicago Press, 1958); Robert Caro, *The Power Broker: Robert Moses and the Fall of New York City* (New York: Random House, 1974); Leroy F. Harlow, *Without Fear or Favor: Odyssey of a City Manager* (Provo, Utah: Brigham Young University Press, 1977); Thomas K. McCraw, *Prophets of Regulation* (Cambridge, Mass.: Harvard University Press, 1984); and David Stockman, *The Triumph of Politics: The Inside Story of the Reagan Revolution* (New York: Harper & Row, 1986). There are several classic social science studies of this subject, including Philip Selznick, *TVA and the Grass Roots: A Study of the Sociology of Formal Organization* (Berkeley: University of California Press, 1949); Herbert Kaufman, *The Forest Ranger—A Study in Administrative Behavior* (Baltimore: Johns Hopkins University Press, 1960); Arthur Maass, *The Army Engineers and The Nation's Rivers* (Cambridge, Mass.: Harvard University Press, 1951); Milton D. Morris, *Immigration: The Beleagured Bureaucracy* (Washington, D.C.: Brookings Institute, 1985); and Paul Light, *Artful Work: The Politics of Social Security Reform* (New York: Random House, 1985).

You should not overlook the rich case studies available through the Inter-University Case Program (P.O. Box 229, Syracuse, N.Y.

13210) as well as the John F. Kennedy School of Government Case Program (Kennedy School of Government, Case Program, Harvard University, 79 JFK Street, Cambridge, Mass. 02138), most of which explore and highlight various dimensions of administrative ecology. The first ICP case book, Harold Stein, ed., *Public Administration and Policy Development: A Casebook* (New York: Harcourt Brace Jovanovich, 1952), contains an especially good introduction by Stein focusing on this topic.

Two short but useful pieces that should be read as well are Herbert G. Wilcox, "The Culture Trait of Hierarchy in Middle Class Children," *Public Administration Review* (March/April 1968), pp. 222–232, and F. E. Emery and E. L. Trist, "The Causal Texture of Organizational Environments," *Human Relations,* 18 (February 1965), pp. 21–32.

Certainly *must* reading for comprehending the whole cultural-social milieu within which American public administration operates remains the two volumes of Alexis de Tocqueville, *Democracy in America* (New York: Vintage, 1945), or for that matter, several of the other historical treatments of the American experience: James Bryce, *The American Commonwealth,* 2 volumes (New York: Macmillan, 1888); Richard Hofstadter, *The American Political Tradition* (New York: Vintage Book, 1948); Michael Kammen, *People of Paradox* (New York: Vintage Books, 1972); Henry Steele Commanger, *The Empire of Reason* (New York: Doubleday, 1977); and Samuel P. Huntington, *American Politics; The Promise of Disharmony* (Cambridge, Mass.: Harvard University Press, 1981). For contemporary trends in the American social, economic, political, and fiscal landscape, read: Aaron Wildavsky, "Ubiquitous Anomie: Public Service in an Era of Idealogical Dissensus, *Public Administration Review* (July/August 1988), pp. 753–755; Harlan Cleveland, "Theses of a New Reformation: The Social Fallout of Science 300 Years After

Newton," *Public Administration Review* (May/ June 1988), pp. 681–686; Robert N. Bellah et al., *Habits of the Heart: Individualism and Commitment in American Life* (New York: Harper & Row, 1985); Paul C. Light, *Baby Boomers* (New York: W. W. Norton, 1988); Tom Peters, *Thriving in Chaos: Handbook for a Managment Revolution* (New York: Alfred A. Knopf, 1987; and Amy Cohen Paul, ed., *Managing for Tomorrow: Global Change and Local Future* (Washington, D.C.: International City Management Assoc., 1990).

# CHAPTER 4

## The Political Environment: The Concept of Administrative Power

*The lifeblood of administration is power.*

*Norton E. Long*

## READING 4

## Introduction

While John Gaus stressed the broad, evolutionary perspective of administrative ecology, Norton E. Long (1910–   ) of the University of Missouri at St. Louis, a contemporary American political scientist and former New Deal civil servant, zeroes in on the immediate environment of public administration, namely, that of administrative power. In his classic essay, "Power and Administration," Long argues that administrative institutions—public agencies, departments, bureaus, and field offices—are engaged in a continual battle for political survival. In this fierce administrative contest bureaucrats contend for limited power resources from clientele and constituent groups, the legislative and executive branches, and the general public to sustain their organizations. As he writes, "The lifeblood of administration is power. Its attainment, maintenance, increase, and losses are subjects the practitioner and student can ill afford to neglect." And yet, "it is the most overlooked in theory and the most dangerous to overlook in practice."

For Long, the concept of power cannot be bottled in a jar and kept safely tucked away for future use; nor can its nature be revealed by simply examining the U.S. Constitution, the legislative mandates, or the formal hierarchy of an organizational chart. It is, rather, an ephemeral substance that is part of the disorderly, fragmented, decentralized landscape of American public administration—a landscape reminiscent more of tenth-century warring medieval fiefs than of twentieth-century modern government. Power in this chaotic terrain is everywhere, flowing "in from the sides of an organization, as it were; it also flows up the organization to the center from the constituent parts."

This fluid situation arises partly, in Long's view, from the failure of the American party system to protect administrators from political pressures and to provide adequate direction and support for government bureaus and agencies. The American party system "fails to develop a consensus on a leadership and a program that makes possible administration on the basis of acceptable decisional premises." Left to their own devices and discretion, public agencies are forced to enter the "business of building, maintaining and increasing their political support."

Administrators seek to build strong public relations and mobilize political support by developing a "wide range of activities designed to secure enough 'customer' acceptance to survive and, if fortunate, develop a consensus adequate to program formulation and execution." If public servants are to succeed, they must understand the political environment in which they operate and the political resources at their disposal. On this point, Long has direct relevance to some of the central political problems faced by administrators in Case Study 1, "The Blast in Centralia No. 5," and in Case Study 3, "Dumping $2.6 Million on Bakersfield."

How can Long's disorderly array of narrow interests weld itself together to develop an overall scheme of the national purpose? Rational schemes of coordination always run counter to "the self-centered demands of primary groups for funds and personnel." Again Long visualizes the power factor as significant in any reorganization plan for government. Improved coordination through any governmental reorganization plan will "require a political power at least as great as that which tamed the earlier feudalism." "Attempts to solve administrative reorganization in isolation from the structure of power and purpose in the polity are bound to prove illusory" and have "the academic air of South American Constitution-making."

In his perceptive essay, Long raises another important issue, namely, that because the decentralized nature of the American political system puts administrators in the midst of numerous competing interest groups, they are plagued with the continual problem, "To whom is one loyal—unit, section, branch, division, bureau, department, administration, government, country, people, world history, or what?" A precise consensus on what should be done and who should be obeyed rarely exists and will not so long as the American system fails to establish organized, disciplined political parties or so long as presidents are unable to find firm and continuing majorities in Congress for their legislative programs. Unlike the Parliamentary system, according to Long, each agency in the American executive branch must fend for itself in the political arena, grasping for its own share of political resources to sustain its programs. Therefore, Long advises American administrators to read Machiavelli, La Rochefoucauld, Duc de Saint Simon, or Madison on the reality of power rather than the classic texts on public administration that often only stress the formal components of public organizations.

The following excerpt from Long's essay, "Power and Administration," is based on his perceptive understanding, his training in classical political philosophy, as well as his practical administrative experiences while working at the local, state, and national levels during the Depression, World War II, and the postwar period, particularly his experience at the National Housing Administration in New York City and the Office of Price Administration in Washington. Long's perspectives on power were also significantly shaped by the "new realism" of such insightful students of governmental administration during the 1930s and 1940s as E. Pendleton Herring, Paul Appleby, and Herbert Simon who, like Long, were sober realists about the nature and substance of administrative power. For some traditionalists, Long may seem uncomfortably iconoclastic and politically cynical in his thinking, offering few simple answers to the questions he poses. Nevertheless, his essay raises several perplexing problems that are still critical in public administration today.

As you read this selection, keep the following questions in mind:

How does Long define administrative power? Why is it important? Are there any differences between political power and administrative power? How is administrative power attained and maintained?

What are the appropriate "ends" or "purposes" of the contest for power in administration?

Will the administrative struggle necessarily, if left unchecked, produce a coordinated, effective, and responsible public policy?

How can better planning and rationality be incorporated into the administrative system?

How does Long's approach differ from Weber's or Gaus's approach?

# Power and Administration

### NORTON E. LONG

There is no more forlorn spectacle in the administrative world than an agency and a program possessed of statutory life, armed with executive orders, sustained in the courts, yet stricken with paralysis and deprived of power. An object of contempt to its enemies and of despair to its friends.

The lifeblood of administration is power. Its attainment, maintenance, increase, dissipation, and loss are subjects the practitioner and student can ill afford to neglect. Loss of realism and failure are almost certain consequences.

This is not to deny that important parts of public administration are so deeply entrenched in the habits of the community, so firmly supported by the public, or so clearly necessary as to be able to take their power base for granted and concentrate on the purely professional side of their problems. But even these islands of the blessed are not immune from the plague of politics. . . . To stay healthy one needs to recognize that health is a fruit, not a birthright. Power is only one of the considerations that must be weighed in administration, but of all it is the most overlooked in theory and the most dangerous to overlook in practice.

The power resources of an administrator or an agency are not disclosed by a legal search of titles and court decisions or by examining appropriations or budgetary allotments. Legal authority and a treasury balance are necessary but politically insufficient bases of administration. Administrative rationality requires a critical evaluation of the whole range of complex and shifting forces on whose support, acquiescence, or temporary impotence the power to act depends.

Analysis of the sources from which power is derived and the limitations they impose is as much a dictate of prudent administration as sound budgetary procedure. The bankruptcy that comes from an unbalanced power budget has consequences far more disastrous than the necessity of seeking a deficiency appropriation. The budgeting of power is a basic subject matter of a realistic science of administration.

It may be urged that for all but the top hierarchy of the administrative structure the question of power is irrelevant. Legislative authority and administrative orders suffice. Power adequate to the function to be performed flows down the chain of command. Neither statute nor executive order, however, confers more than legal authority to act. Whether Congress or President can impart the substance of power as well as the form depends upon the line-up of forces in the particular case. A price control law wrung from a reluc-

tant Congress by an amorphous and unstable combination of consumer and labor groups is formally the same as a law enacting a support price program for agriculture backed by the disciplined organizations of farmers and their Congressmen. The differences for the scope and effectiveness of administration are obvious. The presidency, like Congress, responds to and translates the pressures that play upon it. The real mandate contained in an executive order varies with the political strength of the group demand embodied in it, and in the context of other group demands.

Both Congress and President do focus the general political energies of the community and so are considerably more than mere means for transmitting organized pressures. Yet power is not concentrated by the structure of government or politics into the hands of a leadership with a capacity to budget it among a diverse set of administrative activities. A picture of the presidency as a reservoir of authority from which the lower echelons of administration draw life and vigor is an idealized distortion of reality.

A similar criticism applies to any like claim for an agency head in his agency. Only in varying degrees can the powers of subordinate officials be explained as resulting from the chain of command. Rarely is such an explanation a satisfactory account of the sources of power.

To deny that power is derived exclusively from superiors in the hierarchy is to assert that subordinates stand in a feudal relation in which to a degree they fend for themselves and acquire support peculiarly their own. A structure of interests friendly or hostile, vague and general or compact and well-defined, encloses each significant center of administrative discretion. This structure is an important determinant of the scope of possible action. As a source of power and authority it is a competitor of the formal hierarchy.

Not only does political power flow in from the sides of an organization, as it were; it also flows up the organization to the center from the constituent parts. When the staff of the Office of War Mobilization and Reconversion advised a hard-pressed agency to go out and get itself some popular support so that the President could afford to support it, their action reflected the realities of power rather than political cynicism.

It is clear that the American system of politics does not generate enough power at any focal point of leadership to provide the conditions for an even partially successful divorce of politics from administration. Subordinates cannot depend on the formal chain of command to deliver enough political power to permit them to do their jobs. Accordingly they must supplement the resources available through the hierarchy with those they can muster on their own, or accept the consequences in frustration—a course itself not without danger. Administrative rationality demands that objectives be determined and sights set in conformity with a realistic appraisal of power position and potential. . . .

The theory of administration has neglected the problem of the sources and adequacy of power, in all probability because of a distaste for the disorderliness of American political life and a belief that this disorderliness is transitory. An idealized picture of the British parliamentary system as a Platonic form to be realized or approximated has exerted a baneful fascination in the field. The majority party with a mandate at the polls and a firmly seated leadership in the cabinets seems to solve adequately the problem of the supply of power necessary to permit administration to concentrate on the fulfillment of accepted objectives. It is a commonplace that the American party system provides neither a mandate for a platform nor a mandate for a leadership.

Accordingly, the election over, its political meaning must be explored by the diverse leaders in the executive and legislative branches. Since the parties have failed to discuss issues, mobilize majorities in their terms, and create a working political consensus on measures to be carried out, the task is left for others—most prominently the agencies concerned. Legislation passed and powers granted are frequently politically premature. Thus the Council of Economic Advisors was given legislative birth before political acceptance of its functions existed. The agencies to which tasks are assigned must devote themselves to the creation of an adequate consensus to permit administration. The mandate that the parties do not supply must be attained through public relations and the mobilization of group support. Pendleton Herring and others have shown just how vital this support is for agency action.

The theory that agencies should confine themselves to communicating policy suggestions to executive and legislature, and refrain from appealing to their clientele and the public, neglects the failure of the parties to provide either a clear-cut decision as to what they should do or an adequately mobilized political support for a course of action. The bureaucracy under the American political system has a large share of responsibility for the public promotion of policy and even more in organizing the political basis for its survival and growth. It is generally recognized that the agencies have a special competence in the technical aspects of their fields which of necessity gives them a rightful policy initiative. In addition, they have or develop a shrewd understanding of the politically feasible in the group structure within which they work. Above all, in the eyes of their supporters and their enemies they represent the institutionalized embodiment of policy, an enduring organization actually or potentially capable of mobilizing power behind policy. The survival interests and creative drives of administrative organizations combine with clientele pressures to compel such mobilization. The party system provides no enduring institutional representation for group interest at all comparable to that of the bureaus of the Department of Agriculture. Even the subject matter committees of Congress function in the shadow of agency permanency.

The bureaucracy is recognized by all interested groups as a major channel of representation to such an extent that Congress rightly feels the competition of a rival. The weakness in party structure both permits and makes necessary the present dimensions of the political activities of the administrative branch—permits because it fails to protect administration from pressures and fails to provide adequate direction and support, makes necessary because it fails to develop a consensus on a leadership and a program that makes possible administration on the basis of accepted decisional premises.

Agencies and bureaus more or less perforce are in the business of building, maintaining, and increasing their political support. They lead and in large part are led by the diverse groups whose influence sustains them. Frequently they lead and are themselves led in conflicting directions. This is not due to a dull-witted incapacity to see the contradictions in their behavior but is an almost inevitable result of the contradictory nature of their support.

Herbert Simon has shown that administrative rationality depends on the establishment of uniform value premises in the decisional centers of organization. Unfortunately, the value premises of those forming vital elements of political support are often far from uniform. These elements are in Barnard's and Simon's sense "customers" of the organization and therefore parts of the organization whose wishes are clothed with a very real authority. A major and most time-consuming aspect of administration consists of the wide range of activities designed to secure enough "customer" acceptance to survive and, if fortunate, develop a consensus adequate to program formulation and execution.

To varying degrees, dependent on the breadth of acceptance of their programs, officials at every level of significant discretion must make their estimates of the situation, take stock of their resources, and plan accordingly. A keen appreciation of the real components of their organization is the beginning of wisdom. These components will be found to stretch far beyond the government payroll. Within the government they will encompass Congress, Congressmen, committees, courts, other agencies, presidential advisors, and the President. The Aristotelian analysis of constitutions is equally applicable and equally necessary to an understanding of administrative organization.

The broad alliance of conflicting groups that makes up presidential majorities scarcely coheres about any definite pattern of objectives, nor has it by the alchemy of the party system had its collective power concentrated in an accepted leadership with a personal mandate. The conciliation and maintenance of this support is a necessary condition of the attainment and retention of office involving, as Madison so well saw, "the spirit of party and faction in the necessary and ordinary operations of government." The President must in large part be, if not all things to all men, at least many things to many men. As a consequence, the contradictions in his power base invade administration. The often criticized apparent cross-purposes of the Roosevelt regime cannot be put down to inept administration until the political facts are weighed. Were these apparently self-defeating measures reasonably related to the general maintenance of the composite majority of the administration? The first objective—ultimate patriotism apart—of the administrator is the attainment and retention of the power on which his tenure of office depends. This is the necessary pre-condition for the accomplishment of all other objectives.

The same ambiguities that arouse the scorn of the naive in the electoral campaigns of the parties are equally inevitable in administration and for the same reasons. Victory at the polls does not yield either a clear-cut grant of power or a unified majority support for a coherent program. The task of the presidency lies in feeling out the alternatives of policy which are consistent with the retention and increase of the group support on which the administration

*[margin note: legal structure social structure ethical— the good life]*

rests. The lack of a budgetary theory (so frequently deplored) is not due to any incapacity to apply rational analysis to the comparative contribution of the various activities of government to a determinate hierarchy of purposes. It more probably stems from a fastidious distaste for the frank recognition of the budget as a politically expedient allocation of resources. Appraisal in terms of their political contribution to the administration provides almost a sole common denominator between the Forest Service and the Bureau of Engraving.

Integration of the administrative structure through an overall purpose in terms of which tasks and priorities can be established is an emergency phenomenon. Its realization, only partial at best, has been limited to war and the extremity of depression. Even in wartime the Farm Bureau Federation, the American Federation of Labor, the Congress of Industrial Organizations, the National Association of Manufacturers, the Chamber of Commerce, and a host of lesser interests resisted coordination of themselves and the agencies concerned with their interests. A presidency temporarily empowered by intense mass popular support acting in behalf of a generally accepted and simplified purpose can, with great difficulty, bribe, cajole, and coerce a real measure of joint action. . . . Only in crises are the powers of the executive nearly adequate to impose a common plan of action on the executive branch, let alone the economy.

In ordinary times the manifold pressures of our pluralistic society work themselves out in accordance with the balance of forces prevailing in Congress and the agencies. Only to a limited degree is the process subject to responsible direction or review by President or party leadership. . . .

The difficulty of coordinating government agencies lies not only in the fact that bureaucratic organizations are institutions having survival interests which may conflict with their rational adaptation to overall purpose, but even more in their having roots in society. Coordination of the varied activities of a modern government almost of necessity involves a substantial degree of coordination of the economy. Coordination of government agencies involves far more than changing the behavior and offices of officials in Washington and the field. It involves the publics that are implicated in their normal functioning. To coordinate fiscal policy, agricultural policy, labor policy, foreign policy, and military policy, to name a few major areas, moves beyond the range of government charts and the habitat of the bureaucrats to the marketplace and to where the people live and work. This suggests that the reason why government reorganization is so difficult is that far more than government in the formal sense is involved in reorganization. One could overlook this in the limited government of the nineteenth century but the multi-billion dollar government of the mid-twentieth permits no facile dichotomy between government and economy. Economy and efficiency are the two objectives a laissez faire society can prescribe in peacetime as over-all government objectives. Their inadequacy either as motivation or standards has long been obvious. A planned economy clearly requires a planned government. But, if one can afford an unplanned economy, apart from gross extravagance, there seems no compelling and therefore, perhaps, no sufficiently powerful reason for a planned government.

Basic to the problem of administrative rationality is that of organizational identification and point of view. To whom is one loyal—unit, section, branch, division, bureau, department, administration, government, country, people, world history, or what? Administrative analysis frequently assumes that organizational identification should occur in such a way as to merge primary organization loyalty in a larger synthesis. The good of the part is to give way to the reasoned good of the whole. This is most frequently illustrated in the rationalizations used to counter self-centered demands of primary groups for funds and personnel. Actually the competition between governmental power centers, rather than the rationalizations, is the effective instrument of coordination.

Where there is a clear common product on whose successful production the subgroups depend for the attainment of their own satisfaction, it is possible to demonstrate to almost all participants the desirability of cooperation. The shoe factory produces shoes, or else, for all concerned. But the government as a whole and many of its component parts have no such identifiable common product on which all depend. Like the proverbial Heinz, there are fifty-seven or more varieties unified, if at all, by a common political profit and loss account.

Administration is faced by somewhat the same dilemma as economics. There are propositions about the behavior pattern conducive to full employment—welfare economics. On the other hand, there are propositions about the economics of the individual firm—the counsel of the business schools. It is possible to show with considerable persuasiveness that sound considerations for the individual firm may lead to a depression if generally adopted, a result desired by none of the participants. However, no single firm can afford by itself to adopt the course of collective wisdom; in the absence of a common power capable of enforcing decisions premised on the supremacy of the collective interest, *sauve qui peut* is common sense.

The position of administrative organizations is not unlike the position of particular firms. Just as the decisions of the firms could be coordinated by the imposition of a planned economy so could those of the component parts of the government. But just as it is possible to operate a formally unplanned economy by the loose coordination of the market, in the same fashion it is possible to operate a government by the loose coordination of the play of political forces through its institutions.

The unseen hand of Adam Smith may be little in evidence in either case. One need not believe in a doctrine of social or administrative harmony to believe that formal centralized planning—while perhaps desirable and in some cases necessary—is not a must. The complicated logistics of supplying the city of New York runs smoothly down the grooves of millions of well adapted habits projected from a distant past. It seems naive on the one hand to believe in the possibility of a vast, intricate, and delicate economy operating with a minimum of formal overall direction, and on the other to doubt that a relatively simple mechanism such as the government can be controlled largely by the same play of forces. . . .

It is highly appropriate to consider how administrators should behave to meet the test of efficiency in a planned polity; but in the absence of such a polity and while, if we like, struggling to get it, a realistic science of administration will teach administrative behavior appropriate to the existing political system.

A close examination of the presidential system may well bring one to conclude that administrative rationality in it is a different matter from that applicable to the British ideal. The American presidency is an office that has significant monarchical characteristics despite its limited term and elective nature. The literature on court and palace has many an insight applicable to the White House. Access to the President, reigning favorites, even the court jester, are topics that show the continuity of institutions. The maxims of La Rochefoucauld and the memoirs of the Duc de Saint Simon have a refreshing realism for the operator on the Potomac.

The problem of rival factions in the President's family is as old as the famous struggle between Jefferson and Hamilton. . . . Experience seems to show that this personal and factional struggle for the President's favor is a vital part of the process of representation. The vanity, personal ambition, or patriotism of the contestants soon clothes itself in the generalities of principle and the clique aligns itself with groups beyond the capital. Subordinate rivalry is tolerated if not encouraged by so many able executives that it can scarcely be attributed to administrative ineptitude. The wrangling tests opinion, uncovers information that would otherwise never rise to the top, and provides effective opportunity for decision rather than mere ratification of prearranged plans. Like most judges, the executive needs to hear argument for his own instruction. The alternatives presented by subordinates in large part determine the freedom and the creative opportunity of their superiors. The danger of becoming a Merovingian is a powerful incentive to the maintenance of fluidity in the structure of power.

The fixed character of presidential tenure makes it necessary that subordinates be politically expendable. The President's men must be willing to accept the blame for failures not their own. Machiavelli's teaching on how princes must keep the faith bears rereading. Collective responsibility is incompatible with a fixed term of office. As it tests the currents of public opinion, the situation on the Hill, and the varying strength of the organized pressures, the White House alters and adapts the complexion of the administration. Loyalties to programs or to groups and personal pride and interest frequently conflict with whole-souled devotion to the presidency. In fact, since such devotion is not made mandatory by custom, institutions, or the facts of power, the problem is perpetually perplexing to those who must choose.

The balance of power between executive and legislature is constantly subject to the shifts of public and group support. The latent tendency of the American Congress is to follow the age-old parliamentary precedents and to try to reduce the President to the role of constitutional monarch. Against this threat and to secure his own initiative, the President's resources are primarily demagogic, with the weaknesses and strengths that dependence on mass popular appeal implies. The unanswered question of American government—"who is boss?"—constantly plagues administration.

---

## CASE STUDY 4

# Introduction

In the foregoing essay, Long discusses how critically important it is for public administrators at all levels of government to understand the dynamics and realities of administrative power—its sources, influences, and impacts on their programs and on themselves, as well as the methods for maintaining and effectively using the power. Long's realism about the nature of administrative power, however, was primarily a theoretical study of the subject. But how do Long's ideas apply to actual administrative situations?

Perhaps one of the most insightful recent studies of administrative power—its redirection and application—is found in the following account by James Q. Wilson, "The Changing FBI—The Road to Abscam." Wilson recounts the background of the highly publicized FBI undercover "sting operations" that took place in the early 1980s and were code-named "Abscam." Operation Abscam originated from a tip by an informant who had been useful for several years in locating stolen art works. The Bureau was told by the informant that he could put agents in touch with congressmen who were "for sale." Since the death of J. Edgar Hoover in the early 1970s, the FBI had been prodded by Congress to place greater priority on investigating political corruption and "white-collar crimes" and to move away from its more traditional emphasis on auto thefts and bank robbery cases. Abscam was a case that seemed to fit the new mandates for the Bureau as established by Congress—namely, cracking down on high-level political corruption.

The FBI thus accepted the informant's offer and set up an elaborate Abscam operation by having an FBI agent pose as a wealthy Arab businessman who said he would buy political favors from congressmen to help his businesses. Several members of Congress were then brought individually to a house leased by the Bureau in Washington, D.C., and the negotiations between the congressmen and the mythical Arab businessman were recorded on film by a hidden camera. Abscam ultimately resulted in the arrest and imprisonment of several of these individuals. Although sting operations were and still are fairly commonplace law enforcement activities, as Wilson writes, "What is different is that in this case Congressmen were apparently involved and the operation was leaked to the press before indictments were issued." Wilson not only looks carefully at the development of Abscam, but also probes thoughtfully the reasons for this fundamental shift in FBI priorities, as well as the possible ramifications of the new application for administrative power by the Bureau.

When reading this case, keep in mind the following questions:

Traditionally, why had the FBI stayed away from investigating white-collar crime and high-level political corruption?

What caused the FBI to shift its investigative resources toward these new directions?

In particular, what role did Congress, key subcommittee members, the director of the FBI, and others have in initiating such changes?

How did the FBI agents, individually and collectively, respond to such shifts in the Bureau's priorities? Do you think their responsiveness is characteristic of bureaucrats in other public organizations or is the FBI's political responsiveness unique in several ways?

In general, what does this case say about the nature and use of administrative power? Does the case support Long's ideas on this subject?

# The Changing FBI—The Road to Abscam

### JAMES Q. WILSON

It is inconceivable that J. Edgar Hoover would ever have investigated members of Congress to gather evidence for possible prosecution. Hoover's FBI learned a great deal about congressmen, and may

From "The Changing FBI—The Road to Abscam" by James Q. Wilson, *The Public Interest*, Spring 1980, pp. 3–14. Reprinted by permission of the author.

have gone out of its way to collect more information than it needed, but all this would have been locked discreetly away, or possibly leaked, most privately, to a President or attorney general whose taste for gossip Hoover wished to gratify or whose personal loyalty he wished to assure. The Bureau's shrewd cultivation of congressional and White House opinion, effective for decades, was in time denounced as evidence that the FBI was "out of control," immune from effective oversight.

Today, of course, the Bureau is again being criticized, albeit circumspectly, by various congressmen who complain of the manner (and possibly also the fact) of its investigation of possible legislative bribery. Congressmen wonder whether the FBI is launched on a "vendetta" against its erstwhile allies turned critics. Once again there are angry mutterings that the Bureau is "out of control," this time because it is using its most powerful technique—undercover operations—to discover whether congressmen are corrupt.

It would be tempting to ascribe the changes in the Bureau's relations with Congress to nothing more than personal pique amplified into organizational vengeance. After years of congressional adulation of Hoover and the FBI, the mood suddenly turned nasty with revelations of how far the Bureau was prepared to go in using its investigative powers to maintain political support. The list of Bureau excesses is long, familiar, and dismaying; the wrath visited upon it by several congressional committees combined a proper outrage at abuse of power with a hint of romance gone sour. For the FBI now to turn on those who had turned on it would be precisely the sort of thing one might suppose a Hoover-style agency might relish.

This is not what has happened. No doubt there are some FBI agents who are enjoying the sight of congressmen scurrying for cover, but that was not the motive for "Operation Abscam." The Bureau has in fact changed, and changed precisely in accordance with the oft-expressed preferences of Congress itself. Congressional and other critics complained that the Bureau in the 1960's was not only violating the rights of citizens, it was wasting its resources and energies on trivial cases and meaningless statistical accomplishments. Beginning with Director Clarence Kelley, the Bureau pledged that it would end the abuses and redirect its energies to more important matters. This is exactly what has happened.

This rather straightforward explanation is hard for official Washington to accept, and understandably so. Bureaucracies are not supposed to change, they are only supposed to claim to have changed. It tests the credulity of a trained congressional cynic to be told that a large, complex, rule bound organization such as the FBI would or could execute an about-face.

But the FBI is not just any bureaucracy, and never has been. Next to the Marine Corps, it is probably the most centrally controlled organization in the federal government. Its agents do not have civil service or union protection, its disciplinary procedures can be swift and draconian, and despite recent efforts to decentralize some decision making, the director himself, or one of his immediate subordinates, personally approves an astonishingly large proportion of all the administrative decisions made in the Bureau. Not long ago, a decision to install sanitary-napkin dispensers in women's lavoratories in Bureau headquarters could not be made until Director William Webster endorsed the recommendation. FBI agents have complained for decades about the heavy-handed supervision they received from headquarters; though that has begun to change, the visit of an inspection team to an FBI field office continues to instill apprehension bordering on terror in the hearts of the local staff. The inspectors sometimes concentrate on the minutiae at the expense of the important, but whatever its defects, nit-picking insures that field offices will conform to explicit headquarters directives pertaining to observable behavior.

But even for the Bureau, the change in investigative strategy that culminated in Operation Abscam was no easy matter. For one thing, much of what the Bureau does is not easily observable and thus not easily controlled by inspection teams and headquarters directives. Law enforcement occurs on the street in low-visibility situations that test the judgment and skill of agents but do not lend themselves to formal review. Many laws the FBI enforces—particularly those pertaining to consensual crimes such as bribery—place heavy reliance on the skill and energy of agents and field supervisors who must find ways of discovering that a crime may have been committed before they can even begin the process of gathering evidence that might lead to a prosecution. Relations between an agent and an informant often lie at the heart of the investigative effort, but these are subtle, complex, and largely unobservable. Finally, what the Bureau chooses to emphasize is not for it alone to decide. The policies of the local United States Attorney, who though nominally an employee of the Justice Department is in reality often quite autonomous, determine what federal cases will be accepted for prosecution and thus what kinds of offenses the local FBI office will emphasize.

# Changing the Bureau

Given these difficulties, the effort to change the investigative priorities of the Bureau was a protracted, controversial, and difficult struggle. Several things had to happen: New policies had to be stated, unconventional investigative techniques had to be authorized, organizational changes had to be made, and new incentives had to be found.

As is always the case, stating the new policies was the easiest thing to do. Attorney General Edward Levi and Director Kelley pledged that the Bureau would reduce its interest in domestic security cases, especially of the sort that led to such abuses as COINTELPRO, and in the investigation of certain routine crimes (such as auto theft or small thefts from interstate shipments) that had for years generated the impressive statistics that Hoover was fond of reciting. The domestic security cases were constitutionally and politically vulnerable; the criminal cases that produced evidence of big workloads but few significant convictions were unpopular among the street agents. The man Kelley brought in to close down virtually all the domestic security investigations was, ironically, Neil Welch, then in charge of the Bureau's Philadelphia office and later to be in charge of the New York office and of Operation Abscam. In a matter of months, thousands of security cases were simply terminated; hundreds of security informants were let go; domestic security squads in various field offices were disbanded and their agents assigned to other tasks. New attorney-general guidelines clarified and narrowed the circumstances under which such cases could be opened in the future. The number of FBI informants in organizations thought to constitute a security risk became so small that it was kept secret in order, presumably, to avoid encouraging potential subversives with the knowledge that they were, in effect, free to organize without fear of Bureau surveillance.

Kelley also announced a "quality case program" authorizing each office to close out pending investigative matters that had little prosecutive potential and to develop priorities that would direct its resources toward important cases. Almost overnight, official Bureau caseloads dropped precipitously, as field offices stopped pretending that they were investigating (and in some cases, actually stopped investigating) hundreds of cases—of auto thefts, bank robberies, and thefts from interstate commerce and from government buildings—where the office had no leads, the amounts stolen were small, or it was believed (rightly or wrongly) that local police departments could handle the matter.[1]

Headquarters made clear what it regarded as the "priority" cases that the field should emphasize: white-collar crime, organized crime, and foreign counterintelligence. But saying that these were the priorities, and getting them to *be* the priorities, were two different things. Permitting field offices to stop reporting on high-volume, low-value cases did not automatically insure that the resources thereby saved would be devoted to, say, white-collar crime. For that to occur, some important organizational changes had to be made.

The most important of these was to reorganize the field-office squads. Traditionally, a field office grouped its agent personnel into squads based on the volume of reported criminal offenses—there would be a bank robbery squad, an interstate theft squad, an auto theft squad, and so on. These squads reacted to the incoming flow of reported crimes by assigning an agent to each case. What we now call white-collar crime was typically the province of a single unit—the "accounting squad"—composed, often, of agents with training as accountants, who would handle bank complaints of fraud and embezzlement. Occasionally, more complex cases involving fraud would be developed; many offices had individual agents skilled at detecting and investigating elaborate political, labor, or business conspiracies. But attention to such matters was not routinized because the internal structure of a typical field office was organized around the need to respond to the reports of crimes submitted by victims. Elaborate conspiracies often produced no victims aware of their victimization or enriched the participants in ways that gave no one an incentive to call the FBI. Taxpayers generally suffer when bribes are offered and taken, and innocent investors may be victimized by land frauds, but either the citizen is unaware he is a victim or the "victim" was in fact part of the conspiracy, drawn in by greed and larcenous intent.

Again Neil Welch enters the scene. The Philadelphia office was one of the first to redesign its structure so that most of its squads had the task, not of responding to victim complaints, but of identifying ("targeting") individuals, groups, and organizations for intensive scrutiny on the grounds that they were suspected of being involved in organized crime, major conspiracies, labor racketeering, or political corruption. Though almost every FBI field office would from time to time make cases against corrupt politicians or businessmen, the cases made in Philadelphia were spectacular for their number and scope. Judges, state legislators, labor leaders, businessmen, police officers, and government officials were indicted and convicted. The more indictments that were handed down, the more nervous accomplices, frightened associates, or knowledgeable reporters would come forward to volunteer more information that spurred further investigations.

During the period when Welch and the Philadelphia office were making headlines (roughly, 1975 to 1977), the rest of the Bureau was watching and waiting. Experienced FBI officials knew that under the Hoover regime, the only safe rule was "never do anything for the first time." Taking the initiative could result in rapid promotions but it could also lead to immediate disgrace; innovation was risky. What if the allies of the powerful people being indicted (one was Speaker of the Pennsylvania House of Representatives) complained? Hoover had usually rebuffed such complaints, but you could never be certain. More important, how would Bureau headquarters react to the fact that the *number* of cases being handled in Philadelphia had dropped owing to the reassignment of agents from the regular high-volume squads to the new "target" squads? In the past, resources—money, manpower—were given to field offices that had high and rising caseloads, not to ones with declining statistics.

Kelley's response was clear—he increased the number of agents assigned to Philadelphia and gave Welch even more important responsibilities (it was at this time that Welch was brought to headquarters to oversee the winding down of the domestic security program). There were still many issues to resolve and many apprehensive supervisors to reassure, but the momentum was growing: More and more field offices began to reorganize to give structural effect to the priority-case program, and thus to an aggressive stance regarding white-collar crime.

## Emphasizing Priority Offenses

The incentives to comply with the emphasis on priority offenses came from within and without the Bureau. Inside, the management information system

was revised so that investigations and convictions were now classified by quality as well as number. The criminal offenses for which the FBI had investigative responsibility were grouped into high- and low-priority categories, and individual offenses within these categories were further classified by the degree of seriousness of the behavior under investigation (for example, thefts were classified by the amount stolen). It is far from clear that the statistics generated were used in any systematic way by Bureau headquarters—in the FBI as in many government agencies, such data are often perceived as a "numbers game" to be played and then forgotten—but at the very least these statistics reinforced the message repeated over and over again in the statements of the director, first Kelley and then William H. Webster: Go after white-collar and organized crime.

Outside the Bureau, key congressmen were pressing hard in the same direction. Nowhere was this pressure greater than in the chambers of the Subcommittee on Civil and Constitutional Rights of the House Judiciary Committee, chaired by Congressman Don Edwards of California—who had once been, briefly, a member of the FBI. This Subcommittee had become one of the centers of congressional attacks on the Bureau. Kelley and Webster spent hours answering questions put by its members, who included in addition to Chairman Edwards, Elizabeth Holtzman of New York and Robert Drinan of Massachusetts. The attack on the FBI's performance began with criticism of the domestic security programs, but came to include criticisms of the Bureau's weaknesses in the area of white-collar crime. This latter concern reflected, in part, the Subcommittee members' genuine conviction that white-collar offenses were serious matters. But it also reflected the Subcommittee members' suspicion that the FBI was "soft" on "establishment" crimes while being excessively preoccupied with subversion, and thus inclined merely to go through the motions when investigating the former and to put its heart and resources into inquiries regarding the latter. Thus, getting the Bureau to emphasize white-collar crimes was not only good in itself, it was a way, the Subcommittee seemed to think, of keeping it out of domestic security work.

In 1977, staff members of the Subcommittee toured various FBI field offices and spoke as well to several U.S. Attorneys. Their report sharply criticized the FBI for continuing to devote manpower to street crimes such as bank robberies and hijacking—all of which, in the opinion of the staff, could better be handled by the local police. In some cases, the staff claimed, the FBI's idea of white-collar crime was welfare cheating and other examples of individual, and presumably small-scale, frauds against the government. The staff lamented the "reluctance on the part of FBI personnel, particularly at the supervisory level, to get involved in more complex investigations that may require significant allocation of manpower for long periods of time." And the report criticized the field offices for not mounting more undercover operations.

Whatever shortcomings the FBI may have, indifference to congressional opinion has never been one of them. The pressure inside the Bureau to develop major white-collar-crime cases mounted. The Bureau had always thoroughly investigated reported violations of federal law whatever the color of the collar worn by the suspects. Businessmen, politicians, and labor leaders had been sent to prison as a result of FBI inquiries. But most of these cases arose out of a complaint to the Bureau by a victim, followed by FBI interviews of suspects and an analysis of documents. Sometimes wiretaps were employed. The number, scope, and success of such investigations depended crucially on the skill and patience of the agents working a case. One legendary FBI agent in Boston was personally responsible for making several major corruption cases as a result of his tenacity, his ability to win the confidence of reluctant witnesses and accomplices, and his knowledge of complex financial transactions. But finding or producing large numbers of such agents is difficult at best. Far easier would be the development of investigative techniques that could generate reliable evidence in large amounts without having to depend solely on an agent's ability to "flip" a suspect, who then would have to testify in court against his former collaborators.

## Undercover Operations

One such method was the undercover operation. Narcotics agents in the Drug Enforcement Administration and in local police departments had always relied extensively on undercover agents buying illegal drugs in order to produce evidence. Traditionally, however, the FBI had shied away from these methods. Hoover had resisted any techniques that risked compromising an agent by placing him in situations where he could be exposed to adverse publicity or

tempted to accept bribes. Hoover knew that public confidence in FBI agents was the Bureau's principal investigative resource and that confidence should not be jeopardized by having agents appear as anything other than well-groomed, "young executive" individuals with an impeccable reputation for integrity. From time to time, an agent would pose as a purchaser of stolen goods, but these were usually short-lived operations with limited objectives. For most purposes, the FBI relied on informants—persons with knowledge of or connections in the underworld—to provide leads that could then, by conventional investigative techniques, be converted into evidence admissible in court in ways that did not compromise the informant.

The FBI's reliance on informants rather than undercover agents had, of course, its own costs. An informant was not easily controlled, his motives often made him want to use the FBI for personal gain or revenge against rivals, and either he would not testify in court at all or his testimony would be vulnerable to attacks from defense attorneys. Moreover, it is one thing to find informants among bank robbers, jewel thieves, and gamblers with organized crime connections; it is something else again to find informants among high-level politicians, business executives, and labor leaders. An undercover operation came to be seen as a valuable supplement to the informant system: Though created with the aid of an informant, it could be staffed by FBI agents posing as thieves, fences, or businessmen, carefully monitored by recording equipment, used to develop hard physical evidence (such as photographs of cash payoffs), and operated so as to draw in high-level suspects whose world was not easily penetrated by conventional informants.

In 1974 the Law Enforcement Assistance Administration (LEAA) began supplying money to make possible the now-famous "Sting" operations in which stolen property would be purchased from thieves who thought they were selling to criminal fences. LEAA insisted initially that a Sting be a joint federal-local operation, and so the FBI became partners in these early ventures, thereby acquiring substantial experience in how to mount and execute an undercover effort in ways that avoided claims of entrapment. In 1977, the FBI participated in 34 Sting operations. Soon, however, the requirement of federal participation was relaxed and the Sting became almost entirely a state and local venture (albeit often with LEAA money). After all, most of the persons caught in a Sting were thieves who had violated state, but not federal, law.

The experience gained and the success enjoyed by the FBI in the Stings were now put in service of undercover operations directed at the priority crimes—especially white-collar crimes and racketeering. During fiscal year 1978, the Bureau conducted 132 undercover operations, 36 of which were aimed at white-collar crime. They produced impressive (and noncontroversial) results, and led to the indictment of persons operating illegal financial schemes, trying to defraud the government, engaging in union extortion, and participating in political corruption.

Each of these operations was authorized and supervised by FBI headquarters and by the local United States Attorney or by Justice Department attorneys (or both). Among the issues that were reviewed was the need to avoid entrapment. In general, the courts have allowed undercover operations—such as an agent offering to buy illegal narcotics—as a permissible investigative technique. In *Hampton v. United States,* the Supreme Court held in 1976 that the sale to government agents of heroin supplied to the defendant by a government informant did not constitute entrapment. In an earlier case, Justice Potter Stewart tried to formulate a general rule distinguishing a proper from an improper undercover operation: "Government agents may engage in conduct that is likely, when objectively considered, to afford a person ready and willing to commit the crime an opportunity to do so." It is noteworthy that this formulation appeared in a dissenting opinion in which Stewart argued that the case in question *had* involved entrapment; thus, it probably represents the opinion of many justices who take a reasonably strict view of what constitutes entrapment. As such, it affords ample opportunity for undercover operations, especially those, such as Abscam, in which lawyers can monitor agent activity on almost a continuous basis.

Congress was fully aware that the FBI was expanding its use of undercover operations. The House Appropriations Committee, as well as others, were told about these developments—without, of course, particular cases then in progress being identified. Moreover, Congress by law had to give permission for the Bureau to do certain things necessary for an undercover operation. These prerequisites to FBI undercover operations involve the right to lease buildings or to enter into contracts in ways that do not divulge the fact that the contracting party or the lessee are government agents, and that permit advance payment of funds. Indeed, one statute prohibits a government agency from leasing a building in Washington, D.C., without a specific appropriation for that purpose having first been made by Congress. If that law had been in force, the FBI would not have been able to lease the Washington house in which Operation Abscam was conducted. At the request of the FBI, however, Congress exempted the Bureau from compliance with statutes that might have impeded such operations. The proposed FBI Charter, now before Congress, would specifically authorize undercover operations and would grant a continuing exemption, whenever necessary, from the statutes governing contracts and leases.

Though the FBI learned a great deal about undercover operations by its early participation in Stings, Operation Abscam is not, strictly speaking, a Sting at all. In a Sting, a store is opened and the agents declare their willingness to buy merchandise from one and all. Much of what they buy involves perfectly legitimate sales; some of what they buy is stolen, and when that is established, the ground is laid for an arrest. Operation Abscam followed a quite different route. It resulted from the normal exploitation of an informant who had been useful in locating stolen art works. The informant apparently indicated that he could put agents in touch with politicians who were for sale; the agents accepted, and set up Abscam by having an agent pose as a wealthy Arab interested in buying political favors to assist his (mythical) business enterprises. Several important congressmen, or their representatives, were brought to the house used for Abscam and their negotiations with the agents recorded. The operation is no different in design from those used in many other cases that earned praise for the Bureau. What is different is that in this case congressmen were apparently involved and the operation was leaked to the press before indictments were issued.

## Congress, Law Enforcement, and the Constitution

For congressmen to be in trouble with the law is nothing new. During the 95th Congress alone, 13 members or former members of the House of Representatives were indicted or convicted on criminal charges. Most if not all of these cases resulted from the use of conventional investigative methods—typically, a tip to a law enforcement officer or reporter by a person involved in the offense (bribery, payroll padding, taking kickbacks) who then testified against the official. Law enforcement in such cases is ordinarily reactive and thus crucially dependent on the existence and volubility of a disaffected employee, businessman, or accomplice. Operation Abscam was "proactive"—it created an opportunity for persons to commit a crime who were (presumably) ready and willing to do so.

Congress has never complained when such methods were used against others; quite the contrary, it has explicitly or implicitly urged—and authorized—their use against others. There is no small element of hypocrisy in the complaints of some congressmen that they did not mean a vigorous investigation of white-collar crime to include *them*.

But it is not all hypocrisy. It is worth discussing how such investigations should be conducted and under what pattern of accountability. An unscrupulous President with a complaisant FBI director could use undercover operations to discredit political enemies, including congressmen from a rival party. Hoover was a highly political FBI director, but he saw, rightly, that his power would be greater if he avoided investigations of Congress than if he undertook them. Clarence Kelley and William H. Webster have been sternly nonpartisan directors who would never consider allowing the Bureau's powers to be put in service of some rancid political purpose. But new times bring new men, and in the future we may again see partisan efforts to use the Bureau. What safeguards can be installed to prevent schemes to embarrass political enemies by leaked stories is worth some discussion.

But there is a dilemma here: the more extensive the pattern of accountability and control, the greater the probability of a leak. The only sure way to minimize leaks is to minimize the number of persons who know something worth leaking. In the case of Operation Abscam, scores of persons knew what was going on—in part because such extensive efforts were made to insure that it was a lawful and effective investigation. In addition to the dozens of FBI agents and their supervisors, there were lawyers in the Justice Department and U.S. Attorneys in New York, Newark, Philadelphia, and Washington, D.C., together with their staffs, all of whom were well informed. Any one of them could have leaked. Indeed, given their partisan sponsorship and what is often their background in political activism, U.S. Attorneys are especially likely to be sources of leaks—more so, I should surmise, than FBI agents. If, in order to prevent abuses of the Bureau's investigative powers, we increase the number of supervisors—to include, for example, members of the House or Senate ethics committees—we also increase the chances of leaks (to say nothing of other ways by which such investigations could be compromised).

In the meantime, the debate will not be helped by complaints that the Bureau has launched a "vendetta" against Congress or that it is "out of control." It is nothing of the kind. It is an organization that is following out the logic of changes and procedures adopted to meet the explicit demands of Congress.

## Note

1. A fuller account of these changes can be found in James Q. Wilson, *The Investigators: Managing FBI and Narcotics Agents* (Basic Books, 1978).

## Chapter 4 Review Questions

1. On the basis of your reading of the Long essay and the case study, how would you define the term *administrative power?* Can it be measured? If so, how?
2. Based on the case study, "The Changing FBI—The Road to Abscam," by James Q. Wilson, how did Hoover effectively use the Bureau's administrative power? How did he influence its direction and enhancement of power? Why did he avoid investigating political corruption and white-collar crime?
3. After Hoover's death, what prompted the redirection of Bureau priorities? How did FBI agents respond to these new priorities?

4. In your view, was Abscam a responsible or irresponsible use of FBI administrative power? How can one determine "responsible" or "irresponsible" use of administrative power?
5. Can you list the pros and cons of having the FBI involved in "sting operations" like Abscam?
6. On the basis of Long's essay and your analysis of the case study, can you list the specific factors that can strengthen or detract from an organization's administrative power? Are there specific ways that administrators protect or enhance their power positions? If so, how?

## Key Terms

interest groups
organizational fragmentation
administrative rationality
balance of power

coordination of government
sources of conflict
sources of cohesion
maintaining political support

## Suggestions for Further Reading

The classic works on interest groups and their influence on the governmental process are Arthur F. Bentley, *The Process of Government* (Cambridge, Mass.: Harvard University Press, 1908); E. Pendleton Herring, *Public Administration and the Public Interest* (New York: Russell and Russell, 1936); and David Truman, *The Governmental Process* (New York: Alfred A. Knopf, 1951). The influence of politics on public administration and the general power politics within administrative processes were especially emphasized and popularized by the "new postwar realism" of authors such as Paul H. Appleby, *Big Democracy* (New York: Alfred A. Knopf, 1945) and *Policy and Administration* (University, Ala.: University of Alabama Press, 1949); Robert A. Dahl and Charles E. Lindblom, *Politics, Economics, and Welfare* (New York: Harper and Brothers, 1953); and Herbert Simon et al., *Public Administration* (New York: Alfred A. Knopf, 1950). Of course, Long's numerous essays did much to explore as well as contribute to this topic and they are available in a single volume, *The Polity* (Chicago: Rand McNally and Co., 1962).

The last two decades have witnessed an enormous outpouring of books and articles on this subject. Some of the best that illuminate our understanding of the complex interplay between administration and politics have been more narrowly focused book-length cases of policy dilemmas such as A. Lee Fritchler, *Smoking and Politics*, Second Edition (Englewood Cliffs, N.J.: Prentice-Hall, 1975); Daniel P. Moynihan, *The Politics of a Guaranteed Income* (New York: Random House, 1973); Jeffrey L. Pressman and Aaron Wildavsky, *Implementation*, Second Edition (Berkeley: University of California Press, 1979); and Stephen K. Bailey and Edith K. Mosher, *ESEA: The Office of Education Administers a Law* (Syracuse: Syracuse University Press, 1968), as well as Charles Perrow and Maurio F. Guillén, *The AIDS Disaster: The Failure of Organizations in New York and the Nation* (New Haven, Conn: Yale University Press, 1990). There are many, many more such cases, particularly those available through the Inter-University Case Program (P.O. Box 229, Syracuse, N.Y.

13210), and the John F. Kennedy School of Government Case Program, Kennedy School of Government, Harvard University, 79 JFK Street, Cambridge, Mass. 02138. For recent books about administrative power based on some careful case studies, read: Gary C. Bryner, *Bureaucratic Discretion* (New York: Pergamon Press, 1987); Irene S. Rubin, *Shrinking the Federal Government* (New York: Longman, 1985); and James P. Pfiffner, *The Strategic Presidency* (Chicago: The Dorsey Press, 1988).

Perhaps some of the very best contemporary analyses of the aspects of power influencing administrative actions are found in Harold Seidman and Robert Gilmour *Politics, Position, and Power,* Fourth Edition (New York: Oxford University Press, 1986); Francis E. Rourke, *Bureaucracy, Politics and Public Policy,* Third Edition (Boston: Little, Brown, 1984); as well as Rourke's excellent edited collection entitled *Bureaucratic Power in National Policy Making,* Fourth Edition (Boston: Little, Brown, 1986). The late Stephen K. Bailey's "Improving Federal Governance," *Public Administration Review,* 30 (November/December 1980), pp. 548–553, is also excellent; as well as Frederick C. Mosher, "The Changing Responsibilities and Tactics of the Federal Government," in the same issue, pp. 541–548; and James D. Carroll, A. Lee Fritchler, and Bruce

L. R. Smith, "Supply-Side Management in the Reagan Administration," *Public Administration Review,* 45 (November/December 1985), pp. 805–814.

You should not overlook biographies and autobiographies as offering worthwhile insights, particularly Joseph A. Califano, Jr., *Governing America* (New York: Simon and Schuster, 1981); William Manchester, *American Caesar: Douglas MacArthur, 1880–1964* (Boston: Little, Brown, 1978); Norman Polmar and Thomas B. Allen, *Rickover: A Biography* (New York: Simon and Schuster, 1982); or Robert Caro, *The Power Broker,* cited in Chapter 3; and David Stockman, *The Triumph of Politics,* cited in Chapter 3. For more current "overviews" of national political power, see Hedrick Smith, *The Power Game: How Washington Works* (New York: Random House, 1988); Bradley H. Patterson, Jr., *Rings of Power: The White House Staff and Its Expanding Role in Government* (New York: Basic Books, 1988); A. Lee Fritschler and Bernard H. Ross, *How Washington Works, The Executive Guide to Government* (Cambridge, Mass.: Ballinger, 1987) and at the local level, both Robert J. Waste, *Ecology of City Policy Making* (New York: Oxford University Press, 1989); and James H. Svara, *Official Leadership in the City: Patterns of Conflict and Cooperation* (New York: Oxford University Press, 1990).

# CHAPTER 5

## Federalism, Intergovernmental Relations, and Public Administration: The Concept of "Madison's Middle Ground"

*B*argaining and negotiations, not command and obedience, appear to characterize the practice of intergovernmental programs now as in the past, even if
the past was far more mindful of a tradition called states' rights.

*Martha Derthick*

## READING 5

## Introduction

In most countries, the subject of intergovernmental relations is not a frequent
topic of conversation. Unitary forms of government, found in communist societies, Third World or developing nations, and even modernized traditional Western state regimes, allow for little or no semiautonomous local units of government. Within these unitary models, power flows from the top downward, and
no competition with national sovereignty is tolerated from governmental subunits. Local autonomy is simply unknown.

By contrast, the central framing idea of the U.S. government was federalism.
The federal structure, as designed by the U.S. Constitution, distributes authority among the various levels of federal, state, and local government. In part,
federalism was a pragmatic requirement in 1787. The founders were faced with
the difficult necessity of winning state support for ratification, and thus adopting
a unitary form that would abolish or severely restrict state authority was clearly
out of the question. However, ideological considerations were also important in
opting for federalism. The founders had vivid memories of the dangers from
top-down unitary government of George III's monarchy as well as the loose,
extreme decentralization of the Articles of Confederation (in reality the U.S.'s
first constitution). Neither had produced satisfactory government and so the
founders chose a mixture of both, the novel federal format. Though it is and
remains the central framing idea in the U.S. Constitution, the Constitution on

the specifics of this subject, as in many others, was imprecise and unclear. The details of the wheres and whys of how the various functions of government would be parcelled out among the levels and units are not addressed in the U.S. Constitution beyond the items listed in Article I, Section 8.

In the United States, public administrators, thus, work within an unusual, complex framework in which authority over agency and program activities is frequently shared by various levels, jurisdictions, and units of government. Because of this "scattering" of authority, administrative problems arise, leading in turn to the important study of intergovernmental relations (IGR). IGR involves comprehending the complexities of the federal system based on mutual interdependence, shared functions, and intertwined influence. Morton Grodzins once aptly showed the confusion for public administrators who operate under this system. In the case of a county health officer, called "a sanitarian" in a rural county:

> The sanitarian is appointed by the state under merit standards established by the federal government. His base salary comes jointly from state and federal funds, the county provides him with an office and office amenities and pays a portion of his expenses, and the largest city in the county also contributes to his salary and office by virtue of his appointment as a city plumbing inspector. It is impossible from moment to moment to tell under which governmental hat the sanitarian operates. His work of inspecting the purity of food is carried out under federal standards; but he is enforcing state laws when inspecting commodities that have not been in interstate commerce; and somewhat perversely, he also acts under state authority when inspecting milk coming into the county from producing areas across the state border. He is a federal officer when impounding impure drugs shipped from a neighboring state; a federal-state officer when distributing typhoid immunization serum; a state officer when enforcing standards of industrial hygiene; a state-local officer when inspecting the city's water supply; and (to complete the circle) a local officer when insisting that the city butchers adopt more hygienic methods of handling their garbage. But he cannot and does not think of himself as acting in these separate capacities. All business in the county that concerns public health and sanitation he considers his business. Paid largely from federal funds, he does not find it strange to attend meetings of the city council to give expert advice on matters ranging from rotten apples to rabies control. He is even deputized as a member of both the city and county police forces.[1]

Morton Grodzins's example of the county health officer may be extreme, but it is not uncommon to find public administrators wearing several "governmental hats." Federalism confounds and confuses public administrators' roles and responsibilities to an extreme degree in the United States. Whose the boss? The federal government? State? Locals? Or . . . ? For many administrators, the

[1]Morton Grodzins, "The Federal System," in The American Assembly, *Goals for Americans* (N.J.: Prentice-Hall, Inc., 1960), p. 265.

answer, as that of the county health officer cited by Grozdins, is the ambiguous: "It all depends."

Martha Derthick, the Julia Allen Cooper Professor of Government and Foreign Affairs at the University of Virginia and author of numerous influential writings on federalism and intergovernmental affairs, explores the current dimensions of this subject in the following seminal essay, "American Federalism: Madison's Middle Ground," which appeared in the bicentennial issue of *Public Administration Review*. In honor of the U.S. Constitution's 200th birthday, Derthick assesses the status of federalism and its implications for modern-day administration from both the standpoint of the historical record of the Founding Fathers' ideas as well as its contemporary intergovernmental practices. In framing the Constitution, argues Derthick, James Madison sought "a middle ground" that would provide "due supremacy" to a national government while leaving the states intact so that they might be "subordinately useful." Today, the federal government remains unquestionably supreme, but for domestic purposes it relies pervasively on state cooperation to fulfill many functions. Several new measures had clearly centralizing influences over the past quarter-century, yet even where the urge to centralize was strongest, Derthick emphasizes, such as in income protection and environmental protection programs—state governments in recent years retained a great deal of discretion in policy making and administrative freedom from federal oversight. Derthick further points out how intergovernmental relationships today involve sharing responsibilities among layers of governments. Much of her article explores the reasons for the persistence of state and local discretion in an era of clear national supremacy as well as the nature of "bargaining and negotiations, not command and obedience" that "appear to characterize the practice of intergovernmental programs now as in the past. . . ." Surprisingly, concludes Derthick, "the current debate . . . appears to turn on essentially the issues which divided federalists and anti-federalists 200 years ago. Both sides profess to value liberty and democracy above all. They differ in their judgment of the distribution of governmental power that will best serve those ends." It is thus within this argument over "Madison's middle ground" that modern public administrators must work out solutions to the pressing social, political, and economic questions of our times.

As you read Derthick's essay, reflect on such issues as:

How does she define the term "federalism"? Why does she draw on James Madison, in particular, to understand its contemporary meaning?

Why does Derthick contend that "one wonders if the founders believed their (federal) composition would be stable"? Is it in your view?

What sources does the author cite to draw her conclusion that "bargaining and negotiations, not command and obedience, appear to characterize the practice of intergovernmental programs"? Do you agree?

What does that conclusion mean for public administration practitioners in terms of the training and skills for their work (think about Case Study 3, "Dumping $2.6 Million on Bakersfield," to help draw your conclusions)?

# American Federalism: Madison's Middle Ground

## MARTHA DERTHICK

"Let it be tried . . . whether any middle ground can be taken, which will at once support a due supremacy of the national authority, and leave in force the local authorities so far as they can be subordinately useful."

So wrote James Madison to Edmund Randolph not long before the constitutional convention.[1] Much of American constitutional experience has consisted, as did much of Madison's work in Philadelphia, of a search for that middle ground.

At the convention, even partisans of the states conceded that there must be a stronger central government than the Articles of Confederation provided. And even supporters of national supremacy conceded that the states should not be abolished.[2] So the convention settled on a "composition" or "compound republic," as Madison termed it in *The Federalist*.[3] That is, the new government combined features of federal and purely national forms, most obviously in the structure of its legislature, wherein the states were represented, equally, in one house, and the people directly, in proportion to their numbers, in the other.

Eventually, this creation came to be widely regarded as the prototype of federal government, or at least as the most important and successful example of it. K. C. Wheare, writing

a basic text on federal government in 1953, began by looking to the Constitution of the United States for his definition. The basic principle, he concluded, "is that of the division of powers between distinct and co-ordinate governments."[4] In certain matters, for example the coining of money and the making of treaties, the general government was independent of the state governments, whereas the states, in turn, were independent of the general government in other matters.

One wonders if the Founders believed that their "composition" would be stable. Some evidently doubted it. At the outset of the convention, after explaining the distinction between a federal government as it was then understood ("a mere compact resting on the good faith of the parties") and a national one ("having a complete and *compulsive* operation"), Gouverneur Morris seemed to say that the convention must choose one or the other: "He contended that in all communities there must be one supreme power, and one only."[5] "A National Government must soon of necessity swallow (the states) all up," George Read of Delaware predicted.[6] "Mr. Bedford (also of Delaware) contended, that there was no middle way between a perfect consolidation, and a mere confederacy of the States."[7] In 1828, when the composition was nearly 40 years old and under severe strain, Madison seemed uncertain about its prospects but still hopeful. "It will be fortunate if the struggle (between the nation and states) should end in a permanent equilibrium of powers," he wrote.[8]

As the "composition" approaches 200 years of age, it is still not easy to render a simple, indisputable judgment on the outcome. Surely the national government has proved supreme. It got the better of the states in the original contest, as well as in the major tests of subsequent centuries. The nineteenth century, embracing the great debates over nullification and secession and culminating in the Civil War, virtually disposed of the doctrine that the states have the right to decide disputes over the distribution of governmental power. The twentieth century then proceeded to dispose of the original precept that the powers of the national government are confined to those enumerated in a written constitution—a development that was far enough advanced by the end of World War II to cast doubt even then on Wheare's definition.[9]

On the other hand, even now the national government does not operate alone. State governments survive, not as hollow shells (as their detractors often charge and their defenders always fear), but as functioning entities, with their own constitutions, laws, elected officials and independently-raised revenues. Though Congress has pervasively invaded domains once thought exclusively those of the states and though it very much constrains their conduct with commerce clause regulations applying directly to them and with grant-in-aid conditions, on the whole it has refrained from displacing them—apart, that is, from piecemeal preemptions of regulatory functions under the commerce clause, a practice that is well within the bounds of constitutional tradition and indubitably sanctioned by the supremacy clause. As a general rule, when Congress essays new domestic responsibilities it relies on cooperation of the states, with the result that the two levels of government in our federal system are today massively and pervasively

intertwined—a fact that is of utmost importance for the conduct of public administration.

As it happens, quite apart from the impending bicentennial of the Constitution, the 1980s are an eminently suitable time for taking stock of the federal system for two reasons. First, because the Reagan era has provided surcease from the passage of expansive new federal legislation, we can pause to appraise the changes that took place between 1965 and 1980, a period marked by numerous innovations in intergovernmental relations. Second, within the Supreme Court and between the Court and the Reagan Administration's second attorney general, a rather heated debate has developed over the importance of federalism and the judicial behavior required to preserve it.

## The Practice of Intergovernmental Relations: Shared Programs

For a student of federalism to make sense of the events of 1965-1980 is no easy task. A great deal happened. Grant-in-aid programs proliferated in the customary categorical pattern and then were revised by the introduction of general revenue-sharing and three broad-based grants—two (for community development and employment and training) which the Nixon Administration designed and a third (social services) that developed unintentionally when several powerful, populous states successfully exploited a loophole in the federal law providing for public assistance grants.[10] As of 1984, following attempts by the Reagan Administration to expand block grants and reduce general revenue-sharing, 20 percent of federal grants were classified as broad-based or general-purpose.

Against the decentralization embodied in less-conditioned grants, however, must be set numerous centralizing acts of Congress that occurred in the same period. Congress replaced several public assistance grant programs with a direct federal program of income support (Supplemental Security Income or SSI) and displayed a heightened willingness to try to make national policy for the remaining category of public assistance, Aid to Families with Dependent Children. It experimented boldly and sometimes irresponsibly with a new grant-in-aid technique, what the Advisory Commission on Intergovernmental Relations has called the "cross-cutting requirement."[11] Employed mainly to prevent discrimination in the use of grants, this technique encompasses in one statutory stroke *all* grant programs or some large class of them, in contrast to Congress's earlier practice of attaching conditions specifically to particular categorical programs.[12]

Related to the "cross-cutting requirement," yet clearly distinguishable from it, is another new and bold grant technique, that which ACIR calls the "cross-over sanction."[13] Historically, Congress has confined the sanction of withholding grant funds quite narrowly within grant categories. Withholding would apply only to the activity wherein the recipient's transgression of federal requirements was alleged, but in the 1970s Congress began to threaten sanctions that crossed the boundaries of particular programs. Thus, for example, if states do not meet the pollution control standards of the Clean Air Act, they may be penalized by the withholding of highway aid funds. To assure that the states supplemented federal payments under SSI to the extent that Congress wished, it threatened them with loss of Medicaid grants. Numerous other examples exist. In general, categorical grant-in-aid programs of the 1970s, whether newly enacted or only amended, displayed a much enlarged willingness to intrude in state and local affairs. Statements of federal objectives were often as expansive as grant-in-aid techniques were inventive.

Nor was Congress's inventiveness confined to grant-in-aid programs. In the process of enacting dozens of laws in the 1970s for the regulation of environmental, work-place, and product hazards, Congress repeatedly applied a new technique of intergovernmental relations that has become known as "partial preemption."[14] Very roughly, it is to regulatory programs what the conditioned, categorical grant-in-aid is to spending programs—that is, a way of propounding national objectives and inducing the states to cooperate in pursuing them; the two are often used in tandem. Partial preemption entails the setting of federal regulatory standards but gives the states the option of various forms of participation in the regulatory regime. More often than not, the federal government relies heavily on them for enforcement.

Under the Clean Air Act, for example, Congress sets standards for permissible levels of common pollutants and deadlines for meeting them. States are instructed to adopt implementation plans designed to attain the standards, and the federal Environmental Protection Agency (EPA) reviews the state plans.[15] If a state fails to act or fails to secure EPA's approval of its plan, EPA can develop its own plan for the state. Both the state and federal governments may take action against polluters.

The Surface Mining Control and Reclamation Act uses a similar technique. The act sets forth numerous, detailed performance standards that coal-mining operations must meet. States wishing to assume regulatory responsibility must submit plans for approval by the Office of Surface Mining (OSM) of the Department of the Interior. State laws, regulations, and administrative performance must meet the requirements of the federal act. If a state chooses not to regulate, fails to gain approval of its plan, or fails to implement the plan satisfactorily, OSM is required to take charge.[16]

As a third example, under the Occupational Safety and Health Act of 1970 the Secretary of Labor is required to promulgate standards, but states may regulate those matters that federal regulations fail to address, and they may also assume responsibility in areas where the federal government has acted if their own standards are "at least as effective" as the federal standards.[17]

### The Persistence of State Discretion.

From the perspective of the mid-1980s, one can hardly say that the results of this outburst of congressional activity are clear, but it is perhaps not too soon to say that they are clearly ambiguous. Even where the urge to centralize was strongest—in income support and environmental protection programs—state governments retain a great deal of discretion in policy making and freedom from federal administrative supervision. Despite fears of some partisans of the states that they were being turned into mere administrative agents of an overbearing central government, federalism lives. It is manifest in the persistence of interstate differences in program characteristics and in the ineffectivness of much federal oversight of state administration.

Probably no more striking proof of the persistence of states' individuality exists than the SSI program, in which they are free to supplement the federal minimum payment. Congress in 1973 required supplementation to the extent necessary to hold current recipients harmless against the changes associated with federalization, and some states have also provided optional supplements. Only seven states do not supplement at all, according to a study done in 1984.[18] As of January 1985, the minimum federal payment for an aged individual living alone and having no countable income was $325, but differences in state supplements meant that the actual legal minimum ranged from $325 to a high of $586 in Alaska. Because many recipients have countable income, monthly payments are on average less than these minimums; in August 1985 they ranged from $90.95 per aged recipient in Maine to $252.83 in Alaska.[19]

The persistence of federalism is perhaps

even more vividly demonstrated, though, by the administrative features of SSI. Twenty-seven states administer their own supplements. No federal regulations apply to supplements in these states, which remain free to supplement whomever they please in whatever amounts they please. As one would expect, practices vary widely. At an extreme, Illinois continues to calculate an individual budget amount for each of its nearly 30,000 recipients of state supplements.

Nor is the situation vastly different in those 16 states (plus the District of Columbia) that have accepted Congress's offer to have the Social Security Administration administer supplements for them. Eager to get the program under way with the states' cooperation, SSA at the outset agreed to administer a number of variations in supplementation. Variations are permitted among benefit categories, three geographic divisions within a state, and five different living arrangements. One analyst has calculated that there are about 300 different SSI benefits nationally; he counted 158 state-administered variations and 130 federally-administered variations.[20] Perversely, the result of the "national" takeover has been to burden a national administrative agency, the SSA, with many of the accommodations to local circumstances that ordinarily take place through the medium of state administration. The SSA has found this to be a very large burden indeed, as a history of administrative troubles in SSI shows.

In Aid to Families with Dependent Children, which is still basically a state-run program despite prolonged attempts under both Nixon and Carter to achieve a "welfare reform" that would federalize it, interstate payment differences likewise persist, of course. In the second quarter of 1984, the average monthly payment per recipient ranged from $31 in Mississippi to $217 in Alaska. Twenty-three states were providing AFDC-UP—that is, were using welfare to compensate for parental unemployment as well as the absence of an employed adult from the home—but the rest were not.[21] Encouraged by Congress after 1981 to set up work programs for welfare recipients, the states adopted "a flurry of initiatives," according to a report in *The National Journal*. In most states, however, work and training programs were limited to a few counties and to small subgroups of those eligible because of financial, administrative, or geographical constraints.[22] In short, after a decade or more of the most intense effort in Washington to supplant AFDC, the program survived, interstate and even intrastate variations in it remained the norm, and states were quite conspicuously functioning as "laboratories of experiment."

These laboratories were only lightly supervised by federal administrators. Close, detailed supervision of state administration of welfare, which had been attempted by the Bureau of Public Assistance in the years following passage of the Social Security Act, had collapsed by the end of the 1960s, to some extent destroyed by the growth of caseloads, to some extent deliberately abandoned by leaders of the Department of Health, Education and Welfare who believed that the BPA's administrative style had produced too much red tape while failing to contain the caseloads. In the late 1960s, the very detailed guidance developed by the BPA over decades was cancelled in favor of much more general and permissive regulations.[23]

However, in the face of caseloads which continued to mount along with pressures to contain federal spending, the new permissiveness and simplicity did not last long. HEW in the early 1970s initiated an effort to control error rates in AFDC by designing sample studies, setting performance objectives, and manipulating incentives—rewards *and* penalties—in the fashion of new-style management experts and policy analysts rather than old-style social workers, who had had a more patronizing and less scientific approach to dealing with the states. The idea, incorporated in HEW regulations promulgated at the end of 1972, was that the states would be penalized with the loss of federal funds if they had excessive error rates. But thereafter various secretaries of HEW kept postponing sanctions while various subordinates negotiated with one another and with the states over what would be practicable and acceptable. Eventually, 13 states won a judgment from the U.S. District Court in the District of Columbia that the tolerance levels for error set by HEW were arbitrary and capricious. Negotiations resumed, and weak quality control regulations, with which most states would find it easy to comply, were promulgated in 1979.[24] In the Tax Equity and Fiscal Responsibility Act of 1982, Congress set four percent as an allowable error rate in AFDC payments for 1983 and three percent thereafter, with the proviso that the Secretary of Health and Human Services should make no reimbursements for erroneous payments in excess of that rate. However, the Secretary might waive all or part of the reduction in grants if "a State is unable to reach the allowable error rate . . . despite a good faith effort. . . ."[25]

Bargaining and negotiation, not command and obedience, appear to characterize the practice of intergovernmental programs now as in the past, even if the past was far more mindful of a tradition called states' rights. To these negotiations, states bring some newly-acquired strengths that partially offset Congress's diminished sensitivity to their interests, and federal administrative agencies bring some weaknesses of long standing.

*State Strengths and Federal Weaknesses.* One of the states' strengths consists of organization. Both state and local governments have banded together in various organizations which perform service and lobbying functions on their behalf. When HEW officials were seeking to develop their AFDC quality control program in the 1970s, they negotiated with a group composed of representatives of the National Association of Counties, the National Conference of State Legislatures, National League of Cities/U.S. Conference of Mayors, the National Governors Conference, and the American Public Welfare Association, in which the NGC took the lead. The rise of the "intergovernmental lobby" is well documented, and at least one influential article attributed the passage of general revenue-sharing largely to its existence.[26] A second new-found strength of the states—one not unique to them but widely shared in our society—is their capacity to bring suit. Individually, in *ad hoc* groups or through their formal lobbying organizations, they resort to the courts when they feel that Congress or the executive agencies have transgressed constitutional or statutory bounds.

In general, their constitutionally-based challenges have not succeeded. Courts have found nothing constitutionally impermissible in partial preemptions or the newer grant-in-aid techniques. They typically hold that if a valid national purpose is being served (and under the commerce clause or the power to tax and spend for the general welfare, one always is), and if the states are not being coerced (and under grant-in-aid programs and partial preemptions, the states technically do retain the option of not participating), then the law is valid.

Statutory challenges are another matter, however, as the example of HEW's failed attempt to promulgate strict AFDC quality control regulations shows. Throughout their negotiations with the states, HEW officials in that case were hampered both by intradepartmental differences of view and by a well-founded apprehension over what the courts would permit. Courts are not loathe to find that federal executive agencies have exceeded their statutory authority in promulgating regulations for intergovernmental programs.

Probably the most telling and significant use of the courts' powers of statutory review came in the late 1970s in a set of cases that arose out of the Environmental Protection Agency's promulgation of standards for transportation control plans. Under threat of various civil sanctions, including injunctions,

the imposition of receiverships on certain state functions, and fines and contempt citations for state officials, EPA would have required the states to adopt and enforce such measures as parking bans and surcharges, bus lanes, and computerized carpool matching. Three out of four appellate courts which reviewed these regulations found that they had exceeded Congress's intent and strongly hinted that they violated the Constitution as well. The states could be offered the choice of whether to participate in pollution control and could be fully preempted if they chose not to participate, but they could not be ordered to carry out federal regulations.[27]

If negotiation works well for the states, though, it is not just because they are well organized and sometimes victorious in the courts. It is because federal agencies bring serious weaknesses to the bargaining table. Neither of their principal weapons—to withhold funds in grant-in-aid programs, to take charge of enforcement in regulatory programs—is readily usable.

Withholding funds is self-defeating and risks congressional intervention and reprimand. (The HEW officials who struggled with AFDC quality control issues in the 1970s felt under pressure from Congress to do something yet doubted that Congress would come to their defense if they did anything drastic.) Withholding, though occasionally threatened, is rarely used. When issues arise, the contestants negotiate.[28]

The threat to take charge of administration likewise lacks credibility except in isolated cases because federal agencies generally lack the capacity to supersede the states, and everyone knows it. Congress is unwilling to spend the funds or otherwise to bear the onus of creating a large federal bureaucracy; that is why it chooses to rely so heavily on intergovernmental techniques.

Where partial preemption has been employed, giving states the option of assuming responsibility for enforcement and federal agencies' responsibility for approving state plans and supervising their execution, states in general have opted to participate, and federal agencies have in general made the necessary delegations. Among the new regulatory regimes, only that for occupational health and safety remains overwhelmingly a federal responsibility, and that is only because the AFL-CIO successfully challenged the Department of Labor's criteria for delegation in court during the Ford Administration, raising a set of issues that have since remained unresolved. In practice, about half of the states run their own occupational safety and health programs even if the federal government remains nominally in charge almost everywhere.[29]

When state defiance or default requires federal agencies to assume enforcement responsibilities in regulatory programs based on partial preemption, the results are not invariably felicitous. One consequence of the use of partial preemption has been to demonstrate, through various "natural experiments," that federal administration is not necessarily superior to state administration.

In 1981 the Idaho legislature, irritated by the U.S. Environmental Protection Agency (EPA), voted not to fund the state's air quality program, forcing EPA to administer it. Both state and federal officials concluded after a year that the federal takeover caused more problems than it solved. EPA reportedly spent almost five times as much to maintain the Idaho program that year as the state would have spent to do the same job. In another case, Iowa's environmental budget was cut 15 percent in 1982, causing a loss of federal matching funds. The state then returned responsibility for its municipal water-monitoring program to EPA, which managed to conduct only about 15 percent of the inspections formerly performed by the state.[30]

The Office of Surface Mining in 1984 found it necessary to reclaim responsibility from Tennessee and Oklahoma, but nothing in the administrative performance of the federal agency gives grounds for confidence that it can do much better.[31]

A study by the Congressional Research Service in 1983 sought systematically to compare occupational injury rates in states with federally-run programs with those where state agencies remained in charge, in a tentative test of the effectiveness of programs in the two sets. The study concluded that states with state-run programs had a somewhat better performance record.[32] Organized labor has complained that inspections are fewer in states where the Occupational Safety and Health Administration (OSHA) remains responsible for enforcement, although this has not caused it to reexamine its abiding preference for a federal regime. Current failures of federal performance can be blamed on the Republican administration.[33]

The new regulatory regimes are still new enough that one cannot be sure that they have stabilized. The arrival of the Reagan Administration, committed to a sharp reduction in federal spending and a revival of states' rights—or states' responsibilities, as Reagan officials sometimes insist—accelerated delegations to state governments and correspondingly contracted the size and hence administrative capacities of the federal regulatory agencies. Yet it is doubtful that a future change in the election returns would work more than marginal changes in the administrative arrangements that have emerged. Apparently, these arrangements leave much for the states to do and much room for them to negotiate with their federal-agency supervisors over how and how fast to do it.

## The Role of the Courts

Insofar as centralization has occurred in the past decade or two, the courts have been at least as influential as Congress, arguably much more so. This is not so much because courts have preferred the national side in overt contests between the national government and the states as because federal courts have aggressively pursued the extension of individual rights with little regard for the effect on the states' prerogatives as governments in their own right.[34]

By steadily enlarging the application of the due process and equal protection clauses of the Fourteenth Amendment, the Supreme Court carried into the late 1960s and early 1970s the vigorous extension of the constitutional rights of individuals begun in the 1950s with *Brown* v. *Board of Education* (or, if one prefers, in 1925 with *Gitlow* v. *New York,* in which the Court first read the Bill of Rights into the Fourteenth Amendment). Such celebrated cases as *Roe* v. *Wade* (1973), which struck down state laws prohibiting abortion; *Goldberg* v. *Kelly* (1970), which required that a welfare recipient be afforded an evidentiary hearing *before* the termination of benefits; and *Shapiro* v. *Thompson* (1969), which invalidated state residency requirements for welfare applicants, boldly asserted national power at the states' expense.[35]

In the area of voting rights, statutory construction as well as constitutional interpretation has been the Court's route to a radically altered federalism. Since its decision in 1969 in *Allen* v. *State Board of Elections,* the Department of Justice has had power to review municipal annexations, the redrawing of district lines, and the choice of at-large versus district elections in jurisdictions covered by the Voting Rights Act—power that it has used to increase the probability that minority candidates will win office. Such methods of protecting the franchise of blacks and other minorities to whom the law's protection has been extended are far more problematic and intrusive than those contemplated when it was passed in 1965.[36]

Rather less publicized than Supreme Court decisions, yet arguably at least as intrusive, have been the numerous decisions of lower federal courts in the so-called institution cases, in which state governments were ordered to increase their expenditures on facilities for the

mentally ill or retarded, criminals, and juvenile detainees. The decrees in these cases have mandated massive and often detailed changes in the operation of institutions and their programs— changes involving the physical condition of the facility, staffing, and quality of services.[37]

In some especially intrusive grant-in-aid programs, notably the Education for All Handicapped Children Act of 1975, Congress has been emboldened by courts. That act requires, as a condition of grants-in-aid, that states have in effect a policy assuring all handicapped children between the ages of 3 and 21 the right to a free appropriate public education and that local educational agencies maintain and annually review an individualized program for each handicapped child. This law built upon federal district court decisions of 1971 in Pennsylvania and 1972 in the District of Columbia.[38]

Where newly-sweeping grant-in-aid conditions have been particularly effective, it has ordinarily been because courts have reinforced and elaborated them, in effect working in tandem with the administrative agency. *Together,* the courts and the Office of Education (and then the Office of Civil Rights, after it was separately constituted) brought about the extraordinary desegregation of Southern schools in the late 1960s. Title VI of the Civil Rights Act of 1964, with a "cross-cutting requirement" which prohibited racial discrimination in the use of federal grants-in-aid, when combined with the grants to elementary and secondary schools that were freshly enacted in 1965, complemented *Brown* v. *Board* and the successor decisions. Also, it was crucially complemented by them. As Gary Orfield notes in his definitive study of the application of Title VI to Southern schools, the decisive federal response came in 1968 in a case involving the schools of New Kent County, Virginia. "Once again the work of black attorneys and the response of the judiciary [created] a shield behind which the administrative techniques of HEW could be effectively employed."[39]

The influence of the courts is shown not just in what they have done, but, less directly, in what they have declined to prevent Congress from doing. For a fleeting moment, in *National League of Cities* v. *Usery* (1976), the Supreme Court seemed willing to revive *and apply* the precept that states' sovereignty imposes some limit on Congress's exercise of the commerce clause. In that decision it held that Congress could not use the Fair Labor Standards Act to regulate the states' determination of their employees' wages and hours.[40] Successor decisions, however, rather than building on *National League of Cities,* led to the repudiation of it in *Garcia* v. *San Antonio Metropolitan Transit Authority* in 1985.[41] While the Court has never said that states' sovereignty imposes *no* limit on Congress's commerce clause powers, it has backed away from trying to define one.

It is little wonder that the Reagan Administration's attempt to construct protection for the states had by late 1985 come to focus on judicial appointments. In its own legislative and administrative choices, the Reagan Administration has been far from consistent in its commitment to strengthening the states. When budget reduction and other objectives have conflicted with that aim, the Administration's devolutionary objectives have often been compromised, as Timothy Conlan has shown in a careful analysis.[42] To that, Reagan officials might well reply that for the preservation of the states as a coordinate element of government, it is the federal bench that matters most.

## Current Debates

As of the mid-1980s, the value of federalism was very much at issue within the Supreme Court and between the Court and the Reagan Administration's second attorney general. Today's conservatives profess to value the federal principle highly, whereas liberals, in their preoccupation with perfecting individual rights, are either indifferent to questions of government structure or reflexively prefer national to state action.

The current debate, as yet imperfectly joined for lack of a full exposition on either side, appears to turn on essentially the issues which divided federalists and anti-federalists 200 years ago. Both sides profess to value liberty and democracy above all. They differ in their judgments of the distribution of governmental power that will best serve those ends.

"A substantive issue like abortion is a matter of public or civic morality," Attorney General Edwin Meese has argued, and "should be decided upon through a free and robust discussion at the level [of government] most appropriate to its determination." In his view, that is the level of state and local government, for "big government does not encourage a sense of belonging. . . . An essential sense of community is far more likely to develop at the local level." A proper understanding of federalism, in this view, would permit such matters as abortion, prayer in the schools, pornography, and aid to parochial schools to be deliberated on by state governments and resolved by the sense of the particular community, there to be incorporated in statutes, rather than being treated at the national level as subjects of constitutional doctrine.[43]

Much as Meese in these remarks argued the superior communal qualities of the states, Justice Lewis F. Powell in a dissent to *Garcia* v. *SAMTA* argued the inferior quality of the federal government's policy processes. Federal laws are drafted by congressional committee staffs and federal regulations, often more important than the laws, by the staffs of agencies, he wrote. A realistic comparison of the operation of the different levels of government, in Powell's view, shows state and local governments to be more accessible and responsive, hence more democratic, than the government based in Washington. That government in the national capital would become remote and alienated from ordinary people was one of the fears of the anti-federalists. Their intellectual heirs on the Supreme Court say it has happened.

Perhaps the most important events in the federal system in the recent past are those which bear on the potential power of such arguments as Meese's and Powell's by affecting either the public's receptivity to them or their plausibility. Even as centralization proceeds— indeed, perhaps because it has proceeded so far—the federal government seems to have suffered a decline in popular esteem. Confidence in its performance dropped sharply in the 1970s, and by the mid-1980s it was doing poorly in polls asking the public to compare it to state and local governments.[44] By contrast, scholarly and journalistic accounts of the performance of state governments uniformly judge it much improved over two or three decades ago, enhanced by legislatures more active, more professional, and better-staffed than formerly—*and* more representative of their constituencies, with ironic thanks to the reapportionment decisions of the Supreme Court.[45]

Governmental competence and perceptions of it aside, all discussions of American federalism must henceforth be altered by what is arguably the most important new social and political datum of our times: the end to Southern exceptionalism. Until now, arguments favoring the states' side in any dispute over federalism suffered fatally from the burden of the South's deviant social system. Whether or not blacks have been successfully integrated into American society (a separate question), there can be little doubt that the South as a region has been integrated. That change, even if achieved very largely by the instrumentalities of the federal government, holds the possibility that the case for the states can at last begin to be discussed on its merits.

That case deserves a more careful contemporary exposition than it has yet received, with due regard for the purposes and expectations of the Founders. The Founders did not make a strong argument for the federal aspects of their

"composition." *The Federalist* is "rather inexplicit and ambiguous in its treatment of federalism," for the reason that its authors were at heart nationalists.[46] Madison saw the size of the new republic, not its compound quality, as crucial to the achievement of liberty. His most eloquent and memorable statements were made in support of "extending the sphere."[47] He told the convention that "Were it practicable for the General Government to extend its care to every requisite object without the cooperation of the State Governments, the people would not be less free as members of one great Republic, than as members of thirteen small ones."[48]

Yet Madison's willingness to preserve the states was more than a concession to the fact that their abolition, then as now, was politically unacceptable. Prudent and practical, he thought they would be useful, even if subordinately. He doubted that the national government would be suited to the entire task of governing "so great an extent of country, and over so great a variety of objects."[49]

In this, as in so much else, Madison was very wise. As the burdens of governing grow, the inability or unwillingness of the federal government to bear them alone is manifest.[50] The states therefore remain vigorous, although they are more nearly the subordinately useful governments that Madison anticipated in 1787 than the coordinate ones posited by Wheare's definition.

## Notes

The author is indebted for comments to Wayne Anderson, David R. Beam, Michael D. Reagan, Sarah Ryder, Abigail Thernstrom, and Dwight Waldo.

1. Cited in Irving Brant, *The Fourth President: A Life of James Madison* (Indianapolis: The Bobbs-Merrill Company, 1970), p. 146.
2. "[A] consolidation of the States is not less unattainable than it would be inexpedient," the nationalist Madison wrote, in the same letter to Randolph.

3. The leading statement is No. 39. For an interpretation, see Martin Diamond, "What the Framers Meant by Federalism," in Robert A. Goldwin, ed., *A Nation of States: Essays on the American Federal System* (Chicago: Rand McNally & Co., 1963), pp. 24–41.

4. *Federal Government* (New York: Oxford University Press, 1953), p. 2. Wheare defines the federal principle by reference to the particular features of the United States government, for "The modern idea of what federal government is has been determined by the United States of America," p. 1.

5. *Journal of the Federal Convention Kept by James Madison* (Chicago: Albert, Scott & Co., 1893), p. 74.

6. *Ibid.,* p. 120.

7. *Ibid.,* p. 280.

8. *The Letters and Other Writings of James Madison* (Congress edition: R. Worthington, 1884), vol. III, p. 625.

9. Cf. Edward S. Corwin, "The Passing of Dual Federalism," *Virginia Law Review,* vol. 36 (1950).

10. The Advisory Commission on Intergovernmental Relations (ACIR), in studies of the intergovernmental grant system done in the late 1970s, also counted as block grants those authorized by the Partnership for Health Act of 1966, which had consolidated seven categorical grants, and the Omnibus Crime Control and Safe Streets Act of 1968. See Advisory Commission on Intergovernmental Relations, *Block Grants: A Comparative Analysis* (Washington: ACIR, 1977).

11. Advisory Commission on Intergovernmental Relations, *Regulatory Federalism: Policy, Process, Impact and Reform* (Washington: ACIR, 1984), pp. 8, 71–78.

12. In truth, the technique was not altogether new but had antecedents as old as the Hatch Act, which was amended in 1940 to prohibit partisan political activity by any "officer or employee of any State or local agency whose principal employment is in connection with any activity which is financed in whole or in part by loans or grants made by the United States. . . ." Failure to comply was punishable by the withholding of funds. 54 *Stat.* 767 (1940). Cross-cutting requirements did not become common until the 1960s, however.

13. *Ibid.,* pp. 9, 78–82.

14. *Ibid.,* pp. 9, 82–88. I am much indebted to David R. Beam for enlightenment on the newer techniques of federal influence vis-a-vis the states, derived both from personal conversations and from his work at the ACIR as one of the authors of *Regulatory Federalism.*

15. 84 *Stat.* 1676 (1970). The law says that "Each State . . . shall . . . adopt . . . a plan. . . ."

16. 91 *Stat.* 445 (1977).

17. 84 *Stat.* 1590 (1970).

18. Renato A. DiPentima, "The Supplemental Security Income Program: A Study of Implementation," PhD dissertation (University of Maryland, 1984), p. 80.

19. *Social Security Bulletin,* vol. 48 (October 1985), p. 19, and (November 1985), p. 42. These data published by the federal government cover only those states—slightly more than half of the total—in which the Social Security Administration has responsibility for administering supplemental payments. The SSA lacks comparable data from states that have chosen to administer themselves whatever program of supplementation exists. See the text, *infra,* for further explanation of federal versus state administration of supplements.

20. DiPentima, *op. cit.,* p. 85.

21. U.S. Department of Health and Human Services, *Quarterly Public Assistance Statistics* (April–June 1984), Tables 7 and 15.

22. Julie Kosterlitz, "Liberals and Conservatives Share Goals, Differ on Details of Work for Welfare," *National Journal* (October 26, 1985), pp. 2418–22.

23. Martha Derthick, *The Influence of Federal Grants: Public Assistance in Massachusetts* (Cambridge: Harvard University Press, 1970), pp. 225–29, and *Uncontrollable Spending for Social Services Grants* (Washington: The Brookings Institution, 1975), pp. 15–24.

24. "Controlling AFDC Error Rates," Kennedy School of Government Case C 14-80-302 (copyright by President and Fellows of Harvard College, 1980).

25. H. Rept. 97-760, p. 79.

26. Donald H. Haider, *When Governments Come to Washington: Governors, Mayors, and Intergovernmental Lobbying* (New York: Free Press, 1974); Samuel H. Beer, "The Adoption of Gen-

eral Revenue Sharing: A Case Study in Public Sector Politics," *Public Policy,* vol. 24 (Spring 1976). The impending demise of general revenue-sharing calls into question the hypothesis that the intergovernmental lobby was responsible for its passage, for there is no reason to suppose that the lobby is less well-organized today than it was in the early 1970s.

27. *Brown* v. *Environmental Protection Agency, 521 F. 2d 827 (9th Cir., 1975); Maryland* v. *Environmental Protection Agency, 530 F. 2d 215 (4th Cir., 1975); District of Columbia* v. *Train, 521 F. 2d 971 (D.C. Cir., 1975); Pennsylvania* v. *Environmental Protection Agency, 500 F. 2d 246 (3rd Cir., 1974).*

28. Cf. Derthick, *The Influence of Federal Grants,* chap. 8. However, the willingness of courts since 1970 to discover private rights of action in federal statutes has to some extent offset the weakness of federal agencies in regard to the use of withholding. As R. Shep Melnick has written, "The private right of action has special significance in joint federal-state spending programs. If an alleged beneficiary could only bring suit against a federal administrator for failing to enforce federal standards, the only relief the court could offer successful plaintiffs would be an injunction cutting off federal funds to the state. . . . But when potential recipients can bring suit against the state for failure to comply with federal requirements, the court can compel the state to pay the plaintiff the money owed. The private right of action, thus, significantly alters the balance of power between the federal government and the states." "The Politics of Partnership," *Public Administration Review,* vol. 45 (November 1985), pp. 656–57.

29. On intergovernmental relations in occupational safety and health, see the oversight hearings held annually by the Sub-committee on Health and Safety of the Committee on Education and Labor, U.S. House of Representatives. The most important titles are: *OSHA Oversight—State of the Agency Report by Assistant Secretary of Labor for OSHA,* 97 Cong. 2 sess. (1983), pp. 212–36; *OSHA Oversight—Staffing Levels for OSHA Approved State Plans,* 98 Cong. 1 sess. (1983); and *Oversight on OSHA: State of the Agency,* 99 Cong. 1 sess. (1985), serial no. 99-12.

30. *State of the Environment: An Assessment at Mid-Decade* (Washington: The Conservation Foundation, 1984), p. 458.

31. Rochelle L. Stanfield, "Mine Disaster," *National Journal* (October 12, 1985), p. 2342.

32. U.S. House of Representatives, Committee on Education and Labor, *OSHA Oversight—Staffing Levels for OSHA Approved State Plans,* Hearings before the Subcommittee on Health and Safety, 98 Cong., 1 sess. (1983), pp. 295–327. See also the work of Frank J. Thompson and Michael J. Scicchitano: "State Implementation Effort and Federal Regulatory Policy: The Case of Occupational Safety and Health," *Journal of Politics,* vol. 47 (1985), pp. 686–703, and "State Enforcement of Federal Regulatory Policy: The Lessons of OSHA," *Policy Studies Journal,* vol. 13 (March 1985), pp. 591–598.

33. Michael Wines, "Auchter's Record at OSHA Leaves Labor Outraged, Business Satisfied," *National Journal* (October 1, 1983), pp. 2008–13.

34. For a critique, see Robert F. Nagel, "Federalism as a Fundamental Value: National League of Cities in Perspective," *Supreme Court Review* (1981), pp. 81–109.

35. For a good summary of the Court's use of the Fourteenth Amendment to extend civil liberties, see David Fellman, "The Nationalization of American Civil Liberties," in M. Judd Harmon, ed., *Essays on the Constitution of the United States* (Port Washington, NY: Kennikat Press, 1978), pp. 49–60.

36. Abigail M. Thernstrom, "The Odd Evolution of the Voting Rights Act," *Public Interest* (Spring 1979), pp. 49–76.

37. Gerald E. Frug, "The Judicial Power of the Purse," *University of Pennsylvania Law Review,* vol. 126 (April 1978), pp. 715–794.

38. Erwin L. Levine and Elizabeth M. Wexler, *PL 94-142: An Act of Congress* (New York: Macmillan, 1981), pp. 38–41. In the field of voting rights, statutory amendments and court decisions have interacted to produce the surprisingly far reach of federal action described above. These events are analyzed in detail in a forthcoming book by Abigail M. Thernstrom.

39. Gary Orfield, *The Reconstruction of Southern Education: The Schools and the 1964 Civil Rights Act* (New York: John Wiley and Sons, 1969), p. 262. See also Jeremy Rabkin, "Office for Civil Rights," in James Q. Wilson, ed., *The Politics of*

*Regulation* (New York: Basic Books, 1980), chap. 9.

40. 426 U.S. 833.

41. Slip opinion No. 82-1913, decided February 19, 1985.

42. Timothy J. Conlan, "Federalism and Competing Values in the Reagan Administration," in Laurence J. O'Toole, Jr., ed., *American Intergovernmental Relations* (Washington: CQ Press, 1985), pp. 265–80.

43. Address before the American Enterprise Institute, Sept. 6, 1985.

44. Seymour Martin Lipset and William Schneider, *The Confidence Gap: Business, Labor and Government in the Public Mind* (New York: Free Press, 1968), and Advisory Commission on Intergovernmental Relations, *Changing Public Attitudes on Governments and Taxes: 1984* (Washington: ACIR, 1984).

45. Alan Rosenthal, *Legislative Life: People, Process, and Performance in the States* (New York: Harper & Row, 1981), and William K. Muir, Jr., *Legislature: California's School for Politics* (Chicago: University of Chicago Press, 1982).

46. Martin Diamond, "The Federalist's View of Federalism," in *Essays in Federalism* (Claremont, CA: Institute for Studies in Federalism, 1961), pp. 21–62. The quotation appears at p. 24. It was left to the anti-federalists to make the case for the states at the time of the founding. See Herbert J. Storing, *What the Anti-Federalists Were For* (Chicago: University of Chicago Press, 1981), chap. 3.

47. The classic statement is contained in *Federalist No. 10*.

48. *Journal*, p. 212.

49. *Ibid.* Later, as the author of the Virginia resolution of 1798 protesting the Alien and Sedition Acts, Madison would find the states to be useful more fundamentally, as a medium for resisting unconstitutional acts of the general government. According to his biographer, Irving Brant, this was an instance of putting "political objectives ahead of abstract thought. . . . He had no desire to exalt state sovereignty, but used it as a weapon. . . ." *James Madison: Father of the Constitution, 1787-1800* (Indianapolis: Bobbs-Merrill, 1950), p. 470. As the experience of even this exceptionally thoughtful and principled man shows, positions on federalism (as perhaps on institutional questions generally), are susceptible to change under the impact of new issues and configurations of interest.

50. Cf. Martha Derthick, "Preserving Federalism: Congress, the States, and the Supreme Court," *The Brookings Review*, vol. 4 (Winter/Spring 1986), pp. 32–37.

## CASE STUDY 5

# Introduction

One of the most controversial environmental policy issues today is how to dispose of nuclear waste materials. The Nuclear Waste Policy Act of 1982 (NWPA) gives the U.S. Department of Energy (DOE) considerable flexibility to negotiate with and compensate states in which nuclear waste storage facilities are located. Congress and nuclear experts believed that negotiated compensation plans would be the best way to overcome local resistance to housing nuclear waste facilities in their regions. The following story recounts the events surrounding DOE's monitored retrievable storage (MRS) proposal, the first attempt under the NWPA to site nuclear waste operations in the mid-1980s, and how DOE and Roane County as well as Oak Ridge, Tennessee, agreed on conditions under which they "would willingly accept" an MRS facility. State and regional leaders, however, opposed the project, rather than negotiate with "the Feds." As this case emphasizes, NWPA sought to achieve national goals through intergovernmental cooperation and negotiated agreements, but the controversial nature of the issues involved and multiplicity of local interests can stalemate collective action designed to promote long-term national ends.

As you review this case study, you might want to reflect on the following questions:

Why does "federalism" and "intergovernmental relations" pose serious problems for dealing with nuclear waste disposal? How did NWPA attempt to deal with these problems?

Who were the major "actors" in this case? Why were they motivated to act in the way they did?

What was the "outcome" of the case? Does the story support Martha Derthick's thesis? If so, why?

# Achieving a Negotiated Compensation Agreement in Nuclear Waste Disposal Siting: The MRS Case

## E. BRENT SIGMON

In October of 1985, the legislative bodies of Roane County and Oak Ridge, Tennessee adopted a resolution stating conditions under which they "would willingly accept" a monitored retrievable storage (MRS) facility to consolidate, package, and temporarily store spent nuclear fuel before permanent disposal elsewhere in a geologic repository. That any community would willingly accept spent nuclear fuel is worthy of note; disposition of spent fuel has been one of the more controversial aspects of the civilian nuclear power program. That this proposal involves the first exercise of the siting provisions of the Nuclear Waste Policy Act is even more significant. The exercise has implications for nuclear and non-nuclear hazardous waste management and, more generally, for the broad class of problems involving a facility with negative local impacts but widely dispersed benefits.

## The Siting Dilemma and the Nuclear Waste Policy Act

Nuclear waste management, perhaps more than any other environmental issue, has exceeded the capacity

*Journal of Policy Analysis and Management,* "Achieving a Negotiated Compensation Agreement in Nuclear Waste Disposal Siting: The MRS Case" by E. Brent Sigmon, Vol. 6, No. 2, 170–179. © 1979 by John Wiley & Sons, Inc. Reprinted by permission of John Wiley & Sons, Inc.

of existing institutions and demanded creation of new ones. The Nuclear Waste Policy Act of 1982 (NWPA) was necessary because previous attempts to resolve the spent nuclear fuel disposition issue invariably failed for political reasons. A major issue in the nuclear waste problem is local opposition to site selection. Three features of the Act deserve particular attention in this regard. First, the NWPA authorizes the Department of Energy (DOE) to make grants equivalent to the taxes that would be paid on a repository if it were a privately-owned industrial facility. In contrast with the meager payments-in-lieu-of-taxes typical of federal projects, a repository would be a significant revenue source for local governments. Second, the Act directs DOE to "consult and cooperate with" states in which it is considering sites for a repository or other facility. Further, DOE "shall seek to enter into a binding written agreement, and shall begin negotiations, with such State . . ." The consultation and cooperation (C&C) requirements officially bring affected states into the siting process at an early stage and, through the C&C agreement, provide legal means to incorporate state and local interests in the decision process. Third, affected states are given an opportunity to veto DOE's site selection, subject to override by simple majorities in both houses of Congress.[1]

Gary Downey identified the key institutional innovation of the NWPA to be establishment of a formal adversarial relationship between DOE and prospective repository host states.[2] In his view, the root of the siting problem encountered in earlier attempts lay in the dual role of the federal agencies: they represented both the dispersed population that would benefit from the repository and the local population on whom special costs would or could fall disproportionately. According to Downey, by giving veto authority to prospective host states, the NWPA formally establishes the states as the representatives of local interests. He sees the process as adversarial: DOE and the state represent competing interests and Congress, with its power to override a state's veto, is the final arbiter.

As significant as it may be to shift representation of local interests from the federal level, I believe the more important innovation of the NWPA is its change in the format of the adversarial relationship between local and national interests—from adjudication to negotiation. The significant difference is that adjudication typically yields a winner and a loser while negotiation can produce all winners.

The seemingly intractable problem of facility siting is not limited to nuclear waste, and many analysts have given the problem their attention. Two broad conclusions flow from this analysis of the general siting dilemma. First, determined opposition can almost always stop a project. David Morell and Christopher Magorian talk about "the myth of preemption"—the generally false assumption by governments and project developers that preemptive legal authority carries the political power to override local opposition.[3] Just as the federal government has been unsuccessful at siting a nuclear waste repository, state governments have been similarly thwarted in trying to deal with other hazardous wastes.

Second, the way to break the impasse lies in attempting to accommodate local interests rather than in trying to overpower them. Local opposition generally indicates uncompensated local costs. From this perspective, developers should work toward reducing or compensating for those costs. Appropriate forms of compensation are case-specific but might include compensation in currency or in kind, modification of the project design or operation, guarantees or contingency funds, local authority over operations, and various offsetting benefits. Compensation is not limited to the financial dimension.[4]

In this context the real innovativeness of the NWPA becomes clear: The Act attempts to apply the theoretical prescription for solving the sitting dilemma to the real world problem of radioactive waste. It empowers DOE to negotiate with state and local interests (in reaching a C&C agreement). It empowers DOE to compensate local interests (through impact assistance, tax equivalency, and the C&C agreement). It encourages DOE to be flexible and to act in good faith (by granting the state veto and by requiring a report to Congress on progress toward a C&C agreement). It provides for the information requirements of local interests (through grants for study and monitoring and through the C&C agreement). In short, NWPA establishes a climate for meaningful negotiation between DOE and local interests. The adversarial stage is no longer the courtroom, but the bargaining table.

These features of the act affect the attitude of the DOE toward local interests, but we must also ask whether the NWPA encourages local interests to bargain in good faith. If local interests can always obstruct a project and preserve the status quo, why would they even begin to negotiate? Either they must, at the outset, be able to identify configurations of the proposal that would clearly make them better off or they must be made to doubt that the status quo is defendable. On the first count, tax equivalency is a status-improving incentive. On the second, granting legal authority to the local interests actually weakens local power to obstruct. This paradoxical outcome is explained as follows: local power to obstruct rests on the ability to elicit moral outrage against trampling of local interests; but the NWPA invites local participation in the decision process. Refusal to participate would erode local moral authority and make Congressional override more likely.

The MRS case is the first opportunity to observe the NWPA siting provisions in use and to evaluate whether they adequately promote a siting solution in which local interests are accommodated. Does the NWPA prompt DOE to seek accommodation, and does it give DOE sufficient flexibility to make the necessary compromises? Does the NWPA give states enough incentive to search for workable solutions? The results of this single example suggest that DOE's incentives and flexibility to negotiate are adequate, while state and local incentives are less compelling. The MRS experience also illustrates two important points about the negotiated compensation prescription for siting. First, a successful compensation plan is likely to be a many-faceted arrangement including impact-reducing, authority sharing, and other nonfinancial incentives. Second, local interests may diverge significantly from those of the surrounding region or state, greatly complicating the task of reaching an agreement that will allow the project to proceed. These two complexities apply to all siting controversies, not just those involving nuclear waste.

# The MRS Proposal and the State and Local Responses

The NWPA established, as national policy toward high level waste, immediate development of permanent disposal in a geologic repository, rejecting the more temporary alternative of an engineered storage system. The Act, however, also directed DOE to study the need for engineered temporary storage as a possible addition, not alternative, to a nuclear waste management system centered on geologic disposal. DOE initially viewed engineered storage, termed monitored retrievable storage in the Act, as a fallback position should the geologic repository be delayed. Later, DOE came to the conclusion that an MRS facility integrated into the waste management system could improve the entire system in several important ways. In April 1985 DOE announced its intention, pending further studies, to seek Congressional authorization of an MRS facility to be built at the former Clinch River Breeder Reactor site in the Oak Ridge city limits. Two alternate sites, another in Oak Ridge and one near Hartsville, Tennessee, were also identified.

The MRS facility would receive spent fuel from reactors in the eastern half of the United States (about 85 percent of the total), consolidate, package, store if necessary or desirable, and ship to the repository by unit train. It would cost about one-half billion dollars and employ about 700 people. Spent fuel shipments from reactors to the MRS facility would amount to approximately 3 trucks and 1 train per day; shipments from the MRS facility to the repository would involve only 2 to 3 unit trains per month.[5]

After announcing its tentative MRS plans, DOE gave a $1.4 million grant to the State of Tennessee for the state to study the proposal and develop its position. In turn, the state gave grants ($100,000 each) to the two local communities in which the proposed sites were located. The state and the two communi-

ties took three very different approaches to their studies.

## The Clinch River MRS Task Force

The City of Oak Ridge sits astride the Roane-Anderson county line and both Oak Ridge sites are in the Roane County part of the city. To study the MRS proposal, the Roane County Commission and the Oak Ridge City Council established the Clinch River MRS Task Force. The Task Force included an Executive Committee and three Study Groups: Environmental, Socio-economic, and Transportation. The Executive Committee consisted of the Roane County Executive, his Administrative Assistant, the Oak Ridge Mayor, Oak Ridge City Manager, and the Oak Ridge Assistant City Manager, who also served as Task Force coordinator. Each Study Group had eight members—a Roane County Commissioner, an Oak Ridge City Councilman, and six citizens, three appointed by each jurisdiction.[6]

The Task Force deliberately chose to ignore questions of national policy (e.g., Is an MRS facility needed?) in order to concentrate on the questions of local interest (e.g., How will it affect the local community?) The Task Force also chose to go beyond a yes or no recommendation and to identify conditions that would make the facility more acceptable. These two premises about its role are reflected in the position developed by the Task Force and ultimately adopted by the County Commission and City Council. The Task Force concluded that, as proposed, the MRS facility was detrimental to the interests of the local community and was unacceptable. But it went on to identify how DOE could eliminate, minimize, or compensate for the negative impacts, making the proposal acceptable. None of the Task Force's conditions would materially affect the MRS facility's physical characteristics or its role in the waste management system. Instead, the institutional relationships between DOE and the local community would change.

Task Force concerns fall into several areas, the primary one being health and safety. Although convinced that the transportation, packaging, and storage technologies *permit* safe operation, the Task Force also was aware that technologies do not *guarantee* safe operation. Thus it was unwilling to leave monitoring and enforcement responsibilities entirely in federal hands. Probably the most controversial

Task Force condition, because of its legal ramifications, involves a demand that federal authorities share some monitoring and enforcement power with the local governments.

Economic impacts are another major concern. The Oak Ridge economy is already dominated by DOE facilities paying no taxes and very small payments-in-lieu-of-taxes. These factors hinder desired diversification and growth of the local economy, and the MRS facility would expand the federal presence in Oak Ridge. Negative perceptions about the facility might also hinder growth, especially in the decade between its authorization and operation. To offset these economic impacts, the Task Force specified (1) that the facility should make payments to local governments as if it were a private taxable facility; (2) that those payments should begin with authorization; and (3) that DOE should do business with local private firms whenever possible. (The NWPA grants tax-equivalency only to repositories.)

Other conditions dealing with public perceptions of a nuclear waste facility included linking MRS construction to progress with geologic disposal so the facility would not become or be perceived as a substitute for geologic disposal, and linking MRS construction to cleanup of various environmental problems at existing DOE operations in Oak Ridge to improve the community's negative environmental image and demonstrate DOE's intention to be a better neighbor. A telephone poll by the local newspaper found 2/3 of respondents favoring the Task Force conclusions, 1/6 opposed, and 1/6 undecided.[7]

## Research, Evaluation, Analysis and Liaison Group

Officials in the five counties including and surrounding the Hartsville site chartered an organization, The Five County Research, Evaluation, Analysis and Liaison Group (REAL Group), to study the MRS proposal. Five county executives and six city mayors comprised the Group's membership.[8]

The REAL Group's conclusion—firm opposition—was predictable from the outset. The introduction of the report states, "It was the general opinion of the R.E.A.L. Directors that they did not want the MRS facility located at the Hartsville site . . ." and they were reluctant even to accept the study grant. A telephone survey commissioned by the Group showed 90 percent of the area residents opposed to the project.

## State of Tennessee

Tennessee's legislative and executive branches separately studied the MRS proposal coordinated by, respectively, an ad hoc committee and a cabinet council. The joint legislative committee, three members from each house, was openly hostile to the proposal from the start, as the REAL Group had been. One of the six members, from the Oak Ridge area, tried unsuccessfully to interest the other five in spelling out conditions of MRS acceptability. On February 12, 1986 the committee voted 5-1 to oppose the project and to recommend that the full legislature do likewise.[9]

The governor's cabinet council requested analyses from a number of state agencies and presented findings to the governor, who carefully maintained neutrality until announcing his opposition on January 21. Governor Alexander opposed the project on two grounds: that the facility is not needed and would unnecessarily raise TVA's electric rates in Tennessee, and that it would impose a negative and economically harmful image on the greater region of which Oak Ridge is part. The governor drew support for his position from two surveys—one of business leaders, the other of tourists—in which significant numbers of respondents indicated that an MRS facility would weigh negatively in their own business expansion or tourism plans.[10]

Compensation was considered but ruled out. Supporting material enclosed with the governor's letter to DOE Secretary Herrington suggests that minimum criteria for a compensation plan acceptable to Tennessee would include complete cleanup of past environmental "offenses," plus "regional development assistance." Governor Alexander's own statement, however, says that talk of compensation is inconsistent with opposition, and that he opposes the facility because it is unnecessary and Oak Ridge is the wrong place. Alexander raises the possibility that other sites in Tennessee might be considered acceptable.

## Success and Failure for Negotiated Compensation

Of two state and two local studies, only that by the Roane County/Oak Ridge community approached DOE's MRS proposal as a negotiable proposition.

The other three studies were aimed toward a simple yes-or-no response. Certainly, DOE had indicated a willingness to negotiate. From the start, DOE officials stated their intention to ask Congress to extend the tax equivalency concept to the MRS facility. They also challenged state and local interests to deal creatively with the compensation issue. Finally, DOE accepted virtually all of the Task Force conditions and stated its willingness to be equally responsive to the state.[11] Why, then, was the opportunity to seek a mutually acceptable solution ignored by the state and by the Hartsville locality?

Michael O'Hare and his coauthors discuss why some siting disputes are amenable to a solution involving negotiation and compensation while others are not.[12] They list eight characteristics indicating a favorable situation. A situation is favorable if

1. it involves few parties,
2. potential opponents are geographically defined,
3. potential opponents are cohesive,
4. mutually acceptable outcomes exist,
5. impacts are clearly traceable to the project,
6. impacts are mitigable or reversible,
7. the parties can offer a binding commitment, and
8. the parties are not initially hostile.

These characteristics are relative, not absolute, and a siting conflict need not necessarily possess all eight characteristics for compensation to be a workable solution. But the more nearly a characteristic is present and the more characteristics a situation possesses, then the more amenable it is to such a solution. Characteristic 4, existence of mutually acceptable outcomes, is the only absolutely necessary condition, and even here the characteristic is relative in the sense that the richer the set of mutually acceptable outcomes, the more likely are the parties to find one of them.

Characteristics 1, 2, 3, and 7 can be treated together. In both localities, opinion polls show strong concurrence with the positions of the official study groups and the local political leaders. Thus the REAL Group and the Task Force clearly can speak for their respective constituencies. At the local level two parties exist (DOE vs. the community), and the opposition is geographically localized, cohesive, and effectively represented—all favorable conditions for negotiated resolution. At the state level the situation is more complex, involving the legislative and executive branches as well as the larger regions outside the immediate localities; but the state situation is not strongly polarized or fragmented. Few Tennesseans outside Oak Ridge favor the project, but most do not appear to have intense feelings about it. As for Characteristic 8, both the state and the Oak Ridge community had previous, unhappy dealings with DOE; Hartsville had no prior contact with DOE but it had dealt with TVA and the Nuclear Regulatory Commission.

Evaluating Characteristics 4, 5, and 6 is more complex. The impacts of a large project such as DOE proposes are not predictable with a high degree of confidence, especially as the state and local groups expect the principal impacts to flow from the negative image of nuclear waste. This negative image, they argue, may scare away tourists and discourage businesses from locating in the community or region. MRS-induced loss of economic growth would be nearly impossible to prove and the issue could have become a sticking point between DOE and the local residents. That it did not is testament to DOE's willingness to find a mutually agreeable solution. DOE not only accepted the argument without rebuttal, when first made by the Task Force, but also agreed to the compensating conditions demanded by the Task Force and rewrote its Environmental Analysis to acknowledge the possibility of lost economic opportunities.[13]

If the main impacts are economic, as the state and local groups contend, then these impacts should be compensable and a mutually acceptable outcome should exist. We are back to the original question: Why did only the Oak Ridge community seize the opportunity to negotiate? By the criteria of O'Hare et al., the MRS proposal is a likely candidate for resolution by compensation, and conditions are not substantially less favorable for Hartsville or the state than for Oak Ridge. We must look beyond the MRS proposal itself, to the characteristics of the involved residents.

## Local Attitudes and Backgrounds

Different perceptions of the health and safety risks could explain the divergent approaches to the MRS issue taken by Oak Ridgers and other Tennesseans, but I believe that health and safety concerns were of only minor importance and that different economic perspectives played a greater role. In either case, the background of the Oak Ridge community sets it apart from the rest of the state.

Without question, the nature and history of Oak Ridge differentiate its residents from other Tennesseans. Local residents are generally familiar with nuclear technologies and large government-owned nuclear facilities, as these technologies and facilities are the reason for the city's existence. Many residents played significant roles in developing nuclear technologies and the nuclear power industry. Thus local residents are likely to be comfortable with things nuclear, and no small number of them have a personal interest in the success of the nuclear power industry. Furthermore, a number of Oak Ridgers have wrestled for years with the institutional problem of siting nuclear waste facilities and long ago recognized the value of compensation and negotiation in resolving siting conflicts. Oak Ridgers are convinced that MRS can be safe, they want DOE's nuclear waste program to succeed, and they generally (but not universally) view large energy-related projects as their route to growth and prosperity.

In one important respect the Oak Ridge and Hartsville communities are alike: Both suffered economic setbacks in the early 1980s when nuclear projects were cancelled. The Hartsville MRS site was to have contained TVA's cancelled Hartsville Nuclear Plant. In fact the REAL Group is patterned after an organization formed by the same five counties to deal with TVA on the socioeconomic impacts of that plant. Oak Ridge lost the Clinch River Breeder Reactor and the uranium enrichment business, both centrifuge and gaseous diffusion. The communities differ, however, in their responses to these losses. Oak Ridge eagerly seeks other projects while Hartsville seems to have concluded that more traditional development is less traumatic and uncertain.

Concern about safety is not an obvious factor in Tennesseans' attitudes toward the MRS proposal. Environmental groups tried to make safety an issue, but failed. Neither the Governor nor the REAL Group argues that the MRS project presents unacceptable safety risks; in fact, Governor Alexander expresses confidence that it can be run safely.

On the other hand, Tennesseans may see little to be gained from accommodating DOE. The benefit, 700 jobs, is a decade away and easily discounted,

given the history of the CRBR and similar federal projects. Tax equivalency means little to surrounding cities and counties with no property tax authority at the site. The potential costs are uncertain: How much business location and tourism would be lost and what measures would offset the losses? Especially as the case for adding monitored retrievable storage to the nuclear waste management system is not overwhelming (DOE must convince a skeptical Congress), Tennesseans find it easier to say no and question the need than to devise a compensation package with which they would feel comfortable. "No" is the low effort, low risk response.

Yet another difference between Oak Ridgers' and other Tennesseans' incentives to seek accommodation with DOE is their divergent views of the best route to economic growth. The MRS project fits into Oak Ridgers' plans not only because it is large, federal, and nuclear, but also because it would fulfill their long-sought goal of realizing significant tax income from local employers. On the other hand, Governor Alexander's major effort to establish the East Tennessee region including Knoxville and Oak Ridge as a center of high tech research and manufacturing focuses on strengths in glamor fields such as electronics and biotechnology, combined with amenities such as the nearby Smokey Mountains. Monitored retrievable storage is a misfit on two counts: it is unlikely to foster much growth-inducing spinoff and it may detract from the positive image the state is trying to sell. Even within the Oak Ridge business community, the prevalent and historic growth strategy that stresses the nuclear fuel cycle as the local comparative advantage is under attack.

In other words, while divergent backgrounds and attitudes explain the different approaches taken by Oak Ridgers and other Tennesseans, the differences had little to do with divergent perceptions of health and safety risk and had much to do with divergent opinions about how to achieve economic growth. Governor Alexander believes that the greater Knoxville area can emulate the success of North Carolina's Research Triangle if properly nurtured. Oak Ridgers support the governor's plans but have not forsaken their historic quest for growth in the form of large government projects. Nor can they understand why the nuclear waste business is inconsistent with the Research Triangle model. Beyond the political boundaries of property tax jurisdiction, Tennesseans have little to gain and, according to the non-Oak Ridge viewpoint, potentially much to lose. If the nuclear waste aura were to derail a Research Triangle-style future, it is difficult to imagine an adequate compensation package for the region.

Despite DOE's flexibility on most MRS issues, it has considered the site selection to be nonnegotiable and the entire MRS project is now on hold while a federal court evaluates Tennessee's contention that DOE illegally failed to consult and cooperate with the state prior to site selection. The Act's timetable for MRS actions is confusing, leaving room for several interpretations, but DOE was clearly under time pressures and its interpretation is the expedient one, at least in the short run. Whether earlier consultation and greater site flexibility would have made Tennesseans more receptive to the MRS proposal cannot be known. The other obstacles—controversial project justification, and the difficulty of compensating the larger region surrounding the site—would remain, but a more remote site with little indigenous economic potential would greatly reduce the possibility for regional economic harm, thus easing the regional compensation problem.

## What Have We Learned?

The report of the Oak Ridge Task Force and DOE's response to it indicate that DOE has opportunity and incentive under the Act to negotiate with local interests and to configure its proposals for the mutual benefit of local and nuclear power interests. That the State of Tennessee failed to accept the opportunity to negotiate might be attributed to two factors specific to the MRS proposal—controversy over its justification and controversy over the site selection process. These results do not necessarily indicate that the negotiation and compensation approach to facility siting is impotent nor that the NWPA provisions to encourage negotiation and compensation are fatally flawed. Nevertheless, the MRS results are similar to those noted by Gail Bingham and Daniel S. Miller for the success of negotiation in hazardous waste siting disputes.[14] They report that local reluctance to negotiate and local questioning of need for the facility are common experiences to date. These findings suggest that incentives for local participation may be a generic weakness of the negotiated compensation prescription. This aspect of the problem deserves further study.

The MRS case illustrates that the dichotomy between the local interest and the developer's interest implied in much of the literature on siting is oversimplified. State and regional interests did not coincide with those of the local community in this instance, a situation probably not unique. This fact of life greatly complicates DOE's task and will require far more creativity in designing compensating mechanisms than would a two-party negotiation. For many other siting situations, multiparty negotiations also will be required.

This case also illustrates the multifaceted nature of local concerns that developers must accommodate. For the Oak Ridge community, safety concerns were not with technology but with management, and economic concerns went beyond conventional impacts to questions of image perception and the commitment of DOE to community citizenship. To think of compensation solely in terms of money may be a fatal oversimplification on the part of project developers.

The one clear lesson of the MRS case is that the negotiated compensation prescription offers no easy solution to the sitting dilemma. Successful implementation will require developers to be aggressively creative with incentives and compensation and forceful enough to make defense of the status quo an unattractive state and local response, all the while remaining open, flexible, and politically sensitive.

## Notes

1. For an examination of the NWPA and the history of nuclear waste management, see Office of Technology Assessment, *Managing the Nation's Commercial High-Level Wastes,* OTA-0-171 (Washington, D.C.: U.S. Congress), March 1985.

2. Gary L. Downey, "Federalism and Nuclear Waste Disposal: The Struggle Over Shared Decision Making," *Journal of Policy Analysis and Management,* vol. 5, no. 1, 73-99 (1985). (Of course, an adversarial relationship already existed between the DOE and the Nuclear Regulatory Commission, which must license any repository and represents at least some local interests. The innovation is in the federal government conceding authority to represent local interests to the state, presumably more sympathetic to those local interests.)

3. David Morell and Christopher Magorian, *Siting Hazardous Waste Facilities: Local Opposition and the Myth of Preemption* (Cambridge, Mass.: Ballinger Publishing Company), 1982.

4. Two of the more thorough analyses and prescriptions are Michael O'Hare, Lawrence Bacow, and Debra Sanderson, *Facility Sitting and Public Opposition* (New York, NY: Van Nostrand Reinhold Company), 1983, and S. A. Carnes, E. D. Copenhaver, J. H. Reed, E. J. Soderstrom, J. H. Sorenson, E. Peele, and D. J. Bjornstad, "Incentives and the Siting of Radioactive Waste Facilities," ORNL-5880 (Oak Ridge, TN: Oak Ridge National Laboratory), August 1982.

5. DOE, "Monitored Retrievable Storage Program," briefing package prepared for the State of Tennessee, July 9, 1985. The most recent cost estimates ($2 billion) and project descriptions at this writing are found in DOE, "Monitored Retrievable Storage Submission to Congress," review copy, DOE/RW-0035, 3 volumes, December 1985.

6. Clinch River MRS Task Force, "Recommendations on the Proposed Monitored Retrievable Storage Facility," (Oak Ridge, TN) October 1985.

7. *The Oak Ridger,* November 1, 1985, p. 1, and November 5, 1985, p. 1.

8. Five County Research, Evaluation, Analysis and Liaison Group, "Recommendations on the Proposed Monitored Retrievable Storage Facility at the Hartsville TVA Nuclear Plant Site" (Hartsville, TN), November 1985.

9. *The Oak Ridger,* February 13, 1986, p. 1.

10. Letter from Governor Alexander to Secretary Herrington, February 5, 1986, plus enclosures. Also, interview of Governor Alexander on February 6, published in February 7 edition of *The Oak Ridger,* p. 4.

11. Volume 1, Chapter 4 of DOE's Submission to Congress is a direct and official response to the Task Force recommendations. Earlier indications of DOE flexibility are found in speeches by Ben Rusche, Director of the Office of Civilian Radioactive Waste Management (*The Oak Ridger,* June 28, 1985, p. 1), and Secretary Herrington (*The Oak Ridger,* November 14, 1985, p. 1).

12. Michael O'Hare, Lawrence Bacaw, and Debra Sanderson, *Facility Sitting and Public Opposition* (New York, N.Y.: Van Nostrand Reinhold Company), 1983, pp. 154–157.

13. The Environmental Analysis in Volume 3 of the Submission to Congress was changed from that of an earlier draft circulated in November 1985, to acknowledge that negative perceptions are likely and that these perceptions might cause economic losses.

14. Gail Bingham and Daniel S. Miller, "Prospects for Resolving Hazardous Waste Siting Disputes Through Negotiation," *Natural Resources Lawyer,* v. 17, no. 3, 1984, pp. 473–489.

# Chapter 5 Review Questions

1. Why are federalism and intergovernmental relations so critical to effective program performance in the public sector today? What were the founding fathers' rationale for establishing U.S. government in this federal manner?

2. What has been the recent practice of intergovernmental relations in the United States according to Martha Derthick? The role of agencies? Courts? Congress? The states? How does each bargain in the IGR process? The tools and strategies they use?

3. In what ways did the MRS case study illustrate some of the characteristics and dilemmas of modern federalism?

4. Who were the key IGR actors in this case, and how did they "calculate" to secure their own interests? Do you think that they successfully handled the complex issue?

5. What does the MRS case study say about the role and importance of experts involved in IGR? Who were the experts in this case and how did they derive their professional standards? Is there a problem that their specialized expertise may not always be applied in the public interest? What safeguards are

available to ensure that these experts will be guided by the broad public interest?

6. What does the MRS case study say about the significance of political bargaining and coalition-building in IGR and its role in influencing outcomes? Can these political dimensions of IGR be pointed out in Case Study 3, "Dumping $2.6 Million on Bakersfield"?

7. Do both cases support Derthick's thesis that "bargaining and negotiations, not command and obedience, appear to characterize the practice of intergovernmental programs now as in the past . . ."?

## Key Terms

| | |
|---|---|
| federalism | state discretion |
| intergovernmental relations | Garcia vs. SAMTA |
| categorical grants | grant formulas |
| block grants | federalist/antifederalist debates |
| Advisory Commission on Intergovernmental Relations (ACIR) | intergovernmental lobby |
| | statutory challenges |
| general revenue sharing | withholding funds |
| crosscutting requirements | devolutionary objectives |
| performance standards | Fourteenth Amendment |

## Suggestions for Further Reading

Some of the best up-to-date sources of information on the changing world of intergovernmental relations can be found in the frequent authoritative studies published by the Advisory Commission on Intergovernmental Relations, as well as in the ACIR journal, *Intergovernmental Perspective,* which can be obtained free of charge by writing to the ACIR, Washington, D.C. In addition, the new monthly journal *Governing* is well worth reading on IGR issues. The *National Journal* also contains excellent IGR coverage. Also see Timothy Conlan, *New Federalism: Intergovernmental Reform from Nixon to Reagan* (Washington, D.C.: Brookings, 1988) offers one of the best accounts of IGR during the past two decades and for a current overview, read Deil S. Wright, "Federalism, Intergovernmental Relations and Intergovernmental Management: Historical Reflections and Conceptual Comparisons," *Public Administration Review* (March/April 1990), pp. 168–178.

There are a number of excellent textbooks available, including Parris N. Glendening and Marvis M. Reeves, *Pragmatic Federalism: An Intergovernmental View of the American Government,* 2nd ed., (Pacific Palisades, Calif.: Palisades Publishing, 1984); Deil S. Wright, *Understanding Intergovernmental Relations,* Third Edition (Monterey, Calif.: Brooks/Cole Publishing, 1988); Michael D. Reagan and John D. Sanzone, *The New Federalism,* Second Edition (New York: Oxford University Press, 1981); Richard H. Leach, ed., *Intergovernmental Relations in the 1980s* (New York: Marcel Dekker, 1983); David B. Walker, *Toward a Functioning Federalism* (Cambridge, Mass.: Winthrop, 1981); Thomas J. Anton, *American Federalism and Public Policy: How the System Works* (New York: Random House, 1989);

and Daniel J. Elazar, *American Federalism,* 3rd ed. (New York: Harper & Row, 1984).

The several more scholarly and focused studies of IGR that should be examined as well include James D. Carroll and Richard W. Campbell, eds., *Intergovernmental Administration* (Syracuse, N.Y.: Maxwell School, 1976); Martha Derthick, *The Influence of Federal Grants: Public Assistance in Massachusetts* (Cambridge, Mass.: Harvard University Press, 1970); and Jeffrey L. Pressman, *Federal Programs and City Politics: The Dynamics of the Aid Process in Oakland* (Berkeley: University of California Press, 1975). Serious students of IGR also should read the Kesnbaum Commission Report (June 1955), which contains information still helpful for understanding modern IGR, as well as other basic documents on IGR contained in Richard J. Stillman, *Basic Documents of American Public Administration Since 1950* (New York: Holmes and Meier, 1982).

Laurence J. O'Toole, Jr., ed., *American Intergovernmental Relations* (Washington, D.C.: Congressional Quarterly, 1985); Lewis G. Bender and James A. Stever, *Administering the New Federalism* (Boulder, Colo.: Westview Press, 1986); as well as Deil S. Wright and Harvey L. White, eds., *Federalism and Intergovernmental Relations* (Washington, D.C.: American Society for Public Administration, 1984) offer outstanding collections of current and classic IGR essays. For several recent survey essays on federalism by distinguished scholars in this field, see the entire issue of *The Annals of the American Academy of Political and Social Science* (May 1990), edited by John Kincaid, and entitled "American Federalism: The Third Century."

For a more pragmatic approach to IGR, see Nancy A. Huelsberg and William F. Lincoln, eds., *Successful Negotiations in Local Government* (Washington, D.C.: ICMA, 1985).

# CHAPTER 6

# Internal Dynamics: The Concept of the Informal Group

*F or all of us the feeling of security and certainty derives always from assured membership of a group. If this is lost, no monetary gain, no job guarantee, can be sufficient compensation. Where groups change ceaselessly as jobs and mechanical processes change, the individual inevitably experiences a sense of void, of emptiness. . . .*

*Elton Mayo*

## READING 6

## Introduction

Public administration was never the primary concern of Elton Mayo and Fritz Roethlisberger. Most of their research efforts centered around the study of business enterprises at the Harvard Business School, yet their impact on general administrative thought has been significant principally because from their investigations developed the *human relations* or *industrial sociological school* in organization theory. This school of thought emphasizes understanding and improving the dynamics of the internal human group within complex organizations; it was both a product of and a reaction to the scientific-management movement of the early part of this century. Frederick W. Taylor, an early founder of scientific management, had stressed that from the rational study of industrial organizations, "principles" of efficient, economical management could be derived.

Similarly, Elton Mayo, Fritz Roethlisberger, and a team of researchers from the Harvard Business School set out in 1927 at Western Electric's Hawthorne Electric Plant in Cicero, Illinois, near Chicago, to measure scientifically the effect of changes in the external environment on workers' output; they studied such matters as more or less lighting, shorter or longer lunch breaks, and increased or decreased hours in the work week. Their goal at first, like the goal of scientific management, was to discover the most efficient way to motivate workers. The Hawthorne Plant manufactured phones and telecommunications equipment for American Telephone and Telegraph (AT&T), employing at the time more than 40,000 workers. The company encouraged the Mayo-Roethlisberger experiments as part of its generally considered progressive management practices (progressive at least for that era).

While following the same methods as Taylor's scientific-management research, the Mayo-Roethlisberger team paradoxically arrived at different conclusions and insights from those of Taylor and his followers. The results of five years of intense study at the Hawthorne Plant revealed that the *primary work group* (that is, the relationships between workers and their supervisors and among workers themselves), had as much if not more impact on productivity as the formal physical surroundings and economic benefits derived from the job. For many, the Hawthorne experiment came "as the great illumination," or as Roethlisberger more modestly described it, "the systematic exploitation of the simple and obvious." It underscored a fundamental truth, obscured for some time by scientific-management theories, namely, that the employees of an organization constituted its basis, and that upon their attitudes, behavior, and morale within their primary groups ultimately depended industrial effectiveness and productivity. As Roethlisberger wrote:

> It is my simple thesis that a human problem requires a human solution. First, we have to learn to recognize a human problem when we see one; and second, upon recognizing it, we have to learn to deal with it as such and not as if it were something else.[1]

The Hawthorne investigators shifted the focus of management studies from simply the external elements of organizations to its internal and nonrational aspects. By interviewing techniques and by close observations of the dynamics of primary groups, that is, interrelations between workers, the investigators sought to understand the social codes and norms of behavior of informal work groups that were rarely displayed on the formal organization chart. "They studied the important social functions these groups perform for their members, the histories of these informal work groups, how they spontaneously appear, how they tend to perpetuate themselves, multiply, and disappear, how they are in constant jeopardy from technical change, and hence how they tend to resist innovation." In essence, like Freud and Jung in clinical psychology, they attempted to rationalize the irrational nature of human beings in the organizational context and find cures for the psychotic disorders of industrial institutions.

The Hawthorne experimenters also challenged the prevailing scientific management view of the individual employee, that is, that the greatest motivating factor for the worker was his or her paycheck. Rather, Roethlisberger argued,

---

[1] Fritz J. Roethlisberger, *Management and Morale* (Cambridge, Mass.: Harvard University Press, 1941), p. 7.

"Most of us want the satisfaction that comes from being accepted and recognized as people of worth by our friends and work associates. Money is only a small part of this social recognition. . . . We want the feeling of security that comes not so much from the amount of money we have in the bank as from being an accepted member of a group. A man whose job is without social function is like a man without a country; the activity to which he has to give the major portion of his life is robbed of all human meaning and significance."

After the termination of the Hawthorne Plant experiments Mayo's writings led to broad speculations about administration and the problems of human society. In these later works, *The Human Problems of an Industrial Civilization* (1933), *The Social Problems of an Industrial Civilization* (1945), and *The Political Problems of Industrial Civilization* (1947), his central thesis emphasized that social skills have lagged behind technical skills. While the techniques of specialists, including engineers, chemists, and doctors were important, it was by the leadership of administrators, in particular business people, that human cooperation could be advanced and the problems of organization in society solved. In the deepest sense, Mayo became a social reformer who believed that improving the quality of administrative talent could help to build a better world. In his view, the administrator "becomes the guardian or preserver of the morale through the function of maintaining a condition of equilibrium, which will preserve the social values existing in the cooperative system."

To better understand the following selection by Mayo, it is helpful to know something about his background, which helped to shape the decidedly unique perspective of his writing. Mayo, the senior partner in the Hawthorne research effort, lived from 1880 to 1949 (his assistant, Roethlisberger, lived from 1898 to 1974). Born in Adelaide, Australia, Mayo was the second child in a large, impoverished family of seven. His life was unsettled—while growing up his family moved often, and in trying to find an occupation for himself, he drifted from one job to another. He went from business to publishing, to teaching, and then to medicine, but it was World War I that affected his life the most (as it did the lives of so many of his generation). While working as an interviewer of returning war veterans suffering from shell shock, Mayo learned firsthand about human suffering, dislocation, and tragedy.

Increasingly, thereafter, Mayo was drawn to the study of psychology—particularly the clinical writings of Janet and Freud, as well as the work of social systems theorists like Pareto and Henderson. It was Mayo's unique gift to be able to synthesize the ideas of clinical psychology and develop a grand systems theory into a way that would offer understanding and help for the problems of the worker in the industrial work place. How were people to deal with and adapt to the traumatic upheavals caused by war, technology, and industrialization in the twentieth century? How could the suffering caused by these massive changes in the human condition be alleviated and possibly cured? How could human life for individuals and groups be improved? Mayo wrestled with these and other major philosophical and social issues for most of his life.

Grants from the Rockefeller and Carnegie Foundations brought Mayo to America in the 1920s, first to the University of Pennsylvania and then later to

Harvard University to head the team of researchers at the Hawthorne Plant. There, with his probing mind and inspired personality, along with his emphasis on using rigorous, firsthand field investigations as a way to understand what really was happening inside American industrial life, he was able to give leadership to the overall direction of the Hawthorne experiments. The lasting fame of these experiments in social science and management literature is due in large measure to Mayo. He introduced the modern *team research* concept and indeed inspired other large-scale research efforts such as W. Lloyd Warner's *Yankee City*.

The following selection offers valuable insight into Mayo's views—his unique intuitiveness, his passionate concern for the betterment of human beings, his conviction that close, careful empirical-clinical analysis will yield "the facts" about human problems, and that this analysis can, in turn, lead to resolutions of these problems. Fundamental to all his beliefs is the idea that if only the informal nature of human organizations is recognized and properly dealt with (rather than the scientific, technological, and economic processes), then it is indeed possible to build a better world. This fundamental, reformist conviction spawned much of the human relations literature of post-World War II management thought by writers such as Maslow, Likert, McGregor, Herzberg, and many others who owe a debt to Mayo's writings and the Hawthorne experiments.

Mayo, however, was not without critics: labor unions criticized him for being antiunion, which he denied, and methodologists criticized his work for being unscientific and methodologically unsound, but he never admitted to being a statistician. Most curiously, despite all his work at the Hawthorne Plant, not one of his recommendations was put into practice by the plant's management. Of what importance, then, were Mayo's work and the Hawthorne experiments? Perhaps Mayo's real genius was that he emphatically restated an old truth: human needs, values, and concerns play a primary role in any successful management effort.

As you read this selection, keep the following questions in mind:

Do the informal groups identified by Mayo's experiments in an industrial setting exist in public sector agencies? If so, do they operate in the same way in government as they do in business?

What do you think the similarities, as well as differences, are in the operation of informal group in the public versus private settings?

Are Mayo's suggestions for dealing with the problems of securing the cooperation of individuals and human groups compatible with the goals and practices of public organizations? Where might there be problems in applying his ideas and techniques?

Referring back to Case Study No. 1, "The Blast in Centralia No. 5," or Case Study No. 3, "Dumping $2.6 Million on Bakersfield," identify the primary groups in these cases. Do Mayo's theories and prescriptions apply to these cases?

Compare Weber's and Mayo's views on the human condition. How do the two theorists compare in their conclusions and prescriptions for solving the bureaucratic problems of modern society? For instance, does Mayo emphasize material motives less than Weber does?

# Hawthorne and the Western Electric Company

### ELTON MAYO

I shall make no attempt to describe at length that which has been already and fully described. The interested public is well acquainted with *Management and the Worker,* the official account of the whole range of experiments, by my colleagues F. J. Roethlisberger of Harvard University and William J. Dickson of the Western Electric Company. The same public has not yet discovered *The Industrial Worker,*[1] by another colleague, T. North Whitehead. This is unfortunate, for the beginning of an answer to many problems significant for administration in the next decade is recorded in its pages. I refer to the problems involved in the making and adaptive re-making of working teams, the importance of which for collaboration in postwar years is still too little realized. Assuming that readers who wish to do so can consult these books, I have confined my remarks here to some comments upon the general development of the series of experiments.

A highly competent group of Western Electric engineers refused to accept defeat when experiments to demonstrate the effect of illumi-

From Elton Mayo, *The Social Problems of an Industrial Civilization.* Boston: Division of Research, Harvard Business School, 1945. Reprinted by permission of Harvard Business School Press.

nation on work seemed to lead nowhere. The conditions of scientific experiment had apparently been fulfilled—experimental room, control room; changes introduced one at a time; all other conditions held steady. And the results were perplexing: Roethlisberger gives two instances—lighting improved in the experimental room, production went up; but it rose also in the control room. The opposite of this: lighting diminished from 10 to 3 foot-candles in the experimental room and production again went up; simultaneously in the control room, with illumination constant, production also rose.[2] Many other experiments, and all inconclusive; yet it had seemed so easy to determine the effect of illumination on work.

In matters of mechanics or chemistry the modern engineer knows how to set about the improvement of process or the redress of error. But the determination of optimum working conditions for the human being is left largely to dogma and tradition, guess, or quasi-philosophical argument. In modern large-scale industry the three persistent problems of management are:

1. The application of science and technical skill to some material good or product.

2. The systematic ordering of operations.
3. The organization of teamwork—that is, of sustained cooperation.

The last must take account of the need for continual reorganization of teamwork as operating conditions are changed in an *adaptive* society.

The first of these holds enormous prestige and interest and is the subject of continuous experiment. The second is well developed in practice. The third, by comparison with the other two, is almost wholly neglected. Yet it remains true that if these three are out of balance, the organization as a whole will not be successful. The first two operate to make an industry *effective,* in Chester Barnard's phrase,[3] the third, to make it *efficient.* For the larger and more complex the institution, the more dependent is it upon the wholehearted cooperation of every member of the group.

This was not altogether the attitude of Mr. G. A. Pennock and his colleagues when they set up the experimental "test room." But the illumination fiasco had made them alert to the need that very careful records should be kept of everything that happened in the room in addition to the obvious engineering and industrial devices.[4] Their observations therefore included not only records of industrial and engineering changes but also records of physiological or medical changes, and, in a sense, of social and anthropological. This last took the form of a "log" that gave as full an account as possible of the actual events of every day, a record that proved most useful to Whitehead when he was remeasuring the recording tapes and recalculating the changes in productive output. He was able to relate eccentricities of the output curve to the actual situation at a given time—that is to say, to the events of a specific day or week.

## First Phase—The Test Room

The facts are by now well know. Briefly restated, the test room began its inquiry by, first,

attempting to secure the active collaboration of the workers. This took some time but was gradually successful, especially after the retirement of the original first and second workers and after the new worker at the second bench had assumed informal leadership of the group. From this point on, the evidence presented by Whitehead or Roethlisberger and Dickson seems to show that the individual workers became a team, wholeheartedly committed to the project. Second, the conditions of work were changed one at a time: rest periods of different numbers and length, shorter working day, shorter working week, food with soup or coffee in the morning break. And the results seemed satisfactory: slowly at first, but later with increasing certainty, the output record (used as an index of well-being) mounted. Simultaneously the workers claimed that they felt less fatigued, felt that they were not making any special effort. Whether these claims were accurate or no, they at least indicated increased contentment with the general situation in the test room by comparison with the department outside. At every point in the program, the workers had been consulted with respect to proposed changes; they had arrived at the point of free expression of ideas and feelings to management. And it had been arranged thus that the twelfth experimental change should be a return to the original conditions of work—no rest periods, no midmorning lunch, no shortened day or week. It had also been arranged that, after 12 weeks of this, the group should return to the conditions of Period 7, a 15-minute midmorning break with lunch and a 10-minute midafternoon rest. The story is now well known: in Period 12 the daily and weekly output rose to a point higher than at any other time (the hourly rate adjusted itself downward by a small fraction), and in the whole 12 weeks "there was no downward trend." In the following period, the return to the conditions of work as in the seventh experimental change, the output curve soared to even greater heights: this thirteenth period lasted for 31 weeks.

These periods, 12 and 13, made it evident that increments of production could not be related point for point to the experimental changes introduced. Some major change was taking place that was chiefly responsible for the index of improved conditions—the steadily increasing output. Period 12—but for minor qualifications, such as "personal time out"—ignored the nominal return to original conditions of work and the output curve continued its upward passage. Put in other words, there was no actual return to original conditions. This served to bring another fact to the attention of the observers. Periods 7, 10, and 13 had nominally the same working conditions, as above described—15-minute rest and lunch in midmorning, 10-minute rest in the afternoon. But the average weekly output for each worker was:

Period 7—2,500 units

Period 10—2,800 units

Period 13—3,000 units

Periods 3 and 12 resembled each other also in that both required a full day's work without rest periods. But here also the difference of average weekly output for each worker was:

Period 3—less than 2,500 units

Period 12—more than 2,900 units

Here then was a situation comparable perhaps with the illumination experiment, certainly suggestive of the Philadelphia experience where improved conditions for one team of mule spinners were reflected in improved morale not only in the experimental team but in the two other teams who had received no such benefit.

This interesting, and indeed amusing, result has been so often discussed that I need make no mystery of it now. I have often heard my colleague Roethlisberger declare that the major experimental change was introduced when those in charge sought to hold the situation humanly steady (in the interest of critical changes to be introduced) by getting the cooperation of the workers. What actually happened was that six individuals became a team and the team gave itself wholeheartedly and spontaneously to cooperation in the experiment. The consequence was that they felt themselves to be participating freely and without afterthought, and were happy in the knowledge that they were working without coercion from above or limitation from below. They were themselves astonished at the consequence, for they felt that they were working under less pressure than ever before: and in this, their feelings and performance echoed that of the mule spinners.

Here then are two topics which deserve the closest attention of all those engaged in administrative work—the organization of working teams and the free participation of such teams in the task and purpose of the organization as it directly affects them in their daily round.

## Second Phase—The Interview Program

But such conclusions were not possible at the time: the major change, the question as to the exact difference between conditions of work in the test room and in the plant departments, remained something of a mystery. Officers of the company determined to "take another look" at departments outside the test room—this, with the idea that something quite important was there to be observed, something to which the experiment should have made them alert. So the interview program was introduced.

It was speedily discovered that the question-and-answer type of interview was useless in the situation. Workers wished to talk, and to talk freely under the seal of professional confidence (which was never abused) to someone who seemed representative of the company or who seemed, by his very attitude, to carry authority. The experience itself was unusual; there are few people in this world who have had the experience of finding someone intelligent, attentive, and eager to listen without interruption to all that he or she has to say. But to arrive at this point it became necessary to train interviewers how to listen, how to avoid interruption or the giving of advice, how generally to avoid anything that might put an end to free expression in an individual instance. Some approximate rules to guide the interviewer in his work were therefore set down. These were, more or less, as follows:[5]

1. Give your whole attention to the person interviewed, and make it evident that you are doing so.
2. Listen—don't talk.
3. Never argue; never give advice.
4. Listen to:
   (a) What he wants to say.
   (b) What he does not want to say.
   (c) What he cannot say without help.
5. As you listen, plot out tentatively and for subsequent correction the pattern (personal) that is being set before you. To test this, from time to time summarize what has been said and present for comment (e.g., "Is this what you are telling me?"). Always do this with the greatest caution, that is, clarify but do not add or twist.
6. Remember that everything said must be considered a personal confidence and not divulged to anyone. (This does not prevent discussion of a situation between professional colleagues. Nor does it prevent some form of public report when due precaution has been taken.)

It must not be thought that this type of interviewing is easily learned. It is true that some persons, men and women alike, have a natural flair for the work, but, even with them, there tends to be an early period of discouragement, a feeling of futility, through which the experience and coaching of a senior interviewer must carry them. The important rules in the interview (important, that is, for the development of high skill) are two. First, Rule 4 that indicates the need to help the individual interviewed to articulate expression of an idea or attitude that he has not before expressed; and, second, Rule 5 which indicates the need from time to time to summarize what has been said and to present it for comment. Once equipped to do this effectively, interviewers develop very considerable skill. But, let me say again, this skill is not easily acquired. It demands of the interviewer a real capacity to follow the contours of another person's thinking, to understand the meaning for him of what he says.

I do not believe that any member of the research group or its associates had anticipated the immediate response that would be forthcoming to the introduction of such an interview program. Such comments as "This is the best thing the Company has ever done," or "The Company should have done this long ago," were frequently heard. It was as if workers had been awaiting an opportunity for expressing freely and without afterthought their feelings on a great variety of modern situations, not by any means limited to the various departments of the plant. To find an intelligent person who was not only eager to listen but also anxious to help to express ideas and feelings but dimly understood—this, for many thousand persons, was an experience without precedent in the modern world.

In a former statement I named two questions that inevitably presented themselves to the interviewing group in these early stages of the study:

1. Is some experience which might be described as an experience of personal futility a common incident of industrial organization for work?
2. Does life in a modern industrial city, in

some unrealized way, predispose workers to obsessive response?[6]

And I said that these two questions "in some form" continued to preoccupy those in charge of the research until the conclusion of the study.[7]

After twelve years of further study (not yet concluded), there are certain developments that demand attention. For example, I had not fully realized in 1932, when the above was written, how profoundly the social structure of civilization has been shaken by scientific, engineering, and industrial development. This radical change—the passage from an established to an adaptive social order—has brought into being a host of new and unanticipated problems for management and for the individual worker. The management problem appears at its acutest in the work of the supervisor. No longer does the supervisor work with a team of persons that he has known for many years or perhaps a lifetime; he is leader of a group of individuals that forms and disappears almost as he watches it. Now it is difficult, if not impossible, to relate oneself to a working group one by one; it is relatively easy to do so if they are already a fully constituted team. A communication from the supervisor, for example, in the latter instance has to be made to one person only with the appropriate instructions; the individual will pass it on and work it out with the team. In the former instance, it has to be repeated to every individual and may often be misunderstood.

But for the individual worker the problem is really much more serious. He has suffered a profound loss of security and certainty in his actual living and in the background of his thinking. For all of us the feeling of security and certainty derives always from assured membership of a group. If this is lost, no monetary gain, no job guarantee, can be sufficient compensation. Where groups change ceaselessly as jobs and mechanical processes change, the individual inevitably experiences a sense of

void, of emptiness, where his fathers knew the joy of comradeship and security. And in such a situation, his anxieties—many, no doubt, irrational or ill-founded—increase and he becomes more difficult both to fellow workers and to supervisor. The extreme of this is perhaps rarely encountered as yet, but increasingly we move in this direction as the tempo of industrial change is speeded by scientific and technical discovery.

In the first chapter of this book I have claimed that scientific method has a dual approach—represented in medicine by the clinic and the laboratory. In the clinic one studies the whole situation with two ends in view: first, to develop intimate knowledge of and skill in handling the facts, and, second, on the basis of such a skill to separate those aspects of the situation that skill has shown to be closely related for detailed laboratory study. When a study based upon laboratory method fails, or partially fails, because some essential factor has been unknowingly and arbitrarily excluded, the investigator, if he is wise, returns to clinical study of the entire situation to get some hint as to the nature of the excluded determinant. The members of the research division at Hawthorne, after the twelfth experimental period in the test room, were faced by just such a situation and knew it. The so-called interview program represented for them a return from the laboratory to clinical study. And, as in all clinical study, there was no immediate and welcome revelation of a single discarded determinant: there was rather a slow progress from one observation to another, all of them important—but only gradually building up into a single complex finding. This slow development has been elsewhere described, in *Management and the Worker;* one can however attempt a succinct résumé of the various observations, more or less as they occurred.

Officers of the company had prepared a short statement, a few sentences, to be repeated to the individual interviewed before the conversation began. This statement was designed to assure the worker that nothing he said would be repeated to his supervisors or to any company official outside the interviewing group. In many instances, the worker waved this aside and began to talk freely and at once. What doubts there were seemed to be resident in the interviewers rather than in those interviewed. Many workers, I cannot say the majority for we have no statistics, seemed to have something "on their minds," in ordinary phrase, about which they wished to talk freely to a competent listener. And these topics were by no means confined to matters affecting the company. This was, I think, the first observation that emerged from the mass of interviews reported daily. The research group began to talk about the need for *"emotional release"* and the great advantage that accrued to the individual when he had "talked off" his problem. The topics varied greatly. One worker two years before had been sharply reprimanded by his supervisor for not working as usual: in interview he wished to explain that on the night preceding the day of the incident his wife and child had both died, apparently unexpectedly. At the time he was unable to explain; afterwards he had no opportunity to do so. He told the story dramatically and in great detail; there was no doubt whatever that telling it thus benefited him greatly. But this story naturally was exceptional; more often a worker would speak of his family and domestic situation, of his church, of his relations with other members of the working group—quite usually the topic of which he spoke presented itself to him as a problem difficult for him to resolve. This led to the next successive illumination for the inquiry. It became manifest that, whatever the problem, it was partly, and sometimes wholly, determined by the attitude of the individual worker. And this defect or distortion of attitude was consequent on his past experience or his present situation, or, more usually, on both at once. One woman worker, for example, discovered for herself during an interview that her dislike of a certain supervisor was based upon

a fancied resemblance to a detested stepfather. Small wonder that the same supervisor had warned the interviewer that she was "difficult to handle." But the discovery by the worker that her dislike was wholly irrational eased the situation considerably.[8] This type of case led the interviewing group to study carefully each worker's *personal situation* and attitude. These two phrases "emotional release" and "personal situation" became convenient titles for the first phases of observation and seemed to resume for the interviewers the effective work that they were doing. It was at this point that a change began to show itself in the study and in the conception of the study.

The original interviewers, in these days, after sixteen years of industrial experience, are emphatic on the point that the first cases singled out for report were special cases—individuals—and not representative either of the working group or of the interviews generally. It is estimated that such cases did not number more than an approximate two percent of the twenty thousand persons originally interviewed. Probably this error of emphasis was inevitable and for two reasons: first, the dramatic changes that occur in such instances seemed good evidence of the efficacy of the method, and, second, this type of interviewing had to be insisted upon as *necessary to the training of a skilled interviewer*. This last still holds good; a skilled interviewer must have passed through the stage of careful and observant listening to what an individual says and to all that he says. This stage of an interviewing program closely resembles the therapeutic method and its triumphs are apt to be therapeutic. And I do not believe that the study would have been equipped to advance further if it had failed to observe the great benefit of emotional release and the extent to which every individual's problems are conditioned by his personal history and situation. Indeed, even when one has advanced beyond the merely psychotherapeutic study of individuals to study of industrial groups, one has to beware of distortions similar in kind to those named; one has to know how to deal with such problems. The first phase of the interview program cannot therefore be discarded; it still retains its original importance. But industrial studies must nevertheless move beyond the individual in need of therapy. And this is the more true when the change from established routines to adaptive changes of routine seems generally to carry a consequence of loss of security for many persons.

A change of attitude in the research group came gradually. The close study of individuals continued, but in combination with an equally close study of groups. An early incident did much to set the new pattern for inquiry. One of the earliest questions proposed before the original test room experiment began was a question as to the fatigue involved in this or that type of work. Later a foreman of high reputation, no doubt with this in mind, came to the research group, now for the most part engaged in interviewing, and asserted that the workers in his department worked hard all day at their machines and must be considerably fatigued by the evening; he wanted an inquiry. Now the interviewers had discovered that this working group claimed a habit of doing most of their work in the morning period and "taking things easy" during the afternoon. The foreman obviously realized nothing of this, and it was therefore fortunate that the two possibilities could be directly tested. The officer in charge of the research made a quiet arrangement with the engineers to measure during a period the amount of electric current used by the group to operate its machines; this quantity indicated the over-all amount of work being done. The results of this test wholly supported the statements made by the workers in interview; far more current was used in the morning period than during the afternoon. And the attention of the research group was, by this and other incidents, thus redirected to a fact already known to them, namely, that the working group as a whole actually determined the output of individual workers by reference to a standard, predetermined but never clearly stated, that represented the group conception of a fair day's work. This standard was rarely, if ever, in accord with the standards of the efficiency engineers.

The final experiment, reported under the title of the Bank Wiring Observation Room, was set up to extend and confirm these observations.[9] Simultaneously it was realized that these facts did not in any way imply low working morale as suggested by such phrases as "restriction of output." On the contrary, the failure of free communication between management and workers in modern large-scale industry leads inevitably to the exercise of caution by the working group until such time as it knows clearly the range and meaning of changes imposed from above. The enthusiasm of the efficiency engineer for the organization of operations is excellent; his attempt to resume problems of cooperation under this heading is not. At the moment, he attempts to solve the many human difficulties involved in wholehearted cooperation by organizing the organization of organization without any reference whatever to workers themselves. This procedure inevitably blocks communication and defeats his own admirable purpose.[10]

This observation, important as it is, was not however the leading point for the interviewers. The existence and influence of the group—those in active daily relationship with one another—became the important fact. The industrial interviewer must learn to distinguish and specify, as he listens to what a worker says, references to "personal" or group situations. More often than not, the special case, the individual who talks himself out of a gross distortion, is a solitary—one who has not "made the team." The usual interview, on the other hand, though not by any means free from distortion, is speaking as much for the working group as for the person. The influence of the communication in the interview, therefore, is not limited to the individual but extends to the group.

Two workers in a large industry were recently offered "upgrading"; to accept would mean leaving their group and taking a job in another department: they refused. Then representatives of the union put some pressure on them, claiming that, if they continued to refuse, the union organizers "might just as well give up" their efforts. With reluctance the workers reversed their decision and accepted the upgrading. Both girls at once needed the attention of an interviewer: they had liked the former group in which they had earned informal membership. Both felt adjustment to a new group and a novel situation as involving effort and private discontent. From both much was learned of the intimate organization and common practices of their groups, and their adjustments to their new groups were eased, thereby effectively helping reconstitute the teamwork in those groups.

In another recent interview a worker of eighteen protested to an interviewer that her mother was continually urging her to ask Mr. X, her supervisor, for a "raise." She had refused, but her loyalty to her mother and the pressure the latter exerted were affecting her work and her relations at work. She talked her situation out with an interviewer, and it became clear that to her a "raise" would mean departure from her daily companions and associates. Although not immediately relevant, it is interesting to note that, after explaining the situation at length to the interviewer, she was able to present her case dispassionately to her mother—without exaggeration or protest. The mother immediately understood and abandoned pressure for advancement, and the worker returned to effective work. This last instance illustrates one way in which the interview clears lines of communication of emotional blockage—within as without the plant. But this is not my immediate topic; my point is rather that the age-old human desire for persistence of human association will seriously complicate the development of an adaptive society if we cannot devise systematic methods of easing individuals from one group of associates into another.

But such an observation was not possible in the earliest inquiry. The important fact brought to the attention of the research division was that the ordinary conception of management-worker relation as existing between company officials, on the one hand, and an unspecified number of individuals, on the other, is utterly mistaken. Management, in any continuously successful plant, is not related to single workers but always to working groups. In every department that continues to operate, the workers have—whether aware of it or not—formed themselves into a group with appropriate customs, duties, routines, even rituals; and management succeeds (or fails) in proportion as it is accepted without reservation by the group as authority and leader. This, for example, occurred in the relay assembly test room at Hawthorne. Management, by consultation with the workers, by clear explanation of the proposed experiments and the reasons for them, by accepting the workers' verdict in special instances, unwittingly scored a success in two most important human matters—the workers became a self-governing team, and a team that cooperated wholeheartedly with management. The test room was responsible for many important findings—rest periods, hours of work, food, and the like: but the most important finding of all was unquestionably in the general area of teamwork and cooperation.

It was at this time that the research division published, for private circulation within the company, a monograph entitled "Complaints and Grievances." Careful description of many varied situations within the interviewers' experience showed that an articulate complaint only rarely, if ever, gave any logical clue to the grievance in which it had origin; this applied at least as strongly to groups as to individuals. Whereas economists and industry generally *tend to concentrate upon the complaint and upon logical inferences from its articulate statement* as an appropriate procedure, the interviewing group had learned almost to ignore, except as symptom, the—sometimes noisy—manifestation of discomfort and to study the situation anew to gain knowledge of its source. Diagnosis rather than argument became the proper method of procedure.

It is possible to quote an illustration from a recently published book, *China Enters the Machine Age.*[11] When industries had to be moved, during this war, from Shanghai and the Chinese coast to Kunming in the interior of China, the actual operation of an industry still depended for the most part on skilled workers who were refugees from Shanghai and elsewhere. These skilled workers knew their importance to the work and gained considerable prestige from it; nevertheless discontent was rife among them. Evidence of this was manifested by the continual, deliberate breaking of crockery in the company mess hall and complaints about the quality of the food provided. Yet this food was much better than could have been obtained outside the plant—especially at the prices charged. And in interview the individual workers admitted freely that the food was good and could not rightly be made the subject of complaint. But the relationship between the skilled workers as a group and the *Chih Yuan*—the executive and supervisory officers—was exceedingly unsatisfactory.

Many of these officers—the *Chih Yuan*—have been trained in the United States—enough at least to set a pattern for the whole group. Now in America we have learned in actual practice to accept the rabble hypothesis with reservations. But the logical Chinese student of engineering or economics, knowing nothing of these practical reservations, returns to his own country convinced that the workman who is not wholly responsive to the "financial incentive" is a troublemaker and a nuisance. And the Chinese worker lives up to this conviction by breaking plates.[12] Acceptance of the complaint about the food and collective bargaining of a logical type conducted at that level would surely have been useless.

Yet this is what industry, not only in China, does every day, with the high sanction of State authority and the alleged aid of lawyers and economists. In their behavior and their statements, economists indicate that they accept the rabble hypothesis and its dismal corollary of financial incentive as the only effective human motive. They substitute a logical hypothesis of small practical value for the actual facts.

The insight gained by the interviewing group, on the other hand, cannot be described as substituting irrational for rational motive, emotion for logic. On the contrary, it implies a need for competent study of complaints and the grievances that provoke them, a need for knowledge of the actual facts rather than acceptance of an outdated theory. It is amusing that certain industrialists, rigidly disciplined in economic theory, attempt to shrug off the Hawthorne studies as "theoretic." Actually the shoe is on the other foot; Hawthorne has restudied the facts without prejudice, whereas the critics have unquestioningly accepted that theory of man which had its vogue in the nineteenth century and has already outlived its usefulness.

The Hawthorne interview program has moved far since its beginning in 1929. Originally designed to study the comfort of workers in their work as a mass of individuals, it has come to clear specification of the relation of working groups to management as one of the fundamental problems of large-scale industry. It was indeed this study that first enabled us to assert that the third major preoccupation of management must be that of organizing teamwork, that is to say, of developing and sustaining cooperation.

In summary, certain entirely practical discoveries must be enumerated.

*First,* the early discovery that the interview aids the individual to get rid of useless emotional complications and to state his problem clearly. He is thus enabled to give himself good advice—a procedure far more effective than advice accepted from another. I have already given instances of this in discussing "emotional release" and the influence on individual attitude of personal history and personal situation.

*Second,* the interview has demonstrated its capacity to aid the individual to associate more easily, more satisfactorily, with other persons—fellow workers or supervisors—with whom he is in daily contact.

*Third,* the interview not only helps the individual to collaborate better with his own group of workers, it also develops his desire and capacity to work better with management. In this it resembles somewhat the action of the Philadelphia colonel.[13] Someone, the interviewer, representing (for the worker) the plant organization outside his own group, has aided him to work better with his own group. This is the beginning of the necessary double loyalty—to his own group and to the larger organization. It remains only for management to make wise use of this beginning.

*Fourth,* beyond all this, interviewing possesses immense importance for the training of administrators in the difficult future that faces this continent and the world. It has been said that the interviewer has no authority and takes no action. Action can only be taken by the proper authority and through the formally constituted line of authority. The interviewer, however, contributes much to the facilitation of communication both up and down that line. He does this, first, by clearing away emotional distortion and exaggeration; second, his work manifestly aids to exact and objective statement the grievance that lies beyond the various complaints.

Work of this kind is immensely effective in the development of maturity of attitude and judgment in the intelligent and sensitive young men and women who give time to it. The subordination of oneself, of one's opinions and ideas, of the very human desire to give gratuitous advice, the subordination of all these to an intelligent effort to help another express ideas and feelings that he cannot easily express is, in

itself, a most desirable education. As a preparation for the exercise of administrative responsibility, it is better than anything offered in a present university curriculum. It is no doubt necessary to train young men and women to present their knowledge and ideas with lucidity. But, if they are to be administrators, it is far more necessary to train them to listen carefully to what others say. Only he who knows how to help other persons to adequate expression can develop the many qualities demanded by a real maturity of judgment.

*Finally,* there remains the claim made above that the interview has proved to be the source of information of great objective value to management. The three persistent problems of modern large-scale industry have been stated as:

1. The application of science and technical skill to a material product.
2. The systematization of operations.
3. The organization of sustained cooperation.

When a representative of management claims that interview results are merely personal or subjective—and there are many who still echo this claim—he is actually telling us that he has himself been trained to give all his attention to the first and second problems, technical skill and the systematic ordering of operations; he does not realize that he has also been trained to ignore the third problem completely. For such persons, information on a problem, the existence of which they do not realize, is no information. It is no doubt in consequence of this ignorance or induced blindness that strikes or other difficulties so frequently occur in unexpected places. The interview method is the only method extant[14] that can contribute reasonably accurate information, or indeed any information, as to the extent of the actual cooperation between workers—teamwork—taht obtains in a given department, and beyond this, the extent to which this cooperation includes management policy or is wary of it. The Hawthorne inquiry at least specified these most important industrial issues and made some tentative steps toward the development of a method of diagnosis and treatment in particular cases.

## Notes

1. Cambridge, Harvard University Press, 1938, 2 vols.
2. *Management and Morale,* pp. 9–10.
3. Op. cit., p. 56.
4. For a full account of the experimental setup, see F. J. Roethlisberger and William J. Dickson, *Management and the Worker,* and T. North Whitehead, *The Industrial Worker,* Vol. 1.
5. For a full discussion of this type of interview, see F. J. Roethlisberger and William J. Dickson, op. cit., Chap. XIII. For a more summary and perhaps less technical discussion, see George C. Homans, *Fatigue of Workers* (New York, Reinhold Publishing Corporation, 1941).
6. Elton Mayo, *The Human Problems of an Indus-trial Civilization* (New York, The Macmillan Company, 1933; reprinted by Division of Research, Harvard Business School, 1946), p. 114.
7. Ibid.
8. F. J. Roethlisberger and William J. Dickson, op. cit., pp. 307–310.
9. F. J. Roethlisberger and William J. Dickson, op. cit., Part IV, pp. 379 ff.
10. For further evidence on this point, see Stanley B. Mathewson, *Restriction of Output among Unorganized Workers,* and also Elton Mayo, *The Human Problems of an Industrial Civilization,* pp. 119–121.
11. Shih Kuo-heng (Cambridge, Harvard University Press, 1944).
12. Ibid., Chap. VIII, pp. 111–127; also Chap. X, pp. 151–153.
13. Chap. III, supra.
14. We realize that there are at present in industry many individuals possessed of high skill in the actual handling of human situations. This skill usually derives from their own experience, is intuitive, and is not easily communicable.

---

## CASE STUDY 6

---

# Introduction

The concept of the informal group provides us with several critical insights into modern organizational life and the need for administrators to be realistic about what can and cannot be achieved, given the sentiments, feelings, values, and outlooks of men and women in any particular work setting. Clearly, as Mayo's essay points out, being realistic about the nature and workings of the human group is paramount in any successful administrative undertaking. Human groups present managers with both potentialities and pitfalls for effective internal operations. Whatever happens to organizations, these human groups must be considered.

The following case study by Curtis Copeland illustrates the importance of considering the human element before making any managerial innovations in the public sector. In this case, a city manager in a medium-sized Texas community hired a personnel director to establish a new city personnel department. With speed and efficiency the new director set out to develop a number of new personnel procedures where none had existed before and to make changes he considered necessary improvements for a modern community of its size, such as grievance procedures, performance-based selection procedures, and merit raises tied to annual bonuses.

Although these reforms had been developed by a well-regarded, outside consulting firm, they were proposed without prior employee consultation or involvement. The city employees became upset by the proposals because they were the ones directly affected by these new reforms. A controversy thus ensued involving not only the employees, but the city council and larger community as well, with important lessons for the practice of public administration as a result.

As you read this selection, keep the following questions in mind:

Specifically, what promoted the complaints by the employee groups relative to the newly proposed personnel changes? How were these complaints voiced?

How, in turn, did the personnel director and city manager respond to the complaints?

If you had been either the city manager or personnel director, would you have initiated such reforms in a different manner? As the city manager, how would you have handled the problems caused by the reforms?

Does the foregoing reading by Mayo contain useful ideas for securing worker cooperation with management in achieving organizational goals?

On the basis of your reading of this case study, can you generalize about the importance of informal groups in the public management processes?

# Personnel Changes in City Government*

**CURTIS COPELAND**

Jim Drummond, the city manager of Groveton, Texas, was a worried man. He had held his job for nearly two years, and during that time he and other city administrators had made a number of changes that were of benefit to the city, particularly in the field of personnel management. Those successes, however, were offset by the sometimes adverse reactions of the people affected by the changes. After a series of pitched battles, Drummond was now being pressured by the city council to dismiss the current personnel director, Dan Remmens. Drummond and Remmens had gone through a great deal together, but the dismissal of the personnel director could be the only way to please

Prepared under an IPA federal grant through the Office of Personnel Management and administered at the University of Pittsburgh. Neither the author nor the University of Pittsburgh maintain any rights to this case as it was prepared with federal funding.

*Note: The names of persons and local jurisdictions used in this case are entirely fictitious.

the council. In order to understand Drummond's dilemma, the reader must be given some background as to the setting and how the current situation developed.

## The Setting

The city of Groveton is a typical Texas community of about 60,000 tucked away in the pine woods of the Northeastern part of the state. Like many cities its size in the region, it is basically white and middle-class in nature, but with a poorer black population that has grown rapidly in the past twenty years. The main highway running through the town serves as a man-made boundary line for this racial and economic division, with the eastern portion of the city populated by the more well-to-do white families and the somewhat smaller western section occupied by blacks and other low-income groups. Most of the whites living in the western part of Groveton are older citizens, unable or unwilling to leave the homes in which their children were raised. They endure the steadily worsening conditions of their neighborhoods, hoping that their houses will last as long as they do.

Most of the city's working population is employed in one of wood products is the largest of these, due to the community's proximity to the abundant resources of the East Texas forests. About one-third of the working men in Groveton are employed in the wood-related industry, the companies ranging in size from the numerous small family operations to the giant Nortex plant located just outside the city limits. The other industries in the town may be classified under the general heading of "manufacturing," producing products as varied as Caterpiller tractors and office equipment. Most of these companies are nonunion, largely as a result of a "right-to-work" provision in the state constitution and the relatively high wages paid to the workers in these businesses.

The city grew rapidly when many of these industries arrived in Groveton in the late 1950's and early 1960's, but that growth slowed considerably in the next ten to fifteen years. Growth in the black community more than kept up that pace, however. By 1980, their rate of increase was twice that of the city as a whole. Attracted by the employment opportunities in the local industries, black families continued to migrate to Groveton from smaller communities in the area in the hope of finding a better life. Most of those that did find work, however, were employed in unskilled positions in most companies. By 1980, approximately 25 percent of the city's residents were black and another 5 percent were hispanic.

## Groveton Political Structure and Administration

The city of Groveton is governed and administered under a council-manager form of government. Five council members are selected in nonpartisan elections for staggered two-year terms of office. After each election, the council meets privately and selects one of its own to serve as mayor for the upcoming year. The decision is formalized in the first official council session after the election. The mayor's duties are largely ceremonial, although he is usually the council opinion leader in major decisions.

Prior to 1967, the city had a strong-mayor council form of government. Council members were selected in partisan elections using the place system, with

each portion of the city selecting its own council member to represent its interests and the mayor elected at large. In reaction to excesses of patronage and nonfeasance during the late 1950's and the first half of the 1960's by some members of the council, the citizens of Groveton approved a vastly revised city charter. Many reforms popular during the era were adopted, including the present form of government and at-large election system. Under the current form of government, the city manager is selected by majority vote of the city council and may be dismissed or reprimanded by that body at any time. The city manager, in turn, is the chief executive officer of the city, in charge of all city departments and personnel. He has the authority to hire and fire city personnel and to select department heads. According to newspaper articles published at the time of the reforms, the changes represented an attempt to "bring sound business and management principles to the city's administration."

Actually, however, the city's mode of administration changed relatively little during those years of transition. The city secretary, Jim Taylor, resigned to become the new city manager and continued to perform many of the tasks he had carried out during his seven years at his previous post. (The city secretary is a position required by state law in all Texas cities to perform most of the recordkeeping and official functions in the community. In smaller cities, this job is tantamount to being city manager.) The five city departments (water, streets, sanitation, police, and fire) virtually ran themselves, so all Taylor had to do was perform some minimal coordinative activities and oversee the city finance officer's job.

Taylor had no formal education in public management, although he did attend a few training sessions sponsored by the local regional planning commission over the years. He remained, however, unaware and uninterested in most aspects of modern management, and publicly scorned the new techniques. He often jokingly remarked that "most of the things they teach in those courses either don't work or you can't pronounce them." Nevertheless, the city ran smoothly during his administration and there were few complaints from either the council, the employees, or the city as a whole.

## Personnel Administration in Groveton

The city of Groveton employed nearly 500 people in 1980, but this was only slightly more than were working for the municipal government ten years earlier. Although personnel duties for nonuniformed employees were, according to the new city charter, legaly the providence of the city manager, Taylor had delegated that responsibility in large part to the line managers of the major city departments early in his administration. As was the case under the mayor-council form of government, the line managers in Groveton's municipal departments were each responsible for recruitment, selection and control of the employees within their departments. Although each manager administered a general intelligence test, a major part of the selection process involved an oral interview and a background check. If the applicant had no record or prior arrests and seemed capable of getting along reasonably well with other employees, he or she would probably be hired.

The selection of uniformed personnel, those in the fire and police departments, is governed by a state civil service law. Under the provisions of the law, each city of 10,000 or greater is required to have a civil service commission selected by the city council. The commission is primarily charged with the responsibility of insuring the unbiased selection of fire and police officers and to act as an appeals board to which those officers may complain about unfair treatment. In Groveton, commission members have traditionally been respected businessmen and civic leaders. Over the years, however, the fire and police chiefs (like the managers in the other departments) assumed primary responsibility for recruitment and selection. Most of the time the commission's duties were confined to certification of the top three candidates for open positions (as required by state law) and hearing an occasional appeal from a disgruntled officer.

Since the line managers and the civil service commission performed most of the personnel-related duties, City Manager Taylor did little in the way of actual personnel management. In fact, Taylor liked to refer to his personnel department as the "bottom-right drawers of the big filing cabinet." It was there that a clerk in his office kept records of all employees in separate folders, with such information as the date of their selection, current salary, job title, absences, and supervisor reprimands. Taylor believed the essence of a sound personnel system was the maintenance of accurate records so every employment-related action that occurred in the city was duly recorded. Groveton's personnel system, like other city operations, ran without any

major problems and the city council rarely if ever became involved in its operations.

# City Manager Changes Lead to a New Personnel System

After thirteen years as city manager, Taylor announced his retirement as chief executive officer to "make way for a younger man." The city council reluctantly accepted his resignation and, after a two-month search, decided to hire Mr. Thomas ("Jim") Drummond as the new chief administrator. Drummond had been working as the assistant city manager in San Benedict in West Texas, and was a graduate of a state university not far from Groveton. He was anxious to take the job, not only because he would be moving back to the area in which he had gone to school, but also because he had a strong desire to use the management skills he had acquired as a result of his education and experience in San Benedict. Drummond recognized the political dimensions of his job, however, as he had seen the city manager in San Benedict fired because he disagreed with the will of the city council. But he was equally convinced that sound management practices could be applied in even the most foreboding of environments.

Drummond spent his first month or so in Groveton "learning the ropes." He held meetings with the department heads both separately and as a group to explain his philosophy of management and to hear their suggestions. As a result of these discussions and his own observations, the city's need for an autonomous personnel department became more and more apparent. He realized that if any semblance of coordinated management were to evolve in Groveton, some means of centralized staffing and control would be needed. The city manager decided to discuss the development of a personnel department at the next council work session.

As was mentioned earlier, the council was composed of five city businessmen. Two members of the council were essentially "followers"—that is, they usually voiced their opinions only when asked and even then said very little. The leaders were the Mayor, Earnest Wilson, and Councilmen Calvin Johnson and Albert Hunt. Wilson owned several small businesses in the city and had served on the council for eight years. Johnson owned a real estate agency and Hunt was an industrial engineer at the Nortex lumber plant.

All three men were fiscal conservatives in most matters, and all three were long-term residents of Groveton.

Drummond gave an opening statement at the meeting during which he expressed his belief that the city needed a personnel department, outlined the approximate cost of the change to the city, and waited for the council's reaction. After a somewhat awkward silence, Mayor Wilson's comments clearly indicated he did not share Drummond's enthusiasm for management change.

*Mayor Wilson:* Jim, you know we want you to run this city in a more business-like fashion, and that we respect your ideas and opinions. But I don't think that Groveton really needs a full-fledged personnel department. After all, we have gotten along pretty well without one in the past. And besides, it's not as if this is Dallas or Houston or anything. We've got a small operation here and don't have any immediate plans to put on any new people.

*Councilman Hunt:* I agree, Earnest. Jim Taylor kept this city on an even keel for more years than I would like to remember. He kept good records on each and every employee. He even sent Christmas cards out to each employee every year. And birthday cards too! Now that was coordination! We've never had any real crisis among city employees so I don't see the need for a change right now.

*Drummond:* But gentlemen, we may be leading up to a "crisis" if something isn't done ahead of time. Look, I realize that Jim Taylor did a good job for the city these past thirteen years or so. And I know you all liked and respected what he did for the city. But personnel management has changed a lot in that time, too. It is no longer good enough to "keep good records." This city, like all others, must keep up with the times.

*Wilson:* OK, Jim. We all realize that, but I just don't think we are ready to do something drastic like create a new city department. Why don't we do this. Why don't you get that young assistant of yours to do a study to determine if we need a personnel department, and we will take it up again at next month's work session. Alright?

*Drummond:* But we don't *need* a study, Mayor. It is perfectly obvious. Look at Jacksborough (a city about

the size of Groveton some seventy-five miles away). They have had a personnel department since they adopted the city manager form of government in 1965.

Better yet, look at the major companies in this town. Most of them wouldn't think of operating without a personnel section. And neither should we. If I am to run this city in a more business-like manner, we have to start taking lessons from them.

All you have to do is give me the authority to spend about $30,000 of the money we have left over from the sanitation budget for a director and one staff position. I will make the necessary changes in the administrative regulations, delegating personnel authority to the director, and we can get started. It is as simple as that.

*Hunt:* You know, Earnest, he has a point. Out at Nortex we've got three people working full time in a personnel department and we don't have but about 400 employees all together in the plant.

*Wilson:* All right, Jim, you've made your point. But where will this personnel department of yours be housed? You yourself have said that office conditions are cramped in City Hall already. Won't this be another problem we will have to deal with?

*Johnson:* We could always put them in the basement of the Annex, Earnest. It's not being used for anything but storage right now. We could probably manage it, at least for a while.

After some further discussion, the council finally agreed to fund the new personnel department for a two year period. Formal approval was granted at the next scheduled council meeting the following week. As he drove home from the meeting that evening, however, Drummond could not shake the impression that had he wanted to build a new bridge or road, spend more money on street repair, or even buy a new garbage truck with the sanitation money he would have met with little if any council resistance. These would have been "monuments" to their political eras—physical proof of the good they had done for the city. "Invisible" management changes were different, however. They were of little or no political benefit, and might even backfire.

Drummond realized that this "bricks and morter orientation" was not unique to the Groveton City Council, for he had seen it in San Benedict as well.

The political leaders did not seem to understand that focusing solely upon visible changes was not only an inefficient use of the city's resources, but that it also ignored Groveton's largest resource and expenditures—its personnel. Nearly 75 percent of the annual budget was allocated for personnel costs. Every department and every operation within city government was dependent upon those who would carry out those tasks. Therefore, he concluded, the most important changes are those which determine the quality and effectiveness of those people carrying out the city's business, even though they are "invisible" at times. It was now up to Drummond to prove that philosophy correct.

City Manager Drummond began the search for a personnel director the following morning, and within a few weeks he selected Dan Remmens for the job. Because the personnel director answered directly to the city manager, council approval for Remmen's hire (beyond the allocation of funds) was not required. Remmens had known Drummond at the university they attended some years before, and had been employed as a personnel specialist within the City of Dallas' personnel division for two years. Like Drummond, Remmens was tired of just being a "cog in a big machine" and longed for the greater responsibility and freedom of action that comes with being an administrator in a small city, even though it meant a slight reduction in pay. Both men were convinced that they would make a good working team.

In order for the new personnel director to properly exercise his authority, many of the personnel-related duties performed by the line managers in the departments were transferred to the newly created personnel office. As was mentioned earlier, these managers had exercised virtually complete control over the hiring and promotion processes in their departments during the period Taylor was city manager. The forthcoming diminution in their authority did little to engender support for the new city manager or the personnel director.

Drummond was aware of this reaction, and had even expected it to happen. Shortly after the decision to hire Remmens was announced, the city manager called a meeting of the department heads and the new personnel director to explain the new procedures and to hear their comments. After a brief exchange of pleasantries, the city manager got down to the matter that was on everyone's mind.

*Drummond:* Gentlemen, I realize that you have had to perform many of the personnel functions in this city in the past. You have had people coming directly to you for jobs and you have had to handle all the paperwork pretty much on your own. At the same time, you have had the freedom to select the people you think are best for your departments and this city. What we plan to do in the future will make your jobs easier, but not cut into your authority or the operations of your departments.

From now on, all applications for jobs will be handled by the personnel department, headed by Mr. Dan Remmens. Mr. Remmens will administer examinations where needed and screen out all the "undesirables" before they get to your departments. He will then refer some number of applicants to your department for the interview and final decision. Therefore, you will still have the final word as to who will work for you and how the jobs should be done. All we are trying to do in this area is centralize the operations a bit and take some of the paperwork off your backs.

At this point, let me introduce Dan Remmens.

*Remmens:* Thank you, Jim. First of all, let me say that I am pleased to be in Groveton, and I am sure that we can work together effectively for the good of the city. I concur with what the city manager just said. I am not going to take over your jobs, just make them easier. As I see it, I will just be coordinating personnel duties a little more and making the operations more uniform. You will no longer have to keep track of job applicants or give tests. We can work out some reasonable relationship concerning job referrals, qualifications, and so on. In short, I'd like to think that I can help you manage your departments better. We can discuss the details of all of this at your convenience. I'm looking forward to working with you.

*Drummond:* Any questions?

*Jack Collier (Sanitation Supervisor):* Yeah. I've got a question. When can you start? If my job is going to get easier, I'm ready for you right now!

The brief meeting broke up amiably and Drummond was convinced that it had been a success. The supervisors' suspicions seem to have dissipated considerably when it became clear what the personnel director's (and their) responsibility would be and that they would still be able to make the decisions concerning selections and discipline of employees in their departments.

# The New Personnel Director Takes Over

The following Monday, Remmens officially entered his new job with the City of Groveton. As the city manager had explained the job to him in the interview, it was largely a matter of "interpretation" of applicable city ordinances and state laws. Although he had the authority to write administrative procedure for city personnel, he could not add job titles, hire and fire employees in other departments, or change the ordinances passed by the city council. Before taking any action, however, Remmens felt he should familiarize himself with the city's current personnel "department"—the bottom drawers of the filing cabinets where former City Manager Taylor kept the personnel records.

The contents of that file revealed that the city lacked even the most rudimentary of personnel systems, and as a result the operations of the city as a whole suffered. Almost no data on employee characteristics or performance were maintained. Although job descriptions were noted, they were all over fifteen years old and were clearly out of date since the nature of the jobs in the city had changed a great deal during that period. The selection process, as mentioned earlier, consisted of a general aptitude test given to all applicants, a background check, and an interview. Also, no established grievance system other than complaints to the employee's immediate supervisor existed in the city. Finally, employees were given "merit raises" (bonuses) based upon their annual salaries once per year despite declines in production in virtually every department. Supervisors blamed the performance problems on the "poor quality of new employees," of which there were many. The city's turnover rate for all positions approached 85 percent.

Appalled by what the "filing-cabinet personnel department" revealed, Remmens met with the city manager to discuss the ramifications and how to deal with them. The two men decided that two immediate actions were called for before any other changes could be made. First, a basic social survey of all employees should be conducted, gathering data on personnel characteristics and the nature of their employment.

With these data, the manager and the personnel director believed that they could more clearly see what sort of employees the city had and what jobs they actually performed. Secondly, all city jobs should be analyzed for up-to-date job descriptions and to set job qualifications and performance standards. Although the first of these two actions could be conducted in-house, both Drummond and Remmens recognized that the second required outside assistance.

## Social Survey

Department supervisors were called in and the issue of the social survey was discussed at length. Although all parties agreed that such information would be valuable, the line managers were not quite sure what the city manager and the personnel director had up their sleeves. Their main concern was not the collection process itself or what would be discovered, but to what ends that information would be used once collected. Their suspicions were kept largely to themselves, however, and the social survey was conducted without any major problem.

The data indicated that the city was in even worse shape than either Drummond or Remmens had imagined. Only forty-seven of Groveton's nearly 500 employees were black, and only two were hispanic. All but three of these minority employees were working in either the streets or sanitation departments. No blacks had worked in the police department prior to 1973 and none had ever been employed in the fire department or had been a supervisor in the other departments. Women were similarly underrepresented, particularly in the fire and police departments. In sum, the city of Groveton was ripe for an EEO lawsuit. It was a classic case of "adverse impact" as defined in the Federal Uniform Selection Guidelines.

The fire and police chiefs told the personnel director that they had tried to get "qualified" minorities on their respective forces, but without much success. It seemed that a high percentage of the black and hispanic candidates either failed the aptitude tests given or were screened out by the interviews. Female applicants were often ruled out by the city's height and weight requirements.

## Job Analysis

In order for the job analysis to be conducted properly, both Drummond and Remmens realized it would have to be conducted by qualified professionals. That, of course, meant an expense that would have to be authorized and paid for by the city council. Realizing the councilmen's reluctance to spend city tax dollars on "invisible" changes, the two men sought external help to finance the analysis and to convince the council of its utility.

Remmens had worked with several Intergovernmental Personnel Act (IPA) grants[1] while employed by the City of Dallas, and wrote to the regional office there for information on their availability. With that information and the assistance of the local council of governments, the personnel director was able to obtain the commitment of Federal officials in Dallas to fund one-fourth of the expense of a consultant to conduct the job analysis. Both Remmens and Drummond realized that the more difficult portion of the process was just beginning—to convince the council to allow the expenditure of the city's portion of the study's cost.

The two men, accompanied by a representative from the council of governments, approached the council at the next work session. They explained why the job analysis and position classification were needed and made it clear that much of the city's expense would be absorbed through the provision of in-house services. Although initially skeptical, the enticement of Federal funds for what turned out to be a minimal investment proved to be too attractive to pass up. The city's portion of the expense was agreed to at the next council meeting with a surprising lack of resistance, and the grant application received Federal approval shortly thereafter.

Remmens and his assistant did most of the administrative duties involved in the analysis themselves, and the entire process was completed within a short while. The results provided the personnel director with information he needed concerning the tasks which comprise each city job, the skills needed to perform those tasks, and provided the basis upon which subsequent changes could be made. However, exactly what those changes should be and how they should be administered were in no way clarified. Based upon the information from the survey and the job analysis, Drummond and Remmens finally decided that three changes should be made as soon as possible:

1. codification of employee grievance procedures;
2. begin using valid performance-based selection procedures where possible; and

3. begin a real "merit pay" system by tying annual bonuses to performance evaluations.

# Grievance Procedure Codification

The two men decided that the codification of grievance procedures should be accomplished first, since it required no council action, no expenditure of city funds, and involved only nonuniformed personnel. (Fire and police grievance procedures were codified in the state civil service law.) It was also a change that many municipal employees apparently wanted to take place. Several city workers had approached both Drummond and Remmens about problems they were experiencing with their work assignments. These were particularly aggravating since most of the complaints could have been resolved at a much lower level of supervision.

In addition, many superior employees had reportedly resigned in the past because their complaints never went beyond their supervisors. According to several current employees, City Manager Taylor refused to become involved in these disputes, telling dissatisfied employees to "work it out with your boss." Since many of the complaints concerned their supervisors, the employees either learned to accept the situation or left the organization. Grievances which *were* settled often took over a year to complete, and often resulted in grossly unequal treatment.

The appeals process adopted by executive order was relatively simple and straightforward, copying in form if not in substance the grievance procedure of the nearby city of Jacksborough. Four levels of appeal were delineated, the first of which remained the employee's immediate supervisor (provided that the supervisor was not the subject of the complaint). The next two levels were the department manager and the director of personnel. If the grievance was still not settled, it could then be submitted to the city's Civil Service Commission in accordance with its appeal procedures. The entire process was to be completed within ninety days.

The change in appeals procedures was announced to city employees through notices posted in the departments and information sheets inserted in their pay envelopes. Within a few weeks the new process was running even more smoothly than had been expected. An initial flurry of complaints, stimulated in part by the new procedures, was handled to the satisfaction of most parties, and only a few reached the personnel director. Although Drummond and Remmens were pleased with their progress, they realized the other two innovations were going to be even more difficult, for they posed both real and imagined threats to various segments of the workforce.

## Performance Selection

Drummond and Remmens were particularly anxious to get the new selection methods started, as the city could ill-afford an expensive lawsuit brought about by the currently used aptitude tests, interviews, and background checks. Since many of the entry-level positions in the city were of the unskilled or semi-skilled variety, the use of aptitude tests for these positions was especially questionable. Remmens was enthusiastic about the prospect of change in this area, and discussed the possibilities with City Manager Drummond.

*Remmens:* Jim, I think we have a chance to really make this city a showplace in the area of selection and staffing. We could not only avoid the EEO problems, but could set an example for other cities in the area or even the whole state. Groveton could become a model in the field with the changes we can make.

*Drummond:* Hold on, Dan. What sort of changes do you have in mind? After all, we do have the council to consider. You *do* remember the council, don't you? They haven't exactly been overjoyed with the prospect of spending money, you know.

*Remmens:* These changes won't cost much at all. All it will take is a strong desire on our part to make it work. I think we can set up a modified assessment center here and get rid of those intelligence tests that seem to be our biggest problem. Have you ever seen the system they have in Dallas?

*Drummond:* No, I haven't seen it but I've heard it is pretty complicated.

*Remmens:* Not really. All it involves is the use of the job descriptions in a performance format. For example, if a man's job involved garbage collections, he should be able to lift a can of garbage, dump it in the truck, and follow instructions. A back-hoe operator

should essentially have to demonstrate that he knows how to operate a back-hoe. The same principle could be applied to the selection of managers and in promotional decisions. We can give them an in-basket test of the type of things they need to be able to do on the job and select the ones that are the highest scorers.

*Drummond:* If we are really going to touch all the bases on this thing, won't we have to validate the tests or something?

*Remmens:* Sure. Before we can start using them we have to show they are related to jobs. That is why we need to begin now. According to this EEOC guidebook, the first step should be the publication of our affirmative action program, of which this will be a major part.

*Drummond:* OK, then, let's get started. But be sure to follow those guidelines to the letter. I want to be able to explain the city's actions to the council and others as part of the federal mandate. There are a lot of people that may take offense to this sort of thing. Hopefully, we can explain it to the council *after* it is in place and running smoothly.

After the meeting, Remmens drafted an affirmative action statement based upon the suggestions in the EEOC manual and those he had seen elsewhere. It was a relatively simple document citing the city's poor record of minority hiring in the past and proposing goals for the future. The statement was printed in the local newspaper as pat of a larger article on city hall happenings, along with Remmens' predictions that new professionally developed methods of selection would soon be utilized in Groveton. That process of constructing and validating the exams had not gone very far, however, when it ran into some major obstacles.

About two weeks after the plans were announced, a committee of black citizens confronted the city council at their formal evening meeting and publicly blasted the city for its hiring record. Citing figures they had received from the newspaper and elsewhere, they demanded a speedy end to the pattern of black exclusion from the city's fire and police departments. Unless changes were made immediately, they argued, preparations would be made to seek redress in the courts and at the ballot box. Municipal elections were scheduled to be held in about three months.

Several spokesmen for the fire and police employees also expressed their concern about municipal hiring policies, albeit more privately and in a different direction. They were concerned that the new "performance" tests would be catered to the needs of the black community to too great an extent. As a result, they feared that fire and police trainees selected would be of a lesser quality than required to perform the jobs properly. Plans to select virtually every job through performance tests were met with equal derision. One supervisor in the streets department was quoted as saying, "I'll be damned if I am going to let some guy off the street 'try out' on one of our $40,000 pieces of equipment. No way!"

Although the development of the resentment in each area is a story in itself, one thing had become quite clear. Instead of setting the stage for positive action, the publication of the plan generated a great deal of unexpected controversy and sparked an anger within the community that lay just below the surface. Mayor Wilson and Councilmen Johnson and Hunt held a hurried meeting with Drummond and Remmens shortly after the stormy council session with the black leaders. That meeting proved to be equally tumultuous.

*Wilson:* Dan and Jim, I will admit right off that I don't know as much about personnel management or city management as you do. But I *do* know this community. That "affirmative action plan" of yours has been anything but "affirmative" here. The public is upset, the employees are upset, and frankly I am too.

*Drummond:* I can understand and appreciate your concern, Mayor, but this situation has been brewing for some time. Maybe we had better just proceed with our plan and let the black community and the employees know exactly what is going on. After all, we are not doing anything so different here than is going on all over the United States. And validating these performance tests takes time to do it right.

*Johnson:* Unfortunately this is *not* "all over the United States." This is Groveton, Texas. Do you think the people here understand or care that we are doing this "for their own good" or that "validations take time?" They want action now or else. And if they don't get action, they will take some of their own.

*Remmens:* But we *are* taking action, the kind that this city needs. And if they don't understand it, well then that is just something we will have to explain better in the future. Perhaps if we had done that in the begin-

ning—I mean years ago—we wouldn't have the problems we have today.

*Wilson:* Gentlemen, we could continue placing the blame for this from now until next week. However, I think we had better get on with the solution to this and right away. It is not something that we can allow to go on indefinately.

Dan, can't you just get a validated test used somewhere else and be done with it?

*Remmens:* Written tests can be purchased for some jobs like firemen and policemen, but they need to be locally validated before being used on a wide-scale basis.

*Wilson:* Since most of this flack is coming from the fire and police departments, I suggest that you buy and start using a fire and police exam, announce that it has been validated elsewhere and that it will be valid here too, and that should solve the problem. I would also suggest that it be done *immediately*. You can go ahead with your performance tests in some of the other jobs, but you'd better get this fire and police thing settled *now*.

Although the personnel director and city manager disagreed with the mayor's plan at first, it became clear that the council was adamant. The meeting adjourned with Remmens and Drummond agreeing to make the necessary changes. Generally validated written tests were again the primary selection devices used in the police and fire departments. The black leaders were cautiously pleased with the results, but promised to watch for the tests' effects on black applicants.

In the other departments, the changes were also more modest than expected, due to the negative reactions the proposed changes had generated. Still, the most obvious deficiencies in the earlier system were corrected. Laborers no longer had to pass intelligence tests for work on sanitation trucks or road crews. The changes instituted were painful for some and more limited than hoped for, but they had occurred.

## Merit Pay

About six months after the performance-based examination process was announced, Personnel Director Remmens decided to go forward with the merit pay innovation. As mentioned earlier, the city had had a "merit pay" concept in operation for some time, but made no effort to tie the awards to performance appraisals. In fact, the only performance evaluations attempted were simple "unsatisfactory-satisfactory" employee ratings done by department supervisors, in which virtually all workers were judged to be in the "satisfactory" (i.e., meritorious) category. In some instances, employees were rated "satisfactory," given merit bonuses, and two months later were recommended for suspension or termination.

The new merit bonuses were to be based upon the position descriptions and qualification requirements derived as a result of the earlier job analysis. After developing an evaluation form, Remmens told department and first-line supervisors how to use the new procedures and provided other information about the program. They were also told that, unlike under the earlier system, only 50 percent of the employees in each department would be eligible for merit increases in order to make the awards more competitive. The bonuses would be financed from a percentage of each department's total salary package.

Word of this change in procedure spread rapidly. By the time the plan was made official, virtually every municipal employee knew what was in the offing. Although some city workers were glad to see the advent of a true merit system, the predominate emotion was one of profound mistrust and suspicion. Both supervisors and lower-level employees felt threatened by the change. Supervisors were concerned that they were going to jeopardize the trust and friendship they enjoyed with their employees if they had to exclude onehalf of them from receiving what had become an annual pay supplement. They were also wary of the time and energy required by the new process and how this would affect their every-day supervision. The employees, on the other hand, were not convinced that the new evaluation system was workable or that they would be treated fairly by a process that had been developed without their involvement.

Despite these misgivings, plans were made to put the proposal into effect throughout the city at the start of the new fiscal year. Both City Manager Drummond and Personnel Director Remmens were aware of the grumblings among city employees, but took no overt action to respond to them other than by counseling individual employees. Remmens was convinced that these problems would be short-lived and

that the merit pay plan would be successful by the end of the first year. Such resistance to change was to be expected, he said, but by sticking with the original plan, the complaints would slowly dissipate. Shortly before the official kick-off date for the new performance evaluations, however, Remmens' predictions again proved somewhat less than accurate.

A meeting of city employees was held one evening in which representatives of each city department were selected to talk to Drummond and Remmens about the new pay plan. Before that meeting, Drummond and Remmens met for lunch to discuss the matter at length and present a united front. The two men discussed the complaints they had heard previously and then each gave his impression of what should be done. There, the first real split between them surfaced.

*Drummond:* Dan, I think we should go slow with this new merit pay plan. After all, starting this sort of thing in Groveton would be like moving from the ice age into the space age. You've got to consider where we are coming from. People need time to adjust to something like this.

*Remmens:* Are you saying we shouldn't have real merit pay in this city? Is that annual gratuity for hanging on another year what we really want?

*Drummond:* Of course not. But we probably shouldn't spring it on them all at once, either. Look, I'm as anxious to get this town into the 1980's as much as you are. But this kind of thing can cause all kinds of problems. People feel threatened, and when they do they naturally try to protect their turf. We have got to figure out some way to make it less threatening to them while still making progress. That may mean we will have to take a more subtle tack than we had planned.

*Remmens:* You have something in mind, I hope?

*Drummond:* Well, not exactly.

May be we could do it on a small scale first. You know, kind of try it out on one group and then gradually expand it to all employees.

*Remmens:* And which division do you think will step forward to be first? They are *not* exactly falling over each other to be evaluated, you know.

Look, Jim, things like this are too important to do half-heartedly. If we evaluate one group and not another, then you are *really* going to hear the complaints of unfair treatment. What we need to do is go into this meeting firm in our resolve that what we are doing is right.

The two men failed to agree on a concerted strategy, and left for the meeting without resolving the issue.

That afternoon, representatives from all five divisions sat across the table from the city manager and the personnel director. Remmens again explained the rationale behind the plan, and the employees voiced no strong objections. After a somewhat restrained discussion from all parties, Harold Leavitt, an employee in the streets department, clearly expressed what most city employees were feeling.

*Leavitt:* Look, Mr. Drummond. We don't have any quarrel with being paid for how hard we work. I'm sure that most of the people working for the city feel like they deserve their bonuses and would get them under any fair system. The problem is that we don't think it is a fair system. You've got studies by someone who has never patched a street or driven a truck telling you what it is we do and what is important in the streets department. The same thing is true in all the other departments. I'm sure we could do as good a job as he did or even better.
(Nods and mumblings of agreement from the other employees present.)

*Remmens:* Mr. Leavitt, the study upon which the evaluation forms were designed was done by one of the finest consulting firms in the country. They have done similar job analyses and position descriptions in Dallas, Oklahoma City, St. Louis, and lots of other places.

*Leavitt:* Frankly, I don't care *where* they have done their work before coming here. If you think they are so good at setting these performance standards, why don't you use the ones they developed for *your* job first?

I just don't think that we should be at the mercy of someone who doesn't really know what we do. It's got a lot of people plenty upset. Some of the people are even starting to talk about getting a union started. Now you don't want that and neither do most of us. But something's got to give.

*Drummond:* Harold, let me pick up on something you said a minute ago. You said you thought you

could do as good a job as the consulting firm did. Well, would you like a chance to try?

*Leavitt and Remmens* (simultaneously): What?

*Drummond:* I said, if you think you could do a better job in setting up the evaluations, why don't you give it a shot? You could use the forms that were developed for your jobs as a starting place and work from there. I'm sure we could start the evaluations a little late so we could get your comments. What do you say?

*Leavitt:* Well, I'll have to talk it over with the others but I think that sounds reasonable.

*Drummond:* Good. We'll talk more about it next week, then. Meanwhile, you get back with your people and I'll talk to the supervisors. Together, I think we can still get the program started.

After the meeting, Personnel Director Remmens was livid. He strongly objected to, what he termed, "caving in" to the demands of the employees.

*Remmens:* I can't believe that you are going to let them set their own performance standards. Do you realize what that means? First of all, they will probably come in here with standards that will be so ludicrous that we won't be able to use them. Then we will be worse off than we are now. Also, they now have the impression that they can get whatever they want just by coming in here and making demands. They don't need a union; they've got one already.

*Drummond:* Dan, I know you are upset, but I don't think you realize the nature of the situation we have here. Performance evaluation is an issue that can bring all those people together like no other. And if you think we have trouble from the employees or the council now, just wait until this city gets a union. Then the council will blame you for causing it and will not give you any money for *any* of your ideas.

*Remmens:* Since you are making the decisions, I guess that means you are right. I guess this also means that you plan to run the personnel department from your office from now on, then?

*Drummond:* If I have to.

At that, the two men parted company and did not speak to each other for the remainder of the week.

Drummond negotiated with the line supervisors and arranged a meeting with employee representatives for the following Friday. Remmens continued to operate his department and to perform his regular duties, but refused to alter his position that the job analysis derived performance standards be accepted without change. Any "tampering" with those standards he considered an abrogation of management rights.

Drummond had one more discussion with the employees on this matter, but could not ethically or legally go forward with the development of the performance standards without Remmens involvement. He felt bad about the situation, but decided to allow things to cool off a little more before taking any action.

Mayor Wilson and the other members of the city council heard about the problems the new performance evaluations were causing a short while after the meeting. Although they were unaware of the specifics, the council also knew about the split between the city manager and the personnel director over which standards should be used in the performance appraisals. The one thing they wished to avoid was the establishment of a union in Groveton, and this question of standards was clearly pushing them in that direction. There had even been talk of a petition circulating that would establish a bargaining unit in the city. As a result, two council members—Hunt and Johnson—met privately with City Manager Drummond to discuss the matter. They urged him to dismiss Remmens for insubordination and get on with the process. This, they felt, would cut short any unionization effort and end the major part of the problem.

This, then, was the situation Drummond faced at the beginning of this review. He and Remmens had gone through much together, but it could be that his dismissal would be the only way to appease the council. If Remmens was fired, any subsequent personnel director would, based on past experience, probably be reticent to undertake any such sweeping reforms. That was probably what the councilmen had in mind. Who could have foreseen that such a simple thing as a performance-based bonus system would cause such complex problems?

Drummond scheduled another meeting with the employee representatives to iron out the details of their agreement. Before that meeting, he decided to resolve once and for all the problems between Remmens and himself. He sent a memo to the personnel director asking him to stop by as soon as possible.

## Note

1. Begun in 1971, IPA allows recipients to receive matching funds for personnel changes, technical assistance, temporary mobility assignments between levels of government or academia, and other forms of assistance. The purpose of the IPA program is to develop and strengthen state and local personnel management.

## Chapter 6 Review Questions

1. What is your definition of an informal group in organizations?
2. How are informal groups formed and how do they influence the activities of public organizations?
3. Do informal groups emerge and have an impact on *public* organizations in the same ways as they do upon *business* organizations?
4. If you had been City Manager Drummond or Personnel Director Remmens, would you have initiated such personnel changes any differently? If so, how?
5. Can you see any evidence of the influence of informal groups in organizations with which you are familiar? If so, how did these groups emerge and in what ways do they affect the policies and activities of those organizations?
6. Based on your personal observations of the workings of informal groups, would you modify the Mayo-Roethlisberger concept in any way? For example, could you add more specifics about how to identify informal groups?

Measure their strength? Identify sources of influence in organizations? Reasons for weakness? Methods for achieving the support of management? Ways of communication? Means of motivation?

## Key Terms

informal group
"great illumination"
social structure

Hawthorne experiments
interview program
scientific-technological change

## Suggestions for Further Reading

The best book about the Hawthorne experiments is Fritz Roethlisberger and W.J. Dickson, *Management and the Worker* (Cambridge, Mass.: Harvard University Press, 1939). For a less complicated view, see Fritz Roethlisberger, *Management and Morale* (Cambridge, Mass.: Harvard University Press, 1941). Elton Mayo's broad philosophic interpretations are contained in his "trilogy": *The Human Problems of an Industrial Organization* (New York: Macmillan Co., 1933); *The Social Problems of an Industrial Civilization* (Boston: Graduate School of Business Administration, Harvard University, 1945); and *The Political Problems of an Industrial Civilization* (same publisher, 1947). For an excellent retrospective on Hawthorne, refer to "An Interview with Fritz Roethlisberger," *Organizational Dynamics,* 1 (Autumn 1972), pp. 31-45, and "Hawthorne Revisited: The Legend and the Legacy," *Organizational Dynamics,* 4 (Winter 1975), pp. 66–80.

Two excellent and now classic interpretations of Hawthorne are George Homans, *The Human Group* (New York: Harcourt, Brace, 1950) and Henry Landsberger, *Hawthorne Revisited* (Ithaca, N.Y.: Cornell University Press, 1958). By contrast, to taste a small sampling of the scholarly arguments over Hawthorne, read Alex Carey, "The Hawthorne Studies: A Radical Criticism," *American Sociological Review,* 32 (June 1967), pp. 403–416; and for a review of small group theory applied to public admin-

istration, see Robert T. Golembiewski, "The Small Group and Public Administration," *Public Administration Review,* 19 (Summer 1959), pp. 149–156. For some interesting new perspectives on the psychological dimensions of public management, see Richard L. Schott, "The Psychological Development of Adults: Implications for Public Administration," *Public Administration Review,* 46 (November/December 1986), pp. 657–667; and Larry Hirshhorn, *The Workplace Within: Psychodynamics of Organizational Life* (Cambridge, Mass.: MIT Press, 1991).

The legacy of Hawthorne can be found in numerous examples of the prolific postwar authors associated with the Human Relations School of Management, Chris Argyris, Warren Bennis, Frederick Herzberg, Daniel Katz, Robert Kahn, Rensis Likert, Douglas McGregor, Leonard Sayles, William Whyte, and many, many others who owe a tremendous debt to Hawthorne. In turn, their "spinoffs" and "impacts" on public administration have been profound and numerous but largely uncharted by scholars in the field, though for a useful compilation of many of their writings, refer to Frank J. Thompson, ed., *Classics of Public Personnel Policy,* 2nd ed., (Monterey, Calif.: Brooks/Cole, 1991); Jay Shafritz et al., eds., *Classics of Public Administration,* Second Edition, (Chicago: Dorsey Press, 1987); Thomas H. Patten, *Classics of Personnel Man-*

*agement* (Chicago: Moore Publishing Co., 1979); and Louis E. Boone and Donald D. Bowen, eds., *The Great Writings in Management and Organizational Behavior* (Tulsa, Okla.: The Petroleum Publishing Co., 1980). For a current overview of this topic, read Charles Perrow, *Complex Organizations: A Critical Essay,* Second Edition (Glenview, Ill.: Scott, Foresman, 1979), as well as Larry M. Lane and James El Wolf, *The Human Resource Crisis in the Public Sector: Rebuilding the Capacity to Govern* (New York: Quorum Books, 1991). For a similar point of view, read the Volcker Commission Report, entitled, "The

Report of the National Commission on the Public Service," *Leadership for America: Rebuilding the Public Service* (Lexington, Mass.: Lexington Books, 1990). Interestingly, it is perhaps the success of Japanese business in recent years that has brought renewed attention on the informal group as the basis for effective management by Americans, as reflected in such popular texts as William Ouchi, *Theory Z: How American Business Can Meet the Japanese Challenge* (New York: Avon Books, 1982). Note the heavy influence of Hawthorne thinking in this and other such writings about the Japanese success story.

# CHAPTER 7

## Key Decision Makers in Public Administration: The Concept of the Professional State

*For better or worse—or better and worse—much of our government is now in the hands of professionals. . . .*

*Frederick C. Mosher*

## READING 7

## Introduction

Nearly five million people work for the federal government, and another ten million work in state and local governments in the United States. They may be engineers working on the Panama Canal, foresters in Alaska, city managers in Texas, highway patrol officers in California, or public school teachers in Boston—all are public servants who carry out the varied important and not-so-important tasks that society calls on government to undertake.

Frederick C. Mosher (1913–1990) was a distinguished scholar and practitioner of public administration, who spent more than three decades of teaching in the field, first at the Maxwell School, Syracuse University, later at the University of California, Berkeley, and finally as the Doherty Professor of Government and Foreign Affairs at the University of Virginia. In his brilliant study *Democracy and the Public Service* (now updated in its Second Edition), which won the first Brownlow prize for the outstanding book published in the field, Professor Mosher gives us perhaps the best and most convincing analysis of the character of contemporary American public service. His central argument is that the people who work for government today in appointed positions are increasingly becoming professionalized in terms of their skills and the substance of their work. His statistics show that more than one third of government employees are now engaged in professional or technical pursuits—"three times the comparable proportion in the private sector." The number of professionals working in the public sector has increased since the first quarter of this century, when the U.S.

Classification Act of 1923 established a professional and scientific service, and has continued to increase over the years as civil service ratings have offered increasing incentives for specialized training and advanced skills. The demands for skilled workers have also grown because the tasks of government, particularly since the Depression and World War II, have become increasingly more complex in nature and broader in scope. In short, Mosher characterizes the public service at all levels of bureaucracy as "the professional state."

By *professional* Mosher means: "1) a reasonably clear-cut occupational field, 2) which ordinarily requires higher education at least through the bachelor's level, 3) which offers a lifetime career to its members." These individuals include lawyers and physicians who happen to hold government jobs as well as public professionals such as diplomats or military officers whose professions are generated within government and are dependent solely on public sector employment. Individual professional specialists have come to dominate public agencies, for example, military officers in the Defense Department, physicians in the Public Health Service, and lawyers in the Justice Department.

Mosher identifies several common traits in bureaucracy's public professionalism. One is the desire of professional groups to elevate their status and strengthen their public image as a profession, frequently by defining certain kinds of work as their exclusive domain, thereby protecting career opportunities for their members. There is also an emphasis on "work substance," particularly in terms of training in scientific skills as preparation for their jobs. Another common tendency among professional groups, Mosher contends, is "a built-in aversion between professions and politics." Professional public servants seek continually to escape the control and influence of politicians and concentrate instead on "the correct ways of solving problems and doing things." And if politics are to be avoided, so also are bureaucratic controls. Bureaucracy is viewed as a threat to professional freedoms, for traditional professions such as law and medicine have a high regard for their own autonomy and their control over establishing the rules, fees, and ethics of their profession. Mosher cites various ways in which public service severely restricts the scope of professional autonomy.

Within each public profession, Mosher finds a core of individuals that constitute its professional elite: "it is at the center of the agency, controls the key line positions, and provides the main, perhaps the exclusive, source of its leadership." This elite is also usually the group most closely identified with the central purposes and basic work objectives of the organization—pilots in the Air Force, engineers in the highway department, educators in the Department of Education, geologists in the Geological Survey Office, or scientists and physicians in the National Institutes of Health. Mosher asserts that the real tensions that develop within government occur not between workers and management, but rather "arise between those in different professions (or segments)." "A professional's status is not threatened by his or her secretary, bookkeeper, or janitor. The professional can, and often does, 'go to bat' for them, and they may look upon him or her as their principal advocate. Not so professionals in other segments and professions who are free to challenge the other's competence or judgment." Peer groups, not subordinates or superiors, are chief sources of conflict within administrative agencies.

Professional elites also are the essential decision makers of government, forming the nucleus within professions for determining key personnel policies, hiring criteria, and standards for advancement. Elites sit on promotion boards and draw up job policy and personnel procedures. In general, professional elites in the more established professions exercise greater control over employment practices than those in the newer ones.

Unlike many public administration theorists, Mosher attempts to come to grips with the essential question: who rules the bureaucracy? As he concludes:

> For better or worse—or better *and* worse—much of our government is now in the hands of professionals (including scientists). The choice of these professionals, the determination of their skills, and the content of their work are now principally determined, not by general governmental agencies, but by their own professional elites, professional organizations, and the institutions and faculties of higher education. It is unlikely that the trend toward professionalism in or outside of government will soon be reversed.

As you read this selection, keep the following questions in mind:

How can the appropriate balance be struck between, on the one hand, freedom for professionals to apply expertise in their respective fields of government and, on the other hand, general public control and oversight of their activities?

What ensures that professionals will maintain the broad public view, rather than become narrow special interests seeking only their self-advancement?

What is the appropriate relationship between public professionals and publicly elected officials?

Can you point out the public professionals' influence in any of the cases of Chapters Three and Four? Was professional authority exercised wisely and responsibly?

# The Professional State

### FREDERICK C. MOSHER

There is a curious aura of unreality about much that has been said and done in the last

From *Democracy and the Public Service,* Second Edition, by Frederick C. Mosher. Copyright © 1982 by Oxford University Press, Inc. Reprinted by permission.

half-century with regard to public executives and public managers. A good many otherwise enlightened citizens are not aware of their existence—other than the President, who is of course the chief executive. They know there is a chief of police and a secretary of defense and a county clerk, but these are politicians or bureaucrats, or worse, a combination of the two. They may be aware too that there is a county director of public health, a superintendent of schools, a director of the Forest Service; but these are professionals—a doctor, an educator, a forester. They are not thought of as executives or managers. And a great many of the incumbents of such positions do not think of themselves in those terms either. I have talked with a number of members of the Senior Executive Service who said that they had never thought of themselves as executives. They were engineers, biologists, lawyers, economists. They did not consider themselves managers or executives although they have made or participated in decisions affecting thousands of subordinates, millions of citizens, and sometimes billions of dollars. Some years ago, the president of one of the great universities in the world described himself in these words: "I am first of all a professor."

It may prove over the years that the greatest contributions of the Brownlow Committee on Administrative Management, the two Hoover Commissions, and Carter's personnel reform (as well as a great many other efforts) were to lend credence to the importance of what public executives were doing and therefore to the importance of selecting, preparing, and motivating them for their jobs. The faulty public image and self-image of career public servants are probably a product of developments over the last century or longer toward professionalism in American society. Although its seeds appeared earlier, the professional ethos really began to make its mark in the latter decades of the nineteenth century. It fostered, and was fostered by, a number of parallel social movements: the development of universities (or, in Clark Kerr's apt term, multiversities); increasing occupational specialism; meritocracy; careerism off the farm; the growth of an enormous, fluid, and amorphous middle class; and faith in progress.[1] In the 1960s, Daniel Bell wrote of an emerging new society in which old

values and social power associated with property, wealth, production, and industry are giving way to knowledge, education, and intellect.

To speak rashly: if the dominant figures of the past hundred years have been the entrepreneur, the businessman, and the industrial executive, the "new men" are the scientists, the mathematicians, the economists, and the engineers of the new computer technology. And the dominant institutions of the new society—in the sense that they will provide the most creative challenges and enlist the richest talents—will be the intellectual institutions. The leadership of the new society will rest, not with businessmen or corporations as we know them . . . but with the research corporation, the industrial laboratories, the experimental stations, and the universities.[2]

Viewed broadly, the professions are social mechanisms, whereby knowledge, particularly new knowledge, is translated into action and service. They provide the means whereby intellectual achievement becomes operational.

The extent to which the professions have become dominant in American society has been noted by a number of commentators. Several years ago, Kenneth S. Lynn maintained that "Everywhere in American life, the professions are triumphant."[3] And Everett C. Hughes wrote: "Professions are more numerous than ever before. Professional people are a larger proportion of the labor force. The professional attitude, or mood, is likewise more widespread; professional status more sought after."[4]

In statistical terms, data of the U.S. Census and the Bureau of Labor Statistics reflect the accelerating increase of "professional, technical, and kindred" workers, who grew from 4 to 15 percent of the American labor force between 1920 and 1978. The fastest growth has been since World War II; it continues today and probably will do so well into the future.

# The Professions and Government

The prominent role of American governments in the development and utilization of professions went largely unnoticed for a long time. Governments are the principal employers of professionals. According to estimates of the Bureau of Labor Statistics, about two of every five workers classified as "professional, technical, and kindred" (39.4%) were employed by governments in 1978, a proportion which has been stable since 1970.[5] This category does not include the multitude of engineers, scientists, and others on private rolls who are actually paid from government contracts, subsidies, and grants. Looked at another way, more than one third (36.7%) of all government employees were engaged in professional or technical pursuits, more than three times the comparable proportion in the private sector (10.9%). The governmental proportion is swollen by the education professions, especially elementary and secondary school teachers. But even if education is removed from both sides of the ledger, the percentage of professional and technical personnel in government (21.2%) is nearly double the comparable percentage in the private sector (11.6%).

Leaving aside the political appointees at or near the top of our public agencies and jurisdictions, the administrative leadership of government became increasingly professional in terms of educational and experiential backgrounds. This is not to say that public leadership as such is an administrative profession, rather that it consists of a very wide variety of professions and professionals in diverse fields, most of them related to the missions of the organizations in which they lead.

In government, the professions are the conveyor belts between knowledge and theory on the one hand, and public purpose on the other. The interdependencies of the professions and government are many. Governments are, or have been:

the creators of many professions;

the *de jure* legitimizers of most of those which have been legitimized;

protectors of the autonomy, integrity, monopoly, and standards of those which have such protections;

the principal supporters of their research and of that of the sciences upon which they depend;

subsidizers of much of their education;

among their principal employers and the nearly exclusive employers of some of them; which means also

among the principal utilizers of their knowledge and skills.

For their part, the professions:

contribute to government a very substantial proportion of public servants;

provide most of the leadership in a considerable number of public agencies;

through their educational programs, examinations, accreditation, and licensing, largely determine what the content of each profession is in terms of knowledge, skills, and work;

influence public policy and the definition of public purpose in those many fields within which they operate;

in varying degree and in different ways provide or control the recruitment, selection, and other personnel actions for their members;

shape the structure as well as the social organization of many public agencies.

There is nothing very new about professionalism in government. The principal spawning period for educational programs for many of the professions . . . was the first quarter of this century, and the U.S. Classification Act of 1923 established as the most distinguished segment a professional and scientific service. In all probability the number of professionally educated personnel in all American governments has been rising for the past century. Yet there appears to have been very little recognition of, or concern about, the significance of professionalism in the public service and its leadership until quite recently. For example, the Brownlow report and those of the two Hoover commissions, for all of their emphasis upon administrative management, paid scant attention to professionals in fields other than management as such.

The degree to which individual professional specialisms have come to dominate public agencies is suggested by the small table here. The right hand column indicates both the primary professional field in the agency and the normal professional source of its career leadership.

I define the word "profession" liberally as 1. a reasonably clear-cut occupational field, 2. which ordinarily requires higher education at least through the bachelor's level, and 3. which offers a lifetime career to its members.[6] The professions in government may conveniently be divided into two classes: first, those in fields employed in the public *and* the private sectors and for whom the government must compete in both recruitment and retention. This category, which I shall call "general professions," includes most of the callings commonly understood as professions: law, medicine, engineering, architecture, and many others. I also include among them applied scientists in general and college professors. Second are those employed predominantly and sometimes exclusively by governmental agencies, which I shall call "public service professions." Most of these were generated within government in response

### FEDERAL

| | |
|---|---|
| All military agencies | military officers |
| Department of State | foreign service officer |
| Public Health Service | public health doctors |
| Forest Service | foresters |
| Bureau of Reclamation | civil engineers |
| Geological Survey | geologist |
| Department of Justice | lawyers |
| Department of Education | educators |
| Bureau of Standards | natural scientists |

### STATE AND LOCAL

| | |
|---|---|
| Highways an other public works agencies | civil engineers |
| Welfare agencies | social workers |
| Mental hygiene agencies | psychiatrists |
| Public health agencies | public health doctors |
| Elementary and secondary education offices and schools | educators |
| Higher education institutions | professors |
| Attorneys general, district attorneys, legal counsel | lawyers |

to the needs of public programs, and although there has been a tendency in the direction of increased private employment for many of them, governments are still the predominant employers. They consist of two groups: first, those who are employed exclusively by a single agency such as military officers, Foreign Service officers, and Coast Guard officers; and, second, those employed by a number of different governmental jurisdictions, such as school teachers, educational administrators, social workers, public health officers, foresters, agricultural scientists, and librarians.

Most of those listed above in both categories may be described as "established professions" in the sense that they are widely recognized as professions, and with only a few exceptions their status has been legitimized by formal state action through licensing, credentialing, commissioning, recognizing educational accreditation, or a combination of these.

In addition to these professions, there are many "emergent professions" which have not been so recognized and legitimized but which are valiantly and hopefully pulling themselves up by their vocational bootstraps to full professional status. In this group are included specialists in personnel, public relations, computer technology, and purchasing. Emergent in the "public service" category are governmental subdivisions of all of these and some which are more exclusively governmental: e.g., assessors, police, penologists, employment security officers, air pollution specialists.

The professions—whether general or public service, whether established or emergent—display common characteristics which are significant for democracy and the public service. One of these is the continuing drive of each of them to elevate its stature and strengthen its public image as a profession. In a very few highly esteemed fields, such as law and medicine, the word "maintain" is perhaps more appropriate than "elevate." A prominent device for furthering this goal is the establishment of the clear and (where possible) expanding boundaries of work within which members of the profession have *exclusive* prerogatives to operate. Other means include: the assurance and protection of career opportunities for professionals; the establishment and continuous elevation of standards of education and entrance into the profession; the upgrading of rewards (pay) for professionals; and the improvement of their prestige before their associates and before the public in general.

A second common denominator of the professions is their concentration upon the *work substance* of their field, both in preparatory education and in journeyman activities, and the differentiation of that field from other kinds of work (including other professions) and from work at a lower or subprofessional level in the same field. Accompanying this emphasis upon work substance has been a growing concentration, particularly in preprofessional education, upon the sciences, which are considered foundational for the profession in question, whether they be natural or biological or social (behavioral). This emphasis is an inevitable consequence of the explosive developments of science in the last several decades, and unquestionably it has contributed to the betterment of professional performance in the technical sense.

Partially in consequence of the concentration upon science and work substance there has been a much less than parallel treatment of the *ecology* of the profession in the total social milieu: of the consequences and purposes of the profession and of the constraints within which it operates. There are signs in a good many fields today that attention to these topics is increasing, particularly in the public service professions. Yet much of professional education and practice is still so focused on substance and science as to obscure the larger meaning of the profession in the society. Except for those few professionals who grow beyond their field, the real world is seen as by a submariner through a periscope whose direction and focus are fixed.

One of the most obscure sectors of the real world in professional education and much of its practice is the realm of government and politics. There is a built-in animosity between the professions and politics. Its origin is historical: Most of the professions, and particularly those in the public service category, won their professional spurs over many arduous years of contending against the infiltration, the domination, and the influence of politicians (who to many professionals are amateurs at best and criminals at worst). Compare, for example, the evolution of such fields as the military, diplomacy, social welfare, and city management.

The aversion to politics also has contemporary support. Professionalism rests upon specialized knowledge, science, and rationality. There are *correct* ways of solving problems and doing things. Politics is seen as being engaged in the fuzzy areas of negotiation, elections, votes, compromises—all carried on by subject-matter amateurs. Politics is to the professions as ambiguity to truth, expediency to rightness, heresy to true belief.

Government as a whole comes off not much better than politics in the eyes of most professions, particularly the "general" ones. By definition, it carries the political taint. It also violates or threatens some of the treasured attributes and myths of true professionalism: individual and professional autonomy, and freedom from "bureaucratic" control; service to, and fees from, individual clients; vocational self-government. Among those general professions with large numbers of members employed privately, preservice education usually treats government as an outside agency with or against which one must deal. This seems to be true of most education in law, engineering, accounting, and other business fields, upon which government is heavily dependent. It is also true of medicine and most of its subspecialties. Even in many public service professions—public school education provides an excellent example—there is a considerable aversion to government *in general* and to politics, which may be another word for the same thing. Government is all right in those particular areas in which the specified profession has dominant control; but beyond those perimeters, it is equated with "politics" and "bureaucracy" in their more invidious senses.

I doubt that it is appropriate to speak of "strategies" of the professions in government, because some of their consequences seem to have "just growed" rather than to have been consciously planned. Yet those consequences are fairly consistent, particularly among the established professions, whether of the public service or the general category. And the emergent professions are varying distances down the road. The pattern has these features:

1. the given profession has staked its territory within the appropriate governmental agency or agencies, usually with boundaries approximately coterminous with those of the organization itself;
2. within its organization, it has formed an elite corps with substantial control over the operations of the agency, significant influence on agency policies, and high prestige within and outside the agency;
3. to the extent possible, it has assumed control over employment policies and individual personnel actions for its own members in the agency and also over the employment of persons not in the elite profession;
4. it has provided its members the opportunities, assurances, and protections of a career system of employment.

The following two sections will deal with items 2 and 3 above. . . .

## Professional Elites

Our study and hence our understanding of public administrative organizations have for some time been conditioned by two primary considerations. One is simply the past, when most organizations were not professionalized and when it seemed logical to build on the premise that organization consisted of two essential elements: management and workers. The focus was upon the problems, the skills, the content of management viewed as a single, common task, regardless of the differing activities and objectives of the organizations.[7] The second source of our lore about public organizations derives principally from studies of organizations in the realm of private business, but augmented by cases and analyses about some public or semi-public organizations usually at a fairly subordinate level of operations:

military units, hospitals, mental institutions, prisons, schools, and scientific laboratories. The more recent of the organizational literature has recognized and even dwelt upon a third element of organization: the professionals, usually viewed as *staff.* They are organizationally below management but are often considered to be superior in educational and social terms.

So we begin our organizational analysis from a *trichotomy* which consists of management, workers, and professionals or staff. The professionals are categorized according to whether they are dedicated to their organizations (the "locals") or to their professions (the "cosmopolitans"). There are presumed conflicts of prospects and goals between management and workers, between professionals and workers, and between management and professionals.

One hesitates to generalize as to the validity or usefulness of either the dichotomous or the trichotomous premises in nonpublic organization today. Undoubtedly they are still applicable in many industrial and commercial organizations. They seem quite inapplicable, however, in most of the professionalized agencies of government, and these include the most important ones. In these agencies:

the managers are professionals in the specialized occupational fields of their agencies—but not as managers per se, for few have been trained for management;

most of those designated as staff are also professionals, but typically in fields of specialism different from that of management;

many of the workers—and most of those in middle-management positions—are also professionals, usually in the same professions as management.

Commonly there is a mutually supportive relationship between the professional managers and the professional workers in the same profession. The former see themselves, and are viewed by the latter, as representative of the interests of both.

Further, there may be no conflict between the organization and its objectives on the one hand and the aspirations and standards of its professional workers and executives on the other. In a good many cases, the goals and standards of public agencies, as seen by their officers and employees, are identical with the goals and standards of the professions as they are seen by their members. This is true of most public organizations in fields such as public health, welfare, geology, forestry, education, and military affairs. The public organizations, the bureaucracies, not only heavily influence but actually determine and epitomize the goals of the professions which provide the leaders and many of the workers under them. In other words, the bureaucracies, with their official powers, funds, and activities, and the elite professions which people and often dominate bureaucracies with their educational backgrounds, cultures, standards, and prestige are mutually supportive and have common objectives.[8]

A more useful model of most sizable public organizations in government—at the department level and below in state and local units and at the bureau or service level and below in the federal government—would be one which recognized the internal professional and other vocational groupings and the stratification of these within each agency in terms of both prestige and power. In most public agencies which have been in operation for some time, there is a single occupational group whose knowledge, skills, and orientations are closely identified with the mission and activities of the agency. If the work is seen as requiring intellectual capacity and background education to the level of college graduation—and as we have seen, this is the case in an increasing majority of agencies—the group comes to constitute a professional elite. It is a *corps*—a body of men and women closely associated with each other and with the enterprise—and it is sometimes so designated. It is also a *core:* it is at the center of the agency, controls the key line positions, and provides the main, perhaps the exclusive, source of its leadership. If at the time the elite developed there was no existing profession clearly identified with the activities of the agency, it is likely to be a unique *public service profession*—military, Foreign Service, or public health, for example. If on the other hand there was a clearly related, existing, outside profession or if one subsequently developed, the elite may consist of members of a *general profession*—such as civil engineers in highway departments, psychiatrists in mental hygiene institutions, and lawyers in departments of justice. In some cases, the clearly different nature of the work of the public agencies has occasioned a split-off from an established profession and the birth of a new public service profession, which, however, has retained the educational base of the older one—as in the case of public health doctors and the emerging professions of public works engineers and educational administrators.

There are five principal types of exceptions to the professional elite structure. One is found in relatively new agencies where no existing profession can yet make a clear claim to status as the appropriate elite. A second exception occurs in agencies of the business type, such as the Postal Service and some publicly owned utilities, where the trichotomy of management, staff, and workers may be more descriptive. (In many utility operations, however, line management consists of professional engineers.) A third exception is found in those public agencies whose work does not, or does not yet, require higher education to the graduating level. Police and fire protection are examples of this, though both are moving in the direction of professionalization. Fourth are agencies which are controversial, unstable or temporary, or which, for political reasons, must avoid the appearance of permanence. Professional elitism entails a career orientation. (The Agency

for International Development is a good current example in which the development of a technical assistance elite has been politically inhibited.) Finally, a few agencies were deliberately designed in such a way as to prevent dominance by a single occupation through their multipurpose missions. An historic example is the Tennessee Valley Authority, but interdisciplinary research laboratories offer abundant illustrations.

Professional elites in larger agencies tend to specialize into subdivisions under the general professional canopy. These may be reflections of well-recognized divisions of the profession, determined outside the agency and extending back into educational specialization, as in medicine and engineering. They may be grounded in specializations of work in the agency itself, sometimes highly formalized as in various arms and services of the Army (Engineer, Quartermaster, Infantry, Ordnance). Or they may be based upon continuing kinds of work assignments not formally recognized as separate corps or segments—e.g., the distinctions among personnel officers in activities such as recruiting, examining, classification, labor relations. Among such subgroups there is normally a pecking order of prestige and influence. The most elite of them is likely to be the one which historically was most closely identified with the end purpose, the basic content of the agency—the officers of the line in the Navy, the pilots in the Air Force, the political officers in the Foreign Service, the civil engineers in a construction agency which also employs electrical and mechanical engineers.

No organization of substantial size can consist solely of members of one occupation. There must always be supportive activities, carried on by individuals who are not members of the elite profession. Indeed, the number in the professional elite may constitute only a small minority of all employees; e.g., public health doctors in a local health office, psychiatrists in mental health institutions, social workers in welfare offices. Complex government agencies employ sizable numbers of professionals, specialists, and workers in fields other than the elite one. These may be grouped in the following main categories:

*Supporting Line Professions:* professionals who carry on and contribute to the substantive work of the agency, but are trained and experienced in different fields. Thus in a state mental health department and in state mental institutions the psychiatrists are the elite, but by far the greater numbers are psychologists, psychiatric nurses, and social workers. A forestry operation includes agronomists, botanists, engineers, and many others.

*Staff Professions:* advisers and technicians for their specialized knowledge in areas related to, but not central to, the line work of the agency—as economists, sociologists, legal counsel, design engineers, computer analysts in many kinds of agencies. These are usually few in number and relatively high in grade and position, though not at the very top.

*Administrative Professions:* officials engaged in personnel, budget, finance, communications, purchasing, supply. Some of these can be found in almost every large agency, although in some the positions are filled by members of the elite professions, particularly at the level of leadership. Most of these are "emergent" rather than established professions.

*Workers:* paraprofessionals, supervisors, clerical, service, skilled, and unskilled personnel.

Figure 7.1 is a "still picture" of the composition of a hypothetical public agency, well-established and operating in a professional field. (Hypothetical examples of the schema in particular kinds of agencies are shown in Table 7.1.) The vertical dimension is organizational rank or level of pay, and may be assumed to equate very roughly with the level of day-to-day responsibility of incumbents. The horizontal dimension represents the numbers of persons at each grade. The horizontal lines at the bottom of the figures represent the normal and the sometimes exclusive entering-level of beginners when they are appointed in the various categories. The horizontal lines and points at the top of the various figures represent the highest grade an individual in each category can expect to reach. For an employee to cross lines from one category to another is usually difficult and, where professional standards are high and clear-cut, may be impossible, even illegal. The diamond shapes of the elite profession (2) and of the other professional groups (4 and 5) are typical of most such groups in government where professionals are hired soon after completing their education on a junior basis and advance rapidly to journeyman-level work. The trapezoidal (as distinguished from the familiar pyramidal) shape of the organization as a whole is also representative, although in most agencies the percentage of the total who are professional personnel is much smaller than is represented on the chart. Over the course of time, the normal progress of an employee in any category is upward, but obviously only a few will make it all the way to the top.

At the top of the diagram are represented a small number of political appointees, recruited from outside, who may or may not be professional. With these are included some political appointees drawn from the elite segment of the elite profession. Most of the very top career jobs are also filled from this group, and almost all of such jobs are filled by the elite profession. The incumbents of these jobs constitute very roughly what Morris Janowitz has described as the "elite nucleus."[9]

The diagram suggests that those who make it to the very top, the "elite of the elite," have pursued a more or less orthodox and "proper" type of career. The implication appears to be

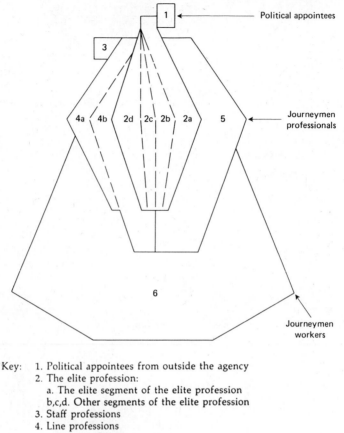

Key:   1. Political appointees from outside the agency
       2. The elite profession:
          a. The elite segment of the elite profession
          b,c,d. Other segments of the elite profession
       3. Staff professions
       4. Line professions
          a. Reserve Officers
          b. Civil Service
       5. Administrative professions
       6. Workers, including supervisors, paraprofessionals, clerical,
          manual, and others

**Figure 7.1**   Schematic diagram of composition of a professionalized government agency. (From *Democracy and the Public Service.* Second Edition by Frederick C. Mosher. Copyright © 1982 by Oxford University Press, Inc. Reprinted by Permission.)

erroneous in some cases and may indeed be widely untrue. Janowitz found a substantial proportion of the military elite nucleus to be individuals who had pursued unorthodox, innovative careers. A study of the U.S. Foreign Service some years ago indicated that among the Foreign Service Officers in executive positions in Washington and overseas, a disproportionate number had entered the service laterally (i.e., unorthodoxly).[10] Whether these findings about the top leadership in the For-

eign Service and the military are typical of professionalized public agencies or arise from certain special circumstances is a significant though largely unexplored question.

Note that the arrangement of professional elites within different agencies does not necessarily reflect the status and prestige of the different professions in the society at large, nor does it reflect the amount of education beyond the bachelor's degree. The determining element is the historic and current identification of the

**Table 7.1  Illustrative but Hypothetical Examples of Social Organizations of Public Agencies**

| | Department of State | Department of Air Force | State Department of Highways | State Department of Mental Health | Local Department of Health |
|---|---|---|---|---|---|
| 1. Political appointees | Secretary, undersecretaries, and some assistant secretaries | Secretary, undersecretaries and assistant secretaries | Department head and deputies | Department head and deputies | Department head |
| 2. Elite profession<br>a. Elite segment<br>b. Other segment<br>c. Other segment<br>d. Other segment | FSO's<br>Political officers<br>Economic officers<br>Consular officers<br>Administrative officers | Air Force officers<br>Flying officers<br>Logistics officers<br>Maintenance officers<br>Administrative officers | Engineers<br>Civil engineers<br>Electrical engineers<br>Mechanical engineers<br>Industrial engineers | M.D.s<br>Psychiatrists<br>Surgeons<br>Pathologists | M.D.s<br>Public health M.D.s<br>Pediatricians |
| 3. Staff professions | Legal advisers<br>Scientific advisers<br>Public relations officers | General counsel<br>Scientific advisers<br>Public information officers | Counsel<br>Economists<br>Public relations officers<br>Real estate appraisers | Counsel<br>Sociologists<br>Statisticians | Counsel<br>Sociologists<br>Biostatisticians |
| 4. Line professions | a. Reserve officers (various fields)<br>b. Civil service (various fields) | Reserve officers (various fields)<br>Civil service (various fields) | Scientists—civil service (various fields)<br>Technicians—civil service (various fields) | Clinical psychologists<br>Psychiatric social workers<br>Psychiatric nurses | Sanitary engineers<br>Public health nurses<br>Social workers |
| 5. Administrative professions | Officers in finance, budget, personnel, training, supply, communications, purchasing, etc.<br>(Civil service and F.S. staff officers) | (Civil service and noncom. enlisted) | (Civil service) | (Civil service) | (Civil service) |
| 6. Nonprofessional employees | Subprofessional, clerical, labor, custodial, etc.<br>(Civil service and F.S. staff) | (Civil service and enlisted) | (Civil service) | (Civil service) | (Civil service) |

specialty with the central content and purpose of the agency's work. Registered nurses are the elite of a visiting nurse association but not of a hospital. Engineers are the elite of a state highway department but not of a scientific laboratory. Masters of social work are elite in a welfare department but not in a mental hospital. Psychiatrists are the elite profession (or a segment if medical doctors are considered a single profession) in a mental hospital but not in a general hospital or in a local, state, or national public health office. Scientists are the elite in a scientific laboratory, but not in a U.S. embassy overseas.

Note also that within large departments there may be a number of different systems of elitism at different levels in the organization. Professionals in a given field tend to form an associational community which is often the basis for formal organizational differentiation. To a considerable extent, therefore, the suborganization of many departments conforms to professional definitions. Within each major unit there is a professional elite, which may not be the same as the elite of the larger organization. Thus architects are likely to be the elite *within* an architectural division which includes many engineers among other professionals; but if the division is a part of a department of public works, the architects yield in elite status to the civil engineers at the departmental level. Similarly, geologists are the elite in the U.S. Geological Survey but not in the Department of Interior.

Thirdly, it may be noted that the elite status of professions in many different public agencies is relatively but not completely stable. The knowledge, technique, and orientation of the older professions tend toward obsolescence in the face of growing science, new kinds of problems, and new understandings about how to deal with them. These tendencies cast the older professional elites in a stance that is defensive and conservative vis-à-vis their positions and their control over agency objectives and programs. The intra-agency structure of elitism is,

in many organizations, a battleground between a professional elite, or an elite segment, and other professions, other segments, and non-professionals. Political leaders desirous of rapid development of new programs may, and frequently do, endeavor to tip the balance against the elite professionals by appointing or selecting for promotion individuals who represent points of view at variance with the elite.

The key zones of potential tension and conflict in agencies of this kind lie not between management and workers, though these are not absent; nor between management and professionals, because most of the managers are themselves professional; nor between professionals and workers as such, since many of the workers are professionals. Rather they are delineated by the vertical lines (solid and dotted) in Figure 7.1. Specifically, they include tensions between:

1. politically appointed officials and the elite profession (or its elite segment), especially if the political leaders are not members of the profession (or segment);
2. different and competing segments of the elite profession;
3. the elite profession (or elite segment) and other professions in the agency, including especially those in line and administrative professions.

My unproven observation is that the most conflictive situations in professionalized but not unionized public agencies arise between those in different professions (or segments) and in different personnel systems who are approximately equal in level of responsibility and pay, but where one is "more elite" than the other. That is, the principal tensions are horizontal and diagonal rather than vertical. Personnel who are clearly subordinate are more likely to look upon their professional superiors as defenders and representatives than as competitors or opponents; and the professional superiors regard their own role in the same somewhat paternalistic fashion. This is less true in programs staffed by unionized employees, and with the growing organization of public employees it has changed substantially in the recent past. Still, a professional's status is not threatened by his or her secretary, bookkeeper, or janitor. The professional can, and often does, "go to bat" for them, and they may look upon him or her as their principal advocate. Not so professionals in other segments and professions who are free to challenge the other's competence or judgment.

Each profession brings to an organization its own particularized view of the world and of the agency's role and mission in it. The perspective and motivation of each professional are shaped, at least to some extent, by the lens provided by professional education, prior professional experience, and professional colleagues. These distinctive views are further molded and strengthened through training and experience in the agency itself; and where the professional corps within the agency is one of long standing, where it operates through a well-entrenched career system, and where there is a vigorously defended stratification between the professional elite and others in the organization, these post-entry forces can be very strong indeed.

The analysis of different public organizations in terms of their professional structure and intraprofessional and interprofessional systems of relationships is basic to a true understanding of how they work. Important decisions are likely to be the product of intraprofessional deliberation, representing the group views of the elite profession in the agency, compromised in some cases to satisfy the demands of other professions and nonprofessionals. Social relationships outside the office usually parallel professional relationships within. Members of the same profession in an agency are "colleagues," like professors in a university; and the flavor of their work is similarly collegial. Toward members of other professions, their behavior is likely to be more formal, sometimes suspicious or even hostile. Toward paraprofessionals and other workers, the relationship may more frequently be paternalistic, patronizing, or dictatorial. Members of the elite profession identify their own work and that of the agency with their profession; the others are a little "outside," they are supplementary or supporting. The "climate" of an organization as well as its view of mission and its effectiveness in carrying it out are in considerable part a product of its professional structure and professional value system.

## The Public Employment of Professionals

As the professional composition of public agencies has substantially revolutionized their internal anatomy, physiology, and nervous systems, so has the emergence of professions revolutionized the precepts and practices of public employment. Both revolutions continue with the development and solidification of new fields and new subspecialties. Although there are large differences in precepts and practices among different jurisdictions of government, the basic directions in public service employment are clear. They also are probably inevitable. They apply to virtually all professional fields, whether or not under civil service laws. They are often at odds with the most central—and most cherished—principles associated with civil service reform in this country: equal opportunity to apply and compete for jobs; competitive examinations for selection and (sometimes) promotion; equal pay for equal work; neutral and objective direction and control of the personnel system.

The most important of the changes is the last one, which involves the direction of personnel activities; it underlies the others. In general, what has happened (and is happening) is a *delegation* of real personnel authority, formal and/or informal, from a central personnel office or civil service commission to the professions and the professionals themselves.[11]

A basic drive of every profession, established or emergent, is *self-government* in deciding policies, criteria, and standards for employment and advancement, and in deciding individual personnel matters. The underlying argument for such professional hegemony is that no one outside—no amateur—is equipped to judge or even to understand the true content of the profession or the ingredients of merit in its practice. This thesis is difficult to challenge, particularly in highly developed, specialized, and scientized fields with which an amateur—or a professional in personnel administration—can have only a passing acquaintance.

The means whereby the professionals assert their control over personnel policies and actions are many and diverse. Some are specified and required by law or regulation; others grow out of gentlemen's agreements within—or in spite of—civil service laws; some reflect a silent abdication by the civil service agencies or a failure to assume an effective role; and some are unintended (or mayhap intended) consequences of others. I shall discuss them under three headings: influence and control by the professional elites within governmental agencies; influence and control by "outside" professions and their organizations; and influence and control by institutions of professional education.

## Professional Elites

The extreme examples of professional control within agencies are provided by the various commissioned corps in the federal government which have never been under a general civil service system. Here one finds the most consolidated mechanisms of internal control by the elite group and particularly by senior members—the *elite cadre,* as Janowitz termed it. They determine the standards and criteria for entrance; the policies and procedures of assignment; the appropriate work content of elite

corps positions; the criteria for promotion. They also set up the machinery for personnel operations, usually including boards, all or a majority of whose members are drawn from the corps itself. They also superintend the policies and operations of personnel management for other employees, including other professionals, who are not in the elite, yielding as little as they must to civil service requirements, to other employee groups, to outside professional interests, and to political pressures.

Much of this personnel control is sanctioned by law. It is significant that personnel matters in the various corps carry such preeminent weight and importance. Historically in the Army the handling of personnel was long entrusted to the staff division known as G-1 (A-1 in the Air Force); today the officers in charge of personnel are first deputy chiefs of staff. In the State Department the Board of Foreign Service has, since its founding, been essentially a personnel board, as the Director General of the Foreign Service has been primarily concerned with matters of personnel. It may be noted too that in these cases the professional elites have assumed control over the administration of agency personnel who are not in the corps: reserve officers, enlisted personnel (or Foreign Service staff), and civil servants.

Among the agencies not dominated by a commissioned corps, professional control over personnel matters has been less conspicuous but still effective. In many cases it is carried out under the canopy of civil service laws and regulations. The professional elites normally have the most influential voice in determining personnel policies, standards, and criteria within broad prescriptions of civil service law. The recent trend toward decentralization, both at the federal level and in other large jurisdictions, has of course facilitated this development. Personnel selection for professionals is in many places left to boards, which are usually dominated by agency professionals. As will be seen later, competitive written and performance examinations in most of the established professional fields have largely been abandoned in favor of evidences of qualification determined outside the agency and indeed outside the civil service system. What is left—normally an "unassembled" examination of the candidates' records and/or an oral examination—is conducted by boards composed principally of members of the agency's elite profession. The same situation pertains to other personnel actions: assignments, promotions, disciplinary actions. In most cases the central influence is that of the agency; and if it is controlled by a professional elite, the basic control lies with that elite. The civil service or personnel agency provides assistance in recruitment, a certain amount of professional personnel guidance, certain procedural requisites, and participation and perhaps inspection to ensure conformance with regulations. The substance of personnel policy and decision rests, however, in the professional elite.

Our studies conducted some years ago of employment practices of federal, state, and local jurisdictions in California in general confirmed the tendency toward professional elite control of policies, standards, and actions within the agencies in which there was a professional elite. There were, of course, variations in the degree of control and in the techniques whereby it was made effective. In general, these variations seemed responsive to two factors: first, the degree to which the professional group had established itself as truly elite within a given agency; and second, the degree to which demand exceeded supply for professionals in the field in question. The better established, more recognized professions had greater control, as did those in which supply was scarcest. In our California studies, we found this to be true at all levels of government in the employment of lawyers, natural scientists, engineers, doctors, social workers, and health professionals. In the federal government, we found it true also for foresters, architects, and some others. In the state of California, it applied to psychiatrists in mental hygiene; among local governments, it applied in varying degrees to recreation workers, city planners, librarians, and some others.

## The Professionals and Their Organizations

Among the established general professions, the practice of licensing practitioners is an old one. Indeed, it is a common index of whether or not a profession is truly "established," and many of the aspiring newer fields are seeking it to give them official and legal sanction. The licensing of professionals, as of craftsmen, is normally accomplished by the legal delegation of state powers to a board, itself composed exclusively or predominantly of members of the profession. It normally requires the passing of an examination, drafted and graded by the board or other professional group. In all of this, the public personnel organization usually plays no part, and the examinations themselves are directed almost exclusively to the knowledge and skills required for private practice, not to governmental policy and managerial problems, nor to those of large organizations of any kind. In well-established fields, such as law, medicine, dentistry, architecture, some kinds of engineering, and school teaching, licensing is normally requisite to practice at the journeyman level. In others, it is essential to advancement to higher levels of responsibility and supervision: accounting and nursing, for example.

Governmental agencies, other than the licensing boards themselves, play little part in the licensing process and have little influence upon or even interest in the content and standards of the examinations. Very probably, the finding of James W. Fesler in his 1942 study *The Independence of State Regulatory Agencies* is still accurate: "Professional licensing boards are virtually the creatures of the professional societies. . . ."[12] Yet it is clear that these examinations significantly affect the education and the qualifications which make for a professional man or woman. The governments by and large accept those qualifications as gospel in their own employment. In some fields (e.g., law, medicine) a license is an absolute requisite to employment at any professional level. In others, while not required, it may be sufficient evidence for hiring—without further evidence of qualification—and a basis for preferential treatment for advancement as well. Professionals who have gained their credentials in most fields are likely to escape any further tests of competence and knowledge if they aspire to enter government employ. For them the governments have abandoned to the professions the testing of merit insofar as it can be determined by examinations of knowledge and skill. Further, the licensing tests are noncompetitive among the candidates. Qualifications are measured only in terms of passing a minimum standard—which may of course be a high one.

But perhaps most important is the effect of the licensing structure upon the content, the dimensions, and the boundaries of the individual professions. As Corinne Lathrop Gilb has observed: "Public administrators generally fail to acknowledge *the extent to which the structure and composition of regulatory boards affect the division of labor and authority in the work world.*"[13] And the "work world" of course includes the administration of government itself.

## Professional Education

Over the long pull, the most profound impact upon the professional public services is that of the universities—their professional schools, their departments in the physical and social sciences which produce professionals, and their faculties in general. Higher education produces the bulk of future professionals. By their images, and by their impressions upon students, the schools have a great influence upon who opts for what fields and what kinds of young people—of what quality, what interests, what values—go where. It is clear too that they influence the choices by students among employ-

ers—whether government or other, and which jurisdictions and agencies of government. By their curricula, their faculties, their teaching, they define the content of each different specialism and the expectations and aspirations of the students in each. These students will of course include the principal operators in government tomorrow and the principal leaders the day after tomorrow.

In most professional fields, governments have accepted, without much question or knowledge, the academic definition of content and the academic criteria of qualification and merit. Most governments, like other employers, rely heavily upon credentials; possession of the sheepskin from an accredited institution is enough. Accreditation itself is normally based upon a review and approval of a given school's program by a committee of a larger organization composed of, or dominated by, professional educators in the same field. It reflects a consensus among academics as to the minimal curricular and faculty requirements necessary to produce qualified practitioners. In some fields accreditation and high academic standing (grade point average) are more important to governmental employers than professional licenses. In fields for which licensing has been provided in only a few states (or in none)—like social work, city planning, or librarianship—accreditation and grades become almost the sole criteria. Accreditation moreover is sometimes a requirement for licensing. Where government employers have any significant choice among candidates for jobs in the recognized professions, their reliance is placed upon 1. whether they come from accredited schools, 2. their grade point averages, and 3. the recommendations of professors. All three are of course academic determinants.

In the main, governments have yielded to the universities and professional educators the significant influences, the criteria, and the choices about public employment. Few of our larger governmental units give any competitive examinations on substance—that is, knowledge and skill—for candidates in professional fields. They leave it largely to the universities to determine what knowledges and skills are appropriate, and who among the graduating students are deserving of appointment. In a few fields, they also rely upon licensing examinations, themselves controlled by practitioners and educators outside of government. Among the agencies dominated by an elite professional corps, personnel decisions are largely dictated by the corps.

It is interesting that the Congress reaffirmed in the Veterans' Preference Act of 1944 its long-standing suspicion of formal academic qualifications for civil service jobs:

> No minimum educational requirement will be prescribed in any civil service examination except for such scientific, technical, or professional positions the duties of which the Civil Service Commission decides cannot be performed by a person who does not have such education.[14]

The Civil Service Commission (now the Office of Personnel Management) has since excepted virtually all of the established and general professional fields, a great many emergent professions including some that are exclusive to government, and a majority of the natural, life, and social scientists. The omissions from the civil service exceptions are more conspicuous than the exceptions themselves. Attorneys are of course omitted since they are not in the classified service anyway. Officials in administrative fields, such as budgeteers, personnel specialists, purchasing officers, tax administrators, and administrative officers are not excepted. None of the fields normally considered among the humanities at universities is excepted; and among social scientists, the political scientists, public administrators, and historians are conspicuous in not being excepted from the Congressional fiat. Anthropologists, economists, psychologists, and sociologists are all excepted.

The professional suspicion and opposition toward politics and government, suggested earlier, are probably even more vigorous among university professors. Here they are strengthened by the creeds of academic freedom and professional autonomy. Apparently, the further one progresses through higher education, the less he or she is enticed by governmental employment; and this must reflect to some extent the influence of university faculties.[15]

. . . We have come full circle. Near the beginning, I discussed the impact of the knowledge explosion upon our society; near the end, I discussed the impact of the universities upon public employment. The latter is a facet of the former. As knowledge has grown and as occupations have been increasingly professionalized, the public services have become more dependent upon the founts of knowledge, the universities. In their own organizations, governments have both reflected and influenced the occupational structure of the society. In so doing they have benefited tremendously through the advancement in the level of knowledge and skill in every field. They may also have suffered in the degree to which the central governments could control and direct operations in the general interest. For in the process, they have yielded a great deal of influence over *who* will conduct and direct individual programs, and how the content of programs will be defined as well.

For better or worse—or better *and* worse—much of our government is now in the hands of professionals (including scientists). The choice of these professionals, the determination of their skills, and the content of their work are now principally determined, not by general governmental agencies, but by their own professional elites, professional organizations, and the institutions and faculties of higher education. It is unlikely that the trend toward professionalism in or outside of government will soon be reversed. But the educational process through which the professionals are produced and later refreshed (in continuing educational programs) can be restudied and conceivably changed. The need for broadening, for humanizing, and in some fields for lengthening professional education programs may in the long run prove more crucial to governmental response to societal problems than any amount of civil service reform.

## Notes

1. There is a growing volume of literature about the growth and effects of professionalism, mostly by sociologists. I have here relied heavily upon Burton J. Bledstein, *The Culture of Professionalism: The Middle Class and the Development of Higher Education in America* (New York, Norton, 1976).

2. "Notes on the Post-Industrial Society," I *The Public Interest,* 6 (Winter, 1967), p. 27.

3. Kenneth S. Lynn, "Introduction," *Daedalus,* 92 (1963), p. 649. This issue of *Daedalus* was wholly dedicated to a discussion of the development of the professions within America.

4. Everett C. Hughes, "Professions," *Daedalus,* 92 (1963), p. 655.

5. Data in this paragraph are drawn from "The 1978 Class of Worker Matrix for the United States," an unpublished table furnished by the Bureau of Labor Statistics. The definition of "professional, technical, and kindred" includes occupations that some might not construe as professional, such as applied scientists, athletic coaches, embalmers, writers, artists, and entertainers. On the other hand, it excludes others that might be considered professional, including all of those who describe themselves as "managers, officials, proprietors" (of whom governments employed some 1,170,000 in 1978), military officers, and police.

6. The definition is unquestionably too loose to satisfy many students of occupations, who would like to add other requisites, such as: professional organization; or eleemosynary or service orientation; or legal establishment; or individual autonomy in performance of work; or code of ethics. In terms of governmental consequences, the liberal usage is more appropriate. For example, in terms of their group behavior in

government, the officers of the U.S. Navy are at least as "professionalized" as are lawyers.

7. For examples see the works of Frederick Taylor, Henri Fayol, or Chester Barnard. Their main tenets were reinforced by the writings of Max Weber.

8. Most of the relevant literature has emphasized the opposition of the professions and their values to organizations and their values, laying stress upon the demands of individual professionals for autonomy against organizational demands for group or social goals. It has ignored the frequent affinity between professions and the organizations which they govern and the organizational efforts, in many cases, to protect the professional autonomy of employees.

9. *The Professional Soldier: A Social and Political Portrait* (Glencoe, Ill., The Free Press, 1964), Chapter 8.

10. John E. Harr, *The Anatomy of the Foreign Service: A Statistical Profile* (New York, Carnegie Endowment for International Peace, Foreign Affairs Study No. 4, 1965), Chapter VI.

11. The word "delegation" is not precisely accurate in a good many fields, since many developed independently of any central personnel office, and there was no real *process* of delegation. But delegation is a reasonably accurate description of the product, whatever the nature of the evolution which preceded it.

12. Chicago, Public Administration Service, pp. 60–61.

13. *Hidden Hierarchies: The Professions and Government* (New York, Harper & Row, 1966), p. 194. (Author's emphasis.)

14. The wording but not the sense of this provision was subsequently modified. See 80 Stat. 89–554, Sept. 6, 1966, p. 419. For an overview and explanation of the rationale for the exception of particular professions from the prohibition against minimum educational requirements see U.S. Office of Personnel Management, *Qualification Standards for Positions under the General Schedule:* Handbook X-118, (Washington, D.C., Government Printing Office, January 1979).

15. On this point, see especially Franklin P. Kilpatrick, Milton C. Cummings, Jr., and M. Kent Jennings, *The Image of the Federal Service* and the accompanying *Source Book* (Washington, D.C., The Brookings Institution, 1964).

# CASE STUDY 7

## Introduction

All "name" economists liked the idea: from liberal economists, Walter Heller and Joseph Pechman, to those "on the right," such as Milton Friedman and George Stigler. "Middle of the road" economists, including Alice Rivlin, then director of the Congressional Budget Office, called it "an economist kind of reform." Or, as Princeton University's Alan Blinder summed it up, "The fine staff of economists and lawyers at the U.S. Treasury knew what was wrong with the tax code and how . . . to fix it."

The following case is about how the 1986 Federal Tax Reform Act, a proposal originally given little chance of success, originated and evolved into one of the major initiatives of President Ronald Reagan's second term. Timothy Conlan, George Mason University, Margaret Wrightson, Georgetown University, and David Beam, Illinois Institute of Technology, recount the difficult process of developing and putting together a comprehensive tax reform package for the president to propose to Congress. The first tax reform plan, called Treasury I, was primarily crafted by professional economists and lawyers within the Treasury Department. The "hows" and "whys" Treasury I became transformed into Treasury II, the proposal that Reagan actually sent to Congress in the mid-1980s and became politically more "saleable," is the focus of this case and relates directly to the role and influence of professionals in modern government discussed by Mosher in the prior essay.

As you review this story, consider some of the following points:

What was the role(s) of expert economists and lawyers in formulating Treasury I? Why were they so influential?

What caused the refashioning of Treasury I into Treasury II?

Does the case support Mosher's thesis?

# Politics, Professionals, and the President: Developing an Executive Tax Initiative

## TIMOTHY J. CONLAN, MARGARET T. WRIGHTSON, AND DAVID R. BEAM

I am asking Secretary Don Regan for a plan for action to simplify the entire tax code, so all taxpayers, big and small, are treated more fairly. . . . I have

From *Taxing Choices: The Politics of Tax Reform* by Timothy J. Conlan, Margaret T. Wrightson, and David R. Beam (Washington, D.C.: CQ Press, 1990), pp. 45–83. Reprinted by permission.

asked that specific recommendations, consistent with those objectives, be presented to me by December, 1984.

—Ronald Reagan, January 1984

As the president uttered those words, derisive laughter burst from Democratic legislators gathered to hear his State of the Union Address. Although they were momentarily intrigued, the December deadline suggested Reagan's plan was an inside joke: bureaucratic studies with postelection due dates are a politician's way of avoiding problems, not solving them.

A year later congressional Democrats discovered that the joke was on them. The Treasury Department had taken its mission very seriously, and by the time of the president's next annual message, tax reform had emerged from its bureaucratic burial ground as Reagan's top domestic priority. Coming on the heels of his forty-nine-state electoral sweep in November 1984, the proposal threatened to make a deep imprint on partisan politics as well as tax policy.

This remarkable transformation stemmed in large part from an unexpected confluence of interests among the different groups who served the president. The tax experts in the Treasury Department viewed reform as an opportunity to implement their professional agenda: improving the tax code by promoting equity among individuals with similar incomes and by removing tax preferences that distort the efficient flow of economic capital. Their ultimate success in defining the parameters of reform demonstrates the power of the bureaucracy to mold policy to fit professional norms and to advance institutional missions. The president's own interest in tax reform was always the promise of lower rates. In this he was egged on by "populist conservatives" for whom tax cuts were the raison d'être of reform. They viewed lower taxes in political terms, as a way to cement the "Reagan Revolution" and solidify Republican electoral gains. Decidedly less enthusiastic were the White House pragmatists, whose job was to evaluate the conflicting demands of interest-group and party politics. This last group was small but close to the president.

As a result of these conflicting interests swirling around the Oval Office, the fate of tax reform was often uncertain. Despite his recurring interest in it. Reagan never stepped in to exert strong leadership. In tax reform as throughout his presidency, when it came to concrete policy decisions the president waited for those in his inner circle to make the first move.

Thus it was not until January 1984, when it appeared that Walter Mondale might make tax reform the economic centerpiece of his presidential campaign, that prospects brightened at the White House. Largely as a way to neutralize the Democratic threat, Reagan announced his intention to "study" the problem.

There ensued a two-stage process, beginning at the Treasury Department. Thanks to a calculated decision to insulate candidate Reagan from possible political liabilities. Treasury Secretary Donald Regan was given free reign over tax reform. Pledged to secrecy by the White House and committed to protect his product from the taint of politics, the former Wall Street maverick harnessed the best talent his department had to offer. By the time of Reagan's smashing electoral victory in November, he and a small group of close aides and tax experts had produced a logically coherent and professionally sound reform plan—dubbed Treasury I.

Initially, its contents generated only heartburn among politicos at the White House. "This steps on every Republican toe in the country," said White House Chief of Staff James Baker when he saw Regan's handiwork. Down Pennsylvania Avenue, the screams of agony were louder still, especially from congressional Republicans. Yet the president needed a bold initiative for his second term, and none had been provided during the 1984 campaign. Moreover, Treasury I was being received favorably by some, especially the all-important media. Then, too, what if tax reform did—as some believed it would—realign the political landscape and end the Republicans' minority status? For all of these reasons, tax reform was off and running at the White House.

Thereafter came a game of cabinet-level musical chairs that astonished Washingtonians but advanced the cause of reform. Newly designated Treasury chief James Baker packed the plan back to the Treasury Department for a political tune-up, while Regan stayed behind as White House chief of staff. This switch put a reformer next to the president's ear and launched a thoroughgoing review of tax reform at Treasury, this time through the lens of pure politics. The result was a much modified proposal (Treasury II), unveiled as the president's own and sent to Capitol Hill.

Thus began the perilous journey of tax reform through the political process. Looking back, it must be said that while politics ascended to the top of a long list of concerns during Treasury II—there to stay through the remainder of tax reform—subsequent decisions were constrained or otherwise influenced by what was accomplished in Treasury I. As this shows, professionals gave tax reform its soul while Reagan's political midwives helped give it life.

## First Stirrings

Arranging deals over a friendly game of golf has long been a corporate tradition, subsidized by the tax code. Thanks to the TRA, though, which put new limits on business deductions such as country club dues, that tradition has become more costly. Thus, it is ironic that tax reform, in the guise of a flat-rate tax, may have received its initial presidential go-ahead on the links.

In David Stockman's recollection, Reagan was first sold on the notion during an amicable round of golf with Secretary of State George Shultz, a former economics professor, in late 1982. Stockman reported. "By the eighteenth hole the president was convinced that [a flat tax] was a way to reduce the deficit without increasing taxes." Shultz "always carried influence" with Reagan, noted the former assistant secretary for tax policy. John (Buck) Chapoton, and he made the idea seem "realistic." Still, not all observers give so much credit to Shultz. Neither tax reform nor the flat tax was new: the Hall-Rabushka plan had established the idea before that, and the Bradley-Gephardt dual-rate bill had been introduced in Congress. Reagan himself had expressed interest some months earlier.[1]

Whatever the immediate cause, the president was enthusiastic. "It was the kind of simple idea that immediately appealed to the president," observed one White House aide. If a flat tax enhanced economic growth, he thought, it would cut the deficit, foreclosing the need for a dreaded tax increase. Moreover, the notion was in keeping with Reagan's deeply rooted, fiercely held opposition to big government. He often remarked that when success as an actor put him in the top World War II tax bracket of 94 percent, he quit making movies! To the president, the lesson was obvious: high tax rates discouraged individual and corporate initiative. Thus, White House adviser Mitch Daniels insisted that "lower rates were the core" of Reagan's interest in tax reform, especially "getting the top rate down as low as possible." This

was, Stockman confirmed, "one of the few things Ronald Reagan deeply wanted."[2]

The idea of flat taxes spun like a top around the corridors of the west wing of the White House in late 1982. "Everyone . . . was talking flat tax," writes the former budget director, "presenting his own version of how it would work."[3] Seeking a bold initiative for 1983, some began drafting language to that effect. The president made mention of the idea for weeks.

In the end, however, a flat-tax proposal was not included in the 1983 State of the Union address. "As [the drafts] came back from the White House . . . the tax-reform paragraphs got watered down step by step," recalled one disappointed Treasury aide. "We were reduced to an afterthought."[4] In part, this was because the necessary consensus on details and definitions never formed. Professionals at Treasury rejected a completely flat-rate tax as regressive and politically unrealistic. Speaking on behalf of his department, Regan objected that, in the aggregate, such a plan would "result in people with annual incomes above $50,000 paying less in taxes, while those with earnings in the middle and lower range would pay $32 billion more!"[5] Treasury wanted tax reform, but according to its own institutional and professional standards, not some ideological icon. Meanwhile, the White House deputy chief of staff, Richard Darman, along with Stockman and Martin Feldstein, the chairman of the president's Council of Economic Advisers, preferred higher taxes, not lower ones. They quietly plotted to turn the president's enthusiasm for flat rates into approval for a "contingency" tax, their not very straightforward plan to solve the deficit problem.

Ultimately, the chief of staff put a stop to it all. A pragmatist, Jim Baker had no special affinity for such reforms, and he worried about the politically dangerous sand traps the golfing twosome had overlooked. As Stockman said: "It meant that we were fixing to cancel the mortgage deduction and tax the welfare checks of blind people. So Shultz' original flat tax idea was packed off to Siberia, in this case a 'deep study mode' at Treasury."[6] Indeed, the study mode was so deep that when the January 1983 address was finally delivered, the president provoked no reaction at all from the Congress. On this occasion, virtually no one outside of Treasury even noticed the one-line request that the department "continue to study ways to simplify the tax code and make it more fair for all Americans."

# Treasury Won: An Economist's Dream

Departmental professionals had noticed, of course, and they used the opportunity to keep their own recipes for reform cooking on the back burner. By December 1983 they were searching for ways to get them back on the menu—"to begin exposing the president to various fundamental reform options" in the words of then-Deputy Assistant Secretary Ronald Pearlman—when presidential politics suddenly turned up the heat. As the 1984 primaries approached, the White House learned that Sen. Bill Bradley was working tenaciously to convince Democrats (especially presidential hopeful Walter Mondale) to endorse the Bradley-Gephardt Fair Tax plan. Standing guard over the president's 1984 electoral interests, Baker wanted a plausible comeback. Should Mondale take Bradley's bait, he reasoned, the president must be able to point to his own work on the subject. A full-fledged Treasury study would fit the bill.

Politics thus explained why tax reform was officially turned over to Treasury in 1984. Baker stated unequivocally: "The true reason that we as an administration undertook an examination of this issue was because we were concerned that the other side would be embracing it and using it against us in the 1984 presidential election." In the terms of one analyst, the political stream had (momentarily) merged with the solutions proposed by Treasury tax experts to form a powerful current of support for an administration tax-reform initiative.[7] Needless to say, it was a combination the president—who still hoped reform might provide a further means of cutting taxes—happily endorsed.

## A Study Is Born

Although Democrats in Congress laughed off the request as "just another study," Treasury officials were delighted at the chance to rekindle their efforts. Old hands recognized the deck was stacked against them. Yet, as former economic staff coordinator Eugene Steuerle reminisced, it was a chance to "really pull together the theories," and to "explore the frontier."

While the economists' enthusiasm was readily understandable, Secretary Regan's motivations were more complex. As the potential domestic policy highlight of Reagan's second term, tax reform piqued his proprietary interests. Yet its selection was by no means ensured, and Baker's initial reactions suggested that the venture would be fraught with political risks. Even so, the Treasury chief eagerly embraced the challenge.

As an officer of Merrill Lynch before heading to Treasury, Regan had earned a reputation as a maverick, a "corporate populist" on Wall Street. Unlike many businessmen, he embraced the economists' belief that the tax system should be neutral in its effects on different and competing industries:

> For most of my career on Wall Street, I chafed under laws and regulations that gave the banking industry tax breaks that brokerage firms were denied. . . . When the same concept is extended to entire industries, the results range from the absurd to the near piratical.

Regan also had strong negative opinions about the individual side of the tax code, which he deemed "complicated" and "inequitable." To convince the president of this, Regan showed him that General Electric (Reagan's old employer) paid less in taxes than the chief executive's personal secretary. All in all, Regan firmly believed, a tax code that "institutionalized tax avoidance" was bad for the country. "I wanted to throw it out and start over," he remembers.[8]

On Wall Street, Regan's blustery style and radical ideas had put him at odds with the financial establishment. Those same qualities also put him on the outskirts of Washington's inner circle. On Capitol Hill and among the city's prestigious law firms and lobbies, the new Treasury secretary was discounted as a neophyte with questionable political skills.

Ultimately, this denigration inspired Regan to fight back via tax reform in the same way that he had earlier revolutionized the securities industry.

During the 1984 State of the Union speech, Regan recalled feeling that the Democratic snickering was directed at him as well as at his president. "My anger rose," he later wrote. "I said to myself, just wait. I'll show you guys."[9]

## A Revolution Afoot

Two weeks later Regan set out to do just that. As he told the chosen few who had been tapped for the task, the aim was to "revolutionize" the tax code. "Be bold," he instructed. "To think . . . compromise [is] to doom the effort." In Regan's memory his core of professionals had "absolute freedom of thought, speech, and action; political considerations were irrelevant. They were to disregard every factor except fairness, simplicity, and efficiency. 'Nothing is sacred,' I told them."[10]

Regan's own preference for order and hierarchy, reinforced by the professionals' training, meant the Treasury I process pursued a classic path of rational decision making, beginning with a careful diagnosis of the tax code's principal problems. Next, alternative schools of reform were identified and a basic approach was agreed to. Finally, the code was divided into its primary components and an exhaustive list of specific options was examined and debated. Decision-making responsibility was assigned to a select "tax strategy group" comprising the secretary, his business community liaison, key assistant and deputy assistant secretaries with responsibility for economic or tax policy, and the chief of the Internal Revenue Service (IRS).[11] Technical responsibility was shared by the Offices of Tax Policy (dominated by lawyers) and Tax Analysis (staffed by economists).

From start to finish the process took nearly a year as analysts reviewed existing law and crafted the best alternatives their professions had to offer. Early on, when tax theory was the focus of discussion, departmental economists led the process. Later, the lawyers joined in as the group combed through the tax code, zooming in on objectionable provisions, devising substitutes, drafting position papers, and preparing summaries.

Each week the tax strategy group met to discuss, debate, and vote on suggested revisions and proposals. The procedure and organization were deceptively routine. Only Regan's choice of participants, his embargo on outside communication, and his decision to hold political considerations at bay gave away the true dimensions of the revolution afoot.

Predictably, the key to this freedom was Regan's willingness to shelter his forces from the winds of politics and interagency haggling. He forbade all such influences from entering Treasury meeting rooms and took measures to prevent outsiders from listening at the doors. Virtually no one else in the department or outside was privy to the process or materials, including other members of the cabinet and emissaries from Capitol Hill. Even the president and his advis-

ers kept themselves on the other side of Treasury's iron fence. Pearlman recalled:

> The secretary made a decision that we would discuss our recommendations with no one. We'd get a call from a cabinet member saying, "What are you doing to *my* constituency?" And, we'd say, "Sorry, we'll talk to you about the *issues,* but we will not talk about what we're going to do." Members of Congress would also call, and we'd say, "Sorry." I remember going up to the Hill and getting beaten over the head by fairly influential members who said, "This is outrageous. You can't do this."

The Treasury Department is known for secrecy, something one observer attributed to its leakproof organizational culture. Career employees often deal with sensitive financial information and with closely guarded presidential initiatives. Yet the code of silence was extreme even by Treasury standards because it suited White House interests as well as Regan's personal style.

Although the secrecy sacrificed a degree of outsider insight, technical advice, and political goodwill, Treasury I would never have emerged as pure without it. In particular, the White House hands-off policy provided freedom to pursue tax reform as the professionals defined it—with far-reaching consequences. Indeed, the president's interest in lower rates *and* no additional taxes was reshaped by experts into the most politically painful and effective discipline in the tax-reform process: revenue neutrality. This tough new standard, which had also been employed in Bradley-Gephardt, said that reform could neither lose nor raise income-tax revenues. Unlike the president, most departmental economists were deeply concerned about enormous federal deficits and were determined not to exacerbate the problem. As Charles McLure put it: "The president said we couldn't raise revenues, and we sure weren't going to lose revenues if I had anything to say about it."

Subsequent to Treasury I—from the preparation of Treasury II to the final passage of H.R. 3838—the contrivance worked to constrain the foes of tax reform and empower its friends. How? By forcing politicians to give up their pet preferences to attain what few of them dared to oppose: lower tax rates. Without the option of raising or losing revenue, base broadening became the principal means to lower rates.

Because base broadening proved to be a highly complex task, policy makers turned to experts and professionals for extra help in crafting proposals. First, politicians had to consider the distributional, sectoral, and revenue implications of their actions, which necessitated reliance on highly skilled revenue estimators and tax economists. Second, when it came to tinkering with details, experts had always been the idea men in tax policy. With so much change in the works, professionals and politicians became locked together as a powerful and ultimately unbeatable duo.

**Always the Same.** If the White House had no detailed tax-reform ideas, the professionals at Treasury certainly did. As Chapoton observed:

> If you give reform to the tax professionals, you're always going to get the same answers, regardless of political party. You'll be moving toward a pure income tax system . . . [one that only] raises revenue . . . and that influences capital flows to a minimum.

Although such remedies are most commonly identified with economists, they were also shared by departmental lawyers and IRS accountants for reasons of organizational culture and mission, as well as for simplicity in tax administration.

Even so, while experts everywhere agreed that the tax code's problems were severe and that "something" should be done to promote horizontal equity, investment neutrality, and a broad tax base, the larger community of tax professionals and economists argued continuously about what that "something" was. Early Treasury action reflected these debates as the strategy group and its staff of experts defined problems and outlined the broad contours of reform.

## Diagnosing the Problem

Looking back, Treasury's assessment of the tax code's principal flaws reflected both its institutional biases and professional assumptions. From a professional perspective, the worst failures were believed to spring from differential treatment of similarly situated individuals and corporations, which produced inequalities, inefficiencies, and lower economic

growth. For example, the Office of Tax Analysis estimated that under existing tax law (with a 5 percent rate of inflation) the effective corporate tax rate varied from—8 percent on some kinds of equipment to +40 percent on most structures. Because different businesses invest in different assets, this meant that effective tax rates varied enormously across industries, most notably between capital intensive operations that were highly favored by the tax code and service industries that were not (see Table 7.2).

Treasury experts pointed to similar inequities on the individual side of the code due to special preferences like employee fringe benefits; state and local taxes; business perquisites for meals, entertainment, automobiles, and "working" vacations; and the explosion of tax shelters. A Treasury Department report counted a 400 percent increase in the number of claims for partnership losses—a common shelter—between 1963 and 1982. "Obviously unfair," instructed the authors of the Treasury report. "Even at moderate income levels, taxpayers with similar incomes can incur tax liabilities that differ by thousands of dollars."[12]

From an institutional perspective, Treasury Department professionals worried about two kinds of per-

**Table 7.2** **Effective Tax Rates on Investments in Equipment and Structures by Selected Industries under Existing Law**

| Industry | Tax Rate (percent) |
|---|---|
| Agriculture | 29 |
| Mining | 13 |
| Logging | 21 |
| Primary metals | 16 |
| Electrical equipment | 26 |
| Motor vehicles | 8 |
| Food | 25 |
| Textiles | 19 |
| Pulp and paper | 12 |
| Petroleum refining | 12 |
| Leather | 30 |
| Transport services | 9 |
| Service and trade | 31 |

*Source:* U.S. Department of the Treasury, Office of Tax Analysis, "Tax Reform for Fairness, Simplicity, and Economic Growth: The Treasury Department Report to the President," *Tax Notes,* December 3, 1984, 916.

*Note:* Assumes equity financing for a corporation in the 46 percent bracket with an inflation rate of 5 percent.

verse effects associated with the complexity of the tax code. First, the IRS argued that the labyrinthian tax code with its jumble of contradictory and overlapping policies was a nightmare to administer. Partly because of the rash of major changes in the tax law in 1978, 1981, 1982, and 1984, the IRS was years behind in issuing regulations.

Second, and more troubling still, Treasury officials believed that this jumbled system threatened the department's central mission: raising sufficient revenues to finance government. Quoting Steuerle:

> I felt that if we got out a good study, we could uphold the tradition and reputation of the Treasury Department. The Department's mission is to stand up for the public interest. Congress and taxpayers always bombard the Treasury with requests for special provisions. Recently Treasury had gotten into the political position of never trying to offend anyone and, therefore, not opposing adequately ideas that were clearly bad for the public interest.

The resulting explosion of tax expenditures during the 1970s and early 1980s had dramatically eroded the income-tax base. By 1982 the amount of revenues forgone because of tax expenditures equaled 73 percent of all income taxes collected.[13] Even worse, department officials feared that a "decline in taxpayer morale" could ultimately reduce voluntary compliance and lead to massive tax avoidance. They pointed to evidence that American taxpayers—like their European counterparts—increasingly under-reported income and overstated deductions and expenses. The Office of Tax Analysis estimated that individual taxpayers failed to report $250 billion in 1981, contributing to a total tax loss of $90.5 billion that year.[14] After adjusting for inflation, this loss was 61 percent greater than it had been only five years earlier.

Thus, despite all the subsequent debate over alternative strategies and options, the general goals of reform were hardly questioned around Regan's table. So many assumptions were shared that Treasury's objectives could be spelled out as soon as the president requested the 1984 tax-reform study:

> [We should] simplify the tax code so that the average person can understand it and fewer wasteful

efforts will be taken to develop "tax deals" that do not promote economic growth . . . ensure more equal treatment of people and families in equal economic circumstances . . . reduce marginal rates to improve economic incentives without raising middle income families' share of the tax burden . . . remove disincentives to savings . . . [and] provide careful transition rules.[15]

## The Limits of Consensus: Choosing a Tax Base

Consensus on goals did not guarantee agreement on means. Economic theory and opinion were divided, and Treasury debates reflected those disagreements. In particular, two different approaches to tax reform existed. One focused on perfecting the existing income-tax system by bringing taxable income into line with true economic income. This could be accomplished with a broad-based, flatter rate income tax indexed to inflation. A single-rate indexed income tax was also an option in deference to the president and other supporters of such an approach. A second approach was to tax consumption instead of income by implementing a national sales or value-added tax (VAT) and a consumed-income tax.

The give-and-take over these options was as stimulating as a civil servant could ask. But although the opportunity to debate truly comprehensive and systematic reform—with a minimum of political interference—was unique, the department's reliance on professional norms and standards to frame the discussion and define policy options was not. As one public administrator has observed, "[professionalism is] the characteristic of public service . . . most significant today."[16]

**Neither Flat nor VAT.** In February 1985 analysts began sorting through the various alternatives.[17] As the work proceeded, two of the four options were quickly rejected as inappropriate. Experts dismissed a purely flat-rate tax, just as they had when the president first expressed enthusiasm for the idea in 1982, and for the same reason. It was unacceptably regressive. According to the Office of Tax Analysis, in order to be revenue neutral, a single flat rate of 16.8 percent would be required. Even with provisions designed to eliminate taxes on very poor families, such a tax would nearly double the share of federal taxes already paid by families earning less than $20,000 and would decrease the share of taxes paid by those earning over $100,000 by almost half. This was unthinkable.

A VAT and a national sales tax received slightly more consideration, as reflected in volume 3 of Treasury's "Report to the President." As that analysis explained, a national sales tax would impose a percentage tax on most or all retail sales, as is currently done in forty-five states. A value-added tax worked less visibly but toward the same end, by applying a tax to the incremental increase in the value of a product at each stage in its production. In the latter instance, no additional taxes were needed at the point of purchase because they were already embedded in the costs of goods themselves.

From the economists' perspective, such taxes had real advantages: because they are paid only when goods are purchased, they would not discourage saving and investment the way income taxes do, and thus they should ultimately enhance economic growth. But such taxes are regressive, they would impose significant administrative burdens and costs, and they would be inflationary. Conservatives also feared that the public's ready acceptance of such taxes, which are paid out in small increments, might provide a powerful new engine for government spending and growth, as had been the case in many European countries. Ultimately, though, most Treasury officials viewed them only as an alternative to true reform. "Although it made some sense for revenue-raising purposes," Pearlman observed, "we didn't want the VAT to be an excuse for not addressing the [problems of] the income tax."

**A Consumed-Income Tax.** The rejection of the flat and the value-added taxes left two important alternatives: a comprehensive income and a consumed-income tax. The latter was more radical.

As its name implies, a consumed-income tax uses consumption, not earnings, as a basis for taxation. Under this concept, to the extent that income is saved rather than borrowed or spent, it could be deducted from taxable income. Many economists favored this approach because it encouraged people to save and because it better measured people's ability to pay taxes.[18]

A consumed-income tax would also simplify complexities that stem from attempting to measure income on an annual basis. The existing income tax required highly complex procedures for handling

long-term investments. In contrast, by allowing businesses to immediately write off costs of purchasing capital assets and inventories, the consumed-income tax could eliminate complexities like depreciation and capital gains differentials in one fell swoop.

Not all economists liked the idea, however Joseph Pechman wrote that it might permit "the accumulation of vast fortunes which would give the owners the ability to exercise great power over the economic and political life of the nation."[19] Others focused on the serious difficulties stemming from the transition to such a system. Since no other countries use a consumed-income tax, would the government have to renegotiate all the nation's tax treaties? Finally, while the consumed-income tax promised to simplify the administration of business taxes, it threatened to complicate personal taxes for anyone borrowing money to make a large capital purchase, most obviously a home or an automobile.[20]

Inside Treasury, resistance came from both the top and the bottom. Although technical problems might have been ironed out, Secretary Regan worried about a greater obstacle—high levels of public confusion and resistance. The specter of widespread public opposition dogged the discussions around the strategy table. Pearlman recalled:

> I remember one Saturday morning when we were talking about this . . . Regan said, "I'll tell you what. The next time you go to a cocktail party, you ask people what they think about a tax system that says borrowings are income and repayments or savings are deductions. They're going to tell you you're crazy!

Although the boss's reluctance might have been enough to block the notion, he was hardly alone. Economist Manuel Johnson recalled widespread rank-and-file resistance to such fundamental change in standard operating procedures and assumptions:

> The tax policy division was institutionally geared to a base-broadening income tax. All the legal expertise in the Tax Policy Division was trained in that direction. . . . IRS was also geared toward that structure. They were intensely concerned about tax shelters and were very strongly in support of broadening the tax base to eliminate all this, what they thought of as useless stuff. That combination

was very formidable. If you wanted to move in another direction, you had to resist the whole institutional structure, and they could be extremely stubborn.

Key decision makers ultimately agreed that the consumed-income tax approach was too risky. As McLure recalled, "We could not afford to get to the end of the process and say, 'We tried but couldn't do it.' We couldn't write a law that didn't work." Moreover, no one wanted to be laughed at. "It was such a change," observed Pearlman, "that we weren't sure people would take it seriously."

Still, "a lot of us were disappointed," lamented Johnson. "It made a heck of a lot of sense," agreed Pearlman. In fact, as Pearlman later acknowledged, the abstract lure of the consumed-income tax meant that Treasury officials "probably made the decision to drop [the idea] later than we should have, in terms of devoting resources." While their professional fascination with the notion was understandable, it was also revealing. The very fact that serious and prolonged consideration was given to such a radical change in the tax system—and one very different from what ordinary citizens imagined when asked about tax reform—illustrates the highly rarefied character of Treasury I's decision-making process and the powerful influence of economic ideas and professional norms at that early stage of tax reform.

**A Comprehensive Income Tax.**  Once the idea of a consumed-income tax was set to rest, the strategy group and its staff of analysts focused on perfecting the existing income tax. The objective was relatively straightforward: to equate *taxable* with *economic* income as fully as possible. For example, if employees received compensation in the form of pension, health, or other fringe benefits rather than wages, the monetary value of these benefits would be taxed. But the legitimate costs of earning income, from the payment of mandatory union dues to the purchase of uniforms, would not. The result would be a broad-based tax with lower, less steeply graduated rates.

Although many thorny technical issues had to be resolved, the task primarily demanded that conventional economic wisdom be distilled into practical proposals. Indeed, Eugene Steuerle, the economist and career bureaucrat who led the economic team charged with generating legislative options, began by compiling and integrating the various ideas and proposals that had accumulated over many years.

> I went through every set of reform proposals that I could find, and I went to every member of the staff, encouraging them to put forward suggestions on how the income tax could be perfected. I wanted to be as comprehensive as possible. In addition, I argued that a general study should be accompanied by a "how to" manual, giving detailed guidance as to how a bill should be drafted. Then members of Congress could vote provisions up or down on a moment's notice—and a moment is often all one gets in the congressional process.

Steuerle's approach had the added advantage of hedging the department's bets on Treasury I. He and others were well aware that the Treasury study's fate was not yet certain and that past reform initiatives had been dismally received in the political arena. He hoped that a catalog of specific, well-crafted proposals could be drawn upon in the future in an incremental fashion if a comprehensive package were not adopted at that time. In his words:

> It wasn't clear that this effort would be anything more than a study. In 1982 and 1984, Bob Dole had been able to achieve some tax reform by simply pulling together a set of proposals that were already well enough developed that they could be voted up or down quickly. Here was our chance to fill the hopper with good ideas.

## Designing a Proposal

Deciding on the basic framework for tax reform had taken five months, from February to June 1984. Yet the group's sojourn ended where it might have begun—in a decision to *improve* rather than *reject* the existing income-tax system. At that point only six months remained until the president's publicly announced due date. Immediately, the tax code was divided into sixteen basic modules, and the economic staff began generating specific reform proposals in each of the areas. The strategy group often began meeting more than once a week.

Just compiling the statistics needed for accurate analysis of the distributional effects of tax law changes was a huge research task.[21] Outside consultants provided some assistance, but the veil of secrecy limited their participation. Even more constraining were the internal limits on staffing and time. Although the tax strategy group devoted unprecedented attention to tax reform, they had competing responsibilities as well—negotiations over DEFRA, the annual economic summit, and the 1984 presidential campaign. Moreover, many of the lawyers in the Office of Tax Policy were occupied with drafting DEFRA and were not readily available to the tax group until August.

Still, it was a hectic and heady experience for all concerned. Regan even compared it to a "dream come true," adding. "The give and take of meetings in which first class minds grappling with a problem that had generally been regarded as insoluble was extremely satisfying. . . . There is no exhilaration like [that] of working all out in the public interest."[22] Others recalled the process in somewhat less idyllic tones: "The tax-policy types went back to all of the ideas they'd ever had in their drawers and presented them in a fairly logical fashion," remarked one. "It was a hell of a lot of work," added economist Beryl Sprinkel. "I never knew the tax code was so vast."

As the exercise progressed, the only major guidelines were that the final product be revenue and distributionally neutral and that it be consistent with the economic logic of a comprehensive income-tax system. Although rate reduction had been the president's primary interest in tax reform from the very beginning. Treasury experts left the issue of tax rates until the very end. Their intention was to expand the tax base as broadly as possible and then reduce tax rates as low as the additional revenues permitted without changing the distribution of the tax burden amont different income classes. To be sure, the group believed that cleansing the code would permit a dramatic lowering of the rates, but no one could be certain.[23] "We were flying blind," acknowledged McLure.

# Reform for Individuals: Implementing Conventional Wisdom

On the individual side of the tax code, the Treasury I process focused on three major issues: broadening the individual tax base; simplifying the taxpaying process; and removing the poor from the tax rolls.

## Broadening the Base

When Ron Pearlman said that improving the current system "*means* base broadening," he was speaking for most tax experts. For them, ridding the tax code of special incentives and preferences, with their inevitable distortions and inequities, was the penultimate goal of reform. Thus, the Treasury proposal recommended unprecedented base-broadening measures, both by including income that was excluded from taxation and by eliminating costly and widely used deductions that reduced taxable income. Although most of these Treasury proposals became enormously controversial in the political arena, they did not go as far as many Treasury economists would have liked. Nor did they raise sufficient revenues to dramatically lower income-tax rates. Ultimately, individual rate reductions had to be financed in part through additional revenues extracted from corporation.

**Excising Exemptions.** Exclusions and exemptions, which allow tax-payers to exclude or subtract money or implicit income before calculating their adjusted gross income (AGI), were one important class of potential base broadeners that Treasury reformers scrutinized in great detail. Some of their resulting recommendations were aimed mainly at the rich, such as tough new restrictions designed to reduce by 80 percent the federal tax revenues lost on interest from tax-exempt municipal bonds.[24] Others directly affected millions of average Americans. Base-broadening reforms hit tax breaks for fringe benefits like life insurance, death benefits, dependent care, education, and legal services. They also targeted special treatment for wage replacements including unemployment, black lung and disability benefits, workmen's compensation, student scholarships, and fellowships. Reformers even played tough with benefits for the nation's war veterans. "Sacred cows were falling like tenpins," commented Don Regan. He recounted the decision to tax the rental value of parsonages provided to clergymen: "The logic of equal treatment that we had imposed on every similar question dictated the answer. "Tax it as income,' I ruled, adding, 'we've mugged everybody else—why should the clergy escape?' "[25]

Still, as bold as it was, the plan did not eliminate all exclusions from income. While some reformers were willing to ignore politics entirely others had no intention of winning professional battles only to lose the legislative war. Thus, health insurance—the largest and politically most revered fringe benefit—was only nicked, not bludgeoned. The plan taxed only values exceeding $70 per month for individuals and $175 for families, leaving 70 percent of families unscathed. Social security benefits remained sacrosanct, and individual retirement accounts (which some administration officials touted as advancing family values) were even expanded, allowing new exemptions for full-time homemakers.

**Downing Deductions.** Deductions from AGI, which lowered taxable income for itemizing taxpayers, were another class of individual preferences targeted by the tax strategy group. Here, too, the economists' goal of horizontal equity played a strong role in weeding out unacceptable items. Once again, however, the base broadening was uneven, combining dramatic proposals to restrict or eliminate popular deductions with some equally striking omissions.

The most extreme Treasury proposal in this area terminated the deduction for state and local income, property, and sales taxes. This recommendation eliminated the single most generous tax break for millions of Americans, one that had been in the tax code since its inception in 1913. Moreover, because the deduction made state and local taxes less painful to citizens, it was vigorously defended by governors, mayors, and public school officials nationwide.

But to reformers, the state and local deduction was simply too big to ignore. In fiscal year 1985 alone this tax deduction was estimated to cost the federal treasury almost $31 billion in revenues forgone.[26] So large an amount would help to lower tax rates significantly. Equally important to Treasury economists, the subsidy was deemed "inefficient" and "unfair," disproportionately benefiting wealthy individuals and communities. Finally, like the interest exclusion on tax-exempt bonds, tax reformers, at Treasury viewed the deduction as just an outmoded vestige of American federalism. As the report declared, "There is no more reason for a federal subsidy for spending by state and local governments than for private spending."[27]

Left wholly unscathed was the entire deduction for mortgage interest expenses on primary residences. This was the largest single departure from economic principles in the Treasury recommendations, and it resulted from one of the few occasions when outside politics directly intervened. Recognizing the reveren-

tial status accorded homeownership and the monumental clout of the real estate, timber, and home-building industries, Treasury economists never considered a full-blown assault on the $25 billion deduction; but they were examining ways to restrict or gradually phase it out. But when the president acknowledged during a meeting with the National Association of Realtors (NAR) in May 1984 that the deduction had not been removed from Treasury's table, the resulting political firestorm forced the White House to publicly declare the deduction off limits. Looking back, a disgruntled McLure called this failure "the achilles heel of tax reform" because the loss made it "impossible to construct a rational and consistent approach to tax treatment of interest."[28]

## Simplifying the Code

For millions of Americans who dread their annual encounter with the 1040 form, simplification was a touchstone of tax reform. Politicians accordingly seized on the symbol, and most reformers paid homage to the goal. Yet Treasury I's authors never gave tax simplification the priority that base broadening received (although the two are not incompatible), nor did Congress later. As in the existing code, simplicity was always the first and easiest goal to be sacrificed.

Nevertheless, Treasury estimates did show that raising the income threshold at which tax liability begins (the so-called zero-bracket amount) would reduce the *size* of the taxpaying population. Moreover, base broadening and a larger personal exemption would cut by one-third the number of taxpayers for whom the time and trouble of itemizing deductions would remain worthwhile. If Treasury I's recommendations were implemented, the department estimated that three-quarters of all taxpayers would submit the IRS short form come April 15.[29] Finally, the authors held out the prospect of creating a "filing-free tax system" for those individuals willing to trust the IRS to calculate their taxes on the basis of employer and financial documents filed with the government. Thus, most Americans could anticipate a simpler tax system as well as a fairer, more efficient one if the Treasury recommendations were adopted.

## Removing the Poor

One additional tax fairness issue that had raised concerns among tax professionals since the late 1970s was the increasingly large federal tax burden on poor and low-income individuals.[30] Three factors were at work. First, pay increases designed to compensate for high inflation were driving low-income wage earners into higher tax brackets or onto the tax rolls for the first time. Second, recent large increases in social security payroll taxes fell on the nation's work force in a regressive manner. Third, the huge individual and corporate tax cuts adopted as part of ERTA in 1981 had produced disproportionate tax savings for the wealthiest Americans and made the federal tax system more regressive than it had been in the 1970s.

Even before Treasury I, there was growing political and professional consensus that this unfair situation needed correction. Joining liberals on the issue were populist conservatives like Rep. Jack Kemp, R-N.Y., whose Fair and Simple Tax (FAST) bill proposed removing 1.5 million poor from the tax rolls.[31]

Treasury I shared the objective of reducing or eliminating income-tax burdens on the poor—a move that became extremely important in the subsequent politics of tax reform because it bolstered Democratic support for the administration's effort and enhanced its image of fairness. Although the president had given no guidance on this matter, he had accepted conservative arguments that expanding the personal exemption would benefit middle-class families. Steuerle explained, "Since the president and the White House began pushing for an increase in the personal exemption long before tax reform got under way, it was easy to combine the desire of some to reduce taxes for the poor with the desire of others to be 'pro-family.' A more perfect liberal-conservative coalition couldn't have existed." The Treasury plan removed many poor individuals and families from the federal income-tax rolls (and also reduced taxes on many of the nonpoor) by almost doubling the personal exemption, from $1,090 to $2,000 annually. Second, it increased the standard deduction for all filers, especially for heads of households. Third, it expanded and indexed for inflation the earned-income credit. Together, these expensive reforms would have increased by one-third the percentage of taxpayers owing no income taxes. Virtually all families with incomes below the poverty line were dropped from the income-tax rolls. According to Treasury estimates, 37 percent of families with incomes below $15,000 would enjoy lower taxes, while only a tiny fraction would see their liabilities increased.[32]

## The Conflict over Corporate Taxation

Having thus applied conventional economic wisdom to the individual side of the tax code, Treasury reformers turned to the more challenging assignment of refashioning corporate taxes. Although the corporate income tax generates a small and declining share of federal revenues, it is far more complex than the individual income tax. Moreover, while economists generally agreed on what a reformed individual income tax should look like, there was far less consensus about the corporate tax. Some proposed the total integration of corporate and individual income taxes, while others favored special treatment for certain forms of investment.

## The Accidental Populists

It was late October 1984 when the tax strategy group sat back to contemplate its accomplishments. Everyone expected to be rewarded for their hard work in the form of lower tax rates. To determine how low, tax reform was handed over to the department's revenue estimators who were reminded of the three ground rules guiding their work. First, the plan should be revenue neutral. There must be no added taxes or revenues forgone. Second, with the exception of the working poor, it should be distributionally neutral across income classes. There must be no windfalls or shortfalls. Third, it should be structurally neutral between individuals and corporations. Such a system of "separate ledgers" meant that final rates for both sides of the tax code would be established independently, according to how broadly the relevant base had been expanded.

The question on everyone's mind was: How low would rates go? Earlier research by Steuerle had shown that marginal income-tax rates during the 1950s and 1960s—before the growth of many of the tax expenditures scheduled for Treasury I's chopping block—had averaged between 20 percent and 22 percent for the vast majority of American taxpayers.[33] McLure and others assumed that the revenue estimators would return with similar figures. But when they reported back with their printouts, the results were far different. As Johnson remembered: "I was apoplectic.

Here it was, October, almost November, and we had done all that work and had brought the [top individual] rate down by only eight points [from 50 to 42 percent]. That was one of the most depressing meetings we had."

Politically, the modest drop in the top rate was disastrous, undermining the entire strategy of building a reform coalition on the appeal of very low, "show-stopper" rates. After all, the Kemp-Kasten proposal offered a flat rate of 24 percent, while the more progressive Bradley-Gephardt proposal's top rate was still only 30 percent. The president would never support such a controversial plan without having more to show for it, nor would supply-siders seeking economic vitality via low tax rates for entrepreneurs. To conventional economists as well, a 42 percent top rate was not low enough to end wealthy taxpayers' craving for tax shelters.

Fortunately, the early estimates were preliminary, and the number crunchers continued working. Distributional neutrality could be defined in somewhat different ways, they found, and this allowed the top rate to come down. Then, too, some additional base broadeners could be added. When these changes were made, the estimators produced a lower three-rate structure of 16-28-37. It was not what economists had hoped for, but it was in the ballpark.

Then a new and equally serious objection reared its head, this time from the department's lawyers. It won't work, they said. Rather than creating a level playing field, the plan would guarantee the creation of a whole new generation of tax shelters. They explained that because there was a nine percentage point difference between the top individual rate of 37 percent and the top corporate rate of 28 percent, partnerships and sole proprietorships (which are taxed as individuals) would be encouraged to convert into corporations. As Pearlman recalled: "When they came back with that rate structure, we *lawyers* said to the secretary. 'We can't have that much disparity. . . . We'll have people deciding whether to go into or stay out of a corporate rate structure based on that rate. We have to reduce the spread.' "

The argument made sense, and Regan listened carefully. Besides he already had a problem with the individual rate structure—16-28-37 had no sex appeal, he complained. It sounded like "a football signal." In the secretary's mind, 15-25-35 was a catchier combination, one with real political potential. And, as he later bragged to the president, 35 percent "exactly halved" the top individual rate in place in 1981. All in all, 15-25-35 was the trio Regan favored, so he turned to his staff and said, in effect, "Do it."

It was easier said than done. Rate reductions of just a few percentage points would cost the treasury tens of billions of dollars once they were applied to tens of millions of taxpayers. But the lawyers provided a solution. To reduce the spread between the top individual and the corporate tax rates, the corporate rate would have to be increased. The resulting revenues could then be used to reduce the highest individual rate and to adjust the lower ones to maintain distributional neutrality. The revenue estimators found that with the proper juggling, a corporate rate of 33 percent, instead of 28 percent, could yield the desired individual rate structure of 15-25-35.

The result satisfied the lawyers and it gave the secretary the marketing edge he desired. But it also did far more. The change in rates altered the very politics of tax reform, converting what had been a modest facade of populism, embodied in the concept of greater tax fairness, into structural pillars that dominated the architecture of reform!

Like the decision on depreciation, the change in rates dramatically reversed past administration policies (which had been championed by Regan) by raising, rather than lowering, taxes on corporations. When combined with corporate base broadening, the decision on rates produced a net corporate tax increase of $165 billion over five years, or an average yearly increase of 30 percent.[34]

To be sure, the resulting increases in corporate taxes were highly relative, exaggerated by the partially unintended generosity of ERTA in 1981. Only the "tyranny of the starting point" made them look so substantial, observed McLure. Moreover, many key policy makers in Congress and the Treasury Department had already concluded that eliminating the costly, on-again off-again ITC was inevitable. Nevertheless, the resulting corporate tax windfall was used to reduce individual tax rates well beyond what could be done on the basis of base broadening alone, adding a populist dimension to the plan that surprised political observers on both the left and the right. Never originally intended, it grew out of professional and technical considerations, reinforced by political insulation. Intended or not, the result dramatically changed the subsequent politics of tax reform by giving a tax cut to millions of Americans. As Pearlman explained:

Our initial reason for doing this had nothing to do with trying to make this a net tax reduction for individuals. But once the politicians saw this they said, "Aha! This is the way we're going to sell tax reform. It's a tax reduction for individuals." Then it got a life of its own.

## To Be or Not to Be

With the tax rates decided, all the major outlines of the Treasury plan were established and the proposal was nearly complete. But it was still just a confidential Treasury proposal. Since the next step belonged to Ronald Reagan, consideration of Treasury I was placed on the president's schedule for November 26, 1984. While the Department hoped for a positive reception, the plan's prospects quickly dimmend when, with the election safely over, news of its contents began to leak from Treasury's high gray walls. Hearing snippets of what they regarded as very bad news, myriad interest groups began to light up the White House switchboards, hoping to head off disaster at the presidential pass. Republican "eagle pins," given in gratitude to wealthy political contributors, began "returning in flocks." Although the president retained his typically detached posture, White House staff, who had not been enthusiastic about tax reform to begin with, sought to insulate him from the negative response as they pondered the fate of Treasury I. Meanwhile, Regan fumed. "Before I briefed the President," he wrote with annoyance, there were news stories of "worried White House aides" who feared "Treasury's tax plan would launch a second term by alienating some of [the president's] staunchest supporters and exciting nobody."[35]

Trying to douse the flames of discontent before they raged out of control, the Treasury chief turned first to reason. Upon releasing the plan, he urged people to evaluate it in its entirety. Lower tax rates for both individuals and corporations, greater fairness, and reduced taxes on the poor were being overshadowed by parochial concerns, he warned. Yet fans of the existing tax code felt no need to read every page of the Treasury manifesto to catch its drift. They knew when their ox was being gored. Nor did most of Washington's political establishment want to be closely associated with it. Indeed, when one congressional wit dubbed it the "biggest trial balloon since the Hindenburg," even the stubborn Regan backtracked. He openly admitted that the plan was "written on a word processor," implying that its provisions could be changed if need be.

Regan's offer notwithstanding, the White House put so much distance between itself and Treasury I during this period that one departmental aide complained, "When [it] was printed up nobody was quite sure where to send it." Indeed, heads were shaking all over the Treasury Department.

### The Doomsayers

For weeks a storm of opposition raged relentlessly through the halls of Congress and the corridors of interest-group power in Washington. A lobbyist for real estate developers said the plan would "devastate" the second-home market and "wipe us out," adding, "Usually we exaggerate to get everyone hyped up, but this is no exaggeration."[36] The president of the National Association of Realtors charged that the plan would "drastically increase taxation of homeownership" and immediately joined forces with the powerful National Association of Home Builders and the Mortgage Bankers Association to oppose it.[37] Lobbyists for capital-intensive industries decried the elimination of accelerated depreciation, while a former Treasury official who helped craft ACRS claimed that tax reform would undermine capital investment and "reinstate the declining productivity growth . . . [of] the 1970s." The head of the AFL-CIO said the taxation of fringe benefits would do "serious and unnecessary harm" to the nation's workers. Public officials in New York said that eliminating the state and local tax deduction would be "ruinous to New York's economy" and formed a bipartisan coalition to oppose it. A study conducted for the nonprofit sector estimated that the Treasury plan would reduce charitable contributions by 15 percent. Banks, life insurance companies, chemical companies, oil producers, steel manufacturers, utilities, restaurants, sports and entertainment facilities, credit-card companies, credit unions, colleges, state and local governments, and veterans' groups all expressed immediate opposition to all or portions of the Treasury proposal.[38]

The negative reaction was not lost on members of Congress, and most rushed to defend particular constituencies or supporters. Although the plan was devised at the president's request, the response among congressional Republicans was particularly hostile.

Sen. Robert Packwood, R-Ore., who had just been selected chairman of the Senate Finance Committee, promised to "defeat" any legislation that sought to tax employee fringe benefits, a preference he had championed for many years.[39] In the House, an aide to Rep. Bill Archer, R-Texas, the second-ranking Republican on the Ways and Means Committee, recalled that "Republicans were livid over Treasury I—there were just so many unacceptable provisions." Even other members of the Reagan cabinet got into the act, expressing everything from concern to outright opposition.

## The Dragon Slayers

In normal times, this chorus of interest-group complaints and congressional reluctance would have been enough to speed Treasury's report to the nearest White House paper shredder. But the postelection period was not a "normal" time at 1600 Pennsylvania Avenue. Reagan's massive forty-nine state sweep on November 6 had elevated the president's "bully pulpit" to an even higher plane. Although no one expected Reagan's second "honeymoon" period to equal his first, the postelection months presented him a golden opportunity to dominate the national agenda with a bold presidential initiative. Yet the vacuous campaign had given the White House nothing suitable to propose. Therefore, when tax-reform proponents spoke up in response to Treasury I critics, White House strategists were more inclined than usual to listen. Here is what they heard.

**Academic Wisdom.** As could be expected, economists were among the most enthusiastic supporters. After all, Treasury I was an unusually pure statement of economic wisdom. "Ninety percent of Treasury I was what I thought it should have been," declared McLure, and economists from Walter Heller and Joseph Pechman on the left to Milton Friedman and George Stigler on the right lent their applause. Said Alan Blinder: "The fine staff of economists and lawyers at the U.S. Treasury knew what was wrong with the tax code and . . . how to fix it." Alice Rivlin, director of the Congressional Budget Office, called it "an economist's kind of reform." Even consumption-tax champions like Harvey Galper and Henry Aaron endorsed the plan as a substantial improvement over the existing system and the best available hope for comprehensive reform.[40] Only a few dissented—

mainly economists with supply-side leanings who advocated greater investment incentives. That group included former administration officials Murray Weidenbaum, Norman Ture, and Martin Feldstein.

**Good-Government Groups.** Well-known public-interest groups, including Common Cause, Citizens for Tax Justice, and the Tax Foundation, also sang the praises of Treasury I. So did a number of Democratic politicians. "It is a superb proposal," declared Arizona governor Bruce Babbitt. "It is so good that the president will not have the courage to endorse it!"[41] Rep. Charles Rangel, D-N.Y., a liberal from Harlem, praised the plan's reduction of taxes on the poor and introduced a modified version of the bill in Congress, calling it a "giant step forward toward a fair and equitable tax system."

**High-Tax Industries.** An equally important, if self-interested, element of support came from sectors of corporate America. Because the Treasury proposal redistributed corporate tax burdens (smoothing out the differences between capital-intensive and service industries) Treasury officials always believed retailers and wholesalers would support the reform. For similar reasons, those sectors were joined by high-tech companies and trade associations that received few tax preferences and paid high corporate tax rates. "We have reservations," said the head of one high-tech coalition, "but we think that . . . it will be very beneficial to our firms." Eighteen different firms and associations endorsed the Treasury plan in December, including IBM, General Mills, Bristol Myers, and the National Retail Merchants Association. Ultimately, these organizations formed the Tax Reform Action Coalition (TRAC), which lobbied actively on behalf of tax reform and undermined claims that reform was antibusiness.

**A Positive Press.** To the president's advisers, the most important tax-reform enthusiasts were the journalists and reporters who occupy the front-row seats at all important policy unveilings. They lavished enormous amounts of attention on Treasury I. During the last week of November and the first two weeks of December, the *Washington Post,* the *New York Times,* and the *Wall Street Journal* together carried more than twenty different news articles and fifteen editorials on various aspects of tax reform. Many other stories appeared in regional and local newspapers, on network news broadcasts, in national news weeklies, and in national business magazines.

Better yet for tax reform, media coverage was generally favorable. Taking their cues from the academics and good-government groups, most stories and editorials accepted the basic claim that the plan would make the tax system simpler, fairer, and better, although some raised questions about political feasibility and substantive details. Journalists also picked up on the new math of reform. "Some 56% of the nation's 91.4 million families would get a tax cut," reported *Time,* especially "low and middle income taxpayers."[42] Altogether, the extensive and favorable media reception helped sway White House opinion. In Steuerle's words, "It was the positive press reaction that got people thinking. 'Hey, maybe we *should* make this a political issue.' "

## Party Time

As White House aides began to give second thoughts to tax reform, they discovered two further political advantages. One was the siren song of history. Although the president's electoral victory gave him a tremendous opportunity to swing for the fences, only bean balls were being tossed around by White House strategists. Among the options then available, none of Reagan's policy advisers wanted to confront the deficit issue with detailed, substantive proposals. Neither did vague suggestions to tackle crime or foreign trade light up any faces around White House strategy tables. But tax reform, if enacted, promised to be the fiscal grand slam of Reagan's second term.

In addition, some were seduced by the hope that tax reform might trigger voter realignment—a once-in-a-generation opportunity to rewrite the ground rules of party competition in the United States. That prospect tugged especially hard on political strategists in the president's employ, whose business, after all, was electoral politics.

As Republicans were painfully aware, the 1930s witnessed the last such realignment. Then, Democrats had become the majority party and acquired a lasting edge in partisan identification among the voters. By late 1984, however, that edge was disappearing. In November 1984, some opinion polls showed a virtual tie in the percentage of people who identified themselves as Republicans and Democrats. To solidify these gains and perhaps precipitate a realignment, Republicans needed the right set of issues. The process of redefining the parties had begun in Reagan's first term, with its emphasis on lower taxes and less government, but history suggested that a "coincident issue" would be needed to solidify voters' attachment to their new party.[43]

Might tax reform be that issue? In absolute numbers, it created more winners than losers. Moreover, it embodied powerful moral symbols like fairness for the middle class. The president's political allies and advisers—Mitch Daniels in the White House, Frank Fahrenkopf, head of the Republican National Committee, and Richard Wirthlin, the president's chief pollster—believed passage of tax reform would help overcome the image of the Republican party as the defender of the rich and privileged and thus benefit all future Republican candidates. Nor were they alone. As reporter Hedrick Smith writes, "[Jack Kemp's] constant refrain in early 1985 was: 'Tax reform is a realigning issue.' " Democratic worries lent credence to Republican assertions. It is "the stuff of realignment," warned Sen. Bill Bradley in his efforts to gain Democratic support for his version of tax reform. "It's clear what's in it for the Republicans, if they support it and the president pushes for it."[44]

Such arguments eventually made headway among reluctant White House aides. In particular, Richard Darman, the administration's preeminent policy strategist, joined the chorus, predicting that tax reform could tap "legions of quiet populists," including many within the "vast world of the 'white collars,' " who were disillusioned with big government and big business.[45] With this vision uppermost in his mind, Darman set to work to enlist the ever-skeptical James Baker. Eventually, he succeeded.

In contrast to all the political agonizing at the staff level, there were no second thoughts within the Oval Office itself. When the issue was finally recommended as the domestic centerpiece of his second term, the president agreed immediately and enthusiastically. Explaining why, one Treasury insider said, "He wanted it more than his staff realized."

From the very start, Reagan was seduced by the allure of lower taxes, both as a symbol and as a means of implementing his philosophy of limited government. Indeed, the prospect of cutting the top marginal tax rate in half during his presidency, from 70 to 35 percent, was simply irresistible. Finally, it must be said that Regan had a way with Reagan. As the following anecdote illustrates, the Treasury secretary and the president seemed to enjoy an unusual and successful "locker-room" relationship. Given his chance, the boisterous Celt from Wall Street pitched the plan precisely right to appeal to his fellow Irishman, beginning by chastising the amiable Reagan for paying his fair share of taxes: " 'Sucker!' I said. 'With the right lawyer and the right accountant and the right tax shelters, you needn't have paid a penny in taxes even if you made more than a million dollars a year—and it would have been perfectly legal.' "[46]

For all his enthusiastic speechmaking and support for the enterprise, by all accounts Reagan was never more than vaguely acquainted with his own proposal. Beyond the basics, Reagan's understanding of the admittedly complex proposal was shallow. For instance, when he was first briefed on the tax plan, despite his obvious enthusiasm, Reagan asked few questions. Out of the entire extraordinary list of far-reaching tax changes, the president focused his concerns on just a few items, such as the proposal to eliminate the business deduction for country club dues.[47]

## Treasury II: Half a Loaf from the Baker

Transforming Treasury's trial balloon into a presidential proposal required balancing the principled integrity of Treasury I (which gathered support from the media, the academic community, and good-government groups) with the need to mollify interest-group opposition (which could spell dismal death in Congress). Yet, this inevitable political transformation was greatly magnified by a switch that stunned political Washington: the decision by White House Chief of Staff James Baker and Treasury Secretary Donald Regan to exchange jobs.

As Regan describes this event, the decision occurred almost by accident. When leaks began springing up about the hitherto secret tax-reform plan, Regan suspected the White House staff of sabotage, and he threatened to resign. Baker, in turn, sought to soothe Regan's ire by explaining the difficulties of controlling competing agendas and egos in the White House. The Treasury chief recounted his response:

"You know what the trouble with you is, Baker? You're tired. . . . You know what we should do,

Jim? We should swap jobs." Our conversation had been half-serious, half joking. I tossed out these words without thinking. But Baker bobbed his head like a man who had been hit with an idea. "Do you mean that?" he asked. I thought for a moment, "I guess I do."[48]

Although virtually unprecedented, the switch made sense to both men. For Regan, it was a chance to be in charge, to create a more businesslike White House operation. Above all, noted Chapoton, it was a chance to get closer to the president: "He was in awe of the presidency. I can remember meetings when his secretary would buzz and say: Jim Baker's on the line God, he'd jump up and take it. And I'd think, 'It's only Jimmy. Leave us alone. We're in a meeting.' But Jim was the president to Regan." Baker, in turn, would exchange the grinding pressures of the White House for the second most important and visible cabinet position in government and the challenge of making history by enacting comprehensive tax reform. A savvy politician, Baker knew that winning this one, against long odds, would secure his reputation for years to come. "[T]aking on this challenge," he allowed, "appealed to me." Accordingly, they presented the idea to the president, and on February 4, 1985, Donald Regan became the new presidential chief of staff, bringing along a coterie of aides from the Treasury Department. James Baker III became the new secretary of the Treasury, appointing his trusted assistant and colleague Richard Darman as deputy secretary.

It was an important development in the chronicle of tax reform, something many saw as a key to its success. "The swap was the best thing that could have happened," said Manuel Johnson. "A terrific stroke of genius or luck," concurred Mitch Daniels:

Jim Baker's as good a congressional handler and negotiator as the administration had, and he was put in a situation of doing that almost full time. And it put down here [in the White House] a person who conceived and believed in tax reform. If you had set out to make second term personnel decisions with only tax reform in mind, you might have decided on that switch.

Not only did Reagan's arrival put a strong proponent of reform in the White House, Baker's departure turned a reform skeptic into an advocate. "Until he got involved, I think his influence would have been negative," maintained Pearlman. "When Baker was at the White House, the staff was so hostile to tax reform. All he was hearing was the bad things. Once he got involved, he appreciated the power of the concept." Yet, the switch was not without its substantive consequences.

## Seeking the Political Fix

According to Regan, when it came to taxation, "the best politics is no politics."[49] In contrast, one Baker confidante noted that the Texan was "imbued with politics." The significance of this difference was—as one who knew all three men summed it up—that "Baker and Darman were much more interested in a political fix to everything."

This is not to say that the group that designed Treasury I had given no thought to its enactment. They had an overarching political strategy based on their goal of broadening the tax base. It was a "hostage strategy," in McLure's terms: "We thought that if we played no favorites, we could hold all the special interests hostage to each other." That is, in a revenue-neutral context, money to restore one group's preference could come only at the expense of others; barring such changes, all would share in the sacrifice.

In keeping with these differences in personal style and approach to policy making, the processes of writing Treasury I and Treasury II differed dramatically. While Treasury I began by defining economic income and expanding the taxable base, Treasury II began, in effect, with dessert. It took as its starting point the low rates that had been developed in the Treasury proposal. Baker and Darman then sweetened the earlier courses as well, making them as politically palatable as possible. Rather than meeting in secret with just a few close aides, Baker flung the doors of the department wide open. Lobbyists for every imaginable interest "wore out his carpet," according to one report.[50] Baker himself went to Capitol Hill to meet with key congressional leaders who would be involved in the legislative process, and he met privately with congressional sponsors of other tax-reform bills, trying to win their endorsement of a common bill.

**Building Coalitions.** The result was a series of important changes in the Treasury plan, retaining its broad outlines but substantially altering many of its provisions. Some were done for largely symbolic purposes, to deal with emotional issues where economic reasoning could not be made persuasive to the average American. For example, the floor on charitable contributions was removed. The parsonage allowance for ministers was restored. And the tax-exempt status of veterans' benefits was continued.

Even more common were changes that were carefully tailored to the task of building a stronger political coalition for reform legislation. The most important involved putting back, and even expanding, incentives for capital investment, including restoring the exclusion for long-term capital gains. Treasury I had proposed eliminating the capital-gains exclusion, which was viewed as one of the key components of many tax shelters. Although the effects of this decision had been softened by indexing the basis of assets to inflation, it shocked many Republican legislators and corporate constituents of the administration. Preferential treatment of capital gains had been a feature of the tax code since 1921, and many high-technology firms argued that it was particularly important for attracting capital to new and risky ventures. Baker and Darman believed that they could ill afford to alienate one of the few potential blocks of business support for tax reform, and a capital-gains exclusion of 50 percent, rather than the original 60 percent, was restored in Treasury II. Because the top rate was reduced to 35 percent, however, even this smaller exclusion yielded a lower capital-gains rate of 17.5 percent, rather than the existing rate of 20.

More costly were the changes made in Treasury I's capital depreciation provisions. The old arguments between McLure and Johnson over expensing and capital incentives were revisited, but this time Johnson emerged victorious on the heels of vociferous complaints by conservative Republicans and capital-intensive industries. Johnson recalled a dramatic change in attitude: "Business depreciation and taxation blew up [politically] more than anything else . . . from a conservative Republican point of view. [Since] Baker and Darman came over determined to make this thing work [and] their concerns were consistent with mine, I gained a lot more influence on restructuring the business side of reform." Treasury I's real cost recovery system (RCRS) was replaced with a capital cost recovery system (CCRS), which retained the favorable inflation indexing provisions of

RCRS but shortened cost recovery periods. The result, according to one business analysis, was a depreciation system "in most cases, more generous than even ACRS."[51]

These changes generally pleased the administration's allies in Congress and solidified a core of business support for tax reform. It is true that most capital-intensive businesses continued to oppose even the revised plan, since it still abolished the ITC and many of the accounting and investment provisions favorable to banks and certain natural resource industries, and it raised overall business taxes by $120 billion over five years. Still, the changes had the intended effect of dividing and to some extent neutralizing business opposition to reform—a key element in Baker's legislative strategy. It was just as one business lobbyist had feared when he warned that "Congress will walk all over us and pick the bones off the carcass," if business failed to provide a united front in opposition to tax reform.[52] High-tech and high-tax industries formed a coalition to support the administration's reform plan, lobbied Congress on its behalf, and prevented consensus-oriented umbrella groups like the Chamber of Commerce from effectively opposing it for many months.

Other changes were aimed directly at the interests of key individuals in Congress. In an effort to gain the support of Senate Finance Committee Chairman Bob Packwood and to mollify opposition by organized labor, taxation of most fringe benefits was dropped from the plan, and Treasury's proposal to tax health benefits was gutted. In place of the original proposal to tax monthly health insurance benefits in excess of $75 ($175 per family), a provision was added to tax only the first $10 ($25 for families) of free health benefits. In contrast to the Treasury I provision, which was designed to discourage this form of untaxed compensation, the new approach was "devoid of policy rationale" observed Chapoton, and it cut the expected revenue gain in half. Yet Baker's substitute did secure a greater degree of cooperation from Packwood.

Likewise, major changes were made in the proposed tax treatment of oil and natural gas. Treasury I had proposed to eliminate or alter provisions that were enormously favorable to some sectors of the oil and gas industry, such as the oil depletion allowance and expensing of intangible drilling costs, which had long been major targets of tax reformers. The changes were removed from Treasury II, however, in

part under the influence of Baker's own policy and political views, stemming from his business and political roots in Texas, as well as the political might of the oil lobby. "The Republican party is going to have to find a new way to finance campaigns in Texas if this goes through," observed one administration official.[53] Such clout gained independent oil producers a meeting with the president himself to discuss their concerns. If anything, though, they were even more strongly represented on the tax-writing committees of Congress, especially the Finance Committee where senators from oil-producing states represented the largest, most senior, and most powerful bloc on the committee. Most observers assumed that any oil and gas reforms left in the president's proposal would be reversed by the Senate. But their deletion from Treasury II reduced expected revenues by $44 billion over five years.[54]

In order to retain Treasury I's rate reductions, not all of its proposed base broadeners could be eliminated. Treasury II recommended many politically daring changes, including repeal of the two-earner deduction (raising $34 billion over five years); taxation of unemployment benefits ($3.8 billion); elimination of the charitable deduction for nonitemizers ($3.1 billion, a less stringent provision than contained in Treasury I); restrictions on business meals and entertainment deductions ($6.9 billion, also less stringent than Treasury I); repeal of income averaging ($18.7 billion); and repeal of the exemption for "private purpose" bonds ($14 billion). Above all, Treasury II continued to call for eliminating the costly investment tax credit ($165 billion), for which there was virtually no support in Treasury, and the equally expensive state and local tax deduction ($149 billion), which was viewed as fiscally unavoidable by Baker, economically inefficient by Treasury staff, and "socialistic" by White House conservatives. Even with the retention of these provisions, however, the costly concessions described above left the plan short of revenues. These were made up in part by revenue-*gaining* changes to Treasury I, including elimination of interest indexing and reduction of the newly proposed deductions for dividends paid from 50 percent in Treasury I to just 10 percent in Treasury II. Both steps would raise tens of billions of dollars over five years. In addition, the minimum tax was strengthened for both corporations and individuals, a step that Treasury economists had earlier said would presage the failure of true reform.

## Mixed Reactions

Such changes did not please everyone, particularly the economists who had shaped Treasury I. They objected to many of the changes on both substantive and political grounds. Although economists could and did disagree about the economic merits of different depreciation schedules, they did not disagree about decisions affecting charitable deductions, fringe benefits, or the oil and gas industry. These were viewed as blatantly political decisions lacking any substantive merit.

Economically, when these revisions were combined with the depreciation changes and dilution of indexing, the net result was to substantially erode the vaunted goal of a neutral and consistent tax system. In the view of McLure, Treasury II was only a "dim shadow" of Treasury I.[55] Moreover, some Treasury officials argued that their chances for obtaining truly comprehensive reform in Congress had been seriously weakened because the revised plan began unraveling the "hostage strategy." As Steuerle argued: "Political compromise was inevitable, but the more quickly we moved from being comprehensive, the more difficult it would be to oppose one interest group on the ground that others had not received special treatment." Treasury staff believed strongly that their role was to send the purest possible bill to Congress, in order to minimize the effects of inevitable legislative compromises. The sentiment was echoed on Capitol Hill, as news of one change after another leaked out of Treasury during the spring of 1985. "Members of the committee said, 'What do they think *we're* going to do?' " recalled one House staff member.

Not all of the reaction was negative, however. Baker believed that the changes he made "represented a vast improvement over current tax policy and did indeed have a chance of being enacted." Although most remained no more than lukewarm to reform, House Republicans did agree that the prospects for Treasury II looked better. In the Senate, Packwood retracted his threats to bottle up the legislation. Moreover, pockets of support in the business community were solidified under Treasury II. Indeed, even outside economists remained generally supportive, if somewhat disappointed. Treasury II was an "ugly duckling" compared to Treasury I, concluded Alan Blinder, but "positively winsome" compared to current law.[56] The same conclusion was reached by leading tax professionals who attended the second Ways and Means Committee retreat in the fall of 1985; when pressed for an up-or-down judgment on the revised Treasury proposal, they favored it 10—2 over the existing system.

## Inestimable Reforms

In late April 1985, believing that Treasury II was virtually complete, Baker briefed the president. Surprisingly, despite his authorship of Treasury I, Don Regan went along with Baker's judgment that the new plan was more viable politically. "Regan was a delegator," explained his top White House aide, and so he swallowed distasteful changes in the treatment of oil, indexing, depreciation, and foreign taxes. With so much agreement before him, President Reagan easily approved Treasury II.

This, as they say, should have been the last word. But, it was not. After the new plan had been approved by the White House and was being prepared for release, the revenue estimators suddenly declared that the plan was a whopping $50 billion short over five years! It was to be only one in a series of revenue-estimating missteps that would haunt the reform process—and sometimes bring it to the brink of disaster—as harried statisticians sought to model the unpredictable effects of dozens of incompletely drafted, last-minute changes. As Johnson recalled the event: "I just lost it. I felt they couldn't have made [an error] that big. I had stressed to Pearlman over and over that the numbers had to be clean before we went to the Man on this. Fifty billion is a big, big number to make up. We were totally destitute."

More important in the long run, this event underscored the enormous difficulty of amending finely balanced, comprehensive tax proposals in a revenue- and distributionally neutral environment. Throughout the Treasury II process, Baker and Darman had encountered unexpected and chronic revenue problems in the process of amending Treasury I. As the $50 billion shortfall illustrated, the expensive additions and subtractions they proposed had been difficult to finance without losing revenues, even with the deletion of interest indexing, large cutbacks in the proposed dividend deduction, and the failure to include funds for costly but unavoidable transition rules. Even so, the problems of maintaining distributional neutrality were often more difficult still. Most of the amendments the duo supported disproportionately aided upper-income individuals, thus distorting the distributional effects of the plan even when revenues were found to cover expenses. "I don't think they understood initially how these constraints were going to interact with what they wanted to do," said one Treasury official. And, in fact, the Treasury II proposal proved to be more generous to the wealthiest taxpayers—those with incomes over $200,000 annually—granting them an average reduction in tax liabilities 22 percent larger than in Treasury I, even though the overall reduction in individual tax liabilities was 18 percent smaller than in Treasury I.

In the end, despite Pearlman's labors, the plan the president sent to Congress was not revenue neutral, as congressional aides quickly discovered, and further changes were subsequently demanded to make it so. Despite this and other eleventh-hour corrections in Treasury II, the first of many revenue crises for tax reform had been weathered. The incident became only a footnote in a far larger and more important story.

## Notes

1. See David A. Stockman, *The Triumph of Politics: Why the Reagan Revolution Failed* (New York: Harper and Row, 1986), 361–62; and "Reagan 'Tempted' by Flat-Rate Tax," *New York Times,* July 8, 1982, A1.
2. Stockman, *The Triumph of Politics,* 229.
3. Ibid., 363.
4. Quoted in Dale Russakoff, "Tracing the Twisted Path of Reagan's Income Tax Revision Plan," *Washington Post,* September 25, 1985, A4.
5. Donald T. Regan, *For the Record: From Wall Street to Washington* (New York: Harcourt Brace Jovanovich, 1988), 196.
6. Stockman, *The Triumph of Politics,* 364.
7. See John W. Kingdon, *Agendas, Alternatives, and Public Policies* (New York: Harcourt Brace Jovanovich, 1984).
8. Regan, *For the Record,* 207, 193.
9. Ibid., 202–3.
10. Ibid., 206.
11. In addition to Secretary Regan, Pearlman, McLure, and Chapoton, who (until he left the department in mid-1984) was the assistant secretary for taxation, the regular participants included Roscoe Egger, the head of the IRS; Dr. Manuel Johnson, a supply-side economist who was dep-

uty and later assistant treasury secretary for economic policy; Bruce Thompson, assistant secretary for legislative affairs; Thomas Dawson, who was Regan's liaison to the business community; and Albert Kingon, assistant secretary for public affairs. This core group was regularly joined by Dr. Beryl Sprinkel, another economist who was assistant secretary for economic affairs until he became head of the president's Council of Economic Advisers.
12. U.S. Department of the Treasury, Office of Tax Analysis, "Tax Reform for Fairness, Simplicity, and Economic Growth: The Treasury Department Report to the President," *Tax Notes,* December 3, 1984, 882, 884, 910.
13. John F. White, *The Politics and Development of the Federal Income Tax* (Madison: University of Wisconsin Press, 1985), 291.
14. Treasury Department, "Report to the President," 884, 911.
15. Regan, *For the Record,* 201.
16. Frederick C. Mosher, *Democracy and Public Service* (New York: Oxford University Press, 1968), 101.
17. Regan, *For the Record,* 206.
18. Henry J. Aaron and Harvey Galper, *Assessing Tax Reform* (Washington: Brookings Institution, 1985).
19. Joseph A. Pechman, *Federal Tax Policy,* 5th ed. (Washington: Brookings Institution, 1987), 211.
20. Treasury Department, "Report to the President," 891.
21. Because existing IRS data compiled from tax returns did not include fringe benefits and other kinds of income that were targeted by reform, a vast new data set was created by merging tax information with census data, and the distribution of existing taxes was recalculated accordingly. See Maureen McCauley, "Treasury Proposal Attempts Improved Definition of Income in Tax Reform Effort," *Tax Notes,* December 24, 1984, 1170–71.
22. Regan, *For the Record,* 209.
23. See Eugene Steuerle and Michael Hartzmark, "Individual Income Taxation 1947–1979," *National Tax Journal* 34 (1981): 145–66.
24. See Margaret Wrightson, "The Road to South Carolina: Intergovernmental Tax Immunity and the Constitutional Status of Federalism," in *Publius: The Journal of Federalism* (Summer 1989).

25. Regan, *For the Record,* 210.

26. U.S. Office of Management and Budget, *Special Analyses: Budget of the United States Government, FY 1987* (Washington: U.S. Government Printing Office, 1987) G-43, 45.

27. Treasury Department, "Report to the President," 893.

28. Charles E. McLure, Jr., "The Tax Treatment of Owner-Occupied Housing: Achilles Heel of Tax Reform?" in *Tax Reform and Real Estate,* ed. James R. Follam Washington Urban Institute, 1986), 222, 230.

29. Treasury Department, "Report to the President," 893.

30. See Mary Bourdette and Jim Weill, "The Impact of Federal Taxes on Poor Families" in U.S. Congress, House, Committee on Ways and Means, *Comprehensive Tax Reform, Hearings,* part 4, 99th Cong., 1st sess., 1985, 2940–96.

31. See Jack Kemp, "Fair and Simple Tax (FAST)," in *A Citizen's Guide to the New Income Tax Reforms: FAIR Tax, Flat Tax, Simple Tax,* ed. Joseph Pechman (Totowa, N.J., Rowman and Allanheld, 1985), 104.

32. Treasury Department, "Report to the President," 879.

33. Steuerle and Hartzmark, "Individual Income Taxation, 1947–79," 156.

34. Calculated from Table 4–2, Treasury Department, "Report to the President," 895.

35. Regan added, "In Wall Street, I had been trained to keep secrets." He was so angered by one White House leak just before the release of Treasury I (which he termed a "treacherous insult") that he attempted to resign from the cabinet. Regan, *For the Record,* 218–19, 251–57.

36. *Tax Notes,* December 3, 1985, 832.

37. Robert Rothman, "Treasury Plan Cuts Real Estate Tax Benefits," *Congressional Quarterly Weekly Report,* December 1, 1984, 3018.

38. See *Tax Notes,* December 17, 1985, 1056, 1154; *Tax Notes,* December 3, 1985, 832.

39. Quoted in Pamela Fessler and Steven Pressman, "Tax Overhaul: The Crucial Lobby Fight of 1985," *Congressional Quarterly Weekly Report,* March 9, 1985, 450.

40. Alan S. Blinder, *Hard Heads, Soft Hearts: Tough-Minded Economics for a Just Society* (Reading, Mass.: Addison Wesley, 1987), 170–71; Alice Rivlin, quoted in "A Forecast of Glad Tidings," *Time,*

December 12, 1985, 37; Harvey Galper, "The Tax Proposals of the U.S. Treasury Department," *Australian Tax Forum* (1987): 191–222; and Henry J. Aaron and Harvey Galper, "The Politics of Tax Reform," reprinted in *Tax Notes,* January 6, 1986, 49–53.

41. Bruce Babbitt, quoted in Dan Balz, *Washington Post,* November 29, 1984, A-5. See also Pamela Fessler, "Treasury Tax Overhaul Excites Little Interest," *Congressional Quarterly Weekly Report,* December 1, 1984, 3017, and *Tax Notes,* December 24, 1984, 1186.

42. "Up Go the Trial Balloons," *Time,* December 10, 1984, 22.

43. Everett Carll Ladd, "On Mandates, Realignments, and the 1984 Presidential Election," *Political Science Quarterly 100* (Spring 1985): 20, 25; James L. Sundquist, *Dynamics of the Party System* (Washington: Brookings Institution, 1973), chap. 13 and p. 297.

44. Hedrick Smith, "Congress: Will There Be Realignment?" in *Beyond Reagan: The Politics of Upheaval,* ed. Paul Duke (New York: Warner Books, 1986), 146; Bill Bradley, quoted in Anne Swardson and Dan Balz, "Simplification Campaign Taxes Public's Interest," *Washington Post,* April 15, 1985, A3.

45. Richard Darman, quoted in Dale Russakoff, "In Taxes, the Impossible Became the Inevitable," *Washington Post,* June 29, 1986, A12.

46. Regan, *For the Record,* 212–13.

47. Paul Blustein, "Tax Plan's Political Growing Pains," *Wall Street Journal,* December 28, 1984, 34.

48. Regan, *For the Record,* 219–20.

49. Ibid., 213.

50. Jane Seaberry, "James Baker an Enigma at Treasury," *Washington Post,* June 2, 1985, F1.

51. Center for the Study of American Business, "The President's Tax Proposal: Implications for Capital Formation," processed, St. Louis, Mo., June 1985, 5.

52. Quoted in Ronald Brownstein, "Wagering on Tax Reform," *National Journal,* February 2, 1985, 247.

53. Ibid.

54. Burt Solomon, "Oil and Gas Hit Paydirt in Reagan Tax Plan," *National Journal,* June 1, 1985, 1310.

55. Charles E. McLure Jr., "Where Tax Reform Went Astray," *Villanova Law Review* 31 (1986): 1657.

56. Blinder, *Hard Heads, Soft Hearts,* 171.

## Chapter 7 Review Questions

1. How would you define *professionalism?* Do you agree with Mosher's definition? In what ways might you expand on his meaning of the term? Is there a difference between public-sector and private-sector professionals?

2. Compare this case study with some of the previous cases such as "The Changing FBI" or "The MRS Case." What were some examples of public professionals in these cases? Where did they derive their sources of influence? Who were "the professional elites"? How did they exercise influence?

3. What are the differences among staff professionals, line professionals, professional elites, administrative professionals, and emerging professionals? Were any of these types of professionals found in this case?

4. According to Mosher, where are "the key zones of potential tension and conflict in agencies"? Were these tensions exemplified in any of the previous case studies?

5. Do you agree with Mosher's conclusion: "For better or worse—or better *and* worse—much of our government is now in the hands of professionals (including scientists)"? Explain why you agree or disagree. Cite some of the problems that may be associated with professionals' control of government.

6. What mechanisms are essential for ensuring that professionals act wisely and in the public interest? Do you agree with Mosher that higher education offers the best route for securing responsible professional actions? Or are there other checks and safeguards that you consider more powerful tools for maintaining professional accountability to the public interest?

## Key Terms

professional associations

professional elites

professional career patterns

professional accreditation

established professions

emergent professions

public service professionals

general professions

supporting line professions

staff professions

administrative professions

key zones of potential tension

## Suggestions for Further Reading

The best book on this subject remains Frederick C. Mosher, *Democracy and the Public Service,* Second Edition (New York: Oxford University Press, 1982), for which the first Louis Brownlow Memorial Book Prize was awarded. Also useful as a companion volume is Frederick C. Mosher and Richard J. Stillman II, eds., *Professions in Government* (New Brunswick, N.J.: Transaction Books, 1982).

Now somewhat dated but nevertheless well worth examining are Corinne L. Gilb, *Hidden Hierarchies: The Professions and Government* (New York: Harper & Row, 1966); Howard M. Vollmer and Donald Mills, *Professionali-*

*zation* (New York: Prentice-Hall, 1966); Burton J. Bledstein, *The Culture of Professionalism* (New York: W. W. Norton, 1976); Guy Benveniste, *The Politics of Expertise,* Second Edition (San Francisco: Boyd & Fraser, 1977); the entire issue of *Daedalus,* 92 (1963), which was devoted to "The Professions," edited by Kenneth S. Lynn; Brian Chapman, *The Profession of Government* (London: Allen & Unwin, 1959); and Mary E. Guy, *Professionals in Organizations: Debunking a Myth* (New York: Praeger, 1985). Students of this topic would do well to study selectively several of the outstanding books on individual professional groups within government such as Samuel P. Huntington, *The Soldier and The State* (Cambridge, Mass.: Harvard University Press, 1957); Morris Janowitz, *The Professional Soldier* (Glencoe, Ill.: Free Press, 1960); John E. Harr, *The Professional Diplomat* (Princeton, N.J.: Princeton University Press, 1969); Richard J. Stillman II, *The Rise of the City Manager* (Albuquerque: University of New Mexico Press, 1974); Don Price, *The Scientific Estate* (Cambridge, Mass.: Harvard University Press, 1965); and William I. Bacchus, *Staffing for Foreign Affairs: Personnel Systems for the 1980s and 1990s* (Princeton, N.J.: Princeton University Press, 1983). For a useful study of ASPA's origins and growth as a key professional organization for public service, read Darrell L. Pugh, *Looking Back, Moving Forward* (Washington, D.C.: ASPA, 1988).

In recent years there have been some fine studies dealing with the relationship between professionals and elected or appointed officials: Hugh Heclo, *A Government of Strangers* (Washington, D.C.: Brookings Institution, 1977); Thomas P. Murphy, Donald E. Nuechterlein, and Ronald Stupak, *Inside Bureaucracy* (Boulder, Colo.: Westview Press, 1978); John W. Macy, Bruce Adams, and J. Jackson Walter, eds., *America's Unelected Government* (Washington, D.C.: National Academy of

Public Administration, 1983); Frederick C. Mosher, *A Tale of Two Agencies* (Baton Rouge, La: Louisiana State University Press, 1984); James H. Svara, *Official Leadership in the City: Patterns of Conflict and Cooperation* (New York: Oxford University Press, 1990); David N. Ammons and Charldean Newell, *City Executives: Leadership Roles, Work Characteristics & Time Management* (New York: State University of New York Press, 1989); as well as several of the articles that appeared in the bicentennial issue of the *Public Administration Review,* "The American Constitution and the Administrative State" (January/February 1987), edited by Richard J. Stillman II, see particularly, Chester A. Newland, "Public Executives: Imperium Sacerdotium, Collegium? Bicentennial Leadership Challenges"; and James P. Pfiffner, "Political Appointees and Career Executives: The Democracy—Bureaucracy Nexus in the Third Century"; as well as Edie N. Goldenberg, "The Permanent Government in an Era of Retrenchment and Redirection," in Lester M. Salamon and Michael S. Lund, eds., *The Reagan Presidency and the Governing of America* (Washington, D.C.: The Urban Institute Press, 1985).

Despite the apparent power and influence of professional groups over the formulation of public policy, there continues a striking dearth of interest in overall assessments of this topic on the part of students of public administration except for pieces such as Richard Schott, "Public Administration as a Profession: Problems and Prospects," *Public Administration Review,* 36 (May/June 1976), pp. 253–259, York Wilbern, "Professionalism and the Public Service: Too Little or Too Much?" *Public Administration Review,* 14 (Winter 1954), pp. 15–21; Beverly A. Cigler, "Public Administration and the Paradox of Professionalism," *Public Administration Review* (Nov/Dec 1990), pp. 637–654; and in the same issue, John Nalbandian, "Tenets of Contemporary Professionalism in

Local Government," pp. 654–662. Also, the entire symposium devoted to this topic is found in the *Southern Review of Public Administration* (Fall 1981) and *Public Administration Quarterly* (Winter 1985). One should not overlook sections of the Volcker Commission Report pertaining to this topic, The Report of the National Commission on the Public Service, *Leadership for America: Rebuilding the Public Service* (Washington, D.C.: privately printed, 1989; and reprinted by Lexington Books, 1990 under the same title).

# PART TWO

The Multiple Functions of Public Administrators: Their Major Activities, Responsibilities, and Roles

**P**ublic administrators must fulfill many functions, often simultaneously. Part Two focuses on several of the important activities performed by public administrators—decision making, administrative communications, management, personnel motivation, budgeting, and implementation. The extent, scope, and capability with which administrators perform these functions vary widely from administrator to administrator, from job to job, and from locale to locale. However, it is safe to say these six functions are considered some of the most critical activities that public administrators must perform if they are to succeed—indeed survive—in their jobs.

As in Part One of this book, in Part Two, chapter by chapter, a single concept is discussed in a reading and its relevance is illustrated in a case study. Although the six major roles of administrators are individually discussed in the following chapters, it should be emphasized that the reality of the administrative processes frequently forces public administrators to assume all these responsibilities at the same time; this makes their work much more complex, less neatly compartmentalized or clear-cut than these individual chapters may suggest. The significant functional concepts discussed in Part Two include:

**CHAPTER 8**
*Decision Making: The Concept of Incremental Public Choice* How are decisions made in the public sector and why do public administrators frequently feel as if they are "flying by the seat of their pants"?

**CHAPTER 9**
*Administrative Communications: The Concept of Information Networks* How does the flow of communications inside organizations influence the way decisions are made and how well (or how poorly) administrators perform their work?

**CHAPTER 10**
*Executive Management: The Concept of the Uniqueness of Public Management* What is a successful management practice for public administrators to adopt? Why is public management often very different from business management?

**CHAPTER 11**
*Personnel Motivation: Theory X and Theory Y* Why is personnel motivation so significant to organizational performance and productivity? How can public administrators most effectively motivate their employees?

**CHAPTER 12**
*Public Budgeting: The Concept of Budgeting as Politics* What is the nature of the budgetary process in government? Why is a knowledge of budgeting so fundamental to administrative survival?

**CHAPTER 13**
*Implementation: The Concept of a Communications Systems Model* What is the best way for administrators to get their jobs done effectively, timely, efficiently, correctly, and responsibly? How can one best conceptualize this approach as a model?

# CHAPTER 8

## Decision Making: The Concept of Incremental Public Choice

*A wise policy-maker consequently expects that his policies will achieve only part of what he hopes and at the same time will produce unanticipated consequences he would have preferred to avoid. If he proceeds through a succession of incremental changes, he avoids serious lasting mistakes. . . .*

*Charles E. Lindblom*

## READING 8

# Introduction

Few concepts are debated in administration more frequently than decision making—how decisions are made; whom they are made by; why they are decided on in the first place; and what impact they have once the choice is made. Gallons of ink have been spilled in academic journals debating whether decision making is an art or a science, how best to construct a decision-making model, or how to arrive at the most rational (or optimal) choice. One point emerges from these seemingly endless discussions: the process by which individuals and groups determine a correct course of action from various alternatives is one of the central functions of an administrator and thus deserves careful consideration by students of public administration.

What is the decision-making function? On one level, we all use decision making daily in confronting a myriad of personal choices, such as when to get up in the morning and what clothes to wear. On the larger and more complicated level of public administration, however, the decisional process involves vital community or societal choices—where to build a new school, when to negotiate an arms limitation treaty, or how to organize a new federal program for poverty relief. The process of choice runs the length and breadth of public administration and involves 4, 40, 400, or 4,000 steps, depending on the complexity and range of variables presented by the problem at hand.

Charles E. Lindblom (1917–   ), a Yale economist and long-time scholar of public policy issues, offers an important conceptual understanding of governmental decision making in his essay, "The Science of 'Muddling Through.'" Lindblom, unlike most economists, has seriously thought about the relationships between economics and politics for many years, an interest evident in his earliest writings with Robert A. Dahl in *Politics, Economics and Welfare* (1953), as well as in his more recent book, *Politics and Markets* (1977). In an effort to realistically analyze the way governmental decisions are made, at the heart of Lindblom's brilliant studies is a model of decision making that he succinctly outlines in the following essay.

Based on earlier writings by Chester Barnard and Herbert Simon, Lindblom's central thesis is that there are two distinct varieties of decision making. One he calls the rational-comprehensive or root method, and the second, the successive limited comparisons or branch method. The first method is found in the classic texts on administration, and the latter is the "real" way decisions are arrived at in government. In the traditional *rational-comprehensive* or *root method* an administrator confronts a given objective, such as reducing poverty by a certain amount. The decision maker, in choosing the best policy to pursue, rationally ranks all the relevant values (or advantages) in attaining this objective, such as improving the health of the poor, reducing crime, improving property values, and eliminating illiteracy. He or she then formulates as many possible alternatives to achieve the stated objective—for example, a guaranteed income plan, direct government subsidies, higher welfare payments, or work-relief programs—and selects from among the options the *best* alternative that serves to maximize the ranked list of values. This approach to decision making is *rational,* because the alternatives and values are logically selected and weighed in relative importance. It is also *comprehensive,* for all the alternatives and values are taken into account by the policy maker.

What *actually* occurs in administrative decision making, argues Lindblom, is quite another process, namely, the *successive limited comparisons* or *branch method.* An objective is established—reducing poverty by a set amount, for example—but in public discussions this objective quickly becomes compromised. It may soon be mixed up with other goals such as educating minority students or providing work relief for the jobless. Administrators tend to overlook or avoid many of the social values that could be derived from their program, concentrating instead on those that they consider immediately relevant. In selecting the appropriate course of action, administrators outline not a broad range of possibilities, but only a few incremental steps that experience tells them are feasible. Furthermore, in practice, policy makers do not rationally select the optimal program that satisfies a clearly delineated list of values. To the contrary, under the successive limited comparisons method, contends Lindblom, public administrators pragmatically select from among the immediate choices at hand the most suitable compromise that satisfies the groups and individuals concerned with the program.

Lindblom sees the first approach, the root method, as wrongly assuming that administrators making decisions have unlimited amounts of time and resources available to them. "It assumes intellectual capacities and sources of information that simply do not exist and it is even more absurd as an approach to policy when the time and money that can be allocated to a policy problem is limited as is always the case." Second, the root method holds that there are always clear-cut values on which all interested parties agree. In fact, argues Lindblom, in a democratic society in which members of Congress, agencies, and interest groups are in continual disagreement over the relative importance of program objectives, policy makers cannot begin to rank explicitly the values derived from any program. There are simply too many groups with too many unknown values. The weight given to their relative importance depends ultimately on personal perspectives. "Even when an administrator resolves to follow his own values as a criterion for decisions, he will often not know how to rank them when they conflict with one another as they usually do." Third, the root method assumes that ends and means in policy choices are distinct, when in fact they are frequently intertwined. Selection of a goal to be accomplished often cannot easily be separated from the means by which it is achieved. For instance, the objective of slum clearance is intrinsically associated with the removal of residents from the neighborhood and the other methods used to achieve the goal, such as the clearing of buildings. Means and ends often become hopelessly confused in public policy choices. Finally, says Lindblom, the choice of a given course of action depends ultimately not on whether it maximizes the intended values (even if the values could be identified and ranked), but rather on whether it serves as a compromise acceptable to all parties concerned. "If agreement directly on policy as a test for the 'best' policy seems a poor substitute for testing the policy against its objectives, it ought to be remembered that objectives themselves have no ultimate validity other than they are agreed upon. . . . Agreement on policy thus becomes the only practicable test of the policy's correctness," argues Lindblom.

Lindblom's view of the reality of administrative decision making contains five characteristics. First, it is *incremental,* for small steps are always taken to achieve objectives, not broad leaps and bounds. Second, it is *noncomprehensive.* In other words, because policy makers' resources are always limited, they cannot take into consideration the full range of policy choices available to them at any given moment, nor can they possibly understand the full effects of their decisions or all of the values derived from any alternative they select. Third, the branch technique of decision making involves *successive comparisons* because policy is never made once and for all, but is made and remade endlessly by small chains of comparisons between narrow choices. Fourth, in practice, decision making *suffices* rather than maximizes from among the available options. "A wise policy maker completely expects that his policies will achieve only part of what he hopes and at the same time will produce unanticipated consequences he would have preferred to avoid." Finally, Lindblom's picture of governmental decision making rests on a *pluralist* conception of the public sector, in which many contending interest groups compete for influence over policy issues, continually forcing the administrator, as the person in the middle, to secure agreement among the competing parties. The political arts of compromise thus become a major part of decision-making methods.

There are two advantages of the branch method, asserts Lindblom. The first is that "if he proceeds through a succession of small incremental changes, the administrator therefore has the advantage of avoiding serious lasting mistakes" as well as permitting easy alterations should the wrong course be pursued. The second benefit of incrementalism is that it fits "hand and glove" with the American political system, which operates chiefly by means of gradual changes, rarely by dramatic shifts in public policies. "Non-incremental policy proposals are therefore typically not only politically irrelevant but also unpredictable in their policy consequences," writes Lindblom. The branch method allows for the art of compromise that American politics demands and produces the gradual changes that American tradition generally favors.

However, from the perspective of the "outside expert" or the academic problem solver, Lindblom points out, this approach seems "unscientific and unsystematic." Indeed, administrators may appear as if they were flying "by the seat of their pants," although in fact the outside theorists do not grasp that administrators are "often practicing a systematic method" of successive limited comparisons. Yet, as Lindblom says, ". . . sometimes decision makers are pursuing neither a theoretical approach nor successive comparisons nor any systematic method."

Lindblom's approach to governmental decision making, which for some may be too descriptive and not sufficiently prescriptive, debunks the classic view of how public choices are made, substituting an incremental model that is peculiarly a product and extension of economic theory of choice (subsequently, much of the language used in decisional theory—words like "optimizing" and "maximizing"—is derived from economics). Kenneth Arrow, Thomas Schelling, Herbert Simon, Edward Banfield, and Robert Dahl are among the major contemporary economists and political scientists who have pioneered the incremental view of decision making in the post-World War II era. Lindblom has fully developed this idea into an elaborate working model in the following article, "The Science of 'Muddling Through.'"

As you read this selection, keep the following questions in mind:

Is Lindblom too pessimistic about the ability of administrators to make profound choices that will significantly alter or reshape their external environment?

What do you see as the benefits and disadvantages of the branch method and are there any remedies for its defects?

How does Lindblom's concept square with any of the previous case studies, such as Case Study 7? Was that tax reform decision made incrementally? Why or why not?

Does Lindblom's "muddling through" idea primarily apply in normal governmental decisions involving simple issues? How about catastrophes such as in Case Study 1 "The Blast in Centralia No. 5"? What decisional methods might have averted the unfortunate choices made in that case?

Do you agree with Lindblom that "the branch method compared to other decisional models often looks far superior," particularly from the perspective of the practitioner?

# The Science of "Muddling Through"

**CHARLES E. LINDBLOM**

Suppose an administrator is given responsibility for formulating policy with respect to inflation. He might start by trying to list all related values in order of importance, e.g., full employment, reasonable business profit, protection of small savings, prevention of a stock market crash. Then all possible policy outcomes could be rated as more or less efficient in attaining a maximum of these values. This would of course require a prodigious inquiry into values held by members of society and an equally prodigious set of calculations on how much of each value is equal to how much of each other value. He could then proceed to outline all possible policy alternatives. In a third step, he would undertake systematic comparison of his multitude of alternatives to determine which attains the greatest amount of values.

In comparing policies, he would take advantage of any theory available that generalized about classes of policies. In considering inflation, for example, he would compare all policies in the light of the theory of prices. Since no alternatives are beyond his investigation, he would consider strict central control and the

abolition of all prices and markets on the one hand and elimination of all public controls with reliance completely on the free market on the other, both in the light of whatever theoretical generalizations he could find on such hypothetical economies.

Finally, he would try to make the choice that would in fact maximize his values.

An alternative line of attack would be to set as his principal objective, either explicitly or without conscious thought, the relatively simple goal of keeping prices level. This objective might be compromised or complicated by only a few other goals, such as full employment. He would in fact disregard most other social values as beyond his present interest, and he would for the moment not even attempt to rank the few values that he regarded as immediately relevant. Were he pressed, he would quickly admit that he was ignoring many related values and many possible important consequences of his policies.

As a second step, he would outline those relatively few policy alternatives that occurred to him. He would then compare them. In comparing his limited number of alternatives, most of them familiar from past controversies, he would not ordinarily find a body of theory precise enough to carry him through a comparison of their respective consequences. Instead he would rely heavily on the record of past experience with small policy steps to predict the consequences of similar steps extended into the future.

Moreover, he would find that the policy alternatives combined objectives or values in different ways. For example, one policy might offer price level stability at the cost of some risk of unemployment; another might offer less price stability but also less risk of unemployment. Hence, the next step in his approach—the final selection—would combine into one the choice among values and the choice among instruments for reaching values. It would not, as in the first method of policy-making, approximate a more mechanical process of choosing the means that best satisfied goals that were previously clarified and ranked. Because practitioners of the second approach expect to achieve their goals only partially, they would expect to repeat endlessly the sequence just described, as conditions and aspirations changed and as accuracy of prediction improved.

## By Root or by Branch

For complex problems, the first of these two approaches is of course impossible. Although such an approach can be described, it cannot be practiced except for relatively simple problems and even then only in a somewhat modified form. It assumes intellectual capacities and sources of information that men simply do not possess, and it is even more absurd as an approach to policy when the time and money that can be allocated to a policy problem is limited, as is always the case. Of particular importance to public administrators is the fact that public agencies are in effect usually instructed not to practice the first method. That is to say, their prescribed functions and constraints—the politically or legally possible—restrict their attention to relatively few values and relatively few alternative policies among the countless alternatives that might be imagined. It is the second method that is practiced.

Curiously, however, the literatures of decision making, policy formulation, planning, and public administration formalize the first approach rather than the second, leaving public administrators who handle complex decisions in the position of practicing what few preach. For emphasis I run some risk of overstatement. True enough, the literature is well aware of limits on man's capacities and of the inevitability that policies will be approached in some such style as the second. But attempts to formalize rational policy formulation—to lay out explicitly the necessary steps in the process—usually describe the first approach and not the second.[1]

The common tendency to describe policy formulation even for complex problems as though it followed the first approach has been strengthened by the attention given to, and successes enjoyed by, operations research, statistical decision theory, and systems analysis. The hallmarks of these procedures, typical of the first approach, are clarity of objective, explicitness of evaluation, a high degree of comprehensiveness of overview, and, wherever possible, quantification of values for mathematical analysis. But these advanced procedures remain largely the appropriate techniques of relatively small-scale problem-solving where the total number of variables to be considered is small and value problems restricted. Charles Hitch, head of the Economics Division of RAND Corporation, one of the leading centers for application of these techniques, has written:

> I would make the empirical generalization from my experience at RAND and elsewhere that operations research is the art of suboptimizing, i.e., of solving some lower-level problems, and that difficulties increase and our special competence diminishes by an order of magnitude with every level of decision making we attempt

to ascend. The sort of simple explicit model which operations researchers are so proficient in using can certainly reflect most of the significant factors influencing traffic control on the George Washington Bridge, but the proportion of the relevant reality which we can represent by any such model or models in studying, say, a major foreign-policy decision, appears to be almost trivial.[2]

Accordingly, I propose in this paper to clarify and formalize the second method, much neglected in the literature. This might be described as the method of *successive limited comparisons.* I will contrast it with the first approach, which might be called the rational-comprehensive method.[3] More impressionistically and briefly—and therefore generally used in this article—they could be characterized as the branch method and root method, the former continually building out from the current situation, step-to-step and by small degrees; the latter starting from fundamentals anew each time, building on the past only as experience is embodied in a theory, and always prepared to start completely from the ground up.

Let us put the characteristics of the two methods side by side in simplest terms.

### Rational-Comprehensive (Root)

1a. Clarification of values or objectives distinct from and usually prerequisite to empirical analysis of alternative policies.
2a. Policy-formulation is therefore approached through means-end analysis: First the ends are isolated, then the means to achieve them are sought.
3a. The test of a "good" policy is that it can be shown to be the most appropriate means to desired ends.
4a. Analysis is comprehensive; every important relevant factor is taken into account.
5a. Theory is often heavily relied upon.

# Successive Limited Comparisons (Branch)

1b. Selection of value goals and empirical analysis of the needed action are not distinct from one another but are closely intertwined.
2b. Since means and ends are not distinct, means-end analysis is often inappropriate or limited.
3b. The test of a "good" policy is typically that various analysts find themselves directly agreeing on a policy (without their agreeing that it is the most appropriate means to an agreed objective).
4b. Analysis is drastically limited:
   i) Important possible outcomes are neglected.
   ii) Important alternative potential policies are neglected.
   iii) Important affected values are neglected.
5b. A succession of comparisons greatly reduces or eliminates reliance on theory.

Assuming that the root method is familiar and understandable, we proceed directly to clarification of its alternative by contrast. In explaining the second, we shall be describing how most administrators do in fact approach complex questions, for the root method, the "best" way as a blueprint or model, is in fact not workable for complex policy questions, and administrators are forced to use the method of successive limited comparisons.

# Intertwining Evaluation and Empirical Analysis (1b)

The quickest way to understand how values are handled in the method of successive limited comparisons is to see how the root method often breaks down in *its* handling of values or objectives. The idea that values should be clarified, and in advance of the examination of alternative policies, is appealing. But what happens when we attempt it for complex social problems? The first difficulty is that on many critical values or objectives, citizens disagree, congressmen disagree, and public administrators disagree. Even where a fairly specific objective is prescribed for the administrator, there remains considerable room for disagreement on sub-objectives. Consider, for example, the conflict with respect to locating public housing, described in Meyerson and Banfield's study of the Chicago Housing Authority[4]—disagreement which occurred despite the clear objective of providing a certain number of public housing units in the city. Similarly conflicting are objectives in highway location, traffic control, minimum wage administration, development of tourist facilities in national parks, or insect control.

Administrators cannot escape these conflicts by ascertaining the majority's preference, for preferences have not been registered on most issues; indeed, there often *are* no preferences in the absence of public discussion sufficient to bring an issue to the attention of the electorate. Furthermore, there is a question of whether intensity of feeling should be considered as well as the number of persons preferring each alternative. By the impossibility of doing otherwise, administrators often are reduced to deciding policy without clarifying objectives first.

Even when an administrator resolves to follow his own values as a criterion for decisions, he often will not know how to rank them when they conflict with one another, as they usually do. Suppose, for example, that an administrator must relocate tenants living in tenements scheduled for destruction. One objective is to empty the buildings fairly promptly, another is to find suitable accommodation for persons displaced, another is to avoid friction with residents in other areas in which a large influx would be unwelcome, another is to deal with all concerned through persuasion if possible, and so on.

How does one state even to himself the relative importance of these partially conflicting values? A simple ranking of them is not enough; one needs ideally to know how much of one value is worth sacrificing for some of another value. The answer is that typically the administrator chooses—and must choose—directly among policies in which these values are combined in different ways. He cannot first clarify his values and then choose among policies.

A more subtle third point underlies both the first two. Social objectives do not always have the same relative values. One objective may be highly prized in one circumstance, another in another circumstance. If, for example, an administrator values highly both the dispatch with which his agency can carry through its projects *and* good public relations, it matters little which of the two possibly conflicting values he favors in some abstract or general sense. Policy questions arise in forms which put to administrators such a question as: Given the degree to which we are or are not already achieving the values of dispatch and the values of good public relations, is it worth sacrificing a little speed for a happier clientele, or is it better to risk offending the clientele so that we can get on with our work? The answer to such a question varies with circumstances.

The value problem is, as the example shows, always a problem of adjustments at a margin. But there is no practicable way to state marginal objectives or values except in terms of particular policies. That one value is preferred to another in one decision situation does not mean that it will be preferred in another decision situation in which it can be had only at great sacrifice of another value. Attempts to rank or order values in general and abstract terms so that they do not shift from decision to decision end up by ignoring the relevant marginal preferences. The significance of this third point thus goes very far. Even if all administrators had at hand an agreed set of values, objectives, and constraints, and an agreed ranking of these values, objectives, and constraints, their marginal values in actual choice situations would be impossible to formulate.

Unable consequently to formulate the relevant values first and then choose among policies to achieve them, administrators must choose directly among alternative policies that offer different marginal combinations of values. Somewhat paradoxically, the only practicable way to disclose one's relevant marginal values even to oneself is to describe the policy one chooses to achieve them. Except roughly and vaguely, I know of no way to describe—or even to understand—what my relative evaluations are for, say, freedom and security, speed and accuracy in governmental decisions, or low taxes and better schools than to describe my preferences among specific policy choices that might be made between the alternatives in each of the pairs.

In summary, two aspects of the process by which values are actually handled can be distinguished. The first is clear: evaluation and empirical analysis are intertwined; that is, one chooses among values and among policies at one and the same time. Put a little more elaborately, one simultaneously chooses a policy to attain certain objectives and chooses the objectives themselves. The second aspect is related but distinct: the administrator focuses his attention on marginal or incremental values. Whether he is aware of it or not, he does not find general formulations of objectives very helpful and in fact makes specific marginal or incremental comparisons. Two policies, X and Y, confront him. Both promise the same degree of attainment of objectives *a, b, c, d,* and *e.* But X promises him somewhat more of *f* than does Y, while Y promises him somewhat more of *g* than does X. In choosing between them, he is in fact offered the alternative of a marginal or incremental amount of *f* at the expense of a marginal or incremental amount of *g.* The only values that are relevant to his choice are these

increments by which the two policies differ; and, when he finally chooses between the two marginal values, he does so by making a choice between policies.[5]

As to whether the attempt to clarify objectives in advance of policy selection is more or less rational than the close intertwining of marginal evaluation and empirical analysis, the principal difference established is that for complex problems the first is impossible and irrelevant, and the second is both possible and relevant. The second is possible because the administrator need not try to analyze any values except the values by which alternative policies differ and need not be concerned with them except as they differ marginally. His need for information on values or objectives is drastically reduced as compared with the root method; and his capacity for grasping, comprehending, and relating values to one another is not strained beyond the breaking point.

## Relations Between Means and Ends (2b)

Decision-making is ordinarily formalized as a means-ends relationship: means are conceived to be evaluated and chosen in the light of ends finally selected independently of and prior to the choice of means. This is the means-ends relationship of the root method. But it follows from all that has just been said that such a means-ends relationship is possible only to the extent that values are agreed upon, are reconcilable, and are stable at the margin. Typically, therefore, such a means-ends relationship is absent from the branch method, where means and ends are simultaneously chosen.

Yet any departure from the means-ends relationship of the root method will strike some readers as inconceivable. For it will appear to them that only in such a relationship is it possible to determine whether one policy choice is better or worse than another. How can an administrator know whether he has made a wise or foolish decision if he is without prior values or objectives by which to judge his decisions? The answer to this question calls up the third distinctive difference between root and branch methods: how to decide the best policy.

## The Test of "Good" Policy (3b)

In the root method, a decision is "correct," "good," or "rational" if it can be shown to attain some specified objective, where the objective can be specified without simply describing the decision itself. Where objectives are defined only through the marginal or incremental approach to values described above, it is still sometimes possible to test whether a policy does in fact attain the desired objectives; but a precise statement of the objectives takes the form of a description of the policy chosen or some alternative to it. To show that a policy is mistaken one cannot offer an abstract argument that important objectives are not achieved; one must instead argue that another policy is more to be preferred.

So far, the departure from customary ways of looking at problem-solving is not troublesome, for many administrators will be quick to agree that the most effective discussion of the correctness of policy does take the form of comparison with other policies that might have been chosen. But what of the situation in which administrators cannot agree on values or objectives, either abstractly or in marginal terms? What then is the test of "good" policy? For the root method, there is no test. Agreement on objectives failing, there is no standard of "correctness." For the method of successive limited comparisons, the test is agreement on policy itself, which remains possible even when agreement on values is not.

It has been suggested that continuing agreement in Congress on the desirability of extending old age insurance stems from liberal desires to strengthen the welfare programs of the federal government and from conservative desires to reduce union demands for private pension plans. If so, this is an excellent demonstration of the ease with which individuals of different ideologies often can agree on concrete policy. Labor mediators report a similar phenomenon: the contestants cannot agree on criteria for settling their disputes but can agree on specific proposals. Similarly, when one administrator's objective turns out to be another's means, they often can agree on policy.

Agreement on policy thus becomes the only practicable test of the policy's correctness. And for one administrator to seek to win the other over to agreement on ends as well would accomplish nothing and create quite unnecessary controversy.

If agreement directly on policy as a test for "best" policy seems a poor substitute for testing the policy against its objectives, it ought to be remembered that objectives themselves have no ultimate validity other than they are agreed upon. Hence agreement is the test of "best" policy in both methods. But where the root method requires agreement on what elements in the decision constitute objectives and on which of these objectives should be sought, the branch method falls back on agreement wherever it can be found.

In an important sense, therefore, it is not irrational for an administrator to defend a policy as good without being able to specify what it is good for.

## Non-Comprehensive Analysis (4b)

Ideally, rational-comprehensive analysis leaves out nothing important. But it is impossible to take everything important into consideration unless "important" is so narrowly defined that analysis is in fact quite limited. Limits on human intellectual capacities and on available information set definite limits to man's capacity to be comprehensive. In actual fact, therefore, no one can practice the rational-comprehensive method for really complex problems, and every administrator faced with a sufficiently complex problem must find ways drastically to simplify.

An administrator assisting in the formulation of agricultural economic policy cannot in the first place be competent on all possible policies. He cannot even comprehend one policy entirely. In planning a soil bank program, he cannot successfully anticipate the impact of higher or lower farm income on, say, urbanization—the possible consequent loosening of family ties, possible consequent eventual need for revisions in social security and further implications for tax problems arising out of new federal responsibilities for social security and municipal responsibilities for urban services. Nor, to follow another line of repercussions, can he work through the soil bank program's effects on prices for agricultural products in foreign markets and consequent implications for foreign relations, including those arising out of economic rivalry between the United States and the U.S.S.R.

In the method of successive limited comparisons, simplification is systematically achieved in two principal ways. First, it is achieved through limitation of policy comparisons to those policies that differ in relatively small degree from policies presently in effect. Such a limitation immediately reduces the number of alternatives to be investigated and also drastically simplifies the character of the investigation of each. For it is not necessary to undertake fundamental inquiry into an alternative and its consequences; it is necessary only to study those respects in which the proposed alternative and its consequences differ from the status quo. The empirical comparison of marginal differences among alternative policies that differ only marginally is, of course, a counterpart to the incremental or marginal comparison of values discussed above.[6]

## Relevance as Well as Realism

It is a matter of common observation that in Western democracies public administrators and policy analysts in general do largely limit their analyses to incremental or marginal differences in policies that are chosen to differ only incrementally. They do not do so, however, solely because they desperately need some way to simplify their problems; they also do so in order to be relevant. Democracies change their policies almost entirely through incremental adjustments. Policy does not move in leaps and bounds.

The incremental character of political change in the United States has often been remarked. The two major political parties agree on fundamentals; they offer alternative policies to the voters only on relatively small points of difference. Both parties favor full employment, but they define it somewhat differently; both favor the development of water power resources, but in slightly different ways; and both favor unemployment compensation, but not the same level of benefits. Similarly, shifts of policy within a party take place largely through a series of relatively small changes, as can be seen in their only gradual acceptance of the idea of governmental responsibility for support of the unemployed, a change in party positions beginning in the early 30's and culminating in a sense in the Employment Act of 1946.

Party behavior is in turn rooted in public attitudes, and political theorists cannot conceive of democracy's surviving in the United States in the absence of fundamental agreement on potentially disruptive issues, with consequent limitation of policy debates to relatively small differences in policy.

Since the policies ignored by the administrator are politically impossible and so irrelevant, the simplification of analysis achieved by concentrating on policies that differ only incrementally is not a capricious kind of simplification. In addition, it can be argued that, given the limits on knowledge within which policymakers are confined, simplifying by limiting the focus to small variations from present policy makes the most of available knowledge. Because policies being considered are like present and past policies, the administrator can obtain information and claim some insight. Non-incremental policy proposals are therefore typically not only politically irrelevant but also unpredictable in their consequences.

The second method of simplification of analysis is the practice of ignoring important possible consequences of possible policies, as well as the values attached to the neglected consequences. If this appears to disclose a shocking shortcoming of successive limited comparisons, it can be replied that, even if the exclusions are random, policies may nevertheless be more intelligently formulated than through futile attempts to achieve a comprehensiveness beyond human capacity. Actually, however, the exclusions, seeming arbitrary or random from one point of view, need be neither.

## Achieving a Degree of Comprehensiveness

Suppose that each value neglected by one policy-making agency were a major concern of at least one other agency. In that case, a helpful division of labor would be achieved, and no agency need find its task beyond its capacities. The shortcomings of such a system would be that one agency might destroy a value either before another agency could be activated to safeguard it or in spite of another agency's efforts. But the possibility that important values may be lost is present in any form of organization, even where agencies attempt to comprehend in planning more than is humanly possible.

The virtue of such a hypothetical division of labor is that every important interest or value has its watchdog. And these watchdogs can protect the interests in their jurisdiction in two quite different ways: first, by redressing damages done by other agencies; and, second, by

anticipating and heading off injury before it occurs.

In a society like that of the United States in which individuals are free to combine to pursue almost any possible common interest they might have and in which government agencies are sensitive to the pressures of these groups, the system described is approximated. Almost every interest has its watchdog. Without claiming that every interest has a sufficiently powerful watchdog, it can be argued that our system often can assure a more comprehensive regard for the values of the whole society than any attempt at intellectual comprehensiveness.

In the United States, for example, no part of government attempts a comprehensive overview of policy on income distribution. A policy nevertheless evolves, and one responding to a wide variety of interests. A process of mutual adjustment among farm groups, labor unions, municipalities and school boards, tax authorities, and government agencies with responsibilities in the fields of housing, health, highways, national parks, fire, and police accomplishes a distribution of income in which particular income problems neglected at one point in the decision processes become central at another point.

Mutual adjustment is more pervasive than the explicit forms it takes in negotiation between groups; it persists through the mutual impacts of groups upon each other even where they are not in communication. For all the imperfections and latent dangers in this ubiquitous process of mutual adjustment, it will often accomplish an adaptation of policies to a wider range of interests than could be done by one group centrally.

Note, too, how the incremental pattern of policy-making fits with the multiple pressure pattern. For when decisions are only incremental—closely related to known policies, it is easier for one group to anticipate the kind of moves another might make and easier too for it to make correction for injury already accomplished.[7]

Even partisanship and narrowness, to use pejorative terms, will sometimes be assets to rational decision-making, for they can doubly insure that what one agency neglects, another will not; they specialize personnel to distinct points of view. The claim is valid that effective rational coordination of the federal administration, if possible to achieve at all, would require an agreed set of values[8]—if "rational" is defined as the practice of the root method of decision-making. But a high degree of administrative coordination occurs as each agency adjusts its policies to the concerns of the other agencies in the process of fragmented decision-making I have just described.

For all the apparent shortcomings of the incremental approach to policy alternatives with its arbitrary exclusion coupled with fragmentation, when compared to the root method, the branch method often looks far superior. In the root method, the inevitable exclusion of factors is accidental, unsystematic, and not defensible by any argument so far developed, while in the branch method the exclusions are deliberate, systematic, and defensible. Ideally, of course, the root method does not exclude; in practice it must.

Nor does the branch method necessarily neglect long-run considerations and objectives. It is clear that important values must be omitted in considering policy, and sometimes the only way long-run objectives can be given adequate attention is through the neglect of short-run consideration. But the values omitted can be either long-run or short-run.

## Succession of Comparisons (5b)

The final distinctive element in the branch method is that the comparisons, together with the policy choice, proceed in a chronological series. Policy is not made once and for all; it is made and remade endlessly. Policy-making is a process of successive approximation to some desired objectives in which what is desired itself continues to change under reconsideration.

Making policy is at best a very rough process. Neither social scientists, nor politicians, nor public administrators yet know enough about the social world to avoid repeated error in predicting the consequences of policy moves. A wise policy-maker consequently expects that his policies will achieve only part of what he hopes and at the same time will produce unanticipated consequences he would have preferred to avoid. If he proceeds through a *succession* of incremental changes, he avoids serious lasting mistakes in several ways.

In the first place, past sequences of policy steps have given him knowledge about the probable consequences of further similar steps. Second, he need not attempt big jumps toward his goals that would require predictions beyond his or anyone else's knowledge, because he never expects his policy to be a final resolution of a problem. His decision is only one step, one that if successful can quickly be followed by another. Third, he is in effect able to test his previous predictions as he moves on to each further step. Lastly, he often can remedy a past error fairly quickly—more quickly than if policy proceeded through more distinct steps widely spaced in time.

Compare this comparative analysis of incremental changes with the aspiration to employ theory in the root method. Man cannot think without classifying, without subsuming one experience under a more general category of experiences. The attempt to push categorization as far as possible and to find general propositions which can be applied to specific situations is what I refer to with the word "theory." Where root analysis often leans heavily on theory in this sense, the branch method does not.

The assumption of root analysis is that theory is the most systematic and economical way to bring relevant knowledge to bear on a specific problem. Granting the assumption, an unhappy fact is that we do not have adequate theory to apply to problems in any policy area, although theory is more adequate in some areas—monetary policy, for example—than in others. Comparative analysis, as in the branch method, is sometimes a systematic alternative to theory.

Suppose an administrator must choose among a small group of policies that differ only incrementally from each other and from present policy. He might aspire to "understand" each of the alternatives—for example, to know all the consequences of each aspect of each policy. If so, he would indeed require theory. In fact, however, he would usually decide that, *for policy-making purposes,* he need know, as explained above, only the consequences of each of those aspects of the policies in which they differed from one another. For this much more modest aspiration, he requires no theory (although it might be helpful, if available), for he can proceed to isolate probable differences by examining the differences in consequences associated with past differences in policies, a feasible program because he can take his observations from a long sequence of incremental changes.

For example, without a more comprehensive social theory about juvenile delinquency than scholars have yet produced, one cannot possibly understand the ways in which a variety of public policies—say on education, housing, recreation, employment, race relations, and policing—might encourage or discourage delinquency. And one needs such an understanding if he undertakes the comprehensive overview of the problem prescribed in the models of the root method. If, however, one merely wants to mobilize knowledge sufficient to assist in a choice among a small group of similar policies—alternative policies on juvenile court procedures, for example—he can do so by comparative analysis of the results of similar past policy moves.

## Theorists and Practitioners

This difference explains—in some cases at least—why the administrator often feels that the outside expert or academic problem-solver is sometimes not helpful and why they in turn often urge more theory on him. And it explains why an administrator often feels more confident when "flying by the seat of his pants" than when following the advice of theorists. Theorists often ask the administrator to go the long way round to the solution of his problems, in effect ask him to follow the best canons of the scientific method, when the administrator knows the best available theory will work less well than more modest incremental comparisons. Theorists do not realize that the administrator is often in fact practicing a systematic method. It would be foolish to push this explanation too far, for sometimes practical decision-makers are pursuing neither a theoretical approach nor successive comparisons, nor any other systematic method.

It may be worth emphasizing that theory is sometimes of extremely limited helpfulness in policy-making for at least two rather different reasons. It is greedy for facts; it can be constructed only through a great collection of observations. And it is typically insufficiently precise for application to a policy process that moves through small changes. In contrast, the comparative method both economizes on the need for facts and directs the analyst's attention to just those facts that are relevant to the fine choices faced by the decision-maker.

With respect to precision of theory, economic theory serves as an example. It predicts that an economy without money or prices would in certain specified ways misallocate resources, but this finding pertains to an alternative far removed from the kind of policies on which administrators need help. On the other hand, it is not precise enough to predict the consequences of policies restricting business mergers, and this is the kind of issue on which the administrators need help. Only in relatively restricted areas does economic theory achieve sufficient precision to go far in resolving policy questions; its helpfulness in policy-making is always so limited that it requires supplementation through comparative analysis.

## Successive Comparison as a System

Successive limited comparison is, then, indeed a method or system; it is not a failure of method for which administrators ought to apologize. None the less, its imperfections, which have not been explored in this paper, are many. For example, the method is without a built-in safeguard for all relevant values, and it also may lead the decision-maker to overlook excellent policies for no other reason than that they are not suggested by the chain of successive policy steps leading up to the present. Hence, it ought to be said that under this method, as well as under some of the most sophisticated variants of the root method—operations research, for example—policies will continue to be as foolish as they are wise.

Why then bother to describe the method in all the above detail? Because it is in fact a common method of policy formulation, and is, for complex problems, the principal reliance of administrators as well as of other policy analysts.[9] And because it will be superior to any other decision-making method available for complex problems in many circumstances, certainly superior to a futile attempt at super-human comprehensiveness. The reaction of the public administrator to the exposition of method doubtless will be less a discovery of a new method than a better acquaintance with an old. But by becoming more conscious of their practice of this method, administrators might practice it with more skill and know when to extend or constrict its use. (That they sometimes practice it effectively and sometimes not may explain the extremes of opinion on "muddling through," which is both praised as a highly sophisticated form of problem-solving and denounced as no method at all. For I suspect that in so far as there is a system in what is known as "muddling through," this method is it.)

One of the noteworthy incidental consequences of clarification of the method is the light it throws on the suspicion an administra-

tor sometimes entertains that a consultant or adviser is not speaking relevantly and responsibly when in fact by all ordinary objective evidence he is. The trouble lies in the fact that most of us approach policy problems within a framework given by our view of a chain of successive policy choices made up to the present. One's thinking about appropriate policies with respect, say, to urban traffic control is greatly influenced by one's knowledge of the incremental steps taken up to the present. An administrator enjoys an intimate knowledge of his past sequences that "outsiders" do not share, and his thinking and that of the "outsider" will consequently be different in ways that may puzzle both. Both may appear to be talking intelligently, yet each may find the other unsatisfactory. The relevance of the policy chain of succession is even more clear when an American tries to discuss, say, antitrust policy with a Swiss, for the chains of policy in the two countries are strikingly different and the two individuals consequently have organized their knowledge in quite different ways.

If this phenomenon is a barrier to communication, an understanding of it promises an enrichment of intellectual interaction in policy formulation. Once the source of difference is understood, it will sometimes be stimulating for an administrator to seek out a policy analyst whose recent experience is with a policy chain different from his own.

This raises again a question only briefly discussed above on the merits of like-mindedness among government administrators. While much of organization theory argues the virtues of common values and agreed organizational objectives, for complex problems in which the root method is inapplicable, agencies will want among their own personnel two types of diversification: administrators whose thinking is organized by reference to policy chains other than those familiar to most members of the organization and, even more commonly, administrators whose professional or personal values or interests create diversity of view (perhaps coming from different specialties, social classes, geographical areas) so that, even within a single agency, decision-making can be fragmented and parts of the agency can serve as watchdogs for other parts.

## Notes

1. James G. March and Herbert A. Simon similarly characterized the literature. They also take some important steps, as have Simon's recent articles, to describe a less heroic model of policy-making. See *Organizations* (John Wiley and Sons, 1958), p. 137.
2. "Operations Research and National Planning—A Dissent," 5 *Operations Research* 718 (October, 1957). Hitch's dissent is from particular points made in the article to which his paper is a reply; his claim that operations research is for low-level problems is widely accepted.

   For examples of the kind of problems to which operations research is applied, see C. W. Churchman, R. L. Ackoff and E. L. Arnoff, *Introduction to Operations Research* (John Wiley and Sons, 1957); and J. F. McCloskey and J. M. Coppinger (eds.), *Operations Research for Management,* Vol. II, (The Johns Hopkins Press, 1956).
3. I am assuming that administrators often make policy and advise in the making of policy and am treating decision-making and policy-making as synonymous for purposes of this paper.
4. Martin Meyerson and Edward C. Banfield, *Politics, Planning and the Public Interest* (The Free Press, 1955).
5. The line of argument is, of course, an extension of the theory of market choice, especially the theory of consumer choice, to public policy choices.
6. A more precise definition of incremental policies and a discussion of whether a change that appears "small" to one observer might be seen differently by another is to be found in my "Policy Analysis," 48 *American Economic Review* 298 (June, 1958).
7. The link between the practice of the method of successive limited comparisons and mutual adjustment of interests in a highly fragmented decision-making process adds a new facet to pluralist theories of government and administration.
8. Herbert Simon, Donald W. Smithburg, and Victor A. Thompson, *Public Administration* (Alfred A. Knopf, 1950), p. 434.
9. Elsewhere I have explored this same method of policy formulation as practiced by academic analysts of policy ("Policy Analysis," 48 *American Economic Review* 298 [June, 1958]). Although it has been here presented as a method for public administrators, it is no less necessary to analysts more removed from immediate policy questions, despite their tendencies to describe their own analytical efforts as though they were the rational-comprehensive method with an especially heavy use of theory. Similarly, this same method is inevitably resorted to in personal problem-solving, where means and ends are sometimes impossible to separate, where aspirations or objectives undergo constant development, and where drastic simplification of the complexity of the real world is urgent if problems are to be solved in the time that can be given to them. To an economist accustomed to dealing with the marginal or incremental concept in market processes, the central idea in the method is that both evaluation and empirical analysis are incremental. Accordingly I have referred to the method elsewhere as "the incremental method."

## CASE STUDY 8

# Introduction

On August 2, 1990, Iraqi President Saddam Hussein invaded his neighbor, oil-rich Kuwait, to the surprise of the United States as well as the entire world. Three days later, Sunday, August 5, U.S. President George Bush, speaking on the White House lawn about the Iraqi invasion, said, "This will not stand." Throughout the crisis, Bush was firm in his conviction that Iraq must completely withdraw from Kuwait. However, what remained in question, at least during the first few months of the ordeal, was the method for achieving that goal. Some favored a "wait and see" approach; others supported a "defer and defend" strategy; others, "economic containment"; and still others argued, "take the offensive!"

The following case study, "The Decision to Liberate Kuwait," an excerpt from *The Commanders* by Bob Woodward, assistant managing editor of the *Washington Post,* describes events from late September to early November 1990 when the decision was made by the United States to go on the offensive and liberate Kuwait. Woodward, of course, is best known as the investigative reporter who, along with Carl Bernstein, broke the Watergate story, which led to the resignation of President Richard Nixon in 1974 (recounted in their books, *The Final Days* and *All the President's Men*). Woodward also has written other well-known "Washington-insider" investigations of the CIA *(Veil: The Secret Wars of the CIA, 1981–87)* and the Supreme Court *(The Brethren,* co-authored with Scott Armstrong).

Woodward explains why he wrote *The Commanders* in the opening "Note to the Reader":

> I initially planned to focus on the military and civilian leadership of the Pentagon, headquarters for one of the world's largest enterprises, the modern American defense establishment. . . .
>
> My initial research emphasized the Pentagon under Bush. . . . The fast-approaching end of the Cold War suggested it could be a quiet time for the military, an opportunity for me to try to understand the Defense Department's subtle intricacies.
>
> "The December 1989 Panama invasion and more importantly, the 1990 Gulf Crisis, changed all that. The military was not going to play a smaller role in the new world (order) . . . . From the time of the Iraqi invasion of Kuwait in August 1990, I concentrated on the evolution of the Persian Gulf Crisis and the decision to go to war against Saddam Hussein.

As the author emphasizes, "It is above all a book about how the United States decides to fight its wars before shots are fired." In particular, "The Decision to Liberate Kuwait" looks closely at how various options facing top Washington policy makers were raised, addressed, and decided on during the Gulf Crisis. In the process of telling this story, Woodward focuses on the top-level participants in the White House, Pentagon, and State Department and offers an insightful narrative about how several key figures thought and acted during these fateful deliberations. He interviewed more than 400 people over 27 months, "some on a regular basis as events unfolded." Nearly all the interviews were done on "a deep background basis"; that is, the sources agreed to speak to Woodward only with the understanding that they would not be identified by name or title. He spoke to some "within the hour or day of events in which they played a role." His account, as he points out, is possibly "somewhere between newspaper journalism and history." This technique nonetheless remains controversial because of his failure to identify sources as well as for his being too close to events after they occurred.

This case tells us much about how decisions are made at the highest levels of government in the 1990s. Therefore, it is well worth reading in relationship to Charles Lindblom's foregoing essay. Think about these questions as you read:

> How did each of the major "players" in this case study perceive of the alternatives in the Gulf Crisis by early Fall 1990? What were their motivations and individual

assumptions concerning how to handle the Iraqi invasion? What were their preferred strategies and method(s) by which they "pushed forward" their own policy agendas?

Why did some options like "containment" and "strangulation" never receive open debate or wide-spread support? Were all options heard and fairly considered, in your opinion?

Who were the "major players" and why were some included and others left out of the discussions? How did the personalities of this group and their interactions influence the type of options raised, debated, and ultimately the way the final decision was reached? Why was "personal chemistry" so critical, according to Woodward?

What major fears were evident involving the policy options? By what means were these uncertainties dealt with? How did the press and instantaneous communications help *and* hinder decision making throughout this case?

Does the case support or contradict Lindblom's incremental model of decision making? Why, at the end of the reading, did General Colin L. Powell, Chairman of the Joint Chiefs of Staff, liken the decisional process to "high stakes poker"? Do you agree that the gambling metaphor is more apt than "incrementalism" to explain how choices were made in the Gulf Crisis?

Do you find this story supports Mosher's concept, described in Chapter 7, regarding the influence of professionals in government? Who were the key professionals in this case? Were they as critical as Mosher suggests to deciding the outcome of governmental decisions in this story?

What were the important policy differences exhibited here between the professionals and politicians? Which group was in charge? What were the sources of these differences? Do you judge such conflicts to be healthy or detrimental to the policy making processes?

# The Decision to Liberate Kuwait

## BOB WOODWARD

On September 21, the sixth week into the U.S. deployment, [Iraqi President] Saddam [Hussein's] Revolutionary Command Council issued a bellicose statement saying, "There is not a single chance for any retreat. . . . Let everybody understand that this battle is going to become the mother of all battles."

Reprinted by permission from *The Commanders* by Bob Woodward (New York: Simon & Schuster, 1991). © 1991 by Simon & Schuster, Inc.

Satellite photos and other intelligence presented to President [George] Bush showed that Iraq was systematically dismantling Kuwait, looting the entire nation. Everything of value was being carried back to Iraq; the populace was being terrorized, starved, beaten, murdered. Kuwait would soon become a perpetual no-man's-land, Bush was told. He could see much of it with his own eyes.

U.S. intelligence claimed that Saddam had 430,-000 troops in Kuwait and southern Iraq. His forces were digging in, moving into even more defensive positions. This made an offensive attack by Saddam into Saudi Arabia less likely. In order to attack, the Iraqis would have to dig out and move into the so-called killing zones—swatches of open desert miles wide—where the United States could obliterate troops and tanks with superior airpower and [General Norman] Schwarzkopf's own ground forces. Though the United States had less than half as many troops in the theater as Iraq, [Secretary of Defense Dick] Cheney and [Chairman of the Joint Chiefs of Staff Colin] Powell told Bush they now felt quite sure the U.S. and allied forces could defend Saudi Arabia.

Friday, September 28, was the Day of the Emir. Bush had the exiled emir of Kuwait, who was visiting the United States for the first time, into the Oval Office for a meeting. Scowcroft joined them for the hour-long meeting. Though the emir did not directly ask for military intervention to liberate his country, [Brent] Scowcroft [National Security Council Director] could see that that was his subliminal message. Bush then took the exiled leader to meet with the cabinet and later to have lunch with the cabinet members in the White House residence. That afternoon, Cheney and Powell met with the emir privately.

Afterwards Bush said that Kuwait was running out of time. It certainly wasn't going to be around as a country if they waited for sanctions to work. The emir himself, the stories of destruction supported by intelligence reports, left an indelible mark on the President, both Cheney and Powell could see. Bush was personally moved. Iraq will fail and Kuwait will endure, Bush said.

At the same time, Powell realized that Schwarzkopf in Saudi Arabia was growing increasingly uneasy. Schwarzkopf had chewed out [Lt. General Thomas W.] Kelly [Director of Operations for the Joint Chiefs of Staff] on the phone once when Powell had requested some information within 30 minutes. Kelly was not afraid, and had barked back that he was just conveying Powell's order: "I didn't give it to you, the Chairman did." But Schwarzkopf had just about everyone else intimidated. Schwarzkopf needed to be consoled not about the hard tasks that might lie ahead but about his uncertainty as to what Washington might order. He was increasingly nervous about the scale of the Iraqi buildup and was asking questions about U.S. objectives and force levels. Though his stated military mission was still only the defense of

Saudi Arabia, Schwarzkopf was aware of repeated presidential statements moving the mission close to the liberation of Kuwait.

At times brooding in his daily secure phone conversations to Powell in the Pentagon, Schwarzkopf was regularly looking for clues, or asking directly, about the next step. Were they going to hold to the defensive mission? Or were they going to build up the forces to do more?

"Norm, I'm working on it," Powell had been telling him.

In their regular 5 P.M. meetings, Cheney and Powell spent much time on these questions.

"You know," Powell told Cheney in early October, "we're going to have to get a decision." The President had to tell them whether to continue deploying forces, or to stop, well before the cut-off date of December 1, when they expected to have in place all the forces and supplies needed for the defensive mission. "When I put the last thing in the funnel, two weeks later it will come out in Saudi Arabia. We need to know when to stop putting things in the funnel." Powell reminded Cheney that he had not participated in a full policy review or a discussion of the options and their merits.

Cheney didn't give much of a response.

Powell started jotting down some notes. He felt that containment or strangulation was working. An extraordinary political-diplomatic coalition had been assembled, leaving Iraq without substantial allies—condemned, scorned and isolated as perhaps no country had been in modern history. Intelligence showed that economic sanctions were cutting off up to 95 percent of Saddam's imports and nearly all his exports. Saddam was practically sealed off in Iraq and Kuwait. The impact could not be measured in weeks, Powell felt. It might take months. There would come a point a month or six weeks before Saddam was down to the last pound of rice when the sanctions would trigger some kind of a response.

Paul Wolfowitz, the undersecretary for policy, told Powell that he felt strangulation was a defensible position as long as it meant applying sanctions indefinitely. Saddam had to know he was facing strangulation forever. To adopt a policy that said, or implied, that sanctions would be in effect for one year or 18 months would give the Iraqi leader a point when he could count on relief. He would have only to tell his people to hold out another so-many months. Wolfowitz said he thought it was a hard call; probably 55 percent of the merit was for one side, 45 percent for the other.

• • •

Powell went to Cheney to outline the case for containment. He had not reduced his arguments to a formal paper; there was no memo, no plan, nothing typed up. All he had were his handwritten notes. Until they were sure sanctions and strangulation had failed, it would be very difficult to go to war, Powell said. If there was a chance that sanctions might work, there might be an obligation to continue waiting—at least to a certain point. To do something premature when there was still a chance of accomplishing the political objectives with sanctions could be a serious mistake.

"I don't know," Cheney responded. "I don't think the President will buy it." Cheney thought that containment was insufficient, and did not see any really convincing evidence that the sanctions were going to guarantee success. The President was committed to policy success. Containment could leave Kuwait in Saddam's hands. That would constitute policy failure. It would be unacceptable to the President.

Powell wanted another dog in the fight. He was concerned that no one was laying out the alternatives to the President. Bush might not be hearing everything he needed to hear. A full slate of options should be presented. Several days later Powell went back to Cheney with an expanded presentation on containment.

"Uh—hmm," Cheney said, noncommittal. "It certainly is another way to look at it."

Powell next went to see [Secretary of State James A.] Baker to talk about containment. The Secretary of State was Powell's chief ally in the upper ranks of the administration. They thought alike on many issues. Both men preferred dealmaking to confrontation or conflict. And both worked the news media assiduously to get their points of view across and have them cast in the most favorable light. Baker was very unhappy about the talk of using or developing an offensive military option. He wanted diplomacy—meaning the State Department—to achieve the policy success. He informed Powell that he had some of his staff working on an analysis of the advantages of containment. This should force a discussion of containment within the Bush inner circle, Baker indicated, or at least it would get out publicly.

But no White House meetings or discussion followed. Powell felt that he'd sent the idea up the flagpole but no one had saluted or even commented. He could see, all too plainly, that the President was consistent and dug in, insisting that Kuwait be freed. Bush had not blinked, and frustrations were obviously mounting in the White House. After more than two months, neither the United Nations resolutions, nor diplomacy, nor economic sanctions, nor rhetoric appeared to be forcing Saddam's hand. Powell had too often seen presidential emotions drive policy; Reagan's personal concern for the American hostages in Lebanon had been behind the Iran-contra affair. Powell decided to go see Scowcroft in the White House.

Scowcroft indicated he was having a difficult time that Powell, as a former national security adviser, would understand. He was trying to manage and control an incredibly active President. Bush was out making statements, giving press conferences almost daily, up at dawn making calls, on the phone with one world leader after another, setting up meetings. Scowcroft found himself scrambling just to catch up. On a supposedly relaxing weekend Bush talked with or saw more people related to his job than most people did in a normal work week.

After listening sympathetically, Powell turned to the question of the next steps in the Gulf. He said he wondered about containment and strangulation, the advantages of economic sanctions.

Scowcroft knew Powell's attitude because Cheney had hinted at it. But now Powell was indirect. He did not come out and say, in so many words, this is my position.

"The President is more and more convinced that sanctions are not going to work," Scowcroft responded. He made it clear that he had a solid read on the President. Bush's determination was undisguised and he had virtually foreclosed any possibility that his views could be changed.

Powell could see that Scowcroft agreed with Bush, and was strongly reinforcing the President's inclinations. As national security adviser, it was his job. As the overseer of the administration's entire foreign policy, he had to mirror the President. But the security adviser also had a responsibility to make sure the range of alternatives was presented.

Scowcroft was substantially more willing to go to war than Powell. War was an instrument of foreign policy in Scowcroft's view. Powell did not disagree;

he just saw that instrument much closer, less a disembodied abstraction than real men and women, faces—many of them kids' faces—that Powell looked into on his visits to the troops. In the West Wing of the White House where Scowcroft sat, the Pentagon seemed far away, and the forces even further away. Powell knew that. He had been there.

Powell told Scowcroft that if there was an alternative to war, he wanted to make sure it was fully considered. If there were any possible way to achieve the goals without the use of force, those prospects had to be explored.

Scowcroft became impatient. The President was doing everything imaginable, he said.

Powell left. He had become increasingly disenchanted with the National Security Council procedures and meetings. Scowcroft seemed unable, or unwilling, to coordinate and make sense of all the components of the Gulf policy—military, diplomatic, public affairs, economic, the United Nations. When the principals met, Bush liked to keep everyone around the table smiling—jokes, camaraderie, the conviviality of old friends. Positions and alternatives were not completely discussed. Interruptions were common. Clear decisions rarely emerged. Often Powell and Cheney returned from these gatherings and said to each other, now what did that mean? What are we supposed to do? Frequently, they had to wait to hear the answer later from Scowcroft or the television.

The operation needed a field marshal—someone of the highest rank who was the day-to-day manager, Powell felt. The President, given his other domestic and political responsibilities, couldn't be chief coordinator. It should be the national security adviser. Instead, Scowcroft had become the First Companion and all-purpose playmate to the President on golf, fishing and weekend outings. He was regularly failing in his larger duty to ensure that policy was carefully debated and formulated.

[White House Chief of Staff John] Sununu only added to the problem, exerting little or no control over the process as White House chief of staff.

As a result, the President was left painted into a corner by his own repeated declarations. His obvious emotional attachment to them was converting presidential remarks into hard policy. The goal now, more than ever, was the liberation of Kuwait at almost any cost.

• • •

"Why don't you come over with me and we'll see what the man thinks about your idea," Cheney said to Powell on Friday. Cheney had a private Oval Office meeting scheduled with the President. It was time reserved for the key cabinet members—"the big guys," as Powell privately referred to them. These included just Bush, a cabinet memeber and Sununu or Scowcroft. Normally, Powell was not included.

At the White House, Cheney and Powell went to the Oval Office to see Bush and Scowcroft. At this meeting Powell made his pitch for containment but pulled away from the brink of advocating it personally.

• • •

Powell's thoughts that containment had not been fully shot down by Bush were soon corrected. Within days, Scowcroft told Cheney that Bush wanted a briefing right away on what an offensive operation against Saddam's forces in Kuwait might look like. This planning was being done by Schwarzkopf and his staff in Saudi Arabia, so Powell passed the word to Schwarzkopf to send someone to Washington.

Over the Columbus Day weekend of October 6–8, Army Chief Carl Vuono flew to Saudi Arabia to see Schwarzkopf. They'd been friends since they were teen-aged cadets together at West Point in the 1950s. Schwarzkopf had been a class ahead, but Vuono had been promoted a little faster, so on three occasions during their careers Schwarzkopf had worked for Vuono. Vuono considered Schwarzkopf one of the most difficult, stubborn and talented men in the Army.

When they went off for a private talk, Vuono could see that Schwarzkopf was upset. The CINC, all 6 foot 3, 240 pounds of him, seemed about to explode out of his desert fatigues. He was precisely halfway through the 17 weeks he'd told the President he would need to put the defensive force in place. Now Washington was beginning to talk offense. Les Aspin had said publicly that the administration was "looking more favorably on an early war option." *The New York Times* had reported that the word around the Pentagon was that the offensive would begin on October 15. Worse, Powell had just told Schwarzkopf in a secure phone conversation that Bush wanted a briefing right away on what an offensive operation against Saddam's forces in Kuwait would look like.

Schwarzkopf was furious. They had to be kidding. He was not ready to present such a plan. He had received no warning, and he didn't want to be pushed prematurely into offensive operations. Now he was afraid some son-of-a-bitch was going to wake up some morning and say, let's get the offense rolling. He had two more months' work to do on defense, and he had told the President in August it would take 8 to 12 months to be ready for offense. That meant next March, but now in October they wanted an offensive plan that they could carry out right away.

Powell had told him that everyone understood it would be a preliminary plan. He gave the Central Command about 48 hours to get someone to Washington with a briefing. Schwarzkopf couldn't leave Saudi Arabia so he would have to send a subordinate.

After listening to Schwarzkopf for four hours, Vuono felt as if he'd been through a psychotherapy session. He could see that his old friend felt very lonely and vulnerable. Vuono promised to do what he could.

On Wednesday morning, October 10, Powell received Schwarzkopf's chief of staff, Marine Major General Robert B. Johnston, at the Pentagon. In the afternoon, Cheney, Wolfowitz, Powell, the other chiefs [of the Army, Navy, Air Force, and Marine Corps] and Kelly went to the Tank. They were all in the most restricted group cleared for top-secret war plans. It was absolutely essential that word not leak out that the Pentagon was considering an offensive operation. It might be an invitation for Saddam to attack before the full defensive force was in place.

Johnston, a stiff, deferential, buttoned-down Marine with extensive briefing experience, began by reminding them that the Central Command had deployed its forces in accordance with the President's deter-and-defend mission. But if the President tells us to go on the offense tomorrow, he said, here's what we would do. Though we haven't had a lot of time to think this through, and we're not prepared to say in detail this is the right plan, this is our best shot at it.

The plan was broken into four phases, he explained. The first three were exclusively an air campaign, and the fourth was a ground attack.

Phase One would be an air attack on Iraqi command, control and communications, attempting to sever Saddam in Baghdad from his forces in Kuwait and southern Iraq. Simultaneously, airpower would destroy the Iraqi Air Force and air defense system. In addition, Phase One would include an air attack to destroy Iraqi chemical, biological and nuclear weapons facilities.

Phase Two would be a massive, continuous air bombardment of Iraqi supply and munitions bases, transportation facilities and roads, designed to cut off the Iraqi forces from their supplies.

Phase Three would be an air attack on the entrenched Iraqi ground forces of 430,000 men, and on the Republican Guard.

The phases would overlap somewhat. As early as a week after the beginning of the first air phase, the Phase Four ground assault would be launched on the Iraqi forces in Kuwait. One of Johnston's slides was a map with three large arrows showing the three attack points where coalition forces would hit the Iraqis. One arrow represented U.S. Marines in an amphibious assault from the Gulf; another was the U.S. Army on the ground attacking directly into Iraqi lines; and the third was an Egyptian ground division, also going straight into enemy forces, while protecting one of the U.S. flanks.

Cheney, Powell and several of the others asked question after question. Could they count on the Egyptians to protect the American ground troops? What about back-up forces if the Iraqis counterattacked?

Powell and Vuono wanted to know if it was possible to move the U.S. forces out to the west along the Iraqi border and then come up on the Iraqi Army from the side and behind. Could the U.S. forces be repositioned fast enough so the Iraqis would not know?

The initial terrain analysis showed that the Iraqi desert was too soft and wet for the support vehicles to carry the necessary supplies, Johnston said.

Kelly was sure that the straight-up-the-middle plan briefed by Johnston was not going to cut it and would not survive a serious review. Two of the main rules of war were "Never attack the enemy's strength" and "Go where they are not." The plan needed mobility.

Cheney felt pretty good about the three phases of the air campaign. The planning looked detailed and complete. Even after the Dugan firing, the Air Force was basically saying they would take care of it all. Cheney didn't believe it, but he could see airpower would have a tremendous advantage in the desert. In addition, the plans anticipated that targets missed on the first run would be hit again and again as necessary.

The Phase Four ground plan, however, looked inadequate to Cheney. The offensive U.S. Army and

Marine units would be sent against a potentially larger defensive Iraqi force, depending on what remained of Saddam's troops after the bombing. Even to a civilian like himself, Cheney reflected, it looked unwise.

Cheney remarked that many of the U.S. forces like the 18th Airborne Corps were lightly armed and might have to fight heavily armored tanks. There were no reserve forces for back-up. He also questioned whether the U.S. ground forces could be kept supplied with food, fuel and munitions for a long period.

He noted that the ground plan called for the U.S. forces to make their assault straight into the Iraqi entrenchments and barricades, the Iraqi strength. Why go right up the middle? he asked.

Johnston deflected most of the questions. The plan was preliminary, he reminded them, and the questions reflected the caveats from Schwarzkopf that were listed in the last slide. By the time Johnston reached the last slide, however, the Phase Four plan was pretty much shredded. That slide said that Schwarzkopf felt an attack now on the Iraqi force twice the size of his, even with U.S. air, naval and technological superiority, was loaded with problems. "We do not have the capability on the ground to guarantee success," Johnston said. Schwarzkopf felt that he would need an additional Army Corps of three heavy armored divisions for a proper offensive option.

Cheney concluded that an attack with the U.S. forces now in place and based on this plan would be a risk of a high order.

Johnston said there was a window of opportunity of some six weeks, from about January 1 to February 15, when offensive action would be most desirable. After that, the weather and Muslim religious holidays would conspire to make combat more difficult. Heavy rains would begin in March and the temperatures could rise to 100 degrees or more. But they could work around the weather. It could not and should not determine their timetable, he said.

On March 17, the Muslims would start the observation of Ramadan, one month of fasting from sunrise to sunset, and in June would be the annual pilgrimage to Mecca, Johnston noted. The timing could present another complication for Arab states in the anti-Saddam coalition.

Cheney recognized that he had an obligation to present this brief to President Bush. The President needed to know exactly where Schwarzkopf was, the status of the deployment, and what might happen if offensive operations were ordered. The President, Scowcroft and Sununu at least had to be educated on the magnitude of the task. Cheney did not want to walk over to the White House one day, months down the road, to say, "Here's the plan, bang, go." The President had to comprehend the stakes, the costs and the risks, step by step.

By now Cheney had come to realize what an impact the Vietnam War had had on Bush. The President had internalized the lessons—send enough force to do the job and don't tie the hands of the commanders. In a September 12 speech in California, Cheney had said, "The President belongs to what I call the 'Don't screw around' school of military strategy."

Though this perhaps was inelegantly stated, Cheney was certain that the President didn't want to screw around. That meant a viable offensive option.

Schwarzkopf, in Saudi Arabia, was unhappy that he would not be there when the President was briefed on a subject of such paramount importance.

The next day, October 11, Johnston made the presentation to Bush at the White House. In the Situation Room, Johnston laid out the same plan. The meeting took nearly two hours. Bush was interrupted several times. He and Scowcroft had many questions on various subjects, such as minefields and weapon systems. When Johnston said Schwarzkopf would need a full corps of three additional heavy divisions to have the capability to attack on the ground, he was asked how long it would take to move that many divisions.

Two to three months to get them in place, Johnston said.

He hoped his briefing proved that the existing forces were inadequate for an offense.

Bush's reaction was similar to Cheney's, particularly on the Phase Four ground plan. The military was not ready for an offensive operation; they didn't have enough strength.

What would be enough? Bush asked.

Cheney promised the President a detailed answer soon.

• • •

On Wednesday, October 24, Cheney was summoned to the White House. The administration had finally reached a budget compromise with the Democrats after a bruising and politically damaging six months, particularly the last two. Now Bush had time to focus on some of the answers to the question he had left with Cheney—how much additional force? The President said he was leaning toward adding the forces necessary to carry out offensive operations to expel Iraqi troops from Kuwait. Nothing could be announced for two weeks, until after the November 6 elections, because any move would be assumed to be an attempt to influence the elections. Cheney said that he was waiting for Powell's report from Saudi Arabia, and they should wait.

It was apparent to Cheney that Bush would be happy with some public hint. Cheney was already scheduled the next day to go on the early morning shows of the three major networks and CNN. He felt that the White House's inept handling of its budget talks with Congress had cast a pall over the entire administration, and raised fundamental questions about whether Bush and the cabinet knew what they were doing. It had affected Bush's standing in the polls and the way people looked at Washington and government, even eroding confidence in the Gulf operation. Cheney also felt that it was best to prepare the public for the likely decision. He had consistently stated that there was no upper ceiling on the troop deployment and had repeatedly warned that the United States was in for the long haul.

Later that day Cheney joined Baker in giving a classified briefing to legislators in the secure room, S-407, in the Capitol. Neither dropped a hint that a reinforcement was being considered.

But in the television interviews the next morning, October 25, Cheney intentionally laid the seed. "We are not at the point yet where we want to stop adding forces," he said on ABC. On CBS he was asked if the Pentagon was getting ready to send another 100,000 troops. Cheney replied, "It's conceivable that we'll end up with that big of an increase."

He repeated this point on NBC, but added that this would not affect the relief of troops already there after six to eight months. "There clearly will be a rotation policy. . . . I would guess we'll end up around six months."

The big news of Cheney's statements reached Powell, who was on a stopover in Europe. "What is going on?" he asked an aide. When it sank in, he told one person, "Goddammit, I'll never travel again. I haven't seen the President on this." There had been discussions but no decision as far as he knew. But there it was in clear language from Cheney, a man who chose his words carefully.

Bush, Scowcroft and Sununu were making decisions again without a full airing of views. Powell was tired of learning of major administration decisions after the fact. Sununu had been advising and urging the President to speak out strongly and to back up his words with a military threat. He or someone else apparently had won.

One thing that could be said for Bush: he had stated consistently that the Kuwait invasion would not stand. Powell, however, felt that the economic sanctions still loomed as the large unknown. When might they work? When would they be deemed to have failed? He was eager to get back to Washington.

In Saudi Arabia, Schwarzkopf also heard Cheney's remarks. Before his own surprise and distress could fully register, the Saudis were on the phone pounding him with questions: What is this? What's going on? Where were the consultations before making such a decision or announcement? Schwarzkopf tried to stumble through with some answers. He was fuming. Not only did he have to learn about something this important from the media, but he had to explain it to the Saudis without any guidance from Washington.

Schwarzkopf gave a long interview to *The Atlanta Journal and Constitution* that week. "Now we are starting to see evidence that the sanctions are pinching," Schwarzkopf said. "So why should we say, 'Okay, gave 'em two months, didn't work. Let's get on with it and kill a whole bunch of people?' That's crazy. That's crazy." He recounted how in Vietnam the United States, unopposed in the air, would pound the villages with bombs and then go in and find the North Vietnamese coming right out of their holes fighting like devils. Schwarzkopf also said, "War is a profanity because, let's face it, you've got two opposing sides trying to settle their differences by killing as many of each other as they can."

Wolfowitz, who visited the Central Commander around this time, felt that Schwarzkopf was making these statements partly for the benefit of his troops, to make it absolutely clear that if there was a war, it would be the civilians who would be taking them there.

Schwarzkopf told Wolfowitz that he had had some discussions with Middle East experts who had convinced him that while war would be damaging to the United States in the region, a failure to go to war would be far more damaging. Schwarzkopf said he felt that a prolonged stalemate would be a victory for Saddam.

Powell arrived back in Washington, but Cheney was going off the next day to do some fishing in Wyoming with Baker. A White House meeting with the President was planned for early the following week to discuss the Gulf options.

• • •

Several times in October, Robert Teeter, Bush's chief pollster, talked with the President about the Gulf policy. Teeter said he thought the administration had too many messages flying around. There was a lack of focus. He suggested that Bush return to the fundamentals that he had stated in August. The two with the strongest appeal were fighting aggression and protecting the lives of Americans, including the more than 900 Americans being held hostage in Iraq and Kuwait. About 100 had been moved to Iraqi military and industrial installations to serve as "human shields" to deter an American attack.

Bush acknowledged the points, but nonetheless seemed confident. The President said that he felt he knew more than anyone about the region, and also about the diplomacy, the military, the economics and the oil. I have been dealing with these issues for 25 years, Bush said. One night he told Teeter it was important that he had served as United Nations ambassador, U.S. envoy to China, CIA director and Vice President. Those experiences allowed him to see all the pieces. Now he could put them together.

Bush described how, since taking office as President, he had been laying the groundwork, building relations with other heads of state. He'd had no specific purpose in mind, just a strategic sense that it was a good idea. Now his good working relationships with the Thatchers, Mubaraks, Fahds and Gorbachevs of the world could be put to use. There might be some rough times, some down times, Bush conceded, but he felt good. "This will be successful," he assured Teeter.

• • •

For months Scowcroft had been concerned that Baker was not a supporter of the Gulf policy. In the inner-circle discussions he seemed to oppose the large deployment of troops, favoring a diplomatic solution almost to the exclusion of the military pressure. But Baker was coming around. Cheney was fishing with him over the weekend and they would have time to talk.

Baker felt the foundation for the Gulf policy was not solid enough. The plight of the emir of Kuwait, his people, aggression and oil were not selling to the American people. The polls showed that the greatest concern was over the American hostages in Iraq and Kuwait. Baker had argued that the focus of the Gulf policy should be shifted to the hostage issue. It was the one issue that would unite Americans and the international community because most nations, including the Soviets, had hostages held in Iraq. It was the one issue that might justify a war.

Scowcroft thought a new emphasis on the hostages would be changing horses in the middle of the stream, but he saw that public opinion polls were showing increasing doubts about the military deployment. Baker wanted to play the hostage card himself in a strong speech. Scowcroft was willing to go along. The national security adviser also realized that Baker saw the handwriting on the wall. The Bush presidency was likely to rise or fall on the outcome of the Gulf policy. Baker, Bush's friend of 35 years, his campaign manager and the senior cabinet officer, had no other choice than to become an aggressive supporter of the policy.

On Monday, October 29, Baker addressed the Los Angeles World Affairs Council. The more than 100 American human shields, he said, "are forced to sleep on vermin-ridden concrete floors. They are kept in the dark during the day and moved only at night. They have had their meals cut to two a day. And many are becoming sick as they endure a terrible ordeal. The very idea of Americans being used as human shields is simply unconscionable."

The Secretary of State added: "We will not rule out a possible use of force if Iraq continues to occupy Kuwait."

• • •

[On the afternoon of October 30], Bush met with Baker, Cheney, Scowcroft and Powell in the Situation Room.

"We are at a 'Y' in the road," Scowcroft began. The policy could continue to be deter-and-defend, or it could switch to developing the offensive option.

Powell was struck once again by the informality of the rolling discussion among these five men who had been friends for years. There was no real organization to the proceedings as they weighed the options. Ideas bounced back and forth as one thought or another occurred to one of them. Bush and Scowcroft seemed primed to go ahead with the development of the offensive option. Baker, less anxious and more cautious, was measured, inquiring about the attitudes in Congress and in the public, but he was no longer reluctant.

Listening, Cheney saw no willingness on Bush's part to accept anything less than the fulfillment of his stated objective, the liberation of Kuwait. The Secretary of Defense was not going to recommend any military action unless they were sure of success. He said that he had a growing conviction that they had to develop the offensive option. The international coalition was too fragile to hold out indefinitely—to outsiders it might look different, but they knew, from the inside, that the arrangements were delicate. Cheney felt it was quite likely that some outside event could absolutely shatter the coalition.

Powell saw that patience was not the order of the day. As in the past, he did not advocate containment. Powell had found the others previously tolerated his broad political advice, but now he sensed that he had less permission to speak up, having already made the case for containment to the President. Now no one was soliciting Powell's overall political advice on this subject.

The meeting had been billed in advance as a chance for the Chairman to report on his discussions with Schwarzkopf.

"Okay, okay, okay," the President finally said, "let's hear what he has to say."

"Mr. President," Powell began, "we have accomplished the mission assigned." The defense of Saudi Arabia had been achieved earlier than expected. He described how Schwarzkopf had moved some of his forces around to accomplish this in light of the continuing Iraqi buildup.

"Now, if you, Mr. President, decide to build up—go for an offensive option—this is what we need." He then unveiled the Schwarzkopf request to double the force. A central feature was the VII Corps so Schwarzkopf would have the high-speed tanks to conduct flanking attacks on the Iraqis. In this way, they could avoid a frontal assault into Iraqi strength.

Scowcroft was amazed that Schwarzkopf wanted so much more. The request for three aircraft carriers in addition to the three he already had especially surprised Scowcroft. Several oohs and ahs were heard around the table, but not from Bush.

Powell said he supported Schwarzkopf's recommendations, if the President wanted an offensive option. He turned to the President. "If you give me more time, say three months, I'll move more troops. It's that important. You can take me to the Savings and Loan bailout account, and we'll all go broke together." Powell's message: it was going to be expensive.

As far as Powell was concerned, the only constraint was going to be the capacity of the transportation system.

Cheney said he supported Schwarzkopf and Powell without conditions. He went even further. It was not a question *if* the President wanted the offensive option; the President should want it and should go ahead and order it, Cheney said. He explained that this would guarantee success if they had to fight. He did not want to be in the position of making another request for more forces come January or February. Saddam was fully capable of responding with more of his own forces. Cheney did not want to be back here in the Situation Room saying then, "Mr. President, I know what we told you back in October, and we put the additional force over there, but we still can't do it."

Finally, Bush said, "If that's what you need, we'll do it."

The President gave the final approval the next day.

● ● ●

Paul Wolfowitz, who as undersecretary for policy was one of few Pentagon civilians granted oversight of war plans, was worried that the administration had transitioned into the decision on the offensive option without a lot of clear thought. There was little or no process where alternatives and implications were written down so they could be systematically weighed and argued. Wolfowitz, a scholarly senior career government official and former ambassador, thought it would have been possible to decide to send additional troops and not say specifically whether they were replacements or an offensive reinforcement. The decision as to their ultimate purpose could be made later. But Wolfowitz didn't have time to get the idea considered.

# Chapter 8 Review Questions

1. What are the key differences between the *root* and *branch* methods of decision making? Summarize the advantages and disadvantages of each method.
2. Does the case study, "The Decision to Liberate Kuwait," exemplify the root or branch method of decision making? Or, another approach? Explain your reasons for your selection by citing examples from the case.
3. How does the case point up the influence of professionals in the decisional process? Which professionals in this case influenced its outcome? In what ways did they impact on the decisional processes? Does the case support Mosher's concept of the professional state discussed in the previous chapter? If so, how?
4. Compare this case involving the Gulf Crisis with the previous case with Case Study 7. Discuss the major differences in the way these two critical national decisions were reached. In particular, consider the number and kinds of people who became involved in the decisional processes, the care and manner by which the options for administrative action were presented and considered, the factors forcing the final decision, and the overall effectiveness of the decisional processes.
5. On the basis of your comparative appraisal of the two cases, can you generalize about how proper timing as well as the general historic time period play important roles in the way these or other public decisions are reached?
6. Also on the basis of your comparison of the two cases, why does who gets involved in the decisional process (or who is left out) play such a critical role in the quality and kind of decisions that are made in government?

## Key Terms

| | |
|---|---|
| incremental decision making | rational comprehensive analysis |
| root method | policy alternatives |
| branch method | maximization of values |
| clarification of objectives | empirical analysis |
| intertwining ends and means | policy outcomes |
| successive limited comparisons | ranking objectives |

## Suggestions for Further Reading

Making good, correct, and efficient decisions in the public interest has been a major concern of public administration literature since the early, "conscious" development of the field. In particular, the writings of Frederick Taylor and his followers about scientific management examined methods of rational decision making in organizations at the lower levels of industrial or business hierarchies. However, the post-World War II writings of Herbert Simon, especially his *Administrative Behavior: The Study of Decision Making Processes in Admin-*

*istrative Organization* (New York: Macmillan, 1947), shifted the focus of administrative thinking to *the decision* as the central focus of study and analysis. The enormous impact of this book (for which Simon won the Nobel Prize in 1978), as well as his other writings on public administration, make it worthy of careful attention by students of the field even today. A recent thoughtful and extensive challenge to the Simonism approach can be found in Roger Penrose, *The Emperor's New Mind* (New York: Oxford University Press, 1989).

Other important writings on this topic include Charles E. Lindblom, *The Intelligence of Democracy: Decision Making Through Mutual Adjustment* (New York: Free Press, 1965), and his book co-authored with David Braybooke, *A Strategy of Decision* (New York: Free Press, 1963). For criticisms of the Simon-Lindblom incrementalist approach see Yehezkel Dror, "Muddling Through—Science or Inertia?" *Public Administration Review,* 24 (September 1964), pp. 154–157, and Amitai Etzioni, "Mixed Scanning: A Third Approach to Decision Making," *Public Administration Review,* 27 (December 1967), pp. 385–392. The debate over incrementalism is hardly over, for an entire symposium in the *Public Administration Review,* 39 (November/December 1979) was devoted to its pros and cons. Pay particular attention to the articles by Charles E. Lindblom, "Still Muddling, Not Yet Through" (pp. 511–516); Camille Cates, "Beyond Muddling" (pp. 527–531); and Bruce Adams, "The Limitations of Muddling Through" (pp. 545–552); plus Amitai Eztioni, "Mixed Scanning Revisited," *Public Administration Review* 46 (January/February 1986), pp. 8–14. By contrast, Aaron Wildavsky, "Toward a Radical Incrementalism" in Alfred DeGrazia, *Congress: The First Branch of Government* (Washington, D.C.: American Enterprise Institute, 1966) pushes the incremental concept about as far as possible; whereas Paul R. Schulman, "Nonincremental Policy Making: Notes Toward an Al-

ternative Paradigm," *American Political Science Review* 69 (December 1975), presents possibly the most searching critique of the incremental model.

Since the 1960s numerous decision models other than incrementalism have been proposed with various degrees of success. The most prominent include the *systems model* as represented in Fremont J. Lyden and Ernest G. Miller, eds., *Planning Programming-Budgeting: A Systems Approach to Management* (Chicago: Markham Publishing Co., 1968); *games theory* as outlined in Thomas C. Schelling, *The Strategy of Conflict* (Cambridge, Mass.: Harvard University Press, 1963); the *bureaucratic model* as represented in Graham T. Allison, *Essence of Decision: Explaining the Cuban Missile Crisis* (Boston: Little, Brown, 1971); *cost-benefit* as found in Edward M. Gramlich, *Benefit-Cost Analysis of Government Programs* (Englewood Cliffs, N.J.: Prentice-Hall, 1981); *personal judgment* approach of Harvey Sherman, *It All Depends* (University, Ala.: University of Alabama Press, 1966); the *Policy analysis method* as discussed in William N. Dunn, *Public Policy Analysis: An Introduction* (Englewood Cliffs, N.J.: Prentice-Hall, 1981); and the *garbage can model,* Michael D. Cohen et al., "A Garbage Can Model of Organizational Choice," *Administrative Science Quarterly* 17 (1972), pp. 1–25. These only scratch the surface of a vast, complex area of decision-making study. You would be well advised to read the current issues of such journals as *Public Administration Review, Administrative Science Quarterly, Journal of Policy Analysis and Management, Public Management,* or *Harvard Business Review* for up-to-date perspectives on decision-making methodology. For two survey textbooks that outline a broad range of public sector quantitative decision techniques, see Michael J. White et al., *Managing Public Systems: Analytic Techniques for Public Administration* (No. Scituate, Mass.: Duxbury Press, 1981); and Richard D. Bingham and Marcus E. Ethridge, eds., *Reaching Decisions in Public Policy and*

*Administration* (New York: Longman, 1982). For an up-to-date scholarly review of various decision-making approaches and where we stand today regarding their application to government, read George W. Downs and Patrick D. Larkey, *The Search for Government Efficiency: From Hubris to Helplessness* (New York: Random House, 1986); James G. March, "Theories of Choice and Decision Making," *Society* 20 (1982); Michael Murray, *Decisions: A Comparative Analysis* (New York: Longman, 1986); David Wilson, *Top Decisions* (San Francisco: Jossey Bass, 1986) and for an excellent collection of applied cases involving local decision making, see James M. Banovetz, ed., *Managing Local Government: Cases in Decision Making* (Washington, D.C.: International City Management Assoc., 1990).

# CHAPTER 9

## Administrative Communications: The Concept of Information Networks

*Blockages in the communications system constitute one of the most serious problems in public administration. They may occur in any one of the three steps in the communication process: initiation, transmission, or reception.*

*H. Simon, D. Smithburg, and V. Thompson*

## READING 9

## Introduction

In arriving at even the most routine policy decisions, the typical public administrator is a prisoner of a seemingly endless communications network that defines the problem at hand and the possible alternatives. Administrators are normally pressed from many sides with informational and data sources flowing into their offices from their superiors, subordinates, other agencies, citizen groups, and the general public. Sometimes the information arrives through routine formal channels; at other times it wells up or trickles down to the administrator via unsolicited routes. Whatever the source, the public decision maker must selectively sort out this information, and, in turn, dispense a substantial quantity of information to people within and outside the organizational structure; this is done by memoranda, reports, conferences, phone conversations, and informal encounters that touch off a new chain of communications and decisions by others. Similar to a telephone switchboard, a policy maker's office acts as a nerve center where the lines of communications cross and are connected and where information is received, processed, stored, assembled, analyzed, and dispensed.

Our conceptual understanding of the importance and complexity of the communications links within public organizations and their critical role in administrative decisions depends to a large extent on the work of Herbert A. Simon (1916–   ). In collaboration with Donald Smithburg and Victor Thompson, Simon wrote the text *Public Administration* (1950); this work, drawing on Simon's earlier writing, *Administrative Behavior* (1947), for which Simon won the Nobel Prize for economics in 1978, offered one of the first integrated behavioral interpretations of public administration. By introducing ideas from sociology, psychology, and political science, Simon and his associates sought to discover "a realistic behavioral description of the process of administration," emphasizing its informal human dynamics.

At the root of public administration, according to Simon, Smithburg, and Thompson, were continual conflicts among contending groups that resulted from such internal pressures as empire-building tendencies, differing individual backgrounds, and varying group identifications, as well as such external pressures as competing interest groups, members of Congress, and other agency heads struggling for scarce resources and influence. Similar to Norton Long's conception of the political power contest surrounding administrative activities (discussed in Chapter 4), the authors envision administrators as people "in the middle of continual conflict" whose actions and activities demand a considerable effort directed toward conflict resolution and compromise. As they write, "public administrators, and particularly those responsible for directions of unitary organizations, are themselves initiators and transformers of policy, brokers, if you like, who seek to bring about agreement between the program goals of government agencies and the goals and values of groups that possess political power." In short, "the greatest distinction between public administration and other administration is . . . to be found in the political character of public administration."

Decisions within this political setting can never be wholly rational but rather, the authors contend, are of a "bounded rational" nature. Instead of insisting on an "optimal solution," the public policy maker must be satisfied with what is "good enough," or as Lindblom suggests more simply in Chapter 8, must "muddle through." The prime ends of a public administrator's efforts are decisions that are not "maximizing" but "sufficing," that have as their goals not efficiency but achieving agreement, compromise, and ultimately survival.

One of the major vehicles for achieving coordination and compromise, in the view of Simon, Smithburg, and Thompson, is the communications network, which they define as the "process whereby decisional premises are transmitted from one member of an organization to another." The communications network acts principally as an integrating device for bringing together frequently conflicting elements of an organization to secure cooperative group effort. Three steps are involved in the communications process: first, "someone must initiate the communication"; second, "the command must be transmitted from its source to its destination"; and third, "communications must make its impact on the recipient." The information travels in two ways: (1) the formal or planned channels such as memoranda, reports, and written communications; and (2) the unplanned or informal ways such as face-to-face contacts, conferences, or phone calls to friends. Simon, Smithburg, and Thompson place considerable emphasis on the informal lines of communications that many refer to as "the grapevine." "In most organizations, the greater part of the information that is used in decision-making is informally transmitted," they observe.

The central problems in communications are the blockages that occur: "Blockages in the communication system constitute one of the most serious problems in public administration. They may occur in any one of the three steps in the communications process: initiation, transmission, or reception. Those who have information may fail to tell those who need the information as a basis of action; those who should transmit the information may fail to do so; those who receive the information may be unwilling or unable to assimilate it."

Seven critical types of communications blockages in public organizations are enumerated by the authors, the first being, simply, *barriers of language*. Words are frequently misinterpreted or understood differently as messages pass from one individual to another within organizations. Second, *frames of reference* differ so that the perception of information varies among individuals. Personal "mental sets" thus often prevent accurate comprehension of the problem at hand. Third, *status distance* can block communications because as information moves upward or downward through the various hierarchical levels of an organization "a considerable filtering and distorting" occurs. Fourth, *geographical distance* impedes the communications process; a far-flung department with many field offices spread over the nation or the world has great difficulty in ensuring prompt and accurate information exchange among its component units. Fifth, *self-protection* of the individual who reports actions plays a role in the informational links. Often "information that will evoke a favorable reaction will be played up; the mistakes and the fumbles tend to be glossed over." Sometimes the deception is conscious and at other times unconscious, but this activity always serves to distort objective reality. Sixth, *the pressures of work* tend to leave important matters overlooked or unreported. Finally, the *censorship* inherent in many governmental activities such as foreign intelligence or military operations limits the accurate flow of information within many public agencies.

These characteristic psychological and institutional communication blockages, suggest Simon, Smithburg, and Thompson, raise the vital question of "where a particular decision can best be made." Selection of the appropriate place for decision making directly depends on how effectively and easily information can be transmitted from its source to a decisional center, and how effectively and easily the decision can be transmitted from the decision maker to the point where action will occur. For instance, a military hierarchy could grant to individual company commanders the authority for deciding on the use of tactical nuclear weapons. This action would reduce the "time costs" associated with communicating to higher headquarters in the event of possible enemy attack and thus would allow for extreme military flexibility at lower echelons, but "local option" in this case might very well increase other costs, such as the likelihood of a nuclear accident. On the other hand, if authority for using these weapons had to be cleared, say, by the president of the United States and by other major Allied powers, the risk of accident might very well be reduced, but the time costs of gaining consent to use these weapons from many sources might make a decision so cumbersome and lengthy that no opportunity for swift retaliatory response would exist. As Simon, Smithburg, and Thompson point out, "Ease or difficulty of communications may sometimes be a central consideration in determining how far down the administrative line the function of making a particular decision should be located." The authors thus view the communications process not only as determining the outcome of particular decisions but as a prime influence on the structure of decision making within organizations. Extreme decentralization may achieve flexibility and initiative at the local level but may exact costs in terms of uniformity and control of response; vice versa, extreme centralization may produce maximum oversight but may reduce organizational responsiveness. Ultimately, the costs associated with delegating such decisional authority within an organizational hierarchy are always relative and are determined by the values and objectives of the organization. In the following selection from Simon, Smithburg, and Thompson's *Public Administration,* many of the enduring and difficult dilemmas of communications within public organizations are outlined.

As you read this selection, keep the following questions in mind:

Can you think of any additional blockages to administrative communications other than those outlined by the authors? For instance, reflect on any communications barriers that might have been apparent to you in the previous cases, "The Changing of the FBI" or "The Decision to Liberate Kuwait."

Is it possible to trace the *formal* network of communications in an organization? The *informal* network? What factors would create or determine a formal informational network? For example, what impact have computers had in recent years?

Can you draw from this essay generalizations concerning the communications process as a means for establishing executive authority and control over an organization? How does fragmentation of executive authority occur in public organizations and how can communications be used effectively "to cure" this problem (think about the first case, "The Blast in Centralia No. 5")?

Finally, consider the following essay in relation to Norton Long's concept of administrative power—do administrative communications influence the patterns of administrative power? How did communications influence the outcomes in the case study in Chapter 3, "Dumping $2.6 Million on Bakersfield"?

# The Communication Process

## HERBERT A. SIMON, DONALD W. SMITHBURG, AND VICTOR A. THOMPSON

The American disaster at Pearl Harbor is one of the dramatic examples in modern times of the possible consequences of failure of an organization communication system. Quite apart from the question of who or what was to "blame" for Pearl Harbor, a large part of the military damage inflicted by the Japanese undoubtedly could have been avoided if two serious breaks in the military communication system had not occurred. The first was the failure to secure proper top-level attention to the intercepted "Winds" message that gave warning an attack was impending. The second was the failure to communicate to the military commander in Hawaii information accidentally obtained from the radar system by an enlisted man that unidentified planes were approaching Pearl Harbor.

Less dramatic, but of equal importance, is the role that communication plays in the day-to-day work of every organization. Without communication, not even the first steps can be taken toward human cooperation, and it is impossible to speak about organizational problems without speaking about communication, or at least taking it for granted.

This process, which is central to all organizational behavior, can be illustrated with the example of a policeman operating a patrol car. He is told to patrol in a particular patrol area; he is provided with a manual of regulations and approved procedures; when he reports for duty in the morning, he may receive specific instructions of things to watch for during the

day. He may be given a list of license numbers of recently stolen automobiles and perhaps a description of a fugitive. As he patrols his beat, a call may come to him from the police radio informing him of a store burglary to investigate.

The patrolman, in turn, becomes a source of communications that influence other organization members. His report on the burglary investigation is turned over to the investigations division where it becomes the basis of further activity by a detective. Certain data from this report are recorded by a clerk and are later summarized for the weekly report that goes to the chief of police. Information contained in this weekly report may lead to a redistribution of patrol areas to equalize work loads. Meanwhile, other data from the report have gone into the pawnshop file where they are used by other detectives who systematically survey local pawnshops for stolen goods.

## Communication and Organization Structure

By tracing these and other communications from source to destination, we discover a rich and complex network of channels through which orders and information flow. Viewing the communication process from a point in an organization where a decision is to be made, the process has a twofold aspect: communications must flow to the decision center to provide the basis for decision, and the decision must be communicated from the decision center in order to influence other members of the organization whose cooperation must be secured to carry out the decision.

The question of where in the organization a

particular decision can best be made will depend in considerable part upon how effectively and easily information can be transmitted from its source to a decision center, and how effectively and easily the decision can be transmitted to the point where action will take place. The decision of a social worker in a public welfare agency in granting or refusing an application for assistance illustrates how these factors enter into the picture. The principal facts and values that have to be brought to bear on this decision are: (1) the economic and social facts of the applicant's situation; (2) accepted principles of casework; and (3) the eligibility regulations and casework policies of the agency. The first set of facts is obtained by interviewing the applicant, by correspondence, and by field investigation. The second set of considerations is derived from the education and training of the social worker and his supervisors. Policies governing the third set of considerations are largely established by the legislative body and the top administrative levels of the agency and communicated downward.

If the decision on the application is to be made by the social worker himself, these three sets of considerations must be communicated to him. The costs of communication here are the time cost of his own investigational activities, the costs of training him adequately in the accepted principles of casework, and the costs of indoctrinating him in agency policies by formal training, instructions, discussion with his supervisor, or otherwise. Once he has made the decision, it must be communicated to the applicant—a relatively simple step—and certain reports on his action must be transmitted to his superiors for supervisory and control purposes.

On the other hand, the decision on the application might be placed in the hands of the casework supervisor, rather than the social worker. This might shorten the communication chain required to bring agency policy to bear on the decision and the chain that reports on the action would have to travel. Further, if the social workers were relieved of this decision, they would probably not need to be as thoroughly trained in casework as if they made the decisions themselves—training efforts could be concentrated on the supervisors. However, in other respects new costs of communication would be incurred. It would be necessary to communicate from social worker to supervisor all the circumstances of the applicant's situation—a very voluminous reporting job and an almost impossible one if intangible impressions received by the social worker in the interview are to be communicated. Moreover, there would be an extra step in communicating the decision on the application to the applicant via the social worker.

Ease or difficulty of communication may sometimes be a central consideration in determining how far down the administrative line the function of making a particular decision should be located (or, as it is usually put, "how far authority should be delegated"). Delegation increases the difficulty of communicating organization policies that are decided at the top and reports from the decision center to the top that are required to determine compliance with policy. Delegation may also involve greater training costs by multiplying the number of persons who have to be competent to make a particular decision. Delegation usually reduces the difficulty of communicating to the decision center information about the particular situation in question, and usually reduces the difficulty of communicating the decision to the point where it is placed into operation. All these factors were illustrated in the previous example.

## Steps in the Communication Process

In the study of communication processes it is convenient to distinguish three steps:

1. Someone must initiate the communication. If the communication is a monthly report, someone must be assigned the task of pre-

paring the report. Many of the most important communications originate outside the organization, or in special "intelligence" units of the organization. Examples of the first would be a fire alarm, a phone call to the police department, or the filing of a patent application or a workman's compensation claim. Examples of the second would be the reports of military reconnaisance aircraft, an information report by an embassy to the State Department on developments abroad, or a compilation of employment statistics by the U.S. Department of Labor.

2. The communication must be transmitted from its source to its destination.

3. The communication must make its impact upon the recipient. The communication has not really been "communicated" when it reaches the desk of the recipient, but only when it reaches his mind. There is a potential gap here 'twixt cup and lip. It will receive attention in later portions of this chapter.

We shall see that costs and difficulties of communication may be encountered at each of these three stages of the process. Before we proceed to a detailed analysis of these costs and difficulties, however, it is necessary to describe in somewhat greater detail the elements that go to make up an organization communication system.

# Elements of the Communication System

Roughly, organizational communications fall in two categories: planned or "formal" communications and unplanned or "informal" communications. Every organization has some formal arrangements whereby knowledge can be transmitted to those who need it. But this formal transmission of information is supplemented by a great deal of communication that springs from the willingness, indeed, the eager-

ness, of employees to share information with one another even when such transmission is not formally authorized, and even when it is forbidden.

## Formal Comunication

The administrative manual of a large organization often specifies who may write officially to whom; who must report to whom and on what occasions; who shall see memoranda on particular subjects; who shall give out information on specified subjects. This attempt to plan and to channel communications can be seen in perhaps its most elaborate form in the armed services, where extremely intricate patterns of communication are incorporated into formal rules and where channels are rigidly enforced.

Where the work of an organization consists of processing applications or claims, the written procedures will usually specify in considerable detail just how the application is to be routed, what information is to be entered on it at each step, and what work is to be performed. Similarly, the form, content, and responsibility for preparation of accounting records is almost always formally determined.

## Informal Communications

. . . The growth of an informal communication system . . . supplements the formal, prescribed system. For example, the unit chief who wants advance information as to whether it is going to be easy or difficult to secure a budget increase for the coming year may find that a friend who is assistant to the bureau chief can give him the desired information long before any formal bulletin flows down through the established channels.

**Method of Informal Communication** The ways in which information is disseminated informally are many. Jones, Smith, and Goldberg who work in different sections lunch together. Each has connections with various parts of the organization, and they swap information. Mrs. Johnson belongs to the same lodge auxiliary as the wife of Mr. Alexander who is administrative assistant to the bureau chief. Mrs. Johnson gets some information which she transmits to her husband who, in turn, passes it on to his section.

But informal communication is not only the inevitable, if somewhat illicit, shop talk and gossip. It includes any kind of information outside the specified channels. Nor is it always easy to define what is meant by "channels"—normally these include communications along the lines of formal authority, or along lines that have been explicitly authorized by the formal hierarchy. In most organizations, the greater part of the information that is used in decision-making is informally transmitted.

## Barriers to Effective Communication

The amount of misunderstanding in the world caused by failure of people to communicate effectively with each other can hardly be exaggerated. Words are tenuous. The failure of human plans and aspirations are all too often bitterly recalled in terms like "if it could have been gotten across," or "if I had said it this way rather than that, he might have understood."

Blockages in the communication system constitute one of the most serious problems in public administration. They may occur in any one of three steps in the communications process: initiation, transmission, or reception. Those who have information may fail to tell those who need the information as a basis of action; those who should transmit the information may fail to do so; those who receive the information may be unwilling or unable to assimilate it.

### The Barrier of Language

Among the barriers to effective communication one of the most serious is the use of language that is not understandable to the recipi-

ent. In a society as specialized as ours there are literally hundreds of different languages which cluster around the various specialties. Many words quite understandable to a physician are Greek to the layman. Many words quite understandable to the skilled machinist are incomprehensible to the doctor. The vocabulary shared by all Americans is meager indeed.

Not only is the shared vocabulary meager, but the words that are shared often mean different things to different people. Philosophers like Ogden and Richards and Carnap have shown how many traps in philosophy have at their base a faulty use of language. At a more popular level, students of semantics have also shown us that many so-called problems are really pseudoproblems which, when correctly formulated, disappear.

Within administration, the written communication is likely to be even more plagued by language difficulties than the oral communication. Most persons in face-to-face contacts try to speak in terms that will be understood by the listener—and if they do not, they will soon be aware of the fact. They can repeat the communication in different terms. They can explain what they "really mean." The author of a written communication has no such an opportunity to assess his audience or to gauge the degree to which his words are being understood.

### Frame of Reference

Very often the communication process is impeded because those giving, transmitting, or receiving the communication have a "mental set" that prevents accurate perception of the problem. The stimuli that fall on a person's eyes and ears are screened, filtered, and modified by the nervous system before they even reach consciousness—and memory makes further selections of the things it will retain and the things it will forget. This selecting process is an important reason why our judgments of people are so often wrong. If we have a favorable impression of a man, we are likely to remember the good things about him that come to our attention and to forget, discount, or explain away the bad things. Only a series of several vivid, undesirable impressions is likely to change our initial estimate of him.

## Status Distance

Communication between persons distant in scalar status most often takes place through a chain of intermediaries. When there is contact between individuals of different status, communication from the superior to the subordinate generally takes place more easily than communication from the subordinate to the superior. If communication were not difficult between persons of widely different status, organizations would not feel the need, as they so often do, to install suggestion boxes that permit low-level employees to bring their ideas to the attention of top executives. And experience with formal suggestion systems shows that even this device is often inadequate to lower the barrier of status difference.

Status differences exert a considerable filtering and distorting influence upon communication—both upward and downward. Upward communication is hampered by the need of pleasing those in authority. Good news gets told. Bad news often does not. The story of Haround al Raschid, the caliph who put on beggar's clothes and went out among his people to hear what they really thought, is the story of the isolation of every high status executive. Most executives are very effectively insulated from the operating levels of the organization. For a number of reasons, pleasant matters are more apt to get communicated upwards than information about mistakes. Subordinates do not want to call attention to their mistakes, nor do they want the executive to think that they can't handle their own difficulties without turning to him. They want to tell him the things he would like to hear. Hence, things usually look rosier at the top than they really are. . . .

## Geographical Distance

One of the most striking and far-reaching phenomena of our era has been the tremendous extension of the mechanical techniques of communication. Changes in the technology of communication have changed both the structure and the problems of administrative organizations. Probably more than any other single factor, the improvement of the means of communication has had a centralizing effect upon administration—centralizing in the sense that a field officer can now be supervised in much greater detail than was previously possible.

Far-flung organizations can now be within hour-to-hour communication with their headquarters. This has enabled central offices to keep a far tighter check rein upon the activities of their agents in the field. Ambassadors who formerly had broad discretion to act in their negotiations with other nations, now can and must constantly check their views with a central office. The operations of widely dispersed field offices can come under the constant scrutiny of central headquarters.

Even where geographical dispersion is not wide, such as in modern police and fire departments, the effect of instantaneous communication has changed the whole pattern of their operations. It has made possible a greater efficiency and greater specialization. The radio police car can be summoned rapidly to an area of trouble. The work of the fire department can be directed rapidly and efficiently.

**Inadequacy of Techniques** But modern communication techniques have not completely overcome the problems of communicating at a distance, and, in addition, they have added new problems of their own. Communication by letter, wire, or telephone, although it may be rapid, is no effective substitute for the face-to-face interchange. As Latham has pointed out:

Impediments to the free exchange of thought are difficult enough to overcome in the same city, building, or even room. They become even more difficult with the increase of distance between the central office and the field. In the same environment, geographical, social, and professional, the common milieu sometimes gives many clues to understanding which precise words could not have spelled out. This element is missing in communications at a distance.[1]

The difficulties of communication at a distance, even with modern means, are several. Oral communication by telephone, while the closest counterpart to face-to-face conference, is by no means a perfect substitute. It is costly, and mechanically imperfect over great distances, and the important overtones of oral communication that are ordinarily conveyed by facial expression and gesture are missing.

Written communication is an even less adequate substitute for the conference. Even in verbal content, a two-page single-spaced letter is the equivalent of only ten minutes' conversation. A division head, with offices adjacent to those of his bureau chief, might confer with his superior individually and in conference a half hour or an hour daily. To communicate the same material in writing would require an interchange of six to twelve single-spaced pages a day. Even then, the letter is much less likely to convey exact ideas than is a conversation, where misunderstanding can be detected and corrected immediately, questions raised, and so forth.

**Insufficient Communication** Moreover, daily personal contact stimulates communication. A man may think to pass on to his superior or subordinate over a luncheon table a piece of information that it would not occur to him to put down in a letter. Where there is geographical separation, the person at each end of the communication line finds it difficult to visualize and keep constantly in mind the needs for information at the other end of the line. A constant complaint of field offices is that they learn from the daily newspapers or from clients things that should have been communicated to them from the central office.

Consider, for example, the problem of communicating a change in rent control regulations. Such a change will probably be publicly announced by the central office at a press conference and instantly transmitted in more or less complete form by newspaper wire services throughout the country. Washington representatives of real estate groups will also advise their local clients of the new regulation, often by telegraph or telephone. To prevent premature disclosure of the regulations, the central office may be reluctant to send them in advance to local field offices, with the result that these field offices may be bombarded by questions from tenants and landlords before they have had any detailed information on the new regulations from the central office. This pattern repeated itself again and again in wartime regulatory programs and was a continual source of friction between central and field offices.

**Excessive Communication** Paradoxically, field offices often complain that they receive too many communications at the same time that they complain that they are insufficiently informed on new developments. The attempt of the central office to supervise closely the operations in the field often results in a steady flow of procedural regulations, instructions, bulletins, and whatnot to the field offices. If too much of this material is trivial, detailed, or unadapted to local problems—and the field office will often feel that it is—it may remain unread, undigested, and ineffective. This problem is not one of geographical separation alone, but applies generally to organization communications.

## Self-protection of the Initiator

We have already pointed out that most persons find it difficult to tell about actions that they believe would put them in a bad light. It is much easier to secure reports about overtime than it is to get reports on the number of times the workers reported late or took extra time for lunch. Furthermore, the ordinary work code demanding loyalty to work groups also prevents the communication of information that would seem to reflect upon one's friends or upon the organization of which one is a part. In consequence, reports flowing upward in the organization, such as reports to Congress, the President, or the public, tend to be "sugar-coated." Information that will evoke a favorable reaction will be played up; the mistakes and the fumbles tend to be glossed over. Information going downward is equally suspect. A casual reading of any house organ will reveal how carefully the higher executives and their actions are "explained" to employees in a way that will show the wisdom of their decisions and their benevolence toward those who occupy the lower levels. In part, this deception is conscious. In part, it is unconscious. These upward and downward distortions make an actual and objective view of the organization difficult to obtain.

### Pressure of Other Work

A person in an ordinary work situation is normally pressed for time. He must establish a system of priorities as to the various demands made upon him. In such circumstances he is likely to respond to the pressures of the immediate work situation while giving lower priority to the more abstract demands of communicating with others. Furthermore, the constant demand for information concerning the details of his work often meets with unspoken resentment because it seems to reflect upon his integrity. If he does not know why he is asked for specific types of information, he is likely to conjure up ideas that the "head office" will use the information against him or that the request has no purpose—that it is mere make-work.

Similarly, the central office is likely to take

an authoritarian view of the communication process and resent the constant inquiries from those lower in the hierarchy or the field. It, too, is likely to slough off the job of communication and to regard it as less important than the task of setting policy. Thus, in many agencies the task of communication is thought of as something basically clerical—a mere stenographic transmittal of decisions. Communication is likely to be shunted into the background.

### Deliberate Restrictions upon Communication

One problem of much government communication is to see that it reaches those who should have the information and yet to prevent it from reaching those who would use it in an undesirable way. There is always disagreement between those individuals who believe that the public should have information concerning every aspect of government policy and policy formulation—particularly those in the press whose business is the dissemination of information—and those in government service who would argue that the compromises which are essential in the formation of public policy would not be possible if every move had to be carried on in the relentless glare of publicity.

Whether or not to have publicity is not a new problem. The founding fathers determined that the only possible way in which agreement could be reached on a new constitution was to conduct the deliberations without continuous publicity. To prevent the publication of the deliberations they even went so far as to establish a guard for the aged, brilliant, but garrulous Benjamin Franklin to see that his disclosures in the neighborhood taverns would not jeopardize the goals of the convention.

### Note

1. Earl Latham, *The Federal Field Service* (Chicago: Public Administration Service, 1947), pp. 8–9.

# CASE STUDY 9

# Introduction

In the foregoing discussion of the concept of administrative communications, Simon, Smithburg, and Thompson illustrated with the story of Pearl Harbor the dramatic importance of effective administrative communications. The Japanese attack caught the American military off-guard largely because of two serious breakdowns in communications: the failure to secure top-level attention to the intercepted "Winds Message," and the failure to communicate to the local base commander the early radar warnings of the approaching enemy aircraft. Both information gaps in military communications had immediate, drastic consequences for American national defense.

In the following case study, the lessons regarding the importance of accurate and timely information are drawn from a more recent wartime situation—Vietnam. This story takes place far from the battlefield—for the most part, inside Central Intelligence Agency (CIA) headquarters near Washington, D.C.—and involves information important for planning the course of the war, estimates of enemy Vietcong (VC) troop strength.

This well-written, compelling story is told in the first person by the principal player, Sam Adams, a mid-level CIA analyst who early in the course of the Vietnam War began to study VC defection statistics. By seriously examining for the first time samples of captured enemy documents in early 1966, Adams made the startling, but relatively simple, deduction that official U.S. data on VC troops were grossly understated. Rather, the real figures on VC troops were at least twice as high as official estimates (at that time, 270,000 personnel).

When he first discovered these serious statistical errors, Adams initially expected his revelations to earn both praise and support from his superiors because it seemed to him that the size of the enemy opposition had a primary, if not the major, role in shaping the overall nature, direction, and level of American response to the Vietnam conflict. What follows in Adams's own words is the unusual but fascinating tale of how the CIA coped with information that it clearly preferred not to hear. Akin to the fable of the messenger who lost his head because he brought bad news to the king, Adams found himself ignored, ridiculed, and ostracized by his superiors, a treatment that in the end forced his resignation from the CIA.

Although part of the story involves how information on enemy troop strength was collected, much of Adams's account focuses on the receptivity, or the lack of receptivity, to new but unwanted information, and the variety of complex "organizational defense mechanisms" that are raised as barriers against data that run counter to ingrained institutional doctrines. The severe career and personal penalties meted out to an individual such as Adams who unflinchingly dared to tell the truth to his superiors, and the promotional rewards that accrue to those who "get along and go along" with the system, are poignant lessons for those who think that communicating truth to the powerful in government agencies may be either easy or simple.

As you read this selection, keep the following questions in mind:

How did Adams arrive at his estimates of VC troop strength? Do you think he used a reasonable and valid approach in gathering this information?

Was the significance of the data, in your opinion, as important as he claimed? Explain why or why not.

What strategies did Adams use to get his information to the top-level war policy planners? Who were his allies and enemies in this effort to gain access to the top-level planners?

What defense mechanisms did the organization use to protect itself from Adams's unwanted statistics?

How did history repeat itself with regard to Adams's information about the Cambodian war?

If you had been Sam Adams, would you have altered your strategies in speaking the truth to your superiors in any way?

On the basis of this case or from your own experience, can you generalize about organizational receptivity to new and perhaps unwelcome information?

How did Simon, Smithburg, and Thompson classify the type or types of barriers to administrative communications that is evidenced in this case? Do you think the authors placed sufficient emphasis on the type(s) of communications barriers? If not, how might you rewrite their discussion of administrative communications to give the problem encountered by Adams adequate attention?

# Vietnam Cover-up: Playing War with Numbers

**SAM ADAMS**

---

In late 1965, well after the United States had committed ground troops to Vietnam, the CIA assigned me to study the Vietcong. Despite the almost 200,000 American troops and the advanced state of warfare in South Vietnam, I was the first intelligence analyst in Washington to be given the full-time job of researching our South Vietnamese enemies. Incredible as it now seems, I remained the only analyst with this assignment until just before the Tet offensive of 1968.

At CIA headquarters in 1965 nobody was studying the enemy systematically, the principal effort being geared to a daily publication called the "Sitrep" (Vietnam Situation Report), which concerned itself with news about the activities of South Vietnamese politicians and the location of Vietcong units. The Sitrep analysts used the latest cables from Saigon, and tended to neglect information that didn't fit their objectives. The Johnson Administration was already wondering how long the Vietcong could stick it out, and since this seemed too complicated a question for the Sitrep to answer, the CIA's research department assigned it to me. I was told to find out the state of enemy morale.

## Good News and Bad News

I looked upon the new job as something of a promotion. Although I had graduated from Harvard in 1955, I didn't join the Agency until 1963, and I had been fortunate in my first assignment as an analyst of the

Congo rebellion. My daily and weekly reports earned the praise of my superiors, and the Vietcong study was given to me by way of reward, encouraging me in my ambition to make a career within the CIA.

Without guidance and not knowing what else to do, I began to tinker with the VC defector statistics, trying to figure out such things as where the defectors came from, what jobs they had, and why they had wanted to quit. In short order I read through the collection of weekly reports, and so I asked for a ticket to Vietnam to see what other evidence was available over there. In mid-January 1966, I arrived in Saigon to take up a desk in the U.S. Embassy. After a couple of weeks, the CIA station chief (everyone called him "Jorgy") heard I was in the building adding and subtracting the number of defectors. He called me into his office. "Those statistics aren't worth a damn," he said. "No numbers in Vietnam are, and, besides, you'll never learn anything sitting around Saigon." He told me I ought to go to the field and start reading captured documents. I followed Jorgy's advice.

The captured documents suggested a phenomenon that seemed incredible to me. Not only were the VC taking extremely heavy casualties, but large numbers of them were deserting. I got together two sets of captured papers concerning desertion. The first set consisted of enemy unit rosters, which would say, for example, that in a certain seventy-seven-man outfit, only sixty men were "present for duty." Of the seventeen absent, two were down with malaria, two were at training school, and thirteen had deserted. The other documents were directives from various VC headquarters telling subordinates to do something about the growing desertion rate. "Christ Almighty," they all seemed to say. "These AWOLs are getting out of hand. Far too many of our boys are going over the hill."

I soon collected a respectable stack of rosters, some of them from large units, and I began to extrapolate. I set up an equation which went like this: If A, B, and C units (the ones for which I had documents) had so many deserters in such and such a period of time, then the number of deserters per year for the whole VC Army was X. No matter how I arranged the equation, X always turned out to be a very big number. I could never get it below 50,000. Once I even got it up to 100,000.

The significance of this finding in 1966 was immense. At that time our official estimate of the strength of the enemy was 270,000. We were killing, capturing, and wounding VC at a rate of almost 150,000 a year. If to these casualties you added 50,000 to 100,000 deserters—well, it was hard to see how a 270,000-man army could last more than a year or two longer.

I returned in May to tell everyone the good news. No one at CIA headquarters had paid much attention to VC deserters because captured documents were almost entirely neglected. The finding created a big stir. Adm. William F. Raborn, Jr., then director of the CIA, called me in to brief him and his deputies about the Vietcong's AWOL problem. Right after the briefing, I was told that the Agency's chief of research, R. Jack Smith, had called me "*the* outstanding analyst" in the research directorate.

But there were also skeptics, particularly among the CIA's old Vietnam hands, who had long since learned that good news was often illusory. To be on the safe side, the Agency formed what was called a "Vietcong morale team" and sent it to Saigon to see if the news was really true. The team consisted of myself, acting as a "consultant," and four Agency psychiatrists, who presumably understood things like morale.

The psychiatrists had no better idea than I'd had, when I started out, how to plumb the Vietcong mind. One of the psychiatrists said, "We'll never get Ho Chi Minh to lie still on a leather couch, so we better think up something else quick." They decided to ask the CIA men in the provinces what *they* thought about enemy morale. After a month or so of doing this, the psychiatrists went back to Washington convinced that, by and large, Vietcong spirits were in good shape. I went back with suitcases full of captured documents that supported my thesis about the Vietcong desertion rate.

But I was getting uneasy. I trusted the opinion of the CIA men in the field who had told the psychiatrists of the Vietcong's resilience. The South Vietnamese government was in one of its periodic states of collapse, and somehow it seemed unlikely that the Vietcong would be falling apart at the same time. I began to suspect that something was wrong with my prediction that the VC were headed for imminent trouble. On reexamining the logic that had led me to the prediction, I saw that it was based on three main premises. Premise number one was that the Vietcong were suffering very heavy casualties. Although I'd heard all the stories about exaggerated reporting, I tended not to believe them, because the heavy losses were also reflected in the documents. Premise two was my finding that the enemy army had a high desertion rate. Again, I believed the documents. Premise three was that both the casualties and the deserters came out of an enemy force of 270,000. An old Vietnam hand, George Allen, had already told me that this number was suspect.

In July, I went to my supervisor and told him I thought there might be something radically wrong with our estimate of enemy strength, or, in military jargon, the order of battle. "Maybe the 270,000 number is too low," I said. "Can I take a closer look at it?" He said it was okay with him just so long as I handed in an occasional item for the Sitrep. This seemed fair enough, and so I began to put together a file of captured documents.

The documents in those days were arranged in "bulletins," and by mid-August I had collected more than 600 of them. Each bulletin contained several sheets of paper with summaries in English of the information in the papers taken by American military units. On the afternoon of August 19, 1966, a Friday, Bulletin 689 reached my desk on the CIA's fifth floor. It contained a report put out by the Vietcong headquarters in Binh Dinh province, to the effect that the guerrilla-militia in the province numbered just over 50,000. I looked for our own intelligence figures for Binh Dinh in the order of battle and found the number 4,500.

"My God," I thought, "that's not even a tenth of what the VC say."

In a state of nervous excitement, I began searching through my file of bulletins for other discrepancies. Almost the next document I looked at, the one for Phu Yen province, showed 11,000 guerrilla-militia. In the official order of battle we had listed 1,400, an eighth of the Vietcong estimate. I almost shouted from my desk, "There goes the whole damn order of battle!"

Unable to contain my excitement, I began walking around the office, telling anybody who would listen about the enormity of the oversight and the implications of it for our conduct of the war. That weekend I returned to the office, and on both Saturday and Sunday I searched through the entire collection of 600-odd bulletins and found further proof of a gross underestimate of the strength of the enemy we had been fighting for almost two years. When I arrived in the office on Monday a colleague of mine brought

me a document of a year earlier which he thought might interest me. It was from Vietcong headquarters in South Vietnam, and it showed that in early 1965 the VC had about 200,000 guerrilla-militia in the south, and that they were planning to build up to 300,000 by the end of the year. Once again, I checked the official order of battle. It listed a figure of exactly 103,573 guerrilla-militia—in other words, half as many as the Vietcong said they had in early 1965, and a third as many as they planned to have by 1966.[1]

## No Official Comment

That afternoon, August 22, I wrote a memorandum suggesting that the overall order of battle estimate of 270,000 might be 200,000 men too low. Supporting it with references to numerous bulletins, I sent it up to the seventh floor, and then waited anxiously for the response. I imagined all kinds of sudden and dramatic telephone calls. "Mr. Adams, come brief the director." "The President's got to be told about this, and you'd better be able to defend those numbers." I wasn't sure what would happen, but I was sure it would be significant, because I knew this was the biggest intelligence find of the war—by far. It was important because the planners running the war in those days used statistics as a basis for everything they did, and the most important figure of all was the size of the enemy army—that order of battle number, 270,000. All our other intelligence estimates were tied to the order of battle: how much rice the VC ate, how much ammunition they shot off, and so forth. If the Vietcong Army suddenly doubled in size, our whole statistical system would collapse. We'd be fighting a war twice as big as the one we thought we were fighting. We already had about 350,000 soldiers in Vietnam, and everyone was talking about "force ratios." Some experts maintained that in a guerrilla war our side had to outnumber the enemy by a ratio of 10 to 1; others said 5 to 1; the most optimistic said 3 to 1. But even if we used the 3 to 1 ratio, the addition of 200,000 men to the enemy order of battle meant that somebody had to find an extra 600,000 troops for our side. This would put President Johnson in a very tight fix—either quit the war or send more soldiers. Once he was informed of the actual enemy strength, it seemed inconceivable that he could continue with the existing force levels. I envisioned the President calling the director on the carpet, asking him why this information hadn't been found out before.

Nothing happened. No phone calls from anybody. On Wednesday I still thought there must have been some terrible mistake; on Thursday I thought the news might have been so important that people were still trying to decide what to do with it. Instead, on Friday, the memorandum dropped back in my in-box. There was no comment on it at all—no request for amplification, no question about my numbers, nothing, just a routine slip attached showing that the entire CIA hierarchy had read it.

I was aghast. Here I had come up with 200,000 additional enemy troops, and the CIA hadn't even bothered to ask me about it, let alone tell anybody else. I got rather angry and wrote a second memorandum, attaching even more references to other documents. Among these was a report from the Vietcong high command showing that the VC controlled not 3 million people (as in our official estimate) but 6 million (their estimate). I thought that this helped to explain the origins of the extra 200,000 guerrilla-militia, and also that it was an extraordinary piece of news in its own right. A memorandum from my office—the office of Current Intelligence—ordinarily would be read, edited, and distributed within a few days to the White House, the Pentagon, and the State Department. It's a routine procedure, but once again I found myself sitting around waiting for a response, getting angrier and angrier. After about a week I went up to the seventh floor to find out what had happened to my memo. I found it in a safe, in a manila folder marked "Indefinite Hold."

I went back down to the fifth floor, and wrote still another memo, referencing even more documents. This time I didn't send it up, as I had the others, through regular channels. Instead, I carried it upstairs with the intention of giving it to somebody who would comment on it. When I reached the office of the Asia-Africa area chief, Waldo Duberstein, he looked at me and said: "It's that Goddamn memo again. Adams, stop being such a prima donna." In the next office, an official said that the order of battle was General Westmoreland's concern, and we had no business intruding. This made me even angrier. "We're all in the same government," I said. "If there's discrepancy this big, it doesn't matter who points it out. This is no joke. We're in a war with these guys."

My remarks were dismissed as rhetorical, bombastic, and irrelevant.

On the ninth of September, eighteen days after I'd written the first memo, the CIA agreed to let a version of it out of the building, but with very strange restrictions. It was to be called a "draft working paper," meaning that it lacked official status; it was issued in only 25 copies, instead of the usual run of over 200; it could go to "working-level types" only—analysts and staff people—but not to anyone in a policy-making position—to no one, for example, on the National Security Council. One copy went to Saigon, care of Westmoreland's Order of Battle Section, carried by an official who worked in the Pentagon for the Defense Intelligence Agency.

By this time I was so angry and exhausted that I decided to take two weeks off to simmer down. This was useless. I spent the whole vacation thinking about the order of battle. When I returned to the Agency, I found that it came out monthly and was divided into four parts, as follows:

| | |
|---|---|
| Communist regulars | About 110,000 |
| | (it varied by month) |
| Guerrilla-militia | Exactly 103,573 |
| Service troops | Exactly 18,553 |
| Political cadres | Exactly 39,175 |
| | That is 271,301 |
| | or about 270,000 |

The only category that ever changed was "Communist regulars" (uniformed soldiers in the Vietcong Army). In the last two years, this figure had more than doubled. The numbers for the other three categories had remained precisely the same, even to the last digit. There was only one conclusion: no one had even looked at them! I decided to do so right away, and to find out where the numbers came from and whom they were describing.

I began by collecting more documents on the guerrilla-militia. These were "the soldiers in black pajamas" the press kept talking about; lightly armed in some areas, armed to the teeth in others, they planted most of the VC's mines and booby traps. This was important, I discovered, because in the Da Nang area, for example, mines and booby traps caused about two-thirds of all the casualties suffered by U.S. Marines.

I also found where the number 103,573 came from. The South Vietnamese had thought it up in 1964; American Intelligence had accepted it without question, and hadn't checked it since. "Can you believe it?" I said to a fellow analyst. "Here we are in the middle of a guerrilla war, and we haven't even bothered to count the number of guerrillas."

The service troops were harder to locate. The order of battle made it clear that these VC soldiers were comparable to specialists in the American Army—ordnance sergeants, quartermasters, medics, engineers, and so forth. But despite repeated phone calls to the Pentagon, to U.S. Army headquarters, and to the office of the Joint Chiefs of Staff, I couldn't find anyone who knew where or when we'd hit upon the number 18,553. Again I began collecting VC documents, and within a week or so had come to the astonishing conclusion that our official estimate for service troops was at least two years old and five times too low—it should not have been 18,553, but more like 100,000. In the process I discovered a whole new category of soldiers known as "assault youths" who weren't in the order of battle at all.

I also drew a blank at the Pentagon regarding political cadres, so I started asking CIA analysts who these cadres might be. One analyst said they belonged to something called the "infrastructure," but he wasn't quite sure what it was. Finally, George Allen, who seemed to know more about the VC than anyone else, said the "infrastructure" included Communist party members and armed police and people like that, and that there was a study around which showed how the 39,175 number had been arrived at. I eventually found a copy on a shelf in the CIA archives. Unopened, it had never been looked at before. The study had been published in Saigon in 1965, and one glance showed it was full of holes. Among other things, it left out all the VC cadres serving in the countryside—where most of them were.

By December 1966 I had concluded that the number of Vietcong in South Vietnam, instead of being 270,000, was more like 600,000, or over twice the official estimate.[2] The higher number made many things about the Vietnam war fall into place. It explained, for instance, how the Vietcong Army could have so many deserters and casualties and still remain effective.

# Nobody Listens

Mind you, during all this time I didn't keep this information secret—just the opposite. I not only told everyone in the Agency who'd listen, I also wrote a continuous sequence of memorandums, none of which provoked the least response. I'd write a memo, document it with footnotes, and send it up to the seventh floor. A week would pass, and then the paper would return to my in-box: no comment, only the same old buck slip showing that everyone upstairs had read it.

By this time I was so angry and so discouraged with the research directorate that I began looking for another job within the CIA, preferably in a section that had some use for real numbers. I still believed that all this indifference to unwelcome information afflicted only part of the bureaucracy, that it was not something characteristic of the entire Agency. Through George Allen I met George Carver, a man on the staff of Richard Helms, the new CIA director, who had the title "special assistant for Vietnamese affairs." Carver told me that I was "on the right track" with the numbers, and he seemed an independent-minded man who could circumvent the bureaucratic timidities of the research directorate. At the time I had great hopes of Carver because, partly as a result of his efforts, word of my memorandums had reached the White House. Cables were passing back and forth between Saigon and Washington, and it had become fairly common knowledge that something was very wrong with the enemy strength estimates.

In mid-January 1967, Gen. Earle Wheeler, chairman of the Joint Chiefs of Staff, called for an order-of-battle conference to be held in Honolulu. The idea was to assemble all the analysts from the military, the CIA, and the Defense Intelligence Agency in the hope that they might reach a consensus on the numbers. I went to Honolulu as part of the CIA delegation. I didn't trust the military and, frankly, I expected them to pull a fast one and lie about the numbers. What happened instead was that the head of Westmoreland's Order of Battle Section, Col. Gains B. Hawkins, got up right at the beginning of the conference and said, "You know, there's a lot more of these little bastards out there than we thought there were." He and his analysts then raised the estimate of enemy strength in each category of the order of battle; instead of the 103,573 guerrilla-militia, for example, they'd come up with 198,000. Hawkins's remarks were unofficial, but nevertheless, I figured, "the fight's over. They're reading the same documents that I am, and everybody's beginning to use real numbers."

I couldn't have been more wrong.

After a study trip to Vietnam, I returned to Washington in May 1967, to find a new CIA report to Secretary of Defense Robert McNamara called something like "Whither Vietnam?" Its section on the Vietcong Army listed all the discredited official figures, adding up to 270,000. Dumbfounded, I rushed into George Carver's office and got permission to correct the numbers. Instead of my own total of 600,000, I used 500,000, which was more in line with what Colonel Hawkins had said in Honolulu. Even so, one of the chief deputies of the research directorate, Drexel Godfrey, called me up to say that the directorate couldn't use 500,000 because "it wasn't official." I said: "That's the silliest thing I've ever heard. We're going to use real numbers for a change." Much to my satisfaction and relief, George Carver supported my figures. For the first time in the history of the Vietnam war a CIA paper challenging the previous estimates went directly to McNamara. Once again I said to myself: "The battle's won; virtue triumphs." Once again, I was wrong.

Soon after, I attended the annual meeting of the Board of National Estimates on Vietnam. Held in a windowless room on the CIA's seventh floor, a room furnished with leather chairs, blackboards, maps, and a large conference table, the meeting comprised the whole of the intelligence community, about forty people representing the CIA, the Defense Intelligence Agency, the Army, the Navy, the Air Force, and the State Department. Ordinarily the meeting lasted about a week, its purpose being to come to a community-wide agreement about the progress of the war. This particular consensus required the better part of six months.

The procedure of these estimates requires the CIA to submit the first draft, and then everyone else argues his group's position. If one of the services violently disagrees, it is allowed to take exception in a footnote to the report. The CIA's first draft used the same 500,000 number that had gone to McNamara in May. None of us expected what followed.

George Fowler from DIA, the same man who'd carried my guerrilla memo to Saigon in September 1966, got up and explained he was speaking for the entire military. "Gentlemen, we cannot agree to this estimate as currently written. What we object to are the numbers. We feel we should continue with the official order of battle." I almost fell off my chair. The official OB figure at that time, June 1967, was still 270,000, with all the old components, including 103,-573 guerrilla-militia.

In disbelief I hurried downstairs to tell my boss, George Carver, of the deception. He was reassuring. "Now, Sam," he said, "don't you worry. It's time to bite the bullet. You go on back up there and do the best you can." For the next two-and-a-half months, armed with stacks of documents, I argued with the military over the numbers. By the end of August, they no longer insisted on the official order of battle figures, but would not raise them above 300,000. The CIA numbers remained at about 500,000. The meetings recessed for a few weeks at the end of the month, and I left Washington with my wife, Eleanor, to visit her parents in Alabama. No sooner had we arrived at their house when the phone rang. It was George Carver. "Sam, come back up. We're going to Saigon to thrash out the numbers."

I was a little cynical. "We won't sell out, will we?"

"No, no, we're going to bite the bullet," he said.

## Army Estimate

We went to Saigon in early September to yet another order-of-battle meeting, this one convened in the austere conference room in Westmoreland's headquarters. Among the officers supporting Westmoreland were Gen. Philip Davidson, head of intelligence (the military calls it G-2); General Sidle, head of press relations ("What the dickens is he doing at an OB conference?" I thought); Colonel Morris, one of Davidson's aides; Col. Danny Graham, head of the G-2 Estimates Staff; and of course, Col. Gains B. Hawkins, chief of the G-2 Order of Battle Section. There were also numerous lieutenant colonels, majors, and captains, all equipped with maps, charts, files, and pointers.

The military dominated the first day of the conference. A major gave a lecture on the VC's low morale. I kept my mouth shut on the subject, even though I knew their documents showed a dwindling VC desertion rate. Another officer gave a talk full of complicated statistics which proved the Vietcong were running out of men. It was based on something called the cross-over memo which had been put together by Colonel Graham's staff. On the second day we got down to business—the numbers.

It was suspicious from the start. Every time I'd argue one category up, the military would drop another category down by the same amount. Then there was the little piece of paper put on everybody's desk saying that the military would agree to count more of one type of VC if we'd agree to eliminate another type of VC. Finally, there was the argument over a subcategory called the district-level service troops.

I stood up to present the CIA's case. I said that I had estimated that there were about seventy-five service soldiers in each of the VC's districts, explaining that I had averaged the numbers in a sample of twenty-eight documents. I briefly reviewed the evidence and asked whether there were any questions.

"I have a question," said General Davidson. "You mean to tell me that you only have twenty-eight documents?"

"Yes sir," I said. "That's all I could find."

"Well, I've been in the intelligence business for many years, and if you're trying to sell me a number on the basis of that small a sample, you might as well pack up and go home." As I resumed my seat, Davidson's aide, Colonel Morris, turned around and said, "Adams, you're full of shit."

A lieutenant colonel then got up to present the military's side of the case. He had counted about twenty service soldiers per district, he said, and then he went on to describe how a district was organized. When he asked for questions, I said, "How many documents are in your sample?"

He looked as if somebody had kicked him in the stomach. Instead of answering the question, he repeated his description of how the VC organized a district.

Then George Carver interrupted him. "Come, come, Colonel," he said. "You're not answering the question. General Davidson has just taken Mr. Adams to task for having only twenty-eight documents in his sample. It's a perfectly legitimate question. How many have you in yours?"

In a very low voice, the lieutenant colonel said, "One." I looked over at General Davidson and Colonel Morris to see whether they'd denounce the lieutenant colonel for having such a small sample. Both of them were looking at the ceiling.

"Colonel," I continued, "may I see your document?" He didn't have it, he said, and, besides, it wasn't a document, it was a POW report.

Well, I asked, could he please try and remember who the twenty service soldiers were? He ticked them off. I kept count. The total was forty.

"Colonel," I said, "you have forty soldiers here, not twenty. How did you get from forty to twenty?"

"We scaled down the evidence," he replied.

"Scaled down the evidence?"

"Yes," he said. "We cut out the hangers-on."

"And how do you determine what a hanger-on is?"

"Civilians, for example."

Now, I knew that civilians sometimes worked alongside VC service troops, but normally the rosters listed them separately. So I waited until the next coffee break to ask Colonel Hawkins how he'd "scale down" the service troops in a document I had. It concerned Long Dat District in the southern half of South Vietnam, and its 111 service troops were broken down by components. We went over each one. Of the twenty in the medical component, Hawkins would count three, of the twelve in the ordnance section, he'd count two, and so forth, until Long Dat's 111 service soldiers were down to just over forty. There was no indication in the document that any of those dropped were civilians.

As we were driving back from the conference that day, an Army officer in the car with us explained what the real trouble was: "You know, our basic problem is that we've been told to keep our numbers under 300,000."

Later, after retiring from the Army, Colonel Hawkins confirmed that this was basically the case. At the start of the conference, he'd been told to stay below a certain number. He could no longer remember what it was, but he recalled that the person who gave it to him was Colonel Morris, the officer who had told me I was "full of shit."

The Saigon conference was in its third day, when we received a cable from Helms that, for all its euphemisms, gave us no choice but to accept the military's numbers. We did so, and the conference concluded that the size of the Vietcong force in South Vietnam was 299,000. We accomplished this by simply marching certain categories of Vietcong out of the order of battle, and by using the military's "scaled-down" numbers.

I left the conference extremely angry. Another member of the CIA contingent, William Hyland (now head of intelligence at the Department of State), tried to explain. "Sam, don't take it so hard. You know what the political climate is. If you think they'd accept the higher numbers, you're living in a dream world." Shortly after the conference ended, another category was frog-marched out of the estimate, which dropped from 299,000 to 248,000.

I returned to Washington, and in October I went once again in front of the Board of National Estimates, by this time reduced to only its CIA members. I told them exactly what had happened at the conference—how the number had been scaled down, which types of Vietcong had left the order of battle, and even about the affair of Long Dat District. They were sympathetic.

"Sam, it makes my blood boil to see the military cooking the books," one of the board members said. Another asked, "Sam, have we gone beyond the bounds of reasonable dishonesty?" And I said, "Sir, we went past them last August." Nonetheless, the board sent the estimate forward for the director's signature, with the numbers unchanged. I was told there was no other choice because Helms had committed the CIA to the military's numbers.

"But that's crazy," I said. "The numbers were faked." I made one last try. My memorandum was nine pages long. The first eight pages told how the numbers had got that way. The ninth page accused the military of lying. If we accepted their numbers, I argued, we would not only be dishonest and cowardly, we would be stupid. I handed the memo to George Carver to give to the director, and sent copies to everyone I could think of in the research branch. Although I was the only CIA analyst working on the subject at the time, nobody replied. Two days later Helms signed the estimate, along with its doctored numbers.

That was that. I went into Carver's office and quit Helms's staff. He looked embarrassed when I told him why I was doing so, but he said there was nothing he could do. I thanked him for all he had done in the earlier part of the year and for his attempt at trying to deal with real rather than imaginary numbers. I thought of leaving the CIA, but I still retained some faith in the Agency, and I knew that I was the only person in the government arguing for higher numbers with accurate evidence. I told Carver that the research directorate had formed a VC branch, in which,

I said, I hoped to find somebody who would listen to me.

## Facing Facts

In November General Westmoreland returned to Washington and held a press conference. "The enemy is running out of men," he said. He based this on the fabricated numbers, and on Colonel Graham's crossover memo. In early December, the CIA sent McNamara another "Whither Vietnam?" memo. It had the doctored numbers, but this time I was forbidden to change them. It was the same story with Helm's New York briefing to Congress. Wrong numbers, no changes allowed. When I heard that Colonel Hawkins, whom I still liked and admired, had been reassigned to Fort Holabird in Baltimore, I went to see him to find out what he really thought about the order of battle. "Those were the worst three months in my life," he said, referring to July, August, and September, and he offered to do anything he could to help. When he had been asked to lower the estimates, he said, he had retained as many of the frontline VC troops as possible. For several hours we went over the order of battle. We had few disagreements, but I began to see for the first time that the Communist regulars, the only category I'd never looked at, were also seriously understated—perhaps by as many as 50,000 men. No one was interested, because adding 50,000 troops would have forced a reopening of the issue of numbers, which everyone thought was settled. On January 29, 1968, I began the laborious job of transferring my files from Carver's office to the newly formed Vietcong branch.

The next day the VC launched the Tet offensive. Carver's office was chaos. There were so many separate attacks that someone was assigned full time to stick red pins in the map of South Vietnam just to keep track of them. Within a week's time it was clear that the scale of the Tet offensive was the biggest surprise to American intelligence since Pearl Harbor. As I read the cables coming in, I experienced both anger and a sort of grim satisfaction. There was just no way they could have pulled it off with only 248,-000 men, and the cables were beginning to show which units had taken part. Many had never been in the order of battle at all; others had been taken out or scaled down. I made a collection of these units, which

I showed Carver. Two weeks later, the CIA agreed to re-open the order-of-battle controversy.

Suddenly I was asked to revise and extend the memorandums that I had been attempting to submit for the past eighteen months. People began to congratulate me, to slap me on the back and say what a fine intelligence analyst I was. The Agency's chief of research, R. Jack Smith, who had once called me "*the* outstanding analyst" in the CIA but who had ignored all my reporting on the Vietcong, came down from the seventh floor to shake my hand. "We're glad to have you back," he said. "You know more about Vietnam than you did about the Congo." All of this disgusted me, and I accepted the compliments without comment. What was the purpose of intelligence, I thought, if not to warn people, to tell them what to expect? As many as 10,000 American soldiers had been killed in the Tet offensive because the generals had played politics with the numbers, and here I was being congratulated by the people who had agreed to the fiction.

In February the Agency accepted my analysis, and in April another order-of-battle conference was convened at CIA headquarters. Westmoreland's delegation, headed by Colonel Graham (now a lieutenant general and head of the Defense Intelligence Agency) continued to argue for the lower numbers. But from that point forward the White House stopped using the military estimate and relied on the CIA estimate of 600,000 Vietcong.

All along I had wondered whether the White House had had anything to do with fixing the estimates. The military wanted to keep them low in order to display the "light at the end of the tunnel," but it had long since occurred to me that maybe the generals were under pressure from the politicians. Carver had told me a number of times that he had mentioned my OB figures to Walt Rostow of the White House. But even now I don't know whether Rostow ordered the falsification, or whether he was merely reluctant to face unpleasant facts. Accepting the higher numbers forced the same old decision: pack up or send a lot more troops.

On the evening of March 31, the question of the White House role became, in a way, irrelevant. President Johnson made his announcement that he wasn't going to run again. Whoever the next President was, I felt, needed to be told about the sorry state of American intelligence so that he could do something about it. The next morning, April 1, I went to the CIA

inspector general's office and said: "Gentlemen, I've come here to file a complaint, and it involves both the research department and the director. I want to make sure that the next administration finds out what's gone on down here." On May 28 I filed formal charges and asked that they be sent to "appropriate members of the White House staff" and to the President's Foreign Intelligence Advisory Board. I also requested an investigation by the CIA inspector general. Helms responded by telling the inspector general to start an investigation. This took two months. The director then appointed a high-level review board to go over the inspector general's report. The review board was on its way to taking another two months when I went to the general counsel's office and talked to a Mr. Ueberhorst. I said, "Mr. Ueberhorst, I wrote a report for the White House about three months ago complaining about the CIA management, and I've been getting the runaround ever since. What I want is some legal advice. Would I be breaking any laws if I took my memo and carried it over to the White House myself?" A few days later, on September 20, 1968, the executive director of the CIA, the number-three man in the hierarchy, called me to his office: "Mr. Adams, we think well of you, but Mr. Helms says he doesn't want your memo to leave the building." I took notes of the conversation, so my reproduction of it is almost verbatim. "This is not a legal problem but a practical one of your future within the CIA," I was told. "Because if you take that memo to the White House, it will be at your own peril, and even if you get what you want by doing so, your usefulness to the Agency will thereafter be nil." The executive director carried on this conversation for thirty-five minutes. I copied it all out until he said, "Do you have anything to say, Mr. Adams?" "Yes sir," I said, "I think I'll take this right on over to the White House, and please tell the director of my intention." I wrote a memorandum of the conversation, and sent it back up to the executive director's office with a covering letter saying, "I hope I'm quoting you correctly; please tell me if I'm not."

A short while later he called me back to his office and said, "I'm afraid there's been a misunderstanding, because the last thing in the world the director wanted to do was threaten. He has decided that this thing can go forward."

I waited until after the Presidential election. Nixon won, and the next day I called the seventh floor to ask if it was now okay to send on my memo to the White

House. On November 8, 1968, Mr. Helms summoned me to his office. The first thing he said to me was "Don't take notes." To the best of my recollection, the conversation then proceeded along the following lines. He asked what was bothering me; did I think my supervisors were treating me unfairly, or weren't they promoting me fast enough? No, I said. My problem was that he caved in on the numbers right before Tet. I enlarged on the theme for about ten minutes. He listened without expression, and when I was done he asked what I would have had him do—take on the whole military? I said, that under the circumstances, that was the only thing he could have done; the military's numbers were faked. He then told me that I didn't know what things were like, that we could have told the White House that there were a million more Vietcong out there, and it wouldn't have made the slightest bit of difference in our policy. I said that we weren't the ones to decide about policy; all we should do was to send up the right numbers and let them worry. He asked me who I wanted to see, and I said that I had requested appropriate members of the White House staff and the President's Foreign Intelligence Advisory Board in my memo, but, frankly, I didn't know who the appropriate members were. He asked whether Gen. Maxwell Taylor and Walt Rostow would be all right. I told him that was not only acceptable, it was generous, and he said he would arrange the appointments for me.

With that I was sent around to see the deputy directors. The chief of research, R. Jack Smith, asked me what the matter was, and I told him the same things I had told Helms. The Vietnam war, he said, was an extraordinarily complex affair, and the size of the enemy army was only—his exact words—"a small but significant byway of the problem." His deputy, Edward Procter, now the CIA's chief of research, remarked, "Mr. Adams, the real problem is you. You ought to look into yourself."

## Permission Denied

After making these rounds, I wrote letters to Rostow and Taylor, telling them who I was and asking that they include a member of Nixon's staff in any talks we had about the CIA's shortcomings. I forwarded the letters, through channels, to the director's office, asking his permission to send them on. Permission was denied, and that was the last I ever heard about meeting with Mr. Rostow and General Taylor.

In early December I did manage to see the executive secretary of the President's Foreign Intelligence Advisory Board, J. Patrick Coyne. He told me that a few days earlier Helms had sent over my memo, that some members of PFIAB had read it, and that they were asking me to enlarge on my views and to make any recommendations I thought were in order. Coyne encouraged me to write a full report, and in the following weeks I put together a thirty-five-page paper explaining why I had brought charges. A few days after Nixon's inauguration, in January 1969, I sent the paper to Helms's office with a request for permission to send it to the White House. Permission was denied in a letter from the deputy director, Adm. Rufus Taylor, who informed me that the CIA was a team, and that if I didn't want to accept the team's decision, then I should resign.

There I was—with nobody from Nixon's staff having heard of any of this. It was far from clear whether Nixon intended to retain the President's Foreign Intelligence Advisory Board. J. Patrick Coyne said he didn't know. He also said he didn't intend to press for the release of the thirty-five page report. I thought I had been had.

For the first time in my career, I decided to leave official channels. This had never occurred to me before, not even when Helms had authorized the doctored numbers in the month before Tet. I had met a man named John Court, a member of the incoming staff of the National Security Council, and through him I hoped for a measure of redress. I gave him my memorandum and explained its import—including Westmoreland's deceptions before Tet—and asked him to pass it around so that at least the new administration might know what had gone on at the CIA and could take any action it thought necessary. Three weeks later Court told me that the memo had gotten around, all right, but the decision had been made not to do anything about it.

So I gave up. If the White House wasn't interested, there didn't seem to be any other place I could go. I felt I'd done as much as I possibly could do, and that was that.

Once again I thought about quitting the Agency. But again I decided not to, even though my career was pretty much in ruins. Not only had the deputy director just suggested that I resign, but I was now working under all kinds of new restrictions. I was no longer permitted to go to Vietnam. After the order-of-battle conference in Saigon in September 1967, Westmoreland's headquarters had informed the CIA station chief that I was persona non grata, and that they didn't want me on any military installations throughout the country. In CIA headquarters I was more or less confined to quarters, since I was no longer asked to attend any meetings at which outsiders were present. I was even told to cut back on the lectures I was giving about the VC to CIA case officers bound for Vietnam.[3]

I suppose what kept me from quitting this time was that I loved the job. The numbers business was going along fairly well, or so I thought, and I was becoming increasingly fascinated with what struck me as another disturbing question. Why was it that the Vietcong always seemed to know what we were up to, while we could never find out about them except through captured documents? At the time of the Tet offensive, for example, the CIA had only a single agent in the enemy's midst, and he was low-level.

At about this time, Robert Klein joined the VC branch. He had just graduated from college, and I thought him one of the brightest and most delightful people I had ever met. We began batting back and forth the question of why the VC always knew what was going to happen next. Having written a study on the Vietcong secret police in 1967, I already knew that the Communists had a fairly large and sophisticated espionage system. But I had no idea *how* large, and, besides, there were several other enemy organizations in addition to the secret police that had infiltrated the Saigon government. Klein and I began to sort them out. The biggest one, we found, was called the Military Proselytizing Directorate, which concentrated on recruiting agents in the South Vietnamese Army and National Police. By May 1969 we felt things were beginning to fall into place, but we still hadn't answered the fundamental question of how many agents the VC had in the South Vietnamese government. I decided to do the obvious thing, which was to start looking in the captured documents for references to spies. Klein and I each got a big stack of documents, and we began going through them, one by one. Within two weeks we had references to more than 1,000 VC agents. "Jesus Christ!" I said to Klein. "A thousand agents! And before Tet the CIA only had one." Furthermore, it was clear from the documents that the thousand we'd found were only the tip of a very big iceberg.

Right away I went off to tell everybody the bad news. I had begun to take a perverse pleasure in my role as the man in opposition at the Agency. The first person I spoke to was the head of the Vietnam branch of the CIA Clandestine Services. I said, "Hey, a guy called Klein and I just turned up references to over 1,000 VC agents, and from the looks of the documents the overall number might run into the tens of thousands." He said, "For God's sake, don't open that Pandora's box. We have enough troubles as it is."

The next place I tried to reach was the Board of National Estimates, which was just convening its annual meeting on the Vietnam draft. Because of the trouble I'd made the year before, and because the meeting included outsiders, I wasn't allowed to attend. By now, Klein and I had come to the very tentative conclusion, based mostly on extrapolations from documents, that the Military Proselytizing Directorate alone had 20,000 agents in the South Vietnamese Army and government. This made it by far the biggest agent network in the history of espionage, and I was curious to know whether this was known in Saigon. I prompted a friend of mine to ask the CIA's Saigon station chief—back in Washington to give another briefing I wasn't allowed to attend—just how many Vietcong agents there were in the South Vietnamese Army. The station chief (a new one; Jorgy had long since moved) was taken aback at the question. He'd never considered it before. He said, "Well, the South Vietnamese Military Security Service has about 300 suspects under consideration. I think that about covers it." If Klein and I were anywhere near right with our estimate of 20,000, that made the station chief's figure too low by at least 6,000 percent.

## New Discoveries

Deciding that we didn't yet know enough to make an issue of the matter, Klein and I went back to plugging the documents. The more we read, the wilder the story became. With a great deal of help from the CIA counterintelligence staff, we eventually found that Vietcong agents were running the government's National Police in the northern part of the country, that for many years the VC had controlled the counterintelligence branch of the South Vietnamese Military Security Service (which may explain why the station chief's estimate was so low), and that in several areas of Vietnam, the VC were in charge of our own Phoenix Program. Scarcely a day passed without a new discovery. The most dramatic of them concerned a Vietcong agent posing as a South Vietnamese ordnance sergeant in Da Nang. The document said that the agent had been responsible for setting off explosions at the American air base in April 1969, and destroying 40,000 tons of ammunition worth $100 million. The explosions were so big that they attracted a Congressional investigation, but the military managed to pass them off as having been started accidentally by a grass fire.

The problem with all these reports was not that they were hidden, but that they'd never been gathered and analyzed before in a systematic manner. Although CIA men in the field were aware of VC agents, Washington had failed to study the extent of the Vietcong network.

This is exactly what Klein and I attempted in the fall of 1969. By this time we had concluded that the total number of VC agents in the South Vietnamese Army and government was in the neighborhood of 30,000. While we admitted that the agents were a mixed bag—most of them were low-level personnel hedging their bets—we nonetheless arrived at an extremely bleak overall conclusion. That was that the agents were so numerous, so easy to recruit, and so hard to catch that their existence "called into question the basic loyalty of the South Vietnamese government and armed forces." This, in turn, brought up questions about the ultimate chances for success of our new policy of turning the war over to the Vietnamese.

In late November Klein and I had just about finished the first draft of our study when we were told that *under no circumstances* was it to leave CIA headquarters, and that, specifically, it shouldn't go to John Court of the White House staff. Meanwhile, however, I had called Court a number of times, telling him that the study existed, and that it suggested that Vietnamization probably wouldn't work. For the next two-and-a-half months, Court called the CIA front office asking for a draft of our memo on agents. Each time he was turned down.

Finally, in mid-February 1970, Court came over to the VC branch, and asked if he could have a copy of the agent memorandum. I told him he couldn't, but that I supposed it was okay if he looked at it at a nearby desk. By closing time Court had disappeared, along with the memo. I phoned him the next morning at the Executive Office Building and asked him if he had it. "Yes, I took it. Is that okay?" he said. It wasn't okay, and shortly after informing my superiors I received a letter of reprimand for releasing the memo to an "outsider." (Court, who worked for the White House, was the "outsider.") All copies of the study within the CIA—several were around being reviewed—were recalled to the Vietcong branch and put in a safe. Klein was removed from working on agents, and told that if he didn't "shape up," he'd be fired.

The research department and perhaps even Helms (I don't know) apparently were appalled by the agent's memo reaching the White House. It was embarrassing for the CIA, since we'd never let anything like that out before. To suddenly say, oh, by the way, our ally, the South Vietnamese government, is crawling with spies, might lead someone to think that maybe the Agency should have noticed them sooner. We'd been in the war, after all, for almost six years.

Court later wrote a précis of the memo and gave it to Kissinger. Kissinger gave it to Nixon. Shortly thereafter, the White House sent a directive to Helms which said, in effect: "Okay, Helms, get that damn agent paper out of the safe drawer." Some months later, the Agency coughed it up, almost intact.

Meanwhile, Klein quit. I tried to talk him out of it, but he decided to go to graduate school. He did so in September 1970, but not before leaving a letter of resignation with the CIA inspector general. Klein's letter told the complete story of the agent study, concluding with his opinion that the White House would never have learned about the Communist spies had it not been for John Court's sticky fingers.

By now my fortunes had sunk to a low ebb. For the first time in seven years, I was given an unfavorable fitness report. I was rated "marginal" at conducting research; I had lost my "balance and objectivity" on the war, and worst of all, I was the cause of the "discontent leading to the recent resignation" of Klein. For these shortcomings I was being reassigned to a position where I would be "less directly involved in research on the war." This meant I had to leave the Vietcong branch and join a small historical staff, where I was to take up the relatively innocuous job of writing a history of the Cambodian rebels.

Once again, I considered resigning from the CIA, but the job still had me hooked, and ever since the coup that deposed Sihanouk in March 1970 I had been wondering what was going on in Cambodia. Within a few weeks of that coup, the Communist army had begun to disappear from the southern half of South Vietnam for service next door, and I was curious to find out what it was up to. When I reported to the historical staff, I began, as usual, to collect documents. This was my main occupation for almost the next five months. I knew so little about Cambodia that I was fairly indiscriminate, and therefore grabbed just about everything I could find. By late April 1971, I had gathered several thousand reports, and had divided them into broad categories, such as "military" and "political." In early May, I began to go through the "military" reports.

One of the first of these was an interrogation report of a Vietcong staff officer who had surrendered in Cambodia in late 1970. The staff officer said he belonged to a Cambodian Communist regional command with a code name I'd never heard of: C-40. Apparently C-40 had several units attached to it, including regiments, and I'd never heard of any of these, either. And, it seemed, the units were mostly composed of Khmers, of whom C-40 had a total of 18,000. Now that appeared to me to be an awful lot of Khmer soldiers just for one area, so I decided to check it against our Cambodian order of battle. Within a month I made a startling discovery: there was *no* order of battle. All I could find was a little sheet of paper estimating the size of the Khmer Communist Army at 5,000 to 10,000 men. This sheet of paper, with exactly the same numbers, had been kicking around since early 1970.

It was the same story as our Vietcong estimate of 1966, only worse. In Vietnam we had neglected to look at three of the four parts of the Vietcong Army; in Cambodia we hadn't looked at the Khmer Communist Army at all. It later turned out that the 5,000-to-10,000 figure was based on numbers put together by a sergeant in the Royal Cambodian Army in 1969.

From then on, it was easy. Right in the same room with me was every single intelligence report on the Khmer rebels that had ever come in. Straightaway I found what the VC Army had been doing in Cambodia since Sihanouk's fall: it had put together the largest and best advisory structure in the Indochina war. Within two weeks I had discovered thirteen regiments, several dozen battalions, and a great many companies and platoons. Using exactly the same methods that I'd used on the Vietcong estimate before Tet (only now the methods were more re-

fined), I came to the conclusion that the size of the Cambodian Communist Army was not 5,000 to 10,000 but more like 100,000 to 150,000. In other words, the U.S. government's official estimate was between ten and thirty times too low.

My memo was ready in early June, and this time I gave a copy to John Court of the White House the day before I turned it in at the Agency. This proved to have been a wise move, because when I turned it in I was told, "Under no circumstances does this go out of the room." It was the best order-of-battle paper I'd ever done. It has about 120 footnotes, referencing about twice that many intelligence reports, and it was solid as a rock.

A week later I was taken off the Khmer Communist Army and forbidden to work on numbers anymore. A junior analyst began reworking my memo with instructions to hold the figure below 30,000. The analyst puzzled over this for several months, and at last settled on the same method the military had used in lowering the Vietcong estimate before Tet. He marched two whole categories out of the order of battle and "scaled down" what was left. In November 1971, he wrote up a memo placing the size of the Khmer Communist Army at 15,000 to 30,000 men. The CIA published the memo, and that number became the U.S. government's official estimate.

## More Distortions

The present official estimate of the Khmer rebels—65,000—derives from the earlier one. It is just as absurd. Until very recently the Royal Cambodian Army was estimated at over 200,000 men. We are therefore asked to believe that the insurgents, who control four-fifths of Cambodia's land and most of its people, are outnumbered by the ratio of 3 to 1. In fact, if we count *all* the rebel soldiers, including those dropped or omitted from the official estimate, the Khmer Rebel Army is probably larger than the government's—perhaps by a considerable margin.

The trouble with this kind of underestimate is not simply a miscalculation of numbers. It also distorts the meaning of the war. In Cambodia, as in the rest of Southeast Asia, the struggle is for allegiance, and the severest test of loyalty has to do with who can persuade the largest number of peasants to pick up a gun. When American intelligence downgrades the strength of the enemy army, it ignores the Communist success at organizing and recruiting people. This is why the Communists call the struggle a "people's war" and why the government found it difficult to understand.

I spent the rest of 1971 and a large part of 1972 trying to get the CIA to raise the Cambodian estimate. It was useless. The Agency was busy with other matters, and I became increasingly discouraged. The Cambodian affair seemed to me to be a repeat of the Vietnam one, the same people made the same mistakes, in precisely the same ways, and everybody was allowed to conceal his duplicity. In the fall of 1972 I decided to make one last attempt at bringing the shoddiness of American intelligence to the attention of someone, anyone who could do anything about it.

Between October 1972 and January 1973 I approached the U.S. Army inspector general, the CIA inspector general, and the Congress—all to no avail. To the Army inspector general I delivered a memorandum setting forth the details of what had happened to the VC estimate before Tet. I mentioned the possibility of General Westmoreland's complicity, which might have implicated him in three violations of the Uniform Code of Military Justice. The memorandum asked for an investigation, but the inspector general explained that I was in the wrong jurisdiction. Of the CIA inspector general I requested an investigation of the Cambodian estimates, but he adopted the device of neglecting to answer his mail, and no inquiry took place. In a last desperate measure—desperate because my friends at the CIA assured me that Congressional watchdog committees were a joke—I even appealed to Congress. To committees in both the House and Senate that watch over the CIA I sent a thirteen-page memorandum with names, dates, numbers, and a sequence of events. A staff assistant to the Senate Armed Services Committee thought it an interesting document, but he doubted that the Intelligence Subcommittee would take it up because it hadn't met in over a year and a half. Lucien Nedzi, the chief superintendent of the CIA in the House, also thought the document "pertinent," but he observed that the forthcoming elections obliged him to concern himself primarily with the question of busing. When I telephoned his office in late November, after the elections had come and gone, his administrative assistant told me, in effect, "Don't call us; we'll call you."

By mid-January 1973 I had reached the end of the

---

## The Moral of the Tale

Readers interested in the question of integrity in American Government might take note of three successful bureaucrats mentioned in this chronicle. All of them acknowledged or abetted the counterfeiting of military intelligence, and all of them have risen to high places within their respective apparats. Lt. Gen. Daniel Graham, who helped to lower the U.S. Army's estimate of Vietcong strength, is now the head of the Defense Intelligence Agency; Edward Procter, who steadfastly ignored accurate intelligence, is now chief of the CIA research directorate; and William Hyland, who conceded the impossibility of contesting a political fiction, is now the head of State Department Intelligence. Their collective docility might also interest readers concerned with question of national security.

—Sam Adams

---

road. I happened to read a newspaper account of Daniel Ellsberg's trial in Los Angeles, and I noticed that the government was alleging that Ellsberg had injured the national security by releasing estimates of the enemy force in Vietnam. I looked, and damned if they weren't from the same order of battle which the military had doctored back in 1967. Imagine! Hanging a man for leaking faked numbers! In late February I went to Los Angeles to testify at the trial and told the story of how the numbers got to be so wrong. When I returned to Washington in March, the CIA once again threatened to fire me. I complained, and, as usual, the Agency backed down. After a decent interval, I quit.

One last word. Some day, when everybody has returned to his senses, I hope to go back to the CIA as an analyst. I like the work.

Editor's Note *In January 1982, CBS Television ran a controversial documentary entitled, "Missing or Uncounting of the Enemy in Vietnam," based largely on the writings of and interviews with Sam Adams, the author of this case study. The program caused an unprecedented amount of discussion and criticism* and led to a $120 million libel suit against CBS by General William C. Westmoreland, the commander of U.S. Army forces in Vietnam during the height of the conflict, who was cast as the major villain in the report. During the course of the ensuing debate over the program (Westmoreland eventually dropped his suit against CBS), an unusual "confession" appeared in print, "Vietnam Anguish: Being Ordered to Lie," Washington Post (November 14, 1982), p. Cl+, by Lt. Col. Gains Hawkins. Beginning in February 1966, Hawkins had served for 18 months in Vietnam in military intelligence and during much of that time was charged with preparing the "Order of Battle," which essentially outlined the nature and strength of the enemy forces. In short, Hawkins was Adams's counterpart within the military in Vietnam, the man on the scene who generated the enemy troop estimates for Westmoreland.

According to Hawkins, when he arrived at his new post he went to work analyzing the numbers of enemy troops and soon had developed figures showing upwards of 500,000 enemy forces, roughly twice the amount of the figures then being used. As Hawkins writes: "When I briefed General Westmoreland on our new figures, he expressed surprise. He voiced concern about the major increase in the irregular forces and political cadres that we had found. He expressed concern about possible public reaction to the new fig-

ures—that they might lead people to think we had made no progress in the war. The general did not accept the new numbers."

"I then reduced them, quite arbitrarily, and returned to General Westmoreland to brief him on my second, lower count. But he rejected it as well."

Adams's story, now over a decade old, remains controversial, but is in large part probably correct as presented here.

### Notes

1. A document was later captured, which showed the Vietcong not only reached but exceeded their quota. Dated April 1966, it put the number of guerrilla-militia at 330,000.
2. This was broken down as follows: Communist regulars, about 100,000; guerrilla-militia, about 300,000; service troops, about 100,000; political cadres, about 100,000.
3. In mid-1968 I had discovered that Agency officers sent to Vietnam received a total of only one hour's instruction on the organization and methods of operation of the Vietcong. Disturbed that they should be sent up against so formidable a foe with so little training, I had by the end of the year increased the hours from one to twenty-four. I gave most of the lectures myself.

## Chapter 9 Review Questions

1. What are the differences between formal and informal channels of communications? Why do public administrators have to be concerned with the informal lines of communications as well as with the formal lines? How does one find out about the formal and informal lines of communications in an organization?
2. Were there both formal and informal methods of communications illustrated in the case, "Vietnam Cover-Up"? If so, what were some of the examples of each? Which were the most important in creating the dilemmas that Sam Adams faced in obtaining and communicating his critical information to the top-level policy planners within the CIA?
3. What types of communication blockages discussed in the Simon, Smithburg, and Thompson reading were illustrated in the Adams case? What strategies did Adams devise in circumventing these blockages? In your estimation, did Adams exhaust all the available routes to get his message to the top-level policy makers?
4. What does the "Vietnam Cover-Up" case study tell us about the interrela-

tionships between organizational norms and values and an organization's receptivity to open communications? Specifically, how did the CIA's doctrine toward the Vietnam War help to create major communications barriers? In your view, what can be done to prevent this problem from recurring?

5. How do communications systems make or break an administrator's ability to control and direct the policies of his or her organization? As an administrator, what techniques would you utilize to ensure that the information you receive is accurate, timely, and *not* distorted by preconceived personal or institutional biases?

6. Can you generalize about the moral dilemmas facing an individual like Adams who works for a public organization and strongly values truthfulness in performing his work? What potential risks does this sort of individual face within the organization given the possibility of censorship of communications? What choices might influence an employee's decision to stay and fight for reforming the system from within—for what he or she values as the truth—versus quitting and going public with the information? Can you identify your own ethical standards that would determine at what point you might be forced to resign in protest over a similar type of issue?

## Key Terms

formal communications
informal communications
deliberate restrictions on communication

language barriers
status differences
geographic differences

## Suggestions for Further Reading

The importance placed on communications processes in shaping governmental and organizational decisions was largely the result of several seminal works. These writings of the following key theorists should be studied with some care: Chester Barnard, *The Functions of the Executive* (Cambridge, Mass.: Harvard University Press, 1938); Herbert Simon, *Administrative Behavior: A Study of Decision-Making Processes in Administrative Organization* (New York: Macmillan, 1947); Karl W. Deutsch, *The Nerves of Government* (New York: Free Press, 1950); Norbert Weiner, *Cybernetics: Or Control and Communication in the Animal and the Machine* (New York: John Wiley & Sons, 1948). For a useful study of

Herbert Simon and his contributions not only to this area but the entire field of public administration, see the whole issue *Public Administration Quarterly* (Fall 1988), especially the opening interview with Simon. Harlan Cleveland, *The Knowledge Executive: Leadership in an Information Society* (New York: E. P. Dutton, 1985), presents a current, lively study of this topic from a leadership perspective. For a recent report on "the payoffs" from computerization, see: Alana Northrop, Kenneth L. Kraemer, Debora Dunkle, and John Leslie King, "Payoffs from Computerization: Lessons Over Time," *Public Administration Review* (September/October 1990), pp 505–514.

For more pragmatic works on the subject,

review Herbert Kaufman in collaboration with Michael Couzens, *Administrative Feedback: Monitoring Subordinates' Behavior* (Washington, D.C.: The Brookings Institution, 1973); Lyman W. Porter and Kathleen H. Roberts, "Communications in Organizations," in Marvin Dunette, ed., *Handbook of Industrial and Organizational Psychology* (Chicago: Rand McNally, 1976), pp. 1527–1551; Lyman W. Porter, "Communications: Structure and Process," in Harold L. Fromkin and John L. Sherwood, eds., *Integrating the Organization* (New York: Free Press, 1974), pp. 237–240; and George C. Edwards III, "Problems in Bureaucratic Communications;" Herbert Kaufman, "Red Tape;" and Francis E. Rourke, "Executive Secrecy," in Francis E. Rourke, ed., *Bureaucratic Power in National Policy Making,* Fourth Edition (Boston: Little, Brown, 1986). The best new practical textbooks on this topic are Fred Knight and Harold B. Horn, *Telecommunications* (Washington, D.C.: International City Management Association, 1982); and David S. Arnold, Christine S. Becker, and Elizabeth K. Kellar, *Effective Communication: Getting the Message Across* (Washington, D.C.: International City Management Association, 1983).

Certainly during the last decade or so the computer revolution has rocked the field of administrative communications, as it will no doubt continue to do. For informative works on this topic, see Lee Spraull and Sara Kiesler, *Connections: New Ways of Working in Network Organizations* (Cambridge, Mass: MIT Press, 1991); Kenneth L. Kraemer et al., *Managing Information System: Change and Control in Or-ganizational Computing* (San Fransisco, Calif.: Jossey Bass, 1989); David F. Andersen and Sharon S. Dawes, *Government Information Management: A Primer and Casebook* (Englewood Cliffs, N.J.: Prentice Hall, 1991); John F. Sacco and John W. Ostrowski, *Microcomputers and Government Management: Design and Use of Applications* (Monterey, Calif.: Brooks/Cole, 1991).

The crisis of war can illuminate problems of administrative communications with unusual clarity. For some excellent examples, see Gordon W. Prange, *At Dawn We Slept: The Untold Story of Pearl Harbor* (New York: McGraw-Hill, 1981); E. B. Potter, *Battle for Leyte Gulf: Command and Communications* (Syracuse, N.Y.: Inter-University Case No. 126); and John W. Spanier, *The Truman-MacArthur Controversy and the Korean War* (Cambridge, Mass.: Harvard University Press, 1959) as well as from the more recent Gulf War, in Bob Woodward, *The Commanders* (New York: simon and Schuster, 1991).

The current studies on communications as related to the world of public administration tend to be highly specialized, focusing on such topics as "The Freedom of Information Act" and "Management Information Systems" as reflected in two recent *Public Administration Review* symposia: Barry Bozeman and Stuart Bretschneider, eds., "Public Management Information Systems," *Public Administration Review* special issue, 46 (November 1986), and Lotte E. Feinberg and Harold C. Relyea, "Symposium: Toward a Government Information Policy—FOI at 20", *Public Administration Review* 46 (November/December 1986).

# CHAPTER 10

# Executive Management: The Concept of the Uniqueness of Public Management

*The debate between the assimilators and the differentiators, like the dispute between proponents of convergence and divergence between the U.S. and the Soviet Union, reminds me of the old argument about whether the glass is half full or half empty. I conclude that public and private management are at least as different as they are similar, and that the differences are more important than the similarities.*

*Graham T. Allison, Jr.*

## READING 10.1

## Introduction

Writings on public management are a comparatively new phenomena; in fact, they are peculiarly products of this century because large-scale formal organizations, both public and private, are modern in origin and existence. Humanity's dependence on massive organizations that span the continent and the globe is therefore recent hence, the comprehensive, detailed analysis of these institutions is also new to scholarly interest. The flood of modern literature analyzing the nature, behavior, and ideal methods for constructing viable human institutions and internal personal relationships has been prompted in part by the need to establish and construct these organizations in ways that effectively cope with problems of the present age.

The central dilemma in studying modern organizations and their management lies in the proper theoretical perspective. As Dwight Waldo reminds us, studying organization is akin to the fable of the blind men and the elephant. "Each of the blind men . . . touched with his hands a different part of the elephant, and as a result there was among them a radical difference of opinion as to the nature of the beast."[1]

[1]Dwight Waldo, *Ideas and Issues in Public Administration* (New York: McGraw-Hill, 1953), p. 64.

A principal cause of the considerable divergence of opinion about organizations thus stems from the specialized vantage points from which observers come to examine human institutions. The economist has a different view than the philosopher, so also the insider versus the outsider and the worker versus the manager. These ideas are not right or wrong; rather, a number of approaches exist for reaching the truth about complex formal organizations. In studying organizations, material that is valid or useful to one individual may not seem so to another.

For one reason or another, very often *one* theoretical perspective in America tends to dominate our understanding of what constitutes good or appropriate public sector organizational practices, namely business perspectives. Not infrequently do we read about political candidates or their appointees promising, "I can make government more businesslike!" or citing as their reason for holding high public office "a successful track-record as a manager in private enterprise." Editorial writers, civic association speakers, and media pundits often echo these refrains in favor of applying entepreneurial talent to public enterprises. Popular opinion generally supports the viewpoint that if only public administrators would simply manage their affairs like business, government—and maybe even the entire country—would run a lot better.

The tendency to identify good management in government with good business management is common even in serious public administration literature. Indeed, discussions of business management methods dominated much of the early development of the conscious study of public administration at the beginning of the twentieth century. Frederick W. Taylor and his business-oriented scientific management concepts served as the core of much of the field of public administration prior to World War II. The Brownlow Committee Report (1937), which some scholars believe was the highwater mark of the influence of public administration thinking on government, largely mirrored the business organization practices of the day. In many respects, this strong influence of business practices on government continues today through such imported private sector techniques as performance budgets, cost-benefit analysis, cost-accounting procedures, performance appraisals, management by objective, zero-based budgeting, and so on. Indeed, you only need to think about the names of major governmental processes and institutions to appreciate the enormous influence of what Waldo calls "our business civilization"—there are government corporations, city managers, efficiency ratings, the contracting out for services, chief administrative officers, and county executives.

Yet, despite the deep-rooted and continuing enthusiasm—on both the popular and the scholarly levels—to make government more business-like, the fundamental issue remains unanswered: is government like business? Can the public sector, in fact, be run like the private sector? Indeed, it is a critical question for the field as a whole, for if public and private management are the same in scope, purpose, and process, why do we have the separate field of public administration and, therefore, public administrators? Why not simply teach and practice "administration" without distinguishing between "public" and "private"? This issue goes to the heart of the intellectual discipline and the professional practice of our field. In many ways, this issue has been a dilemma since the inception of public administration and is of continuing interest to many scholars and practitioners today.

Graham T. Allison, Jr. (1941–     ), formerly dean of the John F. Kennedy School of Government at Harvard University and author of several important books in the field such as *The Essence of Decision* (1971), reflected on this question before a major symposium on public management research agendas sponsored by the Office of Personnel Management. In the following essay, Allison summarizes his remarks on this subject. He takes off on a frequently quoted "law" from the late political scientist Wallace Sayre, which maintains that public and private management are fundamentally alike in all unimportant respects. Allison probes this law from several standpoints: first, by the *personal impressions* of managers who have seen both sides of the fence, for example, John Dunlop; second, by *scholarly surveys* of the literature comparing both public and private management practices and activities; and third, by an *operational perspective* of two actual administrators in action—Doug Costle at the EPA and Roy Chapin at American Motors.

By looking at this issue from a number of angles, Allison is able to draw these important conclusions: (1) while the need for increased governmental efficiency is real, "the notion that there is any significant body of private management practices and skills that can be transferred directly to public management . . . is wrong"; (2) while "performance in many public management positions can be improved substantially," an improvement will not come "from massive borrowing of specific private management skills and understandings"; (3) while it is possible to learn from experiences in public or private settings, "the effort to develop public management as a field of knowledge should start from the problems faced by practicing public managers." Worthy of careful attention, too, are the lists at the end of Allison's essay that outline the specific strategies he sees as necessary for the development of both the professional practice and the academic dimensions of public management.

As you read this selection, keep the following questions in mind:

What essential arguments does Allison put forward in favor of the uniqueness of public management? How does Allison arrive at his conclusions? Do you agree or disagree with Allison's argument and his reasoning?

What model for public management does Allison propose? What are its elements? How does he support its value?

What are the implications of his argument—namely, the uniqueness thesis—for teaching, practice, and scholarship in the field of public management?

# Public and Private Management: Are They Fundamentally Alike in All Unimportant Respects?

### GRAHAM T. ALLISON, JR.

My subtitle puts Wallace Sayre's oft quoted "law" as a question. Sayre had spent some years in Ithaca helping plan Cornell's new School of Business and Public Administration. He left for Columbia with this aphorism: public and private management are fundamentally alike in all unimportant respects.

Sayre based his conclusion on years of personal observation of governments, a keen ear for what his colleagues at Cornell (and earlier at OPA) said about business, and a careful review of the literature and data comparing public and private management. Of the latter there was virtually none. Hence, Sayre's provocative "law" was actually an open invitation to research.

Unfortunately, in the 50 years since Sayre's pronouncement, the data base for systematic comparison of public and private management has improved little. Consequently . . . I, in effect, take up Sayre's invitation to *speculate* about similarities and differences among public and private management in ways that suggest significant opportunities for systematic investigation. . . .

## Framing the Issue: What Is Public Management?

What is the meaning of the term "management" as it appears in Office of *Management* and Budget, or Office of Personnel *Manage-*

Reprinted by permission from pp. 27–38 of *Setting Public Management Research Agendas: Integrating the Sponsor, Producer and User.* Washington, D.C.: Office of Personnel Management. OPM Document 127–53–1. February 1980.

*ment?* Is "management" different from, broader or narrower than "administration"? Should we distinguish between management, leadership, entrepreneurship, administration, policy making, and implementation?

Who are "public managers"? Mayors, governors, and presidents? City managers, secretaries, and commissioners? Bureau chiefs? Office directors? Legislators? Judges?

Recent studies of OPM and OMB shed some light on these questions. OPM's major study of the "Current Status of Public Management Research" completed in May 1978 by Selma Mushkin of Georgetown's Public Service Laboratory starts with this question. The Mushkin report notes the definition of "public management" employed by the Interagency Study Committee on Policy Management Assistance in its 1975 report to OMB. That study identified the following core elements:

1. *Policy Management*  The identification of needs, analysis of options, selection of programs, and allocation of resources on a jurisdiction-wide basis.
2. *Resource Management*  The establishment of basic administrative support systems, such as budgeting, financial management, procurement and supply, and personnel management.
3. *Program Management*  The implementation of policy or daily operation of agencies carrying out policy along functional lines (education, law enforcement, etc.).[1]

The Mushkin report rejects this definition in favor of an "alternative list of public management elements." These elements are:

- Personnel Management (other than work force planning and collective bargaining and labor management relations)
- Work Force Planning
- Collective Bargaining and Labor Management Relations
- Productivity and Performance Measurement
- Organization/Reorganization
- Financial Management (including the management of intergovernmental relations)
- Evaluation Research, and Program and Management Audit.[2]

Such terminological tangles seriously hamper the development of public management as a field of knowledge. In our efforts to discuss public management curriculum at Harvard, I have been struck by how differently people use these terms, how strongly many individuals feel about some distinction they believe is marked by a difference between one word and another, and consequently, how large a barrier terminology is to convergent discussion. These verbal obstacles virtually prohibit conversation that is both brief and constructive among individuals who have not developed a common language or a mutual understanding of each other's use of terms. . . .

This terminological thicket reflects a more fundamental conceptual confusion. There exists no over-arching framework that orders the domain. In an effort to get a grip on the phenomena—the buzzing, blooming confusion of people in jobs performing tasks that produce results—both practitioners and observers have strained to find distinctions that facilitate their work. The attempts in the early decades of this century to draw a sharp line between "policy" and "administration," like more recent efforts to mark a similar divide between "policy making" and "implementation," reflect a common search for a simplification that allows one to put the value-laden issues of politics to one side (who gets what, when, and how), and focus on the more limited issue of how to perform tasks more efficiently.[3] But can anyone really deny that the "how" substantially affects the "who," the "what," and the "when"? The basic categories now prevalent in discussions of public management—strategy, personnel management, financial management, and control—are mostly derived from a business context in which executives manage hierarchies. The fit of these concepts to the problems that confront public managers is not clear.

Finally, there exists no ready data on what public managers do. Instead, the academic literature, such as it is, mostly consists of speculation tied to bits and pieces of evidence about the tail or the trunk or other manifestation of the proverbial elephant.[4] In contrast to the literally thousands of cases describing problems faced by private managers and their practice in solving these problems, case research from the perspective of a public manager is just beginning. . . .[5] But the paucity of data on the phenomena inhibits systematic empirical research on similarities and differences between public and private management, leaving the field to a mixture of reflection on personal experience and speculation.

For the purpose of this presentation, I will follow Webster and use the term management to mean the organization and direction of resources to achieve a desired result. I will focus on *general managers,* that is, individuals charged with managing a whole organization or multifunctional sub-unit. I will be interested in the general manager's full responsibilities, both *inside* his organization in integrating the diverse contributions of specialized sub-units of the organization to achieve results, and *outside* his organization in relating his organization and its product to external constituencies. I will begin with the simplifying assumption that managers of traditional government organizations are public managers, and managers of traditional private businesses, private managers. Lest the discussion fall victim to the fallacy of misplaced abstraction, I will take the Director of EPA and the

Chief Executive Officer of American Motors as, respectively, public and private managers. Thus, our central question can be put concretely: in what ways are the jobs and responsibilities of Doug Costle as Director of EPA similar to and different from those of Roy Chapin as Chief Executive Officer of American Motors?

## Similarities: How Are Public and Private Management Alike?

At one level of abstraction, it is possible to identify a set of general management functions. The most famous such list appeared in Gulick and Urwick's classic *Papers in the Science of Administration.*[6] Gulick summarized the work of the chief executive in the acronym POSD-CORB. The letters stand for:

- Planning
- Organizing
- Staffing
- Directing
- Coordinating
- Reporting
- Budgeting

With various additions, amendments, and refinements, similar lists of general management functions can be found through the management literature from Barnard to Drucker.[7]

I shall resist here my natural academic instinct to join the intramural debate among proponents of various lists and distinctions. Instead, I simply offer one composite list (see Table 10.1) that attempts to incorporate the major functions that have been identified for general managers, whether public or private.

These common functions of management are not isolated and discrete, but rather integral components separated here for purposes of analysis. The character and relative significance of the various functions differ from one time to another in the history of any organization, and between one organization and another. But whether in a public or private setting, the challenge for the general manager is to integrate all these elements so as to achieve results.

## Differences: How Are Public and Private Management Different?

While there is a level of generality at which management is management, whether public or private, functions that bear identical labels take on rather different meaning in public and private settings. As Larry Lynn has pointed out, one powerful piece of evidence in the debate between those who emphasize "similarities" and those who underline "differences" is the nearly unanimous conclusion of individuals who have been general managers in both business and government. Consider the reflections of George Shultz (former Director of OMB, Secretary of Labor, Secretary of the Treasury; now President of Bechtel), Donald Rumsfeld (former congressman, Director of OEO, Director of the Cost of Living Council, White House Chief of Staff, and Secretary of Defense; now President of GD Searle and Company), Michael Blumenthal (former Chairman and Chief Executive Officer of Bendix, Secretary of the Treasury, and now Vice Chairman of Burrows), Roy Ash (former President of Litton Industries, Director of OMB; now President of Addressograph), Lyman Hamilton (former Budget Officer in BOB, High Commissioner of Okinawa, Division Chief in the World Bank and President of ITT), and George Romney (former President of American Motors, Governor of Michigan and Secretary of Housing and Urban Development).[8] All judge public management different from private management—and harder!

**Table 10.1    Functions of General Management**

*Strategy*

1.  **Establishing objectives and priorities** for the organization (on the basis of forecasts of the external environment and the organization's capacities).
2.  **Devising operational plans** to achieve these objectives.

*Managing internal components*

3.  **Organizing and staffing:** In organizing the manager establishes structure (units and positions with assigned authority and responsibilities) and procedures (for coordinating activity and taking action); in staffing he tries to fit the right persons in the key jobs.*
4.  **Directing personnel and the personnel management system:** The capacity of the organization is embodied primarily in its members and their skills and knowledge; the personnel management system recruits, selects, socializes, trains, rewards, punishes, and exits the organization's human capital, which constitutes the organization's capacity to act to achieve its goals and to respond to specific directions from management.
5.  **Controlling performance:** Various management information systems—including operating and capital budgets, accounts, reports and statistical systems, performance appraisals, and product evaluation—assist management in making decisions and in measuring progress towards objectives.

*Managing external constituencies*

6.  **Dealing with "external" units** of the organization subject to some common authority: Most general managers must deal with general managers of other units within the larger organization—above, laterally, and below—to achieve their unit's objectives.
7.  **Dealing with independent organizations:** Agencies from other branches or levels of government, interest groups, and private enterprises that can importantly affect the organization's ability to achieve its objectives.
8.  **Dealing with the press and public** whose action or approval or acquiescence is required.

---

*Organization and staffing are frequently separated in such lists, but because of the interaction between the two, they are combined here. See Graham Allison and Peter Szanton, *Remaking Foreign Policy* (Basic Books, 1976), p. 14.

## Three Orthogonal Lists of Differences

My review of these recollections, as well as the thoughts of academics, has identified three interesting, orthogonal lists that summarize the current state of the field: one by John Dunlop; one major *Public Administration Review* survey of the literature comparing public and private organizations by Hal Rainey, Robert Backoff and Charles Levine; and one by Richard E. Neustadt prepared for the National Academy of Public Administration's Panel on Presidential Management.

John T. Dunlop's "impressionistic comparison of government management and private business" yields the following contrasts.[9]

**1. Time Perspective** Government managers tend to have relatively short time horizons dictated by political necessities and the political calendar, while private managers appear to take a longer time perspective oriented toward market developments, technological innova-

tion and investment, and organization building.

**2. Duration** The length of service of politically appointed top government managers is relatively short, averaging no more than 18 months recently for assistant secretaries, while private managers have a longer tenure both in the same position and in the same enterprise. A recognized element of private business management is the responsibility to train a successor or several possible candidates while the concept is largely alien to public management since fostering a successor is perceived to be dangerous.

**3. Measurement of Performance** There is little if any agreement on the standards and measurement of performance to appraise a government manager, while various tests of performance—financial return, market share, performance measures for executive compensation—are well established in private business and often made explicit for a particular managerial position during a specific period ahead.

**4. Personnel Constraints** In government there are two layers of managerial officials that are at times hostile to one another: the civil service (or now the executive system) and the political appointees. Unionization of government employees exists among relatively high-level personnel in the hierarchy and includes a number of supervisory personnel. Civil service, union contract provisions, and other regulations complicate the recruitment, hiring, transfer, and layoff or discharge of personnel to achieve managerial objectives or preferences. By comparison, private business managements have considerably greater latitude, even under collective bargaining, in the management of subordinates. They have much more authority to direct the employees of their organization. Government personnel policy and administration are more under the control of staff (including civil service staff outside an agency) compared to the private sector in which personnel are much more subject to line responsibility.

**5. Equity and Efficiency** In governmental management great emphasis tends to be placed on providing equity among different constituencies, while in private business management relatively greater stress is placed upon efficiency and competitive performance.

**6. Public Processes Versus Private Processes** Governmental management tends to be exposed to public scrutiny and to be more open, while private business management is more private and its processes more internal and less exposed to public review.

**7. Role of Press and Media** Governmental management must contend regularly with the press and media; its decisions are often anticipated by the press. Private decisions are less often reported in the press, and the press has a much smaller impact on the substance and timing of decisions.

**8. Persuasion and Direction** In government, managers often seek to mediate decisions in response to a wide variety of pressures and must often put together a coalition of inside and outside groups to survive. By contrast, private management proceeds much more by direction or the issuance of orders to subordinates by superior managers with little risk of contradiction. Governmental managers tend to regard themselves as responsive to many superiors while private managers look more to one higher authority.

**9. Legislative and Judicial Impact** Governmental managers are often subject to close scrutiny by legislative oversight groups or even judicial orders in ways that are quite uncommon in private business management. Such scrutiny often materially constrains executive and administrative freedom to act.

**10. Bottom Line** Governmental managers rarely have a clear bottom line, while that of a private business manager is profit, market performance, and survival.

*The Public Administration Review*'s major review article comparing public and private organizations, Rainey, Backoff and Levine, attempts to summarize the major points of consensus in the literature on similarities and differences among public and private organizations.[10]

Third, Richard E. Neustadt, in a fashion close to Dunlop's, notes six major differences between Presidents of the United States and Chief Executive Officers of major corporations.[11]

**1. Time-Horizon** The private chief begins by looking forward a decade, or thereabouts, his likely span barring extraordinary troubles. The first-term President looks forward four years at most, with the fourth (and now even the third) year dominated by campaigning for reelection. (What second-termers look toward we scarcely know, having seen but one such term completed in the past quarter century.)

**2. Authority** over the enterprise. Subject to concurrence from the Board of Directors which appointed and can fire him, the private executive sets organization goals, shifts structures, procedure, and personnel to suit, monitors results, reviews key operational decisions, deals with key outsiders, and brings along his Board. Save for the deep but narrow sphere of military movements, a President's authority in these respects is shared with well-placed members of Congress (or their staffs); case by case, they may have more explicit authority than he does (contrast authorizations and appropriations with the "take-care" clause). As for "bringing along the Board," neither the Congressmen with whom he shares power or the primary and general electorates which "hired" him have either a Board's duties or a broad view of the enterprise precisely matching his.

**3. Career System** The model corporation is a true career system, something like the Forest Service after initial entry. In normal times the chief himself is chosen from within, or he is chosen from another firm in the same industry. He draws department heads et al. from among those with whom he's worked, or whom he knows in comparable companies. He and his principal associates will be familiar with each other's roles—indeed he probably has had a number of them—and also usually with one another's operating styles, personalities, idiosyncrasies. Contrast the President who rarely has had much experience "downtown," probably knows little of most roles there (much of what he knows will turn out wrong), and less of most associates whom he appoints there, willy nilly, to fill places by Inauguration Day. Nor are they likely to know one another well, coming as they do from "everywhere" and headed as most are toward oblivion.

**4. Media Relations** The private executive represents his firm and speaks for it publicly in exceptional circumstances; he and his associates judge the exceptions. Those aside, he neither sees the press nor gives its members access to internal operations, least of all in his own office, save to make a point deliberately for public-relations purposes. The President, by contrast, is routinely on display, continuously dealing with the White House press and with the wider circle of political reporters, commentators, columnists. He needs them in his business, day by day, nothing exceptional about it, and they need him in theirs: the TV Network News programs lead off with him some nights each week. They and the President are as mutually dependent as he and Congressmen (or more so). Comparatively speaking, these relations overshadow most administrative ones much of the time for him.

**5. Performance Measurement** The private executive expects to be judged, and in turn to judge subordinates, by profitability, however the firm measures it (a major strategic choice). In practice, his Board may use more subjective measures; so may he, but at risk to morale and good order. The relative virtue of profit, of "the bottom line" is its legitimacy, its general acceptance in the business world by all concerned. Never mind its technical utility in given cases, its apparent "objectivity," hence "fairness," has enormous social usefulness: a myth that all can live by. For a President there is no counterpart (except *in extremis* the "smoking gun" to justify impeachment). The general public seems to judge a President, at least in part, by what its members think is happening to them, in their own lives; Congressmen, officials, interest groups appear to judge by what they guess, at given times, he can do for or to their causes. Members of the press interpret both of these and spread a simplified criterion affecting both, the legislative box-score, a standard of the press's own devising. The White

House denigrates them all except when it does well.

**6. Implementation** The corporate chief, supposedly, does more than choose a strategy and set a course of policy; he also is supposed to oversee what happens after, how in fact intentions turn into results, or if they don't to take corrective action, monitoring through his information system, acting, and if need be, through his personnel system. A President, by contrast, while himself responsible for budgetary proposals, too, in many spheres of policy, appears ill-placed and ill-equipped to monitor what agencies of states, of cities, corporations, unions, foreign governments are up to or to change personnel in charge. Yet these are very often the executants of "his" programs. Apart from defense and diplomacy the federal government does two things in the main: it issues and applies regulations and it awards grants in aid. Where these are discretionary, choice usually is vested by statute in a Senate-confirmed official well outside the White House. Monitoring is his function, not the President's except at second-hand. And final action is the function of the subjects of the rules and funds; they mostly are not federal personnel at all. In defense, the arsenals and shipyards are gone; weaponry comes from the private sector. In foreign affairs it is the *other* governments whose actions we would influence. From implementors like these a President is far removed most of the time. He intervenes, if at all, on a crash basis, not through organizational incentives.

Underlying these lists' sharpest distinctions between public and private management is a fundamental *constitutional difference*. In business, the functions of general management are centralized in a single individual: the Chief Executive Officer. The goal is authority commensurate with responsibility. In contrast, in the U.S. government, the functions of general management are constitutionally spread among competing institutions: the executive, two houses of Congress, and the courts. The constitutional goal was "not to promote efficiency but to preclude the exercise of arbitrary power," as Justice Brandeis observed. Indeed, as *The Federalist Papers* make starkly clear, the aim was to create incentives to compete: "the great security against a gradual concentration of the several powers in the same branch, consists in giving those who administer each branch the constitutional means and personal motives to resist encroachment of the others. Ambition must be made to counteract ambition."[12] Thus, the general management functions concentrated in the CEO of a private business are, by constitutional design, spread in the public sector among a number of competing institutions and thus shared by a number of individuals whose ambitions are set against one another. For most areas of public policy today, these individuals include at the federal level the chief elected official, the chief appointed executive, the chief career official, and several congressional chieftains. Since most public services are actually delivered by state and local governments, with independent sources of authority, this means a further array of individuals at these levels.

# An Operational Perspective: How Are the Jobs and Responsibilities of Doug Costle, Director of EPA, and Roy Chapin, CEO of American Motors, Similar and Different?

If organizations could be separated neatly into two homogeneous piles, one public and one private, the task of identifying similarities and differences between managers of these enterprises would be relatively easy. In fact, as Dunlop has pointed out, "the real world of management is composed of distributions, rather than single undifferentiated forms, and there is an increasing variety of hybrids." Thus for each major attribute of organizations, specific entities can be located on a spectrum. On most dimensions, organizations classified as "predominantly public" and those "predominantly private" overlap.[13] Private business organizations vary enormously among themselves in size, in management structure and philosophy, and in the constraints under which they operate. For example, forms of ownership and types of managerial control may be somewhat unrelated. Compare a family-held enterprise, for instance, with a public utility and a decentralized conglomerate, a Bechtel with ATT and Textron. Similarly, there are vast differences in management of governmental organizations. Compare the Government Printing Office or TVA or the Police Department of a small town with the Department of Energy or the Department of Health and Human Services. These distributions and varieties should encourage penetrating comparisons within both business and governmental organizations, as well as contrasts and comparisons across these broad categories, a point to which we shall return in considering directions for research.

Absent a major research effort, it may nonetheless be worthwhile to examine the jobs and responsibilities of two specific managers, neither polar extremes, but one clearly public, the other private. For this purpose, and primarily because of the availability of cases that describe the problems and opportunities each confronted, consider Doug Costle, Administrator of EPA, and Roy Chapin, CEO of American Motors.[14]

## Doug Costle, Administrator of EPA, January 1977

The mission of EPA is prescribed by laws creating the agency and authorizing its major programs. That mission is "to control and abate pollution in the areas of air, water, solid wastes, noise, radiation, and toxic substances. EPA's mandate is to mount an integrated, coordinated attack on environmental pollution in cooperation with state and local governments."[15]

EPA's organizational structure follows from its legislative mandates to control particular pollutants in specific environments: air and water, solid wastes, noise, radiation, pesticides and chemicals. As the new Administrator, Costle inherited the Ford Administration's proposed budget for EPA of $802 million for federal 1978 with a ceiling of 9,698 agency positions.

The setting into which Costle stepped is difficult to summarize briefly. As Costle characterized it:

- "Outside there is a confusion on the part of the public in terms of what this agency is all about: what it is doing, where it is going."
- "The most serious constraint on EPA is the inherent complexity in the state of our knowledge, which is constantly changing."
- "Too often, acting under extreme deadlines mandated by Congress, EPA has announced regulations, only to find out that they knew very little about the problem. The central problem is the inherent complexity of the job that the agency has been asked to do and the fact that what it is asked to do changes from day to day."
- "There are very difficult internal management issues not amenable to a quick solution: the skills mix problem within the agency; a research program with laboratory facilities scattered all over the country and cemented in place, largely by political alliances on the Hill that would frustrate efforts to pull together a coherent research program."
- "In terms of EPA's original mandate in the bulk pollutants we may be hitting the asymptotic part of the curve in terms of incremental clean-up costs. You have clearly conflicting national goals: energy and environment, for example."

Costle judged his six major tasks at the outset to be:

- assembling a top management team (six assistant administrators and some 25 office heads);
- addressing EPA's legislative agenda (EPA's basic legislative charter—the Clean Air Act and the Clean Water Act—were being rewritten as he took office; the pesticides program was up for reauthorization also in 1977);
- establishing EPA's role in the Carter Administration (aware that the Administration would face hard tradeoffs between the environment and energy, energy regulations and the economy, EPA regulations of toxic substances and the regulations of FDA, CSPS, and OSHA, Costle identified the need to build relations with the other key players and to enhance EPA's standing);
- building ties to constituent groups (both because of their role in legislating the agency's mandate and in successful implementation of EPA's programs);
- making specific policy decisions (for example, whether to grant or deny a permit for the Seabrook Nuclear Generating Plant cooling system. Or how the Toxic Substance Control Act, enacted in October 1976, would be implemented; this act gave EPA new responsibilities for regulating the manufacture, distribution, and use of chemical substances so as to prevent unreasonable risks to health and the environment. Whether EPA would require chemical manufacturers to provide some minimum information on various substances, or require much stricter reporting requirements for the 1,000 chemical substances already known to be hazardous, or require companies to report all chemicals, and on what timetable, had to be decided and the regulations issued);
- rationalizing the internal organization of

the agency (EPA's extreme decentralization to the regions and its limited technical expertise).

No easy job.

## Roy Chapin and American Motors, January 1977

In January 1967, in an atmosphere of crisis, Roy Chapin was appointed Chairman and Chief Executive Officer of American Motors (and William Luneburg, President and Chief Operating Officer). In the four previous years, AMC unit sales had fallen 37 percent and market share from over six percent to under three percent. Dollar volume in 1967 was off 42 percent from the all-time high of 1963 and earnings showed a net loss of $76 million on sales of $656 million. Columnists began writing obituaries for AMC. *Newsweek* characterized AMC as "a flabby dispirited company, a product solid enough but styled with about as much flair as corrective shoes, and a public image that melted down to one unshakeable label: loser." Said Chapin: "We were driving with one foot on the accelerator and one foot on the brake. We didn't know where the hell we were."

Chapin announced to his stockholders at the outset that "we plan to direct ourselves most specifically to those areas of the market where we can be fully effective. We are not going to attempt to be all things to all people, but to concentrate on those areas of consumer needs we can meet better than anyone else." As he recalled: "There were problems early in 1967 which demanded immediate attention, and which accounted for much of our time for several months. Nevertheless, we began planning beyond them, establishing objectives, programs and timetables through 1972. Whatever happened in the short run, we had to prove ourselves in the marketplace in the long run."

Chapin's immediate problems were five:

- The company was virtually out of cash and an immediate supplemental bank loan of $20 million was essential.
- Car inventories—company owned and dealer owned—had reached unprecedented levels. The solution to this glut took five months and could be accomplished only by a series of plant shutdowns in January 1967.
- Sales of the Rambler American series had stagnated and inventories were accumulating; a dramatic merchandising move was concocted and implemented in February, dropping the price tag on the American to a position midway between the VW and competitive smaller U.S. compacts, by both cutting the price to dealers and trimming dealer discounts from 21 percent to 17 percent.
- Administrative and commercial expenses were judged too high and thus a vigorous cost reduction program was initiated that trimmed $15 million during the first year. Manufacturing and purchasing costs were also trimmed significantly to approach the most effective levels in the industry.
- The company's public image had deteriorated; the press was pessimistic and much of the financial community had written it off. To counteract this, numerous formal and informal meetings were held with bankers, investment firms, government officials, and the press.

As Chapin recalls "with the immediate fires put out, we could put in place the pieces of a corporate growth plan—a definition of a way of life in the auto industry for American Motors. We felt that our reason for being, which would enable us not just to survive but to grow, lay in bringing a different approach to the auto market—in picking our spots and then being innovative and aggressive." The new corporate growth plan included a dramatic change in the approach to the market to establish a "youth-ful image" for the company (by bringing out new sporty models like the Javelin and by entering the racing field), "changing the product line from one end to the other" by 1972, acquiring Kaiser Jeep (selling the company's non-transportation assets and concentrating on specialized transportation, including Jeep, a company that had lost money in each of the preceding five years, but that Chapin believed could be turned around by substantial cost reductions and economies of scale in manufacturing, purchasing, and administration).

Chapin succeeded: for the year ending September 30, 1971, AMC earned $10.2 million on sales of $1.2 billion.

Recalling the list of general management functions in Table 10.1, which similarities and differences appear salient and important?

## Strategy

Both Chapin and Costle had to establish objectives and priorities and to devise operational plans. In business, "corporate strategy is the pattern of major objectives, purposes, or goals and essential policies and plans for achieving these goals, stated in such a way as to define what business the company is in or is to be in and the kind of company it is or is to be."[16] In reshaping the strategy of AMC and concentrating on particular segments of the transportation market, Chapin had to consult his Board and had to arrange financing. But the control was substantially his.

How much choice did Costle have at EPA as to the "business it is or is to be in" or the kind of agency "it is or is to be"? These major strategic choices emerged from the legislative process which mandated whether he should be in the business of controlling pesticides or toxic substances and if so on what timetable, and occasionally, even what level of particulate per million units he was required to control. The relative role of the President, other members of the Administration (including White House staff, Congressional relations, and other agency heads), the EPA Administrator, Congressional committee chairmen, and external groups in establishing the broad strategy of the agency constitutes an interesting question.

## Managing Internal Components

For both Costle and Chapin, staffing was key. As Donald Rumsfeld has observed "the single, most important task of the chief executive is to select the right people. I've seen terrible organization charts in both government and business that were made to work well by good people. I've seen beautifully charted organizations that didn't work very well because they had the wrong people."[17]

The leeway of the two executives in organizing and staffing were considerably different, however. Chapin closed down plants, moved key managers, hired and fired, virtually at will. As Michael Blumenthal has written about Treasury, "if you wish to make substantive changes, policy changes, and the Department's employees don't like what you're doing, they have ways of frustrating you or stopping you that do not exist in private industry. The main method they have is Congress. If I say I want to shut down a particular unit or transfer the function of one area to another, there are ways of going to Congress and in fact using friends in the Congress to block the move. They can also use the press to try to stop you. If I at Bendix wished to transfer a division from Ann Arbor to Detroit because I figured out that we could save money that way, as long as I could do it decently and carefully, it's of no lasting interest to the press. The press can't stop me. They may write about it in the local paper, but that's about it."[18]

For Costle, the basic structure of the agency was set by law. The labs, their location, and most of their personnel were fixed. Though he could recruit his key subordinates, again restrictions like the conflict of interest law and the prospect of a Senate confirmation fight led

him to drop his first choice for the Assistant Administrator for Research and Development, since he had worked for a major chemical company. While Costle could resort to changes in the process for developing policy or regulations in order to circumvent key office directors whose views he did not share, for example, Eric Stork, the Deputy Assistant Administrator in charge of Mobile Source Air Program, such maneuvers took considerable time, provoked extensive infighting, and delayed significantly the development of Costle's program.

In the direction of personnel and management of the personnel system, Chapin exercised considerable authority. While the United Auto Workers limited his authority over workers, at the management level he assigned people and reassigned responsibility consistent with his general plan. While others may have felt that his decisions to close down particular plants or to drop a particular product were mistaken, they complied. As George Schultz has observed: "One of the first lessons I learned in moving from government to business is that in business you must be very careful when you tell someone who is working for you to do something because the probability is high that he or she will do it."[19]

Costle faced a civil service system designed to prevent spoils as much as to promote productivity. The Civil Service Commission exercised much of the responsibility for the personnel function in his agency. Civil service rules severely restricted his discretion, took long periods to exhaust, and often required complex maneuvering in a specific case to achieve any results. Equal opportunity rules and their administration provided yet another network of procedural and substantive inhibitions. In retrospect, Costle found the civil service system a much larger constraint on his actions and demand on his time than he had anticipated.

In controlling performance, Chapin was able to use measures like profit and market share, to decompose those objectives to subobjectives for lower levels of the organization and to measure the performance of managers of particular models, areas, divisions. Cost accounting rules permitted him to compare plants within AMC and to compare AMC's purchases, production, and even administration with the best practice in the industry.

## Managing External Constituencies

As Chief Executive Officer, Chapin had to deal only with the Board. For Costle, within the executive branch but beyond his agency lay many actors critical to the achievement of his agency's objectives: the President and the White House, Energy, Interior, the Council on Environmental Quality, OMB. Actions each could take, either independently or after a process of consultation in which they disagreed with him, could frustrate his agency's achievement of its assigned mission. Consequently, he spent considerable time building his agency's reputation and capital for interagency disputes.

Dealing with independent external organizations was a necessary and even larger part of Costle's job. Since his agency's mission, strategy, authorizations, and appropriations emerged from the process of legislation, attention to Congressional committees, and Congressmen, and Congressmen's staff, and people who affect Congressmen and Congressional staffers rose to the top of Costle's agenda. In the first year, top level EPA officials appeared over 140 times before some 60 different committees and subcommittees.

Chapin's ability to achieve AMC's objectives could also be affected by independent external organizations: competitors, government (the Clean Air Act that was passed in 1970), consumer groups (recall Ralph Nader), and even suppliers of oil. More than most private managers, Chapin had to deal with the press in attempting to change the image of AMC. Such occasions were primarily at Chapin's initiative, and around events that Chapin's public affairs office orchestrated, for example, the announce-

ment of a new racing car. Chapin also managed a marketing effort to persuade consumers that their tastes could best be satisfied by AMC products.

Costle's work was suffused by the press: in the daily working of the organization, in the perception by key publics of the agency and thus the agency's influence with relevant parties, and even in the setting of the agenda of issues to which the agency had to respond.

For Chapin, the bottom line was profit, market share, and the long-term competitive position of AMC. For Costle, what are the equivalent performance measures? Blumenthal answers by exaggerating the difference between appearance and reality: "At Bendix, it was the reality of the situation that in the end determined whether we succeeded or not. In the crudest sense, this meant the bottom line. You can dress up profits only for so long—if you're not successful, it's going to be clear. In government there is no bottom line, and that is why you can be successful if you appear to be successful—though, of course, appearance is not the only ingredient of success."[20] Rumsfeld says: "In business, you're pretty much judged by results. I don't think the American people judge government officials this way. . . . In government, too often you're measured by how much you seem to care, how hard you seem to try—things that do not necessarily improve the human condition. . . . It's a lot easier for a President to get into something and end up with a few days of good public reaction than it is to follow through, to pursue policies to a point where they have a beneficial effect on human lives."[21] As George Shultz says: "In government and politics, recognition and therefore incentives go to those who formulate policy and maneuver legislative compromise. By sharp contrast, the kudos and incentives in business go to the persons who can get something done. It is execution that counts. Who can get the plant built, who can bring home the sales contract, who can carry out the financing, and so on."[22]

This casual comparison of one public and one private manager suggests what could be done—if the issue of comparisons were pursued systematically, horizontally across organizations and at various levels within organizations. While much can be learned by examining the chief executive officers of organizations, still more promising should be comparisons among the much larger numbers of middle managers. If one compared, for example, a Regional Administrator of EPA and an AMC division chief, or two Comptrollers, or equivalent plant managers, some functions would appear more similar, and other differences would stand out. The major barrier to such comparisons is the lack of cases describing problems and practices of middle-level managers.[23] This should be a high priority in further research.

The differences noted in this comparison, for example, in the personnel area, have already changed with the Civil Service Reform Act of 1978 and the creation of the Senior Executive Service. Significant changes have also occurred in the automobile industry: under current circumstances, the CEO of Chrysler may seem much more like the Administrator of EPA. More precise comparison of different levels of management in both organizations, for example, accounting procedures used by Chapin to cut costs significantly as compared to equivalent procedures for judging the costs of EPA mandated pollution control devices, would be instructive.

## Implications for Research on Public Management

The debate between the assimilators and the differentiators, like the dispute between proponents of convergence and divergence between the U.S. and the Soviet Union reminds me of the old argument about whether the glass is half full or half empty. I conclude that public and private management are at least as different as they are similar, and that the differences are more important than the similarities. From this review of the "state of the art," such as it is, I draw a number of lessons for research on public management. I will try to state them in a way that is both succinct and provocative:

- First, the demand for performance from government and efficiency in government is both real and right. The perception that government's performance lags private business performance is also correct. But the notion that there is any significant body of private management practices and skills that can be transferred directly to public management tasks in a way that produces significant improvements is wrong.
- Second, performance in many public management positions can be improved substantially, perhaps by an order of magnitude. That improvement will come not, however, from massive borrowing of specific private management skills and understandings. Instead, it will come, as it did in the history of private management, from an articulation of the general management function and a self-consciousness about the general public management point of view. The single lesson of private management most instructive to public management is the prospect of substantial improvement through recognition of and consciousness about the public management function.

Alfred Chandler's prize winning study, *The Visible Hand: The Managerial Revolution in American Business*,[24] describes the emergence of professional management in business. Through the 19th century most American businesses were run by individuals who performed management functions but had no self-consciousness about their management responsibilities. With the articulation of the general management perspective and the refinement of general management practices, by the 1920s, American businesses had become competitive in the management function. Individuals capable at management and self-conscious about their management tasks—setting objectives, establishing priorities, and driving the organization to results—entered firms and industries previously run by family entrepreneurs or ordinary employees and brought about dramatic increases in product. Business schools emerged to document better and worse practice, largely through the case method, to suggest improvements, and to refine specific management instruments. Important advances were made in technique. But the great leaps forward in productivity stemmed from the articulation of the general management point of view and the self-consciousness of managers about their function. (Analogously, at a lower level, the articulation of the salesman's role and task, together with the skills and values of salesmanship made it possible for individuals with moderate talents at sales to increase their level of sales tenfold.)

The routes by which people reach general management positions in government do not assure that they will have consciousness or competence in management. As a wise observer of government managers has written, "One of the difficult problems of schools of public affairs is to overcome the old-fashioned belief—still held by many otherwise sophisticated people—that the skills of management are simply the application of 'common sense' by any intelligent and broadly educated person to the management problems which are presented to him. It is demonstrable that many intelligent and broadly educated people who are generally credited with a good deal of 'common sense' make very poor managers. The skills of effective management require a good deal of uncommon sense and uncommon knowledge."[25] I believe that the most significant aspect of the Civil Service Reform Act of 1978 is the creation of the Senior Executive Service: the explicit identification of general managers in government.

The challenge now is to assist people who occupy general management positions in actually becoming general managers.

- Third, careful review of private management rules of thumb that can be adapted to public management contexts will pay off. The 80-20 rule—80 percent of the benefits of most production processes come from the first 20 percent of effort—does have wide application, for example, in EPA efforts to reduce bulk pollutants.

- Fourth, Chandler documents the proposition that the categories and criteria for identifying costs, or calculating present value, or measuring the value added to intermediate products are not "natural." They are invented: creations of intelligence harnessed to operational tasks. While there are some particular accounting categories and rules, for example, for costing intermediate products, that may be directly transferable to public sector problems, the larger lesson is that dedicated attention to specific management functions can, as in the history of business, create for public sector managers accounting categories, and rules, and measures that cannot now be imagined.[26]

- Fifth, it is possible to learn from experience. What skills, attributes, and practices do competent managers exhibit and less successful managers lack? This is an empirical question that can be investigated in a straight-forward manner. As Yogi Berra noted: "You can observe a lot just by watching."

- Sixth, the effort to develop public management as a field of knowledge should start from problems faced by practicing public managers. The preferences of professors for theorizing reflects deep-seated incentives of the academy that can be overcome only by careful institutional design.

In the light of these lessons, I believe one strategy for the development of public management should include:

- *Developing a significant number of cases on public management problems and practices.* Cases should describe typical problems faced by public managers. Cases should attend not only to top-level managers but to middle and lower-level managers. The dearth of cases at this level makes this a high priority for development. Cases should examine both general functions of management and specific organizational tasks, for example, hiring and firing. Public management cases should concentrate on the job of the manager running his unit.
- *Analyzing cases to identify better and worse practice.* Scientists search for "critical experiments." Students of public management should seek to identify "critical experiences" that new public managers could live through vicariously and learn from. Because of the availability of information, academics tend to focus on failures. But teaching people what not to do is not necessarily the best way to help them learn to be *doers.* By analyzing relative successes, it will be possible to extract rules of thumb, crutches, and concepts, for example, Chase's "law": wherever the product of a public organization has not been monitored in a way that ties performance to reward, the introduction of an effective monitoring system will yield a 50 percent improvement in that product in the short run. GAO's handbooks on evaluation techniques and summaries suggest what can be done.
- *Promoting systematic comparative research:* management positions in a single agency over time; similar management positions among several public agencies; public management levels within a single agency; similar management functions, for example, budgeting or management information systems, among agencies; managers across public and private organizations; and even cross-nationally. The data for this comparative research would be produced by the case development effort and would complement the large-scale development of cases on private management that is ongoing.
- *Linking to the training of public managers.* Intellectual development of the field of public management should be tightly linked to the training of public managers, including individuals already in positions of significant responsibility. Successful practice will appear in government, not in the university. University-based documentation of better and worse practice, and refinement of that practice, should start from problems of managers on the line. The intellectual effort required to develop the field of public management and the resources required to support this level of effort are most likely to be assembled if research and training are vitally linked. The new Senior Executive Service presents a major opportunity to do this.

The strategy outlined here is certainly not the only strategy for research in public management. Given the needs for effective public management, I believe that a *major* research effort should be mounted and that it should pursue a number of complementary strategies. Given where we start, I see no danger of over-attention to, or over-investment in the effort required in the immediate future.

Any resemblance between my preferred strategy and that of at least one school of government is not purely coincidental.

## Notes

1. Selma J. Mushkin, Frank H. Sandifer and Sally Familton. *Current Status of Public Management: Research Conducted by or Supported by Federal Agencies* (Public Services Laboratory, Georgetown University, 1978). p. 10.
2. *Ibid.,* p. 11.
3. Though frequently identified as the author who established the complete separation between "policy" and "administration," Woodrow Wilson has in fact been unjustly accused. "It is the object of administrative study to discover, first,

what government can properly and successfully do, and, secondly, how it can do these proper things with the utmost possible efficiency . . ." (Wilson, "The Study of Public Administration," published as an essay in 1888 and reprinted in *Political Science Quarterly,* December 1941, p. 481.) For another statement of the same point, see Brooks Adams, *The Theory of Social Revolutions* (Macmillan, 1913), pp. 207–208.

4. See Dwight Waldo, "Organization Theory: Revisiting the Elephant," *PAR,* (November-December 1978). Reviewing the growing volume of books and articles on organization theory, Waldo notes that "growth in the volume of the literature is not to be equated with growth in knowledge."

5. See *Cases in Public Policy and Management,* Spring 1979 of the Intercollegiate Case Clearing House for a bibliography containing descriptions of 577 cases by 366 individuals from 79 institutions. Current casework builds on and expands earlier efforts of the Inter-University Case Program. See, for example, Harold Stein, ed., *Public Administration and Policy Development: A Case Book* (Harcourt, Brace, and World, 1952), and Edwin A. Bock and Alan K. Campbell, eds., *Case Studies in American Government* (Prentice-Hall, 1962).

6. Luther Gulick and Al Urwick, eds., *Papers in the Science of Public Administration* (Institute of Public Administration, 1937).

7. See, for example, Chester I. Barnard, *The Functions of the Executive* (Harvard University Press, 1938), and Peter F. Drucker, *Management: Tasks, Responsibilities, Practices* (Harper and Row, 1974). Barnard's recognition of human relations added an important dimension neglected in earlier lists.

8. See, for example, "A Businessman in a Political Jungle," *Fortune* (April 1964); "Candid Reflections of a Businessman in Washington," *Fortune* (January 29, 1979); "A Politician Turned Executive," *Fortune* (September 10, 1979); and "The Ambitions Interface," *Harvard Business Review* (November–December 1979) for the views of Romney, Blumenthal, Rumsfeld, and Shultz, respectively.

9. John T. Dunlop, "Public Management," draft of an unpublished paper and proposal, Summer 1979.

10. Hal G. Rainey, Robert W. Backoff, and Charles N. Levine, "Comparing Public and Private Organizations," *Public Administration Review* (March–April 1976).

11. From "American Presidents and Corporate Executives" by Richard E. Neustadt from a paper prepared for a meeting of the National Academy of Public Administration's Panel on Presidential Management, October 7–8, 1979. Reprinted by permission of the American Society for Public Administration, 1120 G Street, N.W., Suite 500, Washington, D.C. 20005.

12. *The Federalist Papers.* No. 51. The word "department" has been translated as "branch," which was its meaning in the original papers.

13. Failure to recognize the fact of distributions has led some observers to leap from one instance of similarity between public and private to general propositions about similarities between public and private institutions or management. See, for example, Michael Murray, "Comparing Public and Private Management: An Exploratory Essay," *Public Administration Review* (July–August 1975).

14. These examples are taken from Bruce Scott, "American Motors Corporation" (Intercollegiate Case Clearing House #9-364-001); Charles B. Weigle with the collaboration of C. Roland Christensen, "American Motors Corporation II" (Intercollegiate Case Clearing House #6-372-350); Thomas R. Hitchner and Jacob Lew under the supervision of Philip B. Heymann and Stephen B. Hitchner, "Douglas Costle and the EPA (A)" (Kennedy School of Government Case #C94-78-216); and Jacob Lew and Stephen B. Hitchner, "Douglas Costle and the EPA (B)" (Kennedy School of Government Case #C96-78-217). For an earlier exploration of a similar comparison, see Joseph Bower, "Effective Public Management," *Harvard Business Review* (March–April 1977).

15. U.S. Government Manual, 1978/1979, 507.

16. Kenneth R. Andrews, *The Concept of Corporate Strategy* (Dow Jones-Irwin, 1971), p. 28.

17. "A Politician-Turned-Executive," *Fortune* (September 10, 1979), p. 92.

18. "Candid Reflections of a Businessman in Washington." *Fortune* (January 29, 1979), p. 39.

19. "The Abrasive Interface," *Harvard Business Review* (November–December 1979), p. 95.

20. *Fortune* (January 29, 1979), p. 36.
21. *Fortune* (September 10, 1979), p. 90.
22. *Harvard Business Review* (November–December 1979), p. 95.
23. The cases developed by Boston University's Public Management Program offer a promising start in this direction.
24. Alfred Chandler, *The Visible Hand: The Managerial Revolution in American Business,* Belknap Press of Harvard University Press, 1977.
25. Rufus Miles, "The Search for Identity of Graduate Schools of Public Affairs," *Public Administration Review* (November 1967).
26. Chandler, *op. cit.,* pp. 277–279.

## READING 10.2

# Introduction

Before going on to the next case study, as normally happens in this text's concept-case methodology, which pairs concepts and cases throughout the book, let's look at one more conceptual approach to public management. Robert D. Behn, a professor of public policy at Duke University, conceives of an alternative, "Management by Groping Along" (MBGA). Whereas the Allison essay explicitly finds that a public manager's role involves, to a greater or lesser extent, elements of "strategy," "managing internal components" as well as "external components," Behn makes a compelling case that:

> An excellent manager has a very good sense of his objectives but lacks a precise idea about how to realize them. Nevertheless, the manager does possess some ideas—some deduced from theory, some adapted from past experiences, some based strictly on hunches—about how to achieve his goals. Unfortunately, neither the general theories nor the specific techniques in any manager's repertoire are derived from situations precisely like the current one. From the numerous "lessons" that the manager has learned from the past, he must not only choose those that appear to be the most appropriate, but he must also adapt them to the unique characteristics of the new task he faces.

In short, Behn says, ". . . good managers grope along. But they grope intelligently. They understand their goal and design their groping to move them towards it." Much of the following essay defines the details of this groping process that Behn sees as the primary way in which public managers manage tasks today and why Behn views it as a superior alternative to other methods of explaining the public management process. Particularly, he compares and contrasts MBGA to "strategic planning" outlined by Graham T. Allison or Charles E. Lindblom's "The Science of Muddling Through" (see Chapter 8) as well as other contemporary managerial approaches such as "management by walking around" (MBWA).

As you study Behn's concept, reflect on such problems as:

How does he define MBGA? What are its key elements?

What are the assumptions behind MBGA? Are these clearly outlined by the author in your view?

What are the key differences among the various managerial models discussed by the author? Why does he conclude that MBGA is superior?

Do you find any dangers or weaknesses in Behn's model? Might it be too subjective? Too personalized and not "generalizable"? Or, "teachable"? Not systematic enough as a managerial approach to ensure effective and efficient performance?

What are the implications of adoption of MBGA by practicing public administrators?

# Management by Groping Along

### ROBERT D. BEHN

When Ira A. Jackson was appointed commissioner of the Massachusetts Department of Revenue in 1983, he knew nothing about the management of tax collection. He was not a tax attorney. There was no book on tax administration from which he could learn the business. Nor did his agency's annual report or transition document provide much help. Observed Jackson:

> Sure, we collected taxes and we had something to do with local services, but no one had ever put into "layese" or into English the mission, purpose, strategy, or meaningful outputs, or performance benchmarks of this agency. If you look at those annual re-

ports, and you see a description of the assessing bureau, you wouldn't have a clue as to what it actually does.[1]

So all Jackson could do was grope his way along.

Immediately after being sworn in, Jackson was given the traditional papers to sign delegating authority to various deputy commissioners and bureau chiefs. (All the authority of the department is assigned, by law, to the commissioner. For the department to function, however, the commissioner must delegate much of that authority to the heads of the various divisions and bureaus.) Jackson decided to sign none. Rather, during his first month, he held long interviews with the individuals to whom he would have to delegate authority. These interviews became Jackson's "management vehicle" to learn about every

From *The Journal of Policy Analysis and Management*, Vol 7, No. 4, Fall 1988. © 1988 by John Wiley & Sons, Inc. Reprinted by permission of John Wiley & Sons, Inc.

manager in his department, about the authority to be delegated, and about what, precisely, his agency did. Only after Jackson had "at least a measure of personal confidence that a person was at least capable of doing the job" did he sign the paper delegating authority to that manager.

The resulting days were "exhausting," and these interviews produced more than Jackson had expected. For, he discovered, "it was the way of controlling the entire agency. It was a way of disciplining me to learn what everybody did." And yet, this process was hardly planned carefully from the beginning, nor were its implications fully understood: "I stumbled on[to] that one. And I was very grateful that I had."

Within the first six months, Jackson and his staff took a series of tough enforcement actions designed to prepare the public for the upcoming tax amnesty period and to increase voluntary compliance. First, the department closed restaurants that were delinquent in turning their meals-tax revenues over to the state. Next, it seized yachts whose owners had registered them in Delaware to avoid the Massachusetts excise tax. Then, it went after airplanes that were similarly registered to avoid Massachusetts' taxes.

Yet at the beginning, Jackson and his key executives did not set forth a comprehensive enforcement strategy or even the sequence of seizures. Rather, they developed their strategy as the department's enforcement people tried things, succeeded with some, and failed with others. Jackson knew what he wanted to accomplish: to improve morale, to increase revenues, and to enhance this agency's reputation as being tough on enforcement. He did not, however, know how to do that. But Jackson and his staff did have a number of ideas—various hunches—about how to accomplish their objectives, and they tried them out to see if they would work. Observed Jackson:

It was gratifying to have those insights. God only knows what we missed and continue to

fail to see. But none of that was apparent. . . . Those ideas are radical and clearly novel in this business. So having arrived at them, we're very grateful to have stumbled upon them. They're fairly obvious abstractly and conceptually, but no one served them up on my plate. I had nobody to plagiarize and no Model-II procedure to follow to do it here or in any other damn state.

The value of a succinct statement of mission to the overall management of a business firm[2] or public agency[3] is widely recognized. Yet, when Jackson took office, the department of revenue had none. So he created one: "honest, firm, and fair revenue collection." Again, this clear, concise statement of mission did not emerge from a single, brilliant insight. Rather, it evolved—just as "the speech" of a political candidate evolves during a campaign: There is a sense of the message to be communicated, but no clear idea of what words will achieve that purpose. Thus the candidate gropes along. He or she tests different ideas before different audiences, gauging the reaction to each; then the candidate tries various combinations and permutations until finally the words and phrases that work best take hold.

This process of creating "the speech" for a political campaign provides not only a model for the creation of Jackson's mission statement for the Department of Revenue. It also provides a useful metaphor—groping along—for describing his overall approach for managing his department.

## Most Managers Grope—A Lot

An excellent manager has a very good sense of his objectives but lacks a precise idea about how to realize them. Nevertheless, the manager does possess some ideas—some deduced from theory, some adapted from past experiences, some based strictly on hunches—about how to achieve his goals. Unfortunately, neither the general theories nor the specific techniques in any manager's repertoire are derived from situations precisely like the current one. From the numerous "lessons" that the manager has learned from the past, he must not only choose those that appear to be most appropriate, but he must also adapt them to the unique characteristics of the new task he faces.

Thus, despite years of experience and study, even the best manager must grope along. He tests different ideas and gauges their results. Then he tries different combinations and permutations of the more productive ideas. Rather than develop a detailed strategy to be followed unswervingly, a good manager establishes a specific direction—a very clear objective—and then gropes his way towards it. He knows where he is trying to go but is not sure how to get there. So he tries numerous things. Some work. Some do not. Some are partially productive and are modified to see if they can be improved. Finally, what works best takes hold. That is "management by groping along."

Some might wish to call it "management through experimentation." Indeed, good managers experiment a lot. But the verb "to experiment" gives the wrong impression. Experimentation suggests a pantological process. It is not "management by the scientific method." It is "management by groping along."

Admittedly, "to grope" is not exactly the right verb either. The dictionary's first definition is "to feel or search about blindly, hesitantly, or uncertainly"—hardly the connotation I wish to convey. The manager is not blind. He can see the top of the mountain way off in the distance. But between the trailhead and the summit there are many trails obscured by trees, ledges, and clouds. Thus he is uncertain about which trail to take—or whether to bushwhack. He knows how to use his compass, but, unfortunately, no one has provided him with an up-to-date map of the region. Still, he can pick out its prominent landmarks, and experience has taught him the subtleties of detecting other critical features. He has, of course,

attempted to pick up the folklore of the mountain from the old timers. But no one has ever climbed this mountain before (and, indeed, many of the old-timers say he is foolish to try). He can hire a guide with experience on similar terrain to keep him from falling into hidden ravines, but he will still have to grope his way towards the top. He will not do this blindly, but it will not be scientific either.

Significantly, the experienced manager will not set off directly for the summit. Rather, he will select a nearby plateau with a good view and set out with his team to conquer it. This achieves several purposes: First, it gets the manager's organization closer to its ultimate goal. Second, achieving this intermediate goal develops the capabilities needed to reach the summit. Third, manager and organization together learn a lot—about how to climb mountains, about themselves as a team, and about what additional capabilities they need. Finally, reaching this first plateau is itself an accomplishment. The climb is hard, but (if the manager picked this initial goal wisely) the view is gorgeous. The summit is still a long way off—obscured in the clouds—but it no longer appears unattainable. Indeed, the naysayers are not as vocal, and some new sponsors and workers have signed on with the expedition.

Karl E. Weick advocates such "a strategy of small wins": A small win is a concrete, complete, implemented outcome of moderate importance. By itself, one small win may seem unimportant. A series of wins at small but significant tasks, however, reveals a pattern that may attract allies, deter opponents, and lower resistance to subsequent proposals. Small wins are controllable opportunities that produce visible results. . . . Once a small win has been accomplished, forces are set in motion that favor another small win.[4]

Weick argues, however, that an optimal sequence of small wins cannot be planned:

Small wins do not combine in a neat, linear, serial form. . . . More common is the circumstance where small wins are scattered and cohere only in the sense that they move in the same general direction. . . . Careful plotting of a series of wins to achieve a major change is impossible, because conditions do not remain constant.[5]

To follow a strategy of small wins, the manager gropes along, from one plateau to the next, building on the lessons from the previous climb. "Small wins provide information that facilitates learning and adaptation," writes Weick; "feedback is immediate and can be used to revise theories." Moreover, each new plateau provides a base for the next assent. "[S]mall wins are stable building blocks," argues Weick. "They preserve gains."[6]

In addition, "the psychology of small wins" reduces the risk of the next assent.[7] Indeed, the next target can be chosen to almost guarantee success. And, even if organization does not reach the next plateau, the failure is not fatal. The previous wins still overwhelm this latest loss.

How the nation's governors describe their own approach to management illustrates the process. "We try a number of things, some work and some don't," observed Governor Lamar Alexander of Tennessee.[8] As governor of Utah, Scott Matheson would talk about his "flounder system:"

Some of my political advisors, particularly those whose academic background is political science or public administration, try to dissuade me from talking about my "flounder system." I'm sure that to them it connotes the process of acting clumsily or ineffectively. To me, it represents the natural struggle of government—to move forward and obtain footing in a constantly changing organizational and political climate.[9]

Good managers grope along. But they grope intelligently. They understand their goal and design their groping to move them towards it. For managers with "a bias for action," Thomas J. Peters and Robert H. Waterman, Jr. offer the slogan, "Ready, Fire, Aim."[10] But that misses the mark. A more meaningful permutation of these three words is "Aim, Fire, Ready." The manager knows his target. Rather than get everything ready for a single, big shot, the manager *aims* in the general direction of the target and *fires* a first round. Then based on what his first shot produces, he *readies* his organization for the next round (modifying the sight, getting a new gun, or moving to a better position), aims, and fires again. Maybe the slogan should be "Aim, Fire, Ready. Aim, Fire, Ready. Aim, Fire, Ready . . ." Or perhaps just MBGA.

## Groping Along Versus Strategic Planning

The concept of management by groping along sounds so idiosyncratic, so unscientific, so unreplicable. It offends us—insulting our intellectual abilities, contradicting our desire to plan carefully for the future, and degrading our yearning to be rational. Strategic planning is an attractive concept, for it suggests that we know where we are going *and* that we have a clear notion of how we are going to get there.

Strategic planning[11] is an effort to make management more systematic—more scientific. Borrowing from the concepts behind the mathematics of dynamic programming,[12] strategic planners work backwards from where they want to be in the future to where they are now; the objective is to develop a policy, an "optimal path," for getting from here to there. Implicit in this thinking is the idea that the manager (together with his strategic planners) can determine such an optimal path from an analysis of the organization's resources, its capabilities, and its political, cultural, and economic environment. You have to be smart to do this—an MBA helps—but it can be done.

Then, once the correct strategic plan is developed, the manager can simply follow it to get precisely where he wants to be.

Ironically, while government is becoming enchanted with strategic planning, business is becoming disillusioned with it. "Strategic planning, as practiced by most American companies, is not working very well," writes Robert H. Hayes. This, he argues, is because American firms, rather than seeking "continual incremental improvements," have a " 'strategic leap' mentality." Comparing international business competition to guerrilla warfare being waged in "a swamp whose topography is constantly changing," Hayes describes American business as "a bunch of hares trained in conventional warfare and equipped with road maps [strategic plans]" while the Japanese and Germans are "a bunch of tortoises that are expert in guerrilla tactics and armed with compasses."[13]

(Hayes's swamp dramatizes, in a way that my mountain does not, that the political, economic, and social environment of both business and government is constantly changing. But the metaphor of warfare, while appropriate for business, is not quite right for government. A business firm seeks to defeat its competitors; a government agency seeks to achieve specific policy goals. Admittedly, the political rhetoric emphasizes climbing mountains—e.g., the "strategic leap" of eradicating poverty— but the real goals are more modest—e.g., finding jobs for some welfare recipients. Thus, a better metaphor for public management might be climbing sand dunes. The topography is changing constantly, and the footing never sure. Yet, the objective is not to defeat others in battle, but to scale some modest but still significant heights.)

At a meeting of corporate and gubernatorial CEOs,[14] Governor John Sununu of New Hampshire argued that it is difficult, impossible, and a mistake to develop a comprehensive plan for the future: "You can overplan. You can go too far in your analysis. You can think you know more about the system than you really do." Long-range planning, said Sununu, creates "long-range commitments" that possess "tremendous inertia, sometimes, in allocating resources." Concluded Sununu:

What you may want to do is create a mechanism that is lean and dynamic and responsive as you go along in order to accommodate the response of the system to changes and inputs that you have either no control over or, in fact, can't identify. You develop a strategy. You develop a system that allows you to respond to changing environments, changing needs and changing times. You cannot lay out, today, the script. But you can build the mechanism that is able to adapt, and respond, and reform, and allocate resources, and focus energies. That's all you can do.

That is, you have to design a system so that you can manage by groping along.

Drawing upon his training in mechanical engineering. Sununu outlined two different ways to analyze and predict the thermodynamic processes of a gas:

If you sit down and try to follow all the little bouncing balls [molecules] in a gas, you can't. But you can draw some gross conclusions from an understanding of the overall system that are extremely simple and tell you a lot about it.

Sununu then compared a thermodynamic system with an economic, social, and political system. It is also impossible, he argued, to analyze and predict the behavior of its individual components, although you can develop an understanding of its overall behavior:

There are people who will waste their time trying to deal with the complexities of trying to get a better understanding who don't understand that it is not just hard, it is impossible to analyze the system that way. . . . The complexities . . . are so difficult that it is a waste of time and resources to design strategies that play with all the dials. . . . You can only build a mechanism that as each year comes along you perturb the policy in a dozen different areas to keep bringing it back to the line that you would like it to follow.

Again drawing upon his engineering background, Sununu used the idea of a simple control system[15] to illustrate the kind of policy mechanism he thought worked best:

It's a little like being in the shower. It gets a little too hot, you turn the cold water on. It gets a little too cold, you turn the hot water on. [You do that] instead of trying to design a system that with one setting of the dials would always deliver exactly the right temperature. That is a very difficult task.

Not that Sununu would eschew planning. "I certainly agree that you need to do strategic planning. The worst thing [however] that you can do with strategic planning is [to] allow" an extrapolation of the past into the future "to be what drives the policy development you are going to make." The data from the past may be absolutely accurate, he acknowledged, but any projections are derived by operating on those data with a set of policies whose trends are extrapolated and "assumes that the system itself has no self- or internal-corrective mechanism." A business executive listening to Sununu noted that corporations are "getting away from the word strategic 'planning' and calling it strategic 'management' . . . for many of the reasons you pointed out, John, strategic 'planning' is a bad word."

## Groping Along Versus Muddling Through

In "The Science of Muddling Through," Charles E. Lindblom argued, both descriptively and prescriptively, that "the method of successive limited comparisons" is superior to "the rational-comprehensive method." True strategic planning is impossible, he wrote, because the necessary "means-ends analysis" could not be done. Lindblom argued that the "limits of human intellectual capacities and on available information set definite limits to man's capacity to be comprehensive." Thus, "every administrator," Lindblom continued, "must find ways drastically to simplify," and to do this, the administrator relies upon a "comparative analysis of incremental changes."[16]

This was also necessary because administrators are "unable" he wrote, "to formulate the relevant values first and then choose among policies to achieve them." Consequently, wrote Lindblom, "one chooses among values and among policies at one and the same time."[17] Public policies are selected, Lindblom emphasized, not by comprehensive analysis but through bargaining between differing interests and different philosophical perspectives.

In Hayes's swamp of business competition, those who are muddling through have no compass nor even any real objective. This month, they might try to stave off an attack; next month, they might build a fortress; still later, after discovering an enemy outpost, they might attack it. With no guiding purpose, they bargain amongst each other for the policy of the moment.

In contrast, those managers who are groping along—not groping *around,* but groping *along*—possess not only a good compass. They also know in which azimuth they are headed. Along the way, they learn some things about the ecology of quagmires, about this particular swamp, about the technology of bateaus, and about navigation. Although groping along, the manager has no trouble explaining the purpose of this knowledge: to help him get where he and his organization are going. Such knowledge may also help the manager modify his azimuth, by clarifying what his objectives should be.

"Muddling through" concerns policy-making—the formulation of policies by analysts, and the bargaining over policies by interests. "Groping around" focuses on public management—the leadership of government agencies.[18] Lindblom is interested in how the Lost Patrol in Crock's desert selects the possible routes that it will consider taking, compares their prospects and pitfalls, and bargains among themselves over which one to try. I am interested in how the Lost Patrol's captain leads it back to Crock's fortress.

Indeed, both strategic planning and muddling through are more about policy-making than management. Both emphasize the choice of a policy rather than the management of one; they seem to imply that once the correct policy is selected—through analysis under strategic planning, or through bargaining under muddling through—that the policy's implementation is a minor exercise. The tasks of motivating people and building organizational capacity are not addressed by the concepts of either strategic planning or muddling through.

## Management by Wandering Around

One of the most important contributions that Peters and Waterman have made to the literature on management is "management by wandering around."[19] "MBWA" is not important because it offers some great, new theory of human or organizational behavior. It is not important because it settles through empirical analysis some fundamental debate among intellectual giants. It is not important by any of the standard criteria of social science. In fact, Peters and Waterman did not even coin the phrase; they learned it from one of their excellent companies, Hewlett Packard. Still, the idea of management by wandering around is important for both its descriptive and prescriptive power.

MBWA describes what managers (at least managers of some successful firms) do with a good portion of their time. As with the work of Mintzberg[20] (and others[21]), it helps us understand what managers really do. Henry Mintzberg told us that the work of a manager is "characterized by brevity, variety, and fragmentation."[22] Peters and Waterman told us that the work of a manager is characterized by a lot of wandering around. Of course, the work of Peters and Waterman does not look or sound as scientific as Mintzberg's. *In Search of Excellence* contains no graphs like Mintzberg's for the "frequency distribution of managerial activities by duration (in hours)" showing that desk work averages 15 minutes in duration, telephone calls 6 minutes, scheduled meetings 68 minutes, unscheduled meetings 12 minutes, and tours 11 minutes.[23] Instead, Peters and Waterman simply report that "the name of the successful game is rich, informal communication."[24]

Nevertheless, there are similarities in the messages. Mintzberg reports: "The job of managing does not develop reflective planners; rather it breeds adaptive information manipulators who refer a stimulus-response milieu."[25] Peters and Waterman write that managers of excellent companies have "a bias for action."[26] The literary style is quite different, but there are important similarities in the two descriptions of what managers do.

The concept of MBWA is also important for its prescriptive value. It tells a manager something he can do to be more successful: Spend time with your customers, your suppliers, and your employees. Find out what they are thinking, what problems they confront, what ideas they have. Praise them; reward them; make them feel wanted, respected, and valued.

The concept of MBWA also implies what managers ought not to do. They should not spend all their time behind their desks, reading and dictating memos, or in meetings with their immediate staff and direct subordinates. Managers need to get information more personally and directly from the people affected by their decisions. They need to convey their ideas more personally and directly to the people upon whom their organization is dependent.

Mintzberg's work is primarily descriptive, though he does offer some prescriptions. The work of Peters and Waterman is primarily prescriptive, though their prescriptions are derived from descriptions of what managers in their "excellent" companies do. These different perspectives appear to lead to somewhat different conclusions. Mintzberg's chief executives spent 59 percent of their time in scheduled meetings, 22 percent on desk work, 10 percent on unscheduled meetings, 6 percent on telephone calls, and 3 percent on tours.[27] One of Mintzberg's "propositions about managerial work characteristics" is "Tours provide the manager with the opportunity to observe activity informally without prearrangement. But the manager spends little of his time in open-ended touring."[28]

Peters and Waterman would argue that Mintzberg's managers do not wander around enough; in fact, Mintzberg reaches a similar conclusion: "The surprising feature about this powerful tool [the tour] is that it was used so infrequently."[29] But Mintzberg's perspective is dominantly descriptive, while Peters and Waterman are unabashedly prescriptive.

As a prescription, management by wandering around is not meant to be taken literally. The manager is not supposed to open the dictionary and discover that the first definition of the verb "to wander" is "to move or go about aimlessly." Rather, the prescriptive value of management by wandering around lies in the host of managerial concepts captured and implied by this phrase. MBWA means that managers need to know what their people—customers, employees, and vendors—are doing and thinking. Peters and Waterman concluded that their excellent companies are "close to the customer," and MBWA is one way to establish and maintain this personal rapport. Manage-

ment by wandering around means paying attention to people, listening to them, praising them. It suggests that people are more important than numbers.

Most management concepts are simple. And, to have any impact, these simple management ideas must be expressible in some pithy phrase. Peters and Waterman were not the first to say that managers do and should wander around. But the wandering that these other researchers describe is more abstract and conceptual, less vivid and physical. MBWA is a contribution because it is clever in its wording and compelling in its symbolism. Management by wandering around is important because these four words capture an entire collection of important managerial ideas.

In government, management by wandering around has not acquired the same status that Peters and Waterman gave it in business. When a public manager travels to a district office, a journalist is apt to call it a "junket." Travel funds are often cut for the simple reason that travel is a nonessential activity. When senators and representatives return to their districts to learn what their "customers" are thinking, they are said to be goofing off. House Speaker Thomas P. O'Neill called congressional recesses "district work days," giving journalists more opportunities to make fun and criticize at the same time. Perhaps O'Neill should have called them management by wandering around.

Three days out of a six-day work week, Governor Booth Gardner of Washington practices management by wandering around. He may get on the bus with some children, ride it to school, and then spend the morning talking with teachers, the principal, and more kids. He may get into a state office building (this being no easy trick if he is asked to give his name) and wander around the corridors talking with state employees. He may visit a local welfare office and ask the social workers about their case loads. And he does this alone. He has discovered that if he takes a state trooper or a staff aide with him, people will talk about the weather. If he goes alone, however, they will tell the governor exactly what is on their mind.[30]

The concept of management by wandering around is important for one more reason. It gives managers who are already wandering around (but who are not sure that they should be) a license to keep doing it. Little in the management literature has suggested that managers *ought* to wander around. Managers do strategic planning. They develop information systems. But wander? MBWA is valuable because it can help managers be more analytical and purposeful about what they already do naturally.

## The Value of the Concept of "Management by Groping Along"

Not only do managers wander. They also grope. Yet MBGA does not offer (any more than MBWA does) some new theory of human or organizational behavior. MBGA does not settle some fundamental, intellectual debate. Nor can the importance of MBGA be ascertained by applying the standard procedures of social science. Nevertheless, the idea of management by groping along is important for both its descriptive and prescriptive power.

MBGA describes what successful managers do with much of their time. While they are wandering around, they are also groping along. Good managers have a very good sense of where they are going—or at least of where they are trying to go. They are constantly looking for ideas about how to get there. They know that they have no monopoly on good ideas about how to accomplish their purposes. Thus, given their bias for action, they spend less time analyzing these ideas than experimenting with them. Analysis can be very helpful at eliminating ideas that are way off target. It is not very helpful, however, in determining

*a priori* which of several good ideas will work best[31] (though it can be helpful *a posteriori* in sorting out which did).

The concept of MBGA is also important for its prescriptive value. It tells managers something they can do to be more successful: Establish a goal and some intermediate targets. Then get some ideas and try them out. Some will work; some will not. See which ideas move you towards your goals. You will never really know which ones are productive until you experiment with them.

MGBA also implies what managers should not do: Do not spend your time attempting to plot out carefully your exact course, with all the details. You can never get it right. In fact, you can be sure that, no matter how smart you are, things will not work out as planned. Murphy lurks everywhere.[32]

As a prescription, management by groping along is not meant to be taken literally; managers are not supposed to "search about blindly." Rather, the prescriptive value of management by groping along lines in the collection of managerial concepts captured and implied by the phrase. MBGA means that managers need a clear sense of their objectives but will necessarily be in the dark about how, precisely, to get there. MBGA means that managers have to try lots of different approaches—indeed, that the only way that they will learn how to realize their objectives is through such experimentation. Finally, MBGA means that managers—especially successful managers—will make errors. Groping means taking risks. Groping means making mistakes.

When any management story is told, the emphasis is on premeditated and purposeful action rather than on any groping.[33] The manager hardly wants to portray himself as merely having stumbled onto success—or even into failure. The chronicler, whether a journalist or scholar, is looking for interesting lessons—lessons that can be found in the manager's intelligent and flawless (or misguided and inept) forecasts, decisions, or actions. How can there be a story if all the manager did was grope along?

Little wonder then that management by groping along is frowned upon—particularly in government. If an idea is so good—and to convince all those who control the numerous checks and balances to let you try anything, you have to oversell the idea as very, very good—why should we merely experiment with it? We ought not to deny anyone the benefits of this wonderful new idea. So we enact legislation (or adopt regulations) to make sure that the idea applies to everyone—tomorrow. If the idea of having some "model cities" in a few urban areas is a good one, every city ought to be a Model City.

That is the "legislator's fallacy": that the idea itself—the policy—is all that matters. Implementation is a mere detail. If the legislature gets the idea right, the tasks of motivating people, designing systems, and building capabilities are trivial. But the bargaining inherent in the legislative process (combined with the lack of human prescience) ensures that the policy never comes out right. The final legislation contains ambiguities, contradictions, unreasonable timetables, and inadequate resources. It is unclear which summit the manager is supposed to climb—or whether he is supposed to dam the valley. Yet given the durability of the delusion that we can separate management from policy, little thought is given to the need for the manager to grope along. The political dynamics of initiating policy ideas is biased against experimentation.

The concept of management by groping along is important for one more reason. It gives managers who sense that they are really just groping along (but who are unwilling to confess this even to themselves) a license to keep on groping. Neither cartoons in *The New Yorker* nor the management literature suggests that managers *ought* to grope along. Managers develop strategic plans. Why? Because they will work. Why else? Who ever heard of a manager who just groped along? Thus, MBGA is

important because it can help some managers be more analytical, purposeful, and unashamed about what they already do naturally.

## Groping as Learning

Jerome G. Miller is a minor legend in some public-management circles for doing something that few other public managers have done: terminate a public program. He closed down, completely and quickly, the juvenile reform schools in Massachusetts. Few people have been so "successful" at terminating a public program, and thus his approach warrants study.[34] Other public managers might learn from studying it. So might have Miller.

When Miller was appointed Massachusetts' commissioner of youth services, he immediately started groping. He did not like the performance of the reform schools. He knew what he wanted to accomplish. He wanted to humanize the care given to juvenile offenders—to replace an authoritarian relationship between staff and youth with a more egalitarian one. He wanted to shift from a "custodial model" of youth services to a "therapeutic community model." But he did not know how to do this. So he groped. He tried to get the institutions to adopt new ideas imported from other states and countries.

To prove to others that his state's system of youth services needed reform, he dramatized to the outside world what was wrong with his agency. When he would visit a newspaper editorial board or appear on a television talk show, he would take along a few of the kids from his institutions. Without any prompting, they would easily and dramatically (and perhaps with some exaggeration) tell the world what life was like inside a reform school. Once, when he was giving the governor's wife a tour of an institution, a riot broke out; the resulting publicity of the brutality used to suppress the uprising gave Miller license to close it. He did so quickly.

After two years of groping along, Miller concluded that it was impossible to turn the state's institutions into therapeutic communities. By this time, he had also convinced the political establishment that drastic changes were necessary. So when Miller decided to close all of the reform schools (sending the kids to privately operated facilities or foster homes, or, when this was not possible, simply sending them home) and announced it, he was able to do it very quickly (within weeks) and without much political fuss.

Shortly thereafter, Miller left Massachusetts (in part because he failed to pay as much attention to internal administrative systems as he had to political communication). He took a similar position in Illinois, and later another similar one in Pennsylvania. In both states, he applied the lesson of his Massachusetts success.

But what lesson had he learned? In Massachusetts, Miller had ben able to close the institutions very quickly. Once he made the decision, implementation was simple. He loaded the kids into cars and drove them away. So in both Illinois and Pennsylvania, Miller again acted quickly. He announced major policy changes. These were followed by major political uproars.

Miller had forgotten about the two years that he, the political leadership of Massachusetts, and the state's citizens spent learning about its reform schools. Miller did not come to Massachusetts as a seasoned youth-services professional. So, when he took the Massachusetts job, he automatically started groping. He tried things and learned from them. Moreover, he did something few public managers would even think of doing. He purposefully opened a lot of this groping to scrutiny by the public and the press. So while Miller was learning, so was the public. When Miller decided to close the Massachusetts reform schools, he had convinced the public that this was at least an acceptable idea. His public groping had changed the issue from "What do we do with these bad kids?" to "What do we do with these bad institutions?"

In Illinois and Pennsylvania, however, Miller never thought of groping. He already knew the answers. In Massachusetts, he had learned that therapeutic communities could not be created in large state-run institutions, and (consequently) that it was necessary to replace them with small, privately operated, community-based facilities. He had also learned how to manage change in government: do it quickly. Miller had already done all his learning and was now ready to apply his lessons to Illinois and Pennsylvania. But he failed to learn from his Massachusetts experience that a good manager is a good teacher, and that he needed political support to implement any major change in government (whether it is done quickly or not).

To be successful in Illinois (or Pennsylvania), Miller needed to grope. Such groping would have educated others—demonstrating to political leaders and citizens who are naturally skeptical of any radical change that less drastic solutions simply would not work. (To someone who had already learned this lesson, such groping for others would have been painfully slow.) But this groping would also have educated Miller himself, for the political and organizational situations he faced in Illinois and Pennsylvania were obviously not identical to those in Massachusetts. Maybe Miller knew everything that there was to know about how to take care of kids convicted of a juvenile offense. But he had a lot to learn about the operation of his new agency and about the subtleties of Illinois politics. So even the second and third times around, Miller would have benefited from some intelligent groping along.

In fact, Jerome Miller may be a managerial archetype—someone who proves to be a big winner in his first job, but who is never able to repeat that success in later assignments. And that may simply be because the first time, recognizing his managerial naiveté, the manager is forced to grope his way along. But from all this groping, he learns a collection of managerial lessons that he applies without much discernment to new (and seemingly very similar) tasks. Even the experienced manager will benefit from groping along.

## Managing ET CHOICES by Groping Along

Twenty years after his original article, Lindblom reemphasized "that neither revolution, nor drastic policy change, nor even carefully planned big steps are ordinarily possible."[35] Nevertheless, in the summer of 1983, the Massachusetts Department of Public Welfare, within months after Charles M. Atkins was appointed commissioner, created an employment and training program, ET CHOICES, to place 40,-000 welfare recipients in jobs over five years. Given that the department had little experience finding jobs for welfare recipients, moving into "the jobs business"[36] can certainly be described as a big step or a policy change. If "incrementalism as a political pattern" is, as Lindblom described it, "change by small steps," ET was certainly not incrementalism. Whether it was a drastic policy change depends on your perspective. Yet for a big step it was not particularly carefully planned. The department had a new goal but did not know how to achieve it.

Actually, the *policy* of ET CHOICES was created by muddling through. Lindblom's "successive-limited comparisons" describes well how the ET policy was developed. Goals were not chosen first and then alternatives analyzed to see which best achieved those goals; rather, the package of placement goals and specific training and job-search alternatives was developed simultaneously. Analysis of the policy and its alternatives was drastically limited; there was neither the time nor resources to examine all options. Yet, the final policy was acceptable to liberal advocates for the welfare recipients and to conservatives in President Reagan's Department of Health and Human Services.

But creating the policy was the easy part. How could Atkins find employment for 40,000 welfare recipients? The Massachusetts Department of Public Welfare is a very large organization. In 1983, it had little expertise in helping welfare recipients find jobs; nor had it exhibited much desire to do so. The department functioned as a bank, and its workers as tellers, determining whether families were eligible for assistance (and, if so, for how much) and then processing the appropriate check.

Atkins had several tasks. He had to create capabilities where few existed; his agency knew little about job counseling, training, or placement for welfare recipients. He had to motivate his line workers—"financial assistance workers"; they were not really social workers—to use these new capabilities effectively. Then, he had to motivate welfare recipients to take advantage of these resources. Finally, he had to convince middle management—the people who ran the local welfare offices—that he was serious about ET.

Atkins knew where he wanted to go but not how to get there. (As Jackson and Miller had no experience managing tax collection or youth services, so Atkins had none managing welfare. He had run training and employment programs for the City of Boston but had avoided welfare recipients who were high-risk clients.) So Atkins started groping along. He established a modest placement goal for the first year and subdivided that annual goal into monthly goals for each local office. Then he personally monitored progress towards those goals and rewarded those offices and managers who met their targets. This convinced people that he was serious about the program and the goals, while helping him understand how to modify his agency's capabilities and the specifics of its placement goals.

The department also undertook a marketing campaign to convince welfare recipients to enroll in job-training and placement programs. But, again, it groped along. Its initial marketing efforts emphasized success stories—women who had, through ET, received training, entered employment, and left welfare. Moreover, the department's various marketing materials stressed the feeling of self-worth that employment had given these women. Yet, except for welfare recipients already enrolled in the program, this marketing message was not inspiring. Many recipients simply could not visualize themselves as making it in the marketplace and rationalized that those who had possessed certain advantages (such as a grandmother to take care of the kids).

Thus, the marketing strategy was changed significantly. Now, success stories are used only in the videocassettes that play in the waiting rooms of many local welfare offices; when a former welfare recipient speaks through a medium that dramatizes that the words are her own, her success can have an impact. The print materials have a very different focus. Some, exploiting the mother's pride in her children, center around a theme of "My Mom and ET"; these try to convince recipients to participate in ET not for themselves but for their kids. Others focus on the nuts and bolts of ET—how the program works.

The history of ET can be divided into policy and management phases. First, a policy establishing both ends and means for ET had to be developed. Through a process of muddling through quickly, this was done in less than four months. Then an organization that would use the available means to achieve the stated ends had to be managed. Through a process of management by groping along, this has taken over four years. Indeed, the process of motivating middle managers and line workers, modifying the annual goals, building organizational capabilities, and marketing the program is still going on.[37]

## Survival, Purpose, and Adaptation

MGBA is a sequential process of adaptation in pursuit of a goal. The manager tries some approaches, achieves some successes, adapts the more successful approaches, and continues to pursue his goal. Indeed, scholars of business management have written profusely on adaptation as strategy.[38]

For business, the focus is on coping with the external environment so as to ensure survival. Indeed, for a firm, it makes sense to analyze its management by emphasizing the goal of survival. For one, it makes empirical sense. The manager is, in fact, attempting to ensure the continued survival of the firm. This is not only in the interest of the top executive; it is also in the interest of the stockholders and the firm's other employees (unless survival requires firing half of them). In addition, the survival of the firm is socially useful. Assuming that the firm is not imposing too many of its costs on others, the continued existence of the firm in a free market proves the value of the firm's products or services. Thus, we want the firm to strive for survival (provided it plays by society's rules for the marketplace).

For public agencies, however, the objective is different. In fact, many such agencies are created precisely because the market will not provide its services efficiently (e.g., national defense or public health). For such government agencies, mere survival is not good enough.

Indeed, neither Jackson, Atkins, nor Miller was motivated by the need to ensure his agency's survival. Before Miller became commissioner, the Department of Youth Services had created a cozy political environment that could have ensured the existence of the training schools for many years. Atkins's Department of Public Welfare could simply have continued to determine eligibility and process checks for AFDC, Food Stamps, and Medicaid. Only Jackson's Department of Revenue, which had been rocked by scandal, was under much attack; and even then, would anyone (save the libertarians) have seriously recommended the elimination of the state's agency that collected its taxes?

Jackson, Atkins, and Miller could practice MBGA—a management strategy of adaptation—because each one had a very specific social vision for his agency. Jackson wanted to improve morale, to create a new image for his department, and to generate more revenues to help solve the state's budgetary problems. Atkins wanted to convert welfare recipients into productive citizens. He wanted his agency to be "running one of the most successful employment programs in the country."[39] Miller wanted to provide more therapy and less punishment for delinquent youths. Each one wanted his agency to become a model for the nation. (Each one of them was also interested in establishing his own professional reputation—Jackson and Atkins as effective managers, Miller for his progressive policies. As in business, such ambition can have positive consequences, provided that the goals and the tactics are both socially acceptable.)

A business executive can have a vision too—indeed, possessing a vision is a characteristic of successful firms.[40] But because it is not constrained to be in a particular line of business, a firm can quickly switch product lines—and its vision. The R. J. Reynolds Tobacco Company can diversify into RJR Industries, and then swallow Nabisco Brands to become RJR/Nabisco. It need not depend upon cigarette consumption; it can become a diversified food-products company.[41] Indeed, Hayes argues that a firm's strategic planning should start not by establishing ends but by creating means:

> First, . . . a company should begin by investing in the development of its capabilities along a broad front. . . . Second, as these capabilities develop and as technological and market opportunities appear, the company should encourage managers well down in the organization to exploit matches [between capabilities and opportunities] wherever they occur. . . . Top management's job, then, is to facilitate this kind of entrepreneurial activity. . . . Do not develop plans and then seek capabilities; instead, build capabilities and then encourage the development of plans for exploiting them.[42]

For a firm concerned with its survival, encouraging the creative use of its existing capabilities makes perfect sense.

For a government agency, however, this kind of entrepreneurship (deriving strategy from capabilities) has limitations. Atkins could take his department into the "jobs business" not only because no one else in Massachusetts was in the business of finding jobs for welfare recipients, but also because this activity fits within the general mandate of his agency. But as commissioner of public welfare, he cannot undertake to clean up pollution in Boston Harbor or acquire the city of Springfield. He cannot even seize the opportunity created by his newly acquired job-training and job-placement capabilities to provide these services in Rhode Island or even to provide these services to the general public in Massachusetts.

Because Jackson, Atkins, and Miller were groping toward very specific policy objectives, their processes of adaptation differed from the one described in the literature on business.[43] They were not just adapting their organizations to changes in their environment. Nor were they merely anticipating environmental changes, prospecting continuously for new market opportunities, or attempting to shape the business environment and forcing their competitors to respond. They were interested in more than survival. They each had a very specific mission—for themselves and for their organization—and they were aggressively groping their way towards it.

## Luck and the Manager's Repertoire

Of course, the survival of organizations or the achievement of goals may have nothing to do with brilliant strategic planning or effective bargaining, or intelligent groping along. It may simply be dumb luck. Herbert Kaufman argues this case directly: "The survival of some organizations for great lengths of time is largely a matter of luck."[44] Similarly, the success of some public managers—not those who ensure survival, but those who achieve goals—may be largely a matter of luck.

Maybe it was not that Miller groped along in Massachusetts but failed to do any groping in Illinois or Pennsylvania; maybe he was simply lucky in Massachusetts and not lucky any place else. After all, Miller knew little about management. Why should we believe that he was so strategically clever? Maybe it is only our retrospective analysis that makes him appear to be so.

But perhaps Miller's intelligence in Massachusetts was derived from his recognition that he knew little about either public management or youth services. In Massachusetts, he had to grope. After a few years, he began to develop his own managerial repertoire—patterns of managerial situations and successful actions that can be recalled and applied to new problems.[45] Yet Miller's repertoire was limited and idiosyncratic. It was based on experiences in only one agency. It was not tempered by the study of other managerial situations. Moreover, the repertoire that Miller stored in his longterm memory contained some serious omissions. He had learned to move quickly, but he failed to learn to move quickly *only after* you have convinced the public and the political elite that a serious problem exists.

By contrast, Atkins did not start off groping because he knew nothing about management or about employment and training. He had held several managerial positions in business and government (including some in the employment and training field). And he had studied public management—at least the managerial strategies of his mentor Gordon Chase. Yet rather than develop a multiyear strategic plan, he started off groping along. He recognized that he knew little about his new agency, about welfare recipients, or about the Massachusetts political environment of 1983. Moreover, he understood that no strategic plan—no matter how brilliant—would bring along his senior staff, middle managers, and line workers. They all had to grope along together, while

Atkins motivated them with a series of small wins.

But Atkins did have a large managerial repertoire—much of it developed during his years with Chase: Establish goals, measure results, and reward performance; report frequently to your political superiors on your activities and accomplishments; keep on top of every major project in your agency.[46] Moreover, Atkins used his entire repertoire. He was groping along, but he was not doing it blindly. He knew where he wanted to go, and he had a very good idea how to get there. Still, he had to grope his way along.

At any one time, a good manager is groping in a number of different directions. The better managers—those with the largest and most applicable repertoires—may begin groping in better directions. But they are still groping. They recognize that they do not know precisely how to proceed, though experience and study makes them better at selecting initial directions.

A more important distinction between good and bad managers may be how quickly they learn from their groping. Managers with larger and more diverse repertoires may recognize better the critical patterns and specific lessons (just as a general with more combat experience will understand better the flow of the battle). Also, recognizing success is relatively simple. The difficult task is to read ambiguous results, to recognize when an initial guess is wrong, and to terminate or modify the undertaking before it becomes a disaster. Good managers often start out groping in the wrong direction. But they recognize a mistake more quickly and act to prevent it from becoming calamity.

## Engineers and Laws, Managers and Principles

An engineer's professional repertoire contains thousands of physical laws. The engineer knows all the major ones and remembers how to look up the minor ones. Which physical laws the engineer uses depends upon the problem he faces. All of the laws are correct. The task is to determine which ones are relevant and how they can be applied to the problem at hand. Thus, the engineer's repertoire contains not just the equations for these laws, but also an understanding of the circumstances under which each law is useful. At the beginning, an engineer never knows how he will solve a problem. He has some guesses derived from his engineering repertoire. But he does not know for sure. So he experiments to see how the physical laws he knows apply to this current situation. The engineer must grope along.

The same is true for management. There are thousands of managerial principles:

- "Stick to the Knitting."[47]
- "The degree to which the opportunity to use power effectively is granted to or withheld from individuals is one operative difference between those companies which stagnate and those which innovate."[48]
- "Giving people a role in shaping decisions secures their commitment."[49]

As with the laws of physics, these principles are both prescriptive and descriptive. For example, $F = ma$ describes the relationship between force, mass, and acceleration; it also prescribes how many newtons of force you need to accelerate at 50 meters per second squared a body with a mass of 50 kilograms. Similarly, "stick to the knitting" describes what excellent companies do and prescribes how to become an excellent company.

Unfortunately, the manager must cope with two complications that the engineer does not have. First, the principles of management are less precise. Mass and acceleration are very well defined. The knitting of a firm is not. Second, the principles of management are often contradictory.[50] Peters and Waterman advocate "simple form, lean staff."[51] But Kanter demurs.

To produce innovation, more complexity is essential; more relationships, more sources of information, more angles on the problem, more ways to pull in human and material resources, more freedom to walk around and across the organization.[52]

So how should the manager use the various principles in his managerial repertoire? Is "stick to the knitting" the principle that most applies to this situation? How narrowly should a firm's knitting be defined? And is there some other managerial principle—such as "be alert to new opportunities"—that points in a contradictory direction?

Which managerial principles the manager applies depends upon the particular problem he faces. All of the management principles are correct. Some are applicable in some situations, some in others. The manager's task is to determine which ones are relevant and how they can be adapted to the problem at hand. At the beginning, a manager never knows how he will solve a problem. He had some guesses derived from the thousands of managerial principles in his repertoire. But he does not know for sure. So he experiments to see how the managerial principles he knows apply to this current situation.

The manager must grope along.

## Notes

The author is grateful to the Ford Foundation for its support of the research on the management of ET CHOICES. The author also thanks Alan Altshuler, Eugene S. Bardach, Herman B. Leonard, and the two ubiquitous (yet anonymous) referees for their helpful comments and criticisms on various drafts of this paper. Neither the Ford Foundation nor any of these individuals are responsible for the failures in this article. But then, again, the author is not responsible for the failure, since 1918, of the Boston Red Sox to win the World Series.

1. This quotation and the accompanying chronicle are from Robert D. Behn, "The Massachusetts Department of Revenue" (a public-management teaching case), the Governors Center at Duke University, 1986.

2. Kenneth R. Andrews, *The Concept of Corporate Strategy* (Homewood, IL: Dow Jones-Irwin, 1971).

3. Robert D. Behn, "Leadership for Cut-Back Management: The Use of Corporate Strategy," *Public Administration Review,* 40(6) (November/December 1980): 613–620.

4. Karl E. Weick, "Small Wins: Redefining the Scale of Social Problems," *American Psychologist,* 39(1) (January 1984): 43.

5. *Ibid.*

6. *Ibid.,* p. 44.

7. *Ibid.,* p. 46.

8. From a seminar at Duke University on April 2, 1986.

9. Scott M. Matheson with James Edwin Kee, *Out of Balance* (Salt Lake City: Peregrine Smith, 1986), p. 225.

10. Thomas J. Peters and Robert H. Waterman, Jr., *In Search of Excellence* (New York: Harper & Row, 1982), pp. 119 and 155.

11. Clark Holloway, *Strategic Planning* (Chicago, Nelson Hall, 1986); *Strategic Planning and Management Handbook* (New York: Van Nostrand Reinhold, 1987).

12. Eric V. Denardo, *Dynamic Programming* (Englewood Cliffs, NJ: Prentice-Hall, 1982).

13. Robert H. Hayes, "Why Strategic Planning Goes Awry," *The New York Times* (April 20, 1986).

14. December 12–13, 1985, Stateline, Nevada.

15. In the terminology of control theory, management by groping along is a closed-loop control system; the feedback loop provides information on the behavior of the system that can be used to correct deviations from the desired path. Comprehensive planning would be an open-loop control system; there exists no feedback loop, and once started the system runs completely on dead reckoning.

16. Charles E. Lindblom, "The Science of Muddling Through," *Public Administration Review,* 19(2) (Spring 1959): 81, 84, 86.

17. *Ibid.,* p. 84.

18. Quinn's "logical incrementalism" has a number of similarities to Lindblom's "muddling through." James Brian Quinn, *Strategies for Change: Logical Incrementalism* (Homewood, IL: Richard D. Irwin, 1980). Quinn is concerned primarily about the formulation of the strategy for a corporation, though there is some attention to the implementation of this strategy. Quinn argues that his business executives consider alternatives that are further from the status quo than do Lindblom's public-policy decision makers, and that they "take a much more proactive approach toward change" (p. 100). But compared with Jackson, Miller, and Atkins, Quinn's managers are extremely cautious. Rather than boldly proclaiming that they are going to collect more taxes, treat kids more humanely, or find jobs for welfare recipients. Quinn's business managers prefer to have others suggest what new goals might be, least they get too publicly identified with new directions that the organization will not accept. See also James Brian Quinn, "Managing Strategies Incrementally," *The International Journal of Management Science,* 10(6) (1982): 613–627.

19. Peters and Waterman, *op. cit.,* p. 122.

20. Henry Mintzberg, *The Nature of Managerial Work* (New York: Harper & Row, 1973).

21. For example, Herbert Kaufman, *The Administrative Behavior of Federal Bureau Chiefs* (Washington, D.C.: Brookings, 1981).

22. Mintzberg, *op. cit.,* p. 31.

23. *Ibid.,* p. 33.

24. Peters and Waterman, p. 124.

25. Mintzberg, p. 5.

26. Peters and Waterman, pp. 13 and 14 and Chapter 5.

27. Mintzberg, p. 39.

28. *Ibid.,* p. 52.

29. *Ibid.,* p. 44.

30. Seminar at Duke University, October 8, 1987.

31. Behn's Fifth Law of Policy Analysis states that analysis is much more helpful in exposing the deficiencies of poor options than in determining which option is truly optimal.

32. Robert D. Behn, "Why Murphy Was Right," *Policy Analysis,* 6(3) (Summer 1980): 361–363.

33. Writes Weick, *op. cit.,* p. 43: "A series of small wins can be gathered into a retrospective summary that imputes a consistent line of development, but this post hoc construction should not be mistaken for orderly implementation."

34. Robert D. Behn, "Closing the Massachusetts Public Training Schools," *Policy Sciences,* 7(2) (June 1976): 151–171.

35. Charles E. Lindblom, "Still Muddling, Not Yet Through," *Public Administration Review,* 39(6) (November/December 1979), p. 517.

36. Charles M. Atkins, "An Open Letter to All De-

partment Staff," *Public Welfare News* (January 1986): p. 2.

37. Robert D. Behn, "Managing Innovation in Welfare, Training and Work; Some Lessons. Lessons from ET CHOICES in Massachusetts," presented at the 1987 annual meeting of the American Political Science Association, September 4, 1987.

38. Herbert A. Simon, Donald W. Smithburg, and Victor A. Thompson, *Public Administration* (New York, Knopf, 1950); Dan E. Schendel and Charles W. Hofer, *Strategic Management: A New View of Business Policy and Planning* (Boston: Little Brown, 1979); and Balaji S. Chakravarthy, "Adaptation: A Promising Metaphor for Strategic Management," *Academy of Management Review*, 7(1) (January 1982): 35–44.

39. Atkins, *op. cit.*

40. Richard T. Pascale and Anthony G. Athos, *The Art of Japanese Management* (New York: Simon and Schuster, 1981).

41. "The Consumer Drives R. J. Reynolds Again," *Business Week*, June 4, 1984, pp. 92–95, 98–99; Scott Scredon and Amy Dunkin, "Why Nabisco & Reynolds Were Made for Each Other," *Business Week*, June 17, 1985, pp. 34–35.

42. Robert H. Hayes, "Strategic Planning—Forward in Reverse?" *Harvard Business Review*, 63(6) (November/December 1985): 118.

43. R. E. Miles and C. C. Snow, *Organizational Strategy, Structure and Process* (New York: McGraw-Hill, 1978).

44. Herbert Kaufman, *Time, Chance and Organizations: Natural Selection in a Perilous Environment* (Chatham, NJ: Chatham House Publishers, 1985, p. 67.)

45. Robert D. Behn, "The Nature of Knowledge about Public Management: Lessons for Research and Teaching from our Knowledge about Chess and Warfare," *Journal of Policy Analysis and Management*, 7(1) (Fall 1987): 200–212.

46. Charles Atkins, "Comments," *Gordon Chase, 1932–1980* (Waltham, MA: Brandeis University, 1981).

47. Peters and Waterman, Chapter 10.

48. Rosabeth Moss Kanter, *The Change Masters* (New York: Simon & Schuster, 1983), p. 18.

49. Kaufman, 1981, p. 82.

50. Herbert A. Simon, "The Proverbs of Administration," *Public Administration Review*, 6(1) (Winter 1946): 53–67.

51. Peters and Waterman, Chapter 11.

52. Kanter, p. 44.

## CASE STUDY 10

# Introduction

One of the most explosive urban events of recent decades occurred in Philadelphia on May 13, 1985, when the Philadelphia police confronted the black activist cult MOVE. As the introduction to the following case, "The MOVE Disaster," recounts:

> After massive gunfire, deluges of water and explosive charges failed to dislodge the group from their fortified row house, police dropped plastic explosives from a helicopter onto a rooftop bunker. The bomb ignited an unexpected fire. Believing they could contain the fire, Police Commissioner Gregore Sambor and Fire Commissioner William Richmond decided to let the bunker burn. They miscalculated badly, and the fire raged out of control. Sweeping through three adjoining blocks, the inferno destroyed 61 homes and left 250 people homeless. Of the occupants of the MOVE house, one adult and one child fled through the flames into police custody. In the ashes were found the bodies of six adults and five children.

What caused this tragedy? Several investigative organizations and other observers attributed much of the blame to ineffective management by the city's mayor, W. Wilson

Goode. Ironically, Goode previously had been viewed as a highly successful mayor, not only by those within the city but throughout the nation. This single event severely damaged his reputation as "an effective manager, a rising star in national politics, and a symbol of hope for his city," according to the author, Jack H. Nagel, a professor of political science and public policy and management at the University of Pennsylvania.

In the following case, Nagel focuses on Goode's managerial behavior related to the MOVE decision and explores the causes of why a previously well-regarded public manager should exhibit such an uncharacteristic breakdown in his performance, bordering on what some viewed as irresponsible behavior. The author first explains the background of MOVE as a controversial activist group within Philadelphia and the two central paradoxes of Mayor Goode's behavior in response to MOVE's actions. Though what makes Nagel's case study especially remarkable and insightful is how the author then goes on to probe beneath the surface of Goode's managerial actions related to MOVE. Nagel analyzes three particular psychological problems that the mayor exhibited and relates these mental difficulties to current theories of the psychology of decision making. From this case, the author generalizes important lessons and implications for public management that relate directly and profoundly to the previous readings by Graham T. Allison, Jr. and Robert E. Behn.

As you review the following case, try to reflect on:

What managerial approach did Mayor Goode first attempt to use in response to MOVE's activities? What misconceptions did he have about MOVE? What were the sources of these misconceptions, in your view?

Do you agree with the author that these misconceptions were ultimately rooted in the mayor's "unresolved decisional conflicts that impeded responsible and rational handling of the problem"? What were these "three decisional conflicts" according to the author? How does Nagel support his argument by drawing on the theory of decision making developed by Irving Janis and Leon Mann? What are the assumptions of the Janis/Mann thesis?

Does this case ultimately support the "uniqueness thesis" of Graham T. Allison, Jr.? Or Behn's "groping along" view of public management? Or does Nagel's story suggest an entirely different understanding of the theory and practice of public management? And what are Nagel's implications for public management?

# The MOVE Disaster

JACK H. NAGEL

On May 13, 1985, a confrontation between Philadelphia police and a cult called MOVE resulted in one of the most astounding debacles in the history of American municipal government. After massive gunfire, deluges of water, and explosive charges failed to dislodge the group from their fortified row house, police dropped plastic explosives from a helicopter onto a rooftop bunker. The bomb ignited an unexpected fire. Believing they could contain the fire, Police Commissioner Gregore Sambor and Fire Commis-

"The MOVE Disaster," (Originally titled "Psychological Obstacles to Administrative Responsibility: Lessons of the MOVE Disaster"), by Jack H. Nagel, *Journal of Policy Analysis and Management*, Vol. 10, No. 1, pp 1–23. © 1991 by John Wiley & Sons, Inc. Reprinted by permission of John Wiley & Sons, Inc.

sioner William Richmond decided to let the bunker burn. They miscalculated badly, and the fire raged out of control. Sweeping through three adjoining blocks, the inferno destroyed 61 homes and left 250 people homeless. Of the occupants of the MOVE house, one adult and one child fled through the flames into police custody. In the ashes were found the bodies of six adults and five children.

The MOVE tragedy severely damaged the reputation of Philadelphia Mayor W. Wilson Goode, who until then had been considered an effective manager, a rising star of national politics, and a symbol of hope for his city. In the aftermath of the disaster, a controversial grand jury decided not to bring criminal charges against the mayor and his chief aides, but condemned them for "morally reprehensible behavior" [Philadelphia Court of Common Pleas, 1988, p. 279]. The Philadelphia Special Investigation Commission (PSIC), appointed by the mayor himself, charged that "the Mayor abdicated his responsibilities as a leader," a condemnation shared by most informed observers.[1] With respect to the twelve values Charles Gilbert [1959] identifies with administrative responsibility, Goode and his key subordinates conspicuously failed to satisfy at least seven—responsiveness, consistency, stability, leadership, competence, efficacy, and prudence.

None of the many commentators ever satisfactorily explained why the previously impressive mayor was so irresponsible in this instance and in particular why his behavior contrasted so sharply with his reputation for hands-on management. Many observers subsequently avoided the incongruity by concluding that Goode had simply been "incompetent" all along. Whereas before MOVE he could do no wrong, after the disaster he seldom got credit for doing anything right. This paper will argue instead that, lamentable though it was, the mayor's performance exemplifies universal tendencies well understood by psychologists of decisionmaking. Analysis of the MOVE case therefore can suggest insights that may enable other administrators to recognize and control situations in which they too might otherwise succumb to irresponsible patterns of action and inaction.

The presentation that follows is organized into five sections: (a) a brief history of MOVE and its conflict with the City of Philadelphia; (b) a description of two central paradoxes in Mayor Goode's response to MOVE; (c) an explanation of both paradoxes using a standard theory about the psychology of decision-

making; (d) a closer examination of three decisional conflicts that may explain why Goode had such difficulty dealing with this particular problem; and (e) reflections on lessons the MOVE disaster offers for the education of present and future public managers.

# Move Versus Philadelphia

The origins of MOVE can be traced to the early 1970s in the Powelton Village section of West Philadelphia, near the campuses of Drexel University and the University of Pennsylvania.[2] In this tolerant community, a haven for political and cultural rebels, a charismatic black handyman named Vincent Leaphart developed an anarchistic, back-to-nature philosophy, the main tenets of which were reverence for all animal life, rejection of "the [American] Lifestyle", and absolute refusal to cooperate with "the System." Aided by a white graduate in social work from Penn named Donald Glassey, who transcribed Leaphart's thoughts and taught them in a course at the Community College of Philadelphia, Leaphart attracted a "family" that eventually numbered at least forty members, most but not all of whom were black. At first they called themselves the American Christian Movement for Life, but they later shortened the name to MOVE. Following the example of Leaphart, who now referred to himself as John Africa, all the core members adopted the surname Africa, in honor of the continent where they believed life began.

As they put John Africa's philosophy into practice, MOVE generated frequent tension with landlords and neighbors, who complained about members' grossly unsanitary practices and their harboring of dogs, cats, rats, roaches, and flies. Beyond these spillovers of their peculiar lifestyle, MOVE members courted friction with authorities by confronting "the System" in all its manifestations, from the Philadelphia Zoo to Jimmy Carter. Using bullhorns to demonstrate and disrupt meetings, they perfected a vituperative rhetoric, profane and filled with sexual and racial provocation. When brought to trial, as they were literally hundreds of times, MOVE members acted as their own attorneys and clogged the courts by noncooperative, contemptuous tactics.

During the 1970s, a virtual feud developed between MOVE and the Philadelphia police. The mayor of Philadelphia was then Frank Rizzo, a former police commissioner famous for tough law enforcement. The majority of whites revered Mayor Rizzo's large and aggressive police department as a bulwark against crime and disorder, but political dissidents, blacks, and journalists accused the police of frequent brutality and disregard for civil liberties. As Anderson and Hevenor [1987, p. 11] observe, "MOVE demonstrators were frequently arrested, often harassed, and nearly always regarded with unconcealed disgust and contempt by Philadelphia policemen. With their unwashed, garlic-reeking bodies, dreadlocks, and inpenetrable and obscene harangues, MOVE people were a constant affront to a police force that was (and is) largely white, ethnic . . . and Catholic."[3]

After a melee in March 1976, when MOVE accused the police of causing the death of a MOVE infant, John Africa apparently decided to turn to armed resistance. By this time, core members of MOVE occupied a house owned by Glassey on North 33rd Street. Using loudspeakers fixed in trees, they frequently harangued their neighbors. Responding to complaints, city officials attempted to investigate code violations but were refused admittance. In September 1975, the city began the protracted process of enforcing the code through the courts. A judgment mandating inspections was obtained in July 1976, whereupon MOVE constructed an eight-foot stockage around their compound. Heeding MOVE warnings that they would "cycle" (kill) their own children before submitting to inspections, the city refrained from enforcing the order. On May 20, 1977, mistakenly anticipating a city attempt to enter the premises, MOVE members brandished guns on the platform of their stockade. Shortly afterwards, Donald Glassey was arrested for filing false information when purchasing firearms. Turning informant to save himself, Glassey helped police seize MOVE guns and explosives at a location elsewhere in Philadelphia.

The stalemate in Powelton continued for nearly a year. On March 1, 1978, the city obtained court permission to blockade the MOVE headquarters for nonpayment of utility bills and refusal to admit inspectors. Police cordoned off a four-block area around the house and shut off gas and water. The siege appeared to have succeeded when intermediaries helped negotiate a settlement that was announced on May 3. MOVE surrendered weapons, allowed officials to inspect the Powelton property, and promised to vacate the house by August 1. In return, the city relaxed its blockade, freed eighteen jailed MOVE members on

their own recognizance, and promised to drop all charges once MOVE departed from Powelton.

When August 1 came, MOVE refused to leave, because no one had found a site for relocation they would accept. On August 8, Police Commissioner Joseph O'Neill directed a carefully planned operation to drive the occupants from the house. Announcing each action in advance in order to protect MOVE women and children, whom they regarded as hostages, the police used a bulldozer, ram, and armored truck to breach the walls of the compound. A crane began demolishing the upper stories. Believing that all MOVE weapons had been confiscated in May, authorities were careless about concealing themselves. Suddenly, police saw a gun muzzle protruding from a basement window. After deluge guns flooded the basement, gunfire erupted, killing Officer James Ramp and wounding eight other policemen and firefighters. Following the exchange of shots, police poured in more water and smoke to flush out the occupants. As the MOVE members surrendered, officers beat and kicked Delbert Africa while news photographers recorded the action.

During the next five years, MOVE was visible to most Philadelphians only through a series of trials. In 1980, nine members were sentenced to lengthy prison terms for the murder of Officer Ramp; a tenth followed in 1982. In 1981, three police officers were tried for the beating of Delbert Africa and acquitted.[4] On May 13, 1981, Federal agents arrested John Africa and eight followers in Rochester, New York, where MOVE had owned houses since 1977. (At various times, MOVE also had enclaves in Richmond, Virginia, and Chester, Pennsylvania.) Defending himself and Alphonso Robbins Africa against bombmaking charges, John Africa won acquittal from a jury in Philadelphia in July 1981, after which he dropped out of sight.

As it turned out, the MOVE leader had not gone far. With a group of about a dozen adults and children, he was living in a house owned by his sister, Louise James, at 6221 Osage Avenue in the Cobbs Creek section on the western edge of Philadelphia, three miles from the site of the demolished house in Powelton.

Whereas the 33rd Street house had been a freestanding structure surrounded by a yard and located on a busy street, the new MOVE headquarters was a row house on a narrow, quiet residential street. These physical differences were to prove tactically important during the 1985 confrontation, but events in the two years preceding that catastrophe pivoted around social and political differences between the two neighborhoods. Nonconformist, racially mixed Powelton was a bastion of opposition to Mayor Rizzo. Its residents divided bitterly over whether the cultists or the police were the more distasteful presence in their midst. One can easily imagine Frank Rizzo enjoying some amusement at their discomfort.

In 1980, barred by the City Charter from serving three consecutive terms, Rizzo was succeeded as mayor by the more liberal former Congressman, William J. Green, Jr. Fulfilling a compaign promise to Philadelphia's increasingly powerful black voters, Green appointed W. Wilson Goode as Managing Director, the city's chief appointive official. Goode, a former civil-rights activist, had previously served as executive director of the nonprofit Philadelphia Council for Community Advancement—where he was credited with building more housing than all the city's housing agencies combined [Cohn, 1982, p. 27]—and as chair of the Pennsylvania Public Utilities Commission. As Managing Director, Goode was in charge of ten operating departments, including police and fire. Hard-working, accessible, and highly visible, he soon became hugely popular among blacks and many whites as well. When Green announced in late 1982 that he would not seek a second term, Goode resigned to campaign for the mayoralty. In May 1983, he defeated Frank Rizzo in the Democratic primary, winning the votes of 98% of blacks and 23% of whites. In the November general election, he would face two white opponents.

The Cobbs Creek neighborhood was typical of Wilson Goode's bedrock political base. Its residents, almost all black, were generally stable working- and middle-class families. Most owned their homes and took pride in keeping them pleasant and attractive. By the fall of 1983, MOVE had become an intolerable affliction to this peaceful community. The home of Lloyd and Lucretia Wilson next door was invaded by insects that had spread from 6221. When the Wilsons sought to fumigate, Conrad Africa went berserk. "The bugs are our brothers and sisters. If you exterminate the bugs, you exterminate us," he berated Lloyd Wilson [PSIC, 1985, 10/9 AM, pp. 89–90]. In September 1983, following a dispute over a parking space, a MOVE male struck a neighbor named Butch Marshall to the ground, and three MOVE women bit Marshall on the face, back, and groin. After another assault in

October, the neighbors circulated to city authorities a petition that complained about attacks, garbage, rats, a pigeon coop, animals, and MOVE's blocking of a common driveway behind the row.

As the neighbors "were reaching the breaking point," they met with State Representative Peter Truman.[5] Truman implored them not to do anything that would endanger the election of the city's first black mayor. If they would endure a few months longer, he assured them, Goode would solve their problem. Aided by the arrival of cold weather, which lessened health hazards and reduced outdoor interaction with MOVE, the neighbors waited. In November 1983, Goode won a resounding victory with 55% of the vote.

If Goode's triumph held promise of deliverance for the 6200 block, John Africa saw it as a different sort of opportunity, one that would produce intensified torment for the Osage neighbors. Obsessed with freeing his followers from prison, the MOVE leader believed that the mayor had the power to obtain their release and that the residents of Osage Avenue could persuade him to use that power. MOVE therefore embarked upon a campaign of what Goode later would call "psychological warfare" against their neighbors, holding the block "hostage" in order to obtain as ransom the release of their ten convicted comrades. MOVE launched their campaign on Christmas morning, 1983. Beginning near dawn and continuing for eight hours, their rooftop loudspeakers blared an obscene diatribe that denounced the neighbors, the mayor-elect, and the System, and demanded freedom for MOVE prisoners. Eight days later, Wilson Goode became mayor of Philadelphia.

## Two Paradoxes

Mayor Goode's response to MOVE's challenge can be characterized by describing two patterns, both of which seem paradoxical. First, for sixteen months he avoided any significant action; but when he finally decided to enforce the law, the city mobilized against MOVE in less than a week and tried to execute a hastily prepared plan in the span of twenty-four hours. Second, although he was widely perceived to be an energetic, detail-oriented administrator, when he decided the city should act against MOVE, Goode had minimal personal involvement in both the planning and the execution of the attack.

## Delay Followed by Haste

MOVE's war against the System, by way of their neighbors, continued through 1984 and the spring of 1985. In December 1983, they began fortifying their house by nailing boards across the windows; the ramshackle effect contrasted starkly with the neat white trim and porches of the other houses. In October 1984 they started a rooftop construction that eventually became a bunker made of railroad ties, logs, and steel plates. Similar materials were placed against the interior walls of the house and basement. In May 1984, a hooded MOVE member brandished a shotgun on the roof, and the cultists began the practice of running across the roofs of the row at night, waking frightened residents. Loudspeaker harangues were conducted daily for six to eight hours through the summer and fall of 1984. In these and other communications, MOVE members threatened the lives of President Reagan, Mayor Goode, judges, and any police officers who might try to enforce the law on Osage Avenue. A favorite tactic was to target a particular neighbor for a day, during which the unfortunate individual would be subjected to personal attacks filled with accusations of homosexuality, child molestation, promiscuity, or sexual inadequacy. As Bennie Swans of the Crisis Intervention Network later commented, "MOVE did not let up on those residents. They simply did not let up" [PSIC, 1985, 10/9 AM, p. 68].

Mayor Goode was aware of most of these developments. On March 9, 1984, Commissioner Sambor briefed him about the deteriorating situation on Osage Avenue. On May 28 and July 4, he met at their request with delegations of residents; they found the mayor knowledgeable about their plight and personally familiar with MOVE members, but unwilling to act. In June 1984, District Attorney Edward Rendell provided Goode with a memo outlining a legal strategy for disarming MOVE and abating the nuisance on Osage Avenue. Goode also received several phone calls from block captain Clifford Bond. On August 9, Lloyd Wilson came to City Hall to complain of an assault he had suffered the day before at the hands of Frank James Africa, while police officers watched from the corner. Goode "whisked" Wilson off to a side office, where he had a lengthy but unproductive conversation with Managing Director Leo Brooks and Commissioner Sambor. Subsequently, Wilson and his family abandoned their home, driven out by vermin,

noise, and fear from which their government would not protect them.

During this time, city policy barred operating departments (including Health, Water, Human Services, Streets, and Licenses and Inspections) from carrying out their responsibilities with respect to MOVE, which they were told was "a police matter." For their part, the police maintained surveillance of the 6200 block, but refrained from intervention. They even discouraged state parole officials from serving outstanding fugitive warrants against two residents of the house, Frank James Africa and Larry Howard [Philadelphia Court of Common Pleas, 1988, p. 26]. In response to the neighbors' entreaties, Goode took only two tangible actions: He extended the hours of nearby city recreation centers so residents' children could escape the loudspeakers, and he arranged psychological counseling to help the children cope with chronic tension.

Five of the MOVE Commission's findings describe and condemn this protracted phase of inaction:

3. Mayor Goode's policy toward MOVE was one of appeasement, non-confrontation, and avoidance.
4. The Managing Director and the city's department heads failed to take any effective action on their own and, in fact, ordered their subordinates to refrain from taking action to deal meaningfully with the problem on Osage Avenue. . . .
6. In the first several months of his administration, the mayor was presented with compelling evidence that his policy of appeasement, non-confrontation, and avoidance was doomed to fail.
7. In the summer of 1984, the mayor was told that the legal basis existed at that time to act against certain MOVE members. Yet, the mayor held back, and continued to follow his policy of avoidance and non-confrontation.
8. From the fall of 1984 to the spring of 1985, the city's policy of appeasement conceded to the residents of 6221 Osage Ave. the continued right to exist above the law. [PSIC, 1986, pp. 11–13]

To this indictment should be added two more charges. First, by tolerating MOVE's abuses, the city government for two years abdicated its most basic responsibilities to the law-abiding residents of Osage Avenue. As Clifford Bond put it, "I was placed in a position of feeling not as a citizen" [PSIC, 1985, 10/9 AM, p. 4]. Second, by giving MOVE time to fortify their house, the policy of nonconfrontation made the task of dislodging the cult immensely more difficult when the mayor finally decided to act.

Sixteen months of delay abruptly gave way to fourteen days of hasty action in the spring of 1985. The shift in policy was precipitated by the neighbors. Unwilling to accept another summer of stench and harangues, they organized themselves as the United Residents of the 6200 Block of Osage Avenue and held a public protest meeting on April 25, during which several men announced they would respond to MOVE "in kind." At a May 1 press conference, the United Residents expressed their disgust with the city's inaction and requested intervention by Pennsylvania Governor Dick Thornburgh, a Republican. Coupled with new provocations by MOVE, these actions got the attention of the media, and editorialists demanded that the city meet its responsibilities.

On May 3, Mayor Goode convened a high-level meeting at which he asked District Attorney Edward Rendell to establish a legal basis for city action against the occupants of 6221. On May 5 Rendell's staff interviewed Osage residents in order to prepare warrants. At a second high-level meeting on May 7, Goode directed Commissioner Sambor to develop a plan that was to be carried out under the supervision of Managing Director Leo Brooks, a former Army major general.

Having anticipated action, Sambor had set up a planning group a week earlier. Remarkably low in rank for such a major operation, it consisted of three men who had served under Sambor in his previous post as commander of the Police Academy: Lieutenant Frank Powell, head of the Bomb Disposal Unit; Sergeant Albert Revel, a pistol instructor; and Officer Michael Tursi, the Department's top sharpshooter.

On May 9, with Managing Director Brooks at his daughter's graduation in Virginia, Sambor briefed Goode on the plan the three officers had devised. He recommended that warrants be served on Sunday, May 12, which was Mother's Day. Out of concern for the holiday, Goode authorized Sambor to proceed on May 13. On May 11, a judge issued the warrants, and Sambor again briefed Goode. On the afternoon of May 12, police evacuated the neighborhood. Returning from Virginia that evening, Brooks heard on his car radio that the operation he was to head was underway. He arrived in Philadelphia in time to get a quick briefing from Sambor followed by a few hours' sleep.

At 5:35 a.m. on Monday, May 13, Sambor read an ultimatun to MOVE over a bullhorn, demanding that the four MOVE members named on the warrants surrender within fifteen minutes. MOVE used their own loudspeaker to reject the ultimatum in typical style, telling the police that their wives would be collecting insurance and sleeping with black men that night. When the fifteen minutes had expired, authorities directed water, tear gas, and smoke at the house and its roof. According to the police, MOVE responded with gunfire, and officers retaliated massively, firing many thousands of rounds in the next ninety minutes. The debacle was underway.

As the MOVE Commission and the grand jury pointed out, less hurried planning and execution might have prevented numerous errors and oversights. A full list would occupy many pages, so I shall mention just a few of the more egregious consequences of haste:

- Commissioner Sambor and his planners made little attempt to draw on the resources of other agencies, inside or outside the city government; consequently, they failed to consider alternative strategies and deprived themselves of expertise—such as the use of trained hostage negotiators—that might have resulted in better implementation of their plan.
- Goode, Sambor, and Brooks went ahead with the operation even though they knew that the mayor's directive to pick up the MOVE children before the assault had not been implemented. (MOVE adults usually took the children on daily outings to nearby Cobbs Creek Park, and as late as May 12, two of the children were observed outside the house.) Thus they "clearly risked the lives" of six innocent children, five of whom subsequently died in the conflagration [PSIC, 1986, p. 16].
- The quick, secretive, informal planning process deprived the tacticians of crucial knowledge possessed by others in city government, including surveillance officers. As a result, to take just one example, they did not appreciate the extent of the interior fortifications that foiled their initial strategy of attempting to insert tear gas through the walls.
- Contingency plans were not developed; the final, fatal decision to drop the bomb was the result of ill-considered improvisation. After the primary plan failed, officials were apparently determined

to occupy the house before dark. When Brooks informed Goode of the bomb proposal by telephone at 5 p.m., the mayor paused only thirty seconds before approving the idea.

- Insufficient attention was given to communication systems, resulting in slow, incompatible, or nonexistent communication channels between crucial actors—police and the occupants of the MOVE house, police and fire units, the mayor and managing director, and the managing director and police commissioner. Slow communications may have prevented Goode and Brooks from reversing in time Sambor's and Richmond's decision to let the bunker burn.

## Arms-Length Action by a Hands-on Mayor

Until May 1985, both as Managing Director and as Mayor, Wilson Goode was perceived by the public as an incredibly hard-working, demanding, detail-oriented manager. Contemporary press descriptions give a vivid sense of his style: "He appears to be everywhere. . . . He annoys a lot of people because he continues to ask questions until he gets an answer that makes sense."[6] "He loves to come down hard on details" [Mallowe, 1980, p. 139]. "His zeal is prodigious, his double-digit days are legend . . ." [Javers, 1983]. "Today, in Philadelphia, in the first year of Wilson Goode's first term of office, there is absolutely no doubt about *who* is in charge" [Mallowe, 1984, p. 168]. Indeed, one of the few criticisms of Goode in this happy period was that he delegated too little: "He seeks near-absolute control over his operating departments" [Cohn, p. 21]. "He has an aversion to delegating authority. He tries to do too much on his own" [Mallowe, 1984, p. 226].

Goode's view of himself corresponded to the public image: "I want to know what the problems are in this city. . . . I can't do that sitting on the 16th floor here, I really can't" [Cohn, 1982, pp. 13]. "*Someone* has to be in charge. People through the government must know that the mayor is there giving directions . . ." [Mallowe, 1984, p. 168]. "I'm a nuts-and-bolts person" [Mallowe, 1980, p. 139]. Perhaps his favorite term was "hands-on."

However, after he authorized an armed confrontation with MOVE, Goode was anything but hands-on. He held only two high-level meetings to plan the operation. The May 7 meeting focused on the legal

basis for action, and the May 9 meeting lasted less than thirty minutes. On both occasions, Goode prevented detailed discussion of the police plan. The contrast in styles was pointed out to the MOVE Commission by District Attorney Rendell:

And I turned to the [Police] Commissioner and I said, "Are you going to use tear gas and water?" And he said yes and started to explain a little bit, and the Mayor said . . . , "Look, I will leave that up to you all. It's your plan and execute it." In other words, he cut off discussion. . . .
And I thought it was somewhat unusual. . . . I had known Wilson for the three years that he was Managing Director. I worked very closely with him . . . , and then while he was Mayor I had significant contact with him. Wilson's management style has always been one where he got involved in all—not in all of the details, but in certainly the significant details. And I thought that was . . . a little out of character. . . . [PSIC, 1985, 10/22 AM, pp. 71–72]

Rendell speculated that Goode wished to avoid leaks, that perhaps he "intended as soon as I walked out of the room to sit down and go over it blow by blow with the Police Commissioner" [PSIC, 1984, 10/22 AM, p. 95]. In fact, Sambor did brief Goode about the plan on May 11, but only because Brooks was out of town—at all other times, including May 13, Goode and Sambor strictly followed the chain of command, communicating with each other only through Brooks. Goode seems not to have been deeply engaged in the May 11 meeting, for he recalled it as occurring over the telephone, whereas Sambor testified in detail that he went to Goode's office. Goode's last briefing was by telephone on the evening of May 12, when Brooks called him to relay the discussion he had just had with the Police Commissioner.

On May 13 itself, Goode heeded the advise of his staff and Brooks by staying away not only from Osage Avenue, but also from Brooks' command post four blocks north at the Walnut Park Plaza, the tallest structure in the area. As the operation began, Goode followed developments together with four black elected officials whom he had invited to his home in Overbrook, about two miles from Osage Avenue. Later, in his office at City Hall, he was understandably preoccupied with MOVE. Although the mayor frequently conferred by phone with Brooks, Goode's distance from the scene and the clumsiness of his communication links prevented him from exercising effective control over the terrible events of that day.

In short, as the MOVE Commission concluded, "The mayor failed to perform his responsibility as the city's chief executive by not actively participating in the preparation, review and oversight of theplan" [PSIC, 1986, p. 16].

## Irresponsibility and Decisional Conflict

In 1977, eight years before the MOVE disaster, the psychologists Irving Janis and Leon Mann published a treatise called *Decision Making.*[7] In it, they outlined a model based on psychological conflict that economically explains the two central paradoxes in Wilson Goode's actions, as well as many otherwise puzzling subsidiary aspects of his behavior during this tragic episode.

Janis and Mann premise their theory on the idea that decisionmaking is not merely a cool intellectual process but also involves "hot" emotional influences. The need to make a decision is inherently stressful. Although moderate anxiety improves cognitive functioning, excessive stress can severely impair the quality of decision processes. The greatest stress occurs when all known options threaten to impose severe losses, especially if those losses are not merely "utilitarian" but include "highly ego-involving issues," such as severe social disapproval and/or self-disapproval [Janis and Mann, 1977, p. 46].

When a decision maker is faced with an emotionally consequential, no-win choice, how he or she copes with the problem depends crucially on two factors—hope and time. If the decision maker sees realistic hope of finding a solution superior to any of the risky options that are immediately apparent, then that person's efforts are likely to follow the desirable pattern Janis and Mann call *vigilance*, which is close kin to the familiar rational-comprehensive ideal. The vigilant decision maker canvasses a wide set of alternatives; considers the full range of goals and values involved; carefully weighs costs, risks, and benefits; intensively seeks and accurately assimilates new information; reexamines all alternatives before settling on a final choice; makes detailed provisions for implementing the chosen course; and devotes special attention to contingency plans [Janis and Mann, 1977, p. 11].

If, however, a decision maker loses hope of finding an acceptable option, he or she is likely to fall into either of two patterns of seriously defective search and appraisal. The first and more common syndrome, called *defensive avoidance*, typically occurs when there is no overwhelming pressure to change the existing policy even though its consequences are (like those of all other alternatives) highly unfavorable. The chief symptoms of defensive avoidance are procrastination, passing the buck and other ways of denying personal responsibility, and bolstering [Janis, 1989, p. 80]. "Bolstering" is a process of cognitive distortion in which one "spreads" or exaggerates the value of the chosen course compared to alternatives by avoiding exposure to disturbing information, selective attention and recall, wishful thinking, oversimplification, rationalization, and denial.

Defensive avoidance "satisfies a powerful emotional need—to avoid anticipatory fear, shame, and guilt" [Janis and Mann, 1977, p. 85]. Its emotional benefit is a state of "pseudocalm," resulting from the decision maker's suppression of troubling thoughts and avoidance of stimuli that might evoke the painful dilemma.

When external pressures impose a deadline or threaten an imminent disaster if the existing policy is maintained, the state of pseudocalm is shattered and the underlying conflict breaks through to the surface, arousing unbearable emotional stress. In such circumstances, the decision maker is likely to respond with the pattern of behavior Janis and Mann call *hypervigilance.*[8] Responding to "the strong desire to take action in order to alleviate emotional tension," the hypervigilant decision maker "superficially scans the most obvious alternatives open to him . . . , hastily choosing the first one that seems to hold the promise of escaping the worst danger" [Janis and Mann, 1977, pp. 47, 74]. Like defensive avoidance, hypervigilance involves severely defective search and appraisal:

A person in this state experiences so much cognitive constriction and perseveration that his thought processes are disrupted. The person's immediate memory span is reduced and his thinking becomes more simplistic. . . . [T]he person in a state of hypervigilance fails to recognize all the alternatives open to him and fails to use whatever remaining time is available to evaluate adequately those alternatives of which he is aware. He is likely to search frantically for a solution, persevere in his thinking about a limited number of alternatives, and then latch onto a hastily contrived solution that seems to promise immediate relief, often at the cost of considerable postdecisional regret. [Janis and Mann, 1977, p. 51]

An explanation for the first paradox of Wilson Goode's behavior toward MOVE should now be obvious. His delay/haste pattern is a textbook example of defensive avoidance followed by hypervigilance. The two stages are not really paradoxical, because they resulted from the same underlying decisional conflict. As Janis and Mann [1977, p. 66] observe, a "person's defensive avoidance pattern might abruptly change to hypervigilance if he encounters a new, dramatic danger signal." The mobilization of the Osage neighbors signaled to Goode that a continued policy of nonconfrontation would be fraught with new, unacceptable dangers—a certainty of severe political embarrassment and a high probability of unofficial violence against MOVE. The mayor was forced to act, and in his state of hypervigilance, he accepted the first option presented to him—the ill-fated proposal devised by Sambor's planners.

But why was the MOVE problem in particular so difficult for Wilson Goode to handle, when he had been able to deal effectively with many other issues in a distinguished career of public service? Janis and Mann [1977, p. 75] contend that both vigilant and defective patterns of problem solving are within the repertoire of every decision maker. Anyone, they believe, can fluctuate from one pattern to another depending not only on the objective circumstances of action, but also on the relation of those circumstances to personal values and affiliations, which determine whether actions and outcomes will be conductive to self-esteem and social approval for a particular individual. To explain the second paradox, it will therefore be necessary to look more closely at Wilson Goode, as well as at the finer details of his decision processes with respect to MOVE.

## The Mayor's Decisional Conflicts

Goode's testimony to the MOVE Commission, coupled with other evidence about his personality and values, suggests that the drama on Osage Avenue aroused within the mayor severe conflicts that he was never able to resolve. Instead, he in effect fled from them, with the result that he virtually abdicated his responsibility as the city's chief administrator.[9] The mayor's conflicts may be summarized as three dilemmas: (1) MOVE's intransigence and irrationality appeared to necessitate the use of force that would almost surely end in bloodshed, but Goode saw himself as a peacemaker and a preserver of life; (2) to enforce the law against MOVE would require the mayor to depend on the Philadelphia Police Department, but the police might well be unreliable, among other reasons because his own relationship with them was uneasy and because many of them hated MOVE; (3) as a black committed to a policy of respecting civil rights, Goode felt dissonance about authorizing official coercion of a black group; but MOVE's bizarre behavior must also have aroused in him anger that he would have difficulty acknowledging, given his religious values and self-image as a controlled person.

## Blood on the Hands of a Peacemaker

At first glance, Goode's desire to avoid action against MOVE appears readily understandable. In retrospect, everyone saw Osage Avenue as a no-win situation. If the city refrained from confronting MOVE, the cultists would make life intolerable for their neighbors. If the city attempted to enforce the laws, MOVE would respond violently, producing a high probability of death. District Attorney Rendell described the effect of this realization on the emotions of participants in the crucial meeting:

I have attended a lot of meetings since I have been in public life, but I never ever had attended a meeting that had the impact on me that my meeting on Thursday, May 7, 1985 did, when in fact the plan of action was signed, sealed and delivered; when the arrest warrants and the search warrants were approved, signed by a judge; when we had picked a time and date to act; when we knew it was going to occur. There was almost a dread in that room so thick that you could have cut it with a knife. Because, understand, every one of us in that room knew that someone—there was an extraordinarily high likelihood that someone was going to die. [PSIC, 1985, 10/22 AM, p. 34]

Nevertheless, to some politicians the MOVE problem might have seemed a golden opportunity. Throughout history, leaders have won popularity by unleashing violence against unpopular enemies, foreign or domestic. By 1985, MOVE had alienated virtually everyone in Philadelphia. Confronting them would have cost Goode little if any support among his black political base, because the neighbors who were pleading for relief were not only black but also representative of his most reliable constituency. MOVE instead offered Goode an excellent chance to broaden his already impressive popularity, because forceful action against them in the name of law and order would have appealed most to those whites who were not yet part of his coalition.

Goode himself noted the political value of decisive leadership. Asked at the MOVE Commission hearings whether his staff's advice that he stay away from the scene of action was "substantive or political or both," he replied:

> I thought it was substantive. I don't think that it . . . had anything to do with politics. From my vantage point, both in foresight and hindsight, . . . it is far better for a Mayor to be perceived as being out there on the scene with hands-on than not to be and, therefore, from a political point of view I think I lose points. . . . [PSIC, 1985 10/15 PM, p. 94]

In fact, despite the debacle, polls in the aftermath of May 13 showed strong public support for Goode's decision to act against MOVE. His approval ratings did not drop precipitously until the fall of 1985, when information revealed by the hearings made him appear inept, irresponsible, and evasive [Wilentz, 1985; Stevens, 1985].

True, as 1978 and the aftermath of 1985 showed, the public would be distressed at death to innocent parties—police, firefighters, or MOVE children. Police officers and firefighters do, however, accept mortal risks as part of their jobs; and, forewarned by MOVE's treachery in 1978, they could more carefully protect themselves from gunshots.[10] As for the children, if Goode had insisted on implementation of his explicit order to pick them up before commencing the operation, they probably could have been saved. Thus the people most likely to die in a properly planned and executed operation were MOVE adults. Most Philadelphians perceived them as dangerous,

deranged, and incorrigible; their deaths in resisting legitimate authorities would have been mourned by few and welcomed by many.

Although the conclusion of this cold political logic might not have troubled most citizens, it appears to have been unacceptable for Wilson Goode. Perhaps the most revealing moment of his testimony to the MOVE Commission came when he was asked to describe his emotions as his office television showed the fire raging out of control:

> I went through very deep emotions at that time. I cried because I knew at that point that lives would be lost, and I knew that homes would be destroyed and I knew that despite all of our good intentions, that we had . . . an absolute disaster. And I can't explain to you or to anyone the kind of emotions that I went through, because everything about me is about preserving life and to know that any plan that I've had anything to do with would, in fact, bring about the cessation of life, was very tough. [PSIC, 1985, 10/15 PM, p. 95]

There are independent reasons for believing the sincerity of Goode's statement. Widely regarded as a deeply religious man, he has been a devoted and active member of the First Baptist Church of Paschall since 1955, serving during most of this time as a deacon and lay leader of the congregation. Well into adult life, he seriously considered entering the ministry. On his pastor's advice, he prayed for guidance. "I came away feeling strongly that I *was* called," he said later. "But it was a ministry of a different kind, a ministry of public service." An early profiler wrote, "His whole notion of public service is grounded in his faith, and he approaches his work at City Hall with almost an evangelical fervor" [Cohn, 1982, p. 13].

Indeed, most of Goode's career exhibits a marked inclination toward conciliation and peacemaking. As a community activist in the 1960s and early 1970s, "his low-key manner usually helped keep potentially explosive situations under control" [Cohn, p. 27]. As a politician, he first unified the previously divided black community, then established an effective alliance with white liberals in the Democratic primary, and finally in the 1983 general election, through a series of conciliatory gestures, won the support of Frank Rizzo. Consequently, he carried 27% of the white vote, and Philadelphia during the first year of his term rode a wave of elation, smugly comparing its newfound racial harmony to the bitter divisions in Chicago and other cities. As mayor, many of Goode's early string of triumphs depended on his ability to build consensus and placate opposition. The few criticisms of Goode during this period centered on claims that he was too willing to appease opponents and too reluctant to lead in the absence of consensus. His own view was more positive: "I've had a charmed life as mayor because I've learned the arts of compromise and negotiation" [Wilentz, 1985, p. 22].

A commitment to peacemaking is also consistent with the full pattern of Goode's dealings with MOVE. The disastrously little time and attention he devoted to planning the use of force contrasts strikingly with his extensive involvement in efforts to understand MOVE and to negotiate a solution [Marimow, 1985]. When Managing Director, he met about fifteen times with John Africa's sisters, Louise James and Laverne Sims, both of whom had been involved with MOVE and were also the mothers of MOVE members. "I always had a comfortable relationship with them, when we have shared together, where they have talked with me and I have listened a lot" [PSIC, 1985, 10/15 AM, p. 29]. The open door continued after he became mayor. On July 31, 1984, when city officials were anticipating a confrontation with MOVE on the August 8 anniversary of the Powelton shootout, the two sisters requested a meeting and were given almost instant access. Goode told the MOVE Commission, "I literally jumped at that meeting because for the first time, I thought I had someone that I could talk to that could, in fact, avoid a conflict out there" [PSIC, 1985, 10/15 AM, p. 25]. (Note how the procrastination of defensive avoidance vanishes when hope appears.) As late as May 9, Goode sandwiched in his fateful meeting with Sambor between discussions with community activists, through whom he hoped to arrange a meeting with Gerald Ford Africa:

> I then asked them to go back, to indicate to Gerald Ford Africa that I was willing to meet at any point that he decided, that he decided that he wanted to meet. I would come to his house. I would go to a neutral house. . . . I would personally negotiate with him any type of release from the house that they were talking about, any movement they wanted to make at that time. . . . After the optimism on Thursday, about noon, they got back to me the next day and said that there was a 360 degrees turn in the attitude of Gerald Ford Africa

when they went back, and that he became profane towards them and said he would not meet with me under any circumstances ever for anything. And it was at this point that that hope which I had of bringing about some negotiation in fact fell through. [PSIC, 1985, 10/15 AM, pp. 62–64]

In directing his personal effort concerning MOVE toward negotiation, Goode was clearly playing to the area where he "felt familiar, resourceful, and competent" [Marimow, 1985]. But such skills had probably developed precisely because they were so consistent with Goode's religious motivation and self-image. In contrast, to be "on the scene with hands-on" in managing a police operation against MOVE would be to risk coming away with blood on his hands—blood that might be politically advantageous but personally intolerable.

## Unleashing on Unreliable Force

Thus, when the Osage neighbors precipitated Goode's final stage of hypervigilance, he kept the police operation at arms length, shielding himself from personal responsibility for the onslaught to come by entrusting the planning and execution to the police, whom he described time and again in the hearings as "experts" and "professionals." Goode's seemingly blind trust in his police force prompted this sarcastic interrogation by Commissioner Neil J. Welch, who had once directed the Philadelphia office of the FBI:

*Welch:* Now, we got a Mayor that's been a Mayor for a year or two and before that he was the Managing Director, and certainly isn't the first time he's seen the Philadelphia Police Department and its personnel perform. . . . [W]hat was your judgment as to the professional capability, the dependability, the quality and integrity of the Philadelphia Police Department to execute, to draft a plan and to execute it successfully?

*Goode:* My judgement was that Greg Sambor had the ability within the parameters which I set forth, to go out and to develop a plan. . . . It was my judgment that . . . being the kind of trained professional person and manager he is, that he, in fact, could do that. . . . That when he finished that plan, he was to discuss that with Leo Brooks, who I felt with his 30 years in the armed services, as a Major General, could evaluate appropriately and properly that overall plan. . . . So I left that meeting with full confidence that Greg Sambor and Leo Brooks could, in fact, carry out the assignment given to them.

*Welch:* Mayor, you displayed great confidence in your Police Department and your Police Commissioner, as you have just outlined. This is the same department that has been or would have been under almost continuous federal investigation, had it not, for a period of some time?

*Goode:* That's correct. [PSIC, 1985, 10/15 PM, pp. 119–121]

Having had responsibility for the Police Department during most of the past five years, to admit the department's faults would clearly arouse dissonance for Goode; but it is inconceivable that he did not know, at some level, that his police were an unreliable instrument for this task. The Federal investigations to which Welch referred were not only for corruption, but for brutality and civil rights violations; and the mutual hatred between the police and MOVE was obvious, especially after the death of Officer Ramp and the beating of Delbert Africa in 1978.

In his initial attempt to solve the MOVE problem, Goode in fact sought to bypass the Philadelphia police. On May 30, 1984, just two days after his first meeting with a delegation from Osage Avenue, the mayor led ranking city officials to a session with U.S. Attorney Edward Dennis and representatives of the FBI and Secret Service. They rebuffed his argument that MOVE's threats against President Reagan and violations of their neighbors' rights constituted grounds for U.S. intervention. Although consistent with the buck-passing pattern typical of defensive avoidance, Goode's attempt to enlist Federal authorities can also be interpreted as a prudent effort to find an armed force more detached, disciplined, and reliable than his own police.

Worries about controlling the city police were also present, though not emphasized, in the days before the final confrontation. At the May 7 meeting, prompted by Councilman Lucien Blackwell's strong warning about officers who might seek vengeance for 1978, Goode instructed Sambor to "handpick" the men who would serve in the Osage Avenue confrontation. (Sambor later claimed not to have heard such an order and in any case did not implement it. One of the gas-insertion teams included two officers

who had been accused of beating Delbert Africa [Anderson and Hevenor, 1987, p. 115].) Goode ultimately admitted to the MOVE Commission that he doubted police fire control so much that he feared their bullets might endanger his own life if he went to the scene:

*Commissioner Audrey Bronson:* I understand that you felt that your life would have been at risk—by whom?

*Goode:* Well, I have received a lot of information that simply people said to me, and I will share this candid discussion with you, that I should be careful of, first of all, of people who were MOVE sympathizers in the neighborhood, that with shots going on out there that a shot could easily go awry and hit me, that I should be—I should be—beware of even the potential for police shots going awry on the scene and therefore, there have been, as I was told, instances of the fact that commanders in the Army have, in fact, been mistakenly shot and I should be aware of those kinds of things and the people who talked with me simply persuaded me that, in fact, it would be a risk for me to be in the area. [PSIC, 1985, 11/6 PM, p. 54]

Although not explicit about who were "the people who talked with me," Goode's statement to the Commission is consistent with reports that telephoners purporting to be police officers warned the mayor he might be shot by police if he came to Osage Avenue.

In short, part of Goode's reluctance to act against MOVE must have resulted from doubts, whether conscious or suppressed, that he could sufficiently control the use of force by the police. In the end he made no real attempt to manage the violence he had authorized. Perhaps, as many in Philadelphia believe, Goode rationally calculated that any such effort might fail and therefore deliberately distanced himself from a potential disaster in order to avoid legal or political responsibility. Such motives cannot be ruled out, but they do not adequately explain the string of cognitive distortions by which the mayor apparently avoided appreciating the reality of what his forces were doing. He told his breakfast guests that police were only firing over the roof of the MOVE house; he interpreted explosions he heard from his home as stun grenades; he thought that the "explosive device" would be placed on MOVE's roof rather than dropped from a helicopter; and he mistook "snow" on his television screen for water from firefighters' squirts [PSIC, 1985, 10/15 AM, pp. 74, 97; 10/15 PM, p. 111; 11/6 AM, p. 111; 10/15 PM, p. 31]. Avowing these beliefs—all unsupported by others' testimony—would hardly help against criminal charges, and they only added to Goode's political vulnerability by subjecting him to ridicule. Such a consistent pattern of misperception seems more suited to deceive oneself than to deceive others, and better protection against self-condemnation than against the judgment of courts or voters. It therefore appears likely that deeper sources of ambivalence prevented the mayor from admitting to himself the full import of his decision to unleash official violence against MOVE.

## Black Against Black: Identification and Anger

The foregoing analysis is not meant to portray Wilson Goode as a pacifist or as one whose values are entirely antithetical to those of the police. After completing ROTC at Morgan State University, he served in the U.S. Army from 1961 to 1963, rising to the rank of captain and commanding a unit of 223 military policemen. His military experience made a deep impression on Goode. He has said that he learned more about management in the army than he did earning a master's degree in governmental administration at the University of Pennsylvania.[11] As mayor, he has shown a marked penchant for appointing former military officers to high posts—including Leo Brooks, a major general in charge of the Philadelphia Defense Personnel Support Center before Goode persuaded him to become Managing Director, and Gregore Sambor, a veteran and an officer in the reserves.

To Goode, however, the military seems to represent not so much legitimate violence as it does an organization that develops personal discipline and rewards it, regardless of race—in marked contrast to most of American society in his formative years. Early profiles of Brooks suggest the virtues that Goode most admires:

> [A mutual acquaintance described Brooks as] "made out of the same mold as Wilson." Goode and Brooks shared poor childhoods in the South, Army-officer training and strong religious underpinnings. Brooks' father is a Baptist minister . . .

Brooks also is a black man who, like his new boss, has achieved success by making hard work his credo. [Cooke and Klibanoff, 1983]

> At heart a traditionalist, Brooks believes in the old-fashioned virtues of hard work, self-discipline . . . and taking responsibility for one's own actions. To him, nothing exceeds the importance of family. [Klibanoff, 1984]

To a black man with Wilson Goode's values, MOVE must have aroused deep and intense conflicts.[12] On the one hand, as a former civil rights activist who had himself been twice picked up by police for allegedly creating disturbances [Cohn, 1982, p. 21], Goode must have had some lingering identification with MOVE. In 1978, much of the black and liberal communities had seen the MOVE problem as a racially motivated attack by the Rizzo administration on the rights of a predominantly black group. On one occasion, five thousand demonstrators marched around City Hall to protest the siege in Powelton; their chants linked MOVE with South African blacks as fellow victims of racial oppression. In 1984, U.S. Attorney Dennis, himself black, strongly warned city officials against violating MOVE's civil rights [PSIC, 1985, 10/22 PM, p. 127]. Goode invoked his own concern for minority rights in explaining his reluctance to act:

> I think that if I was a different person, that perhaps I may have acted differently back in 1984. But I . . . do not feel that anyone who holds an office ought to use that office to infringe and violate other people's rights in order to achieve the overall good, and I guess I feel that way because I know that for so long in this country that laws were, in fact, used to deprive blacks and women and Hispanics and others who were different, and therefore, I do not want, as mayor of this city to say to a group: Because you are different, because you don't comply with all the laws, therefore, I have the right, as the mayor, to simply go full speed and trample on you and all your rights. . . . [PSIC, 1985, 10/15 PM, pp. 97–98]

On the other hand, MOVE represented the antithesis of every standard by which Wilson Goode lived. They dwelt in filth; he was always well groomed. They lived communally; he had raised a family. They spewed profanity; he attended church every Sunday. They survived casually; he worked fifteen-hour days. They rejected the system; he aspired to run a major corporation. As they spurned his efforts to negotiate a peaceful solution, as they vilified him and threatened his life, the bizarre cultists must have aroused increasing anger in Goode. The impulse to vent this anger must have been strong, but his religious belief in preserving life and his self-image as a controlled person forbade yielding to it. "I've always felt that I have to be in control of me at all times," he once told an interviewer [Cohn, 1982, p. 27]; and another profiler got "the feeling that the emotion bottled up inside Wilson Goode is always close to eruption. You can see him almost counting to ten, thinking before he responds, calculating each sentence, crafting every phrase, then struggling mightily to reign in what might be rage" [Mallowe, 1984, p. 170].

For a time, the mayor hoped that MOVE itself would assume the moral burden of precipitating violence. After receiving Rendell's memo justifying urgent action in June 1984, Goode delayed until August 8, the anniversary of the Powelton shootout, because reports indicated that MOVE planned a major confrontation with "the System" on that date. At the mayor's direction, the police prepared a plan for capturing the MOVE house,[13] and three hundred officers were assembled near Osage Avenue. Goode's choice of language in describing this incident is revealing:

> The August 8th 1984 plan was a reactive plan, was geared to go into effect only if certain types of aggressive behavior, aggressive steps were taken by MOVE members themselves. And therefore when they did not take any aggressive steps, nothing, in fact, was done at that time. [PSIC, 1985, 10/15 PM, p. 59]

The words "aggressive" and "aggression" recur frequently when Goode refers to the initiation of armed confrontation. It appears that he was willing in 1984 to do battle with MOVE, but only if MOVE were the aggressor, if MOVE bore the responsibility of having clearly initiated violence. To let deaths occur (or appear to occur) merely because of noise, stench, code violations, and unpaid utility bills was, to Goode, a morally unbalanced equation.[14]

On August 8, however, MOVE did nothing except take notes about the police peparations. After that day, Goode and other city officials entered a stage of full-blown defensive avoidance that lasted until May 1985. As the MOVE Commission observed about this period. "The policy of appeasement produced a rule of silence in City Hall, where information on the Osage Avenue situation was not disseminated and where city officials knowledgeable about the problems chose not to speak of them" [PSIC, 1986, p. 13]. Goode and his colleagues were thus able to entertain the wishful hope that the Osage Avenue problem "would disappear" by ignoring the readily available knowledge that MOVE members were vigorously and visibly fortifying their compound [PSIC, 1985, 10/15 PM, pp. 76–7]. Goode justified his policy of nonintervention on the grounds that no action should be taken "until such time as we worked out an overall plan that would be comprehensive in nature," but this argument was a rationalization for avoidance, as is shown by the fact that he did absolutely nothing to force the creation of such a plan [PSIC, 1985, 10/15 PM, pp. 75–80]. Indeed, the mayor had no contact with anyone concerning MOVE from August 9 until the end of April 1985 [PSIC, 10/15 AM, p. 40].

Goode's nine months of pseudocalm were then shattered by the United Residents' initiative, which revived what threatened to be an excruciating inner struggle. Rather than endure the tension during a protracted period of careful search and appraisal, the mayor sought to eliminate his conflict quickly by authorizing the police plan. Although he unleashed the violence of the police and perhaps in part vented his own anger through their vengeance, the use of force in this context was so dissonant with his self-image that he could not accept—psychologically at least as much as politically—the ownership that hands-on management would imply.

To shield himself from personal responsibility for violating crucial values, Wilson Goode thus abdicated his responsibility as an administrator. In so doing, he lost his best chance to control and minimize the inevitable violence. Because he was so reluctant to transgress his values, he permitted a series of events that in the end inflicted on them far greater damage than was necessary. The outcome has the irony of genuine tragedy. The preserver of life bore responsibility for eleven deaths; the builder of homes presided as sixty-one burned; the protector of rights permitted grotesquely excessive official violence.

# Lessons for Present and Future Managers

Perhaps the only consolation we can take from so awful a disaster is the hope that its lessons will help prevent future catastrophes. Thus the MOVE Commission concluded their report with no fewer than thirty-eight recommendations covering such matters as communication systems, assignment of authority and responsibility, policies for controlling weapons and explosives, strategic planning processes, interdepartmental coordinating groups, and so forth. Though the Commission's proposals may be sensible and worthwhile, from the perspective of the analysis offered in this paper, such advice misses the most fundamental lessons of the MOVE debacle.

Organizational systems, policies, and procedures are ultimately controlled and implemented by human beings. Effective communication will not occur when subordinates believe that their superiors cannot bear to hear the truth. Clear allocation of authority will be wasted on executives who, succumbing to painful quandaries, rationalize evasion of responsibility.

Programs for educating public managers should therefore devote much more attention to the psychology of decisionmaking, with a special focus on its prescriptive implications. For example, Janis [1989, ch. 10] concludes his recent book by suggesting twenty sets of leadership practices that might help policy makers avoid pitfalls that often result in defective decisionmaking. As he observes, most of these recommendations will be costly to leaders and their support staffs in time, effort, and stress. Adjusting curricula to sensitize present and future decision makers to psychological factors will also demand new investments by schools, teachers, and students.

Dramatic examples like the MOVE disaster can help motivate such efforts, but in teaching the case during the past several years, I have found that students adopt their own avoidance strategies. Like the general public, their natural reaction is to debate, as one student put it, "whether moral bankruptcy or simple incompetence best explains this disaster." Whichever verdict is chosen, the effect is to distance oneself from the officials who are blamed for the debacle. The observer in effect is saying, "*I* would never be so evil, or so uncaring, or so inattentive, or so blundering as to permit such a horror!"

Interpreting the MOVE case in terms of a general theory such as the Janis and Mann conflict model elevates it from an idiosyncratic failure to a universal warning. Students can then move beyond emotional condemnation of a few officials to a sobering recognition of their own vulnerability to similar errors. The generality of the problem can be further emphasized by exploring parallel cases (though few will be so well documented as the MOVE incident). To take several recent examples, the delay/haste pattern appears to fit the British government's treatment of IRA strongholds in Belfast and Derry during the early 1970s, the Chinese government's response to the 1989 student demonstrations in Tienanmen Square, and the U.S. invasion of Panama to overthrow General Manuel Noriega.[15]

Once managers understand the dynamics of defensive avoidance and hypervigilance, what can they do to protect themselves? Because rationalization, denial, selective perception, and wishful thinking are so insidious, no one can be assured of immunity against defective decision processes. For this reason, Janis and Mann [1977, p. 396] recommend embedding preventive strategies in organizational standard operating procedures,[16] because "if the anti-defensive avoidance procedures are not institutionalized but are rather left to the discretion of the leader or the members, they will be more honored in the breach than in the observance."

Nevertheless, it is not unreasonable to hope that individual awareness will also help. Relying on face validity rather than any systematic evidence of effectiveness, I would suggest the following strategy to managers who wish to reduce their vulnerability.

First, learn to recognize the behavioral symptoms of defective decisionmaking. For defensive avoidance, these include procrastinating, buck-passing, and downplaying danger signals. Symptoms of hypervigilance include grabbing the first available alternative, neglecting contingency plans, and believing that action must be taken under extreme time pressure whether or not compelling deadlines exist. Wise managers will not only monitor themselves for these symptoms, but will also encourage trusted advisors to fight the battle for their minds by calling such tendencies to their attention.

Second, when these symptoms are observed, identify the central no-win dilemma or dilemmas.[17] Conflicts that impede effective decisionmaking are not always obvious and will vary from individual to individual. The desire to avoid responsibility and shield oneself from reality behind a screen of cognitive distortions becomes strongest when one's most central values are threatened, so the manager must heed the ancient injunction to "know thyself."

Third, learn to grasp problems firmly even when all options entail distasteful consequences for important values. The example of Wilson Goode shows that cherished virtues, if excessively protected, can be the source of tragic failure. Though vigilant problem solving and decisive management may induce stress, they are usually rewarded—if not with unequivocal triumph, then at least by controlled damage and the respect that strong leaders are accorded. In contrast, the inferno on Osage Avenue should burn into our memories the lesson that however bad available alternatives seem, potential outcomes can be far worse if avoidance and hasty action permit a though situation to deteriorate into a nightmare.

## References

Anderson, John, and Hilary Hevenor (1987), *Burning Down the House: MOVE and the Tragedy of Philadelphia* (New York: W.W. Norton and Co.).

Assefa, Hizkias, and Paul Wahrhaftig (1988), *Extremist Groups and Conflict Resolution: The MOVE Crisis in Philadelphia* (New York: Praeger).

Bowser, Charles W. (1989), *Let the Bunker Burn: The Final Battle with MOVE* (Philadelphia: Camino Books).

Boyette, Michael, with Randi Boyette (1989), *"Let It Burn!" The Philadelphia Tragedy* (Chicago: Contemporary Books).

Cohn, Roger (1982), "Wilson Goode Has Something to Prove," *Today Magazine, Philadelphia Inquirer* (July 25), pp. 10ff.

Cooke, Russell, and Hank Klibanoff (1983), "Work Is the Credo for New Managing Director," *Philadelphia Inquirer* (November 29), p. 12-A.

George, Alexander L. (1973), "The Case for Multiple Advocacy in Making Foreign Policy," *American Political Science Review* 66, pp. 751–785.

Gilbert, Charles E. (1959), "The Framework of Administrative Responsibility," *Journal of Politics* 21, pp. 373–407.

Goodman, Howard (1989), "Still Haunted by MOVE, Richmond Is Telling His Story," *Philadelphia Inquirer* (May 15), p. B-1.

Janis, Irving L. (1972), *Victims of Groupthink* (Boston: Houghton Mifflin).

Janis, Irving L. (1989), *Crucial Decisions: Leadership in Policymaking and Crisis Management* (New York: The Free Press).

Janis, Irving L., and Leon Mann (1977), *Decision Making: A Psychological Analysis of Conflict, Choice, and Commitment* (New York: The Free Press).

Javers, Ron (1983), "On the Run: Lunch with Wilson Goode," *Philadelphia Magazine* 74 (April), p. 8.

Klibanoff, Hank (1984), "The General," *Philadelphia Inquirer* (May 21), p. 4-B.

Mallowe, Mike (1980), "And Now, the Goode News," *Philadelphia Magazine* 71 (August), pp. 128ff.

Mallowe, Mike (1984), "The No-Frills Mayor," *Philadelphia Magazine* 75 (December), pp. 168ff.

Marimow, William K. (1985), "Two Images of Goode: Activism vs. Delegation," *Philadelphia Inquirer* (October 23), p. 1-A.

Philadelphia Court of Common Pleas (1988), *Report of the County Investigating Grand Jury of May 15, 1986.*

Philadelphia Special Investigation Commission (1985), *Hearings.*

Philadelphia Special Investigation Commission (1986), *Findings, Conclusions, and Recommendations.*

Sharifi, Jahan (1990), Unpublished student paper, University of Pennsylvania.

Stevens, William K. (1985), "Mayor Goode's Once-Solid Path Turns Rocky in Philadelphia," *New York Times* (October 23).

Wilentz, Amy (1985), "Goode's Intentions," *Time* 125 (May 27), p. 22.

## Notes

1. PSIC, 1986, Finding 22; see also Findings 3, 15, 17, and 24, which use comparable language. The PSIC is generally known as "the MOVE Commission."

2. This account draws on the following sources, in addition to the author's knowledge as a resident of West Philadelphia during the period described: PSIC [1986], which includes a chronology; Philadelphia Court of Common Pleas [1988], which includes a history of MOVE; Anderson and Hevenor [1987]; Assefa and Wahrhaftig [1988]; Bowser [1989]; and Boyette [1989]. Charles Bowser and Michael Boyette were, respectively, members of the MOVE Commission and the grand

jury. The eighteen days of hearings the MOVE Commission conductd in October and November 1985 are my principal source [PSIC, 1985]. Transcripts are available in the Government Publications Department of the Philadelphia Free Library and the Urban Archives Center of Temple University. There is a volume for each day of hearings, with pages numbered separately within each volume for morning and afternoon sessions. I supplemented the transcripts by watching videotapes of key witnesses' testimony. (The hearings were televised live by WHYY-TV, the PBS station in Philadelphia.)

3. See also the testimony of Laverne Sims [PSIC, 1985, 10/10 AM, pp. 65–77].

4. District Attorney Edward Rendell later blamed the acquittal on the invective and curses that Delbert directed at the judge and jury [PSIC, 1985, 10/22 AM, pp. 119–120].

5. PSIC, 1985, 10/8 PM, p. 104. In Philadelphia there are 28 districts for the lower house of the state legislature compared with only 10 councilmanic districts; thus the state representative is often the elected official closest to the people of a neighborhood.

6. Cohn, 1982, p. 27. The second sentence is a quotation from Shirley Hamilton, Goode's chief of staff.

7. Janis is better known among students of politics, policy, and management for his earlier work on "groupthink" [Janis, 1972]. Elements of groupthink can be found in various official groups involved in the MOVE problem, but the full-blown syndrome does not appear, perhaps because the mayor's interpersonal style inhibited development of the requisite emotional cohesiveness. (Like other cults, MOVE itself exhibited a virulent form of groupthink.) Janis's work on organizational decisions has developed from the specific to the general. In *Decision Making,* he and Mann depict groupthink as a collective version of the broader phenomenon of defensive avoidance, which in turn is part of a "conflict model" based on psychological stress. In his latest book, *Crucial Decisions* [Janis, 1989], the conflict model becomes a component of a still more general "constraints model." The comprehensiveness of the constraints model is a virtue for some purposes, but I believe the paradoxical features of the MOVE case are explained best

by the conflict model. Thus my account relies more on *Decision Making* than on *Crucial Decisions.*

8. The choice of words is unfortunate, because the authors use "vigilance" for their ideal problem-solving process; thus, "hypervigilance" suggests too much of a good thing. The hypervigilant actor exhibits too much emotional arousal and too much haste, but no true vigilance.

9. Although based as much as possible on published materials, the analysis that follows is necessarily inferential and speculative.

10. On May 13, only one police officer was struck by a MOVE bullet, and a bulletproof vest saved him from serious harm. A policy of protecting firefighters from possible MOVE gunfire was one reason the fire spread so fast and so far. Having vowed that no firefighter would face gunfire, Fire Commissioner William Richmond deliberately chose to sacrifice property in order to save lives [Goodman, 1989].

11. In a conversation with the author in February 1981.

12. Much the same argument can probably be made for Leo Brooks, which may help explain why he too failed to fulfill his responsibility in the MOVE operation. Despite the advantages of similarity in promoting trust and comfortable personal relations, leaders take a great risk in depending excessively on key subordinates who are too much like themselves.

13. This plan, prepared by Sergeant Herbert Kirk of the Police Academy, was the forerunner of the strategy employed the following May [PSIC, 1985, 10/11 PM].

14. Because some of his radical and civil libertarian supporters, both black and white, might have had the same attitude, Goode's calculation can be seen as both political and moral. As Sharifi [1990] observes, successful political leaders often mirror the potential reactions of key constituencies in their own concerns.

15. I owe these and other suggested parallels to an anonymous reviewer for this journal.

16. An example already well known in the policymaking community is the system of multiple advocacy recommended by Alexander George [1973].

17. One device that might help raise conflicts to consciousness is the decisional balance sheet, a kind of expanded cost-benefit analysis that includes

not only utilitarian gains and losses but also the approval and disapproval of reference groups and oneself [Janis and Mann, 1977, ch. 6]. Note that the purpose is to recognize consciously the role of emotional influences, not necessarily to eliminate them.

## Chapter 10 Review Questions

1. Briefly, what arguments does Allison put forward to underscore the uniqueness of public management in comparison with business management? Do you agree with his reasoning? Why or why not?
2. Despite Allison's thesis, there is a repeated public demand—evidenced in the popular press and in political campaigns—that government *should* become more business-like. In your opinion, what are the sources and causes of this repeated public outcry?
3. Does Robert D. Behn's "Management by Groping Along" support or contradict Allison's "uniqueness thesis"? Does he essentially suggest more similarities than differences between public and private management?
4. Does the case "The MOVE Disaster" ultimately support Allison's "uniqueness" thesis or Behn's "groping along" argument? Or, does the author offer a different, more convincing model? How do these still *not* fully explain the problems in the case?
5. If you were charged with constructing a better management system that would prevent such problems as the MOVE disaster from reccurring in the future, what would you recommend?
6. Does this case study support the argument that effective public management is perhaps the most important element in making good public administration a reality today? Explain why or why not. In your view, how does "management" differ from "leadership"? Is this an important distinction?

## Key Terms

Sayre's "law"
common management functions
measurement of performance
personnel constraints on public
  managers
career systems
media relations
terminological tangles

time perspectives of managers
equity and efficiency values
managing internal components
managing external components
implementation strategies
management by groping along
strategic planning
management by wandering around

## Suggestions for Further Reading

Much of the earliest literature on management in this century focused on the role of line managers in business, for example, Henri Fayol, *General and Industrial Management,* translated by Constance Storrs (London: Pitman, 1949); or Frederick W. Taylor, *Scientific Management* (New York: Harper & Row, 1911). Their emphasis on the values of efficiency, rationality, and clear lines of hierarchy was carried over into the public sector by such authors as Henry Bruere, W. F. Willoughby, Frederick Cleveland, Luther Gulick, and others, who pioneered the development of management techniques in the public sector prior to World War II. For a good collection of the works of these writers, see Frederick C. Mosher, *Basic Literature of American Public Administration, 1787–1950* (New York: Holmes and Meier, 1981).

A book that should be read in its entirety is Chester I. Barnard, *The Functions of the Executive* (Cambridge, Mass.: Harvard University Press, 1938), because Barnard stands in marked contrast to the pre-World War II scientific management theorists and because he made an enormous impact on other postwar writers like Herbert Simon, writers who decisively reshaped our whole view of this field. William B. Wolf, *The Basic Barnard* (Ithaca, N.Y.: Institute of Labor Relations, Cornell University, 1974) offers the best available commentary on Barnard's life and work. A good summary of the work of another important figure, Henry Mintzberg, can be found in Henry Mintzberg, *Mintzberg on Management: Inside Our Strange World of Organizations* (New York: Free Press, 1989)

Postwar management thought is aptly described by Harold Koontz as "the management theory jungle," i.e., it is divided into multiple schools and perspectives. To sample some of these diverse points of view, read C. West Churchman, *The Systems Approach* (New York: Dell Publishing, 1968), or Bertram M. Gross, *The Managing of Organizations* (New York: Free Press, 1964), for the *systems approach;* read Harry Levinson, *The Exceptional Executive: A Psychological Conception* (Cambridge, Mass.: Harvard University Press, 1968), or Rensis Likert, *The Human Organization: Its Management and Value* (New York: McGraw-Hill, 1967), for the *human behavioral school;* refer to the several hundred cases available through the Harvard Business School that were instrumental in pioneering the methodology of the *case method;* for the *policy emphasis,*

see Paul Appleby, *Policy and Administration* (University, Ala.: University of Alabama Press, 1949); and the *decision school* of management is well represented in books by Charles E. Lindblom and Herbert A. Simon, Donald W. Smithburg, and Victor A. Thompson (discussed in Chapters 8 and 9).

Where are we today in public management thought? Again, no consensus prevails. The older schools are still very influential. But unquestionably the economic pressures of the 1980s have brought about a new outpouring of ideas on efficiency and cutback management, which are reflected in the practical efficiency-oriented writings of Elizabeth Kellar, *Managing with Less* (Washington, D.C.: International City Management Association, 1979), and Mark W. Huddleston, *The Public Administration Workbook* (New York: Longman, 1987). The new world of the *knowledge manager* is vividly portrayed in Harlan Cleveland, *The Knowledge Executive* (New York: E. P. Dutton, 1985). A more specialized focus on peculiar management problems associated with various levels of government is found in Brian W. Rapp and Frank M. Patitucci, *Managing Local Government for Improved Performance: A Practical Approach* (Boulder, Colo.: Westview Press, 1977); Martha W. Weinberg, *Managing the State* (Cambridge, Mass.: M.I.T. Press, 1977); or, on the federal level, Laurence E. Lynn, Jr., *Managing the Public's Business* (New York: Basic Books, 1981); Barry Bozeman and Jeffrey D. Straussman, *Public Management Strategies: Guidelines for Managerial Effectiveness* (San Francisco: Jossey-Bass, 1990); Steven Cohen, *The Effective Public Manager* (San Francisco: Jossey-Bass, 1988); and John Rehfuss, *The Job of the Public Manager* (Chicago: Dorsey Press, 1989). There are numerous books on management in specialized policy fields like defense, law enforcement, health care, and others. The *effective leadership trait* perspective is emphasized in such recent business-oriented books as Leonard Sayles, *Leadership* (New York: McGraw-Hill, 1979), and John P. Kotter, *The General Manager*

(New York: Free Press, 1982) or public sector leadership, John W. Gardner, *On Leadership* (New York: Free Press, 1990); and Jameson W. Doig and Erwin C. Hargrove, eds., *Leadership and Innovation: Entrepreneurs in Government* (Baltimore: Johns Hopkins University Press, 1990). Humanistic management still remains a vital concern of *new public administration* writers, such as H. George Frederickson, *New Public Administration* (University, Ala.: University of Alabama Press, 1980), and Michael Harmon, *Action Theory for Public Administration* (New York: Longman, 1981). On the opposite side, quantitative, *efficiency-oriented* management is also apparent and popular, as found in Michael J. White et. al., *Managing Public Systems: Analytic Techniques for Public Administration* (No. Scituate, Mass.: Duxbury Press, 1981). *Comparative approaches* also find favor, as in Joseph Bowers, *The Two Faces of Management* (Boston: Houghton Mifflin, 1983), and Donald F. Kettl, *Government by Proxy* (Washington, D.C.: Congressional Quarterly Press, 1988). *Specific management issue/problem* books also are frequently written, such as, John J. DiIulio, Jr., *Governing Prisons: A Comparative Study of Corrections Management* (New York: Free Press, 1987) and David S. Brown, *Management, Hidden Enemy—And What Can Be Done About It* (Mt. Airy, Md. (Lomond Publications, 1987) and Jeffrey S. Luke, et al, *Managing Economic Development* (San Francisco: Jossey-Bass, 1988).

For excellent articles that provide a realistic picture of the recent problems and prospects in public management, see Stephen K. Bailey, "Improving Federal Governance," *Public Administration Review,* 40 (November/December 1980), pp. 548–553; Frederick C. Mosher, "The Changing Responsibilities and Tactics of the Federal Government," *Public Administration Review,* 40 (November/December 1980), pp. 541–548; Herbert Kaufman, "Fear of Bureaucracy: A Raging Pandemic," *Public Administration Review,* 40 (January/February 1981), pp. 1–9; James L. Sundquist, "The Crisis of Competence," in Joseph A. Pechman, ed., *Setting National Priorities: Agenda for the 1980s* (Washington, D.C.: The Brookings Institution, 1980); Richard J. Stillman II, "Local Public Management in Transition," *Public Management,* 64 (May 1982), pp. 2–9; Chester Newland, "Public Executives: Imperium, Sacerdotium, Collegium? Bicentennial Leadership Challenges," *Public Administration Review,* 47 (January/February 1987), pp. 45–56, and in the same issue, James D. Carroll, "Public Administration in the Third Century of the Constitution: Supply-Side Management, Privatization or Public Investment?" pp. 106–114; Charles H. Levine, "The Federal Government in the Year 2000," *Public Administration Review,* 46 (May/June 1986), pp. 191–206; and Louise White, "Public Management in a Pluralistic Arena," *Public Administration Review* (November/December 1989), pp. 522–531. For a recent general overview, see James L. Perry, ed., *Handbook of Public Administration* (San Francisco: Jossey-Bass, 1989).

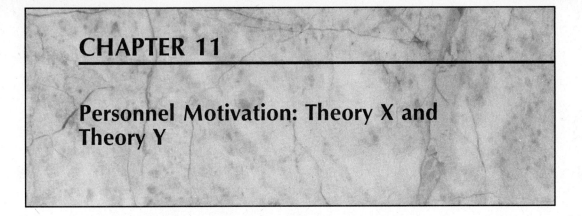

# CHAPTER 11

# Personnel Motivation: Theory X and Theory Y

*M*anagement by direction and control—whether implemented with the hard, the soft, or the firm but fair approach—fails under today's conditions to provide effective motivation of human efforts toward organizational objectives. It fails because direction and control are useless methods of motivating people whose physiological and safety needs are reasonably satisfied and whose social, egoistic, and self-fulfillment needs are predominant.

*Douglas McGregor*

## Introduction

The emphasis on contemporary research in personnel relations has resulted in an impressive subfield of public administration that deals with the many ramifications of the individual in public organizations. Today, most scholars and practitioners of public administration are aware that the handling of personnel issues can be one critical key to the successful management of any public agency.

Chapter 6 explored how our important understanding of the role of the informal group within organizations began. Though concerned primarily with business organizations, Elton Mayo's discoveries in the field of human relations at Western Electric in the 1920s expanded the traditional theories of public administration by showing how critical an impact the human group has on the management process.

However, early researchers in the personnel field tended to accept the basic goals of increased efficiency in organizational activities and actually sought ways by which management could obtain greater productivity from workers. Initially, monotony, alienation, and worker fatigue frequently were problems focused on in personnel studies. These studies often recommended a restructuring of the formal or procedural aspects of the institution as the means of control.

The more contemporary, second-generation personnel specialists like Chris Argyris, Warren Bennis, Rensis Likert, and Douglas McGregor have continued to stress the significance of the problems of the individual in organizations, but frequently with less concern about organizational performance and more careful attention toward helping to achieve worker satisfaction and personal growth on the job. Such writers have de-emphasized traditional administrative goals such as efficiency and, instead, have shown a greater interest in support of individual values and a humanistic environment within organizations.

One of the leading proponents of this school of humanistic thought was Douglas McGregor (1906–1964), a Harvard-trained social psychologist, former president of Antioch College, and professor of industrial management at the Massachusetts Institute of Technology, who throughout much of his writings argued for an alternative philosophy regarding the personnel responsibilities of managers. McGregor criticized the traditional theory of personnel management—which he called Theory X—under which the manager was seen as an active agent for motivating people, "controlling their actions, modifying their behavior to fit the needs of the organization." Proponents of Theory X took a pessimistic view of human nature, portraying people as self-centered, gullible, resistant to change, and reluctant to work.

McGregor's critique of Theory X is based on Abraham Maslow's hierarchy of human needs (discussed at length in McGregor's essay). "The philosophy of management by direction and control—*regardless of whether it is hard or soft*—is inadequate to motivate because the human needs on which this approach relies are today unimportant motivators of behavior. Direction and control are essentially useless in motivating people whose important needs are social and egoistic." McGregor saw the necessity for managers to shift from Theory X—management by direction and control—to Theory Y or "the process primarily of creating opportunities, releasing potential, removing obstacles, encouraging growth, providing guidance." The goal then becomes the creation of a humanistic environment where "people can achieve their own goals best by directing their own efforts toward organizational objectives." Job enlargement, delegation of authority, decentralized responsibilities, and participatory management are several methods by which McGregor thought Theory Y could be practically implemented in organizations. In essence, McGregor searched for ways to create a healthy organization by allowing for maximum growth of human potential. He sought to achieve this through a realistic understanding of human motivation and a fostering of a democratic organizational environment conducive to the development of individual capabilities.

As you read this selection, keep the following questions in mind:

Are McGregor's ideas, primarily oriented toward private business, readily applicable to public organizations? Specifically, can the growth of human potential be *the* central value of public organizations, or might other goals such as representativeness, public service, and efficiency have priorities as well in public enterprises?

Do McGregor's Theory X and Theory Y really differ decisively in terms of their ultimate goals? That is to say, although the traditional and modern personnel management theories may differ in the means whereby their ends are attained, are the final goals of Theory X and Theory Y basically identical, for example, increased organizational performance?

Does Maslow's theory of a hierarchy of human needs as described in the McGregor selection seem a valid theoretical basis for supporting Theory Y? From your own observations, can Maslow's concept be proven or disproven?

How does McGregor's concept compare with the work of Mayo and others involving "informal groups" as described in Chapter 6 or the Simon–Smithburg–Thompson piece in Chapter 9?

# The Human Side of Enterprise

## DOUGLAS McGREGOR

It has become trite to say that the most significant developments of the next quarter century will take place not in the physical but in the social sciences, that industry—the economic organ of society—has the fundamental know-how to utilize physical science and technology for the material benefit of mankind, and that we must now learn how to utilize the social sciences to make our human organizations truly effective.

Many people agree in principle with such statements; but so far they represent a pious hope—and little else. Consider with me, if you will, something of what may be involved when we attempt to transform the hope into reality.

Let me begin with an analogy. A quarter century ago basic conceptions of the nature of matter and energy had changed profoundly

from what they had been since Newton's time. The physical scientists were persuaded that under proper conditions new and hitherto unimagined sources of energy could be made available to mankind.

We know what has happened since then. First came the bomb. Then, during the past decade, have come many other attempts to exploit these scientific discoveries—some successful, some not.

The point of my analogy, however, is that the application of theory in this field is a slow and costly matter. We expect it always to be thus. No one is impatient with the scientist because he cannot tell industry how to build a simple, cheap, all-purpose source of atomic energy today. That it will take at least another decade and the investment of billions of dollars to achieve results which are economically competitive with present sources of power is understood and accepted.

It is transparently pretentious to suggest any *direct* similarity between the developments in the physical sciences leading to the harnessing of atomic energy and potential developments in the social sciences. Nevertheless, the analogy is not as absurd as it might appear to be at first glance.

To a lesser degree, and in a much more tentative fashion, we are in a position in the social sciences today like that of the physical sciences with respect to atomic energy in the thirties. We know that past conceptions of the nature of man are inadequate and in many ways incorrect. We are becoming quite certain that, under proper conditions, unimagined resources of creative human energy could become available within the organizational setting.

We cannot tell industrial management how to apply this new knowledge in simple, economic ways. We know it will require years of exploration, much costly development research, and a substantial amount of creative imagination on the part of management to discover how to apply this growing knowledge to the organization of human effort in industry.

May I ask that you keep this analogy in mind—overdrawn and pretentious though it may be—as a framework for what I have to say. . . .

## Management's Task: Conventional View

The conventional conception of management's task in harnessing human energy to organizational requirements can be stated broadly in terms of three propositions. In order to avoid the complications introduced by a label, I shall call this set of propositions "Theory X":

1. Management is responsible for organizing the elements of productive enterprise—money, materials, equipment, people—in the interest of economic ends.
2. With respect to people, this is a process of directing their efforts, motivating them,

controlling their actions, modifying their behavior to fit the needs of the organization.
3. Without this active intervention by management, people would be passive—even resistant—to organizational needs. They must therefore be persuaded, rewarded, punished, controlled—their activities must be directed. This is management's task—in managing subordinate managers or workers. We often sum it up by saying that management consists of getting things done through other people.

Behind this conventional theory there are several additional beliefs—less explicit, but widespread:

4. The average man is by nature indolent—he works as little as possible.
5. He lacks ambition, dislikes responsibility, prefers to be led.
6. He is inherently self-centered, indifferent to organizational needs.
7. He is by nature resistant to change.
8. He is gullible, not very bright, the ready dupe of the charlatan and the demagogue.

The human side of economic enterprise today is fashioned from propositions and beliefs such as these. Conventional organization structures, managerial policies, practices, and programs reflect these assumptions.

In accomplishing its task—with these assumptions as guides—management has conceived of a range of possibilities between two extremes.

## The Hard or the Soft Approach?

At one extreme, management can be "hard" or "strong." The methods for directing behavior involve coercion and threat (usually disguised), close supervision, tight controls over behavior. At the other extreme, management can be "soft" or "weak." The methods for directing behavior involve being permissive, satisfying people's demands, achieving harmony. Then they will be tractable, accept direction.

This range has been fairly completely explored during the past half century, and management has learned some things from the exploration. There are difficulties in the "hard" approach. Force breeds counter-forces: restriction of output, antagonism, militant unionism, subtle but effective sabotage of management objectives. This approach is especially difficult during times of full employment.

There are also difficulties in the "soft" approach. It leads frequently to the abdication of management—to harmony, perhaps, but to indifferent performance. People take advantage of the soft approach. They continually expect more, but they give less and less.

Currently, the popular theme is "firm but fair." This is an attempt to gain the advantages of both the hard and the soft approaches. It is reminiscent of Teddy Roosevelt's "speak softly and carry a big stick."

## Is the Conventional View Correct?

The findings which are beginning to emerge from the social sciences challenge this whole set of beliefs about man and human nature and about the task of management. The evidence is far from conclusive, certainly, but it is suggestive. It comes from the laboratory, the clinic, the schoolroom, the home, and even to a limited extent from industry itself.

The social scientist does not deny that human behavior in industrial organization today is approximately what management perceives it to be. He has, in fact, observed it and studied it fairly extensively. But he is pretty sure that this behavior is *not* a consequence of man's inherent nature. It is a consequence rather of the nature of industrial organizations, of management philosophy, policy, and practice. The conventional approach of Theory X is

based on mistaken notions of what is cause and what is effect.

"Well," you ask, "what then is the *true* nature of man? What evidence leads the social scientist to deny what is obvious?" And, if I am not mistaken, you are also thinking, "Tell me—simply, and without a lot of scientific verbiage—what you think you know that is so unusual. Give me—without a lot of intellectual claptrap and theoretical nonsense—some practical ideas which will enable me to improve the situation in my organization. And remember, I'm faced with increasing costs and narrowing profit margins. I want proof that such ideas won't result simply in new and costly human relations frills. I want practical results, and I want them now."

If these are your wishes, you are going to be disappointed. Such requests can no more be met by the social scientist today than could comparable ones with respect to atomic energy be met by the physicist fifteen years ago. I can, however, indicate a few of the reasons for asserting that conventional assumptions about the human side of enterprise are inadequate. And I can suggest—tentatively—some of the propositions that will comprise a more adequate theory of the management of people. The magnitude of the task that confronts us will then, I think, be apparent.

Perhaps the best way to indicate why the conventional approach of management is inadequate is to consider the subject of motivation. In discussing this subject I will draw heavily on the work of my colleague, Abraham Maslow of Brandeis University. His is the most fruitful approach I know. Naturally, what I have to say will be overgeneralized and will ignore important qualifications. In the time at our disposal, this is inevitable.

## Physiological and Safety Needs

Man is a wanting animal—as soon as one of his needs is satisfied, another appears in its place. This process is unending. It continues from birth to death.

Man's needs are organized in a series of levels—a hierarchy of importance. At the lowest level, but preeminent in importance when they are thwarted, are his physiological needs. Man lives by bread alone, when there is no bread. Unless the circumstances are unusual, his needs for love, for status, for recognition are inoperative when his stomach has been empty for a while. But when he eats regularly and adequately, hunger ceases to be an important need. The sated man has hunger only in the sense that a full bottle has emptiness. The same is true of the other physiological needs of man—for rest, exercise, shelter, protection from the elements.

*A satisfied need is not a motivator of behavior!* This is a fact of profound significance. It is a fact which is regularly ignored in the conventional approach to the management of people. I shall return to it later. For the moment, one example will make my point. Consider your own need for air. Except as you are deprived of it, it has no appreciable motivating effect upon your behavior.

When the physiological needs are reasonably satisfied, needs at the next higher level begin to dominate man's behavior—to motivate him. These are called safety needs. They are needs for protection against danger, threat, deprivation. Some people mistakenly refer to these as needs for security. However, unless man is in a dependent relationship where he fears arbitrary deprivation, he does not demand security. The need is for the "fairest possible break." When he is confident of this, he is more than willing to take risks. But when he feels threatened or dependent, his greatest need is for guarantees, for protection, for security.

The fact needs little emphasis that since every industrial employee is in a dependent relationship, safety needs may assume considerable importance. Arbitrary management actions, behavior which arouses uncertainty with respect to continued employment or which reflects favoritism or discrimination, unpredict-

able administration of policy—these can be powerful motivators of the safety needs in the employment relationship *at every level* from worker to vice president.

## Social Needs

When man's physiological needs are satisfied and he is no longer fearful about his physical welfare, his social needs become important motivators of his behavior—for belonging, for association, for acceptance by his fellows, for giving and receiving friendship and love.

Management knows today of the existence of these needs, but it often assumes quite wrongly that they represent a threat to the organization. Many studies have demonstrated that the tightly knit, cohesive work group may, under proper conditions, be far more effective than an equal number of separate individuals in achieving organizational goals.

Yet management, fearing group hostility to its own objectives, often goes to considerable lengths to control and direct human efforts in ways that are inimical to the natural "groupiness" of human beings. When man's social needs—and perhaps his safety needs, too—are thus thwarted, he behaves in ways which tend to defeat organizational objectives. He becomes resistant, antagonistic, uncooperative. But this behavior is a consequence, not a cause.

## Ego Needs

Above the social needs—in the sense that they do not become motivators until lower needs are reasonably satisfied—are the needs of greatest significance to management and to man himself. They are the egoistic needs, and they are of two kinds:

1. Those needs that relate to one's self-esteem—needs for self-confidence, for independence, for achievement, for competence, for knowledge.

2. Those needs that relate to one's reputation—needs for status, for recognition, for appreciation, for the deserved respect of one's fellows.

Unlike the lower needs, these are rarely satisfied; man seeks indefinitely for more satisfaction of these needs once they have become important to him. But they do not appear in any significant way until physiological, safety, and social needs are all reasonably satisfied.

The typical industrial organization offers few opportunities for the satisfaction of these egoistic needs to people at lower levels in the hierarchy. The conventional methods of organizing work, particularly in mass production industries, give little heed to these aspects of human motivation. If the practices of scientific management were deliberately calculated to thwart these needs—which, of course, they are not—they could hardly accomplish this purpose better than they do.

## Self-fulfillment Needs

Finally—a capstone, as it were, on the hierarchy of man's needs—there are what we may call the needs for self-fulfillment. These are the needs for realizing one's own potentialities, for continued self-development, for being creative in the broadest sense of that term.

It is clear that the conditions of modern life give only limited opportunity for these relatively weak needs to obtain expression. The deprivation most people experience with respect to other lower-level needs diverts their energies into the struggle to satisfy *those* needs, and the needs for self-fulfillment remain dormant.

Now, briefly, a few general comments about motivation:

We recognize readily enough that a man suffering from a severe dietary deficiency is sick. The deprivation of physiological needs has behavioral consequences. The same is true—although less well recognized—of deprivation of higher-level needs. The man whose needs for safety, association, independence, or status are thwarted is sick just as surely as is he who has rickets. And his sickness will be mistaken if we attribute his resultant passivity, his hostility, his refusal to accept responsibility to his inherent "human nature." These forms of behavior are *symptoms* of illness—of deprivation of his social and egoistic needs.

The man whose lower-level needs are satisfied is not motivated to satisfy those needs any longer. For practical purposes they exist no longer. (Remember my point about your need for air.) Management often asks, "Why aren't people more productive? We pay good wages, provide good working conditions, have excellent fringe benefits and steady employment. Yet people do not seem to be willing to put forth more than minimum effort."

The fact that management has provided for these physiological and safety needs has shifted the motivational emphasis to the social and perhaps to the egoistic needs. Unless there are opportunities *at work* to satisfy these higher-level needs, people will be deprived; and their behavior will reflect this deprivation. Under such conditions, if management continues to focus its attention on physiological needs, its efforts are bound to be ineffective.

People *will* make insistent demands for more money under these conditions. It becomes more important than ever to buy the material goods and services which can provide limited satisfaction of the thwarted needs. Although money has only limited value in satisfying many higher-level needs, it can become the focus of interest if it is the *only* means available.

## The Carrot and Stick Approach

The carrot and stick theory of motivation (like Newtonian physical theory) works reasonably well under certain circumstances. The *means* for satisfying man's physiological and (within limits) his safety needs can be provided or withheld by management. Employment itself is such a means, and so are wages, working conditions, and benefits. By these means the individual can be controlled so long as he is struggling for subsistence. Man lives for bread alone when there is no bread.

But the carrot and stick theory does not work at all once man has reached an adequate subsistence level and is motivated primarily by higher needs. Management cannot provide a man with self-respect, or with the respect of his fellows, or with the satisfaction of needs for self-fulfillment. It can create conditions such that he is encouraged and enabled to seek such satisfactions *for himself,* or it can thwart him by failing to create those conditions.

But this creation of conditions is not "control." It is not a good device for directing behavior. And so management finds itself in an odd position. The high standard of living created by our modern technological knowhow provides quite adequately for the satisfaction of physiological and safety needs. The only significant exception is where management practices have not created confidence in a "fair break"—and thus where safety needs are thwarted. But by making possible the satisfaction of low-level needs, management has deprived itself of the ability to use as motivators the devices on which conventional theory has taught it to rely—rewards, promises, incentives, or threats and other coercive devices.

## Neither Hard nor Soft

The philosophy of management by direction and control—*regardless of whether it is hard or soft*—is inadequate to motivate because the human needs on which this approach relies are today unimportant motivators of behavior. Direction and control are essentially useless in motivating people whose important needs are social and egoistic. Both the hard and the soft approach fail today because they are simply irrelevant to the situation.

People, deprived of opportunities to satisfy at work the needs which are now important to them, behave exactly as we might predict—with indolence, passivity, resistance to change, lack of responsibility, willingness to follow the demagogue, unreasonable demands for economic benefits. It would seem that we are caught in a web of our own weaving.

In summary, then, of these comments about motivation:

Management by direction and control—whether implemented with the hard, the soft, or the firm but fair approach—fails under today's conditions to provide effective motivation of human efforts toward organizational objectives. It fails because direction and control are useless methods of motivating people whose physiological and safety needs are reasonably satisfied and whose social, egoistic, and self-fulfillment needs are predominant.

For these and many other reasons, we require a different theory of the task of managing people based on more adequate assumptions about human nature and human motivation. I am going to be so bold as to suggest the broad dimensions of such a theory. Call it "Theory Y," if you will.

1. Management is responsible for organizing the elements of productive enterprise—money, materials, equipment, people—in the interest of economic ends.
2. People are *not* by nature passive or resistant to organizational needs. They have become so as a result of experience in organizations.
3. The motivation, the potential for development, the capacity for assuming responsibility, the readiness to direct behavior toward organizational goals are all present in people. Management does not put them there. It is a responsibility of management to make it possible for people to recognize and develop these human characteristics for themselves.
4. The essential task of management is to arrange organizational conditions and meth-

ods of operation so that people can achieve their own goals *best* by directing *their own* efforts toward organizational objectives.

This is a process primarily of creating opportunities, releasing potential, removing obstacles, encouraging growth, providing guidance. It is what Peter Drucker has called "management by objectives" in contrast to "management by control."

And I hasten to add that it does *not* involve the abdication of management, the absence of leadership, the lowering of standards, or the other characteristics usually associated with the "soft" approach under Theory X. Much on the contrary. It is no more possible to create an organization today which will be a fully effective application of this theory than it was to build an atomic power plant in 1945. There are many formidable obstacles to overcome.

## Some Difficulties

The conditions imposed by conventional organization theory and by the approach of scientific management for the past half century have tied men to limited jobs which do not utilize their capabilities, have discouraged the acceptance of responsibility, have encouraged passivity, have eliminated meaning from work. Man's habits, attitudes, expectations—his whole conception of membership in an industrial organization—have been conditioned by his experience under these circumstances. Change in the direction of Theory Y will be slow, and it will require extensive modification of the attitudes of management and workers alike.

People today are accustomed to being directed, manipulated, controlled in industrial organizations and to finding satisfaction for their social, egoistic, and self-fulfillment needs away from the job. This is true of much of management as well as of workers. Genuine "industrial citizenship"—to borrow again a

term from Drucker—is a remote and unrealistic idea, the meaning of which has not even been considered by most members of industrial organizations.

Another way of saying this is that Theory X places exclusive reliance upon external control of human behavior, while Theory Y relies heavily on self-control and self-direction. It is worth noting that this difference is the difference between treating people as children and treating them as mature adults. After generations of the former, we cannot expect to shift to the latter overnight.

Before we are overwhelmed by the obstacles, let us remember that the application of theory is always slow. Progress is usually achieved in small steps.

Consider with me a few innovative ideas which are entirely consistent with Theory Y and which are today being applied with some success:

## Decentralization and Delegation

These are ways of freeing people from the too-close control of conventional organization, giving them a degree of freedom to direct their own activities, to assume responsibility, and, importantly, to satisfy their egoistic needs. In this connection, the flat organization of Sears, Roebuck and Company provides an interesting example. It forces "management by objectives" since it enlarges the number of people reporting to a manager until he cannot direct and control them in the conventional manner.

## Job Enlargement

This concept, pioneered by I.B.M. and Detroit Edison, is quite consistent with Theory Y. It encourages the acceptance of responsibility at the bottom of the organization; it provides opportunities for satisfying social and egoistic needs. In fact, the reorganization of work at the factory level offers one of the more challenging opportunities for innovation consistent with Theory Y. The studies by A.T.M. Wilson and his associates of British coal mining and Indian textile manufacture have added appreciably to our understanding of work organization. Moreover, the economic and psychological results achieved by this work have been substantial.

## Participation and Consultative Management

Under proper conditions these results provide encouragement to people to direct their creative energies toward organizational objectives, give them some voice in decisions that affect them, provide significant opportunities for the satisfaction of social and egoistic needs. I need only mention the Scanlon Plan as the outstanding embodiment of these ideas in practice.

The not infrequent failure of such ideas as these to work as well as expected is often attributable to the fact that a management has "bought the idea" but applied it within the framework of Theory X and its assumptions.

Delegation is not an effective way of exercising management by control. Participation becomes a farce when it is applied as a sales gimmick or a device for kidding people into thinking they are important. Only the management that has confidence in human capacities and is itself directed toward organizational objectives rather than toward the preservation of personal power can grasp the implications of this emerging theory. Such management will find and apply successfully other innovative ideas as we move slowly toward the full implementation of a theory like Y.

Before I stop, let me mention one other practical application of Theory Y which—while still highly tentative—may well have important consequences. This has to do with per-

formance appraisal within the ranks of management. Even a cursory examination of conventional programs of performance appraisal will reveal how completely consistent they are with Theory X. In fact, most such programs tend to treat the individual as though he were a product under inspection on the assembly line.

Take the typical plan: substitute "product" for "subordinate being appraised," substitute "inspector" for "superior making the appraisal," substitute "rework" for "training or development," and, except for the attributes being judged, the human appraisal process will be virtually indistinguishable from the product inspection process.

A few companies—among them General Mills, Ansul Chemical, and General Electric—have been experimenting with approaches which involve the individual in setting "targets" or objectives *for himself* and in a *self-*evaluation of performance semi-annually or annually. Of course, the superior plays an important leadership role in this process—one, in fact, which demands substantially more competence than the conventional approach. The role is, however, considerably more congenial to many managers than the role of "judge" or "inspector" which is forced upon them by conventional performance. Above all, the individual is encouraged to take a greater responsibility for planning and appraising his own contribution to organizational objectives; and the accompanying effects on egoistic and self-fulfillment needs are substantial. This approach to performance appraisal represents one more innovative idea being explored by a few managements who are moving toward the implementation of Theory Y.

And now I am back where I began. I share the belief that we could realize substantial improvements in the effectiveness of industrial organizations during the next decade or two. Moreover, I believe the social sciences can contribute much to such developments. We are only beginning to grasp the implications of the growing body of knowledge in these fields. But if this conviction is to become a reality instead of a pious hope, we will need to view the process much as we view the process of releasing the energy of the atom for constructive human ends—as a slow, costly, sometimes discouraging approach toward a goal which would seem to many to be quite unrealistic.

The ingenuity and the perseverance of industrial management in the pursuit of economic ends have changed many scientific and technological dreams into commonplace realities. It is now becoming clear that the application of these same talents to the human side of enterprise will not only enhance substantially these materialistic achievements but will bring us one step closer to "the good society." Shall we get on with the job?

---

# CASE STUDY 11

# Introduction

McGregor's Theory Y characterized a lifetime of thought and work described by Warren Bennis and Caroline McGregor in a collection of McGregor's essays edited after his death as an effort toward "bringing together a creative working truth towards a new consensus."[1] Few public administrators would deny the importance or worth of McGregor's idealistic *new consensus* as expressed in Theory Y, though no doubt many would question whether it could ever be achieved in practice. In short, many would ask: is this concept useful for the working public administrator, or is it another "pie-in-the-sky" theory by an academician?

The following story, "The Curious Case of the Indicted Meat Inspectors," by Peter Schuck, a professor of law at Yale University, provides a unique way of testing the utility of McGregor's Theory X and Theory Y for the public sector, using the demanding situation of a federal meat inspector's job. Reminiscent of the insightful moral issues raised by Case Study 1, "The Blast in Centralia No. 5," the following case tells the story of low-level USDA federal meat inspectors who were indicted by the U.S. Department of Justice for accepting "things of value" from certain Boston-based meat processing companies. To gain a proper perspective on their ensuing trial, the author takes the reader behind the scenes to glimpse the daily frustrations confronting an average USDA meat inspector: the highly unpleasant working conditions, the confusing legal maze of regulations that they are repeatedly asked to enforce, the lack of support or direction from their superiors at the Department of Agriculture, and their woefully inadequate pay combined with continuous offers of "cumshaw" by the very businesses they are asked to regulate.

As you read the case, you may wonder why anyone would want to perform this line of work—under working conditions that are considerably beyond anything McGregor describes as Theory X—even though the work of USDA meat inspectors is clearly vital and necessary to the health and well-being of the general public. Perhaps this is the central irony underscored by the author: that the inspector's job, although vital to the public, is given neither the public recognition nor the remuneration it deserves (ultimately leading to the meat inspectors' vulnerability to federal indictments for what turned out to be very minor infractions of the law).

Moreover, at the same time the meat inspectors went to jail, the businesses they were regulating got off scot-free even though those businesses had offered bribes to the meat inspectors in the first place. Yet, the tale is not just another case of justice denied; on a deeper level it perhaps accurately portrays the demanding, often conflicting, cross-pressures under which many public employees must work day in and day out—frequently enforcing a myriad of complex laws, which at any time, they can be asked to account for by their immediate supervisor, the general public, or even a court of law.

As you read this selection, keep the following questions in mind:

McGregor's Theory Y assumes that employees' potential growth is the main or *only* goal of their employment. In this case study, what were the employers' and employees' main goals? Was personal growth their prime goal?

Given the facts in this case study, could McGregor's Theory Y have been applied to this type of public activity to improve the employment conditions in this case? Discuss why or why not.

If you could redesign the federal meat inspector's job, what reforms would you advocate to enhance its prestige, performance, and effectiveness?

Specifically, what measures would you recommend to keep the inspectors out of jail in the future?

# The Curious Case of the Indicted Meat Inspectors

## PETER SCHUCK

At seven o'clock on the morning of October 8, 1971, Edmund Wywiorski arrived for work at a meat-processing plant in Boston. He entered the plant, waving casually to employees inside the gate, and headed for the U.S. Government office at the rear of the building. As he walked slowly past the long, silent lines of processing machinery being hosed down for another day's work, Wywiorski's thoughts oscillated between his first morning as a U.S. Department of Agriculture meat inspector back in 1929, and the jubilee day, now less than two years off, when he would reach sixty-five and retire. He smiled to himself as he walked, trying to imagine how many carcasses he must have inspected in those forty-two years. The old

"The Curious Case of the Indicted Meat Inspectors" by Peter Schuck, *Harper's Magazine*, 1973, pp. 1–8. Reprinted by permission of the author. © 1972 by Peter Schuck. Peter Schuck teaches at Yale Law School and was Deputy Assistant Secretary for Planning and Evaluation at HEW in 1977 and 1978.

man, unaccustomed to such flights of fancy, broke off the effort as he approached the office door. Glancing at the other inspectors already inside, he knew immediately that something was up.

For most federal meat inspectors, as for Edmund Wywiorski, theirs is a career, a life's work. More than perhaps any other federal career job, however, meat inspection is a grueling, exacting enterprise. Of all blue-collar work in our society, only that of the policeman on the beat begins to compare with meat inspection for the rigor of the intellectual, physical, social, and psychological demands on the job.

The meat inspector works under extremely unpleasant, if not nauseating, conditions. Most meat-processing plants are old, hot, noisy, and noisome. The constant sight and smell of rent flesh, blood, entrails, and offal are sensuous assaults to which the inspector may grow accustomed, but never immune. Twelve-hour work days are common. The inspector must often cover many "houses" in a circuit, traveling from plant to plant at some distance and at odd hours.

What the meat inspector must endure is nothing compared to what he must know. Many inspectors now start at a GS-5 level, earning less than $7,400 per year, yet they cannot perform a day's work without routinely applying vast knowledge of food chemistry, bacteriology, animal pathology, sampling techniques, foodprocessing machinery and technology, plant construction, and industrial hygiene. The regulations, guidelines, and directives the inspector must follow and enforce are so numerous, intricate, and technical that they seem like the bureaucratic equivalent of Mission Control at Cape Kennedy. There are detailed regulations specifying the nature and condition of the salt solutions that may be used on wetting cloths applied to dressed carcasses. There are extensive instructions pertaining to packaging, labeling, and transportation of inspected products. Section 310.10 of the Manual of Meat Inspection Procedures sets forth in fifteen single-spaced pages the requirements for the "routine" (other than final inspection) postmortem inspection of every carcass. A typical excerpt follows:

> Examination of the liver should include opening the large bile duct. This should be done very carefully as cutting through the duct into the liver tissue will interfere with the detection of the small lancet liver fluke. The incision should extend at least an inch through the bile duct dorsally and in the other direction as far as possible. The beef liver should be palpated on the entire parietal surface and within the area of the renal impression. Palpation should be accomplished by exerting sufficient pressure with the hands and fingers to be able to detect deep abscesses or cysts within the liver. . . .

The complex regulations and instructions nevertheless leave the inspector with an irreducible residue of discretion within which he is empowered to impose grave sanctions against the processor, including closing down the plant. In part, this discretion derives from the inability of law to reconcile fully the imperatives of uniformity and diversity. The point at which a "remote product contamination," i.e., a dirty rail, becomes a "direct product contamination," i.e., a very dirty rail, is obviously a matter of degree, and the regulations concede as much. Yet the latter may justify the inspector's closing down production until the

condition is remedied, while the former ordinarily will not.

But the inspector's discretion goes well beyond this. It is a commonplace in the industry, denied only by official USDA spokesmen, that if all meat-inspection regulations were enforced to the letter, no meat processor in America would be open for business. This fact, probably common to all regulated industries, says as much about an agency's tendency to overregulate as about an industry's unwillingness to comply with the law, yet the net result is the same: the inspector is not expected to enforce strictly every rule, *but rather to decide which rules are worth enforcing at all.* In this process, USDA offers no official guidance, for it feels obliged, like all public agencies, to maintain the myth that all rules are rigidly enforced. Unofficially, the inspector is admonished by his USDA superiors to "use common sense," to do his job in a "reasonable way."

Ironically this amalgam of discretion—conferred by law, custom, and necessity—represents to the inspector not power but impotence. For he is obliged to exercise this discretion in a fluid, political context in which he is a pawn of those interests—the processor, its employees, and USDA—with the greatest stake in that exercise. The inspector is the focus, but not the locus, of responsibility.

Most meat processors (or packers) operate on a narrow margin of profitability. In a fiercely competitive industry the incentives to cut costs are practically irresistible. Watered hams, fatty sausages, chicken ingredients instead of beef—these are but a few of the stratagems of the resourceful, cost-conscious packer. A 1 percent increase in the weight of poultry from added water, for example, has been estimated to cost consumers $32 million per year; government studies show excessive watering to be a routine practice. Violations of sanitation and construction standards are also profitable to the packer. There is every reason to delay compliance as long as possible and only one reason to comply at all—the threat that the inspector will stop production until the offending condition is remedied.

To forestall this threat, the packer relies upon a mixed strategy with the inspector, offering the carrot and wielding the stick. The carrots available to the packer are many, and perhaps the most significant is overtime. Since an inspector may earn thousands of dollars annually in overtime to supplement his meager

USDA salary, availability of this perquisite is of crucial importance. The packer decides each day how long the plant will operate and bears the cost of all inspectors required beyond the normal eight hours. Inspectors insist that the subtle offer and withholding of overtime is a mainstay of the system of rewards and punishments by which they are encouraged to be "reasonable."

Another carrot is the gift or favor. Many items are necessary to the inspector's work—boots for the wet floors, freezer coats, pens, office supplies—yet USDA refuses to supply some of them, and scrimps on others. Some packer gifts seem animated by simple goodwill, the oil that lubricates the interactions of people working closely together in the plant day in and day out. A bag of doughnuts for the night shift, a Thanksgiving turkey, a bottle of Scotch at Christmas—these are routinely given to plant employees, and the inspectors are often included. Other gratuities grow naturally out of specific work situations. According to one inspector, "when you have to work overtime, the packer may send out for beer and sandwiches. If you insist on paying, they tell you to go out and get it yourself. It is to the packer's interest to have you eat on the job, so the line can keep running."

To the inspector, a gift of meat is even less suspect. The packer who throws away literally hundreds of pounds of edible product daily for one reason or another—and deducts it as a business expense—does not seem particularly insidious when he asks the inspector, "Need anything for Sunday dinner, Doc?" An inspector observing policemen, firemen, politicians, representatives of veterans groups, hospitals, and other charitable organizations, as well as the packer employees with whom he works, leaving the plant laden with free meat, is hard put to rationalize why he alone should refuse the proffered gift.

The practice is called "cumshaw"—accepting small amounts of product for one's own use at home. Inspectors argue that the pressure to conform to the practice begins from the first day on the job, and comes almost as much from other inspectors as from packers. "We are weaned on the tradition. The old-timers always say, 'It isn't a good inspector who pays for his Sunday dinner.' They tell you that everybody else does it and has always done it, that it has nothing to do with doing your duty, and that if you don't take it, someone else will. I figure the job is hard enough without having the other inspectors suspicious of you." There are unwritten ground rules, moral strictures transmitted from inspector to inspector, and these too are impressed on the new recruit: "Don't accept more meat than your family can use"; "Don't solicit the meat from the packer"; and by far the most important, "Don't let cumshaw influence your judgment or the way you do your job."

To the inspector this distinction between accepting a gratuity and accepting a bribe is clear and morally based. The general federal bribery statutes recognize this distinction and reinforce this morality by making it a crime for a public official to receive anything of value "in return for . . . being influenced in his performance of any official act . . .," or "for or because of any official act performed or to be performed by him."

The inspector readily acknowledges that what appears to be a gift may become a bribe—if it is large enough, takes certain forms, or is given under certain circumstances—but to him, the critical factor is always whether the gratuity induces him not to enforce the regulations in the normal manner. "Sure I'll accept bundles of meat to take home for my family," says one, echoing the sentiments of many. "But that doesn't affect my decisions in the plant one iota, and the packer knows that. The fact of the matter is that if you get on a high horse and *refuse* to take a bundle, it makes it much more difficult to get the job done. Everyone becomes edgy and suspicious. Enforcing the regulations requires reasonableness, cooperation, and flexibility, as USDA is always telling us. If the packer, his employees, or the other inspectors think I look down on them, they are not going to cooperate with me. How can it be morally wrong to do something that hurts nobody and helps me get the job done?"

In addition to the normal urge to self-justification, then, much in the meat inspector's daily life—the pressures of his work routine, temptations by the packer, the job socialization process, the traditions of the industry, the conventional morality of his fellow inspectors, the general bribery statute, and the imperatives of "getting the job done"—tells him that he may accept small gratuities from the packer with a clear conscience. Section 622 of the Wholesome Meat Act, however, tells him something very different. Where the packers are concerned, this section conforms to the traditional ethic—a packer commits a felony in giving something of value to an inspector *only if* it is given "with intent to influence said inspector . . . in the discharge of any duty. . . ." A convicted packer does not forfeit the right to engage in the meat business. The inspector, on the other hand, commits a felony if he receives *anything* of value "given with any purpose or intent whatsoever." And a convicted inspector, in addition to bearing normal criminal penalties, "shall . . . be summarily discharged from office."

The rationale for this double standard is obscure. Federal employees must be held to a high standard of conduct, to be sure, but should it be any higher than that applicable to a packer extensively regulated and certified to do interstate business by USDA? Should one party to an illegal transaction be regarded as guiltless while another is branded a felon? On October 8, 1971, these questions suddenly lost their academic quality.

## The Department of Agriculture: A Case of Nonsupport

Ed Wywiorski, seeing the other inspectors huddled over a newspaper, quickly entered the office and looked at the banner headline in the *Boston Globe*: 40 MEAT INSPECTORS INDICTED IN HUB. A stunned silence lay over the inspectors, each gripped by a private terror. Minutes later, the office phone began its relentless ringing as wives, children, and friends called to ask if it could really be true. Wywiorski cannot recall what he did for the rest of the day or how he made his way back to his West Roxbury home, but his wife recalls that he arrived "in a trance" clutching a notice from USDA suspending him from duty until further notice, effective immediately. "Ed has literally been in a state of shock ever since that day," his wife confides, "and I don't think he will ever get over it."

Later that day, Herbert Travers, then the United States Attorney for Massachusetts and the man who had obtained the grand jury indictments, held a televised press conference in Boston to announce the indictment and suspension of the inspectors, the largest group of federal employees ever indicted at one time, and to assure the public that no impure food had resulted from the inspectors' crimes. The indictments received extensive publicity in the national media, featuring the remark of a USDA spokesman that "We're expecting the worst scandal since meat inspection became mandatory in 1907." Shortly after the

indictments became public, the governor appointed Travers to a Superior Court judgeship.

Several days after he was suspended, Wywiorski and thirty-nine other inspectors, almost two-thirds of the inspectors in the Boston circuit, were arraigned in federal court in Boston under indictments charging some of them with having accepted "things of value," some of them with having accepted bribes, and some of them with having done both. In addition, some were charged with having conspired with certain individuals to defraud the U.S. Government of the full value of their services. Many inspectors were not served with their indictments by the Government until they were arraigned. Judge Charles Wyzanski chastised the prosecutors for finding time to be on TV but not to serve the indictments. The inspectors pleaded not guilty. None had any prior criminal record.

On October 22, the inspectors were summoned to the USDA office in Boston. Each was handed a written advance notice of a proposal to suspend him from duty without pay "until the outcome of the proceedings resulting from the indictment is known." The notice gave them forty-eight hours to respond. USDA refused to give them more time to obtain counsel and prepare their responses, although the forty-eight hours covered a holiday weekend, and Civil Service regulations entitle the employee to "all the time he actually needs to prepare and submit his answer." Five inspectors obtained a federal court order extending their time to respond until November 5. Despite oral assurances by USDA officials that *all* of the inspectors could have the additional time, USDA suspended the other thirty-five inspectors on November 1. This was done by identical form letters, although the inspectors were charged with vastly different crimes, ranging from receiving "a handful of screws" to accepting a bribe of thousands of dollars. Even before the suspensions, USDA had already begun filling the suspended inspectors' positions with permanent replacements.

The inspectors then appealed their suspensions to the Civil Service Commission and USDA, contending that to suspend them before they had even been tried, much less convicted, was illegal, and that USDA had not complied with the procedural requirements for suspension. Twenty-six of the cases are still pending before the Commission. In six other cases, the Commission's Appeals Examiner ordered immediate reinstatement pending trial.

USDA has appealed five of these reinstatement decisions to the Commission's Board of Appeals and Review and refuses to reinstate the inspectors pending the outcome. USDA failed to appeal the case of inspector Frank Cavaleri, yet it refused to reinstate him for seven weeks, and then immediately served him with another notice of suspension. Seven inspectors appealed their suspensions within USDA and won, but USDA rejected the decision of its own hearing examiner as "unacceptable" and appealed to the Commission, refusing reinstatement in the meanwhile.

One union official, surveying the fruits of these hard-won administrative "victories," lamented, "USDA decided from the very beginning to throw these men to the wolves, and it is not going to let due process of law stand in its way." As a result, the inspectors have received no salary since October, and most have been unable to find any work while under indictment. Lack of income, coupled with high legal expenses, has driven all into debt and many to the point of utter financial ruin.

To an old-timer like Ed Wywiorski, who has spent two-thirds of his sixty-three years in USDA, the indifference of the Department to his plight has been profoundly dispiriting. After so many years, he had come to think of the Department possessively and metaphorically: it was "his" Department, it had nurtured him to manhood, it had trained him in a respected career, and it would provide for him in his old age. Now, it seemed, it had suddenly turned on him, almost rushing to condemn him before he had a chance to defend himself.

Many of the younger inspectors, however, see in the situation a confirmation of USDA's true allegiances. To them, the Department is simply a bureaucracy, cold and morally neutral, but possessed of an unerring instinct for political survival. One inspector puts it this way: "Look, we are probably the only regulatory officials who are required to go out among the regulated to do our job. We don't just visit them periodically, we just about marry them. Day after day, night after night, we are in the lion's den alone with the lion. How are we supposed to get along? USDA doesn't tell us. How are we supposed to resist the barrage of threats and temptations the packers constantly direct at us? USDA doesn't tell us. USDA *does* tell us to use our ingenuity to do our job, to use our common sense—but that's not very helpful when you're in the lion's den."

Every inspector has dozens of anecdotes about the failure of USDA supervisors to back him up in disputes with plant management. This pattern of nonsupport is clearly woven in the public records of USDA and outside investigative bodies. The conflict arises from the fact that the inspector, in the words of one old-timer, is "a shock absorber between USDA and the packer. If you tag too many violations, your supervisor will frequently say you are being too antagonistic and rigid. Then when you let some minor violations go, such as allowing 4 percent milk powder in a sausage instead of 3.5 percent, and the supervisor catches them, he blames it on you, not the packer."

Santa Mancina, the top USDA official in the Boston area, readily concedes that most inspector complaints about packer pressures are legitimate. "The packers up here are resistant as hell. I met with their trade association in an effort to communicate. They continually tried to pressure us. Hell, they threatened to go to Washington and cut our appropriations if we didn't play it their way. The packers, of course, complain about the inspectors, but I tend to believe the inspectors most of the time."

USDA files, only recently made public after a Freedom of Information Act suit, are filled with instances of vicious physical and verbal attacks on inspectors by packers or their employees. These assaults, criminal under the Wholesome Meat Act, elicit from USDA little more than gentle reproach and an exhortation to the packer to read the Act. The Act authorizes USDA to withdraw inspection permanently from serious or persistent violators, yet USDA has never invoked that authority. Reports by the General Accounting Office, the investigatory arm of Congress, repeatedly document the low morale of the inspection corps, attributing this in large part to USDA's failure to back up its inspectors.

USDA takes a rigidly legalistic position against the gratuity system while at the same time appearing to ignore—and even contribute to—the vortex of pressures and incentives that nourish this system. Once every year, USDA supervisors meet with inspectors to go over the regulations prohibiting acceptance of things of value from packers. According to many inspectors and supervisors, this is a very tongue-in-cheek affair. "The best analogy I can think of," says one, "is in the Army when they read you the Articles of War or instructions on how to respond to brainwashing. It is all very make-believe, and no one, least of all the supervisors, takes it seriously. If you press them about how to apply these lofty principles in the real world of the plant, they say, 'Oh, it's okay to take a cup of coffee or an occasional meal from the packer.' If you ask how they reconcile that with the regulations, they tell you, 'Use your common sense.' We leave that meeting thinking small gifts are okay so long as they don't affect the way we do our jobs."

USDA enforces these regulations against inspectors with a passion rarely found in its dealings with unregenerate packers. Consider the case of inspector Harry Topol, thirteen years an inspector and a recipient of the USDA Certificate of Merit in 1968 "for sustained superior performance in carrying out assigned responsibilities." One Saturday morning in July 1969, Topol, on duty at a new assignment in Boston, received a telephone call from his brother-in-law, Salvatore Cina, who said he needed about ten pounds of frankfurters, salami, and bologna for a barbecue that afternoon. Cina asked Topol to put in the order for him, and said he would pick the meat up at the plant before closing. The plant closed before Cina arrived, so Topol filled out a purchase slip and took the meat from the order clerk, arranging to pay Monday since no cashier was on duty. On Topol's way out, a USDA supervisor saw the package, stopped him, and ordered him to return the meat. Topol complied and proceeded to forget about the matter.

Three months later, Topol received a letter from USDA charging him with violation of the regulation and proposing that he be fired. Astonished, Topol requested a hearing and received one—before a circuit supervisor in the meat-inspection program. The supervisor recommended that Topol be fired on the ground that he had purchased meat from a plant that had no retail outlet, despite the uncontradicted testimony of at least four individuals that they routinely walked into the plant off the street and bought meat.

Topol appealed and finally obtained a hearing before an official not connected with the meat-inspection program, who found that the plant did sell to the public and that all charges should be dismissed. The resourceful Director of Personnel, however, while accepting these findings, managed to have the last word. Topol had obtained credit for the purchase until Monday, he ruled, "a personal accommodation which was out of the ordinary." He suspended Topol for four weeks without pay. Two weeks after his suspension, Topol suffered a heart attack. Shortly thereafter, his wife had a nervous breakdown that her physician attributed to the strain of the yearlong ordeal.

## The Department of Justice: "It Is More Blessed to Give than to Receive"

In April 1972, Ed Wywiorski's trial began. He had been indicted on eight counts of receiving meat, "a thing of value," in 1967 and 1968. Six of the counts alleged the receipt of a quantity "unknown to the Grand Jury," the seventh stated a quantity of "eight pounds, more or less," and the eighth cited a quantity of "twenty-one pounds and two ounces, more or less." Before trial, the prosecution conceded that Wywiorski had been indicted on three counts he could not possibly have committed, having been on vacation or at different locations at the times alleged. Judge Andrew Caffrey permitted James Krasnoo, the young Assistant U.S. Attorney prosecuting the inspector cases, to drop these counts over the objection of Arnold Felton, Wywiorski's attorney, who argued that the jury should be able to see the kind of evidence on which the prosecution's case rested. A fourth count was dismissed on a technicality.

Krasnoo then offered Felton a deal. "Wywiorski's only a little fish in a big pond," Krasnoo told Felton. "If he pleads guilty before trial, I'll recommend two years probation to the judge." Felton relayed this offer to his client. Wywiorski decided to stand trial on charges of having received four bundles of meat from Jack Satter, Baldwin Vincent Scalesse, and John McNeil. Satter and Scalesse were and are executives of Colonial Provision Company, and McNeil had been a quality-control man with Colonial.

The only damaging witness against Wywiorski was McNeil. He testified that he had no independent memory of transactions with Wywiorski but that when he worked at Colonial he had given bundles of meat to inspectors on behalf of Colonial and had made notations on rack cards for each transaction, usually including the initials of the inspector, the date, and the amount of meat given. He had saved these cards, and he produced four bearing the notation "EdWy."

At the end of the first day of trial, Felton was confronted with an agonizing decision. Reviewing his thought processes, Felton says, "Wywiorski is an old, ineffectual, harmless guy, what people call a 'nebbish.' He would have made a terrible witness, Krasnoo would have made mincemeat of him. I decided he should plead guilty if we could get a favorable disposition." Felton called Krasnoo to ask if his offer to recommend probation on a guilty plea was still open. Krasnoo replied, "Tauro [the new U.S. Attorney] insists that we add on a $2,000 fine as a penalty for your having gone to trial." Wywiorski then called his wife from Felton's office. "I'm going to throw in the towel," he told her. "At least this way, I won't go to jail." Felton, Wywiorski, and Krasnoo then signed a form statement reciting that the determination as to a sentence recommendation "is *always* made after a verdict of Guilty or a Guilty plea has been entered, and *not before*. . . . Any statement relating to a recommendation by an Assistant U.S. Attorney made before a determination of guilt can only refer to his recommendation to be made to the U.S. Attorney, and does not refer to any recommendation to be made to the Court." The statement goes on to say that the final decision on sentence is that of the judge alone. The next day, Wywiorski entered a plea of guilty. Thus the trial ended before Felton could introduce evidence that on March 30, 1967, precisely the period during which McNeil said Wywiorski received meat, Wywiorski reported to his supervisor in writing that he had caught McNeil making entries of reports of laboratory results in official USDA folders without an inspector being present. The report concluded that McNeil left "in an annoyed and resentful manner."

On May 10, Wywiorski appeared before Judge Caffrey for sentencing. Caffrey told Wywiorski that before accepting his guilty plea and sentencing him, he wished to be satisfied that Wywiorski had in fact committed the crimes for which he was admitting guilt. Wywiorski stated that he had not. A surprised Caffrey reminded him that he could not accept a guilty plea unless he was actually guilty. Wywiorski again denied guilt. Caffrey suggested a short recess to resolve the confusion, during which Felton explained that Wywiorski could not plead guilty without admitting guilt, and that if he did not plead guilty, the deal with Krasnoo would be off. When court resumed, Caffrey

once again asked Wywiorski if he was guilty. Wywiorski muttered that he had given McNeil the keys to his car (where McNeil had said the meat was probably placed). Caffrey then asked Krasnoo for his sentence recommendation, and Krasnoo responded with the agreed-upon recommendation. Judge Caffrey proceeded to sentence Wywiorski to one year in prison and a $1,000 fine.

Mrs. Wywiorski recalls the scene. "When the judge pronounced his sentence on Ed, even Krasnoo seemed stunned. Ed was in a trance. He had never for one moment believed that he would go to jail. All he had talked about was retirement, an end to the pressures in the plant. When the U.S. Marshals dragged him away, he still did not seem to know what had hit him. He is a totally broken man. And all this over four bundles of meat."

Wywiorski is now serving his prison sentence.

As of June 1, eight Boston meat inspectors had reached trial and had either been convicted or pleaded guilty. All six who have been sentenced so far have received prison sentences, ranging up to three years. The "bigger fish"—other line inspectors, two subcircuit supervisors, and a circuit supervisor, some of whom are accused of accepting money as well as meat—are still to come.

Krasnoo scoffs at the suggestion that the sentences have been unduly harsh. In his view, the inspectors have not been dealt with harshly enough: "These were public officials invested with a high public trust." (To the inspectors, this view is bitterly ironic. "For years," says one, "we've been pieces of shit, lowly GS-5s and 7s, barely noticed, barely lower middle class. Now, all of a sudden, we are exalted public officials charged with weighty responsibilities and moral leadership.") The young prosecutor told one lawyer that the inspectors were damned lucky that he wasn't prosecuting their wives, who he felt must have had knowledge of their crimes.

Most of the forty inspectors, like Wywiorski, were indicted on the testimony of McNeil, and to a lesser extent Scalesse and Satter, before a federal grand jury first convened in early 1970. The prosecution's case at trial was and is based almost entirely upon the same evidence.

One of the intriguing questions that haunt these trials is why McNeil, who left Colonial in June 1967 to become a USDA inspector, and who is all too familiar with the gratuity system, decided to go before the grand jury and incriminate the inspectors. There is some evidence—based on McNeil's frequently expressed hostility toward Colonial, and on his threats to sue Colonial for compensation for injuries sustained by him and his wife while in Colonial's employ—that he thought his revelations would result in prosecutions not of the inspectors but of the "biggest fish" of all: Colonial Provision Company. Such an expectation would be a natural one, of course, for McNeil's testimony is at least as damaging to Colonial, a company with annual sales of over $50 million, as to a bunch of low-level inspectors, many of whom were charged with receiving small quantities of meat. And while the inspectors could be effectively disciplined administratively—by loss of pay, discharge, or otherwise—Colonial could be punished only by prosecution and public obloquy.

If McNeil's intention was to damage Colonial, he has utterly failed to do so. The Department of Justice has actually contrived the meat-inspection prosecutions in such a way that Colonial has managed to emerge unscathed. That has not been easy to do, given the admissions of McNeil, Scalesse, and Satter that they routinely gave meat, money, and other things of value to numerous inspectors; that McNeil, at Colonial's behest, doctored samples, illegally gained access to the USDA retention cage, and chose dummy samples; that Scalesse lied to the grand jury in at least three sessions; that Satter lied to the grand jury and had tried to bring political pressure to bear from Washington against zealous inspectors. But the ingenuity of a political Department of Justice is not to be underestimated.

According to the Justice Department's own evidence, employees of Colonial and six other Boston area packers routinely and systematically gave meat, money, and other things of value to the forty inspectors on behalf of the packers. *Yet none of these packers or their employees has been, or probably ever will be, indicted for these transactions.* The reason is simple: after lying to the grand jury, Satter and Scalesse finally claimed the Fifth Amendment, refusing to answer further questions. The Department then granted them immunity from prosecution in order to induce them to testify against the inspectors.

When asked why the U.S. Attorney decided to grant immunity from prosecution to Colonial and six other packers and their employees, but not to the inspectors, prosecutor Krasnoo gave three reasons:

1. "I would never grant immunity to a witness who lied before the grand jury." Yet Scalesse and Satter admittedly lied to the grand jury on several occasions prior to being granted immunity.

2. "The inspectors failed to cooperate by giving evidence to the grand jury." But the packer witnesses also failed to cooperate, until they were offered immunity, and there is every reason to believe that the inspectors would have cooperated had *they* been offered immunity. Well before the indictments were issued, at least one attorney representing a group of inspectors told Krasnoo his clients would "sing like canaries" in return for immunity. The offer was refused. To the inspectors, it was clear from their first appearance before the grand jury that they were the targets of the investigation.

3. "I know of no inspector who took the Fifth, so we couldn't offer them immunity." This is incorrect. A number of inspectors took the Fifth, as Krasnoo should certainly have known.

The real reasons that the Department of Justice pursued the minnows while protecting the whales probably lie elsewhere. As one former prosecutor put it: "From the Department's point of view, this was a smart prosecutive decision. By giving immunity to a relatively small number of influential packers who dealt with a relatively large number of inspectors, they could get a large number of convictions, a lot of publicity, and not step on any important toes. If they had prosecuted the packers, they would have had to prove 'intent to influence.' This way, the judge simply charges the jury that in order to convict, they need only find that the inspectors received anything of value. Since McNeil gets up with his cards and says they received, these are very easy cases to win."

The solicitude of the Department of Justice for Colonial, however, goes far beyond immunizing it from prosecution. For the Department has managed to draft indictments against the inspectors, containing well over 2,000 counts, most of which involve gratuities given by key Colonial personnel, without ever mentioning Colonial by name. The same is true of the six other immunized packing companies. The indictments recite that things of value were given, and conspiracies entered into with the defendants, by certain named individuals—Satter, Scalesse, and McNeil in most cases—but they are not identified as employees or agents of Colonial. For all the public knows or *could* know from the indictments, Colonial and the other immunized packers have been pure as the driven snow. Since the mass media have confined their attention entirely to the indictments and the sentences, there has been virtually no coverage of the trials, at which the involvement of Colonial and other packers is brought out.

The Department, to be sure, has secured indictments against three small packers, none of them involved with the forty inspectors. Only one case has been tried, and the outcome is most intriguing and bizarre. As the result of an FBI plant and the use of marked money, inspector Robert Gaff had apparently been caught red-handed immediately after receiving money from a packer, Waters & Litchfield Co. On October 29, 1971, Gaff pleaded guilty to four counts of receiving things of value from two packers. He was sentenced to serve a six-month sentence (half that meted out to Wywiorski for accepting four bundles of meat). After Gaff completed his term and left prison, Waters & Litchfield was brought to trial in April. The Department of Justice, in a most extraordinary and inexplicable maneuver, *waived a jury,* knowing full well that a jury, particularly with the price of meat on their minds, would be far more likely to convict than a judge would be. Then Gaff took the stand as the prosecution's main witness, and his testimony—testimony that had supported his plea of guilty and the grand jury indictment of Waters & Litchfield—was so garbled that the judge directed a verdict of not guilty. So the Department's record remains clean as a hound's tooth: no packers convicted.

Other aspects of the meat-inspector cases also raise the question of whether the lady holding the Scales of Justice in front of the Department's headquarters is actually peeking from under her blindfold. On the day the indictments were returned against the inspectors, Herbert Travers, the then U.S. Attorney, took the extraordinary step in a case of this sort of applying for the issuance of bench warrants for the immediate arrest of the inspectors. This procedure was highly unusual because no inspector had a prior criminal record (this is a condition of being a USDA inspector), and they were obviously unlikely to flee. Travers had arranged for federal agents to sweep through the meat districts and make a dramatic and well-publicized mass arrest and incarceration of the inspectors. The judge, seeing no justification for arrests, refused to issue the warrants.

When the indictments were announced in October to an attentive press, many of the counts against the inspectors were so trivial as to lend comic relief to an otherwise relentlessly depressing affair. One in-

spector indicted for receiving "a thing of value, to wit, a handful of screws," quipped, "I wouldn't mind if I had a big hand, but how many screws can I get in this?" Another inspector was indicted for receiving "a spiritual bouquet," a third for receiving a light bulb. Other "things of value" forming the basis for individual counts were half a can of shoe polish, "the picking up of one photograph," and a car wash. One inspector was charged with accepting a ride home for his daughter from a packer employee.

Many of the counts were not simply trivial, they were demonstrably mistaken. Frank Cavaleri, for example, was indicted on six counts, four of which occurred at times when he was not even working for the Government. Most inspectors had at least some counts of this order of accuracy. After all of the publicity and hoopla had been generated, of course, these counts were dropped by the U.S. Attorney's office, often over the objections of defense counsel who wished the jury to learn how casual the Department had been in securing indictments. The proliferation of counts had another purpose too. As one ex-prosecutor explained, "They threw indictments around like confetti to inundate the inspectors. Then Krasnoo could offer to drop most of the counts in exchange for a plea of guilty. Krasnoo was giving up nothing that was worth anything, of course, but to the inspectors, the offer must have seemed generous."

The Department of Justice has employed other questionable tactics. The indictments contain a large number of counts for accepting bribes—in which there is necessarily an allegation of intent to influence the inspector's official actions—as well as counts of simply receiving things of value, which include no such allegation. *Yet there has been no evidence that inspectors were bribed, and much evidence that they were not.* First, packer employees have admitted at the trials that the inspectors did their jobs and did not relax their application of the regulations. Second, Travers and Krasnoo have both stated publicly that the public has not been exposed to deficient meat products as a result of the indicted transactions. Third, Krasnoo has dropped all bribery counts before trial; he concedes that he has proved only the receipt of things of value by inspectors. Nevertheless, despite requests by defense attorneys not to do so, Krasnoo has used the term "bribery" in summations to the jury on a number of occasions.

The Department, in conjunction with the courts, also consistently penalizes those inspectors who invoke their right to go to trial. This practice is not unique to these cases, of course, but the result is not less unjust for being common. Inspector Hugh McDonald was indicted on 183 counts of receiving money, meat, and liquor; 163 counts were dropped before trial. Then Krasnoo induced him to plead guilty to nine counts of receiving meat and liquor, dropping the others. Krasnoo made no sentence recommendation to the judge. McDonald received one year in prison and a $1,000 suspended fine. Inspector Richard H. Murphy was indicted on 157 counts of receiving money and meat, 147 of which were dropped before trial. Krasnoo offered to make no sentence recommendation if Murphy pleaded guilty. Murphy insisted on going to trial and was convicted on ten counts of receiving money. Krasnoo then recommended a sentence of four years in prison, with a $4,000 suspended fine. Murphy received three years in prison and a $1,000 fine.

It is inconceivable that Murphy would have received so severe a sentence if he, like McDonald several weeks before, had pleaded guilty instead of invoking his right to put the Government to its proof in a trial. As Krasnoo well knows, Murphy's example has not been lost on the thirty-three inspectors still awaiting trial. "I have a strong case," says one "but look at the risk I run by going to trial before jurors angry about the high cost of meat. I will have to plead guilty to avoid paying 'the Murphy premium.'"

With the Department of Justice at the bargaining table, negotiation for guilty pleas can be a nasty business. In the case of one married inspector, the prosecution threatened to show that he had had sexual relations with a female employee of the packer. The Internal Revenue Service, presumably with the connivance of the Department of Justice, has conducted tax audits on a number of inspectors in an effort to show that they were living beyond their means, evidence that would assist the prosecution's case. The IRS, after securing records and cooperation from the attorney for several inspectors, has refused either to return the records or to issue a ruling, thus enhancing the bargaining power of the Justice Department in negotiating with the inspectors for guilty pleas.

The Boston meat-inspector cases raise disturbing questions. A steady stream of inspectors are now entering prison, their careers and reputations irretrievably lost, their families plunged into unspeakable despair. Yet within a mile of the federal courthouse, Colonial Provision Company flourishes, processing millions of pounds of meat daily; Jack Satter drives his Cadillac to his new job as president of Colonial, and Vinnie Scalesse has been promoted to head of a Colonial subsidiary. These admitted perjurers and the other packers who admittedly gave things of value to the inspectors continue to do business as before. John McNeil continues as a USDA inspector, sometimes training new inspectors in their duties, despite having admitted doctoring and switching USDA samples as a Colonial employee and having been a key link in a chain of illegality. The public continues to subsidize this system in several ways—in higher meat prices, reflecting the costs of gratuities, and in higher taxes, reflecting the packers' practice of deducting these gratuities as part of their operational "shrinkage." It is likely, in addition, that the public is getting an inferior product for its money. "How much rigorous inspection do you think is going on today at Colonial or these other houses?" one inspector asks. "These packers bought insurance against strict inspection. How do you think the inspector is going to behave knowing that he can be prosecuted simply on the word of the packer he is supposed to regulate and that the packer will not be touched?"

A society truly concerned about crime must concern itself with those social systems—like the meat plant—in which crime seems to make sense to otherwise moral men. "Cumshaw" is such a system, and it flourishes. While some of its practitioners have been punished, the most powerful have not. For the latter, at least, the system has paid handsome dividends.

### Note

1. Warren Bennis and Caroline McGregor, eds., *The Professional Manager, Essays by Douglas McGregor* (New York: McGraw-Hill, 1967), p. 196.

# Chapter 11 Review Questions

1. In your own words, can you describe McGregor's Theory X and Theory Y? Why do McGregor's Theories X and Y rest on the assumptions of Maslow's

hierarchy of human needs? What is Maslow's hierarchy of human needs? From your experience is such a hierarchy a valid idea?

2. What were the conflicting cross-pressures faced by the federal meat inspectors in their line of work? How did their work environment leave them vulnerable to possible federal indictments? Would you characterize their work situation as Theory X? Or something else?

3. Why did the public demand a higher level of ethics from the meat inspectors than from the meat packers? What were the causes and results of this double standard of public expectations as it affected the public employees? In your opinion, is this double standard typical?

4. Do you think the application of McGregor's Theory Y could have improved the meat inspectors' employment conditions and ultimately prevented their indictment? Would McGregor's Theory Y have been applicable in this case study? Explain why or why not. Specifically, why do the multiple responsibilities of most public employees make it more difficult to adopt McGregor's Theory Y? What were the multiple public responsibilities of the meat inspectors?

5. In human terms, what was the ultimate impact of the working environment on the lives of meat inspectors? Was their working environment healthy or destructive to human growth and development? Was there any possibility of improving their work environment? If so, how and in what direction?

6. In light of the foregoing case study, do you think McGregor's ideas are generally applicable to public sector organizations? Or, are they useful mainly in private business? Can you sum up what conditions might allow for the successful application of Theory Y? Under what conditions may it not be applicable?

## Key Terms

Theory X
Theory Y
hard versus soft management
job enrichment
participatory management
decentralization of control

hierarchy of needs
physiological and safety needs
ego needs
needs of self-fulfillment
management by objectives
consultative management

## Suggestions for Further Reading

Public personnel administration is a field of enormous complexity, specialization, and rapid change, and, therefore, looking at several basic introductory texts is necessary for a good overview: N. Joseph Cayer, *Public Personnel Administration in the U.S.*, Second Edition (New York:

St. Martin's, 1986); Jonathan Beck, *Managing People in Public Agencies* (Boston: Little, Brown, 1984); Gilbert B. Siegel and Robert C. Myrtle, *Public Personnel Administration: Concepts and Practices* (Boston: Houghton Mifflin, 1991); and Steven W. Hays and Richard C.

Kearney, *Public Personnel Administration*, Second Edition (Englewood Cliffs, N.J.: Prentice-Hall, 1990). To supplement these introductions, students should further examine the basic *framing* documents of public personnel, such as the Civil Service Act of 1883, the Hatch Acts, the Civil Service Reform Act of 1978, as well as several others contained in Frederick C. Mosher, ed., *Basic Documents of American Public Administration: 1776–1950* (New York: Holmes and Meier, 1976), and Richard J. Stillman II, ed., *Basic Documents of American Public Administration: Since 1950* (New York: Holmes and Meier, 1982).

For the best history of the American civil service system, see Paul Van Riper, *History of U.S. Civil Service* (New York: Harper & Row, 1958). For an insightful view of personnel practices at the local level, read Frank J. Thompson, *Personnel Policy in the City: The Politics of Jobs in Oakland* (Berkeley, Calif.: University of California Press, 1975); and for a view of its operation at the federal level, see Frederick C. Mosher, *Democracy and the Public Service,* Second Edition (New York: Oxford University Press, 1982); William I. Bacchus, *Staffing for Foreign Affairs* (Princeton: Princeton University Press, 1983); or Hugh Heclo, *A Government of Strangers: Executive Politics in Washington* (Washington, D.C.: The Brookings Institution, 1977). Articles contained in the two volumes of the "classics" series on personnel give readers a useful overview of the scope, diversity, and complexity of this field: Thomas H. Patten, Jr., ed., *Classics of Personnel Management* (Chicago: Moore Publishing Co., 1979), and Frank J. Thompson, ed., *Classics of Public Personnel Policy*, Second Edition (Monterey, Calif.: Brooks/Cole, 1990).

Among the recent articles on federal personnel, some of the more interesting ones include Benton G. Moeller, "What Ever Happened to the Federal Personnel System," *International Personnel Management,* 9 (Spring 1982), pp. 1–8.; Bernard Rosen, "Uncertainty in the Senior Executive Service," *Public Administration Review,* 41 (March/April 1981), pp. 203–207; Norton E. Long, "S.E.S. and the Public Interest," *Public Administration Review,* 41 (May/June 1981), pp. 305–312; as well as the entire symposium on "The Public Service as an Institution," edited by Eugene B. McGregor, Jr., which contains several fine short essays on the subject, in *Public Administration Review,* 42 (July/August 1982), pp. 304–320. James L. Perry and Lois R. Wise, "The Motivational Bases of Public Service," *Public Administration Review* (May/June 1990), pp. 367–373; and Charles H. Levine and Rosslyn S. Kleeman, "The Quiet Crisis of the Civil Service," (Washington, D.C.: National Academy of Public Administration, 1988) are also useful.

For a set of comprehensive essays that explain the "state-of-the-art-of-public personnel administration," see Jack Rabin et al., eds., *Handbook on Public Personnel Administration and Labor Relations* (New York: Marcel Dekker, 1983), as well as several of the essays contained in Frederick S. Lane, ed., *Current Issues in Public Administration*, Fourth Edition (New York: St. Martin's Press, 1990). One would also do well to skim current issues of *Public Administration Review, Harvard Business Review, Public Personnel Management, The Bureaucrat,* and *Public Management* for recent and fast-changing trends in the field of personnel.

Japanese personnel motivation techniques have recently gained wide popularity in the United States; for a balanced introduction to the subject, read William Ouchi, *Theory Z: How American Business Can Meet the Japanese Challenge* (New York: Avon Books, 1982). "Revitalization" themes also are broadly popular in the public service as reflected today by Robert B. Denhardt et al., eds., *The Revitalization of the Public Service* (Columbia, Mo.: University of Missouri and Lincoln University, Extension Publications, 1987).

One should not miss reading the Volcker Commission Report for an updated review of this topic, *Leadership for America,* (Lexington, Mass.: Lexington Books, 1990).

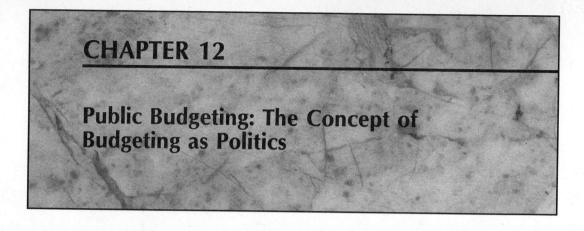

# CHAPTER 12

## Public Budgeting: The Concept of Budgeting as Politics

*The essence of budgeting is that it allocates scarce resources and hence implies choice between potential objects of expenditure. Budgeting implies balance and it requires some kind of decision-making process.*

Irene S. Rubin

## Introduction

Budgets serve many important functions in government. In one sense, budgets are contracts annually agreed on by the executive and legislative branches that allow executive agencies and departments to raise and spend public funds in specified ways for the coming fiscal year (normally running in state and local governments from July 1 to June 30; changed at the federal level by the Congressional Budget Act of 1974 to end on September 30 and to begin October 1 each year). A budget imposes a mutual set of legal obligations between the elected and appointed officers of public organizations with regard to taxation and expenditure policies. A budget is, therefore, a legal contract that provides a vehicle for fiscal controls over subordinate units of government by the politically elected representatives of the people.

Budgets have other purposes as well: they can be planning devices used to translate presently scarce fiscal and human resources in the public sector into future governmental goals and programs. In this respect, budgets are vital instruments for directing what tasks government will perform and how human talent in society and public monies will be used.

In addition, budgets are forces for internal coordination and efficiency in public administration. Budget formulations annually impose choices concerning how public programs should be undertaken, interrelated, and measured in terms of their value, effectiveness, and worth to the general public. Related to the concept of budgets as a coordinating device is the idea that budgets are economic documents. In this role federal budgets are tools of fiscal policy, for they stimulate or slow down national economic growth through increased or decreased taxation or revenue expenditures. Finally, budgets can also be viewed as political documents, reflecting through the allocation of funds the ultimate desires, interests, and power of various groups within the body politic as expressed by elected legislative bodies. In setting up an annual budget, various political participants engage in log rolling, compromises, and bargains to create a document that by and large mirrors the current priorities of the locality, state, or nation. The quality and quantity of government that the citizenry desires and will support at any given time is expressed by the budget.

Our conceptual understanding of these roles of the budget in modern government is comparatively new, being chiefly a twentieth-century phenomenon. In large part, our instituting formal budget documents began in the Progressive Era, when public budgets were developed as vehicles for governmental reform to produce improved economy and efficiency in the public sector and as instruments for imposing greater control over public spending. Many of these ideas and concepts were borrowed from the experience and practices of business management.

Although there remains a strong emphasis on the earlier notions of budgets as vehicles for imposing control, economy, and efficiency in government, a prominent current view of the role of budgets—and a perspective frequently held by political scientists, budgeting specialists, and public administration practitioners—is a political one: budgets are principally governed by considerations of compromise, strategy, and bargaining. Irene S. Rubin, a political scientist and prominent authority on public budgeting at Northern Illinois University, presents the political view of budget making in the opening chapter of her new book, *The Politics of Public Budgeting*. Rubin envisions government budgets as "not merely technical managerial documents" but rather "they are also intrinsically and irreducibly political." Her thesis is that although public budgets share many features of budgeting in general such as presenting choices over possible expenditures and problems of balancing revenues with expenditures, they differ in fundamental ways. The open environments within which budgets are developed, the variety of actors involved, the constraints imposed as well as the emphasis on public accountability, give budgets special and distinctive features in the public sector. These aspects add complexity and unique dilemmas to their formulation, operation, and conceptualization.

Professor Rubin's essay at the outset defines "what is budgeting" and the distinctive features of government budgets. From a local case of budget making in Dekalb, Illinios, she underscores the critical political dynamics of public budgeting processes and the variety of participants that are involved, even within the local setting. The elements of budgetary politics concern, in her view, "separate but linked" decision clusters, specifically five clusters dealing with the revenue process (How much income will be available and from where?); budget process (How to make the budget choices?); expenditure process (Which programs will get what?); the balance cluster (How revenues and expenditures will be balanced?); and <u>budget implementation issues</u> (How the budget will be put into operation?). Her essay concludes with an important distinction between understanding "macrobudgeting," or top-down budget viewpoints, versus "microbudgeting," which focuses on the specific actors and their strategies in putting together budgets.

As you read the following selection, keep in mind such questions as:

Why does Rubin stress throughout her writing the political over the technical or managerial aspects of public budgeting?

What differences are apparent from her perspective between government and business budget-making? Do you agree with her conclusions about these fundamental differences?

How do "macro" and "micro" points of view of budgets differ and yet why are *both* essential for a complete understanding of the budgetary process? What are the advantages and disadvantages of both ways of conceptualizing budgets? Do these perspectives on budgets relate to any of our earlier readings such as Charles Lindblom's "incremental decision-making model"?

Why does Rubin focus on understanding modern budgetary processes as "separate but linked decision clusters"? What are the major clusters of issues apparent in each?

# The Politics of Public Budgets

**IRENE S. RUBIN**

Public budgets describe what governments do by listing how governments spend money. A budget links tasks to be performed with the amount of resources necessary to accomplish those tasks, ensuring that money will be available to wage war, provide housing, or maintain streets. Budgets limit expenditures to the revenues available, to ensure balance and prevent overspending. Most of the work in drawing up a budget is technical, estimating how much it

From *The Politics of Public Budgeting* by Irene B. Rubin (Chatham, N.J.: Chatham House Publishers, 1990), pp. 1–28. Reprinted by permission.

will cost to feed a thousand shut-ins with a Meals on Wheels program or how much revenue will be produced from a 1 percent tax on retail sales. But public budgets are not merely technical managerial documents; they are also intrinsically and irreducibly political.

- <u>Budgets reflect choices about what government will and will not do</u>. They reflect general public consensus about what kinds of services governments should provide and what citizens are entitled to as members of society. Should government provide services that the private sector could provide, such as water, electricity, transportation, and housing? Do all citizens have a guarantee of health care, regardless of ability to pay? Are all insured against hunger? Are they entitled to some kind of housing?

- Budgets reflect priorities—between police and flood control, day care and defense, the Northeast and the Southwest. The budget process mediates between groups and individuals who want different things from government and determines who gets what. These decisions may influence whether the poor get job training or the police get riot training, both as a response to an increased number of unemployed.
- Budgets reflect the relative proportion of decisions made for local and constituency purposes, and for efficiency, effectiveness, and broader public goals. Budgets reflect the degree of importance legislators put on satisfying their constituents and the legislators' willingness to listen to interest-group demands. For example, the Defense Department may decide to spend more money to keep a military base open because the local economy depends on it and to spend less money to improve combat readiness.
- Budgets provide a powerful tool of accountability to citizens who want to know how the government is spending their money and if government has generally followed their preferences. Budgeting links citizen preferences and governmental outcomes.
- Budgets reflect citizens' preferences for different forms of taxation and different levels of taxation, as well as the ability of specific groups of taxpayers to shift tax burdens to others. The budget reflects the degree to which the government redistributes wealth upward or downward through the tax system.
- At the national level, the budget influences the economy, so fiscal policy affects the level of employment—how many people are out of work at any time.
- Budgets reflect the relative power of different individuals and organizations to influence budget outcomes. Budgetary decision making provides a picture of the relative power of budget actors within and between branches of government, as well as the importance of citizens in general and specific interest groups.

In all these ways, public budgeting is political. But budgeting is not typical of other political processes and hence one example among many. It is both an important and a unique arena of politics. It is important because of the specific policy issues reflected in the budget: the scope of government, the distribution of wealth, the openness of government to interest groups, and the accountability of government to the public at large. It is unique because these decisions have to take place in the context of budgeting, with its need for balance, its openness to the environment, and its requirements for timely decisions so that government can carry on without interruption.

Public budgets clearly have political implications, but what does it mean to say that key political decisions are made in the context of budgeting? The answer has several parts. First, what is budgeting? Second, what is public budgeting, as opposed to individual or family budgeting or the budgeting of private organizations? Third, what does *political* mean in the context of public budgeting?

# What Is Budgeting?

The essence of budgeting is that it allocates scarce resources and hence implies choice between potential objects of expenditure. Budgeting implies balance, and it requires some kind of decision-making process.

## Making Budgetary Choices

All budgeting, whether public or private, individual or organizational, involves choices between possible expenditures. Since no one has unlimited resources, people budget all the time. A young child makes a budget (a plan for spending, balancing revenues and expenditures) when she decides to spend money on a marshmallow rabbit rather than a chocolate one, assuming she has money enough for only one rabbit. The air force may choose between two different airplanes to replace current bombers. These examples illustrate the simplest form of budgeting because they involve only one actor, one resource, one time, and two straightforward and comparable choices.

Normally, budgeting does not take place by comparing only two reasonably similar items. There may be a nearly unlimited number of choices. Budgeting usually limits the options to consider by grouping together similar things that can be reasonably compared. When I go to the supermarket, I do not compare all the possible things I could buy, not only because I cannot absorb that number of comparisons, but because the comparisons would be meaningless and a waste of time. I do not go to the supermarket and decide to get either a turkey or a bottle of soda pop. I compare main dishes with main dishes, beverages with beverages, desserts with desserts. Then I have a common denominator for comparison. For example, I may look at the main course and ask about the amount of protein for the dollar. I may compare the desserts in terms of the amount of cholesterol or the calories.

There is a tendency, then, to make comparisons within categories where the comparison is meaningful. This is as true for governmental budgeting as it is for shoppers. For example, weapons might be compared with weapons or automobiles with automobiles. They could be compared in terms of speed, reliability, availability of spare parts, and so on, and the one that did the most of what you wanted it to do at the least cost would be the best choice. As long as there is agreement on the goals to be achieved, the choice should be straightforward.

Sometimes, budgeting requires comparison of different, and seemingly incomparable things. If I do not have enough money to buy a whole balanced meal, I may have to make choices between main dishes and desserts. How do I compare the satisfaction of a sweet tooth to the nourishment of a turkey? Or, in the public sector, how do I compare the benefits of providing shelters for the homeless with buying more helicopters for the navy? I may then move to more general comparisons, such as how clearly were the requests made and the benefits spelled out; who got the benefits last time and whose turn is it this time; are there any specific contingencies that make one choice more likely than the other? For example, will we be embarrassed to show our treatment of the homeless in front of a visiting dignitary? Or, are disarmament negotiations coming up in which we need to display strength or make a symbolic gesture of restraint? Comparing dissimilar items may require a list of priorities. It may be possible to do two or more important things if they are sequenced properly.

Budgeting often allocates money, but it can allocate any scarce resource, for example, time. A student may choose between studying for an exam or playing softball and drinking beer afterward. In this example, it is time that is at a premium, not money. Or it could be medical skills that are in short supply, or expensive equipment, or apartment space, or water.

Government programs often involve a choice of resources and sometimes involve combinations of resources, each of which has different characteristics. For example, some federal farm programs involve direct cash payments plus loans at below-market interest rates, and welfare programs often involve dollar payments plus food stamps, which allow recipients to pay less for food. Federal budgets often assign agencies money, personnel, and sometimes borrowing authority, three different kinds of resources.

## Balancing and Borrowing

Budgets have to balance. A plan for expenditures that pays no attention to ensuring that revenues cover expenditures is not a budget. That may sound odd in view of huge federal deficits, but a budget may technically be balanced by borrowing. Balance means only that outgo is matched or exceeded by income. The borrowing, of course, has to be paid off. Borrowing means spending more now and paying more in the future in order to maintain balance. It is a balance over time.

To illustrate the nature of budget balance, consider me as shopper again. Suppose I spend all my weekly shopping money before I buy my dessert. I have the option of treating my dollar limit as if it were more flexible, by adding the dimension of time. I can buy the dessert and everything else in the basket, going over my budget, and then eat less at the end of the month. Or I can pay the bill with a credit card, assuming I will have more money in the future with which to pay off the bill when it comes due. The possibility of borrowing against the future is part of most budget choices.

## Process

Budgeting cannot proceed without some kind of decision process. Even in the simplest cases of budgeting, there has to be some limit set to spending, some order of decision making, some way to structure comparisons among alternatives, and some way to compare choices. Budget processes also regulate the flow of decisions so they are made in a timely manner.

Back to my shopping example: If I shop for the main course first, and spend more money than I intended on it because I found some fresh fish, there will be less money left for purchasing the dessert. Hence, unless I set a firm limit on the amount of money to spend for each segment of the meal, the order in which I do the purchasing counts. Of course, if I get to the end of my shopping and do not have enough money left for dessert, I can put back some of the items already in the cart and squeeze out enough money for dessert.

Governmental budgeting is also concerned with procedures for managing tradeoffs between large categories of spending. Budgeters may determine the relative importance of each category first, attaching a dollar level in proportion to the assigned importance, or they may allow purchasing in each area to go on independently, later reworking the choices until the balance between the parts is acceptable.

The order of decisions is important in another sense. I can determine how much money I am likely to have first and then set that as an absolute limit on expenditures, or I can determine what I must have, what I wish to have, and what I need to set aside for emergencies and then go out and try to find enough money to cover some or all of those expenditures. Especially in emergencies, such as accidents or other health emergencies, people are likely to obligate the money first and worry about where it will come from later. Governmental budgeting, too, may concentrate first on revenues and later on expenditures, or first on expenditures and later on income. Like individuals or families, during emergencies such as floods or hurricanes or wars, governments will commit the expenditures first and worry about where the money will come from later.

# Governmental Budgeting

Public budgeting shares the characteristics of budgeting in general but differs from household and business budgeting in some key ways. First, in public budgeting, there are always people and organizations with different perspectives and different goals trying to get what they want out of the budget. In individual budgets, there may be only one person involved; and in family and business budgets, there may be only a limited number of actors and they may have similar views of what they want to achieve through the budget.

Second, public budgets are more open to the environment than budgets of families or businesses are. Not only are public budgets open to the economy but also to other levels of government, to citizens, to interest groups, to the press, and to politicians.

Third, budgets form a crucial link between citizen taxpayers and government officials. The document itself may be a key form of accountability. This function does not apply to businesses, families, or individuals.

Fourth, public budgeting is characterized by a variety of constraints, legal limits, perceived limits imposed by public opinion, rules and regulations about how to carry out the budget, and many more. Public budgeting is far more constrained in this sense than budgets of individuals or businesses.

Public budgeting has five particular characteristics that differentiate it from other kinds of budgeting. First, public budgeting is characterized by a variety of budgetary actors who often have different priorities and different levels of power over budget outcomes. These actors have to be regulated and orchestrated by the budget process. Second, in government there is a distinction between those who pay taxes and those who decide how money will be spent—the citizens and the elected politicians. Public officials can force citizens to pay taxes for expenditures they do not want, but citizens can vote politicians out of office. Third, the budget document is important as a means of public accountability. Fourth, public budgets are very vulnerable to the environment—to the economy, to changes in public opinion, to elections, to local contingencies such as natural disasters like floods, or political disasters such as the police bombing of MOVE headquarters in Philadelphia, which burned down part of a neighborhood. Fifth, public budgets are incredibly constrained. Although there is a built-in necessity to make budgets adaptable to contingencies, there are many elements of public budgets that are beyond the immediate control of those who draw up budgets.

## A Variety of Actors

The first characteristic of public budgeting was the variety of actors involved in the budget and their frequently clashing motivations and goals. On a regular basis, bureau chiefs, executive budget officers, and chief executives are involved in the budget process, as are legislators, both on committees and as a whole group. Interest groups may be involved at intervals, sometimes for relatively long stretches of time, sometimes briefly. Sometimes citizens play a direct or indirect role in the budget process. Courts may play a role in budgets at any level of government at unpredictable intervals. When they do play a role in budgetary decisions, what are these actors trying to achieve?

**Bureau Chiefs** Many students of budgeting assume that agency heads always want to expand their agencies, that their demands are almost limitless, and that it is up to other budget actors to curtail and limit their demands. The reasons given for that desire for expansion include prestige, more subordinates, more space, larger desks, more secretaries, and not incidentally, more salary. The argument presumes that agency heads judge their bureaucratic skills in terms of the satisfaction of their budget requests. Successful bureaucrats bring back the budget. Agency expansion is the measure of success.

Recent research has suggested that while some bureaucrats may be motivated by salaries, many feel that one of their major rewards is the opportunity to do good for people—to house the homeless, feed the hungry, find jobs for the unemployed, and send out checks to the disabled.[1] For these bureaucrats, efforts to expand agency budgets are the result of their belief in the programs they work for.

Recent research has also suggested that the bureaucracy has become more professional, which introduces the possibility of another motivation, the desire to do a good job, to do it right, to put in the best machinery that exists or build the biggest, toughest engineering project or the most complicated weapons.

The generalization that bureaucrats always press for budget increases appears to be too strong. Some agencies are much more aggressive in pushing for growth than others. Some are downright moribund. Sometimes agency heads refuse to expand when given the opportunity,[2] suggesting there are some countervailing values to growth. One of these countervailing values is agency autonomy. Administrators may prefer to maintain autonomy rather than increase the budget if it comes down to a choice between the two. A second countervailing value to growth is professionalism, the desire to get the job done, and do it quickly and right. Administrators generally prefer to hire employees who have the ability to get the job done, plus a little, a spare amount of intelligence, motivation, and energy just in case they need to get some extra work done or do it fast in response to a political request.[3] Administrators may refuse to add employees if the proposed employees do not add to the agency's capacity to get things done.

A third countervailing value is program loyalty. Expansion may be seen as undesirable if the new mission swamps the existing mission, if it appears contradictory to the existing mission, or if the program requires more money to carry out than is provided, forcing the agency to spend money designated for existing programs on new ones or do a poor job.

A fourth countervailing value is belief in the chain of command. Many, if not all, bureaucrats believe that their role is to carry out the policies of the chief executive and the legislature. If those policies mean cutting back budgets, agency heads cut back the agencies. Agency heads may be appointed precisely because they are willing to make cuts in their agencies.[4]

Bureaucrats, then, do not always try to expand their agencies' budgets. They have other, competing goals, which sometimes dominate. Also, their achievements can be measured by other than expanded budgets. They may go for some specific items in the budget without raising totals, or may try for changes in the wording of legislation. They may strive to get a statutory basis for the agency and security of funding. They may take as a goal providing more efficient and effective service, rather than expanded or more expensive service.

**The Executive Budget Office** The traditional role of the budget office has been to scrutinize requests coming up from the agencies, to find waste and eliminate it, and to discourage most requests for new money. The executive budget office has been perceived as the naysayer, the protector of the public purse. Most staff members in the budget office are very conscious of the need to balance the budget, to avoid deficits, and to manage cash flow so that there is money on hand to pay bills. Hence they tend to be skeptical of requests for new money.

In recent years, however, there has been a change in the role of budget office. At the national level under President Ronald Reagan, budgeting became much more top-down, with the director of the Office of Management and Budget (OMB) proposing specific cuts and negotiating them directly with Congress, without much scrutiny of requests coming up from departments or bureaus. OMB became more involved in trying to accomplish the policy goals of the President through the budget.[5] At state levels too, there has been an evolution of budget staff from more technical to more political and more policy-related goals. When the governor is looking for new spending proposals these may come from his budget office.

**Chief Executive Officers** The role of chief executive officers (the mayor or city manager, the governor, the President) is highly variable, and hence these executives' goals in the budget process cannot be predicted without knowledge of the individuals. Some chief executives have been expansive, proposing new programs; others have been economy minded, cutting back proposals generated by the legislatures. Some have been efficiency oriented, reorganizing staffs and trying to maintain service levels without increases in taxes or expenditures.

**Legislators** Legislators have sometimes been described as always trying to increase expenditures.[6] Their motivation is viewed as getting reelected, which depends on their ability to provide constituents services and deliver "pork"—jobs and capital projects—to their districts. Norms of reciprocity magnify the effects of these spending demands because legislators are reluctant to cut others' pork lest their own be cut in return. At the city level, a council member described this norm of reciprocity, "There is an unwritten rule that if something is in a councilman's district, we'll go along and scratch each other's back."[7]

For some legislators, however, getting reelected is not a high priority. They view elected office as a service they perform for the community rather than a career, and while they may be responsive to constituents' needs, they are simply not motivated to start new projects or give public employees a raise in order to get reelected. Also, some legislators feel secure about the possibility of reelection, and hence have no urgent need to deliver pork in order to increase their chances of reelections.[8]

Even assuming the motivation to get reelected, holding down taxes may be as important to reelection as spending on programs and projects. The consequence of tax reduction is usually curtailed expenditures. Legislators are bound to try to balance the budget, which puts some constraints on the desire to spend.

The tendency to provide pork is real, but there are counterbalancing factors. Some legislators are more immune to pressures from constituents because they are secure electorally, and legislators can organize themselves in such a way as to insulate themselves somewhat from these pressures. They can, for example, select more electorally secure representatives for key positions on appropriations committees; they can separate committees that deal extensively with interest groups from those that deal with expenditures; they can set up buffer groups to deal with interest groups; they can structure the budget process so that revenue limits precede and guide spending proposals.

Moreover, legislators have interests other than providing pork. Some legislators are deeply concerned about solving social problems, designing and funding defense and foreign aid systems, and monitoring the executive branch. The proportion of federal budget spent on pork-type projects has declined in recent years, despite reforms in Congress that decentralized control and allowed pressure for pork to increase.[9] "Congressmen are not single-minded seekers of local benefits, struggling feverishly to win every last dollar for their districts. However important the quest for local benefits may be, it is always tempered by other competing concerns."[10] The pull for local benefits depends on the program. Some, like water projects, are oriented to local payoffs; others, like entitlements programs for large numbers of people, are not. Programs with local pull account for smaller and smaller proportions of the budget[11] and the trend has accelerated since 1978.[12]

**Interest Groups** Interest groups, too, have often been singled out as the driving force behind budget increases. They are said to want more benefits for their members and to be undeterred by concerns for overall budget balance or the negative effects of tax increases. Moreover, their power has been depicted as great. Well-funded interest groups reportedly wine and dine legislators and provide campaign funding for candidates who agree with their positions.

There is some truth to this picture, but it is oversimplified. Interest groups have other policy goals besides budget levels. In fact, most probably deal with the budget only when a crisis occurs, such as a threat to funding levels. Because they can be counted on to come to the defense of a threatened program, they reduce the flexibility of budget decision makers, who find it difficult to cut programs with strong interest-group backing. But many areas of the budget do not have strong interest-group backing. For example, foreign aid programs have few domestic constituencies. Agencies may even have negative constituencies, that is, interest groups that want to reduce their funding and terminate their programs. The American Medical Association sought for years to eliminate the Health Planning Program.

Often when there are interest groups, there are many rather than one, and these interest groups may have conflicting styles or conflicting goals, canceling one another out or absorbing energy in battles among themselves. A coalition of interest groups representing broad geographic areas and a variety of constituencies is likely to be more effective at lobbying.

Hence coalitions may form, but individual members of the coalition may not go along with measures supported by others, so the range of items lobbied for as a unified group may be narrow. Extensive negotiations and continual efforts are required to get two or more independent groups together for a lobbying effort, and the arrangement can then fall apart. In short, interest groups are often interested in maintaining their autonomy.

**Individuals** Individuals seldom have a direct role in the budget process, as they did in the DeKalb case, but they often have an indirect role. They may vote on referenda to limit revenues, forbid some forms of taxation, or require budgetary balance. They voice their opinions also in public opinion polls, and more informally by calling or writing their elected representatives and giving their opinions. Their knowledge of the budget is not usually detailed, but their feelings about the acceptability of taxation are an important part of the constraints of public budgeting. Their preferences for less visible taxes and for taxes earmarked for specific approved expenditures have been an important factor in public budgeting.

**The Courts** Another budget actor that plays an intermittent role in determining expenditures is the courts.[13] The courts get involved when other actors, often interest groups, bring a case against the government. Suits that affect the budget may involve service levels or the legality of particular forms of taxation. If a particular tax is judged unconstitutional, the result is usually lost revenues. If there are suits concerning levels of service, governments may be forced to spend more money on that service. There can also be damage suits against governments that affect expenditures. These suits are usually settled without regard to the government agencies' ability to pay. The result may be forced cuts in other areas of the budget, tax increases, or even bankruptcy. When the courts get involved, they may determine budget priorities. They introduce a kind of rigidity into the budget that says do this, or pay this, first.

Typical areas in which courts have gotten involved and mandated expenditures for state and local governments are prison overcrowding (declared cruel and unusual punishment) and deinstitutionalization of mentally ill and mentally handicapped patients. In each case, the rights of the institutionalized population required more services or more space, often involving expenditures of additional funds. From the perspective of the courts, the priority of rights outweighs immediate concerns for budget balances, autonomy of governmental units, and local priorities.

**Power Differentials** These various actors not only have different and potentially clashing budgetary goals, but they typically have different levels of power. Thus, at times, the budget office may completely dominate the agencies; at times, the Congress may differ from the President on budgetary policy and pass its own preferences. The courts may preempt the decision making of the executive and the legislature. Some particular interest groups may always be able to get tax breaks for themselves.

The combination of different preferences and different levels of power has to be orchestrated by the budget process in such a way that agreement is reached, and the players stay in the game, continuing to abide by the rules. If some actors feel too powerless over the budget, they may cease to participate or become obstructionist, blocking any agreements or imposing rigid, nonnegotiable solutions. Why participate in negotiations and discussions if the decision will go against you regardless of what you do? If some actors lose on important issues, they may try to influence budget implementation to favor themselves. Or the actors with less budget power may try to change the budget process so that they have a better chance of influencing the outcomes.

## The Separation of Payer and Decider

The second feature of public budgeting is that decisions about how money will be spent are made not by those providing the money but by their representatives. The payers and the deciders are two distinct groups. The payers are not given a choice about whether they want to pay or how much they want to pay. The power of the state may force them to pay. They may protest if they do not like how their money is being spent, and elect new representatives. They cannot, generally, take their money and do something else with it.

The distinction between the payers and the deciders leads to two crucial characteristics of public budgeting: public *accountability* and political *acceptability*. *Accountability* means to make sure that every penny of public money is spent as agreed, and to report accurately to the public on how money was spent. *Acceptability* means that public officials who make budget decisions are constrained by what the public wants. Sometimes they will do precisely what

they think the public wants, even if the results are inefficient or inequitable, and sometimes they will present the budget so that it will be accepted by the public, even if they have not precisely followed public will. This effort may involve persuasion or deception.

Since public demands may not be clearly expressed, and since different segments of the public may make different and competing demands, and since public officials themselves may have priorities, officials may not be able or willing to be bound tightly to public opinion. Nevertheless, if politicians knowingly make decisions that differ from what the public wants, there is pressure to present the budget in a way that makes it appear acceptable. That pressure creates a tension between accountability, which requires nearly complete openness, and acceptability, which sometimes involves hiding or distorting information or presenting it in an unclear fashion.

## The Budget Document and Accountability

Because of the separation of payer and decider, the budget document itself becomes an important means of public accountability. How did the public's representatives actually decide to spend taxpayer money? Did they waste it? Did they spend it on defense or police or on social services? The streets are in terrible shape—how much money did they spend on street repair? Citizens do not typically watch the decision making, but they and the press have access to the budget document and can look for the answers. They can hold the government accountable through the budget, to see that what officials promised them was actually delivered.

But budgets do not always present a complete and accurate picture. One example of how budgets can lose information happened recently in a state university. A university president decided to expand the big-time sports program, in an environment of overall financial scarcity. While some faculty members undoubtedly favored the action, many would have opposed it if they had been asked. The president did not ask their opinions, however; instead, the full costs of the program were disguised to make the budget appear acceptable. Because of progressive underestimates of costs in the sports program, some pundits labeled the sports program the case of the disappearing budget.

To obscure the real costs, the president broke up the costs for the program and scattered them among different portions of the budget. To complicate the picture further, he drew on different pockets of revenue, including student athletic fees, bond revenues, and voluntary donations. When asked, he said money going to the athletic programs was earmarked and could not be spent on other programs, so that professors trying to get more money to teach history or biology would look elsewhere than to sports. The amount of money showing as costs in the athletic program remained constant every year, although the program costs were expanding. Fearing conflict and disapproval, the president hid the costs in the budget.

The more complicated the budget, the more different activities and accounts, the greater the discretion of the administrators. As one university president offered, "Not a day goes by when we do not wish we had a more complex budget." The complexity allows for choice of where to report expenditures, and which revenues to use, to highlight some expenditures and gloss over others.

It would be misleading to suggest that the tension between accountability and acceptability always leads to more distortion or more secrecy. Sometimes the balance tends toward more accountability and budgets become clearer and more representative of true costs. The federal budget, for example, has moved toward clearer and more comprehensive portraits of public expenditures in recent years. But the tension is always present, and each budget represents some degree of selectivity

about what it will present and how. The art of selective revelation is part of public budgeting.

## Openness to the Environment

Public budgets are open to the environment. The environment for budgeting includes a number of different factors including the overall level of resources available (the amount of taxable wealth, the existing tax structure, current economic conditions); the degree of certainty of revenues; and a variety of emergencies such as very heavy snowfall, tornadoes, wars, bridge collapses, droughts, chemical explosions, and water pollution. The environment also includes rigidities resulting from earlier decisions, which may now be embodied in law. For example, rapid inflation in housing prices in California resulted in a citizen referendum to protect themselves from rapidly rising property taxes. The result of the referendum was incorporated in the state constitution, limiting the taxing options of local government. Constitutional restrictions to maintain a balanced budget or limit expenditures or put a ceiling on borrowing operate in a similar manner. Prior borrowing creates a legal obligation for future budgets, an obligation that may press other possible expenditures out of consideration or require higher levels of taxation. The environment in this sense may frame policy issues and limit alternatives. Public opinion is also part of the budgetary environment, and the perception of change in public opinion will be reflected in changing budgets.

The intergovernmental system is also a key part of the environment for budget actors. The legal sources of revenues, limits on borrowing, strings attached to grants, and mandated costs are but a few of the budgetary implications of the intergovernmental system. The requirement that some grants be spent on particular items or that a recipient match expenditures on grants may result in a pattern of spending different from what the state or local government would have preferred.

## 5˙ Budget Constraints

Openness to the environment creates the need for budgets to be flexible. Public officials have to be able to adapt quickly, reallocating funds to meet emergencies, spending more now and making up the difference later, cutting back expenditures during the year to meet sudden declines in revenues or increases in expenditures. But the same openness to the environment that creates the need for flexibility may simultaneously subject budgeting to numerous constraints.

For example, in California, a statewide referendum limited the rate of growth of local assessments, restraining the growth of property tax revenues. Federal grants provide budgetary constraints when they can be spent only on particular programs. The courts may create budgetary constraints by declaring programs inadequate or taxes illegal. Legal obligations to repay debt and maintain public businesses separate from the rest of the budget also create constraints.

The need for flexibility and the number of budgetary constraints contest with one another, creating patterns typical of public budgeting. For example, local officials may press for home rule, which gives more independence and autonomy to local governments to manage their own affairs and adapt to changing conditions. But state officials may erode home rule through continually mandating local costs. State universities may try to squirrel away contingency funds outside those appropriated by the legislature so that they can respond to emergencies; the legislature may then try to appropirate and hence control this new local source of revenues.

# The Meaning of Politics in Public Budgeting

Public budgets have a number of special characteristics. These characteristics suggest some of the ways that the budget is political. Political is a word that covers a number of meanings, even when narrowed to the context of budgetary decision making. The purpose of this book is to clarify the meaning of politics in the context of budgeting by sorting out some key meanings and showing how these meanings apply to different parts of budgetary decision making.

## Concepts of Politics in the Budget

The literature suggests at least five major ways of viewing politics in the budget: reformism, incrementalist bargaining, interest group determinism, process, and policy making.

- The first is a reform orientation, which argues that politics and budgeting are or should be antithetical, that budgeting should be primarily or exclusively technical, and that comparison between items should be technical and efficiency based. Politics in the sense of the opinions and priorities of elected officials and interest groups is an unwanted intrusion that reduces efficiency and makes decision making less rational. The politics of reform involves a clash of views between professional staff and elected officials over the boundary between technical budget decisions and properly political ones.

- The second perspective is the incrementalist view, which sees budgeting as negotiations among a group of routine actors, bureaucrats, budget officers, chief executives, and legislators, who meet each year and bargain to resolution. To the extent that interest groups are included at all in this view, they are conceived of in the pluralist model. The process is open, anyone can play and win, and the overall outcome is good; conflict is held down because everyone wins something and no one wins too much.

- The third view is that interest groups are dominant actors in the budget process. In its extreme form this argument posits that richer and more powerful interest groups determine the budget. Some interests are represented by interest groups and others are not, or are represented by weaker interest groups; the outcome does not approximate democracy. There may be big winners and big losers in this model. Conflict is more extensive than in the incrementalist model. This view of politics in budgeting raises the questions whether these interest groups represent narrow or broad coalitions, or possibly even class interest. To what extent do these interest groups represent oil or banking or the homeless, and to what extent do they represent business and labor more broadly?

- The fourth view of politics in the budget is that the budget process itself is the center and focus of budget politics. Those with particular budget goals try to change the budget process to favor their goals. Branches of government struggle with one another over budgetary power through the budget process; the budget process becomes the means of achieving or denying separation and balance between the branches of government. The degree of examination of budget requests, and the degree to which review is technical or political, cursory or detailed, is regulated by the budget process. The ability of interest groups to influence the budget, the role of the public in budget decisions, the openness of budget decision making—all these are part of the politics of process. In this view of politics, the individual actors and their strategies and goals may or may not be important, depending on the role assigned to individual actors in the budget process, and depending on whether the external environment allows any flexibility.

- The fifth view is that the politics of budgeting centers in policy debates, including debates about the role of the budget. Spending levels, taxing policies, and willingness to borrow to sustain spending during recessions are all major policy issues that have to be resolved one way or another during budget deliberations. Budgets may reflect a policy of moderating economic cycles or they may express a policy of allowing the economy to run its course. Each is a policy. Similarly, budgets must allocate funding to particular programs, and in the course of doing so, decide priorities for federal, state, and local governments. This view of politics in the budget emphasizes tradeoffs, especially those that occur between major areas of the budget, such as social services and defense or police. This view also emphasizes the role of the budget office in making policy and the format of the budget in encouraging comparisons between programs.

These five views of politics have been developed over time, and like an ancient document, the messages have been written over one another. Surely they are not all equally true, and certainly they often contradict each other. Parts of each may still be true, and they may be true of different parts of budgetary decision making, or true of budgetary decision making at different times or at different levels of government.

## Budgetary Decision Making

The focus . . . is to explore the kind of politics that occurs in budgetary decision making. What is budgetary decision making like? We have already discovered that public budgeting is open to environmental changes and deals with policy conflicts. Policy conflicts can delay particular decisions or prevent them from being made at all; other budget decisions must be independent enough to be made without the missing pieces. They can be corrected later when missing pieces fall into place. Environmental emergencies can reorder priorities and alter targets that have already been determined. As a result, public budgeting must be segmentable and interruptible. The need for segmentation and interruptibility is satisfied by dividing budgeting into separate but linked decision clusters: revenues, process, expenditures, balance, and implementation.

Decision making in each cluster proceeds somewhat independently while referring to decisions made in the other clusters, or in anticipation of decisions likely to be made in other clusters. These decision clusters are ultimately interdependent, but do not occur in a fixed sequence. The decision one needs to have in one decision cluster may not be made by another decision cluster in time to use. Then one may guess, or use an old figure, and then change when the new figure is determined. Sometimes decision-making cycles between estimates of revenues, estimates of expenditures, new estimates of revenues and new estimates of expenditures, in an iterative process.

## The Revenue Cluster

Revenue decisions include technical estimates of how much income will be available for the following year, assuming no change in the tax structures, and policy decisions about changes in the level or type of taxation. Will taxes be raised or lowered? Will tax breaks be granted, and if so, to whom, for what purpose? Which tax sources will be emphasized, and which de-emphasized, with what effect on regions, and economic classes, or on age groups? How visible will the tax burden be? Interest groups are intensely involved in the revenue cluster. The revenue cluster emphasizes the scarcity of resources that is an essential element in budgeting and illustrates the tension between accountability and acceptability that is a characteristic of public budgets. Revenues are also extremely sensitive to the environment because changes in the economy influence revenue levels and because the perception of public opinion influences the public officials' willingness to increase taxes.

## The Budget Process

The process cluster concerns how to make budget decisions. Who should participate in the budget deliberations? Should the agency heads have power independent of the central budget office? How influential should interest groups be? How much power should the legislature have? How should the work be divided, and when should particular decisions be made? Normally the legislature takes a key role in establishing budget process, although the chief executive may propose desired changes. Interest groups play a minor role, if any role at all. The politics of process may revolve around individuals or groups trying to maximize their power through rearranging the budget process. This jockeying for power rises to importance when the competing parties represent the executive and legislative branches and involve the definition of the separation and balance between the branches of government. The politics of process may revolve around the policy issues of the level of spending and the ability of government to balance its budget.

## The Expenditure Cluster

The expenditure cluster involves some technical estimates of likely expenditures, such as for grants that are dependent on formulas and benefit programs whose costs depend on the level of unemployment. But many expenditure decisions are policy relevant—which programs will be funded at what level, who will benefit from public programs and who will not, where and how cuts will be made, and whose interests will be protected. Agency heads are more involved in these decisions than in taxation or process decisions, and interest groups are also often active. This portion of the budget emphasizes the element of choice between items of expenditures in the definition of budgeting and illustrates the nature of the constraints on choices that is characteristic of public budgeting in particular.

## The Balance Cluster

The balance cluster concerns the basic budgetary question whether the budget has to be balanced each year with each year's revenues, or whether borrowing is allowed to balance the budget, and if so, how much, for how long, and for what purposes. The politics of balance deals with questions whether balance should be achieved by increasing revenues, decreasing expenditures, or both, and hence reflects policies about the desirable scope of government. Sometimes the politics of balance emphasizes definitions, as the group in power seeks to make its deficits look smaller by defining them away. The balance cluster also deals with questions of how deficits should be eliminated once they occur and their amounts are pinned down. At the national level, because deficits may be incurred during recessions in an effort to help the economy recover, the ability to run a deficit is linked to policies favoring or opposing the role of the budget in controlling the economy and, in particular, the use of the budget to moderate unemployment. These issues—whether budgets should balance, the proper scope of government and level of taxation, and the role of government in moderating unemployment—are issues that the general public cares about. Citizens may participate in this decision cluster through referenda and opinion polls; broad groups of taxpayers and interest-group coalitions representing broad segments of society may be involved in lobbying on this issue. Political parties may even include their policies toward deficits in their election platforms.

## Budget Implementation

Finally, there is a cluster of decisions around budget implementation. How close should actual expenditures be to the ones planned in the budget? How can one justify variation from the budget plan? Can the budget be remade after it is approved, during the budget year? The key issues here revolve around the need to implement decisions exactly as made and the need to make changes during the year because of changes in the environment. The potential conflict is usually resolved by treating implementation as technical rather than policy related. Executive branch staff play the major role in implementation, wich much smaller and more occasional roles for the legislature. Interest groups play virtually no role in implementation. The allowance of technical changes does open the door to policy changes during the year, but these are normally carefully monitored and may cause open conflict when they occur.

# Microbudgeting and Macrobudgeting

The five clusters of decision making outline the nature of the decisions actually being made, but tell little about how and why the decisions are made. On the one hand there are a number of budget actors, who all have individual motivations, who strategize to get what they want from the budget. The focus on the actors and their strategies is called *microbudgeting*. But the actors do not simply bargain with one another or with whomever they meet in the corridor. The actors are assigned budget roles by the budget process, the issues they examine are often framed by the budget process, and the timing and coordination of their decisions are often regulated by the budget process. The budget actors are not totally free to come to budget agreements in any way they choose. Individual actors are bound by environmental constraints. There are choices they are not free to make because they are against the law, or because the courts decree it, or because previous decision makers have bound their hands. The total amount of revenue available is a kind of constraint, as is popular demand for some programs and popular dislike of others. Budgetary decision making has to account not just for <u>budgetary actors but also for budget processes and the environment</u>. <u>This more top-down and systemic perspective on budgeting is called *macrobudgeting*. Contemporary budgeting gives more emphasis to macrobudgeting than exclusively to microbudgeting.</u>

One way of viewing the determinants of budgetary outcomes is as a casual model, depicted in Figure 12.1. In this schema, the environment, budget processes, and individuals' strategies all affect outcomes.

The environment influences budgetary outcomes directly and indirectly, through process and through individual strategies. The environment influences outcomes directly, without going through either budget process or individual strategies, when it imposes emergencies that reorder priorities. Thus a war or a natural disaster preempts normal budgetary decision making.

The environment influences the budget process in several ways. The level of resources available—both the actual level of wealth and the willingness of the citizens to pay their taxes—influences the degree of centralization of budgeting. When resources are especially scarce and there is apparent need to either cutback according to a given set of policies or make each dollar count toward specific economic goals, there is no room for bottom-up demands that result in compromises and a little bit of gain for everyone regardless of need. When resources are abundant, a more decentralized model of process may hold, with less

emphasis on comparing policies and less competition between supporters of different policies.

The environment may influence the format of budget as well as the degree of centralization of decision making. When revenues are growing, there may be more emphasis on planning and on linking the budget to future community goals, to stimulate public demands for new spending. When there is little new money, the idea of planning may seem superfluous. Changing direction, or setting new goals, may seem impossible in the face of declining revenues that make current goals difficult to sustain.

Environment in the sense of the results of prior decisions may also influence process. If there is a huge accumulation of debt and little apparent way to control it, or if the budget has been growing very rapidly for reasons other than war, there may be attempts to change the budget process in an effort to control spending and debt. In contrast, if the environment suggests the need for additional spending, and the current budget process is delivering very slow growth, the process may be changed to make spending decisions quicker and easier.

The level of certainty of funding influences strategies as well. If whatever an agency was promised may never arrive, agency heads are likely to engage in continuous lobbying for their money, and continual rebudgeting internally every time circumstances change. Long-term or future agreements will be perceived as worthless; the possibility of toning down conflict by stretching out budget allocation times will disappear. Attention will focus on what is available now, and going after whatever it is, whether it is what you want or not, because what you really want may never show up and hence is not worth waiting for.

The intergovernmental grant structure is part of the environment that may influence strategies. Because some grant money may seem free, state and local governments may

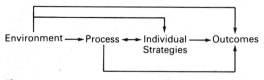

**Figure 12.1**    Decision making: Environment, process, and strategies

focus their energies on getting grants instead of raising local revenues. Or they may seek to decrease the amount of match required for a grant or increase their authority over how the money can be spent. Intergovernmental grants may make some expenditures relatively cheap, and some cutbacks relatively expensive, and hence frame constraints and choices for state and local budget officials.

The legal environment also influences strategies. For example, if public school teachers want tax raises to fund education and there is a provision in the state constitution forbidding income taxes, the teachers must either campaign for a constitutional revision (a time consuming and difficult task) or support a tax they know to be more burdensome to the poor. Thus the environment frames choices and influences strategies.

In Figure 12.1, the budget process influences strategies directly, and to a lesser extent, outcomes directly. But there is a double-headed arrow on the linkage between budget processes and strategies, suggesting that individuals' strategies also influence budget processes.

Budget processes influence strategies in some fairly obvious ways. If the budget structure allows for lengthy detailed budget hearings, open to the public and interest groups, at which decisions are often made, then various actors are likely to concentrate their efforts on making a good impression at these hearings. If the chief executive prepares the budget, which is subject to only superficial scrutiny and pro forma hearings before being approved by the legislature, anyone who wants to influence the budget—including the legislators themselves—must make their opinions heard earlier in the process, before the final executive proposal is put together. Informal discussion with department heads, or even telephone calls to the budget office, may be the route to influence. If the budget is made two or three times, with only the last one effective, then strategies may be to play out the first time or two with grandstand-ing—extreme positions to attract media attention—and more detailed and moderate positions later when the final decisions are made. The budget process orders the decisions in such a way that some of them are critical and determine or influence those that come afterward. Budget strategies naturally gravitate to those key decisions no matter where they are located.

When budget outcomes contradict some group's preference, the group may try to change the budget process to help it get the outcomes it prefers. When coalitions of the dissatisfied can agree on particular changes, fairly substantial changes in process may result. A change in process will bring about a change in outcome if the change in process shifts power from one group of individuals who want to accomplish one goal to another group with different goals.

The final link in the figure is between the strategies of budget actors and outcomes. The effect of different strategies on the outcomes is hard to gauge. It seems obvious, however, that strategies that ignore the process or the environment are doomed to failure. Budget actors have to figure out where the flexibility is before they can influence how that flexibility will be used. Strategies that try to bypass superiors or fool legislators generally do not work; strategies that involve careful documentation of need and appear to save money are generally more successful.

## Summary and Conclusions

Public budgeting shares the characteristics of all budgeting. It makes choices between possible expenditures, it has to balance, and it has a decision-making process. But public budgeting has a number of additional features peculiar to itself, such as its openness to the environment; the variety of actors involved in budgeting, all of whom come to it with different goals; the separation of taxpayers from budget decision makers; the use of the budget document as a means of public accountability; and the numerous constraints typical of public budgeting.

Public budgeting is both technical and political. Politics takes on some special meanings in the context of budgetary decision making. Budgetary decision making must be flexible, adaptive, and interruptible, which leads to a structure of five semi-independent strands of decision making, revenues, process, expenditures, balance, and implementation. Each such strand generates its own political characteristics.

Budget outcomes are not solely the result of budget actors negotiating with one another in a free-for-all; outcomes depend on the environment, and on the budget process as well as individual strategies. Individual strategies have to be framed in a broader context than simply perceived self-interest.

Budgeting is not well described as an annual process with little change from year to year. Budgetary decision making changes over time: interest group power waxes and wanes, competition in the budget increases and decreases, and the budget process itself varies over time. Changes in process take place in response to individuals, committees, and branches of government jockeying for power; in response to changes in the environment from rich to lean, or vice versa; in response to changes in the power of interest groups; and in response to scandals or excesses of various kinds.

## Notes

1. Patricia Ingraham and Charles Barilleaux, "Motivating Government Managers for Retrenchment: Some Possible Lessons from the Senior Executive Service" *Public Administration Review* 43, no. 3 (1983): 393–402. They cite the Office of Personnel Management Federal Employee Attitude Surveys of 1979 and 1980, extracting responses from those in the Senior Executive Service, the upper ranks of the civil service and appointed administrators. In 1979, 99 per-

cent of the senior executives said that they considered accomplishing something worthwhile was very important; 97 percent said the same in 1980. By contrast, in response to the question "How much would you be motivated by a cash award," only 45 percent said either to a great extent or a very great extent.

2. Twelve percent of LeLoup and Moreland's Department of Agriculture requests between 1946 and 1971 were for decreases. See Lance LeLoup, *Budgetary Politics,* 3d ed. (Brunswick, Ohio: King's Court, 1986), 83. For a more recent case study of an agency requesting decreases, see the case study of the Office of Personnel Management, in Irene Rubin, *Shrinking the Federal Government* (White Plains: Longman, 1985). See Irene Rubin, *Running in the Red: The Political Dynamics of Urban Fiscal Stress* (Albany: State University of New York Press, 1982) for an example of a department refusing additional employees.

3. For a good discussion of this phenomenon, see Frank Thompson, *The Politics of Personnel in the City* (Berkeley: University of California Press, 1975).

4. See Rubin, *Shrinking the Federal Government,* for examples during the Reagan administration.

5. U.S. Senate, Committee on Governmental Affairs, *Office of Management and Budget: Evolving Roles and Future Issues,* Committee Print 99-134, 99th Cong., 2d sess., prepared by the Congressional Research Service of the Library of Congress, February 1986.

6. See, for example, Kenneth Shepsle and Barry Weingast, "Legislative Politics and Budget Outcomes," in *Federal Budget Policy in the 1980s,* Gregory Mills and John Palmer, eds. (Washington, D.C.: Urban Institute Press, 1984), 343–367.

7. Rubin, *Running in the Red,* 56.

8. For a vivid account of the relationship between pork-barrel spending and building political coalitions, see Martin Shefter, "New York City's Fiscal Crisis: The Politics of Inflation and Retrenchment," *Public Interest* 48 (Summer 1977): 99–127.

9. See John Ellwood, "Comments," in Mills and Palmer, *Federal Budget Policy in the 1980s,* 368–378.

10. Douglas Arnold, "The Local Roots of Domestic Policy," in *The New Congress,* Thomas Mann and Norman Ornstein, eds. (Washington, D.C.: American Enterprise Institute, 1981), 252, quoted by Ellwood, in Mills and Palmer.
11. Arnold, "Local Roots," 282.
12. Ellwood, in Mills and Palmer, 370.
13. Linda Harriman and Jeffrey Straussman, "Do Judges Determine Budget Decisions? Federal Court Decisions in Prison Reform and State Spending for Corrections," *Public Administration Review* 43, no. 4 (1983): 343–351.

# CASE STUDY 12

# Introduction

Perhaps nothing is more vital to our understanding of public administration than how monies are budgeted to achieve public purposes. This subject, many believe, directly and decisively influences what policies are pursued and how management of public programs is achieved. For some, budgets in reality are what public administration is all about, namely the translation of public purposes into practical actions through the raising and expenditures of government monies. Rubin's foregoing essay therefore offers several stimulating insights into this critical process. It especially shows why this subject should not be viewed as merely a dry, technical document but as something that affects the central fabric of modern democratic society and the choices it faces.

Let's next turn to an actual example of what Rubin's selection addressed by studying the following case, "County Prison Overtime." This case study concerns a dispute over the amount and use of funds for the payment of overtime in a county correctional facility. At first glance, this may seem like a mundane and uninteresting problem. A county budget office staff prods an operating department to cooperate in a cost containment program to reduce the overall level of county spending (seemingly a trivial management task). But this routine administrative matter about overtime pay, which starts out as a simple exchange of memos, turns into an acrimonious confrontation between staff and line personnel and soon involves the county manager, the county board, and other local interests. County administrator George Truly finds himself in the middle of a battle over what Rubin called, "budget implementation decisions" that have important consequences for his workforce and the community at large.

As you read this case, you might reflect on the following points:

What was the basic nature of county government, its structure, workforce, and the politics of the whole community that contributed to the problems raised in this case?

Why is the case about what Rubin refers to in her essay as "budget implementation decisions"? What clusters of issues are involved?

How were these problems first raised in the case and what specific questions did the county administrator, George Truly, confront?

Can you outline the data, methods of analysis, understanding of the community, budgetary policies, and particular sensitivity of people that Truly required to make his decision? What alternatives were presented? Do you think he resolved the issue fairly, creatively, and effectively? Why or why not?

# County Prison Overtime

## TOM MILLS

## Background

Franklin County is a suburban/rural county located in one of the Mid-Atlantic states; it adjoins a large eastern city. Franklin County has a land area of 650 square miles; a population of approximately 500,000; and 45 local governments that consist of boroughs, villages, and townships. The local governments have their own police forces but lack secure holding facilities for defendants arrested and bound over by local magistrates for trial in the county courts.

The county provides all criminal justice system services from the county courthouse located in Franklinville, the county seat. On a tract of county-owned land just outside of Franklinville, the county operates two detention facilities: a small medium-security facility for juveniles and a large, modern medium-security facility for both male and female adult detainees. The latter facility, called the county prison, has a capacity of approximately 340 inmates and is maintained and operated by a staff of 181 employees.

Franklin County's chief lawmaking and administrative authority is the elected county commission, which is vested with both executive and legislative powers. Voters also elect a number of administrative officers—including the sheriff, the controller, and the district attorney—and the judges of the county court, called the supreme court of common pleas.

The county commission consists of three members elected countywide for four-year terms. The county code requires that one of the three commis-

From *Managing Local Government: Cases in Decision Making*, James M. Banovetz, ed. (1990). Reprinted with permission of the International City/County Management Association, 777 North Capitol Street, NE, Suite 500, Washington, D.C. 20002. All rights reserved.

sioners be a member of the opposing, or minority, party. The county is predominantly Republican, and members of that party regularly control the county-wide elective offices. The county commission, perhaps owing to its higher visibility, has occasionally been controlled by a Democratic majority.

The county commissioners appoint a county administrator, all nonelected department heads, and the members of most county boards and commissions. The day-to-day operation of the county is the responsibility of the county administrator, who is a professional local government manager recruited and appointed on the basis of technical competence. The county boasts a commitment to professionalism. The county administrator recruits and hires his or her own staff and has been responsible for securing the appointments of the finance director, the personnel director, and the director of purchasing.

The county code constrains the county commissioners' powers of appointment in some instances. The power to appoint the director of the department of corrections, who oversees both the county prison and the juvenile rehabilitation center, is vested in a prison board. The prison board is composed of the president judge of the supreme court of common pleas or that judge's designee, the district attorney, the sheriff, the controller, and the three county commissioners. Five of the seven members of the board were Republicans at the time this case begins.

## The Case

In the previous election, the Democratic party had won the majority of seats on the county commission by taking what proved to be the more popular position on a critical environmental issue. In hopes of reelection, the Democratic commissioners instituted a cost containment program that, if successful, would enable them to complete their term without raising taxes. The commissioners issued a directive to all department heads instructing them to implement economies wherever possible. The county administrator, George Truly, was given the principal responsibility for implementing the cost containment program. He, in turn, had charged the finance director, Donald Dexter, with much of the operating responsibility for the program.

After monitoring the expenditures of the county prison, Dexter was convinced that overtime expenditures were out of control. He had met on several occasions with Charles Goodheart, the director of corrections, and had called him almost weekly in an effort to reduce overtime costs. In Dexter's view, those contacts had been of little value, since overtime expenditures continued at what he regarded as an excessive rate. Somewhat reluctantly, he decided to go "on record." He dictated what was to be the first in a series of memorandums.

March 12
TO:         Charles R. Goodheart, Director of
            Corrections
FROM:       Donald D. Dexter, Finance Director
SUBJECT:    Excessive Prison Overtime

Pursuant to the county commissioners' directive of January 8 establishing the cost containment program, my staff and I have been closely monitoring the overtime expenditures incurred in the operation of the county prison. We have had several meetings and numerous telephone conversations regarding this matter with both you and your key staff members—all to no avail. Overtime expenditures have continued to rise and might well exceed the budget allocation. This I find to be particularly distressing, since we had every hope that this was one area of your operation in which we could effect significant savings.

I would greatly appreciate it if you would provide me, at your first opportunity, with a detailed justification for the current rate of overtime usage and your plans to keep such expenditures to an absolute minimum.

cc:   George S. Truly, County Administrator
      Frank Friendly, Personnel Director

Before sending this memorandum, Dexter had given the action considerable thought and had concluded that, even if the memorandum was a bit strong, it was warranted in this case.

In the weeks that followed, Dexter continued to scrutinize the prison payroll records but did not observe any reduction in the use of overtime. He was about to schedule yet another meeting with Goodheart when he received the following memorandum.

April 5
TO:         Donald D. Dexter, Finance Director
FROM:       Charles R. Goodheart, Director of
            Corrections
SUBJECT:    Response to Your Request for
            Information Regarding Overtime
            Expenditures

You indicated in your memorandum of March 12 that you felt we were utilizing an excessive amount of overtime. I welcome the opportunity to explain what might appear to be excessive overtime usage, but which really is no more than prudent prison management.

You will recall that during the budget hearings last year, I shared with you information on overtime usage in the four surrounding counties. Each of these counties has a comparable prison system, and, as I noted then, each uses more overtime than we do.

You must remember that I requested $434,400 as an overtime allocation for the current fiscal year (including holiday overtime). The overtime figure that was allocated to this department was substantially less. When budget allocations were announced, there was no explanation for the reduced overtime figure other than a general statement—which certainly is appropriate for you as finance director to make—that times were difficult, money was tight, and every effort must be made to curtail unnecessary expenditures. Although I accept these comments in the spirit in which they were made, I still am held responsible and accountable to the prison board for operating a safe and secure correctional institution. Prisons are potentially very dangerous, and that danger can be averted only by keeping staffing levels at safe and realistic levels.

As we both know, there are many justifiable causes for overtime usage in a prison setting. In the following paragraphs I'll attempt to identify the major causes.

*Turnover* During last year and continuing into this year, we have experienced high levels of turnover among our correctional officers. When staff members leave we are required to fill their posts, which we do through the use of overtime. The problem continues during recruitment for replacements and during the three-week training course to which all recruits are sent. When you add the two-to-four-week delay in filling positions to the three-week training period, you can readily see that a considerable amount of overtime might be involved. Turnover is perhaps our most critical problem. Previously I sent you a detailed commentary on our turnover experience. Over the past several years, I have told everyone willing to listen that there is a strong relationship between turnover in a correctional institution and overtime expenditures.

First of all, entry-level correctional officers are poorly paid, and, as I've told the county commissioners at every budget hearing, that is certainly true in our case. Second, this is a very difficult profession, and prison personnel are continually required to work at very high stress levels. Finally, we enjoy very little public esteem, and the working conditions can on occasion be very unpleasant. Small wonder that there is high turnover not only in our prisons but in prisons all across this country. When a staff member leaves, the need to fill the post continues. Unless the prison board tells me that it does not want me to fill vacant posts, I will continue to do so, and I have no choice but to use overtime.

*Hospital watches* Whenever an inmate requires inpatient treatment in a local hospital, I must provide the necessary security. Recently, two inmates were hospitalized. For each day of hospitalization, we provided two correctional officers per shift, three shifts per day, for a total of forty-eight hours of coverage. As you can see, the time mounts up rapidly. We have no fat in our shift complements; therefore, when a need like this arises, it must be covered with overtime.

*Emergency situations* Whenever there is reason to believe that inmates might be planning an action that could endanger the security of the institution, I adopt an emergency plan that puts all supervisors on twelve-hour shifts. I do not place this institution on an emergency footing for any trivial or illusory cause. Those instances in which I have used emergency overtime have been fully justified, and I stand by my actions.

*Sick leave* Our sick leave usage compares favorably with that of other county departments that enjoy less trying working conditions. Still, when a correctional officer calls in sick, his or her position must be filled, and it is usually filled by the use of overtime. We can't call in a replacement on one hour's notice on the person's day off, upset his or her family life, and worsen a bad morale situation simply to cover an eight-hour shift. We feel that the use of overtime in these situations is the most sensible solution.

*Workers' compensation* I have frequently remarked on this problem in the past. Today we are filling two posts that are vacant as a result of workers' compensation claims against the county. When an employee is injured on the job and a doctor certifies that he or she may not work, I have no choice but to utilize overtime to fill the post. I simply don't have any slack resources that would permit me to do otherwise.

*Reserve duty* Under the laws of this state, all staff members who are members of bona fide military reserve units are authorized to take fifteen days of paid military leave annually. When they depart for their military training, their posts remain, and we are responsible for filling them. The problem is exacerbated by the tendency of both military leave and vacations to cluster in the summer months. Another aspect of military reserve duty also generates overtime. Our correctional officers are scheduled around the clock and frequently are scheduled to work on a weekend when they are expected to attend reserve drills. Under the policy adopted by the county commissioners, the reservists may take "no-pay" time and fulfill their reserve obligations. While the county saves their straight-time pay, I am forced to use overtime to fill their posts.

*Vacations* We do make a concerted effort to schedule vacations so as not to result in overtime expenditures. Unfortunately, as a direct result of our lean staffing, on occasion we must resort to overtime to permit our correctional officers to enjoy the vacations they have eanred.

*Training programs*    Compared to the standard advocated by national authorities, our training efforts are extremely modest. We provide equal employment opportunity training, particularly with respect to our female correctional officers, and some supervisory training. In addition, we provide training in interpersonal communication skills—training I regard as essential in an institution such as ours. Since our shift schedules contain no fat, personnel must be brought in for training on their days off, which, of course, results in overtime.

The major causes of our overtime expenditures are as noted above. I have brought these problems and their causes to the attention of the county commissioners at every budget hearing over the past nine years. Our staff utilization records and overtime documentation are available to anyone who wishes to review them. We have nothing to hide.

I don't mean to be flippant or discourteous, but frankly I'm no wizard. I cannot operate this institution without a reasonable overtime allocation any more than the Jews of antiquity could make bricks without straw. For you to insist that I do so strikes me as being every bit as unreasonable as was the order of the Pharaoh's overseer.

If you can provide specific suggestions regarding policies or methodologies that you feel will assist in overtime reduction without compromising safe and efficient operation of this institution, please be assured that we will be happy to work with you in implementing them. We are open to any thoughtful and constructive recommendations that you or your staff may have. In the meantime, you might consider funding a comprehensive study of our staffing needs, including the need for overtime, by a nationally recognized group specializing in the field of corrections.

cc:    Members of the County Prison Board
       George S. Truly, County Administrator
       Frank Friendly, Personnel Director

Dexter read the memorandum twice, his feelings alternating between anger and frustration. He regarded Goodheart highly, knowing him to be a caring individual and a respected corrections professional.

"But clearly," thought Dexter, "He's no administrator. I asked him for a detailed justification of his use of overtime and his plans to keep those expenditures to a minimum, and what did he do? He offered me a lesson in biblical history and tried to put the monkey on my back with that bit about 'any thoughtful and constructive recommendations' I might have—baloney!" Dexter noted that Goodheart had twice mentioned his accountability to the county prison board and had been ingracious enough to copy the prison board members on the memorandum. "That," thought Dexter sourly, "is just a brazen example of saber rattling. Maybe he thinks that if he can broaden the controversy by bringing in the prison board, he can get me off his case. Not likely!" Still angry, he spun in his chair, picked up the mike of his recording machine, and dictated his reply.

Meanwhile, Jim Kirby, chair of the county commission, was enjoying his new role. He was no stranger to county government; he had been the minority commissioner for eight years under Republican administrations; but that, he felt, was essentially a "naysayer" role. Now, as chairman in a Democratic administration, he was in a position to take the lead on policy decisions, and he was enjoying it. He had founded a very successful business in the county and had called the shots there for more than thirty years. Although Kirby had often mused that government and business were much more different than alike—at least on paper—he relished his leadership role in the county.

Kirby prided himself on his capacity for work and made every effort to keep on top of things. He regretted that he had not read Goodheart's memorandum of April 5 before attending the monthly prison board meeting. He hated to be blindsided! The president judge of common pleas court, Harvey Strickland, who was also president of the prison board, had shown Kirby his copy of the memorandum as well as a copy of Dexter's memorandum of March 12, which had prompted Goodheart's reply. Strickland had been his usual amiable self, but Kirby knew from long experience that with him, you worried not about what he said but about what he left unsaid. The fact that Strickland had brought the memorandums with him to the meeting and his oblique references to "those in this life who are penny-wise and pound-foolish" convinced Kirby that trouble was brewing.

As soon as Kirby got back to his office, he called

George Truly, the county administrator, and asked him to stop by. Truly was the perfect balance to Kirby. Kirby was "born to lead"—an activist by nature, full of ideas and restless energy and impatient with detail. Truly, on the other hand, was a "doer." A professional administrator with substantial background in local government, he disliked the publicity and pressure of policy leadership, preferring instead the satisfaction that came from making policies work and seeing that services were delivered. The two men understood each other and had developed an effective working relationship. Neither one worried about the line between policy and administration; each one understood the overlap between the two activities and freely advised the other about county problems.

As Truly walked through the doorway, Kirby asked him, "Are you familiar with Don Dexter's memo of March 12 and Charlie Goodheart's reply?"

Truly said that he was and that he had already spoken to Dexter about them but that he had been too late.

"What do you mean, too late?" Kirby asked. "This thing looks to me like it can still be salvaged."

"Then," Truly replied, "I guess you haven't seen Don's memorandum of April 7."

April 7
TO:        Charles R. Goodheart, Director of
           Corrections
FROM:      Donald D. Dexter, Finance Director
SUBJECT:   Your Evasive Memorandum of April 5

In a sincere effort to implement the county commissioners' directive establishing a countywide cost containment program, I wrote to you on March 12. In my memorandum I asked you to provide me with a detailed justification for the current rate of overtime usage and your plans to keep such expenditures to an absolute minimum.

In reply, you gave me three pages of generalities and gratuitous comments. You're the prison expert, not me. If I had any good ideas on how you could run your operation more efficiently or economically, you can be sure I'd offer them. But as I see it, that's your job, not mine. My job is to see to the financial well-being of this county, and I can't do my job if I don't get cooperation. That's all I'm asking for—your cooperation in achieving the goals set for all of us by the county commissioners. Your knowledge of the Old Testament is

doubtless better than mine, but I do know that the Pharaoh didn't pay overtime. As far as I am concerned, you can have all the straw you want, but cut down on the overtime.

cc:   George S. Truly, County Administrator
      Frank Friendly, Personnel Director

## The Decision Problem

After Kirby had finished reading Dexter's memo of April 7, he sighed wearily, laid it aside, looked up at Truly, and said, "I see what you mean. Any suggestions?"

Truly was a career administrator who had spent twenty-two years in a series of increasingly demanding city management jobs before being recruited by Kirby to serve as Franklin County administrator. He had been given carte blanche in the recruitment of his administrative staff, and he had picked, among others, Don Dexter. Dexter was extremely bright; he had been the controller for a large manufacturing firm in the county—quite an accomplishment for a man who was not yet thirty. "But," Truly reflected, "he's never swum in political waters before, and there's no question that he's in over his head."

As the two men reviewed the situation, they tried to define the problem specifically, to identify possible courses of action, and to anticipate the probable outcomes of those alternatives.

It was evident that whatever they did, they had to do it quickly. Strickland could not yet have seen Dexter's memorandum of April 7. If he had, he would have had it with him at the meeting, and he would not have been so affable.

The cost containment program was important to Kirby and the other Democrat on the county commission. It was probably their best hope of reelection. If they exempted the county prison from the program for fear of what the prison board might do, the program could be weakened throughout the county. After all, why should the other departments conform if the prison wasn't expected to do its part?

Under the county code, the prison board, not the county commission, was responsible for approving all prison-related expenditures. The board, with its Republican majority, could give Goodheart a blank check if they wanted to, and the commissioners would be able to do nothing about it. "Well not exactly 'nothing,' " groused Kirby. "We could direct the county solicitor to sue the prison board, but since the president of the board is also the president judge, that's more of a theoretical than a practical remedy."

In fact, it was much more likely that the prison board would wind up suing the county commissioners. If the board alleged that an imminent threat to public safety was created by the refusal of the commissioners and their agents to fund the county prison adequately, it could bring an action *in mandamus*. In that event, the prison board would not be likely to limit the action to the question of prison overtime but would, in all likelihood, open a Pandora's box of problems. Goodheart had documented many of these problems in his memorandum of April 5, and that memo would probably be Exhibit A at a trial. Issues most likely to be litigated included the needs for adequate prison staffing levels, proactive strategies to combat the high rate of turnover, and higher salaries for correctional officers.

Kirby knew that if political warfare broke out, the Republicans would move quickly to seize the high ground. They would allege that the Democrats were jeopardizing the safety and tranquility of the community for the sake of a few paltry dollars. Kirby was too old a hand to suppose that arguments of efficiency and economy would carry any weight with the public in such a debate—especially if people were convinced that they were going to be murdered in their beds.

Since all the elected officials in the county were Republicans with the exception of Kirby and the other Democratic commissioner, they could really make things untenable. So far, the elected officials had been cooperating in the cost containment program. If, however, they chose to support the prison board in a confrontation with the commission, the cost containment program would be thoroughly scuttled.

"Don Dexter really put us in a box," remarked Kirby.

"Yes, but he's young and bright; he won't make the same mistake again," replied Truly.

"If the president judge gets him in his sights, he won't have the opportunity," observed Kirby solemnly.

"Funny thing," Kirby continued, "Don was right; that memorandum from Charlie was evasive, but Don should have known better than to say so. More than

that, he shouldn't have written at all. In a situation like that, you go to see the guy. Writing is a very incomplete, very limited way to communicate. It's a lot easier to talk tough to your dictating machine than to an adversary. My rules have always been, never write a letter if you can avoid it, and never throw one away."

After almost an hour of discussion, the two men had identified five alternative approaches to the problem. Unfortunately, none of them were without risk.

1. Exempt the prison from the cost containment program. Under this alternative, Kirby would contact Strickland informally and intimate that the commission would not be unduly concerned if the prison did not achieve its cost containment objectives. The justification offered would be that as a public safety and law enforcement agency, the prison ought not be held to the same standard of cost reduction as other agencies, lest public safety suffer. The main problem with this approach was that party loyalty was paramount in this county, and Strickland was certain to share this information with the other elected officials, especially the district attorney and the sheriff, who headed justice system agencies. Once the commissioners had yielded on the prison, it would be difficult for them to hold the line on other justice system agencies, and the cost containment program would be seriously jeopardized. The result could be that the majority commissioners would be branded as weak men of little resolve, and that could have serious spillover effects in other areas.

2. Fund an in-depth study of the prison by a nationally recognized group specializing in corrections. Since this was a solution proposed by the director of corrections, it would most likely gain the acceptance of the prison board. Apart from the cost of such a study, which could be considerable, its recommendations were not likely to be favorable to the county administration. Through long experience, Kirby and Truly had come to believe that special interest groups of whatever ilk rarely supported anything antithetical to their special interest. Worse yet, a comprehensive study might only document and verify the types of complaints that the director of corrections had been making for years. It was one thing to ignore his complaints; it would be something quite different were the

county administration to ignore the studied recommendations of nationally recognized experts.

3. Conduct an in-house study of the need for prison overtime. This alternative appeared to have a good deal to recommend it. The county had a small management analysis team that reported directly to the county administrator. The supervisor of the team was a thoroughly honest and objective career professional who had been a founding member of the Association of Management Analysts in State and Local Government (MASLIG) and was well respected both within the county and beyond its borders. The problem, of course, was one of credibility. Despite his excellent reputation, his objectivity might be questioned in the partisan political climate that prevailed in Franklin County. Moreover, the prison board might refuse to approve such a study. A study could be undertaken without the prison board's concurrence, as a prerogative of the majority commissioners, but in that event, the prison board might view the study as flawed.

4. Attempt to find an "honest broker" to conduct a study of prison overtime. "Honest" in this context meant someone who would be considered honest in the eyes of the prison board—someone they would perceive as having no ax to grind. Ideally, this person should already work for the county and be known by, and enjoy the confidence of, the prison board. But who? The downside of this alternative, assuming that such a person could be found, was that the "honest broker" might not be all that honest. Should such a person be selected with the prison board's concurrence, that person might very well take the prison board's side, to the considerable embarrassment of the county administration.

5. Invite Strickland to undertake the overtime study with members of his staff. The court's administrative staff included several career professionals in court administration who were graduates of the Institute for Court Management. They were undoubtedly capable of conducting the study, and Strickland and the prison board, which he clearly dominated, would certainly find them acceptable. The question, again, was one of objectivity. Truly favored this alternative, arguing that if, as he believed, they were really professionals, they would be objective. Kirby's response was insightful: "I don't recall book and verse, but somewhere in the

scripture it is written, 'Whose bread I eat, his song I sing,' and those fellows eat court bread."

What really was needed was a dispassionate review of prison overtime usage, the development of sound recommendations that would reduce overtime expenses without endangering the public, and an appraisal of the adequacy of the current budgetary allocation for prison overtime. This last point was particularly important. Goodheart continually reminded the prison board that his overtime request had been cut arbitrarily by the finance department without consultation or even explanation. True, there were other important questions that the study could appropriately consider, such as the adequacy of entry-level salaries for correctional officers and the appropriateness of current staffing levels. But solutions to both of these problems would be likely to cost the county more money. Given a choice, Kirby would prefer to postpone consideration of all problems that might result in increased cost to the county until after the next election.

Fortunately, the collective bargaining agreement with the local union that represented the correctional officers was due to expire in September. The study would certainly be completed well before then, and any recommendations requiring work-rule changes could be negotiated as part of the contract settlement.

Kirby turned to Truly and said, "George, give this some thought—and quickly! See what you can come up with."

Truly knew he had to work fast to answer two questions: (1) Which of the alternatives should be recommended? and (2) If a study were to be undertaken, what kind of person should be given the assignment?

## The Aftermath

Truly's recommendation was a combination of alternatives 3, 4, and 5. He saw no reason to exempt the prison from measures that applied to all other parts of the county government, and he believed that the only way to obtain data for an objective approach to the issue was to commission a study, preferably by an "honest broker." After considering and rejecting several possibilities. Truly recommended that a study be conducted by a team to be headed by Geraldine Eager, administrative assistant to the minority commissioner. Eager was the daughter of the county chair of the Republican party. All of the Republican majority members of the prison board had known her since she was an infant, and all were beholden to her father. Eager had just completed her work for an M.P.A. degree and was looking forward to a career as a professional local government manager. She had interned in Truly's office, and he had established a mentoring relationship with her. She was relatively inexperienced, but that problem could be overcome by having the county's management analysis staff assist her in the study.

Kirby suggested the arrangement to minority commissioner Joe Finley, Eager's boss. He felt reasonably certain that Finley would jump at the idea. Kirby knew that Finley had promised Eager's father to give Eager responsible work and that Finley had thus far been unable to deliver on that promise. Kirby also knew from his own experience that in the commission form of government, minority commissioners, themselves, have little challenging and responsible work to do.

Finley agreed to propose the arrangement to the prison board. The board concurred in the study plan, imposing the condition at Strickland's suggestion that a member of the court administrative staff be on the study team.

The study team reviewed finance department and prison budget files, central payroll records, prison overtime expenditure reports, staffing plans, and shift staffing schedules. By using several different methods of calculating overtime budget estimates, the team determined that a reasonable overtime budget request from the prison would have ranged between $294,200 and $348,600, well below the $434,400 requested by the prison but in line with the finance department's allocation of $319,000.

The study team also found that the prison's estimate of overtime needed for holidays had been overstated by nearly $100,000 and that overtime costs had been inflated because higher-paid employees were working appreciably more overtime than their lower-paid co-workers. Finally, the study team found that 12.5 percent of all nonholiday overtime was occasioned by turnover, thus supporting Goodheart's contention that turnover was a serious problem.

In discussing possible solutions, the team came up with the concept of a correctional officer pool. Under this plan, twenty more correctional officers than were authorized in the budget would be recruited and sent to the three-week training program. On completing their training, they would be placed in a pool from which permanent appointments would be made as vacancies occurred. In the meantime, they would be on call to cover overtime assignments, but at a straight-time rate. In effect, until they achieved their permanent appointments, they would be per diem employees. The start-up costs of the pool were estimated at $16,152, and approval by the collective bargaining agent for the correctional officers was required, since this was a fundamental change in work rules.

The politics of the study worked out as well as the analysis did. The prison board accepted the study and endorsed the the pool concept, which was subsequently implemented. Kirby gave the prison board credit for the $50,000 in annual overtime savings realized by the pool arrangement. Potentially embarrassing aspects of the study were downplayed from the outset. The $100,000 overstatement of holiday overtime requirements was shrugged off by Goodheart with the quip that since he was sure that Dexter was going to cut his overtime request, it was just good budgetary strategy to build in a safety margin. This time, Dexter did not dispute his explanation.

## Chapter 12 Review Questions

1. Why does Irene Rubin at the outset argue that "public budgets are not merely technical managerial documents that they are also intrinsically and irreducibly political"? Do you agree or disagree based on your reading of the case, "County Prison Overtime"?
2. In two or three sentences, summarize how Rubin defines "a public budget." How does it differ from the budget of a private firm?

3. Why does Rubin stress that the chief tension in public budgeting is between public accountability and public acceptability? What does she mean by those terms? Was that tension illustrated in the case study, "County Prison Overtime?"

4. Who are the major participants that Rubin believes are most involved in the public budgetary processes? What are they trying to achieve? Who was involved in the "County Prison Overtime," case and what were the positions they took as well as the strategies they used to achieve their goals?

5. List the five basic "budgetary decision-making clusters" that Rubin's essay outlines. Who are the key actors involved in each cluster? The special pattern of politics in each cluster? Did "County Prison Overtime" represent any one cluster? Does it "fit" Rubin's "cluster model" and if so, why? Or, why not?

6. What are the essential differences between microbudgeting and macrobudgeting according to Rubin? Why is it important to distinguish between the two? Did the case, "County Prison Overtime," represent either or both?

## Key Terms

bureau chiefs
chief executive officers
power differentials
separation of payer and decider
open environment
budget constraints
reform orientation
incrementalist view
revenue cluster
expenditure cluster

balance cluster
budget implementation
microbudgeting
macrobudgeting
legal environment
intergovernmental grant structure
individual strategies
budget outcomes
fiscal year
policy choices

## Suggestions for Further Reading

An excellent way to increase your understanding of budgets is to obtain a current city, county, state, or federal budget (usually the summary document provides all the important information) and read it carefully. Most summaries are written so that the layperson can understand their major contents and proposals. Also, now that public budgets are frequently the subjects of front-page headlines, read the major news coverage devoted to them, particularly in leading newspapers like the *New York Times, Washington Post, Christian Science Monitor, Los Angeles Times, St. Louis*

*Post Dispatch,* and *Wall Street Journal* as well as in news magazines like *Time* and *Newsweek.* The best up-to-date, scholarly survey of budgetary subjects is found in a new, thoughtfully edited journal, *Public Budgeting and Finance.* Each issue contains insightful articles by some of the leading experts in the field. Also do not neglect studying current issues of the *Public Administration Review* or *Governing,* as well as the annual volumes of *Setting National Priorities* published by the Brookings Institution, Washington, D.C.

Although they become dated quickly, introductory texts also offer a useful overview. For the best recent ones, see Robert D. Lee, Jr., and Ronald W. Johnson, *Public Budgeting Systems,* Fourth Edition (Baltimore: University Park Press, 1989); Donald Axelrod, *Budgeting for Modern Government* (New York: St. Martin's Press, 1988); Irene S. Rubin, *The Politics of Public Budgeting* (Chatham, N.J.: Chatham House, 1990); Gerald J. Miller, *Government Financial Management Theory* (New York: Marcel Dekker, 1991); and Aaron Wildavsky, *The New Politics of the Budgetary Process,* Glenview, Ill.: Scott Foresman, Little Brown, 1988). For an outstanding historic collection of several of the best essays written on public budgeting, see Allen Schick, *Perspectives on Budgeting,* revised edition, (Washington, D.C.: American Society for Public Administration, 1987). A handy, free guidebook that explains the difficult and arcane jargon of budgeting is *A Glossary of Terms Used in the Federal Budget Process* (Washington, D.C.: General Accounting Office, 1977). For a useful handbook of synthesizing essays by experts on various aspects of budgeting, see: Jack Rabin and Thomas D. Lynch, eds., *Handbook on Public Budgeting and Financial Management* (New York: Marcel Dekker, 1983) and Allen Schick, *The Capacity to Budget* (Washington, D.C.: Urban Institute, 1990).

Undoubtedly, a profound impact on federal budgetary practices was made by the enactment of the 1974 Congressional Budget Reform Act, which is examined in several scholarly books, including Allen Schick, *Congress and Money* (Washington, D.C.: The Urban Institute, 1980); Dennis S. Ippolito, *Congressional Spending* (Ithaca, N.Y.: Cornell University Press, 1981); Lance T. LeLoup, *The Fiscal Congress* (Westport, Conn.: Greenwood Press, 1980); Rudolph G. Penner, ed., *The Congressional Budget Process After Five Years* (Washington, D.C.: American Enterprise Institute, 1981); and James P. Pfiffner, *The President, the Budget, and Congress* (Boulder, Colo.: Westview Press, 1979). For two thoughtful case studies of federal budgetary

politics in the 1980s, read Paul Light, *Artful Work: The Politics of Social Security Reform* (New York: Random House, 1985); and Irene S. Rubin, *Shrinking the Federal Government* (New York: Longman, 1985); and for an excellent look at where we are today with the application of various budgetary systems, see George W. Downs and Patrick D. Larkey, *The Search for Government Efficiency* (New York: Random House, 1986), especially Chapters 4 and 5, as well as two insightful essays in the *Public Administration Review* 44 (March/April 1984): Hardy Wickwar, "Budgets One and Many," pp. 99–102, and Naomi Caiden, "The New Rules of the Federal Budget Game," pp. 109–117.

For two practical, "how-to" books on budgeting, refer to Edward A. Leham, *Simplified Government Budgeting* (Chicago, Ill.: Municipal Finance Officers Association, 1981), and Richard J. Stillman II, *Results-oriented Budgeting for Local Public Managers* (Columbia, S.C.: Institute of Governmental Research, University of South Carolina, 1982).

A remarkable inside look at modern federal budgeting is William Greider, *The Education of David Stockman and Other Americans* (New York: Dutton, 1981). Also read David Stockman's autobiography, *The Triumph of Politics: The Inside Story of the Reagan Revolution* (New York: Harper & Row, 1986).

Federal budgets today are driven by issues involving debt financing, indexing, and entitlements; three good books relating to these issues are: Robert Heilbroner and Peter Bernstein, *The Debt and the Deficit: False Alarms and Real Possibilities* (New York: W. W. Norton, 1989); R. Kent Weaver, *Automatic Government: The Politics of Indexation* (Washington, D.C.: Brookings, 1988) and Peter G. Peterson and Neil Howe, *On Borrowed Time: How the Growth of Entitlement Spending Threatens America's Future* (San Francisco: Institute of Contemporary Studies, 1988).

Several excellent overview essays on contemporary budgetary issues have appeared in recent years and among those by leading scholars in the field are: Robert D. Lee, "Developments in State Budgeting: Trends of Two Decades," *Public Administration Review* (May/June 1991), pp. 254–262; Irene S. Rubin, "Budget Theory and Budget Practice: How Good the Fit?" *Public Administration Review* (March/April 1990), pp. 179–189; Raphael Thelwell, "Gramm-Rudman-Hollings Four Years Later: A Dangerous Illusion," *Public Administration Review* (March/April 1990), pp. 190–198; Allen Schick, "Budgeting for Results: Recent Developments in Five Industrialized Countries," *Public Administration Review* (January/February 1990), pp. 26–34; Donald F. Kettl, "Expansion and Protection in the Budgetary Process, *Public Administration Review* (May/June 1989) pp. 231–239; and Allen Schick, "Micro-Budget Adaptations to Fiscal Stress in Industrialized Democracies," *Public Administration Review* (January/February 1988), pp. 523–533.

# CHAPTER 13

## Implementation: The Concept of a Communications Systems Model

*O*ur model attempts to make sense of important aspects of the political and administrative behavior associated with the intergovernmental implementation of public policy. The model uses communication theory as the glue that holds the pieces together. Messages, their senders, and the messages' recipients are the critical ingredients. Decoding these messages and absorbing them into agency routine is what implementation is all about.

*Malcolm L. Goggin, Ann O'M. Bowman, James P. Lester and Laurence J. O'Toole, Jr.*

## READING 13

## Introduction

From the very beginning of its conscious development as a field of study, public administration has stressed the importance of "good," "correct," "timely," and "efficient" execution of public objectives. Sound implementation was and perhaps still is "the bottom line" of what the administrative enterprise is all about. As Woodrow Wilson wrote in "The Study of Administration," the first American essay on public adminstration in 1887, "The broad plans of government action are not administration; the detailed execution of such plans is administration."[1]

Although "detailed execution" may well have always been the central preoccupation of public administrators, the last two decades have witnessed an impressive emergence and growth of scholarship directed specifically at exploring this subject. Indeed, by the 1980s implementation scholarship had become a distinct and separate subfield of public administration, political science, and policy studies. Implementation scholarship now boasts its own considerable

[1]Woodrow Wilson, "The Study of Administration," *Political Science Quarterly,* 2 (June 1887), p. 197.

array of professional journals and dedicated scholars, as well as sizable conferences oriented toward discussing various intellectual viewpoints and new methodologies related to this subject.

Much of the original impetus to develop a conscious subfield of study concerning implementation came from what many perceived as the apparent failure of the Great Society Programs. In the mid-1960s President Lyndon B. Johnson succeeded in pushing through Congress in a relatively short period a vast range of new types of social programs designed to alleviate major social problems (such as hunger, delinquency, poverty, unemployment, racial discrimination, and urban decay) as well as other prominent social concerns of the day and aimed at building "The Great Society." As Robert T. Nakamura and Frank Smallwood write, "It was not long before disillusionment began to set in as it became apparent that it might be easier to 'legitimize' social policy by passing ambiguous legislation than to carry out such policy by means of effective program implementation."[2]

By the late 1960s and early 1970s students of public affairs began questioning the value of passing so many laws creating new social programs without paying adequate attention to whether these laws were effectively implemented or carried out at all. Theodore Lowi, in his *The End of Liberalism* (1969), popularized this attack on the broad expansion of governmental activities, which, he argued, had eroded clear standards for administrative accountability and consequently had led to a crisis of public authority over the role and purposes of government in society. As public programs grew into more and more abstract and complex activities, according to Lowi, "it became more difficult to set precise legislative guidelines for execution of public policy."[3] It also opened up government programs to chaotic pluralistic competition. Lowi termed this phenomenon *interest group liberalism.* His solution was to return to a more simplified structure in which Congress and the president make precise laws and the courts formulate strict judicial standards to guide administrative actions, thereby reducing administrative discretion to a minimum. Hence, implementation would become little if any problem for administrators because their choices would be restricted and their direction from policy makers would be well defined and specific.

Meanwhile, other scholars were by then also busily pointing out that the Great Society Programs were not working as planned. Several case studies appeared at this time making much the same point—namely, that the Great Society Social Programs, for various reasons, were not or could not be effectively implemented—such as Martha Derthick's *New Towns In-Town*[4] and Daniel P. Moynihan's *Maximum Feasible Misunderstanding.*[5] Jeffrey Pressman

---

[2]Robert T. Nakamura and Frank Smallwood, *The Politics of Policy Implementation* (New York: St. Martin's Press, 1980), p. 11.

[3]Theodore J. Lowi, *The End of Liberalism* (New York: W. W. Norton, 1969), p. 127.

[4]Martha Derthick, *New Towns In-Town* (Washington, D.C.: Urban Institute, 1972).

[5]Daniel P. Moynihan, *Maximum Feasible Misunderstanding* (New York: Free Press, 1970).

and Aaron Wildavsky's *Implementation* (1973)[6] especially sparked much of the serious academic interest in this topic. Pressman and Wildavsky wrote what was essentially a case study of the Economic Development Administration's effort in the late 1960s to provide jobs for the "hard-core" unemployed in Oakland, California. Their case turned out to be a study in how not to get things done in government. At the end of their book they offered a prescriptive list of warnings about what should *not* be done to accomplish public policy objectives: "Implementation should not be divorced from policy"; "Designers of policy [should] consider the direct means of achieving their ends"; "Continuity of leadership is important"; "Simplicity in policies is much to be desired"; and so on.

After the appearance of the Pressman and Wildavsky book, Edwin C. Hargrove of the Urban Institute called implementation "the missing link" in social theory, and soon an impressive array of new methodological approaches began to search for "the missing link."[7] Several of the more prominent implementation theories that have been put forward during the past decade include the following:

*Implementation as a linear process:*   Donald S. Van Meter and Carl E. Van Horn, in an essay entitled, "The Policy Implementation Process: A Conceptual Framework," which appeared in *Administration and Society* (1975), argue that implementation involves a linear process composed of six variables that link policy with performance: standards and objectives; resources; interorganizational communications and enforcement activities; characteristics of the implementing agencies; economic, social, and political conditions; and the disposition of the implementers.[8] Presumably relationships or changes in any one of these inputs ultimately, according to the authors, can influence the successful performance of the policy objectives.

*Implementation as politics of mutual adaptation:*   In a study of several federal programs by Milbrey McLaughlin in 1975 for the Rand Corporation, the writer concludes, "The amount of interest, commitment and support evidenced by the principal actors had a major influence on the prospects for success."[9] In other words, the political support from the top, according to McLaughlin, was the key to success or failure of program implementation.

*Implementation as gamesmanship:*   Eugene Bardach's *Implementation Game* (1977), as the book's title indicates, sees the subject essentially as a "game," "where bargaining, persuasion, and maneuvering under conditions of uncer-

[6]Jeffrey L. Pressman and Aaron B. Wildavsky, *Implementation* (Berkeley: University of California Press, 1973).

[7]Edwin C. Hargrove, *The Missing Link* (Washington, D.C.: Urban Institute, 1975).

[8]Donald S. Van Meter and Carl E. Van Horn, "The Policy Implementation Process: A Conceptual Framework," *Administration and Society,* 6, no. 4 (February 1975), p. 449.

[9]Milbrey McLaughlin, "Implementation as Mutual Adaptation," in Walter Williams and Richard Elmore (eds.), *Social Program Implementation* (New York: Academic Press, 1976), pp. 167–180.

tainty occur"[10] to exercise control of outcomes. For Bardach, implementation therefore involves all the arts of gamesmanship: learning the rules of the game, devising tactics and strategy, controlling the flow of communications, and dealing with crises and uncertain situations as they arise.

*Implementation as conditions for effectively accomplishing objectives:*  Paul Sabatier and Daniel Mazmanian in "The Conditions of Effective Implementation: A Guide to Accomplishing Policy Objectives," (1979)[13] attempt to forecast what conditions promote or prevent policy implementation. They argue that the likelihood of implementation is enhanced by the existence of a favorable or "optimal" set of conditions. Conversely, in their view, implementation is impeded or altogether prevented when some or all of these conditions do not exist. Much of their essay is devoted to elaborating on the five conditions they consider necessary "that can go a long way toward assuring effective policy implementation if they are met."

*Implementation as a circular policy leadership process:*  By comparison, Robert T. Nakamura and Frank Smallwood perceive implementation as a circular process intricately involved within the entire public policy-making process. In their book *The Politics of Policy Implementation* (1980), the authors argue, "Implementation is but one part of this [policy] process and is inextricably related to, and interdependent with, the other parts."[11] For Nakamura and Smallwood the critical element linking implementation to the rest of the policy process is leadership, which, in their words, is necessary "to coordinate activities in all three environments" (policy formulation, implementation, and evaluation) to achieve program goals.

*Implementation as contingency theory:*  Ernest R. Alexander, by contrast, in "From Idea to Action," in *Administration and Society* (1985), develops a contingency model of policy implementation.[12] He views implementation as a complex "continuing interactive process," one that involves interactions with the environment, stimulus, policy, programs, and outcomes—all very much depending on the specific content, elements, and timing of these interactions.

*Implementation as case analysis:*  As with the Pressman and Wildavsky book, case studies of a single implementation situation remain a popular approach to understanding this subject. They seek to draw specific "lessons" about right—or wrong—approaches to accomplishing public policies within a specific policy field. Charles S. Bullock III and Charles M. Lamb's *Implementation of Civil Rights Policy* (1986) presents a highly sophisticated case analysis of this sort.[14]

[10]Eugene Bardach, *The Implementation Game* (Cambridge, Mass.: M.I.T. Press, 1977), p. 56.

[11]Nakamura and Smallwood, *The Politics of Policy Implementation,* p. 21.

[12]Ernest R. Alexander, "From Idea to Action: Notes for a Contingency Theory of the Policy Implementation Process," *Administration and Society,* 16, no. 4 (February 1985), pp. 403–425.

[13]Paul Sabatier and Daniel Mazmanian, "The Conditions of Effective Implementation: A Guide to Accomplishing Policy Objectives," *Policy Analysis,* Vol. 5, No. 4, Fall 1979, pp. 481–504.

[14]Charles S. Bullock III and Charles M. Lamb, *Implementation of Civil Rights Policy* (Monterey, Calif.: Brooks/Cole Publishing, 1986).

It analyzes in depth five cases in the civil rights field and draws conclusions about the significance of ten specific variables involving the effective implementation of civil rights policies. The authors conclude that five variables in particular are critical for successful policy implementation: federal involvement, specific agency standards, agency commitment, support from superiors, and favorable cost/benefit ratios.

Today the debate among scholars continues over what constitutes the appropriate conceptual framework to best comprehend the implementation of public policy. It remains hardly a settled matter, with theories and counter-theories being put forward at a brisk pace. Certainly, as yet, scholars have not agreed on any *one* model to explain public implementation processes or how models work in government. Nevertheless, it would be worthwhile to look closely at one of the more prominent approaches to this topic to help clarify and understand this topic more thoroughly. The following conceptual framework for viewing implementation by Malcolm L. Goggin, Ann O'M. Bowman, James P. Lester, and Laurence J. O'Toole, Jr., is based on three years of intensive research on this subject involving three major policies: the Resource Conservation and Recovery Act (RCRA) of 1976, Family Planning Services and Population Research Act of 1970, and the 1972 Amendments to the Federal Water Pollution Control Act (commonly called "the Clean Water Act"). Drawing on first-hand, field research of how these federal programs were implemented on the state level, the authors conceptualize what they term as "a third-generation, middle range theory" of how policy objectives are accomplished at the grassroots. Their aim is to build on first- and second-generation research in this field and "to elaborate a theory of how and why we think implementors behave as they do and begin to probe the validity of these notions with systematic observations of how implementation is actually practiced." Their approach thus is based on empirical observation and scientific methodology to build a model of implementation as "is actually practiced." "Communications theory" provides the root of these scholars' third-generation model because, in their words, "the strong features of the model are its dynamism and its synthesis of actions by disparate actors" and because it resists using either "a top-down or bottom-up approach to explain this dynamic process."

As you read this selection, keep the following questions in mind:

What assumptions do the authors make in building their conceptual model of optimal conditions for implementation? Do they assume, for example, that implementation activities take place in an open, democratic, and pluralistic society? One governed by laws? Or what? How do such assumptions shape the concept they put forward?

What implications does their model have for practicing public administrators? Can they use it successfully to predict when conditions are "ripe" for implementing programs or *how* to implement programs?

Are the authors optimistic about the possibilities of understanding all elements to allow for successful implementation of public policies? What are their model's basic elements? And why do the authors favor this approach over others?

Would their ideas have proved useful for the policy makers and administrators designing a program in any of the previous case studies you have read in this text, such as "Dumping $2.6 Million on Bakersfield"? How so?

Does its conceptual framework apply, not just to domestic programs, but also to foreign affairs programs? For example, in Case Study 8, "The Decision to Liberate Kuwait"?

# Implementation Theory and Practice: Toward a Third Generation

MALCOLM L. GOGGIN, ANN O'M. BOWMAN, JAMES P. LESTER, AND LAURENCE J. O'TOOLE, JR.

## The Model and Candidate Theory

Figure 13.1 outlines our Communications Model of Intergovernmental Policy Implementation. It conceptualizes the implementation process at the state level, as well as its product (outputs and outcomes), as resulting from choices made by the state. State choices are not made in a vacuum, however. State policy decisions depend on external government influences as well as intrastate influences. State implementation behavior is a function of inducements and constraints provided to or imposed on the states from elsewhere in the federal system—above or below the state level—as well as of the state's own propensity to act and its capacity to effectuate its preferences. Inducements are fac-

From Malcolm L. Goggin et al. *Implementation Theory and Practice: Toward a Third Generation* © 1990 by Malcolm L. Goggin, Ann O'M. Bowman, James P. Lester, and Laurence J. O'Toole, Jr. Reprinted by permission of HarperCollins Publishers.

tors—conditions and actions—that stimulate implementation; constraints have the opposite effect. Our approach is predicated upon the notion that no single factor can explain differences in implementation.

The national decision that triggers an implementation process affects by its form and content, to varying degrees, the choices and behaviors of agents charged with execution.[2] If this decision were the only factor, implementation would vary little from state to state. But states are discrete units, with their own policy agendas. State responses to federal inducements and constraints vary, depending on the nature and intensity of the preferences of key participants (including, importantly, local-level agents) in the state policy process. Finally, state responses are also influenced by the state's capacity to act.

This synthesizing approach yields the conceptual model displayed in Figure 13.1. Three clusters of variables affect state implementation: inducements and constraints from the

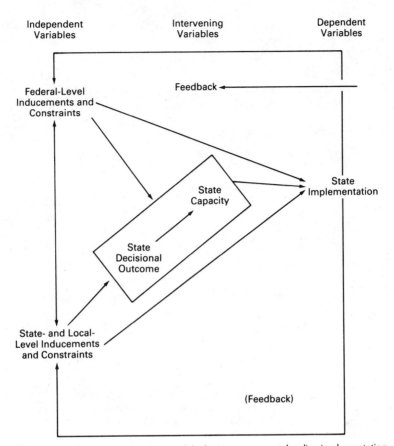

**Figure 13.1**   The communications model of intergovernmental policy implementation

"top" (the federal level), inducements and constraints from the "bottom" (the state and local levels), and state decisional outcomes and capacity. At a given point in time in any state, the interaction of these three clusters determines the course that implementation will take.

The implementation experience sets into motion a feedback process in which agents (subnational politicians and administrators) transmit messages to principals (federal-level policymakers). Policy redesign may result. As noted in the Introduction, the lack of grand theory obfuscates what implementation is and is not. In lieu of a paradigmatic breakthrough, we have adapted a "middle range" communications theory to help link the pieces of the model. We use it here because it helps to inte-

grate a good portion of the extant implementation literature and a wide range of empirical findings.

Communications theory provides a means of understanding the relationships in intergovernmental policy implementation. State-level implementors form the nexus for the communications channels. These implementors are the targets of implementation-related messages transmitted from both federal- and local-level senders. As recipients, state-level implementors must interpret a barrage of messages. The potential for distortion exists. Structuring the interpretation process are the form and content of the message and the legitimacy and reputation of the sender.

Therein lies the key to implementation's

variability. Interpretation is a function of *context*. Therefore, a single message, such as a federal statute, may be interpreted differently in different states. Even within a single state, the pluralistic and interactive nature of local-level policy adoption makes the probability of multiple, conflicting messages high. State-level implementation is correctly conceptualized as the sorting and interpreting of messages by recipients in contextually different settings. The result is a decision that determines the style that implementation takes.

Intergovernmental policy implementation is an exceedingly complex process that takes place in a complex environment. An implementation subsystem full of messages, messengers, channels, and targets operates within a broader communications system. More specifically, our conceptualization of implementation recognizes the joint nature of decisions and actions of interdependent institutions at the subnational level of government. It also incorporates consideration of the bargaining that takes place among the three levels of government. Given the assumptions underpinning our Communications Model of Intergovernmental Policy Implementation, communications theory offers a means of synthesizing the "top-down" and "bottom-up" approaches that dominate (and divide) the implementation literature.

## Model Components

This section introduces the components of the model that operate on federal, state, and local levels. Other aspects of the model, such as feedback and policy redesign, are also discussed.

### State Implementation

State implementation is a *process,* a series of state decisions and actions directed toward putting an already decided federal mandate into effect. State implementation is frequently equated with the state's compliance, or the timely satisfaction of procedural requirements of a law. Also implicit in the notion of compliance is the expectation that the law will be neither modified nor subverted in a way that is contrary to the lawmakers' intent. The essential characteristic of the state implementation process, then, is the timely and satisfactory performance of certain necessary tasks related to carrying out the intent of the law.

This orientation to implementation, which features a focus on the implementation process per se, is the most common in the literature. A conceptual problem arises, however, in the equation of implementation performance with implementation results. We argue that the two cannot be equated. For analytical purposes, it is imperative that the process of policy implementation be distinguished from the policy's results.

For example, a statute may include specific provisions that set up a timetable according to which certain services are delivered to certain clients. If those activities are carried out as specified by law, one could say that implementation has occurred; however, mere occurrence does not mean that the particular problem has been solved or that programmatic objectives have even been partially achieved. Therefore, in our Communications Model state implementation is also defined in two other ways: outputs and outcomes. The term *outputs* refers to the extent to which programmatic goals have been satisfied. *Outcomes* are the changes in the larger societal problem that the program is intended to rectify. Thus, the object of our Communications Model is actually a trio of items: the implementation process, the outputs of the implemented program, and the outcomes that are eventually produced.

Given the dynamic nature of implementation, periodic evaluation of the three factors is the only means of accurately portraying implementation. Not only does the implementation process evolve but outputs and outcomes can change over time. Thus we reject a dichotomous conceptualization of implementation as simply success or failure. . . . at least four different implementation styles exist. Under different conditions, various timing strategies and approaches work differentially. The model implicitly acknowledges this result.

## Federal-Level Inducements and Constraints

The content and form of a national government decision, be that decision a statute, an executive order, a court decision, or an administrative regulation, affect the choices and behaviors of state-level implementors. Federal-level variables, through their objective provisions (such as when the statute contains a penalty for noncompliance) and their subjective impacts (the importance of a penalty to a specific state) influence implementation. The message and the sender matter to the recipients in the contextually different states. One set of variables concerns the substance of the message. The federal-level "content-of-the-decision" variables that are plausible candidates for inclusion in a model of intergovernmental policy implementation include the policy type, the ease with which the problem can be solved, the degree of certainty of effects, the provision for coercion, the arrangement for financing, the anticipated effects on existing power arrangements, and the existence of a provision for citizen participation.

For example, a federal law that provides funds so that a state can devise its own solution to a problem is received very differently than is a federal law that imposes new regulations that are unwanted by powerful state interests. Generally, states prefer a federal program like the General Revenue Sharing (GRS) Act of 1971, which from 1972 to 1980 allocated funds for state governments to use as they pleased. With GRS, there was no five-inch-thick set of rules and regulations, no federally determined remedy; consequently, the program created few messy implementation problems for state governments.

The "form-of-the-decision" variables also affect the way in which a message is received. These variables include items such as the clarity of the provisions of the decision, the consistency of the decision with other policy objectives, and the flexibility of goals and procedures. State governments react differently to federal enactments that are clear and consistent than the same governments respond to enactments that are garbled and irregular. The Highway Beautification Act of 1965, which encouraged the removal of billboards from along major roads, is an example of a mandate that was considered "one of the worst-drafted pieces of legislation" to come out of the U.S. Congress. The unclear, often ambiguous language of the statute complicated interpretation and delayed implementation.

Another set of variables involves the extent of agreement among senders. The federal-level factors likely to affect state implementation include the legitimacy and credibility of officials and agencies. A unanimous Supreme Court decision, a bill that passes Congress with a wide margin, and an executive order of a popular president are actions that, *ceteris paribus*, facilitate implementation. Messages transmitted in this manner carry more weight. Federal agencies that, for example, are under fire in the media are weaker claimants and are likely to find their directives less imposing to recipients. For instance, states inclined to delay implementing the rulings of the U.S. Office of Civil Rights could do so more successfully during the 1970s when the agency was widely acknowledged to be "extremely ill-managed." The "standing" of a sender influences the treatment that a message will receive.

The most salient feature of the model in Figure 13.1 is that it is dynamic. The model considers important political and administrative behavioral changes that happen over time, and across policies and states. Amendments and the promulgation of revised rules can alter the content of a federal-level message. A change in form can result. Nor is the standing of the sender immutable. The potential magnitude of these kinds of changes complicates the task of state implementators as they proceed.

## State- and Local-Level Inducements and Constraints

The inducements and limitations imposed at the state and local levels are a component of the model that emphasizes the importance of state and local politics (the organization of interests at these levels) in understanding how and why implementation occurs the way that it does. This component is oriented toward three interacting institutional clusters: interest groups, state and local elected officials and their associated political institutions, and the focal (implementing) state agency. These clusters, ranging from a simple structure to a complex, polynucleated structure, send messages to state implementors. These messages generate the "receptivity climate"—the context of laws, regulations, and support structure—that the federal enactment encounters in each state. It is not surprising, then, that implementation is seldom simple or automatic.

The essential elements of the state and local subsystem are

- one or more bureau chiefs in each state, who receive federal communications and act instrumentally to ensure agency survival and to enhance their own welfare
- one or more bureaucratic organizations in each state whose organizational structure (and whose quantity and quality of financial and human resources) impinges on individual agent behavior
- spokespersons for organized interests in each of the fifty states, whose main interest is in maximizing benefits for group members and who also communicate their preferences to state-level implementors
- two or more state legislative committee and subcommittee chairs and one governor in

each state whose principal driving force is reelection
- a wide variety of local-level agents with significant levels of interlocal diversity in interest and motive, who also communicate their desires to state-level implementors
- fifty states, each with its own level of capacity to act on its collective preferences
- feedback loops that permit those affected by implementation decisions and actions and distributional consequences of the decisions and actions to communicate their reactions to authorities at both national and subnational levels in the federal system

The seven elements of the subnational system just sketched are interactive, interdependent, and multidimensional. In essence, the implementation decisions made and actions taken at this level in the federal system are jointly produced individual judgments of managers in charge of program operations, the preferences of state elected officials, and the cross-pressures brought to the bargaining table by consumer and provider advocates. These individual judgments are reached, at least partly, as the result of bargaining among various interests. Each interest has its own expectations, goals, resources, stakes, and power. These joint decisions are also constrained by the political, cultural, and economic environment, and the capacity of focal organizations to act on the state's collective choices. . . . these variables have a powerful impact on implementation.

The interdependence of these actors—federal principals (the policymakers with jurisdiction over the program), local interest groups, the governor, state legislators, local elected and appointed officials, and appointed officials in the state's bureaucracy—and their respective institutions is assumed. Finally, individual actors in the Communications Model are constrained by the nature of the decision-making process itself. Each institution is assumed to deal with the problem of the cost, in time and money, of acquiring information by specializing and by dividing tasks. Because of specialization and division of labor, power is usually concentrated in the hands of committee and subcommittee chairs in the legislature, bureau chiefs in state administrative agencies, and the leadership of organizations for consumers and providers of services, as well as direct beneficiaries and cost-bearers.

## Decisional Outcomes and State Capacity

The Communications Model positions state decision makers in a pivotal role. They are the receivers and evaluators of streams of information flowing from the federal and the state and local levels. Even under optimal circumstances in which there is perfect congruence between information from the "top" and the "bottom," two other conditions must exist before implementation can occur. First, a decision to proceed (to implement) must be made. This is no small step. In other words, even though the objective conditions may be identical in state X and state Y, the implementation decision may vary. This variance is a function of the manner in which decision makers interpret the information that they are receiving. Interpretation is related to characteristics internal to the decision makers (such as their psychological predisposition) and external to them (such as interpersonal relations among politicians and representatives of organized interests). This is a little recognized but powerful part of the implementation process. Without the decision to proceed, implementation stalls.

The decision to implement is linked to a second factor: the state's capacity to act. Our model takes into account the important distinction between decisions and actions, suggesting that variations in the capacity to act across states, across programs, or across time also affect the manner or style in which implementation occurs. State actions regarding implementation are influenced not only by federal level and state/local level preferences, but also by the organizational and ecological ca-

pacity of the state to act on those preferences.

*Organizational capacity* refers to an institution's ability to take purposeful action. It is a function of the structural, personnel, and resource characteristics of state agencies. *Ecological capacity* pertains to the contextual environment in which state government operates. It is determined by socioeconomic and political conditions in a state.

The setting for the implementation of a program within a state involves bureaucratic organizations. Information must be converted into action. State capacity, then, is a function of organizational capacity. A vast literature on administration and public organizations testifies to the possible importance of many features of the organizational setting in determining behavior. In our Communications Model, three elements of the setting are paramount: organizational structure, personnel, and financial resources.

Simple structures reduce coordination costs and ease the transmission of information, thus enhancing capacity to act. The implementation process is facilitated by these structures, but they may not improve output and outcomes, depending on the needs of the policy. Similarly, when relevant organizational actors are sufficiently numerous, qualified, and disposed to accept and undertake the course of action, the capacity to act is increased. Finally, agency capacity requires possession of the requisite financial resources to initiate the program successfully. These resources are of two kinds: ones targeted directly to clients and those spent in the process of implementation. Transforming a state preference into action requires both types of resources.

Ecological conditions in a state compose the other aspect of state capacity. The conventional wisdom is that variations in a state's sociopolitical and (especially) economic conditions are systematically related to state implementation behavior, whether it is measured in terms of processes, outputs, or outcomes. A state's capacity to act on its preferences is constrained by these factors. Ecological factors include general characteristics that are constant across policies, including state wealth, policy liberalism, economic conditions, political culture, and public opinion. Also included as ecological factors are specific characteristics that vary across policies, including partisan support, the salience of the problem to the state, and the media attention given to the issue.

In implementing the federal Medicaid program, for example, states make critical decisions about eligibility, benefit levels, and local government involvement. A state's ecology strongly influences the direction of these decisions.

Whereas it is unlikely that massive shifts in a state's ecology occur repeatedly during policy implementation, there is the possibility of some movement. If, for example, a rash of violent crimes breaks out in a state, the salience of criminal justice policy is heightened. If election results produce a change in partisan control of a state legislature, the new party in power usually offers policy alternatives that affect the state's ecology.

### Feedback and Policy Redesign

The constraints and inducements at the national and subnational levels of government are assumed to vary—from program to program and from state to state. Through a process of mutual adaptation and policy learning, the constraints and inducements also vary from one time period to the next. Individuals and their organizations possess both a capacity to learn and an ability to adapt to changing circumstances.

Dissatisfaction with an existing policy may lead to its eventual redesign. For redesign to occur, however, the following actions must unfold:

1. At the outset, elected and appointed state officials have to relay their dissatisfaction to federal-level officials. These state officials, in

all likelihood, are transmitting the dissatisfaction of relevant organized interests, such as clients and attentive publics.

2. As they receive repeated messages expressing similar sentiment, federal officials in the legislative or executive branches may respond by redesigning the policy. This was demonstrated quite vividly in the congressional redesign of the Endangered Species Act of 1973 after construction of the Tennessee Valley Authority's massive Tellico Dam project was halted in order to save the snail darter, a small fish. The importance of redesign has also been underscored by the recent reforms in the welfare program and in Catastrophic Illness provisions for the elderly under Medicare.

A feedback loop is an essential component of an implementation model.

The policy redesign component of the model reflects the fluidity inherent in intergovernmental policy implementation. The complexity of joint action often necessitates coordination and cooperation. However, because of differences between national and subnational priorities—and differences among individuals, institutions, and constraints and inducements—conflict is common. The need for coordination and cooperation, on the other hand, means that those who implement public policy have a strong hand in redesigning it.

## Conclusion

The theoretical argument and its corresponding model offer a vehicle for exploring what Elmore has called "the disorder" that is policy implementation." Our model attempts to make sense of important aspects of the political and administrative behavior associated with the intergovernmental implementation of public policy. The model uses communications theory as the glue that holds the pieces together. Messages, their senders, and the messages' recipients are the critical ingredients. Decoding these messages and absorbing them into agency routine is what implementation is all about.

The strong features of the model are its dynamism and its synthesis of actions by disparate actors. In recognizing that implementation is a dynamic process, the model incorporates policy learning and redesign. It resists the temptation to opt for either a top-down or bottom-up approach and instead synthesizes both approaches into a more comprehensive vision of intergovernmental policy implementation. Such a model facilitates testing propositions, regardless of policy type. In the final analysis, the use of communications theory meets the paramount criterion of a good model in that it approximates reality.

# CASE STUDY 13

# Introduction

As the foregoing essay indicates, serious scholars are spilling a lot of ink over the problems of public sector implementation. Theories about bureaucratic implementation, as a consequence, now abound in books and journals. But from the standpoint of the practicing public administrator on the firing line, how does the work actually get done? How are government objectives achieved in practice? What are the methods used and the problems administrators encounter in the implementation process? Does the theory of implementation square with its "real-life" practice from the standpoint of an administrator?

The following case, "Planning for Early Intervention in HIV Infection: Judith Kurland and the Boston Department of Health and Hospitals," gives us an excellent view from that of an on-the-firing-line practitioner of "real-life implementation dilemmas." In 1989 Judith Kurland was in her second year as Boston Commissioner of Health and Hospitals and learned that the Massachusetts Department of Public Health would encourage early intervention in the treatment of those with the deadly AIDs virus. The state wanted to urge people who were at risk to take an HIV antibody test and, if they tested positive for AIDs, to undergo a new experimental preventive drug-treatment, called AZT, that according to tests at the time, significantly delayed the onset of AIDs for those who had tested HIV positive. That was the state's programmatic goal. Yet, at the same time Massachusetts explicitly sought to encourage local officials such as Kurland to do more in responding to the AIDs epidemic, the state's budget crisis potentially would cause a seven-percent reduction in Kurland's budget. In addition, the state was considering a major reduction in Medicare expenditure, which, at the time, accounted for one-quarter of the funds Kurland had to run Boston City Hospitals. Caught between competing state programmatic goals and fiscal cutbacks, Kurland faced difficult choices about how to carry out a critical health care priority. The following case study outlines the background of this issue, the various alternative choices Kurland faced, as well as the points of view of state planners and policymakers, neighborhood health care providers, and local community advocates. Kurland's choice as to how to proceed, at best, was difficult under such circumstances.

As you study this case, think about the following issues:

What were the chief problems Kurland encountered in implementing the state's programmatic goal for early intervention in HIV infection? The various alternatives she had?

The pros and cons of each? How would you craft an implementation strategy under these conditions?

How does this case study relate to the ideas about implementation discussed in the foregoing reading? Based on your analysis of the case, is the implementation model that is conceptualized by Goggin, Bowman, Lester, and O'Toole a satisfactory explanation of events faced by Kurland? Where might you amend or modify the communications theory model of implementation to better account for events in this case study?

Can you generalize, from the case study as well as the foregoing reading, why implementation in the public sector can often become so frustrating and complicated to those involved? And why it is hardly a clear-cut or simple affair in many instances such as this one?

# Planning for Early Intervention in HIV Infection: Judith Kurland and the Boston Department of Health and Hospitals

## ESTHER SCOTT

[S]cientific breakthroughs mean little unless the health care system can incorporate them and make them accessible to people in need.

National Commission on AIDS
Report to President Bush, December 5, 1989

AIDS is a preventable disease, but we are not treating it as though it is preventable. . . . When things get tough, the money always goes to acute medical care. Acute medical care always eats up the resources and we don't do anything to keep people healthy.

Judith Kurland
Commissioner, Boston Department of Health and Hospitals

In the waning months of 1989, partway into her second year as Boston's commissioner of health

*This case was written by Esther Scott under the direction of Professor Marc J. Roberts for presentation at a March 25–27, 1990 conference, "The Challenge to Care: Meeting the Service Needs of the HIV Epidemic: Access to Ambulatory Care," sponsored by the Harvard AIDS Institute. Funding for this case was provided by the Josiah Macy, Jr. Foundation. Distributed by the Case Program, Kennedy School of Government, Harvard University.*

and hospitals, Judith Kurland learned that the Massachusetts Department of Public Health was about to begin an important new chapter in the handling of AIDS care: it was preparing an advisory that would encourage early intervention in the treatment of people infected with the human immunodeficiency virus. The advisory was being fashioned in response to recent studies indicating that early treatment with the drug AZT significantly delayed the onset of AIDS in people who had tested positive for HIV but as yet exhibited no symptoms (or only mild ones) of the disease. The state was planning to publicize the new findings among health care providers and to urge people who might be at risk of infection to take the HIV antibody test. "Now that there is good evidence that [early treatment] can prolong life for asymptomatic people," Massachusetts Public Health Commissioner David Mulligan said in December, "we're going to be really encouraging more counseling and testing. . . ."

For Kurland, the state advisory could not have come at a worse time. As a result of a Massachusetts budget crisis, which affected state aid to cities and towns, she was facing a seven percent cutback in her budget—already stretched thin—for fiscal year 1991. Equally troubling, the state was looking to limit Medicaid expenditures, which accounted for over a quarter of the reimbursable care provided by the municipally run Boston City Hospital. At a time when the city was about to launch a major construction program to rebuild that hospital, the prospect of thousands of new clients seeking counseling and treatment for HIV infection—at an estimated cost of $10,000 per person (see Exhibit 13.1)—was daunting. Already the hospital was seeing over 300 people a year at its outpatient AIDS clinic, where the volume of visits had tripled in two years' time. But for Massachusetts, conservative estimates put the total number of people with HIV infection at 30,000.[1]

Kurland and her staff had to consider what, if any, response to make to the planned advisory, given increasing criticism of what many saw as the government's unwillingness or inability to provide services to those who learned they were infected with the virus. "It's hypocritical for the government to urge people to get treatment when they aren't willing to provide it," Dr. Marshall Forstein, a psychiatrist and board member of the Massachusetts AIDS Action Committee, told the *Boston Globe*.[2] Forstein worried that people who tested positive would be driven to more destructive behavior and even suicide if they could not find or afford the treatment they needed. On the other hand, some in the minority community argued that wider testing was a moral necessity. "If we wait for health and social systems to be in place,"

argued Wayne Wright of the Multicultural AIDS Coalition in Boston, "I'm afraid we will have an outcry that there is some kind of genocide going on."

# Background: The Department of Health and Hospitals

Kurland had been named head of the Boston Department of Health and Hospitals (DHH) in July 1988, after serving as vice president for strategic planning and corporate affairs at the New England Medical Center, one of Boston's major teaching hospitals, and earlier stints on the staffs of two Democratic congressmen (including House Speaker Tip O'Neill) and of the lieutenant governor of Massachusetts. In her new position, she oversaw the operation of three hospitals—Boston City, Long Island Chronic Care (which housed a shelter for the homeless) and Mattapan Chronic Care—as well as a variety of community and public health services and programs. With the ambitious mission of providing "all people of the City of Boston access to a comprehensive range of high quality, cost-effective medical and nursing services," including prevention, primary, outpatient, acute, chronic and emergency care, and public health services, DHH had to stretch its budget ($183,750,000 for fiscal year 1990) to cover a lot of ground.

**Exhibit 13.1    Early Intervention: Individual Costs**

| | |
|---|---|
| *Pretreatment* | |
| 4 Batteries of blood tests | $300–436 |
| Comprehensive examination | 210–264 |
| 3 Clinic/physician visits | 180–198 |
| 4 Counseling visits | 40–80 |
| Subtotal | $730–978 |
| Median Estimate | $854 |
| | |
| *Treatment* | |
| Drugs | |
| AZT | $4,021–8,042 |
| Aerosal pentamidine or oral drugs | 1,500–2,500 |
| 6–12 clinic/physician visits | 360–792 |
| Blood monitoring (6–12 batteries of tests) | 450–1,308 |
| Counseling (6–12 sessions) | 60–240 |
| Subtotal | $6,391–12,882 |
| Median Estimate | $9,637 |

Source: From "AIDS Treatment Costs Put at $5 Billion a Year," *The New York Times*, September 15, 1989, p. A18. Copyright © 1989 by The New York Times Company. Reprinted by permission.

The major piece of DHH's budget pie (see Exhibit 13.2) went to Boston City Hospital, a sprawling, heavily used acute care facility, most of whose buildings dated back 125 years, with about 356 inpatient beds and a variety of adult and pediatric outpatient clinics that handled about 175,000 visits a year. In addition, the hospital campus was home to, among other things, a methadone clinic, a homeless shelter, a counseling and testing site for drug users and their partners, a residential care program for children with AIDS, and a daycare center for HIV-infected children. One of Kurland's mandates from Mayor Raymond Flynn was to nurse along a $170 million hospital reconstruction project—the single largest capital project ever planned by the city. Boston City had been an important source of medical care in the South Boston neighborhood where Flynn grew up, and the mayor was strongly committed to seeing the hospital rebuilt.

# AIDS Programs at DHH

Even before the testing and early intervention issues arose, the Department of Health and Hospitals was both caring for a large percentage of poor people with AIDS in Boston and struggling with what steps it should take to contain the epidemic. Because of their early interest in research on AIDS—and the availability of experimental drugs being given trials at their clinics—several of the city's major teaching hospitals had developed substantial AIDS caseloads. While Boston City did not treat the greatest number of AIDS patients, it saw a disproportionate share of intravenous drug users and their partners, who represented the fastest-growing AIDS population in the city and in the state as a whole.[3] (See Exhibits 13.3 and 13.4.)

The main vehicle for adult outpatient AIDS ser-

**Exhibit 13.2    Department Budget**

|  | FY 90 Recommended Budget | |
|---|---|---|
| Program Name | Funded Quota | Total Dollars |
| 1. Administration | 228.2 | 9,640,475 |
| 2. BCH operations | 1,132.8 | 65,439,291 |
| 3. Physician services | 437.0 | 21,048,126 |
| 4. Nursing services | 615.8 | 31,495,680 |
| 5. Community health services | 154.0 | 17,191,719 |
| 6. Mattapan Hospital | 298.3 | 14,139,080 |
| 7. Long Island Hospital | 364.0 | 15,641,886 |
| 8. Ambulance services | 184.0 | 8,753,743 |
| Total department | 3,414.1 | $183,350,000 |

Source: Department of Health and Hospitals, FY90 Budget Request.

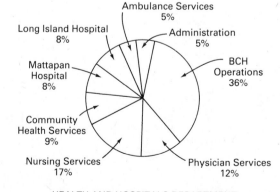

HEALTH AND HOSPITALS DEPARTMENT

Source: From Boston Department of Health and Hospitals, FY90 Budget Request. Reprinted by permission of Boston Department of Health and Hospitals, Public Health AIDS Services.

**Exhibit 13.3    AIDS Statistics: Confirmed Cases According to Reporting Institutions and Year of Report (Massachusetts Department of Public Health and Boston Department of Health and Hospitals; December 1, 1989)**

| Institution | Cumulative Reports | | | | 12-1-88 to 12-1-89 | |
| | as of 12-1-88 | | as of 12-1-89 | | | |
| | No. | % | No. | % | No. | % |
|---|---|---|---|---|---|---|
| Atlanticare | 7 | (0.4) | 10 | (0.4) | 3 | (0.4) |
| Baystate Medical Center | 55 | (2.8) | 79 | (2.9) | 24 | (3.1) |
| Berkshire Medical Center | 11 | (0.6) | 17 | (0.6) | 6 | (0.8) |
| Beth Israel Hospital | 159 | (8.2) | 220 | (8.1) | 61 | (7.8) |
| Boston City Hospital | 171 | (8.8) | 253 | (9.3) | 82 | (10.5) |
| Brigham & Women's Hospital | 133 | (6.9) | 184 | (6.8) | 51 | (6.5) |
| Cambridge Hospital | 12 | (0.6) | 18 | (0.7) | 6 | (0.8) |
| Cape Cod Community Hospital | 11 | (0.6) | 16 | (0.6) | 5 | (0.6) |
| Carney Hospital | 23 | (1.2) | 35 | (1.3) | 12 | (1.5) |
| Charlton Memorial Hospital | 13 | (0.7) | 16 | (0.6) | 3 | (0.4) |
| Children's Hospital | 28 | (1.4) | 32 | (1.2) | 4 | (0.5) |
| Faulkner Hospital | 15 | (0.8) | 22 | (0.8) | 7 | (0.9) |
| Fenway Community Health Center | 27 | (1.4) | 68 | (2.5) | 41 | (5.2) |
| Framingham Union Hospital | 9 | (0.5) | 14 | (0.5) | 5 | (0.6) |
| Harvard Community Health Plan | 55 | (2.8) | 86 | (3.2) | 31 | (4.0) |
| Lahey Clinic | 40 | (2.1) | 49 | (1.8) | 9 | (1.1) |
| Lawrence General Hospital | 6 | (0.3) | 12 | (0.4) | 6 | (0.8) |
| Lemuel Shattuck Hospital | 45 | (2.3) | 65 | (2.4) | 20 | (2.6) |
| Massachusetts General Hospital | 235 | (12.2) | 312 | (11.5) | 77 | (9.8) |
| Mercy Hospital | 5 | (0.3) | 12 | (0.4) | 7 | (0.9) |
| Mt. Auburn Hospital | 39 | (2.0) | 52 | (1.9) | 13 | (1.7) |
| New England Deaconess Hospital | 345 | (17.8) | 404 | (14.9) | 59 | (7.5) |
| New England Medical Center | 73 | (3.8) | 114 | (4.2) | 41 | (5.2) |
| Newton-Wellesley Hospital | 12 | (0.6) | 16 | (0.6) | 4 | (0.5) |
| Quincy City Hospital | 8 | (0.4) | 10 | (0.4) | 2 | (0.3) |
| St. Elizabeth's Hospital | 30 | (1.6) | 43 | (1.6) | 13 | (1.7) |
| St. Luke's Hospital | 23 | (1.2) | 45 | (1.7) | 22 | (2.8) |
| Salem Hospital | 11 | (0.6) | 11 | (0.4) | 0 | (0.0) |
| University Hospital | 45 | (2.3) | 50 | (1.8) | 5 | (0.6) |
| Univ. of Mass. Medical Center | 42 | (2.2) | 70 | (2.6) | 28 | (3.6) |
| V.A. Medical Center | 44 | (2.3) | 62 | (2.3) | 18 | (2.3) |
| Worcester City Hospital | 6 | (0.3) | 10 | (0.4) | 4 | (0.5) |
| Worcester Memorial Hospital | 20 | (1.0) | 26 | (1.0) | 6 | (0.8) |
| Other Boston Hospitals | 23 | (1.2) | 27 | (1.0) | 4 | (0.5) |
| Other Non-Boston Hospitals* | 152 | (7.9) | 257 | (9.5) | 105 | (13.4) |
| | 1933 | (100) | 2717† | (100) | 784 | (100) |

Total as of November 1, 1989    2657
Total as of June 1, 1989:    2269

*Includes 45 Massachusetts residents diagnosed out-of-state
†Includes 394 cases meeting the 1987 revised case definition
AIDS Surveillance Programs of the Boston Department of Health and Hospitals and the Massachusetts Department of Public Health, Massachusetts AIDS Surveillance Monthly Update, December 1, 1989. Reprinted by permission of the Boston Department of Health and Hospitals, Public Health AIDS Services and the Massachusetts Department of Public Health, AIDS Surveillance Program.

vices at Boston City was its immunodeficiency clinic. (The hospital held a separate pediatric infectious disease outpatient clinic twice a week.) Begun in 1986, the clinic had started off as a weekly half-day service, but by 1989 was operating five half-days a week and employing the services of a battery of twenty-five physicians, from a variety of disciplines, as well as nurses, social workers, psychologists, a pastoral counselor, and a nutritionist. During that time, the number of patient visits to the clinic had quadrupled. The clinic carried between 300 and 350 active patients—all of them with symptoms of AIDS or ARC—who

**Exhibit 13.4A    Trends in Massachusetts Resident AIDS Cases by Risk Factor and Year of Diagnosis**

| Transmission Category | Cumulative Cases Reported as of 12/1/89 | | | | | | | | | | | | | |
| | 1984 | | 1985 | | 1986 | | 1987 | | 1988 | | Through 12/1/89* | | Total | |
| | No. | % | No. | % | No. | % | No. | % | No. | % | No. | % | No. | % |
|---|---|---|---|---|---|---|---|---|---|---|---|---|---|---|
| Homosexual/bisexual | 112 | 62% | 136 | 66% | 219 | 67% | 347 | 60% | 374 | 56% | 282 | 53% | 1470 | 59 |
| Intravenous drug user | 22 | 12% | 26 | 13% | 45 | 14% | 110 | 19% | 145 | 22% | 132 | 25% | 480 | 19 |
| Homosexual/IVDU | 11 | 6% | 10 | 5% | 15 | 5% | 16 | 3% | 29 | 4% | 21 | 4% | 102 | 4 |
| Heterosexual contact | | | | | | | | | | | | | | |
| Born in Afr/Car country | 17 | 9% | 14 | 7% | 13 | 4% | 28 | 5% | 32 | 5% | 28 | 5% | 132 | 5 |
| Sex partner of IVDU | 0 | 0% | 4 | 2% | 5 | 2% | 17 | 3% | 21 | 3% | 20 | 4% | 67 | 3 |
| Other heterosexual contact | 1 | 0% | 1 | 0% | 1 | 0% | 5 | 0% | 5 | 0% | 6 | 1% | 19 | 0 |
| All other cases† | 17 | 9% | 15 | 7% | 27 | 8% | 52 | 9% | 66 | 10% | 42 | 8% | 219 | 9 |
| Total | 180 | 100% | 206 | 100% | 325 | 100% | 575 | 100% | 672 | 100% | 531 | 100% | 2489 | 100 |

**Exhibit 13.4B    Trends in Boston Resident AIDS Cases by Risk Factor and Year of Diagnosis**

| Transmission Category | 1984 | | 1985 | | 1986 | | 1987 | | 1988 | | Through 12/1/89* | | Total | |
| | No. | % | No. | % | No. | % | No. | % | No. | % | No. | % | No. | % |
|---|---|---|---|---|---|---|---|---|---|---|---|---|---|---|
| Homosexual/bisexual | 50 | 57% | 66 | 66% | 110 | 71% | 162 | 64% | 179 | 58% | 133 | 59% | 700 | 62 |
| Intravenous drug user | 14 | 16% | 14 | 14% | 23 | 15% | 47 | 19% | 66 | 21% | 43 | 19% | 207 | 13 |
| Homosexual/IVDU | 6 | 7% | 5 | 5% | 7 | 4% | 7 | 3% | 10 | 3% | 7 | 3% | 42 | 4 |
| Heterosexual contact | | | | | | | | | | | | | | |
| Born in Afr/Car Country | 11 | 13% | 10 | 10% | 10 | 6% | 20 | 8% | 20 | 6% | 20 | 9% | 91 | 3 |
| Sex partner of IVDU | 0 | 0% | 1 | 0% | 4 | 3% | 5 | 2% | 9 | 3% | 8 | 4% | 27 | 2 |
| Other Heterosexual contact | 1 | 1% | 1 | 0% | 0 | 0% | 0 | 0% | 4 | 1% | 2 | 0% | 8 | 0 |
| All other cases† | 6 | 7% | 3 | 3% | 2 | 1% | 13 | 5% | 23 | 7% | 11 | 5% | 58 | 5 |
| Total | 88 | 100% | 100 | 100% | 156 | 100% | 254 | 100% | 311 | 100% | 224 | 100% | 1133 | 100 |

*1989 data are incomplete due to reporting delay.

†Includes: Blood transfusion recipients, hemophiliacs, pediatric, and undetermined risk cases

AIDS Surveillance Programs of the Boston Department of Health and Hospitals and the Massachusetts Department of Public Health, Massachusetts AIDS Surveillance Monthly Update, December 1, 1989.

visited the service every two weeks on average; each physician saw an average of five or six patients per clinical session.[4] "So," said Dr. Howard Libman, Boston City Hospital's associate director for clinical AIDS programs, "it's a very intensive, frequent follow-up outpatient clinic, much different from primary care [clinics]." In FY89 AIDS outpatient services expenditures at Boston City Hospital amounted to roughly $943,000; added to that was a share of the $2.8 million in pharmacy costs for AIDS patients at the hospital. The majority of the clinic's clients—anywhere from 75–90 percent—were covered by Medicaid; roughly five to ten percent of the patients were uninsured, and their expenses were ultimately picked up by the state under its "uncompensated" or "free care" pool.[5]

The immunodeficiency clinic was widely regarded as a success, offering multi-disciplinary, high quality care to its patients. "It's worked very well," said Libman. ". . . We have a very difficult patient population and our compliance rate [return for follow-up visits] is very high." Kurland agreed. "I inherited some very good programs," she said. "BCH was doing great programs in AIDS before I got here, in terms of clinical care of AIDS, excellent stuff."

The clinic's success, however, had led to a distinction in the hospital between AIDS and non-AIDS doctors. "Medical residents and even medical staff in primary care have routinely referred patients upstairs to the immunodeficiency clinic for their continuing care," said Libman. "Now, we don't do that for any other medical illness. It's expected that patients with common, particularly chronic, medical illness should be followed in primary care, using subspecialty clinics as places of consultation."

The clinic also found that the city's 25 neighborhood health centers—with a couple of notable exceptions—tended to send AIDS patients to Boston City (and some of the other major hospitals) for their ongoing care. These centers had been reluctant to take on AIDS patients for a variety of reasons—concerns about adequate reimbursement, fears relating to the disease itself or the difficulty of handling the people who were sick with it, and uncertainties about their own technical expertise. At the same time, said Holly Ladd, program director of the Boston AIDS Consortium,[6] some people with AIDS chose not to go to their community health care center because, for example, "they know they're HIV positive and they don't want their neighbor, who happens to be the receptionist there, to know." To help redistribute the caseload, Boston City was participating in a three-year federal demonstration project—the Metropolitan Area HIV Service grant (MAHS), begun in 1987—to provide, among other things, training in AIDS care for neighborhood health center personnel.

Meanwhile, the immunodeficiency clinic was getting close to capacity. So far, the clinic had handled the growing volume—new patients were waiting only a couple of weeks for appointments—but there were concerns about the consequences of greatly increased demand. As Libman put it, "The numbers can't be extraordinary, or we're going to be overtaxed down here."

**Public Health Services** In the area of ongoing education, prevention, and outreach programs, Kurland also found much to admire. DHH had established a counseling and testing center—Project Trust—for drug users and their partners on the grounds of Boston City Hospital; the program accounted for most of the $122,800 the department had specifically allocated to street outreach programs. DHH had also recently hired three street outreach workers, in response to a five-point prevention plan proposed by City Councillor Thomas Menino in 1988. For education and prevention services, the department had allocated $2.28 million, some of which went to programs run out of DHH, and some to support services offered by community-based organizations. (See Exhibit 13.5 for AIDS expenditures at DHH.) The single largest grant—$800,000 in FY89—had gone to support the activities of the Massachusetts AIDS Action Committee, a Boston-based group formed by members of the gay community in 1983. The department had begun giving funds to AIDS Action, said Julie Marston, DHH administrative director of public health AIDS programs, "at a time when [it] was seen as a sole service provider—the only people, for the most part, doing AIDS education and case management." By the late 1980s, the organization had grown enough to employ about 70 full-time staff members and a volunteer base of about 1,200 people, providing, said Marston, "the bulk of the case management that goes on for people with AIDS in the city" and its suburbs. In addition to "client services"—helping people with AIDS with emergency financial assistance, maintaining a "wellness" program, providing

**Exhibit 13.5\*     DHH Expenditures on AIDS, FY89**

| | |
|---|---:|
| *Education and Prevention* | |
| Staff | $128,711 |
| Contracts | 1,014,200 |
| *Street Outreach* | 122,833 |
| *Outpatient Services* | 943,431 |
| *Pharmacy* | 2,828,727 |
| *Medical Supplies†* | |
| Mattapan Hospital | 36,425 |
| Long Island Hospital | 53,842 |
| Boston City Hospital | 606,583 |
| *Administrative and Data Support* | 161,463 |
| Total | $5,896,215 |

\*These figures do not include the cost of inpatient care, such as physician and
nursing services, at any of the DHH facilities.
†Supplies, which are mandated under "universal precaution guidelines," include gloves, gowns, red bags (for infectious wastes), goggles, etc.

advocacy and volunteer services, etc.—AIDS Action
was involved in policy, planning, and resource development for AIDS-related services, and also ran a
number of community education and outreach programs aimed at gay men, the minority community,
women, and IV drug users.

For the most part, said Kurland, she thought the
department's existing public health programs in
AIDS, like the clinical services, were "really quite
good." She was, however, "more concerned about
what we were not doing." What worried her was "a
huge gap or absence of programs in the minority
community." Looking at recent AIDS data when she
first arrived at DHH, she recalled, "I said, wait a minute. This is a minority disease. It isn't yet, in terms of
the number of people who have it, but when you look
at the infection rate, this is a minority disease. . . . It's
becoming a disease of poor minority people on drugs
or connected to drugs, and it's starting to become a
woman's disease." DHH, she believed, was not quite
up to speed on the changes that were occurring: "We
didn't have a plan, and I felt that it was not in our
bones how much the epidemic was shifting. . . . I
thought, my God, we have to be out there with programs, programs that are culturally relevant, programs that are sensitive."

AIDS Action had pointed out, in testimony before
Kurland and the board of trustees of DHH on June
27, 1989, that in reality its caseload was not limited
to the gay community: 27 percent of the 850 families
it served were people of color, and 31 percent of its
clients were IV drug users. "The people we serve,"

said David Aronstein, AIDS Action's director of policy, education, and planning, "reflect who in percentages is sick with AIDS and ARC in Boston." But Kurland had concluded that it was "very important to
work with the minority organizations and institutions
that already existed and get money out to them."

> There are a whole host of health, human services,
> social, fraternal, educational institutions in minor-
> ity neighborhoods, working with all different kinds
> of minority communities that could be, I argued,
> and should be involved in AIDS education and
> outreach. . . . Different groups need to be reached
> in different ways, and I don't believe that this de-
> partment and the people running our programs
> had any knowledge to compare with the knowl-
> edge of people already working with those com-
> munities on how to reach people.

Kurland, a strong believer in the importance of
prevention in containing the AIDS epidemic, was also
concerned that the department's outreach and education activities were "minimal" in areas where the
epidemic was spreading fastest. She planned to combine these two priorities by devoting discretionary
money in the education and prevention budget to the
development of new programs in the minority community. In July 1989, the department allocated
$140,000 which, along with a pledge of $320,000
from the state, helped start up the Multicultural AIDS
Coalition, an organization that distributed funds to
programs and agencies in communities of color. Be-

tween FY89 and FY90, some 13 community-based agencies—including the Multicultural AIDS Coalition, the Latino Health Network, the Haitian Multi-Service Center, and some neighborhood health centers—received DHH funding for education and prevention programs.

At first, Kurland had hoped these new ventures would not come at the expense of existing programs. "When I first came [to DHH] and I thought we would get more money for things," she recalled, "I thought we needed to grow what we weren't doing. But soon after I got here, when Michael Dukakis lost the election, and all of a sudden we're broke and nobody has any money for us, I knew we had to think about shifting [resources]." AIDS Action would now compete through an RFP process with other providers for money for AIDS programs. "I don't think [diversity in providers] is bad," said David Aronstein, "if what that reflects is an understanding that more needs to be done than has been able to be done before. [But] if that reflects a strategy of defunding some people in order to fund other people, then I think it is not good." Aronstein worried about a premature withdrawal of support for gay people who, he noted, made up the majority of the AIDS population and would continue to do so in Boston for at least the next five to 10 years. "The reality," he said, "is there is not enough money." Kurland did not, she stressed, intend to abandon the "gay white male community. . . . I am fighting for lots of programs for them," she said. Nevertheless, she added, "They tend to be a population that has been the traditional focus for services. All of the AIDS populations are underserved, but some groups have far less access than others and are more underserved. We're the place that serves people who are not in the mainstream of current AIDS services."

This was the position from which Kurland and her associates viewed the newly emerging state advisory on early intervention.

## The State Advisory

In the fall of 1989, the financial structure of state-supported medical care in Massachusetts was verging on collapse. Before its budget crisis, Massachusetts had ranked fairly high in its non-Medicaid expenditures on AIDS programs and services: it stood ninth among states in cumulative number of AIDS cases, but, in FY89, sixth in per capita spending ($2.51) and fourth in total state spending ($14,754,-000) on AIDS.[7] Even when Governor Dukakis proposed a FY91 budget that would slash human services spending—unless the recalcitrant state legislature agreed to raise taxes—the HIV/AIDS Office in the Department of Public Health was slated to be level-funded (at $19.4 million). "We're the only [health] line item that's not cut," said Duane Draper, director of the HIV/AIDS Office, "but in the face of a growing epidemic, level-funding is not quite the blessing it could be."

Perhaps more disturbing was the $300 million in proposed cuts in the Medicaid budget, including the elimination of the "medically needy" category, which allowed people with AIDS whose income was in excess of social security disability limits (generally around $500 a month) to receive assistance with their medical bills.[8] For Boston City Hospital in particular, this and other changes in Medicaid coverage held out the prospect of still more needy patients seeking treatment and services that would have to be paid for out of the state free care pool or the city's dwindling funds.

Though aware of the looming Medicaid reductions, the state Department of Public Health decided to proceed with the advisory because, as Duane Draper told reporters, "we can't just quit and go home because there's not enough money."[9] By February 1990, after numerous consultations between the state and AIDS advocates and health care providers, the advisory was ready for release. The document included information on early treatment and guidelines for medical providers on doing risk assessments and on counseling people both before and after testing; it also reiterated Department of Public Health policies on voluntary testing, counseling, and informed written consent. As a result of the advisory's recommendations, said Draper, "we hope all health care providers [will] take a more proactive position on testing, counseling, and early treatment. . . . Our position," he added, "is that people need to know their health status."

As Judith Kurland, like other local public health officials, considered what implications the advisory had for her department, various health care providers, planners, advocates and critics, from what one observer called the "AIDS community," were also developing their positions.

# Viewpoint: Planners and Policymakers

At DHH and elsewhere in the city, the people who would be responsible for planning and implementing programs had a variety of concerns, including confidentiality, the potential volume of patients, coordination of care, and, most acutely, the almost certain inadequacy of funding to meet the new demand.

In the public health division, DHH was talking with the state about setting up post-testing programs, to be funded by money from the federal Centers for Disease Control. The programs, for those who tested positive, were expected to run three weeks or longer. They would provide a bridge between the test results and the start of monitoring blood cell counts, offering clients support and, said Julie Marston, "a place to be able to affect their behavior. . . . We're looking for an environment and a climate [where] we can hopefully work with people, not only to educate them, but help them have some control and effect on their behavior." The aim, explained Marston, was to "offer a program that's useful for people with a history of drug use, something for women, something for adolescents and women of other ethnicities. We're planning to open it up to more than just the traditional gay, white model, who have been predominantly the clients that have shown interest in this service."

Meanwhile, the state was considering establishing treatment and assessment programs, which would offer people with HIV infection T-4 cell monitoring on a regular basis and treatment with aerosol pentamidine and AZT as long as they remained asymptomatic.[10] Patterned after facilities in California and New Jersey, the treatment and assessment programs were, according to P. Clay Stephens, director of state HIV/AIDS services, still "totally in the talking stage." The funding source was not clear, nor was the payment mechanism, but the state was talking about setting up as many as six centers—some of them mobile—throughout Massachusetts.

One thing the state was not talking about, however, was expanding the size of its anonymous testing program. Currently, the state was running 20 alternative test sites (ATS)—some of them open only on a part-time basis—where people could get free and anonymous counseling, testing, and post-test counseling. Money for the ATS's came from the CDC, which was planning to level-fund the program for FY91.

With no expansion of anonymous testing capacity, the state expected health care providers—in private offices, health centers, and clinics—to help take on the expected increase in demand for testing. The fact that these providers would be largely inexperienced in counseling on testing, and that the testing process would be confidential but not anonymous, caused some concern among policymakers and planners. The state hoped to remedy the inexperience problem by providing guidelines on risk assessment and pre- and post-test counseling in its advisory; but some felt that the physician's office or a clinic would not offer the same kinds of careful control found in the ATS's. "What's really happening out there," said Holly Ladd, "is that people are getting a whole pile of papers to sign from their doctors and slipped in among other papers to be signed is the informed consent for HIV testing. They may or may not have their attention drawn to that document separately from the other documents that they're signing. They may or may not get their test results from the physician himself or herself; they may get it from a secretary. They may or may not get it in the physician's office in a confidential setting; they may or may not get it over the telephone. The point is, we have no system right now to monitor the quality of care that's going on around this particular piece of information and the delivery of this information."

The legal protections guarding the confidentiality of HIV test results in Massachusetts were, said P. Clay Stephens, among the strictest in the country (see Exhibit 13.6), but, she acknowledged, they didn't cover every situation. The state's confidentiality requirements meant, she explained, "that if I test [positive] . . . my practitioner . . . can't tell [the results] without my written consent. But that doesn't mean her secretary doesn't get freaked out some day and stand up with the chart in her hand that has my name in big letters across it and say, 'Oh my God, somebody here is . . .' in the middle of the waiting room. So I think the issue is the difference . . . between the legal protections in place, which are quite good . . . versus the comfort level of the community, which is very low, very volatile."

**Planning at BCH** At Boston City Hospital, plans were underway to manage the greater number of HIV patients expected in the wake of the advisory by creating a diagnostic and evaluation unit, which would provide centralized intake services for newly identified HIV-infected patients. Patients would be

## Exhibit 13.6    70F. HTLV-III Test; Confidentiality; Informed Consent

No health care facility, as defined in section seventy E, and no physician or health care provider shall (1) test any person for the presence of the HTLV-III antibody or antigen without first obtaining his written informed consent; (2) disclose the results of such test to any person other than the subject thereof without first obtaining the subject's written informed consent; or (3) identify the subject of such tests to any person without first obtaining the subject's written informed consent.

No employer shall require HTLV-III antibody or antigen tests as a condition for employment.

Whoever violates the provisions of this section shall be deemed to have violated section two of chapter ninety-three A.

For the purpose of this section "written informed consent" shall mean a written consent form for each requested release of the results of an individual's HTLV-III antibody or antigen test, or for the release of medical records containing such information. Such written consent form shall state the purpose for which the information is being requested and shall be distinguished from written consent for the release of any other medical information, and for the purpose of this section "HTLV-III test" shall mean a licensed screening antibody test for the human T-cell lymphotropic virus type III.

Added by St.1986 c. 241.
1986
St.1986, c. 241, was approved July 15, 1986.

---

screened according to the severity of symptoms, T-4 cell counts, and need for services and triaged, explained Howard Libman, "in the best possible world, either to the immunodeficiency clinic or to another primary care site." Those other sites included the hospital's own primary care clinic and "if the system works the way it should work, some of the neighborhood health centers as well."

Libman was hopeful that the new unit and the triage system would prove a workable mechanism for handling a larger volume of patients. "If the unit works the way it's supposed to work, and we get cooperation and participation by the neighborhood health centers," he said, "I think we'll be able to deal with it over time." However, he acknowledged, "we need to find a source of stable long-term funding," and the looming DHH budget cuts made the likelihood of finding that source more remote. "If the commissioner says there is a seven or a 10 percent cutback this coming year," Libman noted, "we can't provide the same services for 10 percent less support."

For Dr. George Lamb, AIDS advisor to Boston Mayor Raymond Flynn and former deputy commissioner at DHH, there were serious questions about the city's ability to handle the treatment of asymptomatic HIV patients even without the budget cutbacks. Lamb worried that the state advisory represented "a premature approach without some mechanisms to deal with" the problems that would arise, or "a system that can do the kinds of things that need to be done reliably." As an example, he pointed to T-4 cell counts which "are not reliably done and take a fair amount of interpretation, and a fair amount of time and effort with the particular [patient]. . . ."

Judgments on whether a T-4 cell count indicated the need for treatment were difficult to make and further complicated by questions about toxicity from AZT and the implications of long-term treatment with the drug. For instance, "if you use it now," Lamb explained, "your bug may become resistant, and yet we're not even sure what your T-4 count is. Those are fairly sophisticated and time-consuming questions that I'm not sure we have enough people yet quite ready [to handle]."

Lamb was also concerned that moving care of asymptomatic HIV patients into primary care clinics, at least in Boston City Hospital's case, would do nobody any good. "The primary care clinic [at BCH] is booked, and you can't be seen quickly," he said. "If you're talking about somebody who has tested HIV positive—and I think most of us are going to be anxious enough that you have to be seen pretty quickly—you'd be waiting six to eight weeks."[11]

Above all, Lamb worried about the consequences of issuing public health information without providing the services that people would seek as a result. In his view, "information alone has never dealt with a problem." If new resources were not added to help the people who tested positive for HIV, he continued,

what I predict . . . is that we'll eat away more and more at preventive services, and that will cost us more in the long run. . . . It may drive people to do more of the health care and not do as much of the preventive. If I'm seeing . . . [patients] in clinic . . . [and] I'm asked to do more, which in essence this new recommendation suggests I do, with the same amount of resources, there's not much question that I'm going to spend more time with those that are positive. That's where this is driving you. If I spend more time with those that are positive, I'm probably going to spend less time with those that are negative, because I don't have more resources. . . . So that the intent to try to give more health care—which I'm not against—may, without more resources, hurt the epidemic.

The "pie," Lamb concluded, "has to get bigger."

## Viewpoint: The Neighborhood Health Centers

Boston's 25 neighborhood health centers, which were expected to take on a larger role in the care of people with HIV infection, were a varied lot, both in their individual character and in their relationship with DHH. "There is a tremendous variety," said Julie Marston, "in the size [of the neighborhood health centers], the scope, the mission, the location, the communities they serve, their specialties." Six of them were directly affiliated with Boston City Hopsital, and in FY89 received $3.3 million in funds from DHH. Despite the affiliation, however, Kurland did not have direct control over these centers, which had independent community boards. In addition, her department provided funding for education and prevention programs in 18 other health centers, either freestanding or affiliated with other hospitals, which were awarded $1.7 million in matching grants in FY89.

For most of the neighborhood health centers, treating people with HIV infection represented a daunting new task under already difficult circumstances. In the past, few centers had sought out people at risk of HIV infection and, when they appeared, most of them were sent on to other hospitals—chiefly, Boston City.[12] A major (though not sole) exception to this was the Fenway Community Health Center, a non-affiliated facility which drew a substantial number of its clients from Boston's gay community. Roughly 75 percent of Fenway's patients were HIV-infected, and the center had been a leader in fighting for better Medicaid reimbursements for community health centers. Patient services at Fenway were "fabulous," said Nurse Practitioner Catherine O'Connor, who worked on the Metropolitan Area HIV Service project. The center was "a model of what we'd like to see happen." But despite its fine services—including a large grant to provide primary care to drug users with HIV—Fenway had found it difficult to attract patients from communities of color, said O'Connor, because they did not want to be "gay-identified."

The Fenway center was participating in the MAHS project, along with Boston City Hospital, by doing "provider education," in an effort to help other neighborhood centers become more proficient and confident in offering HIV care. Health workers from some centers came to Fenway for two to four visits and "shadowed" a physician as he did his HIV rounds. At Boston City, medical personnel (including three medical directors) from four neighborhood health centers visited the AIDS clinic twice a month to get experience in working with HIV patients. To help defray the costs of these visits to BCH—chiefly lost income from services the physicians were not providing at their own health centers—the MAHS grant paid each of the four community facilities $12,000—"a token," said O'Connor.

But, despite these efforts, it would be an uphill battle for many of the neighborhood health centers to take on the care of HIV patients. In many cases, staff and the surrounding communities were fearful of having people with HIV—especially drug users—in their midst. There was "a lost of resistance" from the staff at the Uphams Corner Health Center, noted Executive Director Edward Grimes, to a program for IV drug users that he planned to open at the facility. Uphams Corner, a non-affiliated clinic, served a multiracial population—including hispanics, Cape Verdeans, Southeast Asians, blacks, whites, and Haitians—and handled about 72,000 patient visits a year. The program for drug users would offer addiction services, methadone, and counseling on HIV; the center already housed an alternative test site. The staff members' objections to the program, said Grimes, focused particularly on their feeling that IV drug users were "scary." Staff members also worried about the impact of drug users on the center's other patients. In an effort to allay some of their fears, Grimes had his staff visit Boston City Hospital's methadone clinic, many of whose clients were HIV-infected. "They saw that no one was rowdy," Grimes recalled. "No one was yelling. There was a security guard on the premises." Ultimately, after a "real struggle," the program for IV drug users opened, in July 1989; but, after an initial flurry of visits, the facility did not attract many clients. Grimes had hired an outreach worker with money from the Department of Public Health, but, in his view, the program "needs to signal without scaring [others] away. We have a big prenatal and pediatric clinic. We don't want to literally throw out the baby with the bathwater."

Other neighborhood community health center directors encountered, or anticipated, the same problems. "Right now [treating HIV patients] would affect us negatively," observed Allen Ball, director of the Harvard Street Health Center. "Our people are not educated enough." The center—in one of Boston's poorest neighborhoods—referred all people with HIV infection to Boston City Hospital, with which it was affiliated; any effort to provide care for them at Harvard Street would, Ball predicted, create "an uproar." For Ball, and other neighborhood health center administrators, getting enough training and education on HIV for his staff was a significant problem. "Our staff has asked over and over to be trained to do [counseling on HIV testing]," said Dr. Catherine Samples, director of adolescent services at the Martha Eliot Health Center. While the state offered a three-day course on counseling once a month, it had a long waiting list and provided little advance notice. "We can't afford to send a clinician or a nurse for three days on short notice," Samples explained. "It's hard for us to free up people, especially for education. We need them to produce revenue." The neighborhood health centers, added Catherine O'Connor, "can hardly keep their heads above water. If they send a provider to get training, it means they don't get paid."

Still, the importance of training in the neighborhood centers was inarguable. "You need to educate the receptionist," said O'Connor, "to not treat the [HIV] patient differently, or the patient won't come back. . . . You need a commitment from the medical director all the way down to the person who cleans the floor."

The need for education sprang not only from concerns about how well HIV patients would be treated at the facility, but, equally important, how discreetly. "Addicts have concerns about confidentiality," O'Connor explained. "To be HIV positive in the black or latino community is a very bad thing—you will be completely ostracized. . . . [Addicts] don't want people to know they're substance abusing. [Some are] afraid of losing their kids and their [welfare] benefits if the Department of Social Services finds out." Maintaining confidentiality is "a major problem," despite efforts to protect HIV patients' identities, said Ed Grimes of Uphams Corner. "Here we have secondary files and special codes to protect clients. But our dentists feel they have the right to know [a patient's HIV status]."

For the neighborhood health centers, as elsewhere in the city's health care system, the most intractable problem was money. The centers had very limited resources and struggled to get by with what Grimes called a "patchwork quilt" of funds from the city, the state, Medicaid, and Medicare. Those neighborhood centers that were affiliated with hospitals generally fared better, since they were reimbursed by Medicaid at the higher hospital rate, and were reimbursed for free care as well. (Unaffiliated centers did, however, get some funds that helped defray the costs of free care through the state Department of Medical Security.) Still, most centers were obliged by their financial constraints to see as high a volume of income-generating patients as possible. In that context, it was perhaps not surprising that many neighborhood health centers did not vigorously pursue a policy of counseling patients at risk to test for HIV. "Time is money" for the neighborhood health centers, O'Connor noted; they "need to see patients every 15 to 20 minutes" to bring in enough income, and pretest counseling takes "easily an hour." "We're not able to generate the income we need," agreed Allen Ball of the Harvard Street Center. "Then to have this [HIV care] would be too much. We're already operating short-staffed and with deficits."

For just these reasons, Dr. Catherine Samples of the Martha Eliot center admitted that the prospect of testing and treating HIV patients "scares us a lot because of the immense cost." The Martha Eliot center, which was affiliated with Children's Hospital and Brigham and Women's Hospital, served a largely latino population, many of whom were "totally or functionally illiterate." Samples estimated that 30 to 40 percent of the center's patients had no insurance. The potential for being swamped by new patients needing HIV testing and treatment was enormous. Some estimated that there were 700 HIV-infected people in the center's catchment area. There was not enough staff or resources, Samples believed, to handle the volume or the special needs of so many HIV-infected patients.

Just deciding for whom to urge testing was a delicate, time-consuming task. As Samples explained, "The cultural issue is a major one—there's a lot of stigmatism over homosexuality and bisexuality, especially in the latino community." And there were adverse consequences to consider. "I pushed testing a little more when I first got here," Samples said. But, she observed, women who tested positive sometimes got beaten up, or lost their homes. Without more resources to help them and provide adequate care, Samples was not sure whether "it would be ethical for me to test these clients."

The neighborhood health centers' concerns about resources were expected to be addressed, to some extent, by new Medicaid regulations, which were being readied by the state. Under the planned changes, community health centers would be eligible for "enhanced coverage" for case management services, which would help coordinate HIV patients' medical care, and for physician time for initial assessments of HIV patients, as well as later clinic appointments due to a "significant change" in symptoms.[13] Still, with such high percentages of their clients not covered, it was not clear how much these changes would help mitigate the financial impact of testing and treating the asymptomatic HIV population.

Moreover, as Allen Ball observed, his center was already dealing with overwhelming needs in the population it served. "Our infant mortality rate," Ball said, "is higher than in some third world countries. [Our patients] need a lot of time already. . . . Our people outside everybody." Looking at the existing need for services that the Martha Eliot center faced, Catherine Samples likewise wondered where the time and resources would come from to meet the new demand. "We have a lot more people dying of other things than AIDS," she added.

## Viewpoint: The Advocates

Among those who worked with, or for, people with HIV infection as advocates or outreach workers, there was general agreement that urging testing and early intervention was fine in an ideal world, but views differed as to what to encourage in a world of scarce resources. David Aronstein of the AIDS Action Committee argued that an "across-the-board" policy encouraging anyone at risk to test for HIV "doesn't recognize the need to make this decision individually and in a context. . . . There is a difference between telling people to get tested and giving them information and helping [them] . . . to be able to make a good decision for themselves at that point in time."[14] Once the test results come in, Aronstein added, people would need more individual attention to help think through the implications.

There needs to be support for people when they find out their antibody status—whether they are

positive or negative, because that has implications in relationships as well, when you are negative, for behavior maintenance, whether it is safer sex or clean needle use. It means helping people get linked up to good health care services, and that doesn't just happen because you tell somebody to go get a piece of information—people need to know where to get tested, where their anonymity can be guaranteed so that they can get health care.

"Frankly," he concluded, "it is all going to be totally ridiculous if the cuts in Medicaid go through the way they have been talking about."

Marshall Forstein, a member of the board of the AIDS Action Committee and a psychiatrist whose practice included HIV-infected people, worried about the effects of "advising people to take a test for which you then don't provide the resources to do anything about." Finding out their HIV status, he argued, "generates [in some] a kind of anxiety at a deep emotional level that forces them, in fact, to deny their risk behavior and become more entrenched in the kinds of problems that may contribute to the transmission of AIDS."

Forstein's concerns were shared by Kattie Portis of Project WARN, a federally funded education and prevention program that provided outreach services for women at risk of AIDS. Portis, whose work included doing outreach on the street, in homeless shelters, and welfare hotels, found the idea of urging testing on a wide-scale basis "scary. Once people find out that they're infected," she said, "the treatment won't be there. . . . We don't need people out in the street freaking out." As Portis noted, "The women I work with haven't had access to health care, period."

Dianna Christmas, AIDS coordinator at the Dimock Community Health Center—a health center serving a black and latino community and, like Fenway, offering a wide range of services for people with AIDS—said the staff workers at the facility "have a lot of mixed feelings about whether to push testing or not." Testing for HIV might be a good idea for "someone independent, who has insurance, but . . . a population that depends on other systems to pay costs and make decisions" might not fare so well. There were a "lot of people [at Dimock] who are under the court system or a [state] hierarchy they basically don't trust," she continued. "What will it cost them as welfare recipients to be known as somebody who has AIDS?"

For some who worked with the poorest populations at risk of HIV, there were questions as to the utility of testing at all, in view of the immensity of their other problems. Marshall Forstein illustrated:

> You hear, for instance, women who are married to IV drug users, or living with IV drug users, and who have kids, say, "How do I worry about AIDS when I need my boyfriend or husband or lover to put food in my kids' mouths. If I talk about condoms, he beats me up and kicks me out of the house. What's more important—feeding my kids and having a roof over their heads, or having a condom in my pocket?"

But some in the minority community felt strongly that widespread testing, as well as education about AIDS, was essential for survival. Wayne Wright of the Multicultural AIDS Coalition argued for "aggressive testing and helping people in our communities who are disenfranchised understand that they have more alternatives available to them than they know. . . . [E]ducating people about the risks that they're running forces them to be empowered in ways they have never been before. . . . And so if we empower people to realize they have alternatives and they do become educated, they do begin to motivate themselves in other ways. If we don't give people an opportunity for that empowerment, then in my opinion that's real genocide."

The Multicultural AIDS Coalition, Wright added, aimed to help provide that empowerment by supporting programs and agencies within communities of color. "We here at the Multicultural AIDS Coalition," he commented, "don't see ourselves doing outreach. We are in fact the community, so we're not reaching outside ourselves to include someone. We're reaching into ourselves to create something."

Speaking for himself—the coalition had not yet adopted a policy on testing—Wright said, "I believe that we have to be very aggressive about testing for a number of reasons. One of them is that the resources are not increasing; they're getting smaller. My feeling is they're getting smaller because we have not made the case for a real epidemic." The consequences of not making that case were; for communities of color, especially severe, Wright argued. Looking back at past failures of society to respond to the pleas of the community for help with education, teenage parenting, and drugs, Wright saw the same pattern with the AIDS crisis. "We're dealing with an emergency here," he said. "I can't sit around and wait and trust that people are going to put into place a system that has never been in place, that there is no evidence that it will ever be in place for my people." It was possible, he acknowledged, that an aggressive testing program could do harm to some:

> But either people are going to die in this thing as a result of us taking no action, or at least we can empower other people with a sense of action. I can't just sit idly by and have people say to me, "Well, we shouldn't test because the systems aren't in place." The fact is that the AIDS Action Committee, the Boston AIDS Consortium, the Multicultural AIDS Coalition, the Latino Health Network—we're all going to see those people one way or another. Either we're going to see them as people who are asking us to help them secure a system that allows them to get AZT, or they're going to be people who come to us, mere frames of what they were, so involved in the AIDS disease that the only thing that we can do is sit and hold their hands.

Apart from the need for more money, some activists were concerned by what they perceived to be a lack of proper planning. "The city, the state, and the government agencies, and the private community groups need to work better together," David Aronstein said. He saw little evidence, outside the work being done by the organizations involved in the Boston AIDS Consortium, of any comprehensive planning for AIDS services. It was, he felt, "a reflection of no resources. But, as a result, I get concerned that we end up with patched-together programs from 1985 rather than the start of growing programs that are going to be needed in 1995."

Marshall Forstein saw the same problem.

> I think clinicians are struggling extraordinarily hard and I think that the communities are working very, very hard to get people whatever services are available—just kind of scrambling as we're sliding down a hill of sand that's falling apart under our feet. . . . We're doing things in the short term that seem to make sense—struggling hard just to get through day by day. But nobody's taking a look at where we want to be five years from now. What are the numbers we're going to be dealing with? What do we have to put in place now and in-

crease a little bit at a time to get there? That kind of long-term planning [is needed]—this is not an epidemic that's going to go away.

For Wayne Wright, political commitment was as necessary as planning. "I feel that the Department of Health and Hospitals has been a real partner to us," he said, ". . . [but] it is only one department of many." The city of Boston, he continued, "has got to recognize that if in fact this is an epidemic, it means throwing its full weight behind it. It means that there is a role for the office that deals with housing, . . . that there is a role for the police department, that there is a role for the firemen. I don't see that unified plan as to what every department will be doing to put its weight behind this epidemic." DHH, Wright felt, had been "doing something that no one else in this community is willing to do, and that is to address the fact that in an environment of limited resources, it sometimes means shifting priorities. It sometimes means taking away from some and giving to some others because it is an epidemic and that is where the most important emergency is." But, he continued, the resources DHH "brings to the table [are] not enough. It's nowhere near enough. . . ."

## Viewpoint: Judith Kurland

For Judith Kurland, the state advisory on testing and early intervention raised a host of questions, practical and philosophical, that she felt needed addressing both within DHH and by society as a whole. On a purely practical level, she worried that the testing outlined in the advisory would primarily affect "a connected group. You are not going to get the IV drug user who is living in a crack house," she said, "to come in and get voluntary testing, so you are still going to get a bias. . . . [It will likely be someone] who is already involved with a health care system where there is some social support. The people that are going to benefit from this model . . . are still going to be the people who are connected to the system."

Kurland wondered whether "the whole conversation about testing [should] get opened up. . . . Should everybody who is at risk or should everybody in the world be tested, so that we can do things about it that are appropriate and good—not do things like segregate people on Devil's Island, but appropriate things like education, like early AZT. If we found out by testing that twice as many or ten times as many

youngsters are already HIV positive, wouldn't that change our public policy?"

Kurland's interest in the issue sprang in part from her concern that the focus on acute care in the nation's health care system slighted the importance of prevention in the battle against AIDS. In her view, a strong commitment to prevention programs could hold the key to eliminating the disease altogether. "My belief about AIDS," she said, "is very simple."

We could stop it now, except for those people already infected. We know that. Theoretically, you could end AIDS . . . without a vaccine. You stop people from sharing needles. You stop people from certain sexual behaviors, unprotected sexual practices. We could stop it, we know that. So why would you shift from prevention to care? Our whole medical system always does that. When things get tough, the money always goes to acute medical care. . . . Acute medical care always eats up the resources, and we don't do anything to keep people healthy.

Surveying the health care system in the US, Kurland saw a structure heavily weighted toward diagnosis and treatment. Recalling arms negotiator Paul Warnke's observation that once an arms system became technologically feasible it became politically inevitable, she saw an analogous trend in the medical field. "Once [something] becomes technologically feasible [in medicine]," she argued, "you have to have it, you have to do it." And "once you diagnose it, you have to do something about it, which is why I think the health companies put all their money into [creating] diagnostic tools. If you have a means to find out if people have x, . . . then of course you have to spend a hell of a lot of money on fixing them up once you've found out what's wrong with them." Once people are diagnosed with asymptomatic HIV, she continued, "there is phenomenal stress on the system to treat them, so we will keep seeing the concentration of money on acute medical care and not on prevention once again." Kurland added that "now that we know that people can be treated successfully when they are asymptomatic, we ought to try to treat them. . . . I think we have an obligation to do something about it." Nevertheless, she was concerned that the program the state recommended would do little to help the population that DHH served, or that no one was presently serving, and that, by focusing on treatment, early intervention would have little effect on the people in danger of infection.

"My dilemma is this," she said. "There is protection of people who have a disease, and there's protection of people who don't have the disease. . . . I would like to know where is the best expenditure of what I have to assume is limited money."

Kurland had similar questions as she surveyed the problems of the people who came to Boston City Hospital seeking care. It was possible, she believed, for the demand for HIV care to transform Boston City into "an AIDS hospital, if we [aren't] careful about it." For a variety of reasons, Kurland argued, BCH should resist that trend, chiefly because of the other services it provided the poor. "There are a lot of poor people," she noted, "who have lots of problems and need excellent care, and they're only going to get it here. If we disappear as a general service acute care hospital for the poor, they will not get service. So this [hospital] has to continue to have strong obstetrics, great neonatal care, pediatrics, other adult medicine, and a strong adolescent program. People need these programs."

By the same token, Kurland did not consider expanding the size of the hospital a workable solution to the problem posed by the growing AIDS population.[15] She had resisted, for example, suggestions that the new facility—which was scheduled to begin construction soon—should have more beds to meet the new demand from people with AIDS. For one thing, the project plan she inherited already called for the rebuilt hospital to remain at its current level of 356 beds; to try to negotiate a new number, Kurland said, would mean delays of up to two years. Moreover, she was convinced that, with AIDS becoming more of a chronic disease, it made little sense to increase the number of acute care beds. Boston City had, in fact, once had a much larger capacity, but from a peak of 2,200 in the World War I era, the number of beds had steadily declined, particularly after Medicare and Medicaid began providing coverage for the poor in private hospitals. Medicaid and Medicare, Kurland argued, had made some of the poor—such as elderly people, pregnant women—"attractive to private hospitals, so the need for the number of beds at BCH dropped. I think our number [of beds] now shows what the private hospitals are willing to do. They're not willing to take care of the people we now take care of, for the most part. And I think if we got too big, and times got bad, the private hospitals would dump."

Kurland's concern about "dumping" by private hospitals reflected her belief that "it is very wrong for public hospitals or any public institutions to be the only

place that poor people go." In company with other observers, she had spotted what she considered a disturbing trend among even the few hospitals that handled the majority of Boston's AIDS patients. "For two months in a row," she said, "BCH has had the largest new caseload of AIDS in the city." A couple of other hospitals had more cases cumulatively, she noted, "but you can see that we are coming up, because we take care of IV drug users, we take care of people of color, we take care of poor women and their babies." The private hospitals "loved AIDS when it was neat and clean with lots of research money from NIH," Kurland added. ". . . But the nature of the epidemic [now] is that we're going to pick up a disproportionate share, and we should not be the only place in town. The other hospitals have to do more."

It would be, admittedly, an uphill battle to change the way patient care was distributed in Boston. As Mayor Flynn noted in a January 1990 letter to Governor Dukakis (arguing against Medicaid reimbursement reductions for BCH), Boston City Hospital provided 25 percent of free care in the state, and 50 percent in the city, even though it housed only six percent of the city's hospital beds.[16] The commissioner of health and hospitals, as Kurland freely acknowledged, had little power to force Boston's private hospitals to take on a larger share of the poor AIDS population. "She's got pitifully little in her black bag to pull out and make them do what they don't want to do," said Holly Ladd. Some, like Ladd, argued that it was the mayor's job to create the climate that would induce private hospitals to provide more free care, but Kurland felt that beyond using its powers of persuasion and moral authority, there was not much the city could do. It was the state, she pointed out, that licensed hospitals. Boston had some leverage: hospitals had to go to the city for building permits to expand, but in view of Massachusetts' slumping economy, Kurland noted, it was unlikely that they would be denied. The state "is the only one who has clout," said Kurland. "But the state hasn't gotten to the point of realizing that we [Boston City] can't do it all. I mean, the state isn't where we are."

Meanwhile, where Kurland was at the moment was in the midst of a fiscal crunch that could result in serious cuts in her budget for FY91. While the budget figures were still a matter of debate, pending final state action, the human statistics, such as an almost two percent jump in the mortality rate for black infants in Massachusetts,[17] were unalterable facts that Kurland had to consider in her planning for treatment for people with asymptomatic HIV infection. "One-fifth of all the babies born here [at BCH]," she said, "are born to women who have used cocaine within the previous 48 hours. One-fiftieth are HIV positive. Think of what we could do in terms of preventing AIDS by doing outreach education, spending a lot of time with those women, and all the women that come here, with the amount of money we need to spend on acute care and drug therapy for asymptomatic AIDS patients."

Both she and Mayor Flynn were committed, Kurland asserted, to increasing AIDS clinical and outreach programs "even though money is tight." Kurland said she planned, for example, to beef up outreach throughout DHH by incorporating education and prevention efforts into the activities of a broad range of programs where AIDS was not the primary focus. In addition, Kurland said, she had launched an "aggressive strategy" to develop new grant-funded efforts for AIDS prevention and treatment, and intended to submit supplemental budget requests to the city for AIDS services. Of course, it was not clear how much new money either of these efforts would produce. In this context, the state advisory certainly complicated already difficult issues. Kurland felt sure of one thing: it was not going be easy to expand AIDS services significantly. "Every other program is also full and has waiting lists," she said, "but without additional money, I would have to take from something else [to expand], and there is nothing sufficiently unworthy that is easy for me to take from."

# Epilogue*

In response to the HIV epidemic in the city of Boston, the Boston Department of Health and Hospitals (DHH) continues to play a key role in monitoring the status of the epidemic, funding local prevention, education and client service programs, conducting research, and overall citywide planning around issues presented by the epidemic.

The prevalence of HIV continues to grow among populations served by DHH. These populations include women, drug users, TB patients, and incarcerated men. Patients with HIV disease and patients at high risk for HIV disease continue to be seen and treated through Boston City Hospital's inpatient and

outpatient services. In addition to the clinics discussed in the case, BCH's primary care, STD, neurology, Women's Center, and Adolescent Center clinics have introduced programs to deal with special issues around HIV and infected patients. Mattapan Hospital has introduced services and clinics as well. A continuing need exists to better integrate the care and manage the services of patients seen throughout the hospital, through the DHH system, and through services in the community. The human and financial resources at Health and Hospitals devoted to AIDS and HIV disease, although appearing significant, have only begun to address these needs. In fiscal year 1990, DHH expenses for AIDS related services totalled $14,790,000 of which $4 million were not reimbursed. In addition, a substantial portion of clinical services are also grant supported.

Efforts to provide AIDS education through the Division of Public Health and Clinical AIDS Program expanded in 1990 to include HIV education for agencies serving the general public and special populations; an AIDS information line staffed by public health nurses in the Communicable Disease Control (CDC) program, and a range of educational services to individuals and groups; AIDS education for IV drug users through Addiction Services and Project TRUST; education and counseling through the Public Health clinic (which continues to host a state sponsored Alternative Testing Site); continuing social services and counseling offered through the Immunodeficiency Clinic at Boston City Hospital; provider education and training through the Metropolitan Area HIV Services (MAHS) grant; and a CDC funded cooperative agreement with the Boston Public Schools to provide AIDS education. These internal DHH efforts are complemented by existing contracts with 18 community based organizations for fiscal year '91, which will grow to 22 agencies in fiscal year '92.

Since the case study was completed, the variety of testing potions for patients and providers, changes in available treatment for HIV infection, and growth of services available to HIV positive clients have necessitated a review of policies concerning HIV testing. A subcommittee of the AIDS Planning Task Force, established by Deputy Commissioner Alonzo Plough, is underway to conduct this review. HIV testing for clinical purposes is confidential and is usually integrated into clinical care, in order to obtain differential diagnoses or assess appropriate treatment. Public Health AIDS Services has recently hired an HIV Counseling and Testing Coordinator who has established a pro-

*Epilogue, Spring 1991. Reprinted by permission of the Boston Department of Health and Hospitals, Public Health AIDS Service.

gram for citywide training of counselors to support community health efforts. In addition, the Coordinator will further develop a multi-session post-test counseling support program that has proven highly successful in providing client education. This program also empowers newly diagnosed individuals to make choices regarding care options. The Coordinator will also provide group supervision and support to counselors throughout the DHH system.

In addition to these existing initiatives, Public Health AIDS Services at the request of the Commissioner is acting on behalf of the Mayor and Commissioner to distribute and monitor new funds coming to Boston under the Ryan White Comprehensive AIDS Resources Emergency Act of 1990, (C.A.R.E. Act). The C.A.R.E. Act provides federal support for comprehensive health and social services for people living with AIDS and HIV disease. Title I provides "disaster relief" grants to meet the needs identified by HIV planning councils in localities disproportionately affected by the HIV epidemic. Through application for these emergency relief dollars, DHH will distribute and administer approximately $2 million (1991–1992) in awards to community based providers.

## Notes

1. According to Richard Knox, reporting in the *Boston Globe,* at least 70 percent of the 1.5 million people estimated to be infected with HIV nationwide did not know they carried the virus.
2. *Boston Globe,* December 10, 1989, p. 1.
3. Roughly 60 percent of the AIDS patients at the clinic were IV drug users; 33 percent of the clinic's clients were women. According to December 1989 statistics from the AIDS Surveillance Programs (a joint venture of DHH and the state Department of Public Health), IV drug users made up 19 percent of the AIDS population in Boston; women, 11 percent.
4. Physicians in the immunodeficiency clinic usually saw patients there for one or two of its five weekly sessions, devoting the rest of their time to duties in other clinics.
5. The AIDS clinic had a much lower rate of uninsured patients than the rest of the hospital; overall, 46 percent of Boston City's patient population was uninsured.
6. Founded in the spring of 1988, the Boston AIDS Consortium was an umbrella planning organization with over 100 members representing health care providers and service agencies in the private and publc sector.
7. Mona Rowe and Rita Keintz, "National Survey of State Funding for AIDS," *Intergovernmental AIDS Reports,* September-October 1989.
8. Holly Ladd of the Boston AIDS Consortium estimated that 50 percent of people with AIDS in Massachusette were receiving Medicaid benefits—a figure that could go as high as 65 percent by mid-1990. AIDS patients alone, of course, would not be hurt by eliminating the medically needy category, which covered anyone with chronic disease (such as diabetes) and large medical bills. Over 50 percent of the state's Medicaid expenditures covered the expenses of the medically needy. The state was also planning to freeze its insurance program for uninsured or underinsured working adults.
9. *Boston Globe,* February 1, 1990, p. 26.
10. On January 30, 1990, a federal advisory committee recommended that the Food and Drug Administration approve AZT treatment for HIV-positive people whose T-4 cell count fell below 500 for each milliliter of blood; AZT was already being administered to people with T-4 cell counts under 200, almost all of whom would be symptomatic.
11. According to Howard Libman, Boston City's primary clinic was "booked in the sense that it takes two months to get an appointment." But because of its relatively high no-show rate, "particularly for interns and junior residents," Libman believed "there is a way that more patients could be incorporated into the primary care clinic."
12. Apparently, some of Boston's major hospitals did not apprecitae HIV or AIDS referrals from neighborhood centers affiliated with them. One health care provider said of her hospital affiliate, "It's hard to refer to them. [The hospital] has not done a lot with HIV—it's not anxious to be seen as an AIDS center."
13. Community health centers were already receiving higher rates for administering aerosol pentamidine.
14. The AIDS Action Committee underscored its point in a "Statement on HIV Antibody Testing" it issued on January 3, 1990, in anticipation of the forthcoming state advisory.
15. As part of an effort to contain costs, Kurland was also planning to cut mid-level staff at the hospital by several hundred people. The hospital's staff-to-patient ratio (10 to 1) was higher than average.

16. *Boston Globe,* January 2, 1990, p. 21
17. According to figures from the Massachusetts Department of Public Health, the black infant mortality rate went from 15.5 percent in 1987 to 17.2 percent in 1988. The rate for white infants from 6.6 to 7.1 percent over the same time period.

## Chapter 13 Review Questions

1. How do you define the word "implementation"? In what ways does "implementation" differ from "management" or "administration"? What are the similarities and differences among these terms?
2. Can you outline how the concept of implementation draws on other ideas concerning decision making, communications, politics, budgeting, intergovernmental relations, public professional expertise, and the general environment that have been discussed earlier in this text? How does the concept of implementation both use and build on these other concepts?
3. Why has implementation become such a major concern for students and practitioners of public administration and public policy in recent decades? What was responsible for its development as a recent focus of scholarly research? Do you think there is a valid need for studying implementation in the public sector and, if so, why?
4. What are the essential elements of the implementation model that Malcolm L. Guggins et al. propose? What are its basic assumptions and utility for practicing public administrators? Can you define in your own words its basis for understanding the processes? Is it applicable to all situations, such as in foreign affairs? Or, just in local issues?
5. From your reading of this case, "Planning for Early Intervention in HIV Infection," what conditions contribute to complications in effective program implementation? How should they be dealt with in your view?
6. Consider the key administrator in "Planning for Early Intervention in HIV Infection" and evaluate whether or not she was successful at implementing this program under crisis conditions. By what standards can we judge whether or not administrators are successful at the task of program implementation?

## Key Terms

communications model
state implementation
state capacity

decisional outcomes
feedback/policy redesign
inducements and constraints

## Suggestions for Further Reading

The book that started much of the contemporary theorizing about this subject is now in its second edition and is still well worth reading, Jeffrey L. Pressman and Aaron B. Wildavsky, *Implementation,* Second Edition (Berkeley, Calif.: University of California Press, 1978) as well as several of the case studies that criticized the implementation of Great Society programs and also stimulated early research in this field, especially Martha Derthick, *New Towns In-*

*Town* (Washington, D.C.: Urban Institute, 1972); Daniel P. Moynihan, *Maximum Feasible Misunderstanding* (New York: Free Press, 1969); Stephan K. Bailey and Edith K. Mosher, *ESEA: The Office of Education Administers a Law* (Syracuse: Syracuse University Press, 1968) as well as Beryl A. Radin, *Implementation, Change and the Federal Bureaucracy* (New York: Teachers College Press, 1977).

Serious students of implementation theory should review carefully the major conceptual approaches cited in the introduction to this chapter as well as other important contributions such as: Martin Rein and Francine F. Rabinovitz, "Implementation: A Theoretical Perspective," in Walter D. Burnham and Martha W. Weinberg, eds., *American Politics and Public Policy* (Cambridge, Mass.: MIT Press, 1978) and also in the same book, Michael M. Lipsky, "Implementation on its Head"; Carl E. Van Horn, *Policy Implementation in the Federal System* (Lexington, Mass.: Lexington Books, 1979); A. Dunsire, *Implementation in Bureaucracy* (New York: St. Martin, 1979); Walter Williams, *The Implementation Perspective* (Berkeley, Calif.: University of California Press, 1980); J. S. Larson, *Why Government Programs Fail* (1980); Helen M. Ingram and Dean E. Mann, eds., *Why Policies Succeed or Fail* (Los Angeles: Sage, 1980); R. D. Behn, "Why Murphy was Right," *Policy Analysis* (Summer 1980); G. C. Edwards, *Implementing Public Policy* (Washington, D.C.: Congressional Quarterly Press, 1980); Susan Barrett and Colin Fudge, eds., *Policy and Action: Essays on Implementation of Public Policy* (London: Methuen, Inc., 1981); Dennis J. Palumbo and Marvin A. Harder, eds., *Implementing Public Policy* (Lexington, Mass.: Lexington Books, 1981); Daniel A. Mazmanian and Paul A. Sabatier, eds., *Effective Public Policy Implementation* (Lexington, Mass.: Lexington Books, 1982); B. Hjern and D. O. Porter, "Implementation Structure," *Organization Studies* (1981); Randall B. Ripley and Grace A. Franklin, *Bureaucracy and Policy Implementation* (Homewood, Ill.: Dorsey Press, 1982); Walter Williams, et al., *Studying Implementation: Methodological and Administrative Issues* (Chatham, N.J.: Chatham House, 1982), and B. Hjern and C. Hull, eds., "Implementation Beyond Hierarchy," Special Issue, *European Journal of Political Research.* For a helpful reader, see George C. Edwards III, ed., *Public Policy Implementation* (Greenwich, Conn.: JAI Press, 1989).

During the 1980s greater attention has been paid by scholars to careful case analyses of implementation within the context of particular policy fields such as M. K. Marvel, "Implementation and Safety Regulation: Varieties of Federal and State Administration Under OSHA," *Administration and Society* (May 1982); S. L. Yafee, *Prohibitive Policy: Implementing the Federal Endangered Species Act* (Cambridge, Mass.: MIT Press, 1982); Donald C. Menzel, "Implementation of the Federal Surface Mining Control and Reclamation Act of 1977," *Public Administration Review* (March/April 1981); Dean E. Mann, ed., *Environmental Policy Implementation* (Lexington, Mass.: Lexington Books, 1982); Charles S. Bullock III and Charles M. Lamb, *Implementation of Civil Rights Policy* (Monterey, Calif.: Brooks/Cole, 1984); David L. Kirp and Donald N. Jensen, eds., *School Days, Rule Days* (Philadelphia, Pa.: Taylor & Francis, 1986); Gary C. Bryner, *Bureaucratic Discretion* (New York: Pergamon Press, 1987); Donald F. Kettl, *Government by Proxy* (Washington, D.C.: Congressional Quarterly Press, 1988); Joan W. Allen et al., *The Private Section in State Service Delivery: Examples of Innovative Practices* (Washington, D.C.: The Urban Institute, 1989) and Lester M. Salamon, ed., *Beyond Privatization: The Tools of Government Action* (Washington, D.C.: The Urban Institute, 1989). For an up-to-date summary of where we are today with implementation studies, read Malcolm L. Goggin, Ann O'M. Bowman, James P. Lester, and Laurence J. O'Toole, Jr., *Implementation Theory and Practice: Toward a Third Generation* (Glenview, Ill.: Scott, Foresman and Co., 1990); see especially its excellent bibliography.

# PART THREE

Enduring and Unresolved
Relationships: Central Value
Questions, Issues, and Dilemmas of
Contemporary Public Administration

**P**art Three focuses on three key persistent and pressing relationships in the field of public administration today: the problems of political-administrative relationships; the public and the private sector; and ethics and the public service. All of these relational issues are new in the sense that they have come to the forefront of recent discussions and controversies in public administration. Yet, these issues have certainly been part of the problems and perplexities of public administration since its inception as an identifiable field of study after the turn of the twentieth century. Indeed, the topics of political-administrative relationships, the problems of ethics, and relationships between public and business administrations were central themes of the writings of many early administrative theorists, such as Woodrow Wilson, Frederick Taylor, Luther Gulick, Louis Brownlow, and Leonard White. No doubt one could even trace the origins of these topics back to the classic writings of Plato, Aristotle, Moses, and Pericles. But for a variety of reasons, we are witnessing the reemergence of these older issues as very real dilemmas for public administrators today. Readings and cases in Part Three therefore address these critical issues:

**CHAPTER 14**
*The Relationship Between Politics and Administration: The Concept of Issue Networks* What are the current trends and practices in political oversight and control of administration? What are the implications for public administration and the governance of America?

**CHAPTER 15**
*The Relationship Between the Public and Private Sectors: The Concept of Pillars of Success for Mixed Undertakings* What is the relationship between public and private sectors? How have new forms of public action through sharing government authority with a host of "third parties" affected performance of government? What are the advantages and disadvantages of using different tools to accomplish public policy goals? What does this "new reality" of public management practices mean for contemporary public administrators?

**CHAPTER 16**
*The Relationship Between Ethics and Public Service: The Concept of the Moral Ambiguities of Public Choice* How are ethical choices involved in contemporary decisions facing public servants? What is an appropriate conceptual model for understanding how ethical choices are involved in public administrators' choices? How can these choices be made in a more responsible manner?

# CHAPTER 14

## The Relationship Between Politics and Administration: The Concept of Issue Networks

*T*he iron triangle concept is not so much wrong as it is disastrously incomplete. And the conventional view is especially inappropriate for understanding changes in politics and administration during recent years. . . . Looking for the closed triangles of control, we tend to miss the fairly open networks of people that increasingly impinge upon government.

*Hugh Heclo*

## READING 14

## Introduction

Perhaps no issue has been more controversial or more discussed in public administration since its inception as a self-conscious field of study than the appropriate relationship between the politically elected representatives of the legislature and the permanent bureaucracy of the executive branch. Indeed, as was pointed out in Chapter One, the first essay on the subject of public administration written in the United States, "The Study of Administration," prepared by a young political scientist named Woodrow Wilson in 1887, essentially wrestled with the problem of the proper relationship between these two spheres of government: politics and administration.[1] Wilson wrote his essay at a time when civil service reform had recently been instituted in the federal government (the Pendleton Act had been passed in 1883). Wilson sought to encourage the development of the newly established merit system and the emergence of a field of academic study—public administration—because in his words, "It is getting to be harder to run a constitution than to frame one." The new complexities of government—both in terms of widening popular participation of the citizenry in democratic government and the rising technological problems of organizing

[1]Woodrow Wilson, "The Study of Administration," *Political Science Quarterly,* 2 (June 1887), 197–222.

public programs—created, in Wilson's view, the urgent need for developing effective administrative services free from congressional "meddling."

Generally, the drift—both in terms of intellectual thought and institutional reform in the United States during the century after Wilson's writing—until the 1970s was toward a realization of the Wilsonian argument in favor of greater administrative independence from legislative oversight. War, international involvements, economic crises, and a host of other influences (including public administration theorists) supported the claims for administrative independence from detailed legislative control. In particular, as political scientist Allen Schick notes, three factors led to congressional acquiescence. The first factor was the massive growth in the size of government. "Big government weakened the ability of Congress to govern by controlling the details and it vested administration with more details over which to govern. In the face of bigness Congress could master the small things only by losing sight of the important issues." This was bolstered by the message of public administration theorists "that a legislature should not trespass on administrative matters inevitably registered on Congressional thinking about its appropriate role, especially because the theme was so attractively laced with the promise of order and efficiency in the public service and carried the warning that legislative intrusion would be injurious to good government."[2]

Nonpartisanship in foreign affairs also played a powerful role in checking congressional intrusion in executive affairs by conveying "the assurance that unchecked executive power would be applied benevolently in the national interest of the United States." Pluralism, a third factor in fostering congressional retreat, according to Schick, furthered administrative independence by the convincing certainty that wider administrative discretion over executive agencies would be in fact used "to provide benefits to powerful interests in society to the benefit of everyone."

In retrospect, perhaps these assumptions were naive, but they were generally accepted as truths until the early 1970s. Suddenly the abuses of Watergate, the disastrous consequences of Vietnam, the failure of numerous Great Society social programs, combined with an unusually high turnover of congressional seats, brought about a dramatic revival of congressional interest in the problems of Congress's control over executive activities. A variety of new laws were enacted to achieve more control: for example, widening the requirement of Senate approval of presidential appointees to executive offices; creation of the Congressional Budget Office to act as a legislative fiscal watchdog; the passage of the Freedom of Information Act to provide Congress and the general public with greater access to executive activities; and the War Powers Resolution, which restricted presidential initiative in foreign military involvements.

Concomitant with the rise of congressional oversight in the 1960s and 1970s, it became fashionable to argue that governmental policies emerged from *iron triangles*—three-way interactions involving elected members of Congress, par-

[2]Allen Schick, "Congress and the 'Details' of Administration," *Public Administration Review,* 36 (Sept./Oct. 1976), pp. 516–528.

ticularly key committee and subcommittee chairpersons; career bureaucrats, particularly agency heads or senior staffers; and special interest lobbies, particularly powerful lobbies in specialized fields such as health, welfare, education, and defense. From this closed triad of interests, so the theory goes, governmental policies emerge by means of members of Congress writing and passing favorable legislation, bureaucrats implementing these congressional mandates in return for bigger budgets, and special-interest groups backing (with re-election monies and other support) the helpful members of Congress: In all, a tidy and closed relationship.

Is this how the political-administrative relationships in government actually work today? In the following essay Hugh Heclo (1944–   ), currently distinguished Robinson University professor, takes issue with the iron triangle conception of modern political-administrative relationships. He emphasizes, "The iron triangle concept is not so much wrong as it is disastrously incomplete." "Unfortunately," writes Heclo, "our standard political conceptions of power and control are not very well suited to the loose-jointed play of influence that is emerging in political administration. We tend to look for one group exerting dominance over another, for subgovernments that are strongly insulated from other outside forces in the environment, for policies that get 'produced' by a few 'makers.' " Instead, says Heclo, in "looking for the few who are powerful, we tend to overlook the many whose webs of influence provoke and guide the exercise of power. These webs, or what I will call 'issue networks,' are particularly relevant to the highly intricate and confusing welfare policies that have been undertaken in recent years."

Note that in Heclo's view of the *issue networks,* unlike the iron triangle concept, which assumed a small identifiable circle of participants, the participants are largely shifting, fluid, and anonymous. In fact, he writes, "it is almost impossible to say where a network leaves off and its environment begins." Whereas iron triangles are seen as relatively stable groups that coalesce around narrow policy issues, Heclo's issue networks are dispersed and numerous players move in and out of the transitory networks, without anyone being clearly in control over programs or policies. Although the "iron triangles at their roots had economic gain as an interest of all parties concerned," Heclo believes "any direct material interest is often secondary to intellectual or emotional commitment involving issue networks." Passion, ideas, and moral dedication replace, to a significant degree, material and economic gain from policy involvement.

The profound influence of the rise of these issue networks on government is manifold, Heclo thinks, especially in adding new layers of complexity to government. First, networks keep issues, potentially simple to solve, complex instead, primarily to gain power and influence by virtue of their own specialized expertise. Second, rather than fostering knowledge and consensus, issue networks push for argument, division, and contention to "maintain the purity of their viewpoints," which in turn sustain support from their natural but narrow public constituencies. Third, issue networks spawn true believers who become zealots for narrow interests rather than seekers of broad mandates of consensus, support, and confidence for public programs. Finally, rather than pushing for closure of debate, issue networks thrive by keeping arguments boiling and disagreements brewing. They survive by talking, debating, and arguing the alternatives, and not by finding common grounds for agreement and getting down to making things happen.

As you read this selection, keep the following questions in mind:

How does Heclo's issue network concept differ from the notion of iron triangles as the basis for political-administrative relationships?

What examples does Heclo give to support his new conceptualization of this relationship?

Do you find his arguments reasonable and correct on the basis of your experience or your reading of the case studies in this text?

What impact does the rise of issue networks have on democratic government in general and public administration in particular?

What new roles must public administrators assume, given the growth of issue networks today? Specifically, in your opinion, how can an administrator prepare or be trained for assuming these new roles?

# Issue Networks and the Executive Establishment

## HUGH HECLO

The connection between politics and administration arouses remarkably little interest in the United States. The presidency is considered more glamorous, Congress more intriguing, elections more exciting, and interest groups more troublesome. General levels of public interest can be gauged by the burst of indifference that usually greets the announcement of a new President's cabinet or rumors of a political appointee's resignation. Unless there is some White House "tie-in" or scandal (preferably both), news stories about presidential appointments are usually treated by the media as routine filler material.

"Issue Networks and the Executive Establishment" by Hugh Heclo from *The New Political System,* edited by Anthony King, 1978, pp. 87–124. Reprinted with permission of The American Enterprise Institute for Public Policy Research, Washington, D.C.

This lack of interest in political administration is rarely found in other democratic countries, and it has not always prevailed in the United States. In most nations the ups and downs of political executives are taken as vital signs of the health of a government, indeed of its survival. In the United States, the nineteenth-century turmoil over one type of connection between politics and administration—party spoils—frequently overwhelmed any notion of presidential leadership. Anyone reading the history of those troubled decades is likely to be struck by the way in which political administration in Washington registered many of the deeper strains in American society at large. It is a curious switch that appointments to the bureaucracy should loom so large in the history of the nineteenth century, when the federal government did little, and be so completely discounted in the twentieth century, when government tries to do so much.

Political administration in Washington continues to register strains in American politics and society, although in ways more subtle than the nineteenth-century spoils scramble between Federalists and Democrats, Pro- and Anti-tariff forces, Nationalists and States-Righters, and so on. Unlike many other countries, the United States has never created a high level, government-wide civil service. Neither has it been favored with a political structure that automatically produces a stock of experienced political manpower for top executive positions in government.[1] How then does political administration in Washington work? More to the point, how might the expanding role of government be changing the connection between administration and politics?

Received opinion on this subject suggests that we already know the answers. Control is said to be vested in an informal but enduring series of "iron triangles" linking executive bureaus, congressional committees, and interest group clienteles with a stake in particular programs. A President or presidential appointee may occasionally try to muscle in, but few people doubt the capacity of these subgovernments to thwart outsiders in the long run.

Based largely on early studies of agricultural, water, and public works policies, the iron triangle concept is not so much wrong as it is disastrously incomplete.[2] And the conventional view is especially inappropriate for understanding changes in politics and administration during recent years. Preoccupied with trying to find the few truly powerful actors, observers tend to overlook the power and influence that arise out of the configurations through which leading policy makers move and do business with each other. Looking for the closed triangles of control, we tend to miss the fairly open networks of people that increasingly impinge upon government.

To do justice to the subject would require a major study of the Washington community and the combined inspiration of a Leonard White and a James Young. Tolerating a fair bit of injustice, one can sketch a few of the factors that seem to be at work. The first is growth in the sheer mass of government activity and associated expectations. The second is the peculiar, loose-jointed play of influence that is accompanying this growth. Related to these two is the third: the layering and specialization that have overtaken the government work force, not least the political leadership of the bureaucracy.

All of this vastly complicates the job of presidential appointees both in controlling their own actions and in managing the bureaucracy. But there is much more at stake than the troubles faced by people in government. There is the deeper problem of connecting what politicians, officials, and their fellow travelers are doing in Washington with what the public at large can understand and accept. It is on this point that political administration registers some of the larger strains of American politics and society, much as it did in the nineteenth century. For what it shows is a dissolving of organized politics and a politicizing of organizational life throughout the nation. . . .

Unfortunately, our standard political conceptions of power and control are not very well suited to the loose-jointed play of influence that is emerging in political administration. We tend to look for one group exerting dominance over another, for subgovernments that are strongly insulated from other outside forces in the environment, for policies that get "produced" by a few "makers." Seeing former government officials opening law firms or joining a new trade association, we naturally think of ways in which they are trying to conquer and control particular pieces of government machinery.

Obviously questions of power are still important. But for a host of policy initiatives undertaken in the last twenty years it is all but impossible to identify clearly who the dominant actors are. Who is controlling those actions that go to make up our national policy on abortions, or on income redistribution, or consumer protection, or energy? Looking for the few who are powerful, we tend to overlook the many whose webs of influence provoke and guide the exercise of power. These webs, or what I will call "issue networks," are particularly relevant to the highly intricate and confusing welfare policies that have been undertaken in recent years.

The notion of iron triangles and subgovernments presumes small circles of participants who have succeeded in becoming largely autonomous. Issue networks, on the other hand, comprise a large number of participants with quite variable degrees of mutual commitment or of dependence on others in their environment; in fact it is almost impossible to say where a network leaves off and its environment begins. Iron triangles and subgovernments suggest a stable set of participants coalesced to control fairly narrow public programs which are in the direct economic interest of each party to the alliance. Issue networks are almost the reverse image in each respect. Participants move in and out of the networks constantly. Rather than groups united in dominance over a program, no one, as far as one can tell, is in control of the policies and issues. Any direct material interest is often secondary to intellectual or emotional commitment. Network members reinforce each other's sense of issues as their interests, rather than (as standard political or economic models would have it) interests defining positions on issues.

Issue networks operate at many levels, from the vocal minority who turn up at local planning commission hearings to the renowned professor who is quietly telephoned by the White House to give a quick "reading" on some participant or policy. The price of buying into one or another issue network is watching, reading, talking about, and trying to act on particular policy problems. Powerful interest groups can be found represented in networks

but so too can individuals in or out of government who have a reputation for being knowledgeable. Particular professions may be prominent, but the true experts in the networks are those who are issue-skilled (that is, well informed about the ins and outs of a particular policy debate) regardless of formal professional training. More than mere technical experts, network people are policy activists who know each other through the issues. Those who emerge to positions of wider leadership are policy politicians—experts in using experts, victuallers of knowledge in a world hungry for right decisions.

In the old days—when the primary problem of government was assumed to be doing what was right, rather than knowing what was right—policy knowledge could be contained in the slim adages of public administration. Public executives, it was thought, needed to know how to execute. They needed power commensurate with their responsibility. Nowadays, of course, political administrators do not execute but are involved in making highly important decisions on society's behalf, and they must mobilize policy intermediaries to deliver the goods. Knowing what is right becomes crucial, and since no one knows that for sure, going through the process of dealing with those who are judged knowledgeable (or at least continuously concerned) becomes even more crucial. Instead of power commensurate with responsibility, issue networks seek influence commensurate with their understanding of the various, complex social choices being made. Of course some participants would like nothing better than complete power over the issues in question. Others seem to want little more than the security that comes with being well informed. As the executive of one new group moving to Washington put it, "We didn't come here to change the world; we came to minimize our surprises."[3]

Whatever the participants' motivation, it is the issue network that ties together what would otherwise be the contradictory tendencies of, on the one hand, more widespread organizational participation in public policy and, on the other, more narrow technocratic specialization in complex modern policies. Such networks need to be distinguished from three other more familiar terms used in connection with political administration. An issue network is a shared-knowledge group having to do with some aspect (or, as defined by the network, some problem) of public policy. It is therefore more well-defined than, first, a shared-attention group or "public"; those in the networks are likely to have a common base of information and understanding of how one knows about policy and identifies its problems. But knowledge does not necessarily produce agreement. Issue networks may or may not, therefore, be mobilized into, second, a shared-action group (creating a coalition) or, third, a shared-belief group (becoming a conventional interest organization). Increasingly, it is through networks of people who regard each other as knowledgeable, or at least as needing to be answered, that public policy issues tend to be refined, evidence debated, and alternative options worked out—though rarely in any controlled, well-organized way.

What does an issue network look like? It is difficult to say precisely, for at any given time only one part of a network may be active and through time the various connections may intensify or fade among the policy intermediaries and the executive and congressional bureaucracies. For example, there is no single health policy network but various sets of people knowledgeable and concerned about cost-control mechanisms, insurance techniques, nutritional programs, prepaid plans, and so on. At one time, those expert in designing a nationwide insurance system may seem to be operating in relative isolation, until it becomes clear that previous efforts to control costs have already created precedents that have to be accommodated in any new system, or that the issue of federal funding for abortions has laid land mines in the path of any workable plan.

The debate on energy policy is rich in examples of the kaleidoscopic interaction of changing issue networks. The Carter administration's initial proposal was worked out among experts who were closely tied in to conservation-minded networks. Soon it became clear that those concerned with macroeconomic policies had been largely bypassed in the planning, and last-minute amendments were made in the proposal presented to Congress, a fact that was not lost on the networks of leading economists and economic correspondents. Once congressional consideration began, it quickly became evident that attempts to define the energy debate in terms of a classic confrontation between big oil companies and consumer interests were doomed. More and more policy watchers joined in the debate, bringing to it their own concerns and analyses: tax reformers, nuclear power specialists, civil rights groups interested in more jobs; the list soon grew beyond the wildest dreams of the original energy policy planners. The problem, it became clear, was that no one could quickly turn the many networks of knowledgeable people into a shared-action coalition, much less into a single, shared-attitude group believing it faced the moral equivalent of war. Or, if it was a war, it was a Vietnam-type quagmire.

It would be foolish to suggest that the clouds of issue networks that have accompanied expanding national policies are set to replace the more familiar politics of subgovernments in Washington. What they are doing is to overlay the once stable political reference points with new forces that complicate calculations, decrease predictability, and impose considerable strains on those charged with government leadership. The overlay of networks and issue politics not only confronts but also seeps down into the formerly well-established politics of particular policies and programs. Social security, which for a generation had been quietly managed by a small circle of insiders, becomes controversial and politicized. The Army Corps of Engineers, once the picturebook example of control by subgovernments, is dragged into the brawl on environmental politics. The once quiet "traffic safety establishment" finds its own safety permanently endangered by the consumer movement. Confrontation between networks and iron triangles in the Social and Rehabilitation Service, the disintegration of the mighty politics of the Public Health Service and its corps—the list could be extended into a chronicle of American national government during the last generation. The point is that a somewhat new and difficult dynamic is being played out in the world of politics and administration. It is not what has been feared for so long: that technocrats and other people in white coats will expropriate the policy process. If there is to be any expropriation, it is likely to be by the policy activists, those who care deeply about a set of issues and are determined to shape the fabric of public policy accordingly. . . .

## The Executive Leadership Problem

Washington has always relied on informal means of producing political leaders in government. This is no less true now than in the days when party spoils ruled presidential appointments. It is the informal mechanisms that have changed. No doubt some of the increasing emphasis on educational credentials, professional specialization, and technical facility merely reflects changes in society at large. But it is also important to recognize that government activity has itself been changing the informal mechanisms that produce political administrators. Accumulating policy commitments have become crucial forces affecting the kind of executive leadership that emerges. E. E. Schattschneider put it better when he observed that "new policies create new politics."[4]

For many years now the list of issues on the public agenda has grown more dense as new policy concerns have been added and few

dropped. Administratively, this has proliferated the number of policy intermediaries. Politically, it has mobilized more and more groups of people who feel they have a stake, a determined stake, in this or that issue of public policy. These changes are in turn encouraging further specialization of the government's work force and bureaucratic layering in its political leadership. However, the term "political" needs to be used carefully. Modern officials responsible for making the connection between politics and administration bear little resemblance to the party politicians who once filled patronage jobs. Rather, today's political executive is likely to be a person knowledgeable about the substance of particular issues and adept at moving among the networks of people who are intensely concerned about them.

What are the implications for American government and politics? The verdict cannot be one-sided, if only because political management of the bureaucracy serves a number of diverse purposes. At least three important advantages can be found in the emerging system.

First, the reliance on issue networks and policy politicians is obviously consistent with some of the larger changes in society. Ordinary voters are apparently less constrained by party identification and more attracted to an issue-based style of politics. Party organizations are said to have fallen into a state of decay and to have become less capable of supplying enough highly qualified executive manpower. If government is committed to intervening in more complex, specialized areas, it is useful to draw upon the experts and policy specialists for the public management of these programs. Moreover, the congruence between an executive leadership and an electorate that are both uninterested in party politics may help stabilize a rapidly changing society. Since no one really knows how to solve the policy puzzles, policy politicians have the important quality of being disposable without any serious political ramifications (unless of course there are major symbolic implications, as in President Nixon's firing of Attorney General Elliot Richardson).

Within government, the operation of issue networks may have a second advantage in that they link Congress and the executive branch in ways that political parties no longer can. For many years, reformers have sought to revive the idea of party discipline as a means of spanning the distance between the two branches and turning their natural competition to useful purposes. But as the troubled dealings of recent Democratic Presidents with their majorities in Congress have indicated, political parties tend to be a weak bridge.

Meanwhile, the linkages of technocracy between the branches are indeliberately growing. The congressional bureaucracy that has blossomed in Washington during the last generation is in many ways like the political bureaucracy in the executive branch. In general, the new breed of congressional staffer is not a legislative crony or beneficiary of patronage favors. Personal loyalty to the congressman is still paramount, but the new-style legislative bureaucrat is likely to be someone skilled in dealing with certain complex policy issues, possibly with credentials as a policy analyst, but certainly an expert in using other experts and their networks.

None of this means an absence of conflict between President and Congress. Policy technicians in the two branches are still working for different sets of clients with different interests. The point is that the growth of specialized policy networks tends to perform the same useful services that it was once hoped a disciplined national party system would perform. Sharing policy knowledge, the networks provide a minimum common framework for political debate and decision in the two branches. For example, on energy policy, regardless of one's position on gas deregulation or incentives to producers, the policy technocracy has established a common language for discussing the issues, a shared grammar for identifying the major points of contention, a mutually familiar rhet-

oric of argumentation. Whether in Congress or the executive branch or somewhere outside, the "movers and shakers" in energy policy (as in health insurance, welfare reform, strategic arms limitation, occupational safety, and a host of other policy areas) tend to share an analytic repertoire for coping with the issues. Like experienced party politicians of earlier times, policy politicians in the knowledge networks may not agree; but they understand each other's way of looking at the world and arguing about policy choices.

A third advantage is the increased maneuvering room offered to political executives by the loose-jointed play of influence. If appointees were ambassadors from clearly defined interest groups and professions, or if policy were monopolized in iron triangles, then the chances for executive leadership in the bureaucracy would be small. In fact, however, the proliferation of administrative middlemen and networks of policy watchers offers new strategic resources for public managers. These are mainly opportunities to split and recombine the many sources of support and opposition that exist on policy issues. Of course, there are limits on how far a political executive can go in shopping for a constituency, but the general tendency over time has been to extend those limits. A secretary of labor will obviously pay close attention to what the AFL-CIO has to say, but there are many other voices to hear, not only in the union movement but also minority groups interested in jobs, state and local officials administering the department's programs, consumer groups worried about wage-push inflation, employees faced with unsafe working conditions, and so on. By the same token, former Secretary of Transportation William Coleman found new room for maneuver on the problem of landings by supersonic planes when he opened up the setpiece debate between pro- and anti-Concorde groups to a wider play of influence through public hearings. Clearly the richness of issue politics demands a high degree of skill to contain expectations and manage the natural dissatisfaction that comes from courting some groups rather than others. But at least it is a game that can be affected by skill, rather than one that is predetermined by immutable forces.

These three advantages are substantial. But before we embrace the rule of policy politicians and their networks, it is worth considering the threats they pose for American government. Issue networks may be good at influencing policy, but can they govern? Should they?

The first and foremost problem is the old one of democratic legitimacy. Weaknesses in executive leadership below the level of the President have never really been due to interest groups, party politics, or Congress. The primary problem has always been the lack of any democratically based power. Political executives get their popular mandate to do anything in the bureaucracy secondhand, from either an elected chief executive or Congress. The emerging system of political technocrats makes this democratic weakness much more severe. The more closely political administrators become identified with the various specialized policy networks, the farther they become separated from the ordinary citizen. Political executives can maneuver among the already mobilized issue networks and may occasionally do a little mobilizing of their own. But this is not the same thing as creating a broad base of public understanding and support for national policies. The typical presidential appointee will travel to any number of conferences, make speeches to the membership of one association after another, but almost never will he or she have to see or listen to an ordinary member of the public. The trouble is that only a small minority of citizens, even of those who are seriously attentive to public affairs, are likely to be mobilized in the various networks.[5] Those who are not policy activists depend on the ability of government institutions to act on their behalf.

If the problem were merely an information gap between policy experts and the bulk of the population, then more communication might help. Yet instead of garnering support for policy choices, more communication from the issue networks tends to produce an "everything causes cancer" syndrome among ordinary citizens. Policy forensics among the networks yield more experts making more sophisticated claims and counterclaims to the point that the nonspecialist becomes inclined to concede everything and believe nothing that he hears. The ongoing debates on energy policy, health crises, or arms limitation are rich in examples of public skepticism about what "they," the abstruse policy experts, are doing and saying. While the highly knowledgeable have been playing a larger role in government, the proportion of the general public concluding that those running the government don't seem to know what they are doing has risen rather steadily.[6] Likewise, the more government has tried to help, the more feelings of public helplessness have grown.

No doubt many factors and events are linked to these changing public attitudes. The point is that the increasing prominence of issue networks is bound to aggravate problems of legitimacy and public disenchantment. Policy activists have little desire to recognize an unpleasant fact: that their influential systems for knowledgeable policy making tend to make democratic politics more difficult. There are at least four reasons.

## Complexity

Democratic political competition is based on the idea of trying to simplify complexity into a few, broadly intelligible choices. The various issue networks, on the other hand, have a stake in searching out complexity in what might seem simple. Those who deal with particular policy issues over the years recognize that policy objectives are usually vague and results difficult to measure. Actions relevant to one policy goal can frequently be shown to be inconsistent with others. To gain a reputation as a knowledgeable participant, one must juggle all of these complexities and demand that other technocrats in the issue networks do the same.

## Consensus

A major aim in democratic politics is, after open argument, to arrive at some workable consensus of views. Whether by trading off one issue against another or by combining related issues, the goal is agreement. Policy activists may commend this democratic purpose in theory, but what their issue networks actually provide is a way of processing dissension. The aim is good policy—the right outcome on the issue. Since what that means is disputable among knowledgeable people, the desire for agreement must often take second place to one's understanding of the issue. Trade-offs or combinations—say, right-to-life groups with nuclear-arms-control people; environmentalists and consumerists; civil liberties groups and anti-gun controllers—represent a kind of impurity for many of the newly proliferating groups. In general there are few imperatives pushing for political consensus among the issue networks and many rewards for those who become practiced in the techniques of informed skepticism about different positions.

## Confidence

Democratic politics presumes a kind of psychological asymmetry between leaders and followers. Those competing for leadership positions are expected to be sure of themselves and of what is to be done, while those led are expected to have a certain amount of detachment and dubiety in choosing how to give their consent to be governed. Politicians are supposed to take credit for successes, to avoid any appearance of failure, and to fix blame clearly on their opponents; voters weigh these claims and come to tentative judgments, pending the next competition among the leaders.

The emerging policy networks tend to reverse the situation. Activists mobilized around the policy issues are the true believers. To sur-

vive, the newer breed of leaders, or policy politicians, must become well versed in the complex, highly disputed substance of the issues. A certain tentativeness comes naturally as ostensible leaders try to spread themselves across the issues. Taking credit shows a lack of understanding of how intricate policies work and may antagonize those who really have been zealously pushing the issue. Spreading blame threatens others in the established networks and may raise expectations that new leadership can guarantee a better policy result. Vagueness about what is to be done allows policy problems to be dealt with as they develop and in accord with the intensity of opinion among policy specialists at that time. None of this is likely to warm the average citizen's confidence in his leaders. The new breed of policy politicians are cool precisely because the issue networks are hot.

## Closure

Part of the genius of democratic politics is its ability to find a nonviolent decision-rule (by voting) for ending debate in favor of action. All the incentives in the policy technocracy work against such decisive closure. New studies and findings can always be brought to bear. The biggest rewards in these highly intellectual groups go to those who successfully challenge accepted wisdom. The networks thrive by continuously weighing alternative courses of action on particular policies, not by suspending disbelief and accepting that something must be done.

For all of these reasons, what is good for policy making (in the sense of involving well-informed people and rigorous analysts) may be bad for democratic politics. The emerging policy technocracy tends, as Henry Aaron has said of social science research, to "corrode any simple faiths around which political coalitions ordinarily are built."[7] Should we be content with simple faiths? Perhaps not; but the great danger is that the emerging world of issue politics and policy experts will turn John Stuart Mill's argument about the connection between liberty and popular government on its head. More informed argument about policy choices may produce more incomprehensibility. More policy intermediaries may widen participation among activists but deepen suspicions among unorganized nonspecialists. There may be more group involvement and less democratic legitimacy, more knowledge and more Know-Nothingism. Activists are likely to remain unsatisfied with, and nonactivists uncommitted to, what government is doing. Superficially this cancelling of forces might seem to assure a conservative tilt away from new, expansionary government policies. However, in terms of undermining a democratic identification of ordinary citizens with their government, the tendencies are profoundly radical.

A second difficulty with the issue networks is the problem that they create for the President as ostensible chief of the executive establishment. The emerging policy technocracy puts presidential appointees outside of the chief executive's reach in a way that narrowly focused iron triangles rarely can. At the end of the day, constituents of these triangles can at least be bought off by giving them some of the material advantages that they crave. But for issue activists it is likely to be a question of policy choices that are right or wrong. In this situation, more analysis and staff expertise—far from helping—may only hinder the President in playing an independent political leadership role. The influence of the policy technicians and their networks permeates everything the White House may want to do. Without their expertise there are no option papers, no detailed data and elaborate assessments to stand up against the onslaught of the issue experts in Congress and outside. Of course a President can replace a political executive, but that is probably merely to substitute one incumbent of the relevant policy network for another.

It is, therefore, no accident that President Carter found himself with a cabinet almost none of whom were either his longstanding political backers or leaders of his party. Few if any of his personal retinue could have passed through the reputational screens of the networks to be named, for example, a secretary of labor or defense. Moreover, anyone known to be close to the President and placed in an operating position in the bureaucracy puts himself, and through him the President, in an extremely vulnerable position. Of the three cabinet members who were President Carter's own men, one, Andrew Young, was under extreme pressure to resign in the first several months. Another Carter associate, Bert Lance, was successfully forced to resign after six months, and the third, Griffin Bell, was given particularly tough treatment during his confirmation hearings and was being pressured to resign after only a year in office. The emerging system of political administration tends to produce executive arrangements in which the President's power stakes are on the line almost everywhere in terms of policy, whereas almost nowhere is anyone on the line for him personally.

Where does all this leave the President as a politician and as an executive of executives? In an impossible position. The problem of connecting politics and administration currently places any President in a classic no-win predicament. If he attempts to use personal loyalists as agency and department heads, he will be accused of politicizing the bureaucracy and will most likely put his executives in an untenable position for dealing with their organizations and the related networks. If he tries to create a countervailing source of policy expertise at the center, he will be accused of aggrandizing the Imperial Presidency and may hopelessly bureaucratize the White House's operations. If he relies on some benighted idea of collective cabinet government and on departmental executives for leadership in the bureaucracy (as Carter did in his first term), then the President does more than risk abdicating his own leadership responsibilities as the only elected executive in the national government;

he is bound to become a creature of the issue networks and the policy specialists. It would be pleasant to think that there is a neat way out of this trilemma, but there is not.

Finally, there are disturbing questions surrounding the accountability of a political technocracy. The real problem is not that policy specialists specialize but that, by the nature of public office, they must generalize. Whatever an influential political executive does is done with all the collective authority of government and in the name of the public at large. It is not difficult to imagine situations in which policies make excellent sense within the cloisters of the expert issue watchers and yet are nonsense or worse seen from the viewpoint of ordinary people, the kinds of people political executives rarely meet. Since political executives themselves never need to pass muster with the electorate, the main source of democratic accountability must lie with the President and Congress. Given the President's problems and Congress's own burgeoning bureaucracy of policy specialists, the prospects for a democratically responsible executive establishment are poor at best.

Perhaps we need not worry. A case could be made that all we are seeing is a temporary commotion stirred up by a generation of reformist policies. In time the policy process may reenter a period of detumescence as the new groups and networks subside into the familiar triangulations of power.

However, a stronger case can be made that the changes will endure. In the first place, sufficient policy-making forces have now converged in Washington that it is unlikely that we will see a return to the familiar cycle of federal quiescence and policy experimentation by state governments. The central government, surrounded by networks of policy specialists, probably now has the capacity for taking continual policy initiatives. In the second place, there seems to be no way of braking, much less reversing, policy expecta-

tions generated by the compensatory mentality. To cut back on commitments undertaken in the last generation would itself be a major act of redistribution and could be expected to yield even more turmoil in the policy process. Once it becomes accepted that relative rather than absolute deprivation is what matters, the crusaders can always be counted upon to be in business.

A third reason why our politics and administration may never be the same lies in the very fact that so many policies have already been accumulated. Having to make policy in an environment already crowded with public commitments and programs increases the odds of multiple, indirect impacts of one policy on another, of one perspective set in tension with another, of one group and then another being mobilized. This sort of complexity and unpredictability creates a hostile setting for any return to traditional interest group politics.

Imagine trying to govern in a situation where the short-term political resources you need are stacked around a changing series of discrete issues, and where people overseeing these issues have nothing to prevent their pressing claims beyond any resources that they can offer in return. Imagine too that the more they do so, the more you lose understanding and support from public backers who have the long-term resources that you need. Whipsawed between cynics and true believers, policy would always tend to evolve to levels of insolubility. It is not easy for a society to politicize itself and at the same time depoliticize government leadership. But we in the United States may be managing to do just this.

## Notes

1. Hugh Heclo, *A Government of Strangers: Executive Politics in Washington* (Washington, D.C.: Brookings Institution, 1977).
2. Perhaps the most widely cited interpretations are

J. Leiper Freeman, *The Political Process* (New York: Random House, 1965); and Douglass Cater, *Power in Washington* (New York: Vintage, 1964)

3. Steven V. Roberts, "Trade Associations Flocking to Capital as U.S. Role Rises," *New York Times,* March 4, 1978, p. 44.

4. E. E. Schattschneider, *Politics, Pressures and the Tariff* (Hamden: Archon, 1963), p. 288 (originally published 1935).

5. An interesting recent case study showing the complexity of trying to generalize about who is "mobilizable" is James N. Rosenau, *Citizenship Between Elections* (New York: The Free Press, 1974).

6. Since 1964 the Institute for Social Research at the University of Michigan has asked the question, "Do you feel that almost all of the people running the government are smart people, or do you think that quite a few of them don't seem to know what they are doing?" The proportions choosing the latter view have been 28 percent (1964), 38 percent (1968), 45 percent (1970), 42 percent (1972), 47 percent (1974), and 52 percent (1976). For similar findings on public feelings of lack of control over the policy process, see U.S. Congress, Senate, Subcommittee on Intergovernmental Relations of the Committee on Government Operations, *Confidence and Concern: Citizens View American Government,* committee print, 93d Cong., 1st sess., 1973, pt. 1, p. 30. For a more complete discussion of recent trends see the two articles by Arthur H. Miller and Jack Citrin in the *American Political Science Review* (September 1974).

7. Henry J. Aaron, *Politics and the Professors* (Washington, D.C.: Brookings Institution, 1978), p. 159.

# CASE STUDY 14

# Introduction

Professor Heclo in the foregoing reading advances an important conceptualization, or rather reconceptualization, of political-administrative relationships. Note, however, that the context and examples from which he drew this idea were centered in the federal level of U.S. government. Does his concept apply locally as well? Or, do political-administrative relationships operate fundamentally differently on other levels? How do they function at the grassroots?

In the following story we look at a mayor and his style of governance in one of the largest and most difficult cities to run today. "Mayor Dinkins: Every Day a Test," by Sam Roberts, an urban affairs reporter for the *New York Times,* examines the work of the mayor of New York City, David Dinkins. In one sense, this study is *not* a typical case study as others in this text that recount a series of events with a clear beginning and end. Rather, Roberts draws for us more of a character study of the man and his job, sort of "a day in the life" portrait of how Mayor Dinkins struggles to govern New York under very demanding and complex conditions. From this angle, Dinkins emerges as "the man in the middle" of multiple, contending interests, or "issue networks," in Heclo's terminology. He must calculate his actions precisely because his margin for error is thin, razor thin, according to Roberts. How he battles every day to balance and deal with these seemingly endless, conflicting demands relates directly to several of Heclo's themes. What emerges from Roberts' story is a fascinating character study of persistence, skill, attention to details, and no small amount of good luck, even though from the outside, Dinkins' personality at times seems "rambling," "indecisive," and "muddled."

As you read the "Mayor Dinkins" case, think about the following issues:

What sort of issue-network demands does Mayor Dinkens face and what are the various strategies or means he uses to deal with them?

Are these interests that he must contend with, in your view, best termed as "pressure groups," "iron triangles," "issue networks," or something else? How would you characterize the method that the mayor uses to balance political-administrative relationships? What are the implications of his methods?

Based on this case, do you believe Heclo's concept applies to the local level as well as the federal level? If so, why? If not, what's a more realistic conceptualization for understanding this key relationship?

# Mayor Dinkins: Every Day a Test

## SAM ROBERTS

On a blustery afternoon last month, two of New York's top labor leaders mounted the steps of City Hall to blast the Mayor they had helped elect. "The head stinks," said Stanley Hill, leader of the city's largest municipal union. Barry Feinstein, president of the teamsters' local that represents city workers, exploded: "This administration is going into the toilet."

New York politics is often indistinguishable from theater, but on this day the anger was genuine. The city's union leaders, a keystone in the coalition that brought David N. Dinkins to office, had just been humiliated before their own members. Philip R. Michael, the city budget director, had privately assured the financial community that the city was negotiating to have the unions defer part of their newly won wage increases. The word got out, and now the unions were howling for Michael's scalp.

They didn't get it. Instead, three days later, Dinkins summoned his labor commissioner, Eric J. Schmertz, to Gracie Mansion, the restored 18th-century coun-

try home on the Upper East Side that serves as the Mayor's official residence. Schmertz, it turned out, had suggested to Michael that wage deferrals might indeed be in the offing. And Dinkins had decided that Schmertz, who had been organized labor's favorite for the job, would take the fall—not Michael, recruited from Wall Street. "I think," Schmertz recalls Dinkins saying solemnly, "your usefulness is at an end."

Those eight words marked a defining moment for this Mayor and his administration. Dinkins couldn't recall ever having dismissed anyone before. In choosing Michael over Schmertz to vindicate his administration, he signaled that his immediate priority would be to establish fiscal credibility rather than to please his natural consistency and the fragile coalition that had elected him.

The ouster of Schmertz, and the agonized balancing of interests that led to that decision, also underscored what may be the most important single fact about David Dinkins: he is a minority mayor. The word resonates on several levels. First, Dinkins is acutely conscious of his precarious position as a black man being judged by a white society. Second, he won the slimmest of victories in the mayoral election by carefully holding together a coalition of minority interests. Finally, he governs a city of minorities, seeking to apportion its diminishing resources equitably among the myriad racial and ethnic groups that form the New York he likes to call a "gorgeous mosaic."

No decision is made at City Hall without passing through this complicated layering, as if through a triple filter. In surveying the five boroughs of New York, Dinkins sees an infinitely complex, restive concatenation of competing groups and special pleaders, whose interests he must weigh, balance and respond to. "You are my base," he once told a group of black supporters at Sylvia's, a soul-food landmark in Harlem, "but I have to be Mayor of all the people of the city of New York."

David Dinkins was elected in 1989 as New York's first new mayor in 12 years and its first black mayor ever. Although it was the narrowest victory since 1905, his election was a milestone, a powerful symbol of change in a city where non-Hispanic whites, although they still control the levers of economic power, no longer constitute a majority. Belatedly—New York was the last of America's 10 largest cities to elect a mayor who was black, female or Hispanic—the city's politics had caught up to its demographics.

Unusually for a large American city, no single racial or ethnic group in New York constitutes a majority. Blacks, who make up about a quarter of the population, are nearly outnumbered by Hispanic residents. Newer groups are jockeying for supremacy or, in some cases, simple recognition. When Dinkins greeted the Indian consul general in February, it was suggested that the traditional political itinerary for New York office-seekers—Ireland, Italy and Israel—be expanded to include a fourth "I," India. The Mayor, who has already visited Italy and Israel, politely explained that he had accepted an invitation to tour Africa first.

Dinkins was chosen as the instrument to defeat Edward I. Koch, the three-term incumbent, not in spite of his race, but largely *because* of it. As the most prominent black city official—he served as Manhattan Borough President—he was uniquely positioned to unite a coalition embracing organized labor, liberal whites, and black and Hispanic New Yorkers, an alliance that had signaled its potential just the year before by delivering the city to the Rev. Jesse Jackson in the Democratic Presidential primary. The voter-registration campaign that had been mounted for

Jackson set the stage for Dinkins's victory; a final boost came when Gov. Mario M. Cuomo, a week before the 1989 mayoral primary, coyly hinted that whichever candidate could best bring a racially divided city together would win.

Dinkins was a touch-and-feel politician, a product of the Democratic clubhouse whose secret weapon was his Rolodex. As a party regular he had shaken so many hands over the years—especially in the quasi-ministerial post of borough president—that, despite his race, he emerged almost as a candidate of the status quo. "No Jewish politician has gone to more Jewish events," says Ken Sunshine, who last year held the thankless job of arranging the Mayor's schedule. "Eighty percent of success is showing up," Woody Allen once said. "David," says Basil A. Paterson, a close friend and former law partner of the Mayor, "was always showing up."

But when Dinkins began showing up as Mayor, he seemed to be a stranger in two worlds. The white establishment, which he had cultivated for years, was wary of a black mayor with a progressive agenda. And, as recession forced him into the no-win position of allocating losses, his own constituency became estranged, particularly poor blacks, embittered that hard times were deferring their dreams. Moreover, a revised City Charter required him to tolerate a newly assertive City Council, which gained enhanced powers over the city budget, land use and other mayoral prerogatives.

Still, during 15 months as Mayor, Dinkins has bridged a mammoth budget gap, laid the groundwork for a vastly expanded police force and revolutionary strategies for deploying it, cajoled commodities exchanges to remain in New York, snared next year's Democratic National Convention for his city and organized a hero's welcome for Nelson R. Mandela.

Yet those brief celebratory moments have been muffled by a painfully deliberate, measured style. An asset in the race against the loud, combative Koch, that style has often made Dinkins look indecisive and reluctant to lead, aloof and out of touch with the passions that move his city. Dinkins contrasts his style with Koch's. "It's easy to get angry," he says. "It's a lot more difficult to maintain composure in the face of difficult circumstances, and I, frankly, don't think people want to see a mayor out of control." Yet in trying to project self-restraint and a dignified aura, and to adhere to his own timetable, the Mayor has often appeared so detached from events that it seemed he was not *in* control.

In one particularly chaotic week last October, he adopted stances that might have been defensible individually but, taken together, seemed bewildering, naïve and reactive. Only days after negotiating a surprisingly generous raise for the city's school teachers, his administration hinted that as many as 15,000 city workers would have to be laid off. At the same time Dinkins announced his plan for an expanded police force. During a crime wave last summer, the public had become fixated on the goal of hiring 5,000 more police officers, but Dinkins, in what seemed a remarkable display of obstinacy, refused to commit himself to any specific figure until a review of the department's needs had been completed. Dinkins lamely suggested that his apparent reticence on the issue was intentional: by stalling, he helped create a constituency for positions he had wanted to advance anyway.

It's a bitter commentary that a Mayor who has begun what could be the biggest police-force expansion in New York's history, in a city for which crime is the top priority, has been reduced to pleading for credit—financial credit from Wall Street, and approval from the New Yorkers he governs.

With potential challengers thinking they smelled the blood of a lame duck, Dinkins's political hold seemed so tenuous only a year into his first term that he felt compelled last month to declare that he would be a candidate for reelection in 1993. He also issued an unusually pointed appeal, as guest host on a black radio station to galvanize his base: "There are a lot of folks who are not pleased that I am Mayor," he said. "There are a lot of folks who don't want me to be right nohow under any circumstances." Beleaguered and reeling, the Mayor of all the people was pleading for understanding from his bedrock constituency in his hour of need.

The gentlemanly demeanor and reticence that helped elect Dinkins but now threatens to undo him as Mayor was shaped, in part, by a calculated strategy: how to survive on white terms in a largely white world. "David learned a long time ago, that as a black person you couldn't afford to get angry if you're going to exercise power," says Percy E. Sutton, a mentor and a predecessor as Manhattan Borough President.

For the same reason, Dinkins has scrupulously avoided casting himself as a victim because of his race. When asked if he thinks he is held to a different standard because he is black, he says, "You could stick needles under my fingernail; you would not get me to respond in the affirmative to that, because that will be seen by many as hiding behind color."

Yet race remains the prism through which many New Yorkers view their Mayor, and through which the Mayor sees himself and his city. According to Koch, it has shielded Dinkins from tough assessments from whites: "We tiptoe around criticism because we're afraid of hurting his feelings or the feelings of his black constituents."

Blacks tend to see the matter differently. Representative Charles B. Rangel, whose district includes Harlem, says Dinkins has been regarded with suspicion and subjected to tougher standards because of his race. He compares him to a white basketball player coming to Harlem, where spectators would say, "Sure he should be given a chance, but let's watch him very carefully."

Although some of the Mayor's wounds have been self-inflicted, Rangel's remark rings true. While the new Mayor was no more irresolute about his budget than President Bush was about *his* budget last fall, nobody asked whether Bush was up to the job, as they did about Dinkins.

But it's not only whites who are scrutinizing the Mayor. Blacks, who expected Dinkins to be "a superman," according to Basil Paterson, are watching closely too, fearful lest the Mayor decide to appease the financial community by cutting services rather than raising taxes. Dinkins, "has to do some demonstrable things to show he's not just cutting everything to satisfy the Wall Street people," says Dr. Roscoe C. Brown Jr., president of Bronx Community College, who is black.

So intense is the scrutiny, so heated the competition for scarce money, that at times, evenhandedness can be seen as inherently unfair. "It's not the same to please the Wall Street community coming out of a decade of excess as to please the lady from the Bronx who has no health care," says Dennis Rivera, head of the hospital workers' union.

Indeed, the effort to treat all New Yorkers equally, to please everyone and offend no one, has on occasion produced a kind of moral gridlock. When blacks boycotted a Brooklyn grocery store owned by Korean immigrants, the Mayor seemed so reluctant to slight either group that he alienated both. His failure suggested naïvete in assuming that black militants had an investment in his success and contradicted one of his most appealing campaign claims: that he was a conciliator who could keep the peace. (His administration speedily settled a subsequent boycott in Queens, though.)

Race is also the lens through which Dinkins has privately filtered criticism, whether aimed at his handling of the budget, the handcarved headboard his wife chose for Gracie Mansion, or his passion for tennis. He tends to interpret negative press coverage as having a racial component but stoically subdues his indignation, wrapping his feelings in a protective layer of bland verbiage and baroque syntax. (Despite his formality and his avuncular profile, he can be testy and curt in private, peppering his remarks with the occasional expletive.)

Reporters need the persistence of a picador to pierce Dinkins's thick protective hide. But on rare occasions he hints at his irritation. Perhaps, Dinkins says of the press's early obsession with his tennis game, people "would react differently if I shot basketball hoops."

Race has undeniably been a variable in any number of mayoral equations—even in controversies that were not overtly racial. One factor in Dinkins's eagerness to show financial discipline, Paterson says, was that "blacks have not been associated with fiscal concerns, but with taking care of people." Last fall, when Governor Cuomo broached the possibility that the state's Financial Control Board might usurp authority from the city's first black mayor, Dinkins cautioned a businessman: "If the F.C.B. tries to take over, the Korean boycott would be nothing compared to that."

Earlier, Dinkins had been criticized for apparently capitulating to disgruntled correction officers who blockaded the city's jail complex on Rikers Island. He later explained privately that he had feared violence if mostly white police officers were deployed against predominantly black and Hispanic guards.

Race even figured in Dinkins's decision to attend the United States Open tennis tournament in Queens rather than fly to Utah for the funeral of a white tourist slain in a Manhattan subway station. "Expectations are raised about what I should do," he said. "What is the message I send to the families of other people who got killed?"—meaning the black and Hispanic families whose sons constitute the majority of murder victims in the city. "When he errs," says Deputy Mayor Milton Mollen, whom Dinkins

dispatched to the funeral instead, "he errs on the side of decency."

So complex have New York's racial and ethnic politics become, that even a visit to Israel, a matter of course for Koch, became a political mine field for his successor. In January, responding to a request from the Jewish Community Relations Council, Dinkins flew to Israel as a gesture of solidarity with the Jewish state, then under siege from Iraqi missiles. It was emblematic of the dilemma of a minority mayor that not everyone was delighted with his decision. A number of blacks, including some who opposed the Persian Gulf war altogether, complained that he was catering to the Jewish community again; some Jews suggested the Mayor was guilty of pandering. Arab-Americans demanded that he visit Jordan, too. Dinkins responded that he was demonstrating solidarity not only with Jews in Israel, but also with American soldiers in the Middle East—nearly a third of them black. One week later, the scribbled message he inserted in Jerusalem's Western Wall covered all bases: "I pray for peace here and everywhere in the world," he wrote, "and for freedom in South Africa."

If war was hell for Dinkins, peace wasn't much better. When a radio reporter handed him the opportunity to announce a homecoming parade for American troops, the Mayor balked. The city couldn't afford it, he said. Moreover, he cautioned that encouraging private benefactors to subsidize a celebration would only invite complaints that the money could better be spent on enduring projects like libraries. This was the response of a junior accountant, not a mayor in tune with the mood of his city. "Millions for Mandela, but not one cent for American heroes," a white civic leader said tartly. Once again, Dinkins lagged behind a public desperate for leadership or, at least, for diversion. Four days after the radio interview, the Mayor reversed himself. He announced that, solely through private philanthropy, returning troops would receive a hero's—and, as he made sure to mention, a *"she-ro's"*—welcome in the city's greatest official greeting ever.

In tennis, a dink is a deceptively weak shot. In Gaelic, it's an elegant dresser. Growing up in Trenton and, briefly, in Harlem, serving in the Marine Corps, and attending Howard University, David Norman Dinkins was called Dink, and the nickname was prophetic. The Dinkins style of governing is a direct extension of his tennis game. He prefers singles "because it's all you—you don't have to worry what your partner's doing." The Mayor, says Sid Davidoff, a lobbyist and sometime court rival, "has a weak serve and not a very good backhand. You don't get the killer shot. But he stands there and goes from side to side. And, if you play his baseline game, he'll lull you and finally wear you out."

That is the Mayor's game plan. Having defied the skeptics by winning office, Dinkins, stubborn and at times sanctimonious, follows his personal convictions now more than ever. He loathes critical advice. Even Rangel, Paterson and Sutton, the members of Harlem's old guard who were his mentors and under whom he served perhaps too long an apprenticeship, have been reluctant to second-guess him. Paterson, a skilled mediator, was stunned that he was never asked to help resolve the Brooklyn grocery boycott. The decision seemed to reflect Dinkins's burning desire for personal vindication—to stand on the shoulders of those who had come before, as the Rev. Dr. Martin Luther King Jr. put it, but without holding anyone else's hand.

After a quarter-century in public life, however, Dinkins has remarkably unsophisticated political instincts. He has also been slow to transcend his previous job, in which reaching a decision loomed as an end in itself, and to shed a management style in which moderation sometimes seemed to be a goal rather than a consequence of good government. There are signs of late, though, that he has turned a corner, that feeling more self-assured, he has begun to project some of the decisiveness and leadership that he has displayed behind closed doors—qualities I saw when, for this article, the Mayor overcame his antipathy to letting the press see him in an unscripted setting and allowed me to accompany him for two full days in private and in public. At times, his performance fully lived up to the expectations of his critics: detached, uncommunicative and perpetually late. But another Dinkins emerged, a decisive and demanding Mayor who demonstrated flashes of potential—tantalizing pulses that, if sustained, could propel him from being the right candidate at the right time to being the right Mayor as well.

Dinkins's first public appearance is at St. Barnabas Hospital in the Bronx for a breakfast meeting of the 48th Precinct community conference. The Mayor's mantra is children; this speech provides another opportunity to promote his "cops and kids" anti-crime agenda before this racially mixed audience. But the Dinkins style can be so stultifying that, after earnestly

expressing the sentiment that "kids are our future," and promising 30 more officers for the precinct, he pauses to say plaintively, "You all are supposed to applaud to indicate that you agree."

After looking to the future, Dinkins turns to his own past: he shares some rare personal reminiscences with his audience, reflecting on his strict upbringing and sense of discipline. This is the message that many of the whites who voted for Dinkins hoped he would bring to his black and Hispanic constituents. But while he acknowledges that many poor children lack the discipline that was imposed on him by his mother and grandmother, both dollar-a-day domestics for white families, he shuns the term "underclass" and avoids lecturing. This disappoints critics who believe a black mayor, in particular, has a special responsibility to confront the problems of welfare dependency. Today he recounts the now-familiar story of how his mother and grandmother beat him after he was caught stealing a reflector off a license plate, but he adds a new wrinkle: the only time he had been slapped by his mother before was when he addressed an adult by her first name on the street.

After the speech, Dinkins heads to City Hall for a full day of meetings. His formal first-floor office is dominated not by the traditional portrait of an eminent predecessor, but by photographs of Nelson Mandela and Paul Robeson. A narrow staircase, lined with photographs of the Mayor posing with sports and entertainment figures, leads to a more fuctional basement hideaway. Wooden blinds, nearly always drawn, and a leather couch the color of ruby Port lend it a vaguely English atmosphere, somehow appropriate to Dinkins's Victorian elocution and personal manner.

He is meeting today with his "mini-cabinet": his five Deputy Mayors; George B. Daniels, his counsel; Albert Scardino, his press secretary (soon to resign); and Victor A. Kovner, a onetime Koch confidant, active in Jewish and liberal causes, who was chosen as Corporation Counsel even before Election Day to reassure jittery New Yorkers that a Dinkins administration would not turn City Hall upside down. (As it turned out, three of the five Deputy Mayors, like Kovner, are Jewish.)

Dinkins's full cabinet is considered largely unexceptional but competent, despite early complaints that talent and experience had been sacrificed to diversity and a determined housecleaning of Koch holdovers. Nobody reports directly to the Mayor, but some Commissioners enjoy special stature and access, notably Lee P. Brown in Police, Betsy Gotbaum in Parks and Mark Green in Consumer Affairs. Three of the five Deputy Mayors—Bill Lynch, Barbara J. Fife and Sally Hernandez-Pinero—are alumni of Dinkins's borough presidency. Their intimacy with the Mayor has prevented the usually assertive First Deputy Mayor, Norman Steisel, a former Sanitation Commissioner and investment banker, from presiding as effectively as he might over key players who are putatively on the same team but don't always wear a common uniform.

At the top of the agenda today is the Board of Education's proposal to help prevent the spread of AIDS by distributing condoms to high-school students on request—a controversial program for which Dinkins has announced his support. Analyzing the condom vote, Dinkins seems confident—just as he was when he jauntily emerged from a secret meeting in a midtown hotel room last fall with Schools Chancellor Joseph A. Fernandez, who had been resisting budget cuts demanded by City Hall. How had Dinkins persuaded Fernandez to back down? The Mayor, referring to the fact that he and his allies had corralled the votes on the Board of Education, ventured an unusually blunt reply: "He can count."

Dinkins displayed a similar toughness earlier that day in a meeting with his mini-cabinet to discuss strategy for dealing with the City Council. The Council Speaker, Peter F. Vallone, wants to begin the bargaining over the Mayor's anti-crime plan with the Council's more modest version, which included fewer preventive services for children and would require smaller tax increases. "I'm not going to do that," Dinkins declares. "I say we should work for the product *we* have, which is eminently superior to what they put together. The battle you've got to win for me is, work from *our* document, not theirs. If it develops that we can't get it, it sure as hell is going to be pretty clear who doesn't want it." Subsequent negotiations produce a compromise that is closer to Dinkins's version than to the Council's.

So pronounced is the difference between the Dinkins who can dominate in private and ramble obliquely in public that, after viewing both versions during the "urban summit" that Dinkins convened in New York last fall, San Francisco's Mayor, Art Agnos, asked Bill Lynch in disbelief: "Does your Mayor have two personalities? Does he think that's the way a mayor is supposed to behave?"

Seated at an oval conference table, Dinkins often seems distracted. He peruses his mail, fingers a silver letter opener and vets speech texts. (He interrupts another meeting to call his speech writer to insert several paragraphs about bias-related violence, moments before he is to deliver an address at a gay and lesbian celebration of African-American History Month.)

At one point, the Mayor interrupts the condom debate to ask Fife, "Has 'Miss Saigon' cleaned up its act?" The British musical almost didn't make it to Broadway because of a dispute over the casting of an English actor as a Eurasian, but Fife attests to the show's racial rectitude. Dinkins telephones his wife, Joyce, and tells her to accept an invitation.

Dinkins can be attentive and exacting, demonstrating a methodicalness and math major's obsession with detail that make occasional personal lapses all the more unfathomable. "Is it logical?" he implies as he counterpunches each parry from his appointees. He wields his watch— an $1,800 black stainless-steel-and-gold Concord Mariner SG, which he won in a charity tennis tournament—as a management tool and an escape hatch. "I'm due at the Mariners' Temple at noon, so why don't we cut to the chase?" he announces at 11:40 to officials who have gathered to explore solutions to another looming crisis, prison overcrowding. "Give me my piece of it in 10 minutes."

Dinkins's meetings are heavy on good intentions. But a subtext seems to be: Tomorrow we've got to get organized. To that end, the Mayor just recruited a chief of staff, John Flateau, a campaign alumnus whose duties and authority over other appointees remain ill defined. He has his work cut out for him. Disorganization among the Deputy Mayors pushed Bill Lynch to the verge of leaving earlier this year; he changed his mind when Dinkins warned that his defection would only fuel disaffection among the civic, religious, political and labor leaders from outside Dinkins's Harlem base who were closer to Lynch than to the Mayor.

After lunch, Dinkins is briefed on the impact of pending Congressional bills and on a meeting with West Side legislators pressing for a highway detour. He greets visiting Soviet dignitaries, the sort of ceremonial occasion that often occupied him as borough president. He still attends so many black-tie affairs that some disillusioned handlers refer to him as "Waldorf Dave." Yet, with this Mayor, some ceremonies assume a symbolic value that many whites overlook, just as they did the importance of Jesse Jackson's candidacy for American blacks. "The value of being an African-American mayor is not limited to things a mayor can do," Dinkins says. "These things translate." They translate more slowly among New York's white establishment where, Dinkins says, "if you look at the corporate boards, the law firms, you find very few people like me." When he paid a courtesy call last fall at the headquarters of a major bank, top officials complained about the paper work involved in monitoring minority recruitment. Defending the fundamental fairness behind such requirements, Dinkins said stiffly: "Some people don't understand the city is here for all of us."

No translation is necessary during the Mayor's midday speech at the Mariners' Temple Baptist Church on the Lower East Side. Introducing Dinkins, the pastor, Dr. Suzan D. Johnson, recalls the biblical David as "a shepherd boy whom everybody kept overlooking." "The David we know," she says, had also challenged a giant. Dinkins, grandson of a minister and son of a barber, reminds visiting schoolchildren that they can grow up to be anything if they stay in school. "You *know* that you can be mayor," he says. After the service, as a beaming 9-year-old, Dana Thorpe, poses for a picture with Dinkins, the young man's mother whispers: "You have been an enormous motivation to my son."

This is the kind of event that Dinkins believes the "general press," as he refers to non-black newspapers, largely overlooks, depriving him of balanced coverage. (This distrust of the press was reinforced by Albert Scardino.)

"I'll tell you what makes me angry, or at least annoyed," Dinkins says, and cites recent news coverage suggesting that blacks are dissatisfied with some of his positions, but neglecting to report that he had been enthusiastically received at a black church's fund-raising dinner (the appearance had not been listed on his public schedule). "I think I'm misjudged by some, but I don't like to dwell on it because it comes out like I'm whining and complaining," he says. "But in many instances, what people perceive is what the press tells them. It's the first-nighters: the critics can kill a show."

"Problems don't go away when you elect a black," Harold Washington warned before he was elected Mayor of Chicago. Dinkins agreed, but suggested during his own campaign that even raised expectations were better than none. "Our cause is about

change," he promised. But Act 1 of his mayoralty was largely a struggle to maintain continuity in the face of unprecedented budget gaps coupled with growing demands for government services. "We worked hard and finally got a victory," says the Rev. Herbert Daughtry, the black minister from Brooklyn, "so we thought the Messiah had come."

Dinkins has been in no position to perform miracles, though. Last year, he claimed credit for adding no more than $60 million to the city budget—mostly for drug treatment and social services for children. That's about two-tenths of 1 percent of the city's $29 billion budget, and he may have even less impact in the budget he submits this month. "It may be that you affect things at the margins," he says, "but when things get tight, the margins matter a hell of a lot."

And many of Dinkins's critics may be missing the main event. "The fundamental message is that we are becoming the pluralistic society we always thought we were," said Albert Scardino shortly before leaving as press secretary. "The people who are in charge are not exactly enthusiastic about that change. The miracle of David Dinkins, if he's able to perform it, will be to make that happen peacefully."

The difficulty of that challenge was sharply illustrated last month, when Dinkins agreed to march with the St. Patrick's Day parade's first gay and lesbian contingent. The newcomers were the targets of taunts from spectators, as well as several beer cans. "It was like marching in Birmingham," Dinkins later said, pointedly comparing the mean-spirited response of spectators to civil rights demonstrations in the Alabama city. Dinkins, as it happened, has never been in Birmingham, but by marching in the parade, shillelagh in hand and resplendent in a green blazer, the Mayor looked like a leader, even though he gave up the traditional position at the front of the parade. This was a matter of profound personal conviction, not political calculation (though the decision probably cost him fewer votes than it restored to his coalition). Similarly, the Mayor recalled that he hadn't weighed how his visit to Israel would be perceived because he believed that he was doing the right thing. "You ought not," he says, pausing to lick his index finger, "test the wind."

For years, Dinkins doggedly kept his eye on the prize—not the mayoralty, but the borough presidency, which he finally won in 1985 after failing twice. When he reluctantly relinquished that job to run for mayor, he did so to pursue a progressive agenda—not just to balance the budget or expand the police force. Symbolism aside, he acknowledges, "my election is of no moment to the guy who was not eating two years ago and is still not eating."

Many of Dinkins's white voters had hoped that he might stifle black militants (he was "strong enough to hold the line," one campaign slogan said ambiguously). Or that he might cement the jagged edges of the city's ethnic and racial mosaic. Some thought he would be uniquely situated to preach self-help, to sensitively apportion the pain demanded by an austerity budget and to inspire blacks who had never tasted prosperity or empowerment. Perhaps expectations were too high. But Dinkins *did* get 3 in 10 white votes, an electoral milestone. "If you're right," the Mayor said, about my premise that he was elected largely *because* he is black, "you could argue that people *were* coming together."

That was a major hurdle. So was balancing his first budget. But Dinkins wonders how many more tests he must pass. "I'm not saying we ought to be entered into the Fiscal Hall of Fame, but look at what we achieved," he says. "Since we did all the things they said we couldn't do, they ought to be saying, 'Wow.' Just maybe, the time will come when people will be a trifle more patient and say, perhaps he does know what the hell he's doing."

In last month's Inner Circle lampoon, a reporter playing Scardino sang, "You're Just an Ordinary Mayor." Ordinary isn't going to be good enough during fiscal and social crises—just as it wasn't in the mid-1970's when Abraham D. Beame, New York's first Jewish mayor, was widely viewed as being in over his head. If the dismissal of Eric Schmertz defined the end of an agonizingly long first act of the Dinkins administration, then Act 2 will feature new players and new props. Its success still depends, though, primarily on whether its leading man manages to project greater presence.

After Dinkins got rid of his Labor Commissioner,

he promised a more hands-on administration. But he offered only an ambiguous explanation about "reassessment" and a promise to place himself "in the loop sooner"—the same sort of grudging concession he made last summer when he promised to sound angrier about surging crime if that's what it would take to get reporters off his back.

"David Dinkins should resolve to rush the net," says the Bronx Borough President, Fernando Ferrer. It would go against his grain to do so, but there is recent evidence that Dinkins is at least inching forward. Ten days after Schmertz was dismissed, Dinkins himself proposed give-backs from organized labor and forcefully acknowledged that the city faced a "structural deficit" because it had been spending more on services than it had been receiving from taxes. That same night, Barry Feinstein and Stanley Hill, among other labor leaders, attended a party that raised $800,000 for the Mayor's re-election campaign—suggesting that Dinkins may have been right when he told Wall Street contributors during the campaign that he could persuade organized labor to accept sacrifices. "They'll take it from me," he said.

"What's important here in general is not to, quote, 'be politically right,'" Dinkins says. "What's important is to do the right thing. And that does take some courage and conviction. I understand the whole business of form and substance and whatnot. You can get out the smoke and mirrors and do things and, hell, Ronald Reagan was damn good at it. But that did not make him right. And I'm not going to be a part of that kind of crap."

The mandate he gave his deputies, Bill Lynch recalls, was direct if somewhat detached: "I want to be right—you've got to make sure I'm effective." Lynch says: "The last administration was often perceived as effective. History will determine whether or not we were right." David Dinkins's challenge is to be both.

# Chapter 14 Review Questions

1. How does Heclo conceptualize the current relationship between politics and administration? What are the basic elements of his *issue network* idea and how does the idea differ from the *iron triangle* notion of political-administrative relations?

2. Did you find this issue network concept evident in the foregoing case study? If so, in what ways? What sort of on-the-job demands did Mayor Dinkins face? What strategies and means does he use to deal with these contending pressures?

3. Heclo primarily applied the issue network notion to the federal level of government. Is it possible to apply it to state and local levels as well? Describe why or why not based on your reading of the Dinkins case.

4. In what ways does the issue network concept pose serious dilemmas for democratic government in general and public administration in particular?

5. What implications does the issue network theory hold for the practical functions and training of public administrators? Does it essentially alter the types of jobs, tasks, and roles they perform?

6. On the basis of your analysis of the foregoing reading and case study, what general recommendations would you make to improve the relationships between administration and politics in America? Be sure to think carefully about the *value implications* of any new reform measures you may advocate.

## Key Terms

politics-administration dichotomy
issue networks
iron triangles
policy makers
proliferation of interests
think tanks
technopols

trade and professional associations
public policy processes
issue specialization
issue watchers
single-issue organizations
presidential appointees
professional-bureaucratic complex

## Suggestions for Further Reading

You would do well to compare and contrast Heclo's ideas with those of earlier theorists who argued for a clearer, more distinct separation of politics and administration (what is termed the political-administrative dichotomy), especially Woodrow Wilson, "The Study of Administration," *Political Science Quarterly*, 2 (June 1887), pp. 197–222; Frank J. Goodnow, *Politics and Administration* (New York: Macmillan, 1900); or the later writers who discovered the interest groups involved with administrative processes and gave roots to the iron triangle concept, particularly Paul H. Appleby, *Policy and Administration* (University, Ala.: University of Alabama Press, 1949); E. Pendelton Herring, *Public Administration and the Public Interest* (New York: Russell and Russell, 1936); and David B. Truman, *The Governmental Process* (New York: Alfred A. Knopf, 1951).

Today, of course, because of the sheer size, complexity, and power of American government, new and more complicated political-administrative relationships have arisen, described by several astute observers, including Hugh Heclo, *A Government of Strangers: Executive Politics in Washington* (Washington, D.C.: The Brookings Institution, 1977); Don K. Price, *The Scientific Estate* (Cambridge, Mass.: Harvard University Press, 1965); Frederick C. Mosher, *Democracy and the Public Service,* Second Edition (New York: Oxford University Press, 1982); Emmette S. Redford, *Democracy in the Administrative State* (New

York: Oxford University Press, 1969); Francis E. Rourke, *Bureaucracy, Politics and Public Policy,* Third Edition (Boston: Little, Brown, 1984); Harold Seidman and Robert Gilmour, *Politics, Position and Power,* Fourth Edition (New York: Oxford University Press, 1986); Lawrence C. Dodd and Richard L. Schott, *Congress and the Administrative State* (New York: John Wiley & Sons, 1979); Louis Fisher, *The Politics of Shared Power: Congress and the Executive* (Washington, D.C.: Congressional Quarterly Press, 1981); and Herbert Kaufman, *The Administrative Behavior of Federal Bureau Chiefs* (Washington, D.C.: The Brookings Institution, 1981).

Both the *National Journal, Governing,* and *Congressional Quarterly* serve to provide timely insiders' views of this topic. You should give particular attention to the writers who discuss the changes in the presidency, Congress, and interest groups that have decisively altered political-administrative relationships in recent years: see Samuel Beer, ed., *The New American Political System* (Washington, D.C.: The American Enterprise Institute, 1979); Lawrence C. Dodd and Bruce I. Oppenheimer, *Congress Reconsidered,* Second Edition (Washington, D.C.: Congressional Quarterly Press, 1981); Randall B. Ripley and Grace A. Franklin, *Congress, The Bureaucracy and Public Policy* (Chicago: Dorsey Press, 1984); Norman J. Ornstein and Shirley Elder, *Interest Groups, Lobbying and Policymaking* (Washington, D.C.: Congressional Quarterly Press, 1978); and Harrison W. Fox, Jr., and Susan W. Hammond, *Congressional Staffs* (New York: Free Press, 1977).

Several excellent book-length case examinations of various policy fields provide further insights into this subject. See Robert J. Art, *The TFX Decision* (Boston: Little, Brown, 1968); Stephen Bailey and Edith K. Mosher, *ESEA: The Office of Education Administers a Law* (Syracuse, N.Y.: Syracuse University Press, 1968); A. Lee Fritschler, *Smoking and Politics* (Englewood Cliffs, N.J.:

Prentice-Hall, 1975); Richard J. Stillman II, *The Integration of the Negro in the U.S. Armed Forces* (New York: Praeger Publishers, 1968); Daniel P. Moynihan, *The Politics of the Guaranteed Income* (New York: Random House, 1973); Milton D. Morris, *Immigration: The Beleaguered Bureaucracy* (Washington, D.C.: Brookings Institution, 1985); Charles L. Schultze, *The Politics and Economics of Public Spending* (Washington, D.C.: The Brookings Institution, 1968); I. M. Destler, *U.S. Foreign Economic Policy-Making* (Washington, D.C.: The Brookings Institution, 1978); Martha Derthick, *Policy-Making for Social Security* (Washington, D.C.: The Brookings Institution, 1978); Barbara J. Nelson, *Making an Issue of Child Abuse* (Chicago: University of Chicago Press, 1984); Paul Light, *Artful Work: The Politics of Social Security Reform* (New York: Random House, 1985) and Frederick C. Mosher, *A Tale of Two Agencies* (Baton Rouge, La.: Louisiana State University Press, 1984). For a good collection of essays, many dealing with various aspects of this topic, read Francis E. Rourke, *Bureaucratic Power in National Policy Making,* Fourth Edition (Boston: Little, Brown, 1986). See also several of the essays contained in the bicentennial issue of the *Public Administration Review* (January/February 1987), edited by Richard J. Stillman, II; particularly, Chester A. Newland, "Public Executives: Imperium, Sacerdotium, Collegium? Bicentennial Leadership Challenges"; James P. Pfiffner, "Political Appointees and Career Executives: The Democracy-Bureaucracy Nexus in the Third Century"; and James D. Carroll, "Public Administration in the Third Century of the Constitution: Supply-Side Management Privatization or Public Investment"; as well as several essays contained in new books published by the Urban Institute, Washington, D.C.: John L. Palmer, ed., *Perspectives on the Reagan Years* (1986); and Lester M. Salamon and Michael S. Lund, eds., *The Reagan Presidency and the Govern-*

*ing of America* (1985); plus G. Calvin MacKenzie, ed., *The In and Outers* (Baltimore: Johns Hopkins University Press, 1987); and James P. Pfiffner, *The Strategic Presidency* (Chicago: The Dorsey Press, 1988); Hendrick Smith, *The Power Game: How Washington Works* (New York: Random House, 1988); John W. Gardner, *On Leadership* (New York: Free Press, 1990); James H. Svara, *Official Leadership in the City: Patterns of Conflict and Cooperation* (New York: Oxford University Press, 1990).

# CHAPTER 15

## The Relationship Between the Public and Private Sectors: The Concept of Pillars of Success for Mixed Undertakings

*In the mixed economy nothing seemed purely public, nothing purely private. And within such a context, no status—public, private, or mixed—was in and of itself a route to legitimacy. Instead, a series of new criteria arose that transcended the public-private question.*

*Thomas K. McCraw*

## READING 15

## Introduction

There once was a time, as Frederick C. Mosher reminds us, when government "was responsible for and expended money for what it did by itself through its own personnel and facilities." Consequently, much of the public management lore, like that of private enterprise, according to Mosher, "was based upon the premise that efficiency rested upon the effective supervision and direction of its own operations." Rather, recent decades have witnessed "exploding responsibilities of the national government in virtually all functional fields and its carrying out of those responsibilities through, and interdependently with, non-federal institutions and individuals."[1]

Data tend to support Mosher's point. Although the federal budget between 1949 and 1991 grew 29 times, from approximately \$39.0 billion to 1,091.4 billion, payment for services of federal employees and goods that the federal government purchased directly rose as a percentage of the GNP from 8 percent in 1949 to 16 percent in 1953. Since that time, this figure has steadily declined to less than 7 percent today. In addition, two thirds of these payments for "in-house" employees and services were spent in *defense-related purposes*, leaving 2.4 percent for civilian needs (compared with 2.8 percent in 1949). Except

[1]Frederick C. Mosher, "The Changing Responsibilities and Tactics of the Federal Government," *Public Administration Review*, 40, no. 6 (Nov./Dec 1980), p. 541.

for the Korean War and Vietnam War eras, when the federal work force rose quickly and then declined sharply, the total number of civilian federal employees has remained roughly 3 million during the last 40 years (3.1 million in 1990). As a total percentage of the U.S. population, civilian and military employees grew from 25 per 1,000 in 1947, to 31 per 1,000 in 1957, to 37 per 1,000 in 1970, but has since declined steadily to 27 per 1,000 in 1990.

The conclusion that students of government and public administration draw from these data is that federal expenditures and responsibilities (and to a large extent state and local ones as well) are increasingly shifting in new directions. The traditional in-house performance of public activities by government has given way to five different types of government action. First, a substantial portion of this activity consists of *contracts* and *grants* to do the work of the public sector outside the formal bounds of public agencies through private businesses, universities, and nonprofit enterprises—even foreign governments. Much domestic research and many overseas public works projects are accomplished in this manner at numerous federal agencies like the National Aeronautics and Space Administration and the Agency for International Development. At the state and local levels, garbage collection, computer facilities, and many other such services are often handled through contractual arrangements. Increasingly, government is turning to "third parties" to accomplish much of its responsibilities and tasks. But there are other forms of indirect public action as well.

Second, a fast growing and very large portion of federal expenditures today goes to *direct transfer payments* to individuals. These direct benefits and reimbursements for individuals rose from 21 percent of the federal budget in 1954 to 46 percent in 1990. Most of these payments ($505 billion in 1990) go to individuals for income support through such programs as Social Security, Medicare, unemployment benefits, veterans benefits, and retirement programs.

Third, *aid to state and local governments,* although declining from a high of $109.7 billion in 1978 (in constant 1982 dollars) to $100.9 billion in 1990, accounts today for approximately 11 percent of federal budget outlays. Two thirds of these monies in reality go to individuals through intergovernmental transfer payments to state and local governments that administer these programs in such fields as housing, Medicaid, nutrition, welfare, and education.

Fourth, *regulation* is yet another indirect route used to promote public action in recent years. Although regulatory power has been around for some time (since 1887 on the national level, when the federal government established the Interstate Commerce Commission to regulate railroads), it has been extended during the past three decades into new fields through the use of government contracts and state and local aid requirements. Federal regulations now apply to such areas as equal employment opportunity, environmental protection, energy conservation, occupational health and safety, and consumer protection.

Finally, in the 1980s, *tax incentives and loan guarantees* are used pervasively to promote various kinds of public actions in the name of the public interest. In general, they are used to provide incentives to people to do what government wants them to do without formal regulatory controls or direct governmental action. Tax credits, tax deductions, tax exemptions, and corporate loan guarantees are examples of such forms of indirect public action. Tax incentives and loan guarantees often seek to encourage or discourage public investment in certain economic fields such as home ownership, international trade, energy conservation, family farms, and small businesses.

Although these "third-party" forms of government action—for example, private instruments used to achieve essentially public policies—increasingly seem to be a common attribute of U.S. government, what serves to give them legitimacy? The United States, unlike the rest of the world, traditionally views government intervention, of any form, in the private sphere with hostility and thus erects a uniquely sharp separation between public and private activities, the former viewed generally negatively and the latter seen more often in positive terms. In practice, however, "a mixed economy" has evolved in the late twentieth century that is "an American Original," and which is mutually supportive for both private and public enterprises.

In the following selection, "The Public and Private Spheres in Historical Perspective," Thomas K. McCraw, a professor of business history at Harvard University's Graduate School of Business Administration and author of the Pulitzer Prize-winning book, *Prophets of Regulation,* examines the relationship between public and private sectors in a comparative historical context. He argues convincingly that compared to other nations, "The United States at the present time is at one extreme among market economies." ". . . in cross-national perspective, [it] is surely valid to say the American private economy receives less direction from government than do economies of most other countries." Yet, at the same time, says McCraw, "The economy of the United States has become so interdependent with others that we cannot isolate ourselves from economic tendencies elsewhere." International pressures from abroad, especially the quest for international markets and protections for our own workers' employment "tends powerfully to promote the rise of government influence within national economies, even those that stop short of state ownership." Thus there is a constant tug of war between more and less intervention by government in the private sphere. In the following essay, McCraw traces the unique U.S. historical background of the sharp split in public-private spheres with its resulting adversarial tendencies. "In Europe and Japan," according to McCraw, "both government and big business today enjoy a presumptive legitimacy that is simply lacking in the United States." In his view the legitimacy question is central to achieving effective public-private partnerships. Based on historical analysis, McCraw outlines the six "pillars of success" for promoting "mixed" undertakings as well as barriers to their achievement.

As you read the following essay, reflect on such questions as:

What sources in American culture gave rise to the sharp split in public-private spheres according to McCraw?

Do these conditions persist in the 1990s in your view?

Why does McCraw stress "the legitimacy issue" as being so central in establishing effective public-private partnerships?

What six conditions does he conclude are important for promoting public-private collaboration and why? What are some of the chief barriers today for achieving this collaboration?

Can you summarize some of the implications for practicing public administrators from McCraw's arguments?

# The Public and Private Spheres in Historical Perspective

### THOMAS K. McCRAW

Throughout American history, the proper relationship between the public and private spheres has been a theme of prickly debate. In our own time it underlies much research and commentary on such topics as regulation, industrial policy, and corporate governance. Proposals for deregulating industries, for "getting the government off the backs of the people," and for the "reprivatization of public functions" all reflect the characteristic belief of our time that the public-private relationship is somehow out of whack and must be restored to proper balance.

As soon as one begins to think systematically about this question, it becomes apparent that the ground is very slippery. Definitional problems abound. Does "public" mean simply governmental and "private" nongovernmental? If so, then in what sector should such entities as defense contractors be placed? When the Reagan administration increased the defense budget, did the public sector grow? Or did private companies such as General Dynamics merely record higher sales? And what is the impact on the public-private split when such "in-and-outers" as John J. McCloy, Cyrus Vance, Caspar Weinberger, and George Shultz change jobs? Is there any effect at all? Are these persons men of the public sector, or of the private?

Ambiguities of this sort are not new in our history. They have persisted from the beginning of the American republic, though in different forms at different times. For approximately the last century, Americans have been especially concerned about having a clear demarcation between public and private activities. During this same period, we as a people have developed certain abiding criteria for legitimacy that apply to both public and private behavior. These same criteria attach as well to that growing list of activities and organizations that cannot easily be classified as either public or private but which loom large in the mixed economies characteristic of modern democratic capitalism.

This addresses these issues by orienting the American experience comparatively: first across countries, then within the United States

From "The Public and Private Spheres in Historical Perspective," by Thomas K. McCraw in *Public Private Partnership: New Opportunities for Meeting Social Needs*, edited by Harvey Brooks, Lance Liebman, and Corinne S. Schelling. Published by Ballinger Publishing Company. Copyright 1984 by Ballinger Publishing Company, a division, of HarperCollins Publishers, Inc. Reprinted by permission.

itself across time. The premise is that we cannot see our present situation clearly without the light shed by the experience of other democratic market economies as well as by our own past. In the latter part, I will explore the indexes of legitimacy within mixed public-private institutions in America, set forth some of the pillars of success in such undertakings, and comment on the performance of public functions by private corporations.

## The United States in Comparative Perspective

One relevant index of American attitudes toward the public and private spheres is the extent of public ownership of industry. The United States at the present time is at one extreme among market economies, as shown in Figure 15.1.

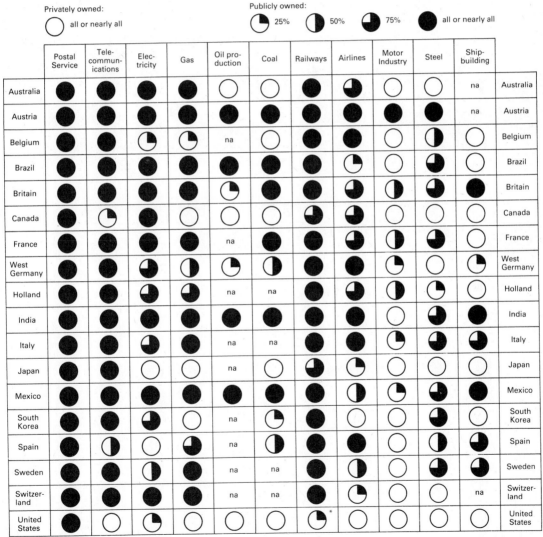

na - not applicable or negligible production

*including Conrail

**Figure 15.1**   Who owns how much? From *The Economist,* December 30, 1978. Reprinted by permission of The Economist Newspaper Group.

The facts depicted in this chart speak mostly for themselves. The United States is the only country besides South Korea with a completely private airline industry. We are the only country with an all-private telecommunications network, and one of a handful with no public enterprises in oil, gas, and steel. Furthermore, the trend over the last decade in most countries other than the United States has been toward more state ownership.[1]

One perhaps unexpected characteristic of this chart is the absence of a clear correlation between extent of state-owned enterprise on the one hand and national economic performance on the other. Some economies that grew rapidly over the last twenty years (Germany, Brazil) had substantial public ownership, while others (Japan) relatively little. Some slow performers (Canada, the United States) had few state enterprises, others (Britain) a great many.[2]

Of course, public ownership in these industries, which include utilities as well as manufacturing, is only one measure of public involvement in a nation's economy. Another type of index is the degree and growth rate of government spending. Table 15.1 shows these numbers, which include all public spending on all levels.

Here again the story is the same: the United States has a low percentage of government spending among the industrialized market economies. And by a very wide margin it has the smallest recent growth rate in public spending. Recent rhetoric about the rampant growth of government spending in the United States would seem to have little foundation when viewed beside statistics for comparable countries. Only if the United States is abstracted from the world economy and considered in isolation can the proposition of rapid growth in public spending be defended.

**Table 15.1     Government Spending as a Percentage of Gross Domestic Product**

| Country | Government spending as a percentage of GDP, 1979 | Increase in government spending as a percentage of GDP, 1960–1963 average to 1970–1973 average | Increase in government spending as a percentage of GDP, 1970–1973 average to 1977–1979 average |
|---|---|---|---|
| Sweden | 59.7 | 13.1 | 14.4 |
| Netherlands | 57.7 | 11.9 | 10.2 |
| Norway | 51.3 | 11.3 | 8.0 |
| Denmark | 51.1 | 13.8 | 8.1 |
| Belgium | 49.2 | 7.8 | 10.5 |
| Ireland | 49.0 | 9.0 | 9.4 |
| Austria | 49.0 | 5.5 | 8.7 |
| Germany | 46.4 | 5.1 | 7.2 |
| France | 45.0 | 2.2 | 6.5 |
| Italy | 44.8 | 6.9 | 6.5 |
| Britain | 43.8 | 5.8 | 4.1 |
| Canada | 40.3 | 6.8 | 3.9 |
| Switzerland | 40.1 | 5.9 | 9.7 |
| Finland | 39.1 | 5.0 | 6.8 |
| Greece | 34.6 | 5.6 | 5.1 |
| United States | 33.4 | 3.5 | 1.2 |
| Australia | 31.7 | 3.1 | 5.4 |
| Japan | 30.5 | 2.5 | 9.5 |
| Spain | 28.5 | 5.1 | 5.5 |

*Source:* Cameron (1982: 49), derived from OECD publications. Annals of the American Academy of Political and Social Science.

Government expenditures as a percentage of a national economy can be calculated in different ways, of course. One careful study using several methods was done in 1980 for the National Bureau of Economic Research. Each method pointed to the same conclusion: with the important exception of transfer payments, there has been no substantial growth of government spending in the United States as a percentage of gross national product since 1952. Government purchases of goods and services as distinct from Social Security and other transfers have followed a pattern characterized not by growth but by a decided shift away from federal and toward state and local government spending. Recent proposals to shift public functions to these lower levels, therefore, express a desire for something that in large measure has already occurred.

The apparent inconsistency between Table 15.1 (which shows total government spending in the United States at 33.4 percent) and Table 15.2 (which shows it at nearer 20 percent) derives from the exclusion from the second table of transfer payments. The dramatic rise in transfer payments over the last two decades can be seen in the shifting disposition of the federal budget dollar (Table 15.3).

Several points are clear from the foregoing chart and tables. First, speaking compara-

**Table 15.2    Government Purchases of Goods and Services as a Percentage of Gross National Product (Current Dollars)**

| Year | Federal (percent) | State and local (percent) | All government (percent) |
|------|-------------------|---------------------------|--------------------------|
| 1952 | 15.1 | 6.7 | 21.8 |
| 1955 | 11.1 | 7.6 | 18.8 |
| 1960 | 10.6 | 9.2 | 19.8 |
| 1965 | 9.8 | 10.3 | 20.1 |
| 1970 | 9.7 | 12.5 | 22.3 |
| 1975 | 8.0 | 14.1 | 22.1 |
| 1976 | 7.6 | 13.5 | 21.1 |
| 1978 | 7.3 | 13.3 | 20.6 |
| 1980 | 7.5 | 13.0 | 20.0 |
| 1981 | 7.8 | 12.5 | 20.3 |

*Source:* Break (1980: 622). *Stat. Abstract* (1982: 419).

**Table 15.3    The Federal Budget Dollar, 1960–1979**

| Year | Defense (percent) | Nondefense (percent) | Transfers (included in nondefense) (percent) |
|------|-------------------|----------------------|-----------------------------------------------|
| 1960 | 49.0 | 51.0 | 24.8 |
| 1965 | 40.1 | 59.9 | 25.7 |
| 1970 | 40.0 | 60.0 | 30.4 |
| 1975 | 26.2 | 73.8 | 43.7 |
| 1976 | 24.4 | 75.6 | 45.7 |
| 1977 | 24.2 | 75.8 | 45.3 |
| 1978 | 23.3 | 76.7 | 43.3 |
| 1979 | 23.2 | 76.8 | 43.2 |
| 1980 | 23.6 | 76.4 | 43.1 |
| 1981 | 24.3 | 75.7 | 44.3 |

*Source:* Break (1980: 637); *Stat. Abstract* (1982: 250).

tively, the United States has an extremely small amount of state ownership of enterprise. Similarly, the size and recent growth rate of its government expenditure are quite small measured against those of other democratic market economies. As a percentage of gross national product, public expenditures in America have remained almost constant over the last two decades. But in two respects dramatic changes have occurred. One is in the rapid rise of transfer payments, as the United States—like other Western nations but unlike most Asian market economies—has determined that the welfare function will be a public responsibility with an extremely heavy call on public funds. The second change is a rapid shift from expenditures by the federal government to those by the states and local communities, largely through the mechanism of revenue sharing.

To be sure, a government's influence on a national economy cannot be measured solely by such percentages. Regulatory measures of many types cause private-sector expenditures that otherwise would not have occurred and that do not show up in calculations such as those outlined. Enormous investments in pollution abatement, reports to agencies, tax returns, and a host of other expensive requirements mandated by government constitute a hidden dimension of the public sector's impact on expenditures. In addition, tax laws often have decisive effects on private-sector investment decisions.

Here again, however, in cross-national perspective it is almost surely valid to say that the American private economy receives less direction from government than do the economies of most other countries. For example, to ignore government planning, promotion, and overall economic influence in such countries as Germany, Japan, and Brazil during their periods of "miracle growth" would be to leave out what most scholars regard as the most important elements. I can think of no serious scholar who would argue that the level of general government influence on the national economy is greater in the United States than it is in these other countries.

Many would argue, of course, that the kinds of influence and the goals of public policy differ dramatically across countries. The common perception that other governments tend to promote and encourage the development of business enterprise while we in the United States tend to regulate and restrain it is, by and large, an accurate position. Despite numerous exceptions, there is little question that in cross-national comparison the United States does not promote business enterprise to the degree that its international competitors do or that the United States itself did earlier in its history (Vogel 1981; Johnson 1982).[3]

A comparative framework for these questions is essential not only for the sake of intellectual perspective, but for immediate practical reasons as well. The economy of the United States has become so interdependent with others that we cannot isolate ourselves from economic tendencies elsewhere. Nor can others insulate themselves from events here. This is who looked after the bank's interests in return. The young J. Pierpont Morgan, it was now discovered, had earned his first fortune by selling defective rifles to the Union Army.

These peccadilloes, progressive scholars wrote, were mere preludes to what happened in the last third of the nineteenth century. In that sordid era, such Robber Barons as John D. Rockefeller, Jay Gould, and James B. Duke rode roughshod over the public interest in pursuit of their private fortunes. Mark Twain had given this period its sobriquet, "The Gilded Age," in a spirit not entirely pejorative. Later on, one of the most eminent of progressive scholars, Vernon Louis Parrington, called it "the Great Barbecue." The cook at the Great Barbecue was big business, the carcass the American public (Josephson 1934).

In the 1920s, attacks on big business quieted down. But the Crash of 1929 and the ensuing Great Depression seemed to confirm the view that private business, which by common consent had caused the depression, was indeed rotten. Accordingly, it must be disciplined by an aroused people acting through a much-enhanced public sector; as Franklin D. Roosevelt called it, "a New Deal for the American people." Along with banishing fear, FDR's first inaugural called for driving the "money changers" from the American temple. And by the middle of the twentieth century, the functional separateness of the public and private sectors had become a mainstay of the American liberal creed. Within the academy, the climax of progressive scholarship came with Arthur M. Schlesinger, Jr.'s great books on Jacksonian Democracy and on the New Deal. In the stirring prose emblematic of progressive writing, Schlesinger cast both these movements in terms of their resolute opposition to the business community. As he put it in a famous statement that by now was so self-evident in liberal circles that he hardly needed to make it at all, "Liberalism in America has been ordinarily the movement on the part of the other sections of society to restrain the power of the business community" (Schlesinger 1945:505).

Self-evident in the middle of the twentieth century, such a generalization would have been incomprehensible in the middle of the nineteenth. The great leaders of that period—Clay, Webster, Calhoun, Jackson, Lincoln, Douglas—did not habitually posit a dichotomy between the interests of business and those of the American people. Instead, these were seen to go hand in hand. Granted there were plenty of quarrels between warring economic interests: southern planters versus northern textile magnates, industrialists versus labor unionists, merchants versus sharecroppers, shippers versus railroads. But there was no basic division between business on the one hand and the people on the other. In fact, the nineteenth-century political economy was characterized by widespread public assistance to business enterprise through the promotion of canals, railroads, and other "internal improvements" (Goodrich 1960; Heath 1954; Hartz 1948; Handlin and Handlin 1947; Scheiber 1969; Lively 1955).

What changed it all, what brought about the seismic shift in the American viewpoint toward the public-private issue, was probably the sudden rise of big business. This profound movement began with the railroads in the 1850s and matured with the revolution in manufacturing and distribution between about 1880 and 1910. Prior to this period, no single enterprise, indeed no entire industry, was sufficiently large to threaten a substantial number of people. Even major factories usually employed no more than a few hundred workers. Before the 1870s, even the largest manufacturing companies were usually capitalized at less than $1 million (Chandler 1977, pt. 1).

Within a single generation, all this changed. By 1890 each of several railroads employed more than 100,000 workers. By 1900 John D. Rockefeller's Standard Oil Company had grown into a huge multi-national corporation capitalized at $122 million. James B. Duke's American Tobacco Company completed a series of mergers and internal expansions that took it from a capitalization of $25 million in 1890 to one of $500 million in 1904. And in 1901 the creation of the United States Steel Corporation climaxed a $1.4 billion transaction. This sum, far beyond the imagination of most contemporary citizens, became a symbol of the new giantism in the American economy (Chandler 1977, pts. 2–4; Moody 1904).

With the rise of big business, the term *private enterprise* acquired a different meaning. Where once it had meant liberty and freedom, it now meant danger as well. It menaced America. It brought, without any question, that very centralized power against which the Founding Fathers had fought their revolution. Small wonder that in its train came a new way of interpreting American history and a new insistence on separating the public sphere from the private.

As big business emerged, the size of the public sector was changing as well, though not nearly so rapidly. In 1871, on the eve of the creation of the first great business trusts, only 51,020 civilians worked for the federal government. Of these, 36,696 were postal employees. The remaining 14,324 governed a nation whose population exceeded 40 million. The subsequent trend in federal employment, further broken down with respect to those working in the national capital, was as shown in Table 15.4.

In the thirty years from 1871 to 1901, rapid growth is evident, but from a tiny base figure. Even by 1901, the year of the U.S. Steel merger, the ratio of federal employees to the national population was only 1 to 751, compared with 1 to 102 in 1980. As the table suggests, the largest absolute growth in federal employment occurred just where one would expect to find it: in the years of the New Deal, World War II, and the Great Society.

What do these numbers have to do with the relationship between the public and private spheres? Simply this: *In the United States, alone of all major market economies, the rise of big business preceded the rise of big government.* In Britain, France, Germany, and Japan, a substantial civil bureaucracy was embedded in the culture long before the appearance of big business. In addition, each of these other nations had a feudal heritage stretching back for several centuries, together with a well-defined

**Table 15.4   Population, Federal Employment (Nonpostal), in Washington, D.C., and Ratios**

| Year | U.S. population (thousands) | Nonpostal federal employees | Located in Washington, D.C. | Population per federal employee | Population per employee in Washington, D.C. |
|------|------|------|------|------|------|
| 1871 | 40,938 | 14,324 | 6,222 | 2,858 | 6,580 |
| 1901 | 77,584 | 103,284 | 28,044 | 751 | 2,767 |
| 1925 | 115,829 | 268,495 | 67,563 | 431 | 1,714 |
| 1940 | 132,122 | 718,939 | 139,770 | 184 | 945 |
| 1950 | 151,684 | 1,476,019 | 223,312 | 103 | 679 |
| 1970 | 204,879 | 2,240,316 | 327,369 | 91 | 626 |
| 1980 | 227,700 | 2,215,852 | 366,000 | 102 | 654 |

*Source:* Bureau of the Census. U.S. Department of Commerce (1975: 8, 1102–1103); *Stat. Abstract* (1982: 6, 264, 266–7).

locus of national sovereignty. In the United States, however, big business came first. And when it did come, no countervailing force existed to soften its impact: no aristocracy, no mandarin class, no guild tradition, no labor movement, no established church. This is one reason why the business revolution proceeded so much more rapidly here than elsewhere, why extremely large enterprises came so much earlier, and why the political reaction was so much stronger (Keller 1979; McCraw 1981:1–19).

The United States was the only nation to enact regulatory legislation directed specifically against big business at very early dates. Congress passed the Interstate Commerce Act in 1887, the Sherman Antitrust Act in 1890, and the Federal Trade Commission and Clayton Acts in 1914. We were the only country to attempt such a thoroughgoing regulation of railroads as was contemplated under the Hepburn Act (1906). Elsewhere, such laws were regarded as unnecessary. In the case of railroads, either the government itself owned the enterprise or the size of the company was not so great as in the United States, with its vast distances and correspondingly large railroad corporations. And the antitrust laws were simply inappropriate for Europe. Although practices varied from one country to the next, in general the European polities encouraged guilds and cartels, both of which tended to protect small business and to aid those countries' efforts to promote their exports (Keller

1979; McCraw 1981:1–19; Cornish 1979; Hannah 1979; Chandler 1980).[5]

In the United States, by contrast, small enterprises were often threatened, displaced, or even absorbed by the integrative measures typical of American big business, either through horizontal integration (absorption by merger and acquisition) or through vertical integration (displacement of small wholesalers and retailers by forward-integrating giant firms). The injuries suffered by small businesses in these often brutal procedures thrust the question of big business immediately into national politics. Bewildered owners of small businesses joined with angry farmers in demanding that the government do something about the new menace.

In this manner, a new political agenda emerged, and the adversarial business-government relationship in America was born. It is important to note that this adversarial character is strictly between American government and *big* business. Throughout the last century, small businesses have attempted to exploit the relationship as a means of protecting themselves. Their success has varied according to many different conditions: the ebb and flow of national prosperity, the involvement of the country in wars, and their own attitudes toward government (McCraw 1981:25–55).

Of course, generalizations of the sort just set forth are very problematical. They require careful specification and are subject to many exceptions and qualifications. But the main point is simple and straightforward: The nature of the relationship between government and big business in the United States is difficult to specify in any absolute sense, but measured comparatively against the same relationship in other democratic capitalist countries, it is clearly more adversarial. Further, the character of this relationship derived in part from a reverse sequence of institutional growth. Whereas in most nations big government (or, more precisely, a powerful and well-developed state apparatus) preceded the coming of big business, in the United States alone, with its antistatist traditions, big business came first. The pattern resembled a three-stage evolution (see Figure 15.2).

Obviously, this chart is only a rough depiction of the differential growth rates of the public sector on the one hand and big business on the other. The size of the figures only crudely expresses their relative strength. And the chart leaves out other institutions such as the church, the aristocracy, and the military, all of which served in Europe and Japan as additional counterweights to undue influence by business. In the United States, where no such counterweights existed, nothing appeared to stand between big business and the kind of centralized power Americans had so long abhorred. (A refinement of the chart might also show broad overlaps of the figures for the other countries. Business-government cooperation sometimes became so close that portions of the public and

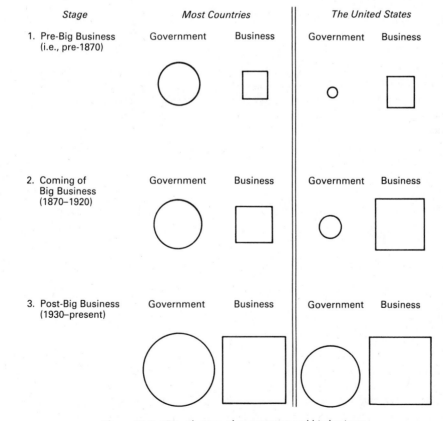

**Figure 15.2**  Growth rates of government and big business

private sectors could enter relationships of symbiosis or even merger.)

In the United States alone, big business was seen as the initial threat to liberty, since it occupied the field uncontested and since many of the early railroads and "trusts" did indeed abuse their great power. They unilaterally decided questions that affected whole communities and often made little secret of their "public be damned" attitude. The fact that they also brought technological innovations, economic growth, and low prices to consumers could not entirely offset the bad reputation they were making for themselves.

From the business perspective, on the other hand, when government finally did begin to grow, *it* was seen as the threat—as a new challenger and pretender to the power that business had grown accustomed to enjoying alone. Eventually, in a development full of irony, the rise of big government in stage 3 was perceived by both big and small business as an illegitimate incursion by Washington into the autonomy rightfully exercised by private enterprise. In the rise of big government, business saw, quite accurately, a reduction in its own freedom of decision.

Without the comparative perspective, it is difficult and perhaps impossible to understand this process. But in the differential growth rates between government and big business, the American experience has been more exceptional than we often think. In other countries, business executives seldom experienced the autonomy characteristic of their American counterparts. Few European or Japanese business managers took it for granted that they could make important investment decisions without consulting the state. American executives, by contrast, thought it outrageous when the U.S. government first did claim such a role during the New Deal. And within another generation, their feelings had hardened into a virtual ideology. As one student of this question has recently commented, "The most characteristic, distinctive and persistent belief of American

corporate executives is an underlying suspicion and mistrust of government. It distinguishes the American business community not only from every other bourgeoisie, but also from every other legitimate organization of political interests in American society" (Vogel 1978).

To this day foreign business executives envy American managers their high social status, as well as the degree of autonomy they still possess in making decisions. Europeans would like very much to have the freedom their American counterparts enjoy from attacks by powerful Marxist groups and to some extent from claims by trade unions for a major voice in business decisions. Even the domestic cultures of Europe and the United States reflect the difference. Seldom in American history did business managers suffer the vaguely unseemly station characteristic of their counterparts in Europe, lower in the social pecking order than church officials, the landed aristocracy, or the military. Being "in trade" did not disqualify Americans from making a good marriage. Indeed, such American aristocracy as did develop grew primarily not from a landed gentry but from a business gentry.

European and Japanese managers emphatically do not, however, envy American executives their relationship with government. Instead, they often express wonder and bafflement at the adversarial character of that relationship. They have difficulty understanding the mutual hostility between two sets of players whom foreign executives tend to regard as natural allies.[6]

## Legitimacy and Performance in the Mixed Economy

In Europe and Japan, both government and big business today enjoy a presumptive legitimacy that is simply lacking in the United States. Historically speaking, America's absence of a feudal heritage and its early conditions of openness and mobility meant that almost nothing except individualism and personal freedom did have legitimacy. In such a setting business enterprise, nearly all of which was small scale, appeared most often as a manifestation of individual autonomy, as well as the commonest means of upward mobility. It therefore shared in the legitimacy of individualism. But the rise of big business in the late nineteenth century partly undermined the presumptive legitimacy of private enterprise and separated business into two camps: small business, which retained legitimacy, and big business, which never quite acquired it. Whenever big business did seem to have gained legitimacy, some new scandal or other event undermined it once more.

The culmination came in the 1930s, when the Great Depression destroyed the legitimacy that big business had managed to gain through its remarkable record in promoting economic growth. At the same time, the initial failure of Herbert Hoover's government to deal with the economic crisis began to call into question the legitimacy of government itself. The issue of government legitimacy was complicated still further, though in a very different way, by the presidency of Franklin D. Roosevelt. FDR's New Deal appealed deeply to most Americans, but it angered corporate executives and wealthy shareholders more than any other event since the beginnings of big business itself. With the onset of the New Deal, the rise of big government began in earnest, and the whole question of the proper relationship between the public and private spheres took on new meaning.

The emergency of World War II temporarily mooted some of these issues, but the pattern had been set. Out of the combined upheavals of the Great Depression and the war emerged the modern mixed economy, in which the business-government relationship in America was far more complex than it had ever been before. The new situation did not offer a relevant setting for the old conceptual separation of the public and private spheres. The proliferation of huge government contracts—with defense industries, with private companies doing work unrelated to defense, and with universities both public and private—blurred the issue as never before. In the mixed economy nothing seemed purely public, nothing purely private. And within such a context, no status—public, private, or mixed—was in and of itself a route to legitimacy.

Instead, a series of new criteria arose that transcended the public-private question. Later in this [article], these criteria or pillars of legitimacy are discussed in detail. First, however, the relevancy to the present discussion of both these criteria and the concept of legitimacy itself should be made more explicit.

The reason why the legitimacy question is so important is that it underlies whatever changes different groups may wish to make in the business-government relationship. These include, among other things, proposals for deregulation, for "getting the government off the backs of the people," and for the "reprivatization of public functions." In order to clarify such issues and estimate the likely degree of their fulfillment, it is appropriate not only to place the American experience in cross-national and historical perspective, as this [article] has done up to now. It is also necessary to examine the boundaries of legitimacy in some of the institutions that have been developed under the recent regime of the mixed economy.

A premise of this approach is that a question such as "Which types of activity belong in the public sector and which in the private?" is slightly off the mark. A better way to get at the important issues is to ask "What are the conditions of legitimacy in modern America for different types of public, private, and mixed undertakings?"

Often, new medical principles are discovered by researchers who look at uncommon pathologies or mutations. By much the same route, we can get a clearer idea of modern institutional legitimacy by examining the performance of organizations that combine public and private roles in some unusual way in the mixed American economy. It is likely that the American polity holds public, private, and mixed organizations alike accountable for the fulfillment of the conditions of legitimacy and that in some respects it makes little difference which of these institutions carries on a given activity.

For each, the conditions of legitimacy seem to be a complex amalgam of efficiency, fairness, and shared power. Often we tend to associate the first with the private sector and the next two with the public. But long-term legitimacy in America for any institution, whether public, private, or mixed, requires satisfactory performance on all three counts. To illustrate let us examine briefly the experiences of two mixed institutions that grew out of the new Deal. The examples are, first, the Tennessee Valley Authority, a public corporation with a variety of functions; and second, the public-private corporate regulatory system constructed under the aegis of the Securities and Exchange Commission.

## The Tennessee Valley Authority

The TVA was created in 1933 as a multiple-purpose river project intended to raise the standard of living in a depressed area of about 40,000 square miles and about 2.5 million population. The new agency was to construct dams, develop an inland waterway, control the river's chronic flooding, develop new forms of fertilizer, and bring electricity to farms, only 3 percent of which had it at the time in this region. The TVA was a controversial undertaking, primarily because of the provisions about electricity. Privately owned power companies were already serving the area, and they would have to be coopted or displaced. President Herbert Hoover had vetoed earlier legislation to do these tasks. His veto message expressed the characteristic American concern about keeping public and private affairs separate. For the

government to enter into a competitive situation with private companies, said Hoover, "is not liberalism. It is degeneration" (U.S. President 1931).

President Franklin D. Roosevelt, on the other hand, regarded public ownership of utilities as a legitimate function of government, given certain circumstances. In the case of the Tennessee Valley, he showed no hesitation. Just before FDR signed the TVA Act, Senator George Norris of Nebraska, who had sponsored both this legislation and the bill Hoover had vetoed, put a question to him: "What are you going to say when they ask you the political philosophy behind TVA?" Roosevelt answered with typical blandness, good humor, and unconcern about mixed enterprise: "I'll tell them it's neither fish nor fowl, but, whatever it is, it will taste awfully good to the people of the Tennessee Valley" (Goldman 1952: 339).

The TVA has remained controversial to this day. But in the years since 1933 it has also achieved an extraordinarily high reputation, both in the United States and even more so abroad, for the efficient performance of its multiple functions. Eventually it became the largest electric utility in the United States. It pioneered such innovations as the declining-block utility rate structure, the coordinated management of water reservoirs, and creative methods of personnel management. And it succeeded brilliantly in its overall strategy of a unified development of the Tennessee River system into a waterway whose flow can be controlled almost like a kitchen tap. That in the process of doing all these things the TVA forced a major privately owned utility out of business did not appreciably detract from the agency's overall reputation for success (McCraw 1971: ch. 8).

It was not until the 1960s and 1970s that the TVA ran into real trouble. In those decades, the agency's halo not only began to tarnish, but ultimately fell to the ground. The new problems had to do, first, with the pollution caused by its gigantic thermal power plants, which fouled the air and used huge quantities of strip-mined coal. Environmentalists protested against the spectacle of a government agency's doing no better on environmental issues than the privately owned utility industry was doing.

A second wave of problems struck in the 1970s, as the perceived dangers of nuclear power and the skyrocketing cost of both fuel and capital all hit simultaneously. When these blows fell, TVA's public-sector status afforded it no immunity. The agency was very adversely affected, just as were its counterparts in the investor-owned part of the industry. (The public sector accounts for about 20 percent of the electric power industry in America [McCraw 1976: 1372–1380]).

The significance of the TVA story to the present discussion falls into three parts. First, the multiple-purpose job accomplished by this public agency could not have been done by a private company or even a consortium of companies. Public ownership was sine qua non. Only a part of the enterprise was even potentially profitable, and this part initially was regarded as incidental to the harnessing of the river and the general uplift of living standards. There simply would have been no way to "privatize" all of TVA's multiple functions.

Despite its acknowledged success, the TVA experiment has never been duplicated in the United States. When Senator Norris introduced a bill in 1937 for "seven little TVA's" to be built in other parts of the country, the proposal did not even receive Roosevelt's support and did not come close to passage. In the American system, one TVA was enough, even in the depression atmosphere of the 1930s. The nation did not need additional yardsticks to measure the efficiency of the private utilities. Indeed, it is clear that without the crisis of the Great Depression, there would not have been even one.

Finally, when the TVA encountered intractable problems beginning in the 1960s, public-sector status not only failed to shield it from attack but actually compounded its problems. The pressures it received from environmentalists and from its own customers who were outraged at the rapid rise in its rates for electricity were all the stronger because TVA was perceived as part of the government.

In all these ways, the TVA's experience is a useful litmus test for the elements of institutional legitimacy in modern America. Its odyssey suggests that in some fundamental ways, it makes little difference whether an organization is wholly public, wholly private, or mixed in nature. If the organization is to maintain its legitimacy, it must be perceived as performing its tasks efficiently, fairly, and without too many unpleasant side effects. There is no immunity from these requirements.

## Corporate Control and the Securities and Exchange Commission

A second revealing story of a mixed system began with the passage of the Securities Act of 1933 and the Securities Exchange Act of 1934. In the years since this legislation, the Securities and Exchange Commission, which administers both laws, has developed a reputation as the most effective regulatory agency in the federal government (Heffron 1971:188; U.S. Senate 1977:I, 270; SEC Presidential Transition Team 1980:I, 9). It might even be argued that without the SEC, business corporations in America would not now enjoy the legitimacy they do. The agency promotes the disclosure of information in an unusually thoroughgoing yet noncoercive way. Nearly all business executives have a well-founded respect for it. But it is the strategy behind the SEC's achievement in a mixed public-private system, in addition to the success itself, that is of interest here (McCraw 1982).

Confronted in the 1930s with a national economic depression and a discredited, moribund securities market, the SEC could easily have construed its mission as a punitive attack on unpopular giant corporations. Instead of wreaking vengeance, however, the agency set out to restore legitimacy to Wall Street's essential function of channeling investment capital into enterprise. In order to do this, the architects of the SEC's laws and policies emphasized disclosure and publicity of corporate affairs much more than the hunting down and punishing of miscreants. The strategy looked forward rather than back and focused on new reports rather than on past sins. The SEC did not, for example, dwell on corporate America's role in bringing on the Depression. The legislation, very carefully drawn (which was atypical for regulatory laws), required corporations to report annually to the SEC on a host of intimate details of their business.

In a crucial decision, the SEC opted for enforcement of these provisions not by a huge Washington bureaucracy but by a mixed public-private regulatory system. The agency worked hand-in-hand with the American accounting profession in order to promote accurate and useful reports. In effect, private-sector accountants were made the linchpin of the scheme of regulation. The accountants themselves cooperated enthusiastically once their panic over personal liability was assuaged. The size of their profession multiplied rapidly in order to meet the SEC-mandated requirements for accounting services. What is significant is that the SEC deliberately used private agents to serve public functions.

A similar strategy underlay the SEC's management of its relationship with the organized exchanges, especially the one in New York. Rather than take over the New York Stock Exchange, as it might well have done given the disgraceful record of Wall Street in policing itself, the SEC pursued a policy of encouraging reform-minded insurgents within the exchange organization. This approach achieved complete success within a few years, despite several contrary forces: opposition to cooperation

from militant SEC staff members, stonewalling by the ruling oligarchs of the stock exchange, and frequent carping from the *New Republic* and other liberal organs, which argued that the SEC was contaminating itself by association with wrongdoers. Implicitly, the *New Republic* was insisting that the public and private spheres must be kept separate, that mixed systems of this nature were illegitimate.

The final brick in the SEC's edifice of public-private regulatory structures came in 1938, when the agency helped to organize a privately run regulatory body for the so-called over-the-counter portion of the securities industry. This new institution, the National Association of Securities Dealers, Inc., looked like an ordinary trade association. In fact, it became an effective regulatory force for the industry. The association did not hesitate to discipline erring members through fines, suspensions, and expulsions. Expulsion from the association meant removal from the industry. And the beauty of the system was that as a private institution the association was not constrained by the procedural red tape that delayed implementation of sanctions by public regulatory agencies.

The SEC achieved its remarkable success primarily by encouraging and involving third-party groups from the private sector. These players, in turn, supported both the process and the SEC itself. The litigation, delay, and adversarial posturing so characteristic of other regulatory proceedings were thereby finessed.

Both the TVA and SEC stories are a good deal more complicated than suggested in these synopses, and the precise nature of bureaucratic "success" remains subjective and obscure. Such success as each of the two agencies did achieve was not gained without internal bickering within the organization, serious attacks from without, and perennial problems with Congress. In each agency, moreover, success could not have come without first-rate talent. Such men as Arthur E. Morgan and David E. Lilienthal of the TVA, James M. Landis and

William O. Douglas of the SEC, were not just good public servants. They were topflight strategists who would have made their marks in many other lines of work in either the public or private sector.

To understand the likely fate of proposals for public-private partnerships or for the re-privatization of public functions, it is necessary to comprehend both the pillars of and barriers to success in mixed undertakings.

## Pillars of Success

### 1. A Sense of Crisis

The most creative experiments in mixed undertakings have come during economic crisis, wartime, or intense international competition. The TVA and SEC during the Great Depression, the Manhattan Project and mobilization of the private sector during World War II, NASA and the moon shot during the post-Sputnik competition with the Soviet Union, all come to mind as instances of successful public-private collaboration in mixed institutions for the purpose of meeting some crisis. The perception of crisis is not a sufficient condition for success, and it may not even be essential. But it is certainly helpful. For example, a form of Medicare was introduced as early as the Truman administration, but not until the Great Society was the public perception of a crisis in health care sufficiently powerful to push through the required legislation.

### 2. The Opportunity of a Positive-Sum Game

In the examples just cited, almost every player ended up better off. There were few clear losers. Even in the TVA story, the principal loser on the private side, Mr. Wendell Willkie of Commonwealth and Southern Corporation, parlayed his loss into the Republican nomination for the presidency in 1940. In the SEC case, Wall Street regained a measure of legiti-

macy, the accounting profession acquired new functions and hordes of new members, and the over-the-counter brokers and dealers gained power over the fly-by-night operators who were giving their industry a bad name. The Manhattan Project offered physicists and other scientists an enormous budget and relatively attractive working conditions. War mobilization presented the opportunity for the making of great private fortunes without profiteering. NASA was profligate with public funds during its heyday in the 1960s. And Medicare, with all its faults, finally passed Congress once the medical profession perceived it as an economic boon as well as an alternative to something more drastic.

### 3. A Coherent Strategy Implemented by First-Rate Talent

Most of these successful experiments were carried out by unusually able architects of the original strategies and by capable administrators who believed in the justice of the cause. The TVA and SEC leadership has already been described. In addition, there were Robert Oppenheimer and Leslie Groves of the Manhattan Project, James Webb of NASA. Robert Moses of the New York Port Authority, Lucius Clay of the interstate highway system, and Hyman Rickover of the Navy's nuclear power program. Each one of these leaders understood the necessity for a coherent strategy and for getting the right subordinates to carry it through.

### 4. High-Percentage Initial Steps

The first thing TVA did was build a great dam. Working round the clock, it employed four six-hour shifts of workers in order to alleviate unemployment in the depressed region. Given the engineering talent the agency was able to attract (in large part because private construction was languishing at the time), there was hardly any way its first project could fail. The initial success led to others and infused the whole organization with a spirit that became its trademark. Much the same thing happened with the SEC. And NASA took extraordinary pains to make its initial manned rocket launchings not only successful in the technical sense, but the occasions for national media spectaculars.

## 5. An Identifiable Measure of Success Other than Profit

On a cost-benefit calculus, nearly all of the achievements listed so far become less clearly successful. Yet each project tended to be either self-justifying through its fulfillment of noneconomic criteria (making the atomic bomb; reaching the moon), or was financially self-sustaining (the TVA power program through customers' revenues, the SEC through requirements that private accountants be paid by their corporate clients).

In the absence of severe crisis, this pillar is perhaps the most difficult of all to put in place. If no clear proof of success is available, the issue returns to the bottom line of the income statement. And if that is to be the criterion, then the very nature of capitalism's allocation of resources is not going to be helpful on a broad scale to any undertaking except the investments of first choice as defined by capital markets.

## 6. Some Means of Controlling the Agenda and Limiting the Number of Players

Almost any mixed-function enterprise or public-private collaboration depends, if it is to succeed, on the orderly implementation of a coherent strategy. If the agenda of a given undertaking is up for grabs and the number of participants is unlimited, then the likelihood of success is small.

Because of the upheavals in American society over the last twenty years, one can argue that insuperable barriers to the control of important public agendas now exist. The number of interest groups that now scramble for attention to their own narrow goals—whether economic, political, racial, social, sexual, or whatever—makes it clear that cozy bilateral business-government relationships, even on an ad hoc basis for admirable purposes, may often be doomed. The revolution in judicial standing, which makes it possible for all sorts of players to delay almost any new undertaking through exploitation of the court system, has already killed numerous projects that in an earlier time would have sailed through. One cannot avoid wondering whether some of the successes listed could have survived had they been born in the media-dominated, litigious atmosphere characteristic of American public life today. Several commentators have expressed doubt, for example, that the interstate highway system could have been built had it been proposed in the 1970s rather than the 1950s. Yet it is equally clear that without the revolution in judicial standing and the opening up of access to power, the civil rights movement and other social achievements of the last generation could not have occurred. The old dilemmas remain, and as usual there are no easy solutions.

Despite such problems (and the list could be much longer), one salient trend of the 1980s suggests that the barriers to successful public-private collaboration might be breached. This is the trend toward viewing countries as competitors, or toward viewing competition from abroad as a threat to domestic jobs. Today, as more and more of the American people begin to understand their economic vulnerability to the superior industrial efficiency of foreign producers, they might well begin to see that business-government hostility within the United States compounds the problem and delays the adjustment. As in the past, so too in the present: A sense of crisis can redefine legitimacy in any society. In the face of crisis, customs that seem entrenched or even sacred today might tomorrow become very flexible indeed. This is just the kind of thing that happened during

World War II, when the issue of national survival made adversarial relationships within the American polity suddenly inappropriate, even irrelevant.

The history of the corporation itself illustrates the same point. That history began not in an adversarial but a cooperative context. It would probably surprise many American business managers today to discover that the roots of corporate development lie deep within the political state. The pattern in the early nineteenth century was to allow the incorporation of only those enterprises regarded as helpful to the public good. Bridges, turnpikes, and banks were the favored fields. The numerous special charters that characterized early-nineteenth-century business history reflected a conception of the corporation as agent of the state. The chartered companies would perform functions that were necessary but that the miniscule state did not wish to perform for itself. In this sense proposals in our own time for private companies to assume public functions resonate with the origins of the business corporation in America (Handlin and Handlin 1945).

During the last part of the nineteenth century, however, state governments adopted laws permitting free incorporation without special legislative action. This ushered in the familiar modern era in which almost anyone could start a company for almost any business purpose. Yet neither here nor in the earlier period did a coherent theory of corporate legitimacy develop, aside from the original notion of incorporation as a privilege bestowed in exchange for the discharge of some public purpose. In the twentieth century, corporate legitimacy has rested almost entirely on the demonstrated ability of the device as a means of mobilizing capital for a growing economy. For good or ill, therefore, the legitimacy of the business firm has been entirely utilitarian. When it has performed poorly, as during the Great Depression, it has tended to lose legitimacy (Hurst 1970).

Seen against this complex historical background, the "reprivatization" movement raises perplexing issues. Suppose, for example, it is suggested that inner cities be revitalized through the employment of ghetto youth by profit-making corporations whose payrolls are to be subsidized by government. Such experiments have succeeded on a small scale, as we know. But consider the odds against widespread replication of these happy outcomes. Suppose that the arrangement became so successful in the financial sense that the corporation began to make a large profit. How long would the experiment be perceived as legitimate? For the public image of the undertaking, would it not be disadvantageous if the sponsoring company were a big business? But would not such a powerful company be the only kind able to afford the experiment in the first place? Assuming a large profit by a big business, how long would it be before an enterprising journalist wrote a convincing story that the company was enriching itself at the expense of taxpayers by taking advantage of loose public purse-strings? How long before "60 Minutes" brought the scandal to the attention of a national television audience?

Or consider the opposite financial performance. Suppose the undertaking lost money year after year. How long before complaining shareholders put a stop to it? Is it not illegitimate for companies deliberately to lose money, however worthy the cause? Given this damned-if-you-do, damned-if-you-don't situation, thoughts on the theme of "reprivatization" evoke a bit of hope, but some pessimism as well.

## Notes

1. Renato Mazzolini, *Government Controlled Enterprises* (New York: Wiley, 1979). The pie chart depicted in the present essay in some respects understates the extent of state-owned enterprise. Canada, for example, established a stateowned oil company in 1975 and has continued to nationalize elements of that industry, even though the chart shows no public ownership of oil in

Canada. On the U.S. situation, see Annmarie Hauck Walsh, *The Public's Business* (Cambridge, Mass.: MIT Press, 1978).

2. The growth rates of national economies can be traced in the pages of the *Economic Report of the President* (Washington, D.C.: U.S. Government Printing Office), various years. For the 1982 *Report,* see Table B-109 on p. 355.

3. I do not wish to be misleading on this point. There is in America a long history of government-business interpenetration, occasionally even symbiosis. The relationship between the Defense Department and its thousands of contractors, the American system of price supports and research assistance to agriculture, and numerous other examples attest to the dangers of any easy generalization about American business-government relations. The many works of the historians James Willard Hurst and Ellis W. Hawley are especially helpful on this point. See also Harry N. Scheiber, "Law and Political Institutions." Gerald D. Nash, "State and Local Governments," Thomas K. McCraw, "Regulatory Agencies," and Byrd L. Jones, "Government Management of the Economy," all in volume 2 of *Encyclopedia of American Economic History,* edited by Glenn Porter (New York: Scribner's, 1980). A useful and comprehensive text is H. H. Liebhafsky, *American Government and Business* (New York: Wiley, 1971).

4. I have in mind here Alexis de Tocqueville, M.G. Jean de Crevecoeur, Mrs. Trollope, and other articulate foreign observers of the American scene. For a sample covering a wide spectrum of time, see *America in Perspective: The United States through Foreign Eyes,* edited by Henry Steele Commager (New York: c. 1947, New American Library Edition, 1961).

5. The argument I am making in this section about the differential growth rates of big business and government in the United States, including some of the numbers about federal employment, was first articulated by Alfred D. Chandler, Jr., in an essay called "Government versus Business: An American Phenomenon," in *Business and Public Policy,* edited by John T. Dunlop (Boston: Harvard Graduate School of Business Administration, 1980), pp. 1–11.

6. These comments are based on my own conversa-

tions on this subject with European and Japanese business executives.

7. These favorable judgments of the SEC are typical, but such judgments are of course not unanimous. It is within the context of other regulatory agencies, not against some ideal standard, that I am positing the SEC's success.

## References

Beard, Charles A. 1913. *An Economic Interpretation of the Constitution of the United States.* New York: Macmillan.

Break, George F. 1980. "The Role of Government: Taxes, Transfers, and Spending." In *The American Economy in Transition,* edited by Martin Feldstein. Chicago: The University of Chicago Press.

Bureau of the Census, U.S. Department of Commerce, 1975. *Historical Statistics of the United States.* Washington, D.C.: U.S. Government Printing Office.

Cameron, David R. 1982, "On the Limits of the Public Economy," *Annals of the American Academy of Political and Social Science* 459 (January).

Chandler, Alfred D., Jr. 1977. *The Visible Hand: The Managerial Revolution in American Business.* Cambridge, Mass.: Harvard University Press.

———. 1980. "Government versus Business: An American Phenomenon." In *Business and Public Policy,* edited by John T. Dunlop. Boston: Harvard Graduate School of Business Administration.

Commager, Henry Steele, ed. 1961. *America in Perspective: The United States through Foreign Eyes.* New York: New American Library.

Cornish, William R. 1979. "Legal Control over Cartels and Monopolization 1880–1914: A Comparison." In *Law and the Formation of the Big Enterprise in the 19th and Early 20th Centuries,* edited by Norbert Horn and Jurgen Kocka. Gottingen: Vandenhoeck and Ruprecht, pp. 280–303.

Goldman, Eric F. 1952. *Rendezvous with Destiny: A History of Modern American Reform.* New York: Knopf.

Goodrich, Carter. 1960. *Government Promotion of American Canals and Railroads, 1800–1890.* New York: Columbia University Press.

Handlin, Oscar, and Mary F. Handlin. 1945. "Origins of the American Business Corporation," *Journal of Economic History* 5 (May).

———. 1974. *Commonwealth: A Study of the Role of Government in the American Economy, Massachusetts, 1774–1861.* New York: New York University Press.

Hannah, Leslie. 1979. "Mergers, Cartels, and Concentration: Legal Factors in the U.S. and European Experience." In *Law and the Formation of the Big Enterprise in the 19th and Early 20th Centuries,* edited by Norbert Horn and Jurgen Kocka. Gottingen: Vandenhoeck and Ruprecht, pp. 306–314.

Hartz, Louis. 1948. *Economic Policy and Democratic Thought: Pennsylvania, 1776–1860.* Cambridge, Mass.: Harvard University Press.

———. 1955. *The Liberal Tradition in America.* New York: Harcourt, Brace.

Heath, Milton Sydney. 1954. *Constructive Liberalism: The Role of the State in Economic Development in Georgia to 1860.* Cambridge, Mass.: Harvard University Press.

Heffron, Florence Ann. 1971. "The Independent Regulatory Commissioners." Ph.D. dissertation, University of Colorado, Boulder.

Hurst, James Willard. 1970. *The Legitimacy of the Business Corporation in the Law of the United States 1780–1970.* Charlottesville: The University Press of Virginia.

Johnson, Chalmers. 1982. *MITI and the Japanese Miracle: The Growth of Industrial Policy, 1925–1975.* Stanford, Calif.: Stanford University Press.

Jones, Byrd L. 1980. "Government Management of the Economy." In *Encyclopedia of American Economic History,* vol. 2, edited by Glenn Porter. New York: Scribner's.

Josephson, Matthew. 1934. *The Robber Barons: The Great American Capitalists.* New York: Harcourt, Brace.

Keller, Morton. 1979. "Public Policy and Large Enterprise: Comparative Historical Perspectives." In *Law and the Formation of the Big Enterprises in the 19th and Early 20th Centuries,* edited by Nobert Horn and Jurgen Kocka. Gottingen: Vandenhoeck and Ruprecht, pp. 515–531.

Liebhafsky, H.H. 1971. *American Government and Business.* New York: Wiley.

Lively, Robert A. 1955. "The American System: A Review Article." *Business History Review* 29: 81–96.

Mazzolini, Renato. 1979. *Government Controlled Enterprises.* New York: Wiley.

McCraw, Thomas K. 1971. *TVA and the Power Fight, 1933–1939.* Philadelphia: Lippincott.

———. 1976. "Triumph and Irony—the TVA." *Proceedings of the Institute of Electrical and Electronics Engineers* 64 (September): 1372–1380.

———. 1980. "Regulatory Agencies." In *Encyclopedia of American Economic History,* vol. 2, edited by Glenn Porter. New York: Scribner's.

———. 1981. "Rethinking the Trust Question." In *Regulation in Perspective: Historical Essays,* edited by Thomas K. McCraw. Boston: Harvard Graduate School of Business Administration.

———. 1982. "With Consent of the Governed: SEC's Formative Years." *Journal of Policy Analysis and Management* 1: 346–370.

Moody, John. 1904. *The Truth about the Trusts.* New York: Moody.

Nash, Gerald D. 1980. "State and Local Governments." In *Encyclopedia of American Economic History,* vol. 2, edited by Glenn Porter. New York: Scribner's.

Scheiber, Harry N. 1969. *Ohio Canal Era: A Case Study of Government and the Economy, 1820–1861.* Athens, Ohio: Ohio University Press.

———. 1980. "Law and Political Institutions." In *Encyclopedia of American History,* vol. 2, edited by Glenn Porter. New York: Schribner's.

Schlesinger, Arthur. 1945. *The Age of Jackson.* Boston: Little, Brown.

Securities and Exchange Commission. Presidential Transition Team. 1980. "Final Report." December 22.

*Statistical Abstract of the United States, 1982–83.* 1982. Washington, D.C.: U.S. Bureau of the Census.

U.S. President. 1931. *Veto Message Relating to Disposition of Muscle Shoals.* Senate Document 321, 71st Cong., 3rd sess: 1–3. Washington, D.C.: U.S. Government Printing Office.

U.S. Senate. 1977. *The Regulatory Appointments Process.* Committee on Government Operations, 95th Cong., 1st sess. Washington, D.C.: U.S. Government Printing Office.

Vogel, David. 1978. "Why Businessmen Distrust Their State: The Political Consciousness of American Corporate Executives." *British Journal of Political Science* January: 45.

———. 1981. "The 'New' Social Regulation in Historical and Comparative Perspective." In *Regulation in Perspective: Historical Essays,* edited by Thomas K. McCraw. Boston: Harvard Graduate School of Business Administration, pp. 155–185.

Walsh, Annmarie Hauck. 1978. *The Public's Business.* Cambridge, Mass.: MIT Press.

Walters, Kenneth D., and R. Joseph Monsen. 1981. "The Spreading Nationalization of European Industry," *Columbia Journal of World Business* Winter: 62–72.

---

## CASE STUDY 15

---

# Introduction

At the end of Thomas McCraw's foregoing essay, "The Public and Private Spheres in Historical Perspective," six "pillars of success" for sustaining the legitimacy of mixed public-private enterprises were enumerated: "a sense of crisis," "the opportunity of a positive-sum game," "a coherent strategy implemented by first-rate talent," "high-percentage initial steps," "an identifiable measure of success other than profit," and "some means of controlling the agenda and limiting the number of players." McCraw draws these "pillars" from a close reading of the past records of such initiatives, in most part from national level experiences. But do such broad precepts for giving legitimacy to sustain mixed undertakings apply to the local level as well? And in the 1990s? Or, does their success turn on other factors not accounted for in broad-brush historic overviews at the national level? And what do these general precepts mean for the practicing public administrator engaged in "making things happen" in local government? Can they be applied in his or her working world?

To judge their application and worth in creating viable public-private partnerships at the grassroots level, let us turn to the following case study, "Close Encounters: Or How to Create a Workable Partnership in Downtown," by Margaret F. Reid, a political scientist professor at the University of Kentucky at Louisville. Professor Reid's case, unlike several in this text, is a success story in public administration that describes carefully and clearly the twenty-year story about how Trinity City (a fictitious name of a real city—the same is true for the case's characters also), faced with a deteriorating central business district (CBD) in the early 1970s, undertook an innovative planning and redevelopment project through the effective use of a public-private partnership. From its conception through "finished product," however, as this case demonstrates, a public-private partnership is no easy matter to put together. Such mixed enterprises, even in a local community of moderate size, involve many complex factors for their successful creation and implementation: for example, supportive local interests, state legislative approval, federal funding, astute community leadership, administrative planning, not to mention plenty of good luck and the right timing. As the author stresses throughout, a cooperative and mutually supportive attitude by all the parties involved is vital.

Some questions you should think about as you review this case are:

How did the idea of using a public-private partnership in Trinity City originate? And why was it seen as the preferable alternative to others for center city redevelopment?

Who were the major "players" involved with its formation and why? Were any left out and for what reasons?

Can you describe and analyze the coalition-building process that you observed in this case? What criteria guided each actor's strategies and assessment of success or failure?

What three options confronted the city manager in selecting the role his office should play in the creation of this project? The constraints as well as opportunities that were available? What option did the city manager select and why?

What does the case say regarding why public-partnerships succeed? Does this case support or contradict McCraw's findings outlined in the foregoing essay?

# Close Encounters or How to Create a Workable Partnership in Downtown[1]

## MARGARET F. REID

In 1990 Trinity City, Inc. (TCI), the nonprofit downtown management group of Trinity City, looked with pride yet anxious anticipation to the next decade. During the group's decade of existence a lot had been accomplished, but the future of Trinity City's work in downtown redevelopment, as that of many other larger cities, remains uncertain. Only recently, three major retailing establishments left town. Still, over a million square feet of new or planned construction is under way, including residential construction. The units in residential complex were already purchased before its completion and more are planned. So are a new cinema, restaurants, bars, and new entertainment. A new corporate headquarters building has been ingeniously converted from a former downtown garage building. The county is constructing a new criminal courts building. The cultural district is also taking shape and a waterfront project can possibly be added in the future. There is a new vibrancy to the place with a sense of accomplishment and yet, can it be made to last? Can the momentum of cooperation between the city and business firms be sustained if the economy sours? Can a strategic vision be created that will allow Trinity City to continue to compete with its larger competitors in the region?

The answer to these questions can be found if Trinity City is able to respond to the challenges of the economic environment of the nineties. The tendencies of some local businesses to rely on recipes of old are increasingly questioned as inadequate to deal with the cyclical swings Trinity City's local economy has been exposed to, making meaningful long-range planning very difficult. Forward-looking entrepreneurs and political leaders acknowledge that the private sector will continue to play a major role in determining priorities but that without a directing role of the public sector, increasingly diverse economic interests may not be reconcilable.

Policymakers and private firms are willing to take a chance that such an approach can be made to work. After all, too much is at stake for both sides. The economic policies in Washington with their concomitant loss of federal funding for urban areas have placed Trinity City, similar to many other cities across the country, in a predicament that defies easy resolution. Increasingly, recognition of the necessity of a viable downtown area, the legacy of ill-fated policies of earlier decades that created massive flight to the suburbs, leaves urban policy makers scrambling for answers. Trinity City does not differ much in this respect.

## Lessons of the Seventies

The planning and development processes in Trinity City could be characterized by what Stephen Elkin refers to as "entrepreneurial political economy."[2] Ac-

An original essay written for this text and published by permission of the author, Professor Margaret F. Reid, University of Louisville, Department of History, 1991.

cording to Elkin's thesis, such an environment ac-
cords leading business representatives a privileged
position while at the same time encouraging public
sector professionalism. Elkin describes such a system
in his discussions of Dallas as follows:

> Organized businessmen were able to create and
> foster a political system that was directed at pro-
> moting a greater Dallas. This was done, not by
> corrupting the system, but by excluding "politics",
> by which was meant the pulling and hauling of
> various neighborhood and other interests and
> politicians who spoke for these interests and who
> could act to further their own pocketbooks. . . .
> Instead, the aims were to professionalize the city
> bureaucracy.[3]

Administrative officials in Trinity City echoed similar views. They believed it was up to TCI, which represented views of downtown merchants and businesses, or the chamber of commerce to approach the
city if it felt strongly enough about an issue:

> I question that it's the city's responsibility to estab-
> lish [goals]—I see it more a cooperative situa-
> tion—not just the city's.

The city has always been open to initiatives from
the private sector—not having pride of ownership—but seeing ourselves as facilitator.

Our city has a business oriented council many of
whose members have offices or businesses in
downtown. In Trinity City we've been fortunate to
have various segments that are very energetic.
They have a feeling that they have an open door
at City Hall and that we are responsive to suggestions from outside.

In other words, there existed a strong bond between
the administration, city council and the business community in the downtown area. Business representatives were to articulate their preferences and the administration was to bring these concerns to the city
council.

The emphasis on the Central Business District
(CBD) reflected in the genesis of downtown planning

since the seventies became the basis for the current
CBD planning. The downtown had received priority
consideration only quite recently. According to one
administrator the very active neighborhood movements outside the CBD focused much of the council's attention on other areas of the city:

> I don't think there is [currently] a very strong
> vision of what the downtown is supposed to be.
> . . . With the economy turning up, however, and as
> we see additional interest in the downtown . . . the
> focus will come back again to downtown.

The same administrator, however, also suggested:

> It is important for any community to have a
> vibrant downtown.

And the former planning director mentioned:

> We are very lucky with our citizenry. They con-
> sider it their downtown, the focal point, a focal
> point that is important to them. They shop there,
> they go there for entertainment. Even if they don't
> live there many work there, we have 45,000 that
> work in the downtown area.

The need to revitalize the downtown was echoed
by almost everyone with any interest in the downtown. The former planning director continued:
"Downtown is such a unique place in terms of the
services needed. But the needs of the city change all
the time and the plans need to change with the social
and economic configuration of the downtown."
Eventually, it was feared, Trinity City would be unable to compete successfully with other major cities
for conventions and tourism, or for headquarters of
businesses. To address this predicament, Trinity City
introduced a planning concept referred to as *Sector
Planning*. It was first applied by the city council in
1968 to develop a comprehensive land use plan for
the city and found its most noted manifestation in L.
Halperin & Associates *CBD Sector Report* in 1971.
Under this program the city was divided into eleven
planning units, or "sectors." In each of the eleven
sectors, an organization representing interested parties was established to provide for feedback and to
communicate problems or needs in that sector. The

experimentation with such extensive citizen participation was still considered an innovation in the early seventies. The former director of planning points out: "When we first started it back in the seventies, it was unique at that time. We tried to get key leaders of the community. We had a good mix . . . But in order to keep those people involved you had to use their time very efficiently."

With improvements in the economy in the late seventies and early eighties, a building boom ensued in Trinity City. The downtown began to turn around as well. Within the span of a few years about four million square feet of new space was developed. Private sector investments of over $500 million were complemented by an additional $50 million of public funds, much of it raised locally. In addition UDAG monies (Urban Development Action Grant) by the federal government helped to add needed parking space to the downtown. There was a general consensus among leading representatives of both the public and the private sector that upgrading the CBD sector plan was critical. The sector plan for the CBD had framework character and did not address implementation issues in great detail. In the words of the authors:

> This document is intended to be an action-oriented management plan. The specific purpose of this plan is to provide guidance strategies and a flexible framework for shaping the CBD under the very real opportunities and pressures of the time. [emphasis in original].

To assist the city administration in its efforts to better implement the plan in the downtown sector an advisory committee, the CBD Planning Council, was created. It was made up of about thirty civic, political, and business representatives at that time. It received technical assistance from various city departments and a private consultant team that had been hired to develop insights into opportunities and problems of the CBD and to deal with some of the design aspects of the plan. The CBD Planning Council met a dozen times over nearly a one and a half year period. On the city's side, the entire process occupied two planning professionals full time in addition to the considerable time spent by the planning director. Recommendations by the Planning Council were then translated

into more specific action plans to serve as frames of reference for various agencies, public and private, throughout the city.

Although the new CBD plan was sufficiently detailed in spelling out implementation options including an assessment district, its goals were obsolete almost the minute they were approved in 1981. Soon after its passage, the plan encountered a severe recession from which the state began to recover only by the mideighties. A renewed debate over the future of the CBD resumed and came to a head when some members of the CBD Planning Council advanced a proposal for a Special Assessment or Improvement District (SID). It reflected the recognition among members of the administration and the Planning Council of the greater restrictions placed on them by the changes in the financial environment. The cooperation between private and public representatives that had been successful in the implementation of the downtown sector plan during the seventies was tested again to address the novel needs of the eighties and nineties.

## Setting the Stage: Saving a Little Bit of Downtown, Maybe a Little Bit More

TCI became a viable actor when three or four members of the CBD Planning Council began to seriously contemplate the formation of a nonprofit CBD management corporation in 1981.

Initially, TCI members saw their main contribution to assist in the coordination of public and private interests in the CBD during the implementation phase of the CBD plan and to help refine future visions for downtown. Several administrators admitted: "I don't know that we have clearly identified the goals. I question that it's the city's responsibility to establish them single-handedly. I see it more of a cooperative effort," and "I don't think there is a clear vision of what the downtown should be. The council's focus has not always been on the downtown." One participant, Mr. Van de Holtz, commented that TCI's primary role was to "keep the public sector's feet to the fire" to continue its commitment to the CBD development process.

TCI became operational in 1982 when a steering

committee was selected and a strategic planning process commenced. The original statement of TCI's mission capsulized its role in the downtown:

increase activity in the downtown area

offer to serve as a liaison between city, county, and the business community

support the implementation of the city's Central Business District Plan as the vehicle for long-term improvements in the CBD.

Its contributions became focused further when the discussion of the possibility of an assessment or improvement district surfaced. For a self-imposed fee, member organizations of the district would receive additional services over and above those currently provided by the municipality. They would be able to target services for which there was a perceived need or deficit for which general fund monies would be difficult to get.

## The Decision to Pursue Adoption of a Special Assessment District

The idea of a special assessment district was first addressed in the implementation section of the CBD plan as one of several financing options. However, special assessments were not yet legal instruments that Trinity City could use in the early 1980s. The city council was hesitant to look at this option as it was never tried in the state. Both TCI and the city staff believed it was an effort worthwhile pursuing if the city council could be convinced it would benefit them politically. One member of the administration commented: "You have council members who always are concerned about taxes and to them this appeared to be a new tax. So, you have to deal with the benefits and it had to be made clear that this was a project brought to the administration *not* originated by it." Exogenous factors worked in the city's favor as well. Faced with rising fiscal problems and dwindling federal support that had been the mainstay of urban renewal in previous decades, Trinity City, like other cities across the nation, was forced to look inward. The most natural place to start was its downtown.

Promoting office and retail growth appeared to be the only reasonable entry point for the revitalization of other city neighborhoods. New York, Boston, Cleveland, Pittsburgh, and Cincinnati had all succeeded at it. Why shouldn't it work here as well?

At about the same time the TCI Board, a steering group composed of local business leaders, had decided that it was necessary to further strengthen the organization's role and provide it with clearer direction. This was accomplished by the formation of a Long Range Planning Committee in 1984 as an effort to enhance TCI's strategic planning capacity. Trinity City's Planning Department staff was invited to assist TCI in formulating its new objectives for the downtown sector. TCI board members hoped that if public and private interests could be brought into sync, acrimonious confrontations over goals could be avoided later.

To further their understanding of the functioning of an assessment and maintain a vibrant CBD in Trinity City based on a vision, good programs, and an ambience of a healthy city.

The *New Directions Report* was approved by TCI's general membership in March 1985. Later that month Mr. Van der Holtz was hired to become Director of Programs charged with the design and implementation of the assessment district project. Like many other staff members of TCI including its director, Van der Holtz had joined the organization because he believed in the idea. He had been a member of Trinity City's planning department but had served as a volunteer for TCI for several years. Similarly, TCI's director who had been a private business man joined TCI for the challenge it offered. Both wanted TCI to succeed.

In a second phase of planning some forty interviews with downtown businesses, public officials and other influential decision makers resulted in a needs assessment matrix, which attempted to target strength and weaknesses of the CBD. Trinity City was aware of problems with its image. Articles in the largest newspaper commented on it repeatedly when Trinity City searched for a new executive director of its Convention and Visitors Bureau two years earlier. The needs assessment interviews identified the following major weaknesses:

lack of a national image of Trinity City

absence of headquarters of national companies

lack of diversified entertainment

*perceived* lack of security, parking

concerns over appearance of downtown

lack of participation of businesses in local government

The assessment report and the increasing emphasis on the downtown created a climate described by one participant:

We felt it was necessary to create an environment in which there would be continued attention paid to the downtown—a forum or platform, if you will, that would hold interest focused on the downtown, by bringing all involved together to discuss needs of the CBD and how to meet them.

## Public Entrepreneurialism?

It became evident that public sector officials' willingness to entertain innovative solutions depended on the leadership of the city manager. Trinity City's managers during the seventies and eighties had supported efforts toward revitalization of the CBD. As the urgency for a downtown agenda grew they set the tone for the administration by creating a climate of cooperation and by freeing up enough of the city's personnel to work on special projects. Both, Bob Hilger, manager during the early phases of the SID, and John Douglass, the manager who succeeded him, committed themselves to downtown redevelopment. Given the political culture of the city, the administration's way was not to aggressively push such projects. In an "entrepreneurial urban regime" (Elkin) a tax oriented mindset was unacceptable as well. In the absence of federal or state dollars, the city had to find other methods of financing to accomplish the desired goal. Using the assessment method would minimize the visible involvement of the administration and minimize possible opposition from the city council while allowing it a voice in the negotiations. One member of the administration reflected:

The first public presentation of the issues [concerning SID]—as I recall—the creation of the awareness of the issues was pretty well handled by TCI. We did not want it to appear it was a staff project—something that we had cooked up.

What position the administration would assume in the SID debate depended on the following calculations:

How much staff time are the manager's office and other department willing to devote to this effort given that other priorities existed?

How much resistance will they encounter from these departments, primarily the legal department and public works, which would carry the brunt of the work?

Are there any perceived risks (political primarily) associated with committing to SID that would make council opposition likely?

How much support will TCI provide, and what could happen if the process got started and TCI was not able to establish sufficient credibility with the business owners who had trusted that TCI could represent them adequately?

What will it take to convince the council of the feasibility of the assessment district?

When TCI was formed and approached the city for help, Hilger and some planning staff members began to meet with them as early as 1983. At that time, Van der Holtz was still working for the Planning Department, volunteering some of his time for TCI, and so did the planning director, who left his position in 1985 to form his own company.

Hilger and later Douglass considered it critical that they define the city's role in this process. They sensed that if the city lent its support to the SID, then the project might work successfully. If their support was lukewarm, then the SID would likely be delayed, which in turn could result in serious damage to the city's image.

Trinity City, supported by other communities in the state, spearheaded an effort to get assessment legislation passed by the state legislature in 1983, known as the *Public Improvement District Act* (see box). Trinity City's legal department and especially its city attorney, Walter Addison, were critical players in this effort as was acknowledged by all participants:

The City Attorney was involved from day one— perhaps to assure that the city was protected— but also so that things would be done right, that is, that the Council would give its approval. Also given our (TCI's) staffing situation, we would have been forced to hire an attorney. To avoid prolonged debates and cost we felt it was best this way. Also, remember Trinity City was the first city to try an assessment district—so there was some apprehension whether we could pull it off—politically, operationally and financially. The only way it could be done was together.

Naturally, TCI and the administration had their differences in the process of negotiation. Frustrations resulting from the length of the procedures occasionally strained business leaders' patience. Many managers underestimated the extent and detail of the discussions needed and the duration of the process to bring the matter before the city council.

## Pledging Local Resources: The Decision to Go Off-Budget

The city manager's office at this time sought to determine what role the administration would or should

### Public Improvement District Assessment Act of 1983

The Act includes the following provisions and requirements:

1. A city may set up a *clearly defined district* for purposes of service delivery or improvements such as landscaping, lighting, street and drainage improvements, parks construction, parking facilities, and management services related to these improvements.
2. A *petition* must be signed and submitted by the property owners within the boundaries of the district representing more than fifty percent of the assessed value of the property and representing a majority of the property owners *or* representing a majority of the taxable land area in the district.
3. The city may require that a *feasibility study* be made (TCI anticipated this requirement by conducting the needs assessment study).
4. There must be *hearings* held on the nature of the district, the method of assessment, and the apportionment of the costs between the district and the city as a whole.
5. The *district can be dissolved* at any time if a specified number of owners on record so request it.
6. An *advisory body* should be created composed of the property owners in the district.

assume in this process. It saw itself confronted with three choices:

1. leave the matter to TCI and let it struggle to convince the legislature of the feasibility of the SID
2. take on the project by itself at the risk of generating opposition from the city council, downtown businesses, and other property owners
3. pursue a public-private partnership as expression of a long-term commitment to the downtown and its economic vitality

The first option entailed that TCI would perform all the legal work, as well as the coordination and coalition building by itself with assistance of the downtown business owners. The administration would simply negotiate the city's portion of the assessments with TCI and leave the rest up to the city council to determine.

The second choice envisioned a more aggressive stance of the city. Knowing that TCI was severely understaffed and fearing that the entity would be incapable to handle matters in an appropriate fashion, the city manager's office would essentially direct the operations. TCI's role would be reduced to maintaining contact with their constituents and assuring their continued support for the project.

The last option, by contrast, was the most complicated of the three. Each participant group made a commitment to contribute its expertise to a team effort, with the ultimate purpose being the creation of a better downtown. It required a long-term commitment of all the players. Unlike traditional development efforts, which were typically *ad hoc* and designed for short-term cooperation, a partnership of this type would extend involvement years beyond the day that the district would be officially approved. For such a partnership to be successful, participants would have to look beyond the "bottom line," the economics of the venture. Partnerships are not business deals in the traditional sense but represent a bundle of responsible economic, social, and political decisions that make the downtowns and neighborhoods of tomorrow.

The decision to pursue an SID and not some other option rested primarily in the conviction that TCI's experience of working with downtown business owners for nearly half a decade could be pooled with the city's need for a viable downtown. TCI's primary concern was the degree of control they could exercise over the district. The proposed SID involved all larger downtown businesses and some at the periphery of the district. At the same time, the wording of the assessment legislation guaranteed enough accountability to persuade even a suspicious council.

First and foremost funding would be needed for staffing TCI and for covering program costs. More traditional vehicles such as UDAG (Urban Development Action Grant) and CDBG (Community Development Block Grant), or bond issues were either not available anymore (UDAGs were eliminated in 1987) or would likely raise major opposition from taxpayers. Like TIF (Tax Increment Financing) SIDs have the advantage that they produce tangible effects that often transcend the immediate area they benefit while avoiding politically unpopular tax increases.

# Where There is a Will There Must be a Plan

## Plan Preparation for the SID

During 1985 and 1986, two years of intense work was involved for all parties. TCI was pressuring to get the district set up. Its own timetable had envisioned about one year until it would submit their proposal to the council. The process turned out to be much more complicated as unexpected obstacles emerged. Three areas stood out in the memories of participants:

1. preparation of the legal document and other requirements
2. determination of the city's share of the assessments
3. design and dissemination of the petition.

Given the inexperience of all involved, the following comment by one participant aptly summarized the feelings of many others:

> If we had known in advance that it was going to be as complicated and as time consuming, we'd probably become disillusioned. Not that we had given up on the project. Just we'd probably hadn't stayed quite as enthusiastic pursuing it, dealing with the little problems as we should.

And complicated it was. The proposed SID involved all larger downtown businesses and some at the periphery of the district. "Securing their cooperation [for example, businesses at the periphery of the proposed SID] was the most difficult," Van der Holtz recalled. "They felt that their assessments would not be complemented by services received from the SID." While this may have been true in a few individual cases, by and large the revitalization would trigger long-term effects that likely would offset any assessments paid. TCI was also careful not to overextend the boundary of the district to keep service cost in manageable proportions and to maintain service quality.

Another problem that hit TCI quite unexpectedly—especially given its small staff—was the absentee owner group. Not only were the owners difficult to track down, but many cared little about the downtown, as they considered their properties as mere investments. In the words of Van der Holtz, "sucking away from the downtown, but not giving anything back to it."

Multiple property ownership turned out to be another headache for TCI. Some properties were held by thirty or more heirs in common. By law, each person must be notified by letter. Many reacted with skepticism or worse. Being unfamiliar with the downtown situation, they saw no good reason for the establishment of an SID. TCI and city officials spent long hours in explaining the purpose of the district. Karen Longfellow was the designated administrative official in charge of the assessment hearings. She commented: "We sent letters out—repeatedly—and telephoned them telling them that it was not a tax. We explained the purpose of the district to them and the benefits it would generate to their property if they signed the petition for the SID." Both TCI and the administration believed that the petition needed to be signed by a large number of property owners to send a strong enough signal to the city council. "We wanted an overwhelming majority. We were going down uncharted territory," Van der Holtz recalled.

Finally, TCI saw itself confronted with several smaller business owners who expressed concern that their views would not be heard; "Downtown Tax District Draws Vocal Opposition," read one of the headlines in the local newspaper. Many felt dwarfed by the "big guys" and their political and financial clout. The same local newspaper cited some of the more outspoken business owners: "There are no services to us, but TCI expects us to pay away. I am not against the idea. What I oppose is the way it was put together. TCI has called every shot." Van der Holtz and city administrators had little understanding for this attitude. In some cities, Van der Holtz recalled, assessments were made on a volunteer basis with the result that the large businesses would carry an disproportionately large share of the assessments. In Trinity City

> . . . we wanted that everyone was assessed their fair share. It benefits the small property owners in the long run and some even in the short run. I don't have a lot of sympathy for the nay sayers, not just because I work for this organization. I have worked as a public servant as well. TCI gives almost instantaneous service, something the city could never provide and that is probably priceless.

## Planning by Consensus?

The success of the project hinged on the close cooperation between TCI and legal staff because the draft had to assure that all legal requirements were met, and that each party (city and property owners) would assume its respective responsibilities. TCI membership insisted that preliminary service arrangements between TCI and the city contained a provision that held the city to perform at least a standard level of services in the CBD until a final contract could be drawn up after the approval of the SID. Property owners insisted that the draft also include an appendix detailing city-wide administrative costs applied to the CBD. Since no separate records were kept for some services covering the CBD, uncounted staff time was spent to make reasonable estimations of the costs. While the process was described as "smooth" by all participants, they did not deny that "we ran into some rough spots during the negotiations." Van der Holtz also added that the process would have been probably much more protracted had each side furnished its own attorneys.

The second issue, the city's share of the assessments, primarily involved TCI and the city manager's office. The outcome of these negotiations was also critical. Not only would the city agree to pay substantial fees to a future management group and thus provide a considerable portion of its revenues, it also

sent a signal to the rest of the property owners that the city was making a good faith gesture to meet its fair share of obligations. Karen Longfellow explained: "An organization has to build credibility. Everyone was taking 'a wait and see' attitude. We had to convince them [TCI, the property owners, the city council] that we were serious, that we meant business." No one knew whether TCI would win the bid to become the management group for the SID—an issue to be determined if and when the council had decided the SID issue. It was quite reasonable to expect that there could be problems during the transition time until the future management group had hired subcontractors to perform the maintenance. In other words, the city would probably for a period of several months pay the assessment fees *and* continue to do the maintenance of the CBD. The manager's office, however, accepted this fact as inevitable.

Finally, an unforeseen problem occurred when TCI had difficulty in locating some of the property owners despite all the efforts it undertook. Here again, city staff was made available by the city manager to assist in this process due to the fact that TCI's staff consisted of only three full-time members.

## The Budget—The Top Priority

Understandably, budget development assumed top priority for TCI staff. For one thing, it highlighted the programmatic range planned for downtown services. Secondly, it was needed to document rationale and level of fees to be assessed to downtown business owners. TCI's budget was based on a time horizon of five years as required by state law and included yearly increases averaging about five percent, unless a new program or service was proposed for that year or a project completed, in which case the budget was lowered.

The budget summary shown above reflects TCI's proposed expenditures for the first year only as the composition of the budget did not change much in the following years.[4] Revenues were derived primarily from the city's service sharing contract and from the assessments on the city's and private property. The county did not pay any assessments for its properties in the SID. Promotions revenues are a result of the sponsors involved in a variety of events hosted by the SID.

**Proposed Special Improvement District Budget Summary (1985/6)—Year One**

| Programs | Expenses | Revenues |
|---|---|---|
| 1. Maintenance and landscaping | $506,236 | $60,000 |
| 2. Downtown promotions | $98,313 | $34,400 |
| 3. Security enhancement | $19,147 | $-0- |
| 4. Parking and transportation | $2,000 | $11,000 |
| 5. Administration | $141,888 | $-0- |
| Totals | $767,584 | $105,400* |

*Revenues include city payments for services provided by the future downtown management organization. The remaining expenses would be covered by $577,186 of assessments.

Paralleling TCI's stated objectives in the *New Directions Report,* the budget's priority was maintenance and landscaping. TCI staff was convinced that through enhancing the outward appearance of the CBD, some of the security concerns also would be addressed. Maintenance and cleaning crews would be present nearly all day. This introduced a full-time official presence resembling in some ways a neighborhood watch program. Maintenance crews would also carry brochures, maps, and other useful materials to guide visitors to attractions in the downtown.

## Testing the Waters: How Much Political Support?

With the resolution of these issues and the development of a budget, TCI and city officials could not wait for a mandate from the city council to act since neither party had much time in preparing the required documents. Consequently, the council had to be kept abreast of developments informally and contact be maintained with the council leadership. City manager Douglass designated Joanne Smith, an assistant city manager, to assume this important liaison role. He had great confidence in her administrative and negotiating skills. She had also served under the previous city manager and was familiar with the genesis of the project being a veteran administrator. Her role was to make sure that all the important deadlines were met, that TCI prepared the appropriate documents, and that council leadership was informed at all times. Serving as liaison between the administration and

council, she also provided Douglass with important feedback on the "mood" of the council that could be used to better time the decision.

Several other staff members contributed significantly to the preparation of TCI's district proposal. One of the most critical tasks was performed by the legal department where the city attorney Walter Addison and his staff worked out the details of the SID draft legislation. The enormity of the project is difficult to portray and was duly acknowledged by all as a major milestone.

Another "selling point" TCI staff designed into their proposal was the hiring of minority firms that would perform the maintenance. TCI believed that the council, particularly its minority members, would be receptive to such an approach. Other members of the council saw it as an effort to give small businesses an opportunity.

To convince the council members of the feasibility of the project, TCI invited council members to their quarterly meetings or approached them in informal meetings to answer their questions and concerns. TCI prepared a slide show documenting the history of the SID proposal, its rationale, and its benefits to be used in council hearings and for general educational purposes. Joanne Smith recalled: "We worked in small groups with the council members, briefing them, sitting down with TCI, and with business people. This enabled us to answer all their questions, some of which they would not ask in open sessions."

## County Gets a Free Ride

Efforts to involve the county in the process failed. Under state legislation the county is exempt from assessment fees unless it engages voluntarily in a self assessment. For TCI this response came not unexpectedly but was nevertheless a disappointment. Although the county's property would be included in the landscaping and maintenance rotation, other downtown properties would essentially subsidize the county because the county did not feel obliged to pay its share of the expenses. Similarly, the convention center, a county facility, would also benefit. For the county, however, conventions do not represent a major source of revenues, they do not generate a hotel-motel tax. "There are no financial incentives for them to do anything in the downtown," as one administrator summarized the situation. Moreover, the county commissioners do not have much control over the management of the convention center because it is run by an independent board. Consequently, their interest was not very high.

The county's refusal ultimately was attributable to its traditional interest in the surrounding communities rather than the much more sparsely populated CBD. There was only one commissioner whose district included the downtown. He was easily outvoted. One of the administrators put it quite succinctly:

> Based on our experience with them [the county] on other issues, we have a series of conflicts and there is nothing we can do to have them assume their responsibility. . . . We say, rather than spending our time on it, it's not worth it. . . . There are only a few counties in this state—though their number is steadily growing—that go beyond the traditional 'we build roads' attitude.

In retrospect, the president of TCI was not quite as pessimistic but conceded that they probably had made a mistake in not pushing the county harder:

> Looking at it from hindsight, we should have pressured them to make their contribution. Given the size of their property and our limited budget, we are now paying for this mistake. The county's contribution would help us significantly to do other projects or the ones we do better.

## The Decision

The council essentially adopted a wait-and-see attitude from the start. They simply felt that their role was to listen to all parties to make sure that they would not adopt anything that would later backfire. Even though they were faced with new legal territory here, prior assessment hearings for other projects had prepared them for a variety of reactions. Therefore, the protests of some smaller property owners after the petition had been presented favorably surprised many. They surprised even city staffers who had prepared the council meetings. Over sixty percent of the property owners on record had signed the petition. The local newspaper, however, sensationalized this incident in that these protests represented a small minority. Despite repeated efforts by TCI the cover-

age of the SID and its purpose prior to these events had been rather spotty—except when council-mandated hearings required public notice. TCI and city staff worked feverishly prior to the July 22, 1986, decision to assure a favorable outcome. About half of the nine-member council appeared favorably inclined toward the project. Some council members were business owners themselves and had an interest in a viable downtown. The remaining members had not openly committed themselves for or against with two members appearing negatively disposed toward the SID. They saw themselves representing the small or minority interests on the council. TCI and city staffers were worried: "We had invested so much time and energy to make the SID a top priority, just to see it all wasted because of a few small business owners . . ."

Their worries were quieted when the council approved the proposal for an SID by 6 to 1, with two members absent (at least one of them had opposed the adoption of the district in the past). The opposing council member had not been convinced by the arguments of TCI that the concerns of small business interests and those on the periphery of the district were properly taken into consideration. On the whole, however, TCI's and the administration's preparations had paid off. Only a few changes were recommended in the SID draft prepared by the legal department. They also included some compromises that had surfaced during the negotiating process between the city and TCI. Most of the initial disagreements stemmed from the novelty of the situation and the need to clarify the respective responsibilities of city departments and TCI crews. Costs were not entirely clear, nor were some of the legal issues, such as liability and negligence should one of the parties fail in its obligations. Council members, while generally favorable, did not want to overcommit themselves to a project that had never been tried. They recommended that:

> the district would be established for a period of three years rather than the five years TCI had favored

> the assessment fee was limited to a maximum of 8.5 cents per $100 of assessed value

> TCI would not be awarded the contract outright but would have to bid on it following the adoption of the district

**Appendix A   Improvement District Budget Projections 1985–1995**

| Program Area | 1985–86 | 1986–87 | 1987–88 | 1988–89 | 1989–90 | 1990–91 | 1991–92 | 1992–93 | 1993–94 | 1994–95 |
|---|---|---|---|---|---|---|---|---|---|---|
| *Expenses* | | | | | | | | | | |
| Maintenance and landscaping | 506,236 | 503,947 | 502,512 | 483,708 | 445,000 | 425,912 | 446,000 | 446,800 | 476,800 | 489,181 |
| Promotions and Marketing* | 98,313 | 108,305 | 103,229 | 152,502 | 113,257 | 85,000 | 110,316 | 118,340 | 118,340 | 122,478 |
| Marketing | 0 | 0 | 0 | 0 | 56,743 | 53,000 | 56,743 | 60,677 | 60,677 | 62,885 |
| Security enhancement | 19,147 | 20,004 | 221,604 | 22,684 | 23,818 | 21,000 | 23,818 | 25,932 | 25,932 | 26,653 |
| Transportation and parking | 2,000 | 3,000 | 4,333 | 4,550 | 4,550 | 4,005 | 4,650 | 5,470 | 5,470 | 7,045 |
| Administration | 141,888 | 148,250 | 150,222 | 155,627 | 150,073 | 152,760 | 156,918 | 158,731 | 161,238 | 171,428 |
| Totals | 767,586 | 783,506 | 781,900 | 819,071 | 793,441 | 741,677 | 798,441 | 835,950 | 848,450 | 888,670 |
| *Revenues* | | | | | | | | | | |
| Various city payments | 85,000 | 89,250 | 145,000 | 145,000 | 153,265 | 133,000 | 153,265 | 153,265 | 153,265 | 160,927 |
| Assessments | 577,186 | 573,556 | 610,176 | 610,176 | 610,176 | 546,677 | 605,176 | 641,185 | 651,185 | 683,743 |
| Other | 20,400 | 31,450 | 25,000 | 64,000 | 30,000 | 62,000 | 40,000 | 41,500 | 44,000 | 44,000 |
| Totals | 682,585 | 697,585 | 780,176 | 819,176 | 793,441 | 741,677 | 798,441 | 835,950 | 848,450 | 888,670 |

*Promotions & Marketing were treated as one item from 1985 to 1989.
From 1989 onwards both items were separated.

an advisory board to be principally composed of property owners would oversee the district's activities

In December 1986 the last stage of the three-phase process was concluded with the assessment hearings. The hearings almost duplicated those held in June and July, with a few smaller property owners protesting their assessments. Also the assessed value was lowered from 8.5 cents to 8 cents per $100 of assessed value. These assessment fees were supported by all of the largest businesses. One of the larger owners agreed to pay close to $60,000 in assessment levies, while one of the smaller merchants protested his yearly assessment of $60.

The compromise that was worked out with the help of the city manager's office included a proposal to consider only the frontage of the building, thus assessing the property at merely fifty percent of its total value. Several other valuations were reduced to twenty-five percent.

The assessments and amendments passed unanimously by a vote of 9 to 0. TCI was awarded the management contract for the SID later in 1986 and subcontracted, as agreed earlier, much of the maintenance and cleaning work to minority businesses. The details of the contract, specifically the allocation of responsibilities between city and contractor crews, again involved much work by the city's legal department. It was crucial that each party understood what its respective responsibilities were so that services during the transition time from city crews to TCI subcontractors would not be disrupted. These businesses have, by all accounts, done an excellent job in performing their assigned duties and were rehired for another contract year.

# Epilogue: Development or Dalliance?

Three years later TCI in cooperation with the administration and city legislators had accomplished most what it set out to do. According to assessments of city staffers, the transition period from city-provided services to subcontractors created a number of minor and major problems. Public Works provided much of

the services for several months until the contractors were ready to assume their tasks.

TCI's management contract was up for renewal in September 1989. The SID was unanimously reestablished for five more years. Council members were convinced that the assessment district route was a viable option for downtown revitalization and was politically defensible. SID's broad support is further evidenced by TCI's general membership that has now increased to approximately 100 members. Seventy-five TCI-sponsored promotional events are registering record attendance.

There is general agreement, that as long as the downtown property owners are committed and willing, the council will continue its support of the SID. One of the major problems that TCI must address is people's forgetfulness. TCI's president as well as administrators involved with the district suggested that not enough people understand why their downtown is looking so much better and who is behind all of those events they enjoy attending. After several years of looking at the current CBD cityscape people tend to forget its appearance before these efforts were initiated. They have to be reminded that all of these accomplishments are and remain possible only with continued commitment of public and private individuals and organizations.

Trinity City obviously is not an isolated case. Jurisdictions at all levels are currently looking at similar problems: attempting to reconcile "the traditional American hostility to government with recent American fondness for the services that modern society has increasingly required government to provide."[5] Whether these efforts exhaust themselves in symbolism and rhetoric or lead to "true" development depends on the attitudes of the actors. Such efforts must adopt new approaches that rest on a combination of bargaining, persuasion, commitment, and willingness to cooperate beyond the "deal."

Since cooperation of actors with such diverse interests is not easily established, we should not look for quick fixes—attitudes are not easily changed. Urban environments with a longstanding history of business domination probably are better off to start with projects of a more symbolic nature to give everyone time to adjust and build a foundation for future efforts.

In the case of Trinity City this question has yet to be answered. Of its legacy of hands-off government (or behind-the-scenes government with a legislature listening primarily to big business interests or other constituents outside the downtown), Van der Holtz was right when he said: "Our role is to hold the city's feet to the fire." TCI has done that by entering into new cooperative ventures that will attempt to generate enough momentum to keep the process growing and expanding. A recent such project between TCI and the city involved the establishment of a Retail/Entertainment Task Force to study possibilities to strengthen retailing downtown (January 1988). The importance of this theme was further reiterated in a "visioning workshop" conducted by TCI in April 1990. The purpose of the workshop was to identify priorities for the downtown and to continue the cooperation that was begun in the SID.

Whether one agrees with the beneficial effects of public-private cooperation, legislators, administrators, businesses, and, yes, citizens' groups have all begun to look for a more creative way of "muddling through." As Thomas McCraw (in the reading in this chapter) and this case suggested, some key factors must be in place to make such efforts workable:

a shared vision to give legitimacy to the effort

a broad-based involvement/participation of affected constituents

an identifiable structure to assure performance and accountability

and groups and individuals to provide leadership to sustain the effort beyond the time horizon of election cycles

As one participant mentioned, the issue at stake is the future of the urban areas in this country: "I don't think there is a clear vision of what the downtown is all about. . . . The focus has been on the suburbs, the CBD, or a city district. We have lost the view of 'the city'."

## Notes

1. All names have been changed to protect the identity of public and private actors. Upon request, the author can provide a contact address for the downtown management group.
2. Elkin, S.L. (1987) "State and Market in City Politics: Or, The "Real" Dallas." In C.N. Stone and H. T. Sanders, eds., *The Politics of Urban Development.* (Lawrence, Kan.): University Press of Kansas.
3. Elkin, p. 39.
4. For a complete overview of budget projections until 1995, see Appendix A.
5. Salamon, L. M. (1989) "The Changing Tools of Government Action: An Overview." In L. M. Salamon, ed., *Beyond Privatization: The Tools of Government Action.* (Washington, D.C.: Urban Institute Press) p. 11.

# Chapter 15 Review Questions

1. What does McCraw mean by "public sphere" and "private sphere"? Why does McCraw argue, "the United States at the present time is at one extreme among market economies"? How does it effect public administration?
2. Do you agree with McCraw that "the legitimacy issue" is central in establishing effective public-private partnerships"? What does he mean by that term? How does it influence the tasks and responsibilities of public administrators as well as educational preparation necessary to fulfill their career assignments in the future?
3. What are the pillars of and barriers to success for mixed undertakings in general? Do you believe that in the 1990s we will see more public-private collaboration? Why?
4. In the case study "Close Encounters," what key problems confronted Trinity

City? Why did they use public-private partnerships to solve these problems? How did they go about planning for and implementing this decision? What "pillars of success" or "barriers of success" from McCraw's reading were evidenced in the case study?

5. Much of the selection by Thomas McCraw was oriented toward the *federal level,* whereas the case study by Margaret Reid was about *local level* issues involving government. Do you think McCraw's "pillars of success" concept can be applied properly to the local or state levels? Or do they have to be modified in some ways? If so, how?

6. Specifically, does the case support or contradict McCraw's thesis that when survival is at stake "adversarial relationships between business and government are inappropriate, even irrelevant"?

## Key Terms

| | |
|---|---|
| market economy | positive-sum game |
| mixed public-private undertakings | reprivatization |
| institutional legitimacy | public organizations |
| TVA | pillars of/barriers to mixed |
| SEC | undertakings |

## Suggestions for Further Reading

The issue of "public vs. private" sectors to do the work of government tends in public administration literature over the last decade to divide itself into those strongly favoring it and those equally opposed to it. The advocates include E. S. Savas, *Privatizing the Public Sector: How to Shrink Government* (Chatham, N.J.: Chatham House, 1982), as well as his *Alternatives for Delivering Public Services Toward Improved Performance* (Boulder, Colo.: Westview Press, 1977); Vincent Ostrom, *The Intellectual Crisis in American Public Administration,* revised edition (University, Ala.: The University of Alabama Press, 1974), as well as his and Elinor Ostrom's, "Public Choice: A Different Approach to the Study of Public Administration," *Public Administration Review,* 31 (March/April 1971), pp. 203–216. As well as Presidents Commission on Privatization, *Toward More Effective Government* (Washington, D.C.: privately printed, March 1988). David

R. Morgan and Robert E. England, "The Two Faces of Privatization," *Public Administration Review* (November/December 1988) pp. 979–987. For a useful collection of writings, pro and con on this topic see, Barry J. Carroll, Ralph W. Conant and Thomas A. Easton, eds., *Private Means—Public Ends: Private Business in Social Delivery* (New York: Praeger, 1987). By contrast, critics of this approach include Donald F. Kettl, *Government by Proxy: [Mis?] Managing Federal Programs* (Washington, D.C.: Congressional Quarterly Press, 1988); Gordon Adams, *The Iron Triangle: The Politics of Defense Contracting* (New York: Council on Economic Priorities, 1981); Douglas W. Ayres, "Municipal Interfaces in the Third Sector: A Negative View," *Public Administration Review,* 35 (Oct./Sept. 1975), pp. 459–463; Charles Wolf, Jr., "A Theory of Non-Market Failures," *The Public Interest,* 55 (Spring 1979), pp. 114–133.

For a more balanced treatment of this topic, see Bruce L. R. Smith and D.C. Hague, eds., *The Dilemma of Accountability in Modern Government: Independence Versus Control* (New York: St. Martin's Press, 1971); Phillip J. Cooper, "Government Contracts in Public Administration," *Public Administration Review,* 50 (September/October 1980), pp. 459–468; Clarence Danhof, *Government Contracting and Technological Change* (Washington, D.C.: The Brookings Institution, 1968); Ruth Hoogland DeHoog, *Contracting Out for Human Services* (New York: State University of New York Press, 1984); Donald Fisk, Herbert Kiesling, and Thomas Muller, *Private Provision of Public Services: An Overview* (Washington, D.C.: The Urban Institute, 1978); Frederick C. Mosher, "The Changing Responsibilities and Tactics of the Federal Government," *Public Administration Review,* 40 (November/December 1980), pp. 541–547; Donald F. Kettl, "The Fourth Face of Federalism," *Public Administration Review,* 41 (May/June 1981) pp. 366–373; Charles E. Lindblom, *Politics and Markets* (New York: Basic Books, 1977); Ted Kolderie, "The Two Different Concepts of Privatization," *Public Administration Review,* 46 (July/August 1986), pp. 285–291; and James D. Carroll, "Public Administration in the Third Century of the Constitution: Supply Side Management, Privatization or Public Investment?" *Public Administration Review,* 47 (January/February 1987) pp. 106–114.

The subject of regulation has been dealt with extensively and separately in a variety of new books—many also strongly "pro" or "con"—appearing in the 1980s: Michael S. Baram, *Alternatives to Regulation* (Lexington, Mass.: Lexington Books, 1981); George C. Eads and Michael Fix, *Relief or Reform? Reagan's Regulatory Dilemma* (Washington, D.C.: Urban Institute Press, 1984); A. Lee Fritschler, *Smoking and Politics,* Third Edition (Englewood Cliffs, N.J.: Prentice-Hall, 1983); Florence Heffron with Neil McFeeley, *The Administrative Regulatory Process* (White Plains, N.Y.: Longman, 1983); Robert E. Litan and William D. Nordhaus, *Reforming Federal Regulation* (New Haven, Conn.: Yale University Press, 1983); Kenneth J. Meier, *Regulation: Politics, Bureaucracy, and Economics* (New York: St. Martin's Press, 1985); Michael D. Reagan, *Regulation: The Politics of Policy* (Boston: Little, Brown, 1987); Michael Pertschuk, *Revolt Against Regulation* (Berkeley, Calif.: University of California Press, 1982); Robert W. Poole, Jr., *Instead of Regulation: Alternatives to Federal Regulatory Agencies* (Lexington, Mass.: Lexington Books, 1981); and James Q. Wilson, ed., *The Politics of Regulation* (New York: Basic Books, 1980).

# CHAPTER 16

# The Relationship Between Ethics and Public Service: The Concept of the Moral Ambiguities of Public Choice

*There is no public decision whose moral effect can be gauged in terms of what game theorists refer to as a 'zero sum' result: a total victory for the right and a total defeat for the wrong. This ineluctable fact is not only because 'right' and 'wrong' are incapable of universally accepted definition. It is because an adequate response to any social evil contains the seeds of both predictable and unpredictable pathologies. . . . One mark of moral maturity is in the appreciation of the inevitability of untoward and often malignant effects of benign moral choices.*

*Stephen K. Bailey*

## READING 16

## Introduction

Long before the Iran-Contra affair, leading thinkers in public administration recognized that the critical issues of government ultimately involved moral choices. The definitive policy decisions made by public officials often have at their base conflicting ethical issues, such as whether to give precedence to the public interest or to the narrower demands of profession, department, bureau, or clientele. The ambivalent position in which public officials often find themselves has led some sensitive administrative theorists like Chester Barnard to say that the chief qualification of an executive is the ability to resolve these competing ethical codes—legal, technical, personal, professional, and organizational codes. In Barnard's view, the strength and quality of an administrator lies in his or her capacity to deal effectively with the moral complexities of organizations without being broken by the imposed problems of choice: ". . . neither men of weak responsibility nor those of limited capability," writes Barnard, "can endure or carry the burden of many simultaneous obligations of different types. If they are 'overloaded' either ability, responsibility, or morality or all three will be destroyed. Conversely, a condition of complex morality, great activity, and high responsibility cannot endure without commensurate ability."[1]

For Paul Appleby, another administrative theorist, the institutional arrangements in government provide the most effective safeguards for ensuring ethical administrative behavior. Appleby, in his book *Morality and Administration in Democratic Government,*[2] contends, however, that the traditional constitutional arrangements, such as checks and balances, federalism, or the Bill of Rights, do not supply this protection against immorality. Rather, two institutional safeguards are the best guarantees of administrative morality: (1) the ballot box, and (2) hierarchy. By means of the *ballot box* the electorate judges direct the performance of government at periodic intervals. Through *hierarchy* important decisions are forced upward in the administrative structure where they can receive broader, less technical, and more political review. Appleby equates the application of broad, disinterested, and political judgment with responsible and ethical administration.

In the following selection written as a memorial essay to Appleby, Stephen K. Bailey (1916–1982), a political science professor and former dean of the Maxwell School, draws on Appleby's writings to develop some further insights into the essential qualities of moral behavior in the public service. At the core of Bailey's essay is his emphasis on three moral qualities in public administration: "optimism, courage, and fairness tempered by charity." *Optimism,* in the author's view, is the ability of a public servant to deal with morally ambiguous situations confidently and purposefully. *Courage* is the capacity to decide and act in the face of situations when inaction, indecision, or agreement with the popular trend would provide the easy solution. *Fairness tempered by charity* allows for the maintenance of standards of justice in decisions affecting the public interest.

Bailey emphasizes the high ethical content of most important public questions. He points out how the varied complexities of public service add enormous complications to moral behavior so that the resolution of public issues can never be black or white. The "best solution," writes Bailey, "rarely is without its costs. . . . And one mark of moral maturity is in the appreciation of the inevitability of untoward and often malignant effects of benign moral choices." A strain of pessimism appears in Bailey's writing, for he observes that public policies rarely lead to a total victory for the "right" and a total defeat for the "wrong." Indeed, policy solutions themselves often create new policy problems.

As you read this selection, keep the following questions in mind:

Does Bailey's essay, in your estimation, offer some valuable advice to practicing public servants?

[1]Chester I. Barnard, *The Functions of the Executive* (Cambridge, Mass.: Harvard University Press, 1938), p. 272.

[2]Paul H. Appleby, *Morality and Administration in Democratic Government* (Baton Rouge, La.: Louisiana State University Press, 1952).

Does Bailey provide some reasonable standards for ethical conduct in government?

Can you visualize how Bailey's ideas might be applied, for example, in any of the previous cases, such as "The Decision to Drop the Atomic Bomb" or "The Blast in Centralia No. 5"?

Does Bailey give enough credit to the importance of structure and procedure in maintaining ethical conduct in public administration?

# Ethics and the Public Service

## STEPHEN K. BAILEY

When Paul Appleby was asked to deliver the Edward Douglass White lectures at Louisiana State University in the Spring of 1951, he chose as his topic *Morality and Administration in Democratic Government.* He preferred the term "morality" because he did not wish to suggest his lectures were "either a treatment in the systematic terms of general philosophy or a 'code of administrative ethics'."[1] His attempt instead was to cast the light of his uncommon wisdom upon what he considered to be the central ethical and moral issues of the American public service. These issues centered upon the felicitous interaction of moral institutional arrangements and morally ambiguous man.

In some ways *Morality and Administration* is a disconcerting book. The essays are discontinuous. Each one is chocked with insight, but in the collection viewed as a whole, theoretical coherence and structure emerge implicitly rather than explicitly. Some inherently ambig-

uous terms like "responsibility" are clarified only by context. The final chapter, "The Administrative Pattern," is not the logical fulfillment of the preceding chapters. It stands beside the other essays, not on top of them. Furthermore, in spite of the highly personal connotation of the word "morality," Appleby spent most of his time discussing the effect of the governmental system upon official morality rather than vice versa. He saw in the American governmental system a series of political and organizational devices for promoting ethical choices. The most serious threats to the "good society" came, in his estimation, not from the venality of individuals but from imperfections in institutional arrangements.

His normative model ran somewhat as follows: politics and hierarchy force public servants to refer private and special interests to higher and broader public interests. Politics does this through the discipline of the majority ballot which forces both political executives and legislators to insert a majoritarian calculus into the consideration of private claims. Hierarchy does it by placing in the hands of top officials both the responsibility and the necessity of homogenizing and moralizing the spe-

"Ethics and the Public Service" by Stephen K. Bailey in *Public Administration and Democracy,* edited by Roscoe C. Martin. Syracuse, N.Y.: Syracuse University Press, 1965, pp. 283–298. Reprinted with permission. Quotations from *Morality and Administration in Democratic Government* by Paul H. Appleby. Baton Rouge, L.A.: Louisiana State University Press, 1952. Reprinted by permission.

cial interests inevitably represented by and through the lower echelons of organizational pyramids.[2] Both politics and hierarchy are devices for assuring accountability to the public as a whole. The public makes its will known in a variety of ways and through a variety of channels, but its importance is largely in its potential rather than in its concrete expressions. "Its capacity to be, more than its being, is the crux of democratic reality."[3] Politics and hierarchy induce the public servant to search imaginatively for a public-will-to-be. In this search, the public servant is often a leader in the creation of a new public will, so he is in part accountable to what he in part creates. But in any case the basic morality of the system is in its forcing of unitary claims into the mill of pluralistic considerations.

The enemies of this normative model, then, are obvious: they are whatever disrupts politics and hierarchy. For whatever disrupts politics and hierarchy permits the settlement of public issues at too low a level of organization—at too private a level, at too specialized a level. As Madison saw in Federalist 10, bigness is the friend of freedom. But Appleby saw more clearly than Madison that bigness is freedom's friend only if administrative as well as legislative devices exist to ensure that policy decisions emerge out of the *complexity* of bigness rather than out of the simplicity of its constituent parts. The scatteration of power in the Congress, the virtual autonomy of certain bureaus and even lesser units in the executive branch, an undue encroachment of legal and other professional norms upon administrative discretion, the substitution of the expert for the generalist at the higher levels of general government, the awarding of statutory power at the bureau rather than at the department level, the atomized character of our political parties—these, according to Appleby, are the effective enemies of morality in the governmental system. They are the symptoms of political pathology. "Our poorest governmental performances, both technically and morally," he

wrote, "are generally associated with conditions in which a few citizens have very disproportionate influence."[4] He felt that "the degradation of democracy is in the failure to organize or in actual disintegration of political responsibility, yielding public interest to special influence."[5]

Here, then, is the grand design. Government is moral in so far as it induces public servants to relate the specific to the general, the private to the public, the precise interest to the inchoate moral judgment. Within this context, a moral public decision becomes one in which "the action conforms to the processes and symbols thus far developed for the general protection of political freedom as the agent of more general freedom; . . . leaves open the way for modification or reversal by public determination; . . . is taken within a hierarchy of controls in which responsibility for action may be readily identified by the public; . . . and embodies as contributions of leadership the concrete structuring of response to popularly felt needs, and not merely responses to the private and personal needs of leaders."[6]

It is no disparagement of Paul Appleby's contributions to a normative theory of democratic governance to point out that he dealt only intermittently and unsystematically with the moral problems of the individual public servant. The moral system intrigued him far more consistently than the moral actor. All of his books and essays contain brilliant flashes of insight into the moral dilemmas of individual executives, administrators, and legislators, but there emerges no *gestalt* of personal ethics in government. One can only wish that he had addressed himself to a systematic elaboration of the personal as well as the institutional aspects of public ethics. For the richness of his administrative experience and the sensitivity of his insight might have illuminated uniquely the continuing moral problems of those whose business it is to preserve and improve the American public service.

Perhaps, without undue pretention, this memorial essay can attempt to fashion a prolegomenon to a normative theory of personal ethics in the public service—building upon and elaborating some of the fragments which Appleby scattered throughout his writings and teaching.

Appleby's fragments suggest that personal ethics in the public service is compounded of mental attitudes and moral qualities. Both ingredients are essential. Virtue without understanding can be quite as disastrous as understanding without virtue.

The three essential mental attitudes are: (1) a recognition of the moral ambiguity of all men and of all public policies, (2) a recognition of the contextual forces which condition moral priorities in the public service, and (3) a recognition of the paradoxes of procedures. The essential moral qualities of the ethical public servant are: (1) optimism, (2) courage, and (3) fairness tempered by charity.

These mental attitudes and moral qualities are relevant to all public servants in every branch and at every level of government. They are as germane to judges and legislators as they are to executives and administrators. They are as essential to line officers as to staff officers. They apply to state and local officials as well as to national and international officials. They are needed in military, foreign, and other specialized services quite as much as they are needed in the career civil service and among political executives. They, of course, assume the virtue of probity and the institutional checks upon venality which Appleby has so brilliantly elaborated. They are the generic attitudes and qualities without which big democracy cannot meaningfully survive.

## Mental Attitudes

The moral public servant must be aware of the moral ambiguity of all men (including himself) and of all public policies (including those recommended by him). Reinhold Niebuhr once

stated this imperative in the following terms: "Man's capacity for justice makes democracy possible, but man's inclination to injustice makes democracy necessary."[7] American public ethics finds its historic roots in the superficially incompatible streams of Calvinism and Deism. The former emphasized a depravity which must be contained; the latter emphasized a goodness which must be discovered and released. The relevance of this moral dualism to modern governance is patent. Any law or any act of administrative discretion based upon the assumption that most men will not seek to maximize their own economic advantage when reporting assets for income tax purposes would be quite unworkable. But so would any law or any act of administrative discretion which assumed that most men would use any and every ruse to avoid paying taxes at all. Similarly, any administrative decision threatening the chances of reelection of a powerfully placed Congressman almost inevitably invokes counterforces which may be serious both for the decision-maker and for the program he or his agency espouses. But administrative decisions fashioned totally out of deference to private ambitions and personal interests can negate the very purposes of general government and can induce the righteous reaction of a voting public.

The fact is that there is no way of avoiding the introduction of personal and private interests into the calculus of public decisions. As James Harvey Robinson once wrote, "In all governmental policy there have been overwhelming elements of personal favoritism and private gain, which were not suitable for publication. This is owing to the fact that all governments are managed by human beings, who remain human beings even if they are called kings, diplomats, ministers, secretaries, or judges, or hold seats in august legislative bodies. No process has been discovered by which promotion to a position of public responsibility will do away with a man's interest in his own welfare, his partialities, race, and prejudices. Yet most books on government neglect these conditions; hence their unreality and futility."[8] The most frequently hidden agenda in the deliberations of public servants is the effect of substantive or procedural decisions upon the personal lives and fortunes of those deliberating. And yet the very call to serve a larger public often evokes a degree of selflessness and nobility on the part of public servants beyond the capacity of cynics to recognize or to believe. Man's feet may wallow in the bog of self-interest, but his eyes and ears are strangely attuned to calls from the mountaintop. As moral philosophy has insistently claimed, there is a fundamental moral distinction between the propositions "I want this because it serves my interest," and "I want this because it is right."

The fact that man is as much a rationalizing as a rational animal makes the problem of either proving or disproving disinterestedness a tricky and knotty business. "I support the decision before us because it is good for the public," may emerge as a rationalization of the less elevated but more highly motivational proposition: "I support the decision before us because it will help reelect me, or help in my chances for promotion, recognition, or increased status." But the latter may have emerged, in turn, from a superordinate proposition: "Only if I am reelected (or promoted) can I maximize my powers in the interests of the general citizenry." Unfortunately, no calipers exist for measuring the moral purity of human motivations.

But, in any case, few would deny the widespread moral hunger to justify actions on a wider and higher ground than personal self-interest. In fact, the paradox is that man's self-respect is in large part determined by this capacity to make himself and others believe that self is an inadequate referent for decisional morality. This capacity of man to transcend, to sublimate, and to transform narrowly vested compulsions is at the heart of all civilized morality. That this capacity is exercised imperfectly and intermittently is less astounding than the fact that it is exercised at all. Man's capac-

ity for benevolent and disinterested behavior is both a wonder and a challenge to those who work below, beside, and above him. It is in recognition of this moral reality that Appleby wrote in one of his most eloquent statements that "the manner and means of supporting one's own convictions, including inventiveness in perceiving how high ground may be held, are one measure of skill in the administrative process."[9]

But appeal to high morality is usually insufficient. It is in appreciating the reality of self-interest that public servants find some of the strongest forces for motivating behavior—public and private. Normally speaking, if a public interest is to be orbited, it must have as a part of its propulsive fuel a number of special and particular interests. A large part of the art of public service is in the capacity to harness private and personal interests to public interest causes. Those who will not traffic in personal and private interests (if such interests are themselves within the law) to the point of engaging their support on behalf of causes in which both public and private interests are served are, in terms of moral temperament, unfit for public responsibility.

But there is a necessary moral corollary: a recognition of the morally ambivalent effect of all public policies. There is no public decision whose moral effect can be gauged in terms of what game theorists refer to as a "zero-sum" result: a total victory for the right and a total defeat for the wrong. This ineluctable fact is not only because "right" and "wrong" are incapable of universally accepted definition. It is because an adequate response to any social evil contains the seeds of both predictable and unpredictable pathologies. One can, in the framing of laws or decisions, attempt to anticipate and partly to mitigate the predictable pathologies (although this is rarely possible in any complete sense). But one mark of moral maturity is in the appreciation of the inevitability of untoward and often malignant effects of benign moral choices. An Egyptian once commented that the two most devastating things to have happened to modern Egypt were the Rockefeller Foundation and the Aswan Dam. By enhancing public health, the Rockefeller Foundation had upset the balance of nature with horrendous consequences for the relationship of population to food supplies; by slowing the Nile, the Aswan Dam had promoted the development of enervating parasites in the river. The consequence of the two factors was that more people lived longer in more misery.

The bittersweet character of all public policy needs little further elaboration: welfare policies may mitigate hunger but promote parasitic dependence; vacationing in forests open for public recreation may destroy fish, wildlife, and, through carelessness in the handling of fire, the forests themselves. Unilateral international action may achieve immediate results at the cost of weakening international instruments of conflict resolution. Half a loaf *may* be worse than no loaf at all. It also may be better in the long run but worse in the short run—and vice versa.

Awareness of these dilemmas and paradoxes can immobilize the sensitive policymaker. That is one of the reasons why both optimism and courage are imperative moral qualities in the public service. At best, however, awareness of moral ambiguity creates a spirit of humility in the decision-maker and a willingness to defer to the views of others through compromise. Humility and a willingness to compromise are priceless attributes in the life-style of the generality of public servants in a free society. For they are the preconditions of those fruitful accommodations which resolve conflict and which allow the new to live tolerably with the old. Humility, however, must not be equated with obsequiousness, nor willingness to compromise with a weak affability. As Harold Nicolson once wrote, "It would be interesting to analyze how many false decisions, how many fatal misunderstandings have arisen from such pleasant qualities as shyness, consideration, affability or ordinary good

manners. It would be a mistake . . . to concentrate too exclusively upon those weaknesses of human nature which impede the intelligent conduct of discussion. The difficulties of precise negotiation arise with almost equal frequency from the more amiable qualities of the human heart."[10]

Men and measures, then, are morally ambiguous. Even if this were not a basic truth about the human condition, however, moral judgments in the public service would be made difficult by the shifting sands of context. An awareness of the contextual conditions which affect the arranging of moral priorities is an essential mental attitude for the moral public servant.

The moral virtues of the Boy Scout oath are widely accepted in the United States. But, as Boy Scouts get older, they are faced time and again with the disturbing fact that contexts exist within which it is impossible to be both kind and truthful at the same time. Boy Scouts are trustworthy. But what if they are faced with competing and incompatible trusts (e.g., to guard the flag at the base and to succor a distant wounded companion)? Men should be loyal, but what if loyalties conflict?

To the morally sensitive public servant, the strains of establishing a general value framework for conducting the public business is nothing compared to the strains of re-sorting specific values in the light of changing contexts. The dilemmas here are genuine. If value priorities are shifted with every passing wind, the shifter will suffer from his developing reputation as an opportunist. If value priorities are never adjusted, the saints come marching in and viable democratic politics goes marching out. To be consistent enough to deserve ethical respect from revered colleagues and from oneself; to be pliable enough to survive within an organization and to succeed in effectuating moral purposes—this is the dilemma and the glory of the public service.

In general, the higher a person goes on the rungs of power and authority, the more wobbly the ethical ladder. It is not the function of the junior civil servant in a unit of a branch of a bureau to worry about congressional relations—except on specific mandate from above. But a bureau chief, an assistant secretary, undersecretary, or secretary of a department may find himself contextually conditioned to respond frequently to congressional forces whose effect it is to undermine the integrity of the hierarchical arrangements in the executive branch. The heroic proportions of the Presidency become clear when one recognizes that the winds are fiercest and most variable above the timber line. The very fact that the President has fewer moments in the day than there are critical problems to be solved, and that crises often emerge unheralded, means an unevenness in the application of his time and attention to adjusting or influencing the moral niceties of any single issue. Appleby understood this when he wrote, "On many matters he [the President] will appear rather neutral; beyond enumerating items in messages and budgets he can expend his time and energies on only a few things. On as many matters as possible he normally yields for the sake of larger concerns."[11] The crucial word is "yields." Put in another way, if the President had more time and staff assistance he would "yield" to far fewer private and petty claims than he presently supports tacitly or openly.

During the Kennedy administration, the President called together a small group of top legislators, cabinet officers, and executive office staff to advise him on whether he should support the extension of price supports for cotton. His staff reminded him of the bonanza which price supports gave to the biggest and wealthiest cotton farmers. Legislative and cabinet leaders reminded him that a Presidential veto on an important agricultural bill could mean forfeiting key and critical legislative support on subsequent domestic and international matters of overriding importance to the nation's security and welfare. The President agreed not to veto the bill, but the moral torment was there.

According to one witness, he stared at the wall and mumbled to himself, "There is something wrong here. We are giving money to those who don't need it. If I am reelected in 1964, I'm going to turn this government upside down."

President Eisenhower was an honorable chief executive. Yet he publicly lied about the U-2 affair. The context was the crucial determinant.

If the heat in the ethical kitchen grows greater with each level of power, no public servant is immune from some heat—some concern with context. As Appleby has written, "A special favor, in administration even—as by a traffic policeman to a blind person or a cripple—would be regarded as a political good when it appears an act of equity compensating for underprivilege."[12]

There is not a moral vice which cannot be made into a relative good by context. There is not a moral virtue which cannot in peculiar circumstances have patently evil results. The mental attitude which appreciates this perversity can be led, of course, into a wasteland of ethical relativity. But this is by no means either inevitable or in the American culture even probable. Where this attitude tends to lead the mature public servant is toward a deep respect for the inconstant forces which swirl around public offices, and toward a deeper understanding of the reasons why moral men sometimes appear to make unethical public decisions. An old American Indian proverb is relevant: "Do not scoff at your friend until you have walked three miles in his moccasins." Because it is not easy for any man to place himself empathetically in the arena or moral dilemmas faced by another man, charity is a difficult moral virtue to maintain with any constancy. But as we shall review more fully below, charity is an essential moral quality in the public service of a democracy.

The third mental attitude which the public servant of a free society must cultivate is a recognition of the paradoxes of procedures. Justice Frankfurter once wrote, "The history of American freedom is, in no small measure, the history of procedure."[13] Rules, standards, procedures exist, by and large, to promote fairness, openness, depth of analysis, and accountability in the conduct of the public's business. Those who frequently by-pass or short-cut established means are thereby attacking one aspect of that most precious legacy of the past: the rule of law. Official whim is the enemy of a civilized social order. Not only does it sow the seeds of anarchy in organization, it denies to a new idea the tempering which the heat of procedural gauntlets normally provides. John Mills' "market place" is of little utility if an idea is never allowed to enter the town at all.

But, alas, if procedures are the friend of deliberation and order, they are also at times the enemy of progress and dispatch. Furthermore, there are procedures and procedures. There are apt procedures and inept procedures. The only really bitter comments in *Morality and Administration* are reserved for those members of the legal profession who believe that administration should be circumscribed by precise legal norms, and that a series of administrative courts should be the effective arbiters and sanctioners of administrative discretion.[14] And this, of course, is only one aspect of the problem. Juridic procedures aside, both administration and legislation are frequently encumbered by rules and clearances which limit both responsiveness and the accountability they were presumably designed to enhance. The Rules Committee of the House of Representatives is not only the guardian of orderly procedures, it is the graveyard of important social measures. The contract and personnel policies of many agencies—federal, state, and local—have frequently led to what Wallace Sayre has termed "the triumph of technique over purpose." Anyone who has been closely associated with reorganization studies and proposals knows that every shift in organization—in the structural means for accomplishing governmental ends—is pregnant with implications for the ends themselves. Only a

two-dimensional mind can possibly entertain seriously the notion that the structural and procedural aspects of government are unrelated to competing philosophies of substantive purpose.

The public servant who cannot recognize the paradoxes of procedures will be trapped by them. For in the case of procedures, he who deviates frequently is subversive; he who never deviates at all is lost; and he who tinkers with procedures without an understanding of substantive consequence is foolish. Of all governmental roles, the administrative role is procedurally the most flexible. But even here procedural flexibility in the public interest is achieved only by the optimistic, the courageous, and the fair.

## Moral Qualities

If mental attitudes related to the moral ambiguities, contextual priorities, and procedural paradoxes of public life are necessary prerequisites to ethical behavior on the part of public servants, they are insufficient to such behavior. Attitudes must be supported by moral qualities—by operating virtues. A list of all relevant virtues would be a long one: patience, honesty, loyalty, cheerfulness, courtesy, humility— where does one begin or stop? One begins beyond the obvious and ends where essentiality ends. In the American context, at least, the need for the virtue of honesty is too obvious to need elaboration. Although Appleby has a chapter on "Venality in Government," he properly dismisses the issue with a single sentence: "Crude wrong doing is not a major, general problem of our government." And he continues with the pregnant remark, "Further moral advance turns upon more complicated and elevated concerns."[15]

The three *essential* moral qualities in the public service are optimism, courage, and fairness tempered by charity.

Optimism is an inadequate term. It connotes euphoria, and public life deals harshly with the euphoric. But optimism is a better word than realism, for the latter dampens the fires of possibility. Optimism, to paraphrase Emerson, is the capacity to settle with some consistency on the "sunnier side of doubt." It is the quality which enables man to face ambiguity and paradox without becoming immobilized. It is essential to purposive as distinct from reactive behavior. Hannah Arendt once commented that the essence of politics was natality not mortality. Politics involves creative responses to the shifting conflicts and the gross discomfitures of mankind. Without optimism on the part of the public servants, the political function cannot be performed. There is no incentive to create policies to better the condition of mankind if the quality of human life is in fact unviable, and if mankind is in any case unworthy of the trouble.

Optimism has not been the religious, philosophical, or literary mood of the twentieth century. But in spite of a series of almost cataclysmic absurdities it has been the prevailing mood of science, education, and politics. It is the mood of the emerging nations; it is the mood of the space technologist; it is the mood of the urban renewer. Government without the leavening of optimistic public servants quickly becomes a cynical game of manipulation, personal aggrandizement, and parasitic security. The ultimate corruption of free government comes not from the hopelessly venal but from the persistently cynical. Institutional decadence has set in when the optimism of leadership becomes a ploy rather than an honest mood and a moral commitment. True optimism is not Mr. Micawber's passive assumption that something will turn up; true optimism is the affirmation of the worth of taking risks. It is not a belief in sure things; it is the capacity to see the possibilities for good in the uncertain, the ambiguous, the inscrutable.

Organic aging and the disappointments and disaffections of experience often deprive mature individuals of the physical and psychic vitality which in youth is a surrogate for optimism. That is why optimism as a moral virtue—as a life-style—is one of the rare treasures sought by all personnel prospectors whose responsibility it is to mine the common lodes for extraordinary leadership talent. Thus is true in all organizations; it is especially true in the public service. What else do we mean, when we speak disparagingly of "bureaucratic drones," than that they are those who have entered the gates of Dante's Hell and have "abandoned all hope"?

In the midst of World War II when crises were breaking out at every moment and from every quarter, an ancient White House clerk was caught by a frenetic Presidential aide whistling at his work. The aide asked, "My God, man, don't you know what's going on?" The clerk replied, "Young man, you would be terrified if you knew how little I cared." A sprinkling of such in the public service can be tolerated as droll. If a majority, or even a substantial minority of public servants become jaded, however, especially at leadership levels, an ethical rot settles in, which ultimately destroys the capacity of a government to function effectively in the public interest.

The second essential moral quality needed in the public service is courage. Personal and public life are so shot through with ambiguities and paradoxes that timidity and withdrawal are quite natural and normal responses for those confronted with them. The only three friends of courage in the public service are ambition, a sense of duty, and a recognition that inaction may be quite as painful as action.

Courage in government and politics takes many forms. The late President John F. Kennedy sketched a series of profiles of one type of courage—abiding by principle in an unpopular cause. But most calls upon courage are less insistent and more pervasive. In public administration, for example, courage is needed to ensure that degree of impersonality without which friendship oozes into inequities and special favors. Appleby relates a relevant story about George Washington. Washington told a friend seeking an appointment: "You are welcome to my house; you are welcome to my heart. . . . My personal feelings have nothing to do with the present case. I am not George Washington, but President of the United States. As George Washington, I would do anything in my power for you. As President, I can do nothing."[16] Normally it takes less courage to deal impersonally with identifiable interest groups than with long-standing associates and colleagues upon whom one has depended over the years for affection and for professional and personal support. This is true in relationship to those inside as well as those outside the organization. Part of the loneliness of authority comes from the fact, again in the words of Paul Appleby, that "to a distinctly uncomfortable degree [the administrator] must make work relationships impersonal."[17] Appleby was quick to see that impersonality invites the danger of arrogance, but he also saw that the courage to be impersonal in complicated organizational performance is generally valuable as far as the affected public is concerned. "Its tendency is to systematize fair dealing and to avoid whimsy and discrimination—in other words to provide a kind of administrative due process."[18]

The need for this kind of courage on a day-to-day basis is probably greater, and more difficult to conjure, in the legislative than in either the executive or the judicial branches of government.

A second area for consistent courage in the public service is to be found in the relationship of general administrators to experts and specialists. It takes quite as much courage to face down minority expert opinion as it does to face down the majority opinion of a clamoring crowd. In some ways it takes more, for relationships with experts are usually intimate in the decisional process, whereas relations with the crowd are often distant and indistinct. Both courage and wisdom are reflected in the words of Sir Winston Churchill: "I knew nothing

about science, but I knew something about scientists, and had had much practice as a minister in handling things I did not understand."[19]

Perhaps on no issue of public ethics is Appleby more insistent than on the necessity of experts being kept in their proper place—subordinate to politicians and general administrators. "Perhaps," he wrote, "there is no single problem in public administration of moment equal to the reconciliation of the increasing dependence upon experts with an unending democratic reality."[20] The expert, whether professional, procedural, or programmatic, is essential to the proper functioning of a complex and highly technical social system. But the autonomous or disproportionate power of experts, and of the limited worlds they comprehend, is a constant threat to more general consideration of the public good.

During World War II, a 25-year-old civil servant in the soap division of O.P.A. found himself, because of the temporary absence of superiors, dealing directly with the president and legal staff of Lever Brothers. After a few minutes of confrontation the president of Lever Brothers turned scornfully to the government employee and asked, "Young man, what do you know about soap?" A strong voice replied, "Sir, I don't know much about soap, but I know a hell of a lot about price control."

This is the courage needed by a Budget Bureau examiner in dealing with the Pentagon; this is the courage needed by an Assistant Secretary of Health, Education, and Welfare in dealing with the Surgeon General; this is the courage needed by a transient mayor in dealing with a career engineer in the public works department; this is the courage needed by a Congressman faced with appraising the "expert" testimony of an important banker in his district.

Perhaps the most essential courage in the public service is the courage to decide. For if it is true that all policies have bittersweet consequences, decisions invariably produce hurt. President Eliot of Harvard once felt constrained to say that the prime requisite of an executive was his willingness to give pain. Much buck-passing in public life is the prudent consequence of the need for multiple clearances in large and complex institutions. But buck-passing which stems from lack of moral courage is the enemy of efficient and responsible government. The inner satisfactions which come from the courage to decide are substantial; but so are the slings and arrows which are invariably let loose by those who are aggrieved by each separate decision. The issues become especially acute in personnel decisions. Courage to fire, to demote, to withhold advancement, or to shift assignments against the wishes of the person involved, is often the courage most needed and the most difficult to raise.

The third and perhaps most essential moral quality needed in the public service is fairness tempered with charity. The courage to be impersonal and disinterested is of no value unless it results in just and charitable actions and attitudes. Government in a free society is the authoritative allocator of values in terms of partly ineffable standards of justice and the public weal. It requires the approximation of moving targets partly camouflaged by the shadows of an unknowable future. The success or failure of policies bravely conceived to meet particular social evils is more frequently obscured than clarified by the passage of time. As R. G. Collingwood once pointed out, "The only thing that a shrewd and critical Greek like Herodotus would say about the divine power that ordains the course of history is that . . . it rejoices in upsetting and disturbing things."[21]

What remains through the disorder and unpredictability of history is the sense on the part of the public and of working colleagues that power for whatever ends was exercised fairly and compassionately. The deepest strain in our ethical heritage is "man's sense of injustice." The prophetic voices of the Old Testament repaired time and again to this immemorial standard. "Let Justice roll down like waters. . . ." Hesiod, speaking for generations of ancient Greeks, wrote "Fishes and beasts and fowls of the air devour one another. But to men Zeus has given justice. Beside Zeus on his throne Justice has her seat."[22] Justice was the only positive heritage of the Roman World. The establishment of justice follows directly behind the formation of union itself in the Preamble to the American Constitution.

But the moral imperative to be just—to be fair—is a limited virtue without charity. Absolute justice presupposes omniscience and total disinterestedness. Public servants are always faced with making decisions based upon both imperfect information and the inarticulate insinuations of self-interest into the decisional calculus. Charity is the virtue which compensates for inadequate information and for the subtle importunities of self in the making of judgments designed to be fair. Charity is not a soft virtue. To the contrary, it involves the ultimate moral toughness. For its exercise involves the disciplining of self and the sublimation of persistent inner claims for personal recognition, power, and status. It is the principle above principle. In the idiom of the New Testament, it is the losing of self to find self. Its exercise makes of compromise not a sinister barter but a recognition of the dignity of competing claimants. It fortifies the persuasive rather than the coercive arts. It stimulates the visions of the good society without which government becomes a sullen defense of existing patterns of privilege.

The normative systems of politics and organization which Appleby elaborated in his writings are umbilically related to the mental attitudes and moral qualities of the individual moral actor in the public service. They nourish these attitudes and qualities. They condition and promote public morality. But the reverse is also true. Without proper mental attitudes and moral qualities on the part of the public servant, Appleby's normative systems could neither exist nor be meaningfully approximated.

The intermeshing of the mental attitudes and moral qualities of the individual moral actor with the institutional arrangements elaborated by Paul Appleby produces in effect a working definition of the public interest. Men of good will may disagree on what amalgam of commonly shared interests of the nation's several publics constitutes a *substantive* public interest. What this essay attempts to suggest is that normative, procedural, institutional, attitudinal, and moral standards do exist which preserve and promote a public interest far more fundamental than any set of transient policies can possibly preserve or promote.

Bureaucracy and technology are the pervasive realities of modern civilization. Together they have made possible order, prosperity, and mobility in unprecedented magnitudes; but unfortunately they have demonstrated a perverse tendency to drain from man the blood of his essential humanity. The nobility of any society is especially encapsulated and made manifest to the world in the personal example of its public leaders and public servants. Perhaps, therefore, Appleby's writings about morality and government—no matter how wise and how provocative—were of less importance than the lessons of his example as a public servant. For in selecting the mental attitudes and moral qualities of the moral public servant, I have been guided far more by my memories of Paul Appleby than by my perusal of his writings. Appleby in his public career demonstrated an uncommon understanding of the moral ambiguities, the contextual priorities, and the paradoxes of procedures in ethical governance. Of all men of my acquaintance in public life, he was the most completely endowed in the moral qualities of optimism, courage, and fairness tempered by charity. While his wisdom illuminated everything he observed and experienced, his example shone even more brilliantly than his wisdom.

The Spanish philosopher Unamuno, thinking of Goethe's dying words, "Light, light, more light," declared passionately, "No! warmth, warmth, more warmth, for we die of cold, not of darkness. It is not the night that kills, but the frost."[23]

Without denigrating the richness of his intellectual contributions, Paul Appleby's charity of spirit was perhaps his fundamental contribution to ethics and the public service.

## Notes

1. Paul H. Appleby, *Morality and Administration in Democratic Government* (Baton Rouge, La.: Louisiana State University Press, 1952), p. vii.
2. The intellectual as distinct from the moral implications of hierarchy have been suggested by Kenneth Underwood in his contention that "the policy-making executive is to be distinguished from the middle management-supervisor levels most basically in the excessively cognitive, abstract dimensions of his work." See his paper, "The New Ethic of Personal and Corporate Responsibility," presented at the Third Centennial Symposium on *The Responsible Individual*, April 8, 1964, University of Denver.
3. Appleby, p. 35.
4. *Ibid.,* p. 214.
5. *Ibid.,* p. 211.
6. *Ibid.,* p. 36.
7. *The Children of Light and the Children of Darkness* (New York: Scribners, 1944), p. xi of Foreword.
8. *The Human Comedy* (London: The Bodley Head, 1937), p. 232.
9. Appleby, p. 222.
10. Quoted by James Reston, in *The New York Times,* April 11, 1957.
11. Appleby, p. 127.
12. *Ibid.,* p. 65.
13. Felix Frankfurter, *Malinski v. New York,* 324, U.S. 401, 414, 1945.
14. See especially Appleby, Chapter 4.
15. Appleby, p. 56.
16. *Ibid.,* p. 130.
17. *Ibid.,* p. 221.
18. *Ibid.,* p. 149.
19. *Life,* February 28, 1949, p. 61.
20. Appleby, p. 145.
21. R.G. Collingwood, *The Idea of History* (Oxford: Clarendon Press, 1946), p. 22.
22. Quoted in Edith Hamilton, *The Greek Way* (New York: W. W. Norton, 1930), p. 292.
23. Douglas V. Sheere, "The Golden Rule," in R. M. McIver, ed., *Great Expressions of Human Rights* (New York: Harper & Bros., 1950), p. 55.

## CASE STUDY 16

# Introduction

The regulation of banks and savings and loan (S&L) associations has long been a subject associated with accountants—hardly an exciting subject, and more accurately considered a bit boring, even somewhat beneath concerns of serious students of public administration. Who would think that by the 1990s the "underwhelming," neglected topic of effective bank/S&L audits and enforcement would involve the most serious financial disaster the U.S. federal government has ever suffered? The cost of the S&L bailout is an estimated $500 billion nationally, but no one yet knows the full magnitude of the crisis.

The following account of the S&L scandal, "The $150 Billion Calamity," (written in 1989 when the cost of the bailout was figured to be "merely" $150 billion) focuses on the S&L industry in Texas and its oversight problems in the 1980s. Texas suffered some of the earliest and most difficult S&L failures. In 1983 there were 287 thrifts operating in Texas; less than six years later there were only 140, with an estimated 70 finally surviving the financial collapse. It leaves not only financial ruin and personal loss for many, but as the Justice Department's William C. Hendrick says, "as big a systematic criminal problem as I have ever seen." The authors, David Maraniss and Rick Atkinson of the *Washington Post* argue that much of the source for the calamity came from "the general mentality . . . that the regulator was to be deregulated into oblivion."

The story is primarily about two of the principal regulators of the S&L industry during the 1980s who had to address the thrift problems in Texas: Edwin John Grey, Chair of the Federal Home Loan Board, the chief regulator of the S&L industry; and Harry Joe Selby, chief thrift regulator in Texas and four other sunbelt states. Ironically, both men were products of the S&L industry, chosen for their assignments because they were viewed initially as its "friends," but their *public* roles soon put them at odds with the industry, their fellow S&L executives, key congressmen, and interest groups. As regulators, they became intense objects of vilification and hatred shortly after their appointments—for merely carrying out their assignments of effective regulatory enforcement. Their work turned into a fight for their survival, physically, mentally, and emotionally. Soon they became "men in the middle" of serious ethical and moral choices affecting the public interest, themes very much central to Bailey's foregoing thesis.

Think about some of the following issues as you study this piece:

What were the sources of the S&L crisis and how did both Grey and Selby deal with these problems at first?

Can you outline the choices that confronted them in coping with the crisis in Texas?

How did Texan interests in Congress and other special interests attempt to exert pressure on Grey and Selby?

Did they resist these pressures effectively in your opinion? Were they successful or were there strategies and methods they should have followed to push regulatory enforcement of the thrift industry more strictly? What would you have done if you had been in their shoes?

Does the Bailey essay offer any helpful advice for public servants who face such dilemmas? Or, would you recommend other approaches such as "going public to the media" or "resignation in protest" to "make their case"?

# The $150 Billion Calamity

DAVID MARANISS AND RICK ATKINSON

Ed Gray, ensconced in the back seat of a regal blue Rolls Royce, concluded that the stereotype was accurate: Texans were brash, gregarious, larger than life. A different breed, they displayed a raffish gusto for making and spending money.

Gray glanced across the seat at his host. Spencer H. Blain Jr., beau ideal of the new high-rolling Texas thrift executive, seemed a case in point, right down to his $5,000 Rolex.

Not that 47-year-old Edwin John Gray had anything against making money. As the new chairman of the Federal Home Loan Bank Board, part of his job as chief regulator of the savings and loan industry was to give the nation's thrifts an opportunity to earn an honest buck. In Texas, it was clear to Gray on this Tuesday evening, June 7, 1983, they were seizing that opportunity with both hands. As the car glided toward the dollar-green neon skyline of downtown Dallas, Gray couldn't resist tweaking Blain.

"You know," Gray said dryly, "I don't know any S&L operators who drive Rolls Royces."

"Oh, well," Blain replied. "We're just very profitable down here in Texas."

Years later, when Texas was no longer bold and unbowed, when the nation faced its worst financial catastrophe since the Great Depression and the Texas thrift industry had become a virtual ward of the federal government, Gray recalled one other peculiar scene from that night.

A band of Lone Star thrift executives, who like Gray had come to Dallas for the Texas S&L industry's annual convention, met for a party in Blain's penthouse atop the Registry Hotel. They hooted and hollered and danced around the ornate fireplace and the mock 18th century French furniture. An odd, guitar-picking duo provided the music: L. Linwood Bowman III, the lanky, sedate Texas savings and loan commissioner, and chubby, ribald Durward Curlee, lobbyist

From "The $150 Billion Calamity" by David Maraniss and Rick Atkinson from The Washington Post, June 14–17, 1989. Copyright © 1989 The Washington Post. Reprinted by permission.

for the industry that Bowman was responsible for regulating. The two crooned for more than an hour, serenading Gray with "I'm Walking the Floor Over You" and "Lovesick Blues."

Sometimes people look but do not see, hear but do not listen. So it was for Gray during that first visit to Texas. Perhaps the setting was wrong, or the timing, or his frame of mind. Context is the filter for everything. Whatever the reason, the Rolex and the Rolls became fixed in Gray's mind, but he brushed aside a disturbing message, delivered during the same trip, about Spencer Blain and his operation at Empire Savings & Loan in nearby Mesquite.

Commissioner Bowman privately described for Gray how Empire, once a conservative thrift in suburban Dallas, was growing at an astonishing rate, doubling and redoubling in just a few months. Then he outlined a quick-cash scheme known as a "land flip" in which Empire and several other thrifts repeatedly sold a piece of property back and forth, pocketing big fees for each transaction. Finally, Bowman told Gray of Empire's mind-boggling condominium projects east of town, thousands of units. Strange things are going on out there, Bowman warned; someone has been dragging cars out from a junkyard to make the projects look occupied.

This warranted closer inspection by federal regulators, but Gray did not pursue the matter. When his focus was elsewhere, an aide once remarked, Gray had the attention span of a doorknob. After all, Gray reflected later, he had not gone to Dallas to sniff out misdeeds. He had been on a different mission: To urge the Texas S&L operators to take advantage of new federal legislation that unshackled the industry, removing the traditional constraints on how thrifts could attract deposits and lend money.

As a former publicist for a California thrift and a long-time press aide to Ronald Reagan, Gray accepted the prevailing ideology of the time—that free markets and deregulation were salves for economic hard times. This applied especially to the savings and loan industry, which had been mired in a three-year slump triggered by increased competition from newfangled financial enterprises that paid higher interest rates than a Plain-Jane S&L account. What the industry needed was less regulation from Washington, Gray believed, and more opportunity to grow out of its problems, "A Sure Cure for What Ails You" as he had called his speech to the Texas conventioneers.

But at the very moment that Chairman Gray and the band of Texans met in Dallas, they unwittingly stood on the brink of a disaster, one in which both the Texas economy and the deregulated S&L industry went down the tubes together, tugging and clawing at each other during a long, nasty and corrupt descent. Now, as the decade nears its end, here is the result:

The Texas savings and loan industry lies in ruins. Six years ago the state boasted 287 thrifts; today, there are 140 and the number is expected to dwindle to as few as 70. Federal investigators, meanwhile, are pursuing 7,000 criminal referrals across the country in what the Justice Department's fraud section chief, William C. Hendricks III, calls "as big a systematic criminal problem as I have ever seen." Even the hundreds of thrifts innocent of wrongdoing have suffered, as an anxious and suspicious public withdraws $1.5 billion in deposits every month. Finally, the nationwide bailout plan before Congress is expected to cost more than $150 billion.

Like light years and nanoseconds, $150 billion suggests a unit of measure not easily comprehended. Perhaps the best way to think about the sum—to pare it to human scale—is to consider what else the money might have bought. It could have financed the U.S. Food for Peace program at its current level for 136 years or the Drug Enforcement Administration for 262 years or federal prenatal care programs for 717 years. It could have purchased, at current prices, 47 nuclear-powered aircraft carriers or 4,717 F-15 jet fighters. It could have built 53,571 miles of Interstate highway.

Four of the men who gathered in Spencer Blain's penthouse suite that night six years ago each contributed to the calamity in a different way. Each was forever changed by it. Bowman, forced out as commissioner of the Texas Savings and Loan Department, ended his career with remorse and self-recrimination. Curlee, his lobbying days over, saw his fortune disintegrate in a bankruptcy sale on the courthouse steps. The flamboyant Blain, stripped of his S&L and permanently barred from the thrift business, is on trial on fraud and racketeering charges, which he has denied.

But no one changed more than Ed Gray, and it was his transformation that told a larger tale of human frailty and the search for moral courage.

## A Fatal Flaw

Ed Gray was neither an economist nor a businessman by profession, but rather a born pitchman and cheerleader. After a brief episode as a reporter, working in the Madrid bureau of United Press International during the early 1960s, he went into public relations and made a career of saying positive things about his employers.

This decidedly average man—brown hair, square face, medium height and build—instinctively shunned controversy and conflict. He saw himself as the quintessential nice guy. His favorite sport was not tennis, but fly-fishing, alone, in the high country of his native California. He liked reading history, particularly accounts of the Dark Ages in Europe. He was seen as a close friend of the S&L industry, and when the Federal Home Loan Bank Board chairmanship opened in 1983, the industry pushed his candidacy.

Gray's attachment to Reagan began in 1966, when he helped run the press operation for Reagan's first inauguration as governor of California. When Reagan needed a Bible for the swearing-in, Gray was dispatched to Carmel to fetch the 200-year-old holy book used by missionary Junipero Serra. Gray served Gov. Reagan in Sacramento, then took his skills into private enterprise as an S&L executive.

At first glance these causes—Reagan and savings and loans—might not seem easily linked, but they fit together neatly in Gray's romanticized world view. He shared the thrift industry's self-image as the enabler of the American dream. From its inception in suburban Philadelphia in 1831, the business had portrayed itself as the benefactor of American home ownership. Nearly a century ago the thrift industry's principal trade association coined the slogan: "The American Home, the Safeguard of American Liberties."

To Gray, Reagan embodied wholesome American virtues, and that value system held the dream of home ownership. Gray thought of Reagan not so much as spokesman for corporate America but more as an average fellow, similar to the character Jimmy Stewart played in the 1946 Hollywood classic, "It's a

Wonderful Life"—a small-town thrift executive who was patient and forgiving of his mortgage customers during hard times.

The industry that Gray joined in the mid-1970s had not changed much since the era portrayed in the movie. It remained a relatively simple business dedicated to making mortgage loans on single-family residences. Federal law capped the interest rates an S&L could pay its depositors, but thrifts lived comfortably on the consistent, seemingly immutable, profit spread of 2 or 3 percentage points between deposit and loan rates. Furthermore, since 1934, the system had been virtually risk free, with deposits guaranteed by the Federal Savings and Loan Insurance Corp. (FSLIC). Hence the industry's lighthearted motto: "Three Six Three"—pay depositors 3 percent interest, lend at 6 percent, and hit the first tee at the country club by 3 in the afternoon.

As the 1980s began, thrift executives were still playing golf—they would never relinquish the game, nor their framed pictures of Billy Casper and Arnold Palmer, nor their fairway lingo (Newark, one executive quipped, is "two woods and a nine iron from New York")—but their world had become more complicated and uncertain. The creation of money market accounts and other investment opportunities, offering higher interest rates and easily available to consumers, eliminated the advantage that thrifts had enjoyed for many decades. From a zenith in 1978, when S&Ls reported record profits, the industry went into a stunning tailspin: 18 straight months in which Americans withdrew more money than they deposited.

The first federal response, near the end of Jimmy Carter's presidency, was to remove restrictions on banks and savings and loans, eventually allowing them to offer any interest rate they desired. At the same time, Congress more than doubled the amount the FSLIC would insure in deposits, from $40,000 to $100,000.

This change was of more than passing interest to Gray. After working in Reagan's 1980 presidential campaign, he had moved to the White House domestic policy staff, where his territory included the savings and loan industry. Gray and others soon realized that deregulating the interest ceiling on deposits had a fatal flaw. Thrifts now had no trouble attracting new deposits, but they were still losing money faster than ever. The thrifts were caught in a "negative spread," paying high interest on their deposits while collecting relatively low interest on the long-term mortgage loans that provided most of their income.

In Texas, inevitably, this condition was converted into an Aggie joke. Negative spread, one Austin economist said, was "like the Aggie service station owner who bought fuel at 50 cents a gallon, sold it at 45 cents, and hoped to make up the difference on volume."

## A Profound Revolution

But how to respond? That is where the first fissure appeared in the Reagan team. While the administration agreed that the financial world should be deregulated, there was no consensus on what to do specifically about the savings and loan industry.

Survival was as much an issue for the industry at the dawn of the '80s as it is now, at the end. A remarkable aspect of the calamity is that after so much activity—so many proposed solutions, so many transmutations, so much mismanagement, so much venality, so many delusions, so many failures of the regulatory system—there was a problem then and there remains a problem now.

Donald T. Regan, Reagan's first Treasury secretary, who had a large voice in the administration's economic policy, held less sway when it came to the S&L issue. Despite Regan's misgivings, Gray and the U.S. League of Savings Institutions succeeded in getting their candidate appointed chairman of the Federal Home Loan Bank Board in 1981. He was Richard Pratt, finance professor at the University of Utah, a fullback of a man with a thick neck, a deep rolling voice and a commanding presence; while he did not share Gray's romantic notions of the goodness of thrifts, Pratt did believe in their utility. Above all, he believed in the value of a free market.

In Pratt's perfect world, the savings and loan industry would be neither regulated nor protected with federal insurance. He sermonized on how deposit insurance, while reassuring to customers, provided S&L operators with a perverse incentive to take risks. But eliminating the insurance was too radical even in the free market fervor of the time, so Pratt went for what he could get: legislation and rules that had the eventual effect of provoking even more risk-taking. Deregulation was his shibboleth. When recruiting Robert Mettlen of the University of Texas for chairman of the regional Federal Home Loan Bank responsible for Texas, Pratt began: "Let me ask you one question. Do you fundamentally believe in deregulation?"

Working with a troop of assistants known as the "Mormon Mafia," Pratt sought to resolve the negative spread dilemma by easing restrictions on how thrifts could be run, who could run them, and how money could be invested. Central to this effort was the Garn-St Germain Depository Institutions Act of 1982, which encouraged thrifts to move away from the home mortgage business and toward riskier—but potentially more profitable—commercial and real estate loans, development loans, and subsidiary enterprises.

At the same time, Pratt's bank board issued an equally important set of rule changes. Accounting procedures for S&L examinations were eased. Thrift owners were required to put less of their own cash in a reserve fund intended to hedge against losses. The definition of cash, or capital, for that reserve fund was liberalized to include such assets as raw land. And the requirement that thrifts have at least 400 stockholders was eliminated, wiping out the concept of community involvement.

Yet, Pratt later recalled, there were "no substantive conversations" in the early '80s about beefing up the regulatory side of the operation. Ed Gray, from his vantage point at the White House, summed up the philosophy: "The general mentality was that the regulator was to be deregulated into oblivion."

The industry underwent a swift and profound revolution. From coast to coast, consultants held seminars on how to take advantage of the new commercial opportunities in the thrift business. In Los Angeles, a law firm put out a brochure raising the question, "Why Does It Seem Everyone is Buying or Starting a California S&L?" Among the answers: Developers operating under the thrift umbrella could tap cash resources and seize favorable deals while competitors were looking for financing.

When Pratt left office, replaced on March 24, 1983, by industry cheerleader Gray, the feeling in Washington and around the country was that Pratt had worked wonders. Nearly 750 thrifts had closed shop during his tenure, victims, mostly, of negative spread. But those that survived reported good profits, even astounding profits. Pratt was credited with leading the industry out of the 19th century and preparing it for the 21st.

And no place in the world was more eager for the 21st century than Dallas. Oil prices had stabilized after a dizzying rush two years earlier and the energy centers of the Sun Belt—Houston and Midland—had flattened out a bit. But the whole world still seemed eager for a piece of Texas, and Dallas, real estate capital of the Southwest, was in a veritable land frenzy. Before 1983 was over, nearly 20,000 residences would be built there, the most of any metropolis in the nation. Building permits in Texas quadrupled over the number issued in the late 1970s. Much of that enterprise was financed with cash borrowed from Texas thrifts.

The Washington of Ronald Reagan was ascendant as well. Interest rates had eased and inflation dropped to the lowest level in 15 years. Much of the country was emerging from a recession and the White House was willing to take credit for it. Reaganomics had been transformed in many minds from a dirty word to a magic one.

There was, then, in the spring of 1983, an unusual convergence of two worlds—freewheeling Texas and free-market Washington—at a time when each was thought to have reached a pinnacle of economic access. In Texas, boom times were taken as something more than mere luck or geographic circumstance. They were seen as a confirmation of Lone Star values: pioneer spirit, frontier ethic, anti-government bias and entrepreneurial style.

But in hubris there is self-deception. In this case it was monumental.

## A Cautionary Step

Back in Washington in the fall of 1983, Chairman Gray began to receive troubling reports from his staff at the Home Loan Bank Board. At the October meeting of the enforcement staff, he learned that thrifts around the country—especially those in Texas—had shown explosive growth in the previous four months. The suddenly resurgent S&Ls were using their newfound cash to make risky development loans, Gray was told.

By the end of the year, Gray had heard enough to take a mild, cautionary first step: requiring new thrifts to increase their cash reserves as a protection against loan losses. This provoked a harsh reaction from his friends at the U.S. League, as Gray later recounted the episode. Several league officials suggested that imposing restrictions on new thrifts would hurt the organization, which needed all the new members it could get.

The last thing Gray wanted was to displease the industry. League president William B. O'Connell, an occasional lunch partner and Gray enthusiast, had mentioned that the chairman might be a leading candidate to succeed him someday. The salary of $275,-000 a year rang loud in Gray's mind. He had spent his career being a nice guy. He wasn't used to being jostled, knocked around, criticized, especially by his friends. These guys have never seen the other side of me, he thought to himself, but then neither have I.

This insight troubled him, in no small measure because he realized that he wasn't going to be able to make everybody happy.

• • •

Harry Joe Selby hardly cast an imposing shadow when he walked through the double doors of the Federal Home Loan Bank of Dallas on May 1, 1986. Plump and pink-cheeked, with snow-white hair and a fondness for bird-watching, he had a milquetoast demeanor that belied the image of the Hammer—which is what he called himself—and the Angel of Death, which is what his many enemies would soon call him.

Yet Joe Selby was a man with a mission: to restore law and order to the savings and loan industry in the Southwest. After 32 years serving the federal agency that regulates national banks, he had agreed to leave Washington to become the chief federal thrift regulator in Texas and the four other Sun Belt states of District 9.

Dallas appealed to Selby for two reasons. The first was money. Rejecting an offer of $150,000 a year—twice his salary in Washington—he held out for $165,000. Both Roy Green, the Dallas Home Loan Bank president who had recruited Selby, and Edwin J. Gray, the Federal Home Loan Bank Board chairman, considered the deal a bargain. "I want to send a message to Texas that we mean business," Gray told his staff. Joe Selby, the Hammer, would be the messenger.

The other factor influencing Selby was the chance to return to his native Texas. He had grown up in Ganado, one of a string of villages—most featuring women's names—along Highway 59 in the oil and cattle country of the gulf plains. Traveling salesmen, Selby joked, liked to spend the night in Ganado so they could boast of sleeping between Edna and

Louise. Selby's father, a prominent burgher who owned the local bank, often took young Harry Joe along to banking conventions. By the time his son was in seventh grade, the senior Selby had put him to work, first at the dreary task of filing canceled checks, later as a part-time teller on Saturdays when the cotton farmers walked in to deposit their weekly earnings.

At age 55, Joe Selby had come home. Although an expert on banks, he knew little about the savings and loan business; he knew even less about the industry in Texas, except that it had grown 1,200 percent in the past quarter-century. Before leaving Washington, he had heard of only one specific thrift in all of District 9. "You've got an institution down there," a banking acquaintance said one day, "called Vernon Savings. I hear they're over in Taiwan soliciting deposits." Puzzled but intrigued, Selby tucked the information away for future reference.

As he settled into the cramped temporary office assigned him on the third floor of the Dallas bank, he also was puzzled by the rumors that had preceded his arrival. The Joe Selby being whispered about by anxious thrift executives was a 10-foot-tall bogeyman with fangs, bent on destroying their industry.

Selby liked the image, hoping to put it to good use. "This is probably the best thing that can happen," he assured Roy Green. "I'm going to be the bad guy, cleaning up the system, getting rid of the crooks." You, he told Green, can be the good cop to my bad cop; we'll make a terrific team.

## "Let God Sort 'Em Out"

There were, to be sure, disquieting portents. Selby was astonished to find that his examiners not only lacked computers, they even wanted for typewriters. Despite a $30 million annual budget for regulatory activities in District 9, all 300 examinations then under way were scratched out in pencil and carried to a typing pool, just as they had been in the 1950s.

Selby also found that the bank was undergoing a $12 million renovation. The place was bedlam. Scores of workers were adding a wing, complete with five-story garage, child-care center and health club; other workers clumped about the old building, noisily bolting new granite facing to the walls and installing a sprinkler system. Consultants and lawyers besieged the bank, selling their services whenever another thrift tottered toward insolvency.

Most alarming to Selby was the prevailing coziness between the savings and loan industry and regulators. Banks and thrifts, he soon concluded, were different creatures. Bankers would not dare refer to the federal insurance fund as "our FDIC" as thrift owners referred to "our FSLIC." Selby was appalled to learn that some Dallas supervisors had accepted mortgage loans from institutions they were overseeing. He also had the bank's general counsel fire a barrage of conflict-of-interest warning letters to former regulators who had quit the Dallas bank so they could take jobs with the Texas thrifts they once supervised.

Selby, soon working 12 to 15 hours a day, helped establish a triage system that gave priority to the sickest of the sick thrifts. Examiners evaluated a thrift's health on a 1-to-5 scale, but the system had become almost meaningless because a majority of Texas savings and loans now rated an unhealthy 4 or 5. (By March 1987, 191 S&Ls in District 9 would be classified as 5s.) Determined to send his own message to the industry, Selby created an "investigation unit" with a half-dozen gumshoes assigned to work with the U.S. attorney and Federal Bureau of Investigation. "We need to put somebody behind bars," he demanded again and again.

He urged his regulators to be tough-minded, aggressive. Gone were the days when a regulator could assume that if a questionable practice wasn't specifically forbidden, it was therefore permissible. Ed Gray's new rules for evaluating an S&L's true financial plight had to be applied rigorously, Selby insisted.

Equally frustrating for Selby was the pedestrian pace of state regulators, who often resented the feds for their imperious manner and apparent presumption that a Texas regulator was an inferior species. Selby shared the view, prevalent at the Bank Board in Washington, that the Texas Savings and Loan Commission had long been an underpaid, understaffed handmaiden of the industry. Yet he couldn't help but like the gregarious commissioner, L. Linwood Bowman III; Selby laughed heartily when Bowman presented him with a black T-shirt, inscribed "Kill 'Em All and Let God Sort 'Em Out."

To many thrift industry executives, Selby indeed seemed determined to "kill 'em all." Their initial whispers of alarm turned into rancorous maledictions. Selby was viewed as vengeful and arbitrary, "sinking

ships to get the captains," as one former S&L executive put it.

One afternoon in the late summer of 1986, the telephone went dead at the home of supervisory agent Bill Churchill. When a repairman arrived, he found a three-inch black box clipped to the line outside; the device was a transmitter—a bug—that had malfunctioned and caused the phone to stop working. The matter was reported to the FBI, but never resolved. (A more ominous incident occurred earlier when a gunman shot out the windshields of two unoccupied Chrysler LeBaron station wagons owned by the Texas S&L Commission and parked outside the agency's suburban Dallas office. Local police investigated, to no avail.)

After discovery of the Churchill bug, the Dallas bank conducted regular sweeps for listening devices in the bank and at the homes of Selby, Roy Green and other senior officials. An elaborate security system was installed at the district bank, along with new procedures for entering and leaving the building after hours.

Bank officials began to worry about more sinister threats—particularly after hearing rumors of a plot to kidnap Selby. A security firm installed expensive burglar alarms in the homes of the bank's top executives. The systems included intruder detectors, special phone lines that notified police if the line was cut, and small, portable "panic buttons" that would trip an alarm if pushed. Keep one button hidden near the toilet in your house, the security consultants advised, since most kidnappers will let you use the bathroom before abducting you.

Only a few months after returning home, Joe Selby began to have second thoughts about the benefits of being the federal bogeyman, the "bad cop," the Hammer. The stakes—billions of dollars—were enormous enough to compel desperate men to act desperately. What, he wondered, have I gotten myself into?

## "Long Days and Hard Work"

Within weeks of his arrival in Texas, Selby began hearing a great deal more about that thrift supposedly peddling its services in Taiwan: Vernon Savings and Loan. What was happening at Vernon had happened in Texas and elsewhere a hundred times with varying degrees of stupidity, misjudgment, fraud and bum luck. Regulators had a nickname for Vernon: They called it Vermin.

Vernon, Texas, is a town of 13,000, two hours northwest of Dallas. Originally called Eagle Flats, it once straddled the old cattle trail leading to Doan's Crossing, where 6 million beeves had splashed across the Red River. Renamed in honor of George Washington's home, Vernon now boasted, among other local industries, a factory outside town that stitched Boy Scout uniforms.

Vernon Savings, one of the town's two thrifts, was founded in May 1960 by R.B. Tanner, who had been a bank examiner during the Depression and knew the virtue of caution. For 22 years, the S&L lived within its means on the profits earned by making home mortgage loans in Wilbarger County. In January 1982, Tanner sold out to a local boy turned Dallas real estate developer, Donald R. Dixon, son of Vernon's newspaper publisher. Promising to give something back to the community, Dixon took control of the $83 million institution by putting up $1 million in cash and another $4.7 million in promissory notes.

Dixon expanded Vernon full bore. He moved the main office to Dallas and lured new deposits in the form of "jumbo" certificates of deposit—$100,000 each—with high interest rates. He promoted his thrift aggressively; in 1983, one of Vernon's ads bested 750 competitors to win a national advertising prize. The winning entry showed a photograph of a Stetson, cowboy boots and work clothes heaped next to a bathtub: "Relax. A relaxing end to a hard day. We all need that, especially when we're putting our best efforts into our work. Vernon Savings employees understand long days and hard work. . . . Relax with that assurance." The ad prominently displayed the logo of the Federal Savings and Loan Insurance Corp.

Within four years, Dixon had increased Vernon's assets by more than 1,000 percent, to $1.3 billion. He also increased Vernon's liabilities by 1,500 percent, according to Bank Board documents. In 1982–83, Vernon made $700 million in construction loans in an effort to earn enough cash to pay the high interest it was offering on deposits. Dixon declined to be interviewed for this series. His attorney, R. Stan Mortenson, said criticisms of Vernon are made with "20/20 hindsight. . . . Most of the problems here have to do with the regulators and the economy and over-reaction."

In a pattern repeated by other highfliers, according

to federal officials, Vernon often took all the risk by financing not only the purchase price of the land and construction project, but also closing fees and future interest costs. It frequently skimped on collateral, as in a $24 million loan secured by a 99-acre tract, one-third of which was underwater, according to Bank Board documents. By 1985, the Bank Board documents conclude, 70 percent of the thrift's interest and fee income was "self-generated." In other words, Vernon was paying itself.

Vernon paid itself in other ways, too, as later documented by Bank Board investigators. The S&L bought a hunting club and three beach houses, including the $2 million Del Mar "cottage" in California where Dixon and his wife lived for 18 months, running up a $761,000 entertainment and expense tab. Vernon spent $6 million for a fleet of five planes and six pilots, the so-called Vernon air force. Another $5.5 million went to buy artworks for the thrift's offices.

The conspicuous consumption included pleasures of both palate and flesh: a two-week, $22,000 "Gastronomique-Fantastique" dining spree through Europe; the flying of comely young women to board meetings in California for "sexual payoffs" that eventually led to the bribery conviction of a Vernon vice president; and the purchase of a luxury yacht, the High Spirits, which often plied the Potomac, carrying members of Congress and other officials who were wined and dined lavishly.

Vernon Savings also demonstrated how comfortably the foxes and chickens lived with one another in Texas. State S&L Commissioner Lin Bowman—who believed that proximity to thrift highfliers helped him keep tabs on them—had accepted a ride to California with the Vernon air force and had twice gone pheasant hunting in Kansas with Dixon. He also had an ongoing condominium development partnership—Cottonwood Investments—with Patrick G. King, who had left his post as state director of S&L supervision to work at Vernon; Bowman has defended the investment, which began when King still worked for the state, saying it did not influence his actions as a regulator.

## Grounding the Air Force

Within a few months of Dixon's 1982 takeover, regulators began to pick up hints of Vernon's questionable practices. In November of that year, a federal examiner lowered Vernon's rating from 1 to 2, noting several rule violations and "loan documentation deficiencies." A state examination in January 1983 observed that Vernon was accepting virtually all of the risk in construction loans. Another federal exam in October 1983 downgraded Vernon to a 4, citing "unsafe and unsound lending practices." In August 1984, Vernon's directors promised to reform, but a year later, examiners found that 29 of the 31 reform agreements had been violated. "Out of control," the examiners wrote on Aug. 2, 1985, and slapped Vernon with a 5, the lowest possible rating.

That should have triggered immediate regulatory action, yet nothing happened. Somewhere between the examiners' red warning flags and the Dallas supervisors' responsibility for acting on those warnings, Vernon slipped between the cracks. "I wish I had a good answer to why we didn't do anything," one Dallas supervisor lamented recently. "Vernon didn't get the attention it should have. It was one of the herd, one of the many."

In late summer of 1986, Joe Selby entered the Vernon fray. He discovered that the thrift had a bonus plan—euphemistically known as the "bean program"—that had paid Dixon and others nearly 5 million "beans." "Gentlemen," Selby declared in a meeting with several Vernon officials and his own regulators, "the bean program is dead."

Because Vernon was state-chartered, the Texas Savings and Loan Commission could, in some respects, move more quickly than its federal counterpart. In September, the state seized supervisory control of Vernon with a team headed by Deputy Commissioner Earl Hall. To make a statement about who was in charge, Hall moved into Dixon's former office but promptly tripped near the ornate desk and broke his leg. Hobbling about in a cast for six weeks, Hall tried to take command. He grounded the Vernon air force—"Fire the damned pilots!"—and refused to pay $12,000 to international playboy Philippe Junot for services in arranging the Gastronomique-Fantastique.

Yet Joe Selby suspected that more radical action was necessary, perhaps a federal takeover—or closing the institution altogether. Vernon was hundreds of millions of dollars in the red, a staggering potential loss to the federal insurance program.

The debacle at Vernon Savings made Joe Selby angry. Many regulators had gone about their business determined to see, hear and speak no evil. As they used 1950s techniques—scratching reports with lead pencils—so they displayed a 1950s mentality. Selby was determined to bring them into the '80s.

But many in the Texas thrift industry saw things differently; Selby was willing to run roughshod over everyone, solvent and insolvent, innocent and guilty, autocratically dictating how their businesses would be run. To Durward Curlee, who lobbied in Washington for 20 Texas thrifts, including Vernon, Selby resembled a fireman who demanded to know who had been playing with matches before he'd fight the conflagration. "Joe Selby," another lobbyist complained, "wants to close up every association in Texas."

By autumn, Texans were looking to Washington for a redress of their grievances. On Oct. 21, 1986, House Majority Leader Jim Wright, the Texas Democrat who was about to ascend to House speaker, arrived for a luncheon meeting and gripe session at the Ridglea Country Club in Fort Worth. Wright expected perhaps 15 real estate and S&L executives to show up; instead, 150 awaited him. More than a dozen recounted tales of what they considered to be arbitrary and capricious actions by the federal regulators. Wright listened attentively and, as the luncheon drew to a close, publicly asked his friend and business partner, George A. Mallick, to draft a report outlining "the real story" on District 9's problems.

News of Wright's interest spread quickly and his Washington office was bombarded with phone calls from others eager to recount their "horror stories." On Oct. 23, two days after the Ridglea meeting, Wright met in San Antonio with W.W. "Bo" McAllister, president of the Texas Savings and Loan League.

"I am convinced," McAllister subsequently reported in the league's magazine, "that Congressman Wright is taking this issue very much to heart and is dead serious about insuring that Texas financial institutions are given every opportunity for survival."

• • •

Ed Gray cupped the telephone receiver against his ear, nodding more in courtesy than agreement. For several minutes, the Bank Board chairman listened attentively, saying little beyond a few perfunctory "uh-huhs." He'd heard it all before: once again, House Majority Leader Jim Wright was complaining about how heavy-handed regulators were making life miserable for the savings and loan industry in Texas.

Chief of staff Shannon Fairbanks sat next to Gray's desk, eavesdropping on his end of the conversation. Calls from important members of Congress had become so commonplace that Fairbanks had worked out a routine for fielding them. As usual on this mid-November afternoon in 1986, she had walked into Gray's office, shut the door and announced that Wright was on the line.

Five minutes into the call, Gray's countenance changed. He stopped nodding. His features tightened. "No," he interjected. "I was the one who recruited him. I think very highly of him. He is doing what I want him to do. He is being a tough regulator."

Gray hung up and wheeled toward Fairbanks, his face flushed. "No way!" he declared. "No way!"

The chairman summoned several other staffers who listened intently as Gray poured out his version of the phone call: Jim Wright wanted Joe Selby fired. Wright, a Texas Democrat, had claimed that Selby, the hard-nosed chief regulator for the Home Loan Bank of Dallas, was homosexual, and had established a "ring of homosexual lawyers" in Texas who got preferential treatment in handling S&L legal matters. "Isn't there anything you can do to get rid of Selby, or ask him to leave or something?" Gray quoted Wright as saying.

It was nearly 6 P.M., but Gray called the comptroller of the currency's office, where Selby had worked for 32 years before taking the Dallas job in 1986. Have you ever heard anything about Joe Selby giving special treatment to homosexuals? Gray asked. No, he was told, nothing like that.

Suddenly, Ed Gray felt dirty. He had grown accustomed to queries and complaints from Capitol Hill about regulatory matters. On occasion, he even brought district bank officials to Washington so they could explain to this congressman or that senator why actions had been taken against a particular thrift. Yet Wright's call, Gray thought, went too far, even for someone as persistently eager as Jim Wright to insert himself into the regulatory world. Congressional investigators later reached the same conclusion and recommended that Wright be charged with conduct unbecoming a House member; for his part, Wright denied asking Gray to fire Selby.

Just a month before this phone call, Gray had met with Wright to explain the dilemma the Bank Board faced: how the Federal Savings and Loan Insurance Corp. (FSLIC), which guaranteed deposits, was heading toward bankruptcy because of the rising tide of

S&L failures; how the FSLIC fund had dwindled to $2 billion, with hundreds of thrifts—holding nearly $100 billion in additional deposits—in serious trouble; how regulators could not close even the most insolvent institution because the insurance fund was dangerously low.

But Wright, Gray was convinced, did not hear. Instead, he petitioned the Bank Board on behalf of his Texas thrift constituents, including Thomas M. Gaubert, whose Independent American Savings Association was nearly half a billion dollars in the red. Gray also believed Wright had demonstrated his displeasure with the Bank Board by blocking a bill that would have injected $15 billion into FSLIC. Now Congress had adjourned and new legislation would have to wait at least six weeks until the 100th Congress convened in January 1987.

If Ed Gray felt dirty, he also felt exhausted. For nearly four years as chairman, he had fought one battle after another, against the thrift industry, against Congress, against his enemies in the Reagan administration. Aides noticed that his hands often trembled now; he seemed distracted, jittery, graceless under pressure, a far cry from the hail-fellow public relations executive who had come to the job four years earlier. Chain-smoking, Gray hunched over his Selectric III typewriter far into the night, pounding out his own speeches and congressional testimony, pausing only long enough to order a pizza for supper or dash out to McDonald's.

Hardly audacious by nature, he drew strength from his heroes. Winston Churchill was a particular favorite, and, alone at night, Gray often pulled out "History of the English Speaking People" or listened to tapes of the great statesman's speeches. Seeking a moral azimuth to guide himself, he often wondered, "How would Ronald Reagan make this decision?" As often as several times a week, he called Paul Volcker at the Federal Reserve for advice and sympathy, dragging on his cigarettes and pouring out his troubles while the Fed chairman worked his ubiquitous cigar at the other end of the line.

For someone with a public relations background, Gray managed to garner unbelievably bad press for himself. Shortly after Wright's call regarding Shelby, thrift executives leaked word to the press that Gray enjoyed an imperial lifestyle whenever he traveled. That triggered inquiries leading to stories such as this one in The Washington Post: "Bank Board Lived Well Off S&Ls—Industry Picked Up Tab." Gray, for example, had stayed in a $649-a-night room at the Waldorf Astoria. He and board members Mary Grigsby and Don Hovde had run up a $4,000 limousine bill in Dallas, as well as a $5,000 hotel bill in California, all paid for by the industry through its financial support of the district banks.

The revelations humiliated Gray and damaged his credibility, further weakening his clout on the Hill and in the administration. How could he campaign against profligate thrift executives if he appeared profligate himself? While acknowledging his own mistakes, he railed against the industry for disclosing his travels, sounding so bitter that a close aide admitted he sounded "wacko . . . . off the deep end."

To make amends, Gray voluntarily repaid $28,000 in personal expenses. Supporting two homes, he mailed his paycheck to his family in California and lived alone in a small, $500-a-month flat near the Bank Board. Increasingly strapped for cash, Gray raided his daughter's college tuition fund, borrowed $15,000 from his mother, and eventually plunged $80,000 in debt.

His relations with the industry that had once championed him slid from bad to dreadful. The California thrifts, formerly the core of his support, passed the word that Ed Gray was not welcome at the state's 1986 convention. "Ed," one S&L executive explained, "they don't want to hear you."

## The Texans Fight Back

In Texas, the hostility toward Gray built to a fever pitch. He was seen as Gray the Unfair, Gray the Lightweight, Gray the Re-Regulator, the man who wanted to shackle the industry with a new set of draconian rules. After flying home to La Jolla for Christmas in 1986, Gray received yet another call from Jim Wright. The majority leader had a particular problem. The owner of Vernon Savings, Donald Dixon, was complaining that regulators were depriving him of the chance to find new capital to save his S&L.

Wright had met Dixon aboard his yacht, "High Spirits," but he was calling Gray at the urging of Rep. Tony Coelho (D-Calif.), who had become a regular aboard Vernon's corporate jets and on the yacht, which he used for fund-raising parties. Coehlo sent Wright a memo, noting Dixon's concerns and reporting with a touch of apparent sarcasm that "a Joe Selby, with the Dallas Trouble Home Loan Bank Board, was specifically mentioned as desiring that [Vernon and Sunbelt Savings] be shut down."

In phoning Gray, Wright told the chairman that Dixon has "a week or three or four days that he can save [Vernon] and avoid foreclosure. Why don't you look into it?"

Once again, Gray was baffled by Wright. Vernon Savings, which had been under state supervision since September, was perhaps $600 million in the red and was losing another $10 million a month. Dixon had collected at least $1 million in bonuses and millions more in dividends, as his institution slid ever faster toward insolvency, according to a subsequent federal lawsuit.

Vernon deserved to be shut down, Gray thought, but that would require FSLIC to pay depositors a mind-boggling $1.6 billion. As Gray later informed Wright's office, he could not afford to close Vernon; instead, regulators wanted a voluntary agreement, placing the thrift under federal control.

What is it about these Texans? Ed Gray asked himself. Since his first meeting with the state's thrift executives back in June 1983, he had known that they were different somehow, oversized in their ambition to make money. But now they seemed to lack any sense of discipline. Much of the thrift business in Texas seemed obsessed with racking up colossal profits and letting the devil take the hindmost—all in the name of American entrepreneurship. Gray didn't buy it; the word "corrupt" came to mind frequently now.

The Texans had a different view. Durward Curlee, who lobbied in Washington on behalf of 20 Texas thrifts, thought Gray possessed a wide streak of the tyrant. "Why did Hitler go into Russia?" Curlee would demand, smiling slyly at the analogy. The chairman was five years too late and now seemed intent on strangling every thrift in the state.

The only hope for relief appeared to be through Congress, and it was Jim Wright, about to become speaker of the House, who seemed most receptive to the Texans' pleas. Wright sympathized with businessmen who stood on the verge of ruin because of the slumping economy; explaining the plight of such constituents to federal regulators, he believed, was a big part of his job.

On Jan. 6, 1987, as the 100th Congress convened, a bill to inject $15 billion into FSLIC was introduced in the House. This "recapitalization" proposal immediately drew fire from the industry, which feared that $15 billion in Ed Gray's hands would permit him to close thrifts willy-nilly and sell off their holdings, depressing real estate prices. The U.S. League of Savings Institutions endorsed a $5 billion plan, with "forbearance" provisions that required regulators to ease up on "well-managed institutions in trouble due to local economic conditions."

Desperate to shore up the insurance fund, the Bank Board summoned top officials from the district banks to testify at hearings scheduled before the House Banking Committee on Jan. 21 and 22. The thrift industry's biggest guns also showed up, the regulators and the regulated often perched elbow-to-elbow in the audience. Dallas bank president Roy Green, sitting with Joe Shelby, greeted a familiar figure in a nearby chair.

"Joe," Green said, "have you met Durward Curlee?"

"Oh, yeah," Curlee quipped as he shook Selby's hand, "I've heard of you through a mutual friend. From what I understand, he's the only friend you've got."

As Selby and Green entered Wright's antechamber on Feb. 10, they were surprised to find a familiar face from Texas already there. It was George Mallick, the Fort Worth developer, Wright's friend and business partner. The regulators had brought along a sheaf of inside information to explain their actions against thrifts that had gotten Wright's attention. But there was no way they could go into details with Mallick in the room. So much for Plan A, Green thought to himself.

## "The Speaker Hates Us"

After the morning testimony, several thrift executives, including W.W. (Bo) McAllister of San Antonio, Texas Savings and Loan League president Tom S. King and U.S. League president William O'Connell met for lunch with Wright and other members of the Texas delegation. "Speaker Wright indicated to us that he was considering 'slowing up' the FSLIC recap until he was satisfied with efforts toward forbearance," McAllister wrote in the Texas League's magazine two months later. "We encouraged him to take this action and that is exactly what happened." Wright later de-

nied "holding hostage" any legislation, saying the bill went through "normal legislative channels" and that he later supported the full $15 billion proposal.

In early February, the regulators decided to meet with Wright to make their case. The idea came from Selby and Green, who wanted to make peace with the speaker. Gray, though less sanguine, appreciated the session's importance, and made sure he was represented by two of his top aides. Gray thought Wright was ducking him, and he instructed his secretary to call the speaker's office every 15 minutes for a week. If nothing else, Gray wanted to show that if the two men weren't communicating, it was not his fault.

Wright sat behind his desk, facing a semicircle of regulators. To the sides stood George Mallick; Mallick's son, Michael, and a line of congressional assistants. Green began by outlining the general state of Texas thrifts and what the Dallas bank was doing to help them. He said regulators were trying to be lenient, but this was counterproductive in the long run. Sick thrifts could attract depositors only by offering high interest rates; healthy ones followed suit, reducing their profits and threatening their stability.

Selby spoke next. This was the first and only time in his life he would meet Jim Wright, his one chance to talk to the man who two months earlier had called him a homosexual and allegedly sought his removal.

"I just wanted to come and show you in person that we don't have horns," Selby said.

Wright let it pass, but later in the meeting he turned to Selby and said: "And you, you are the most feared man in the state of Texas. You carry the biggest hammer. Institutions tremble when they hear your name."

Much of Wright's information about Selby and the regulators in Dallas came from a report he had asked Mallick to prepare. That report reinforced Wright's perspective during the meeting.

Federal regulators in Texas, Mallick wrote, had been abusing their powers, making threats that they could close any thrift—insolvent or not. Why were they so tough on Texans, Mallick wondered, when New York bankers were being instructed to go easy on Third World debtors? Sick institutions were not offered the chance to get well, to "weather the real estate markets."

Mallick painted a picture of oppression: "A systematic thread of horror stories that involve unfair, unjust, intimidating, unduly expensive and illegal tactics has been the modus operandi of the regulatory agents in District Nine." He closed with an appeal to Wright as a champion of oppressed peoples and "people who are the single-family homeowners, the developers, the appraisers and the thrift owners themselves."

Wright took the floor. In two of the S&L matters that he had studied, Wright said, he found the regulators' behavior unsatisfactory. Particularly in the case of Vernon Savings, which one of the regulators had noted earlier, Wright said, Ed Gray had misled him by saying the institution would not be shut down.

William K. Black, one of Gray's top assistants, couldn't let that statement go unchallenged. The regulators hadn't shut down Vernon, he told Wright; its managers had signed a voluntary agreement placing it under federal control.

That, responded Wright, is a distinction without a difference. Black began to reply, and Wright lost his temper. His trademark bushy eyebrows twitched. His face reddened. "Wait just a goddamn minute!" he shouted. "I waited patiently for you and heard you represent your case. Now you listen to me! You're giving me a bunch of goddamn semantics!"

His outburst lasted 20 seconds, followed by a long silence. For all practical purposes, the meeting was over. What a disaster, thought Joe Selby.

Gray's aides, Black and William Robertson, had the same feeling. In the cab ride back to the bank board office, Robertson worked himself into a nervous frenzy. "What are we going to do now?" he asked. "The speaker hates us! Recap is show. We'll all get fired!"

When Ed Gray heard about the meeting, he concluded that his dealings with Wright were over. No more appeasing the speaker to win support for the FSLIC legislation. But that decision did not free Gray; he was too depressed to feel free. His term as chairman was about to expire. If the federal insurance fund was to be saved, he realized, it would be after his departure.

He shifted his focus from the shadows of the moment—Jim Wright, the Texans, leaders of an industry that had once loved him—to safeguarding his place in history. He had been the bank board chairman during the most calamitous period in the history of American thrifts. His name would be attached to that, one way or another.

He began collecting every speech he had ever delivered, every piece of testimony he had ever written, every article he could find on his tenure. "Every-

thing is for history," he told Fairbanks, his chief of staff. He organized his works into a chronology, and placed them inside blue bindings. The anthology eventually reached 12 volumes. He was convinced that he had done the right thing, but that no one would recognize his accomplishments until he was gone. "Joe, one day we're going to be proved right," he told Selby. "We're going to be proved exactly right."

## A Bitter Victory

In the gloom of his final six months, Gray found joy for one day—Feb. 27, 1987, the day his nemesis, Donald T. Regan, was fired as White House chief of staff. Calling his staff to his office, the chairman popped open three bottles of champagne and they celebrated into the night. "I'm very proud I didn't give in to that guy," Gray said. "He wanted me to bow and scrape, and I wouldn't do it."

The next month Gray won another bitter victory of sorts. On the morning of March 20, more than 200 of his regulators entered the main office and 10 branches of Vernon Savings and Loan, seized the records, and placed the thrift into federal receivership. Vernon, the institution that provoked Jim Wright's call to Gray three months earlier, now had legal exposure on sour deals of more than $6 billion.

A certain symmetry was at play. The regulators planned the seizure the night before at the Grand Kempenski Hotel in north Dallas. Formerly called the Registry Hotel, this was where Ed Gray had stayed in the spring of 1983 during his first visit to Texas as the new, optimistic bank board chairman. It was there that S&L operator Spencer Blain, now permanently barred from the S&L business, had taken him for a spin in his blue Rolls Royce.

Gray stayed on the job three more months—he would not leave until the final minute of his final day, June 30—but there were no more battles for him to win. A compromise bill pumping $10.8 billion into FSLIC, the issue that had consumed him for more than a year, would not be signed into law until Aug. 10. In his final days, Gray spent his time compiling his version of history. His internal turmoil seemed to manifest itself physically. His clothes became increasingly disheveled, and his face became more pallid and drawn. "It was horrible," chief of staff Fairbanks later recalled. "There was no lightness to him."

On his final day, Fairbanks had to drag him away from his typewriter for a meeting in the second-floor auditorium. When they arrived, the place was packed—some 700 members of the bank board staff had gathered for a farewell party.

As Ed Gray, his clothes rumpled, his soul tormented, walked through the throng, Kenny Rogers' "The Gambler" pounded through a set of giant stereo speakers: "You got to know when to hold 'em, know when to fold 'em, know when to walk away. And know when to run."

• • •

So this is what you get, Joe Selby thought to himself. This is the thanks you get for doing your job as the chief supervisor here, for being the toughest regulator in the nation. You get fired. Your proteges get canned along with you. No phone calls of gratitude, no thank you letters, not one director of the Federal Home Loan Bank of Dallas expressing a hint of appreciation for the two years you devoted to purging the bad guys from the savings and loan industry in Texas.

At breakfast two days earlier, in the coffee shop of a downtown Washington hotel, Selby had faced his executioner: George Barclay, the new president of the Dallas district bank. "Joe," Barclay told him, "the process is not working the way it should. One of us is going to have to leave, and I would prefer it not be me." Forty-eight hours later, on Thursday morning, April 28, 1988, the two men were back in Dallas. One was packing. It was not Barclay.

The toughest regulator in the nation cleaned out his office. First, he packed the small figurine of a gun-toting muscleman in a space suit; mounted on a walnut base, the statue was a gift from a Texas thrift executive who had inscribed a moniker on the brass plaque: *H. Joe Rambo Selby.* Second, he put away a framed $3 bill with the motto "In Don We Trust," a promotional gimmick immortalizing Donald Dixon, head of a savings and loan Selby had cracked down on despite intervention by then-Speaker of the House Jim Wright (D-Tex.). Third, came a gift from another savings and loan association manager with a sense of humor—the gauntlet from a suit of armor. Finally, Selby packed the black T-shirt given him by Linwood Bowman, the good-natured Texas state regulator: *Kill 'em All and Let God Sort 'em Out.*

As he moved through his third-floor office for the last time, carefully placing the mementoes in cardboard boxes, Selby pondered his fate. When Ed Gray had chaired the regulatory system in Washington and Roy Green presided over the regional staff in Dallas, Selby felt secure. His bosses not only encouraged him, they also protected him from intense political and industry pressure. But Gray had been gone for a year, and Green for several months. Perhaps it was inevitable that Selby would not survive without them.

Who had done him in? When Barclay fired him, the Dallas bank president had accepted 30 percent of the responsibility and ascribed 70 percent to Gray's successor at the Federal Home Loan Bank Board, M. Danny Wall. Yet Selby believed a third factor had influenced the decision.

"Jim Wright got me, didn't he?" he asked Barclay repeatedly. In November 1986, Wright had asked Gray to fire Selby. The chairman refused. Now, with Gray gone, Wright had triumphed after all, Selby believed.

No, Barclay replied, it wasn't just Wright. The larger problem was that Selby seemed to demand that the staff be more loyal to him than to Barclay. Besides, his administrative talents left something to be desired. He had done an admirable job under difficult circumstances, Barclay explained, but times had changed. This was the dawn of a more optimistic era, and Harry Joe Selby had the taint of the bitter old one.

## Ducking the Hard Decisions

As the spring of 1988 yielded to a brutally hot summer in Texas and Washington, no one more personified that new epoch of optimism than Melvin Danny Wall. A one-time urban renewal czar—first in Fargo, N.D., then in Salt Lake City—Wall had migrated to Washington in 1976 on the staff of newly elected Sen. Jake Garn (R-Utah).

When Garn became chairman of the Senate Banking Committee in 1981, Wall became the panel's staff director. Months before Gray's term as Bank Board chairman expired, Wall began campaigning for the job so ardently that the bank staff lampooned him in their Christmas 1986 skit, belting out "If I Were a Chairman" to the tune of "If I Were a Rich Man" from the musical "Fiddler on the Roof."

Now, after a year in office, Wall was being lampooned publicly—ridiculed might be a better description—for his buoyant proclamations that the S&L crisis was less bleak than some experts claimed. After predicting that the Texas mess could be be cleaned up for $7 billion, Wall had since been forced to double that estimate. "His optimism for the business outstripped even the industry itself," said Tom S. King, president of the Texas Savings and Loan League, which presented the balding Wall with a gigantic comb as a symbol of his eternal hopefulness. Wall's House Banking chairman, Rep. Henry B. Gonzalez (DS-Tex.), began referring derisively to the "Wall-number-of-the-Month"; within the agency he headed, he became known as M. Danny Isuzu, an allusion to the chipper prevaricator in a popular television commercial.

Such gibes, Wall believed, were deeply unfair. The Bank Board was making the best of a bad situation, he felt. Estimating the damage was nearly impossible, particularly in oil patch states like Texas, where the plummeting economy acted as a dead weight on the thrift industry. To stanch the bleeding in Texas, the board devised its so-called Southwest Plan, closing or merging more than 100 insolvent thrifts and attracting new owner-investors with federal subsidies and tax breaks. Water cooler wits dubbed the plan "McDeal."

Slowly, painfully, the American public was beginning to sense the magnitude of the fiscal calamity that had befallen the nation. Yet truly grasping what had happened was difficult, given the reluctance of politicians in both parties to confront the issue other than with occasional finger-pointing obfuscation.

Even that took place late in the presidential campaign. On Sept. 29, 1988, Democratic presidential nominee Michael S. Dukakis blamed the Reagan administration for permitting the disaster to unfold. Dukakis charged that Vice President George Bush, the Republican nominee, "could have headed off" the crisis as head of an earlier task force on financial deregulation, but instead had "walked away from a ticking time bomb [and] now, four years later, Mr. Bush's inattention will cost tens of billions of dollars."

For a day or two, Republicans and Democrats traded salvos. Then the guns fell silent and the savings and loan crisis largely vanished as an issue in the '88 campaign. Both parties, recognizing their vulnerability on the subject, tacitly decided to leave the hard decisions to the next president.

On Feb. 6, 1989, less than three weeks after taking office, President Bush unveiled his 500-page bailout package. Now working its way through the House and Senate, with a compromise version likely to land on Bush's desk later this summer, the legislation would dismantle the 57-year-old Federal Home Loan Bank Board system, transplant oversight responsibility to the Treasury Department, and fold the bankrupt Federal Savings and Loan Insurance Corp. (FSLIC) into the Federal Deposit Insurance Corp. (FDIC), which safeguards bank deposits. Estimated costs for the plan range from the breathtaking to the astronomical: $157 billion, according to the administration; $285 billion, according to the General Accounting Office.

The dollar figures are hardly more than guesses now, and so too are the estimates on how many thrifts will be left once the dust settles. Some analysts say another 800 to 1,200 savings and loans may topple in the next few years, leaving perhaps 1,500 S&Ls of the 4,000 that existed at the beginning of the 1980s. One critical factor—and an issue of bitter debate on Capitol Hill—is how much capital thrifts should keep on hand to be considered solvent. A prime element in the S&L debacle was the adoption of rules permitting high-rollers to control a thrift's assets despite risking very little of their own money; current efforts by S&L lobbyists to whittle away the capital requirements strikes some members of Congress as an invitation to replay the disaster.

On another level, the nation's lawmakers are grappling with several fundamental issues regarding commerce and government in the United States. In retrospect, it seems incontrovertible that deregulation cannot mean *no* regulation, at least when the full faith and credit of the U.S. Treasury is at stake. What deregulation should mean, however, is less clear, particularly in industries where the market seems to be faster, or smarter, or at least slicker than the regulators.

The crisis has spawned a cottage industry of civil litigation and criminal prosecution. An estimated 11,-000 lawsuits have been filed by regulators, stockholders, directors and virtually everyone else whose ox was gored in the thrift industry. The Home Loan Bank Board has augmented its staff of 60 lawyers with attorneys from 100 outside firms. "The only profession to come out of this smelling like 20 acres of roses is the lawyers," said Robert Mettlen, former Dallas bank chairman.

Yet recouping even a modest fraction of the lost

billions is unlikely. For one thing, reconstructing a paper trail is often difficult at best; FSLIC investigators involved in a suit against Lamar Savings of Austin, which once proposed opening a branch office on the moon, have identified 350,000 potentially relevant documents.

Even when the government's claim seems solid, collecting can be problematic. Spencer Blain, the flamboyant former owner of Empire Savings and Loan, agreed to repay FSLIC $100 million as part of a civil lawsuit in which he acknowledged no wrong-doing. But federal officials hardly expect to recoup that amount since Blain's contribution to the settlement consists largely of his share in 132 Texas oil wells. Blain is on trial in Texas, charged in an 88-count indictment with systematically looting his thrift.

Bank Board officials estimate that some 170 officers, borrowers and other individuals connected to the thrift industry have been convicted of fraud and other criminal charges in the past six years. Much of the federal prosecution effort has centered on Texas. A special Justice Department task force thundered into Dallas two years ago and has notched 27 convictions. But compared to the hundreds of thrifts nationwide where past criminal activity is at least suspected, the public's thirst for vengeance—voiced daily on television and radio talk shows—may not be quenched soon.

"These are hard cases," said William C. Hendricks, chief of the Justice Department's fraud section. "Very few of these people have prior convictions. . . . They're people who have lovely wives, lovely children and terrific character witnesses."

## "The Black Hole"

Nowhere is the wreckage of the American thrift industry deeper than in Texas. The decade there dawned bright with the promise of limitless growth and now sets with the state mired in a profound depression. Property values have dropped 70 percent in places; office vacancy rates in places like Austin and Houston are among the nation's highest, with landlords collecting rents that are half of what they were just two years ago. Officials considering potential nominees to the Texas Business Hall of Fame find themselves drawn to the dead or retired because of concern about picking a Lone Star businessman who will turn out to be crooked, bankrupt, or both.

In 1987 and 1988, the S&L industry in Texas lost $16 billion; about half of the state's thrifts went out of business in those two years. Of the ten U.S. thrifts suffering the most egregious losses, five were in Texas, which Bank Board chairman Wall calls "the black hole of the FSLIC." The Dallas Home Loan Bank now estimates it will cost at least $45 billion to resolve the mess in Texas; one pundit has suggested it would be cheaper to give the state back to Mexico.

Attempts by Texans to understand what happened have been fitful, half-hearted. The governor appointed a special task force, which delivered a detailed study on the crisis in January 1988; yet task force members had to pay for their own stenographer, as well as the cost of printing the report.

Likewise, attempts by Texans to improve the state regulatory machinery have been fitful, half-hearted. A 1987 bill that would have doubled the number of state examiners and increased their paltry salaries died in committee. "I did not realize at the time," committee chairman Charles Evans explained in a recent interview, "that the industry was going under like it was." At the time, the industry was losing $750,000 an hour.

## Epilogue: Four Lives

### Durward Curlee

"Nobody did everything right. Everybody made mistakes. Horrible mistakes," said Durward Curlee, dragging on a cigarette in the shadows of a booth at the Night Hawk restaurant in Austin. His life is proof enough of that. Only four years earlier, he was the Washington lobbyist for 20 Texas thrifts; all of them have gone out of business or merged with other S&Ls.

In his heyday, Curlee earned half a million dollars a year. Now he is broke, his business ventures defunct and his personal holdings auctioned in a recent bankruptcy sale on the courthouse steps. High Flyers Inc. Gone. Side Deals Inc. Long gone. Many of his old clients are on trial or are under investigation by the federal government. The man who once likened Ed Gray to Adolf Hitler, who called the Dallas regulators the Gestapo, still feels that his good old boys in Texas have been wronged. But there is no hatred left in his voice, not even bitterness, only a sense of loss and regret and, as always in Texas, hyperbole.

If oil prices hadn't crashed, Curlee laments, "Donald Dixon would be Donald Trump. If the oil boom hadn't gone bust, these guys they're now trying to put in jail would be secretary of the Treasury."

## L. Linwood Bowman III

"It happened on my watch. I can't blame it on anyone else," said L. Linwood Bowman III, offering up each word in a slow drawl punctuated by deep sighs. For five crucial years, from 1982 to 1987, Bowman was the chief S&L regulator for the state of Texas. As he readily acknowledges, the calamity unfolded before his eyes, which in a figurative sense, sometimes seemed wide-open, sometimes half-closed.

Bowman watched a troop of his employees—close friends, business associates—leave his agency to work for the thrifts they regulated. Several now find themselves in trouble. Last month his former assistant, Pat Malone, pleaded guilty to funneling corporate money illegally to Texas politicians. Two weeks ago, Bowman's business partner and former deputy, Patrick King, was indicted on similar charges.

Since he left state service two years ago, Bowman has hovered around the edges of the S&L wreck, helping insolvent thrifts manage their bad assets. He works in the Millennium Building, originally built by a savings and loan association that later went bankrupt; now the Millennium belongs to the federal government. From his headquarters in the western hills above Austin, Bowman overlooks what may be the most overbuilt city in the nation. "We just turned out," he sighs, "to be the graveyard instead of the New Jerusalem."

## H. Joe Selby

"I feel good about myself. I have nothing to be ashamed of," said H. Joe Selby on the morning of April 19, 1989. This is a pivotal day in his life, the day the House ethics committee makes public a 279-page report on Speaker Wright. The document includes a detailed account of the congressman's telephone call to Ed Gray in which he suggested that Selby was homosexual and, as the chief federal regulator in Dallas, gave preferential treatment to "a ring of homosexual lawyers."

Accounts of that phone call had been published before, but never with Selby's name attached. Now, Selby knew, his 89-year-old father and other relatives in Ganado, Tex., would read about the episode.

That's unfortunate, Selby muses, but the story has taken on a life of its own, transcending his circumstances and his privacy.

After his firing last year, Selby sought to remove himself from the savings and loan scene. He began working as a financial consultant, living in Dallas but occasionally traveling to the Caribbean and Far East on jobs. Asked to run the Texas S&L department, he turned down the offer with a terse "never again." The damage had been done; the important battles fought. The entire experience still sickens him, he said, especially what he views as the ethical laxity, the incestuousness between regulators, Congress and the industry.

"My biggest surprise was that an entire industry could be raped and pillaged like it was," he added, voice rising in indignation. "Especially in my home state. It's still inconceivable to me that could have happened."

## Edwin J. Gray

"If I had tried to be the good guy, the good old boy, right now people would be trying to lynch me around the country," said Ed Gray.

His voice on this warm spring evening in Miami has the urgency of a man trying to convince himself as much as his listeners. Since leaving Washington two years ago, Gray has mellowed in many respects: He stopped smoking; his depression lifted; his finances improved; he found more time for his wife and daughters.

But when it comes to the S&L disaster, Ed Gray remains a man possessed, a man, as Joe Selby puts it, "on a holy mission." Voluble, fervent, tireless, he portrays himself as a man more sinned against than sinning, acknowledging past mistakes—such as living a royal lifestyle at industry expense—but brushes them aside as inconsequential in the larger catastrophe.

He devours newspaper articles about the bailout bill moving through Congress. Reading of the enduring influence of the savings and loan lobby, Gray said, takes him back to the days when he felt locked in a life and death struggle with his former friends at the U.S. League, a time when, in his words, "I made myself an ass to the industry."

"They're still doing what they did then," he observed. "They're still powerful. They're still going up there with 600 local executives, trying to make it look like righteousness is on their side. Only now everyone knows what they're doing. You read about it every day. When I was there no one knew. No one knew what I had to fight."

Gray is speeding down Biscayne Boulevard at midnight, heading toward his office at Chase Federal Bank F.S.B., the only one of the nation's 3,000 thrifts to offer him a job after he left the Bank Board. The others, he said, "hate my guts."

"You have to understand," he keeps saying, voice rising, body turning away from the steering wheel to look squarely at his listeners. "You have to understand." Again he plunges back in time, recollecting in half sentences, his mind jabbing and sparring with shadows of the past:

"I was saying to myself, I'll probably go down in flames, but somehow, some way, history will say. . . . I knew I had tried, I had been warning, I had gone so many miles beyond anything expected of me . . . I took the position, what do I have to lose? So I went all the way . . . Now people in Congress are coming up to me. They say, 'Ed, you've been vindicated.'

"Thank God I did those things. Now I can look myself in the mirror."

## Chapter 16 Review Questions

1. How would you sum up the advice about ethical behavior in the public office suggested in Bailey's essay? How do his views on the subject differ from those of Paul Appleby, to whom Bailey refers in his essay? Whose approach to ethics in government—Appleby's or Bailey's—do you find the more persuasive? Explain your answer.

2. What factors caused the S&L crisis and how did both Grey and Selby at first deal with these problems? What norms or values influenced their actions? Were their choices fundamentally moral and ethical?

3. Do you think their behavior in office met the ethical standards for public officials as outlined by Bailey's essay? For instance, in their ability to resist Texan S&L lobbiest interests in Congress? On the basis of your reading of the case study, would you add any points to Bailey's essay regarding other criteria or standards for correct moral behavior by public officials?

4. Why do issues that arise in government always contain some degree of ethical or moral choice? In your opinion, are similar moral choices apparent in decision making in the private sector? Explain your answer.

5. Some observers argue that it is impossible to teach individuals who are preparing for public service careers to be moral and ethical—in other words, family background, religion, personal attitudes, and upbringing have more to do with a person's ethical orientation than does formal educational training. Do you agree? Or, are there ways formal education can inculcate ethical behavior in those persons who may someday fill government posts? If so, explain how, based on examples from "The $150 Billion Calamity".

6. Compare and contrast Case Study 1, "The Blast in Centralia No. 5," with Case Study 16 from the standpoint of their ethical lessons for public administrators. Can you extract from the cases a specific list of important lessons for practicing public administrators?

# Key Terms

moral issues
ethical dilemmas
administrative responsibility
mental attitudes
public interest
moral sensitivity
contextual priorities
complexity of bigness

personal ethical codes versus
   organizational ethical codes
normative theory
higher law
predictable pathologies
moral virtue versus
   moral vice
paradoxes of procedures

# Suggestions for Further Reading

Despite the enormous concern recently expressed about this topic, perhaps the most sensitive treatments remain those by earlier theorists: Chester Barnard, *The Functions of the Executive* (Cambridge, Mass.: Harvard University Press, 1938)—especially Chapter 17; Paul H. Appleby, *Morality and Administration in Democratic Government* (Baton Rouge, La.: Louisiana State University Press, 1952); and Frederick C. Mosher, *Democracy and the Public Service,* Second Edition (New York: Oxford University Press, 1982)—especially Chapter 8.

The classic scholarly debate over this subject (though it is couched in terms of responsibility instead of ethics) is between Carl J. Friedrich, "Public Policy and the Nature of Administrative Responsibility," *Public Policy,* 1 (Cambridge, Mass.: Harvard University Press, 1940), pp. 3–24 and Herman Finer, "Administrative Responsibility in Democratic Government," *Public Administration Review,* 1 (Summer 1941), pp. 335–350. Along with the Friedrich-Finer arguments, which remain highly germane even today, you should also read John M. Gaus, "The Responsibility of Public Administration," in Leonard D. White, *The Frontiers of Public Administration* (Chicago: University of Chicago Press, 1936), pp. 26–44, as well as Arthur A. Maass and Law-

rence I. Radway, "Gauging Administrative Responsibility," *Public Administration Review,* 9 (Summer 1949), pp. 182–192.

For more recent writings that have addressed this subject with varying degrees of success or failure, see John Rohr, *Ethics for Bureaucrats*, Second Edition (New York: Marcel Dekker, 1988); Sissela E. Bok, *Lying* (New York: Random House, 1979), and *Secrets* (New York: Pantheon, 1983); John P. Burke, *Bureaucratic Responsibility* (Baltimore: The Johns Hopkins Press, 1986). Terry L. Cooper, *An Ethic of Citizenship for Public Administration* (Englewood Cliffs, N.J.: Prentice Hall, 1991); William L. Richter, et al., *Combating Corruption/Encouraging Ethics: A Sourcebook for Public Service* (Washington: D.C.: American Society for Public Administration, 1990); Terry L. Cooper, *The Responsible Administration: An Approach to Ethics for the Administrative Role,* 3rd edition (San Francisco: Jossey-Bass, 1990); David H. Rosenbloom and James D. Carroll, eds., *Towards Constitutional Competence: A Casebook for Public Administrators* (Englewood Cliffs, N.J.: Prentice Hall, 1990); Kathryn G. Denhardt, *The Ethics of Public Service: Resolving Moral Dilemmas in Public Organizations* (New York: Greenwood, 1988). Mark T. Lilla, "Ethos, 'Ethics' and Public Service," *The Public Interest,* 63 (Spring 1981), pp.

3–17, or, in the same issue, Thomas C. Schelling, "Economic Reasoning and the Ethics of Policy," pp. 37–61. For other essays, see York Wilbern, "Types and Levels of Public Morality" *Public Administration Review* 44 (March/April 1984), pp. 102–108; Barbara S. Romzek and Melvin J. Dubnik, "Accountability in the Public Sector: Lessons from the Challenger Tragedy," *Public Administration Review* 47 (May/June 1987), pp. 227–238; Terry L. Cooper, "Hierarchy, Virtue, and the Practice of Public Administration: A Perspective for Normative Ethics" *Public Administration Review* 47 (July/August, 1987), pp. 320–328; Dennis F. Thompson, "The Possibility of Administrative Ethics," *Public Administration Review* 45 (September/October 1985) pp. 555–561. James S. Bowman, "Ethics in Government, A National Survey of Public Administration," *Public Administration Review*, 50 (May/June 1990), pp. 345–353; J. Patrick Dobel, "Integrity in the Public Service," *Public Administration Review*, 50 (May/June 1990) pp. 354–366 and Lloyd G. Nigro and William D. Richardson, "Between Citizen and Administration: Administrative Ethics and *PAR*," *Public Administration Review*, 50 (November/December 1990), pp. 623–635.

Any in-depth review of this subject should include study of the Ethics in Government Act of 1978, as well as the enabling legislation and debates over such seminal oversight mechanisms as the War Powers Resolution of 1973, Freedom of Information Act 1967 (with 1974 amendments), Privacy Act (1974), the Inspector General's Office (1976), and the various ombudsman offices instituted within state and local governments. For many of these recent documents, see Richard J. Stillman II, ed., *Basic Documents of American Public Administration Since 1950* (New York: Holmes and Meier, 1982).

Many novels focus on the role of ethics in public life. For an excellent discussion of how they contribute to our understanding of the subject, see Dwight Waldo, *The Novelist on Organization and Administration: An Inquiry into the Relationship Between Two Worlds* (Berkeley, Calif.: Institute of Governmental Studies, June 1968), or Marc Holzer, Kenneth Morris and William Ludwin *Literature in Bureaucracy* (Wayne, N.J.: Avery Publishing, 1979).

For two useful applied casebooks on this topic, read: William M. Timmins, *A Casebook of Public Ethics and Issues* (Monterey, Calif.: Brooks/Cole, 1990) and Mark H. Moore and Malcolm K. Sparrow, *Ethics in Government: The Moral Challenge of Public Leadership* (Englewood Cliffs, N.J.: Prentice-Hall, 1990).

# Topic Index

# Citizens' Rights and Participation

# Communications in Administration

## The Legislature and Congress

## Decision Making

## Ethical Issues

## Health and Human Services

# Implementation

# Intergovernmental Programs, Policies, and Relationships

# National Defense and International Relations

# Organizational Behavior

# Organization and Management

# Personnel and Civil Service

# Presidency

# Regulation, Rule Enforcement, and Law Enforcement

## State and Local Government

## The Study of Public Administration as a Discipline

## Third-party Government

# Subject Index